World's Largest Countries by Population

Rank	Country	[illegible]
1	China	1 284
2	India	1 046
3	United States	281
4	Indonesia	232
5	Brazil	176
6	Pakistan	148
7	Russia	145
8	Bangladesh	133
9	Nigeria	130
10	Japan	127

Source: US Census Bureau, International Database.

World's Most Expensive Countries

Rank	Country
1	Japan
2	South Korea
3	Russia
4	Taiwan
5	Norway
6	Hong Kong
7	Switzerland
8	Denmark
9	Argentina
10	China

Source: ECA International.

World's Highest Unemployment Rates

Rank	Country	Unemployment Rate (%)
1	Liberia	70.0
2	Djibouti	50.0
3	Kenya	50.0
4	Zambia	50.0
5	Zimbabwe	50.0
6	Lesotho	45.0
7	Mayotte	45.0
8	Reunion	42.8
9	Botswana	40.0
10	Bangladesh	35.2

Source: CIA – World Factbook 2002.

PRINCIPLES OF MacroEconomics

FOURTH EDITION

John E. Sayre • **Alan J. Morris**

Capilano College and Western Washington University

Capilano College

Toronto Montréal Boston Burr Ridge, IL Dubuque, IA Madison, WI
New York San Francisco St. Louis Bangkok Bogotá Caracas
Kuala Lumpur Lisbon London Madrid Mexico City Milan
New Delhi Santiago Seoul Singapore Sydney Taipei

The McGraw-Hill Companies

Principles of Macroeconomics
Fourth Edition

ISBN: 0-07-091455-9

1 2 3 4 5 6 7 8 9 10 TRI 0 9 8 7 6 5 4

Printed and bound in Canada

Vice President, Editorial and Media Technology: Patrick Ferrier
Executive Sponsoring Editor: Lynn Fisher
Economics Editor: Ron Doleman
Developmental Editor: Maria Chu
Copy Editor: Susan James
Proofreader: Eugenia Canas
Production Coordinator: Jennifer Wilkie
Marketing Manager: Kelly Smyth
Cover and Interior Design: Pronk&Associates Inc.
Electronic Page Makeup: Pronk&Associates Inc.
Cover Image: Antonio Mo/Taxi/Getty Images
Printer: Tri-Graphic Printing

National Library of Canada Cataloguing in Publication

Sayre, John E., 1942–
Principles of macroeconomics / John E. Sayre, Alan J. Morris. — 4th ed.

Includes index.
ISBN 0-07-091455-9

1. Macroeconomics. I. Morris, Alan J. (Alan James) II. Title.

HB172.5.S29 2003 339 C2002-905052-9

With love to Clélie, who
will always be a friend
(JES)

and

To the ones I love:
Brian, Trevor, and Jean
(AJM)

About The Authors

John E. Sayre earned a B.S.B.A. at the University of Denver and an M.A. from Boston University. He began teaching principles of economics while in the Peace Corps in Malawi. He came to Vancouver to do Ph.D. studies at Simon Fraser University and ended up teaching at Capilano College for the next thirty years. In the summer of 2001, he joined the faculty at Western Washington University and now lives in Bellingham, Washington. John is an avid golfer who also enjoys cycling and listening to a wide range of music.

Alan Morris, though loath to admit it, first worked as an accountant in England, where he became an Associate of the Chartered Institute of Secretaries and obtained his first degree in 1971 in Manchester, U.K. He subsequently obtained his Master's degree at Simon Fraser University, B.C., in 1973. He worked on his doctorate at Leicester University, U.K., and returned to work in business in Vancouver, B.C., until his appointment at Capilano College in 1988. He currently resides in North Vancouver with his wife and two sons and is an avid devotee of classical music, mountaineering, soccer, and beer. To his knowledge, he has never been an adviser to the Canadian government.

Brief Contents

Contents

Preface

To the Students

So, you may well ask, why take a course in economics? For many of you, the obvious answer to this question is: "Because it is a requirement for the program or educational goal that I have chosen." Fair enough. But there are other good answers to this question. It is a simple truth that if you want to understand the world around you, then you have to understand some basic economics. Much of what goes on in the world today is driven by economic considerations, and those who know nothing of economics often simply cannot understand why things are the way they are. In this age of globalization, we are all becoming citizens of the world and we need to function effectively in the midst of enormous changes that are sweeping across almost every aspect of the social/political/economic landscape. You can either be part of this, and all the opportunities that come with it, or not be part of it because you can't make any sense of it.

It is quite possible that you feel a little apprehensive because you have heard that economics is a difficult subject. Though there may be a grain of truth in this, we are convinced that almost any student can succeed in economics. But it will require some real work and effort on your part. Here are some tips on the general approach to this course that you might find helpful. First, read the **Economics Toolkit** that appears at the beginning of the book. The section titled "Canadian Reality" offers basic information on Canada and its economic picture. "Graphing Reality" gives a quick lesson on graphs, which are an essential part of economics. These two sections will give you a solid foundation on which to build your knowledge of economics.

Second, before each lecture, quickly look over the chapter that will be covered. In this preliminary survey you don't need to worry about the glossary boxes, the self-test questions, or the integrated Study Guide. Third, take notes as much as you can in the lecture, because the process of forcing yourself to express ideas *in your own words* is a crucial stage in the learning process. Fourth, re-read the chapter, again taking notes and using your own words (don't just copy everything word for word from the text). While doing this, refer to your classroom notes and try to integrate them into your reading notes. After you finish this, you will be ready to take on the Study Guide. As painful as it may be for you to hear this, we want to say loud and clear that you should do *all* of the answered questions and problems in the Study Guide. You may be slow at first, but you will be surprised at how much faster you become in later chapters. This is a natural aspect of the learning process. It might be helpful for you to get together with one or two other students and form a study group that meets once or twice a week to do economics Study Guide questions. You will be amazed at how explaining an answer to a fellow student is one of the most effective learning techniques there are. If you ever come across a question that you simply can't understand, this is a sure sign that you need to approach your instructor (or teaching assistant) for help. Don't get discouraged when this happens, and realize that it will probably happen more at the beginning of your process of learning economics than later on in the term. We are convinced that if you follow this process consistently, beginning in the very first week of class, you will succeed in the course—and not only succeed, but most likely do well. All it takes is effort, good time management, and consistent organization.

Finally, a great deal of what becoming educated is all about involves gaining self-confidence and a sense of accomplishment. Getting an A in a "tough" economics course can be a great step in this direction. We wish you all the best.

To the Instructors

General Philosophy

Over the years, we have become increasingly convinced that most economics textbooks are written to impress other economists as much as to enlighten beginning students. Such books tend to be encyclopedic in scope and intimidating in appearance. Small wonder, then, that students often emerge from an economics course feeling that the discipline really does earn its reputation of being daunting and unapproachable. We agree that the study of economics is challenging, but our experience is that students can also see it as intriguing and enjoyable if the right approach is taken. It is our belief that this right approach starts with a really good textbook that is concise without sacrificing either clarity or accepted standards of rigour.

In writing this text we attempted to stay focused on four guiding principles. The first is to achieve a well-written text. We have tried to write as clearly as possible, to avoid unnecessary jargon, to speak directly to the student, and to avoid unnecessary abstraction and repetition.

Of equal importance, and our second principle, is a focussed emphasis on student learning. Many years of teaching the principles courses have convinced us that students learn economics "by doing economics." To this end, both review questions and self-test questions are positioned throughout each chapter. This encourages students to apply what they have just read and gives them continuous feedback on their comprehension of the material being presented. Further, we feel that we offer the most comprehensive and carefully crafted Study Guide on the market, which has evolved over the years as a result of continued use in our own classes. In addition, each chapter's Study Guide contains a Chapter Summary as well as a section of Study Tips for the students.

Our third principle has been to avoid an encyclopedic text. It seems that in an effort to please everyone, textbook authors often include bits and pieces of almost everything. The result is that students are often overwhelmed and find it difficult to sort out the more important material from what is less important.

The fourth principle is to avoid problems of discontinuity that can occur when different groups of authors do separate parts of a total package. To this end, we are the sole authors of the entire package of material—text, Study Guide, instructor's manual, and test bank. We have tried to ensure that as much care and attention goes into the ancillary materials as goes into the writing of the text.

Few things are more satisfying than witnessing a student's zest for learning. We hope that this textbook adds a little to this process.

Fourth Edition Changes

The changes to the fourth edition have resulted largely from feedback provided by our many users and reviewers. Several chapters have been re-organized and the integrated Study Guide has been completely overhauled to provide even better structure for our students. Important changes to individual chapters are listed below, and the re-organization to the Study Guide is described in detail in the next section of the preface.

In **Chapter 1** we re-organized the topics to create a stronger narrative flow. We have tried to ensure that the concept of "scarcity-choice-cost" is at the heart of the chapter and we now introduce the topic of trade immediately after the discussion of opportunity cost. We do this by way of a simple arithmetic example that is very easy to understand and yet clearly demonstrates the gains from trade. We have also re-organized the section on economic goals. Each goal is now highlighted by the use of much clearer graphics and contrasted with the performance of other countries. The goal of a livable environment has been replaced with the simple one of improving and maintaining a high standard of living, which we believe encompasses that goal.

In **Chapter 2** we use more straight-line demand and supply curves. We made this change at the suggestion of some reviewers who felt that our third edition curves were a little "kinky"! There was a reason why the shapes were the way they were, but we agreed that it might make sense to change the data in our tables mid-chapter and thereafter use only simple straight-line curves.

We have removed the sections on the sources of economic growth and the causes of the business cycle from **Chapter 4** and placed them in Chapter 5. Thus, the fourth edition discussion of economic growth now focuses on its measurement and on some of its benefits and costs. In this way, the discussion parallels the coverage of unemployment and inflation. As a result, we feel that the chapter is much tighter.

Chapter 5, which has been moved forward in the text, is a revision of the old Chapter 6 on aggregate demand and supply. The major change is that we no longer make a distinction between long- and short-run aggregate supply. Instead, we label the long-run aggregate supply, "potential GDP." Potential GDP is thus regarded as a benchmark for the economy and, as such, highlights what the economy is capable of producing at full employment. We also explain potential GDP by way of making an analogy with the production possibilities curve and demonstrate (with a diagram) that economic growth without a change in potential GDP is not likely to be sustainable in the future. By doing this, we are able to emphasize the importance of productivity. We then look at the factors that cause a change in potential GDP (by bringing in the material on sources of economic growth from Chapter 4 of the previous edition). Next we look at aggregate supply, which is simply labelled AS. We then explain that although potential GDP is usually on a steady upward course, the growth of actual GDP is much more volatile (by taking a look at business cycles—material from the previous Chapter 4). The causes of these fluctuations lie in (short-run) changes in aggregate demand, which we then look at in detail. Most of the rest of the chapter is unchanged, apart from the discussion of Classical and Keynesian schools of thought, where we contrast the two, not in terms of disagreements over the short-run versus the long-run (as in previous editions), but in terms of the differing views on (the shape of) AS.

In **Chapter 6**, we introduce the algebraic equations as we complete each section: a consumption function, an investment function, a net export function, etc. (They can easily be omitted by instructors who do not wish to cover the algebra.) Once we have completed the discussion of each element of expenditures, it then becomes simply a matter of adding up each function to obtain an aggregate expenditure function and then calculating equilibrium.

In addition to this, we have added the appropriate graphing as we cover each function. So, unlike the last edition, in which we postponed the graphical coverage until we had discussed every element of spending and then put all the functions on a single graph, in this edition we graph each function as we go along. Another important change is that we no longer present the algebra in general forms (such as C = a + bY) but always put in actual numbers (for the Canadian economy, when it makes sense to do so). This means that we no longer derive the multiplier in general form, but rather simply explain the multiplier equation and show how to do the calculations. It all makes things a lot simpler.

In **Chapter 9** we introduce a simple numerical example to enable students to see and quickly calculate the gains from trade. We have also written an Added Dimensions box on open-border trade policies in the post-September 11th era.

In **Chapter 12** we have changed the terminology a little by categorizing the approaches to monetary policy as "activist" and "non-activist." All other chapters have been appropriately updated to reflect this change.

Textbook Features

As an initial review and a resource to return to, the book opens with the **Economics Toolkit**. The first section, Canadian Reality, offers basic information on Canada and its economy. The second section, Graphing Reality, provides the student with a primer on how to interpret and create tables and graphs. We have provided a number of features to help the student come to grips with the subject matter.

Learning Objectives, listed at the beginning of each chapter, form a learning framework throughout the text, with each learning objective repeated in the margin at the appropriate place in the main body of the chapter. Each chapter opens with a vignette that provides a context and overview for each chapter.

CHAPTER FIVE

Aggregate Demand and Supply

LEARNING OBJECTIVES

This chapter will enable you to:

LO1 Understand the concept of *potential GDP.*

LO2 Explain what is *aggregate supply.*

LO3 Understand the concept of *aggregate demand.*

LO4 Explain the concept of macroeconomic equilibrium.

LO5 Understand the causes of recessions and inflationary booms.

What's ahead...

This is an important chapter in which we develop the AD/AS model and look at the factors which explain changes in the level of GDP. In later chapters, we will use this model extensively to examine various economic policies and problems. In this chapter we look separately at how aggregate demand and aggregate supply are determined and then explain the factors that cause them to change and how this will affect the economy. Finally, through the eyes of two opposing schools of thoughts, we look at the question of whether the economy is self-adjusting or needs the active intervention of government.

A QUESTION OF RELEVANCE...

Which of the following acts do you think will improve economic conditions more: you buy a new CD player for $300, or you increase your work productivity effort by 20 percent? Aside from your obvious objection that neither act will have much impact on the whole economy, you probably would opt for the second one, since it seems to involve real production. After all, if we all became 20 percent more productive at our work, then the economy would surely be more wealthy than if people simply bought more things. Surprisingly, in the short run, the two acts will have about the same effect on the economy. In the longer run, however, a sustained productivity increase will make for a healthier economy.

5.2 Aggregate Supply

LO2
Explain what is aggregate supply.

Aggregate supply refers to the total quantity of goods and services that firms in the economy would be willing and able to produce at various prices. While most firms have little control over the market demand for their products, they can and do try to exercise as much control

Glossary terms indicate the first use of any term that is part of the language of economics. The term itself is in bold print and the definition is provided in the margin. The page number where the definition appears is supplied at the end of the chapter for quick and easy reference, and a complete glossary of terms appears at the end of the book.

Review boxes contain very straightforward questions—often definitional—that cover the most basic material within each chapter. Students should be able to answer these questions directly from the text and thus are encouraged to master the language of economics before tackling the more abstract concepts, which are at the heart of the discipline.

REVIEW

1. What are the four *factors of production*?
2. What is the payment to each factor of production?
3. Distinguish between the *product market* and the *factor market*.
4. Define the term *loanable funds*.
5. Distinguish between *savings* and *investment*.
6. List the three leakages and the three injections.
7. What does the word *equilibrium* mean?
8. Define the term *aggregate expenditure*.

Self-Test question boxes appear at important points throughout the main body of each chapter. Their purpose is to give students immediate feedback on how well they understand the more abstract concept(s) discussed. In doing this, we have tried to establish what we believe to be a minimum standard of comprehension that all students should strive to achieve. Students can check their own progress by comparing their answers with those in the Answer Key, which is available online at the Sayre and Morris Web site, **www.mcgrawhill.ca/college/sayre**.

SELF-TEST

1. If the economy is in disequilibrium because total income exceeds aggregate expenditure, what must be happening to inventories?
2. Does the term "consumption" refer to spending by households on domestically produced goods and services only? Does the term "investment" include the purchase of stocks and bonds?

Added Dimension boxes identify material that is either general information or supplementary material that we hope adds a little colour to the student's reading.

ADDED DIMENSION

The World after September 11, 2001

In the aftermath of the Second World War, the free nations of the world negotiated a series of trade agreements that reduced tariffs and other trade restrictions and increased the amount of trade between nations. This was done under the auspices of GATT (General Agreement on Trade and Tariffs), which has since been replaced by the WTO (World Trade Organization). As a result of this increased trade, nations have become more interdependent and the flow of people, as well as of goods, between countries has greatly increased. For Canada, the culmination of this trend was the NAFTA agreement with the U.S.A. and Mexico, which has dramatically increased Canadian exports and created hundreds of thousands of jobs within our borders. In the aftermath of the tragic events of 9-11-01, we may wonder whether this trend will reverse itself as borders become more difficult for goods and people to penetrate because of increased security concerns. If this does occur, then the events of that infamous day will reach far into the future and affect the entire world community.

Highlighted Concepts. Throughout the text, important ideas are pulled out and presented in a highlighted box—signalling to students that this material is particularly relevant and critical for their understanding.

> **An increase in demand causes the price to increase and the quantity traded also to increase.**

Simple, clear and uncomplicated **visuals** are found throughout the text. These are supported by captions that thoroughly explain the concepts involved.

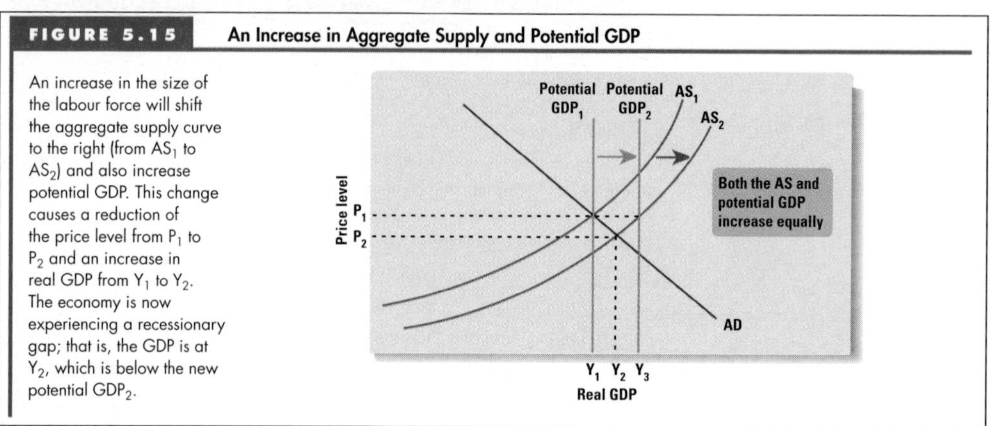

FIGURE 5.15 An Increase in Aggregate Supply and Potential GDP

An increase in the size of the labour force will shift the aggregate supply curve to the right (from AS_1 to AS_2) and also increase potential GDP. This change causes a reduction of the price level from P_1 to P_2 and an increase in real GDP from Y_1 to Y_2. The economy is now experiencing a recessionary gap; that is, the GDP is at Y_2, which is below the new potential GDP_2.

@-conomics boxes are brief snippets designed to give a glimpse of what is becoming known as the "new economy."

@-CONOMICS

Re-inventing the Market

Capitalism, as we know it today, first emerged and began to spread about 250 years ago as commerce moved out of the occasional village markets of Europe into the age of factory-centred manufacturing, which was then combined with widespread systems of wholesaling and retailing. However, this transformation also introduced a less predicable chain of supply and demand. While the seller in the village market was in direct contact with the buyer, the evolution of capitalism's mass markets and mass production techniques imposed vast gulfs in time and space between the two. Producers became much less sure of what the demand for their product was and buyers were never sure if there wasn't a better deal somewhere else. In response to this, sellers used the blunt tool of a fixed price list and adjusted output accordingly, while buyers just did the best they could. The phenomenon of the Internet is re-inventing commerce as the seller's market horizon expands, buyers have more information, real-time sales become routine, and the need to stockpile inventory diminishes. In short, supply-chain bottlenecks are being eradicated. What is emerging is far *more efficient markets* and the rise of dynamic pricing based on constantly fluctuating demand and supply.

Integrated Study Guide Features

As expressed earlier, we believe that answering questions and doing problems should be an active *part of the students' learning process*. For this reason, we chose to integrate a complete **Study Guide** within the covers of this text. Thus a Study Guide section, with pages screened in colour, immediately follows each chapter. We were careful to write the questions in the Study Guide to cover all the material, but *only* the material, found in the text itself. We have chosen a colourful, user-friendly design for the Study Guide sections, and we hope this will encourage significant student participation.

The **Study Guide** has been re-organized into three main sections: a *Review section*, a set of *Answered Questions and Problems*, and then a set of *Unanswered Parallel Problems*.

The ***Review*** *section* contains the *Chapter Summary*, *New Glossary Terms*, and *Key Equations*, as well as *Study Tips*, which are suggestions to help students manage the material in the chapter.

STUDY TIPS

1. The material covered in this chapter contains very little theory; the chapter is mostly descriptive or institutional. This does not mean that it is unimportant, but it probably does mean that you don't need to study it quite as much as some of the other chapters. If you have gained a sense of the limitations of the measurements, this is very good.
2. In a very real sense, growth, unemployment, and inflation are subjects of the entire course that we call macroeconomics. This chapter is meant to be an introduction to these topics and not the final word. Therefore, you should not be concerned at this point if you are still unclear about questions like what is the cause of unemployment and what are the solutions to inflation. We still have a long way to go.

The ***Answered Questions and Problems*** *section* includes true/false questions and multiple-choice questions. The multiple-choice questions have been grouped into three learning levels: Basic, Intermediate, and Advanced. In addition, there are a set of problems, each of which has a twin in the Unanswered Parallel Problems section.

Answered Questions

Indicate whether the following statements are true or false.

1. **T or F** Frictional unemployment is likely to be greatest in sunset industries.

2. **T or F** The natural rate of unemployment is the unemployment rate at full employment.

Basic (Questions 11–21)

11. What is the real rate of interest if the nominal rate of interest is 10 percent and the rate of inflation is 4 percent?
 a) 6 percent.
 b) 14 percent.
 c) 10 percent.

Students can judge their progress by working through the Answered Questions and Problems, and checking their answers with those in the Student Answer Key available for download at the Student Online Learning Centre **www.mcgrawhill.ca/college/sayre**.

Parallel Problems

ANSWERED PROBLEMS

26. **Key Problem** The data in **Table 4.11** shows the total output (a mixture of consumer, capital, and government services) and the prices of each product for the distant country of Vindaloo. (All figures are in billions and the base year is 2000.) Complete the table and answer the questions which follow (to one decimal place):

TABLE 4.11

1	2	3	4	5	6	7	8	9	10	11	12	13	14
	2000			2001					2002				
Item	Qty	Prices Year 2000	Nominal GDP	Qty	Prices Year 2001	Nominal GDP	Prices Year 2000	Real GDP	Qty	Prices Year 2002	Nominal GDP	Prices Year 2000	Real GDP
Hot dogs	50	2	100	55	2.40				58	2.50			
CDs	10	12	120	12	13				14	13.50			
Farm tractors	3	100	300	4	95				4	110			
Parking meters	4	50	200	4	60				5	70			
Totals			720										

a) What is the value of nominal GDP in:
2001: $ ________; 2002: $ ________.

b) What is the value of real GDP in:
2001: $ ________; 2002: $ ________.

c) What is the value of the GDP deflator in:
2001: $ ________; 2002: $ ________.

d) What is the inflation rate (using the GDP deflator) in:
2001: $ ________; 2002: $ ________.
2002: $ ________.

h) Converting the cost of each bundle into a consumer price index, what is the value of each bundle using 2000 as the base year:
2000: $ ________; 2001: $ ________;
2002: $ ________.

i) What is the inflation rate using this price index?
2001: $ ________% 2002: $ ________%

Answers to the problems in the Unanswered Problems section can be found in the Instructor's Manual. The authors hope that instructors will use the Unanswered Problems to prepare assignments or exams, knowing that students have had exposure, as well as answers, to very similar problems.

Finally, the **Web-Based Activities** are included to give students the opportunity to apply what they've learned using the World Wide Web.

Web-Based Activities

1. Draw a picture of the circular flow of income. Now, go to **www.statcan.ca/english/econoind/gdpexp.htm** and fill in the dollar amounts for consumption, investment, government, and net exports in your diagram.

2. From the data found on the following Web pages, do leakages equal injections? Illustrate and explain.
www.statcan.ca/english/econoind/gdprev.htm
www.statcan.ca/english/econoind/gdpexp.htm
www.statcan.ca/english/econoind/indic.htm

Supplements For Students

Student Online Learning Centre

Prepared by Chris McDonnell and Raimo Marttala of Malaspina University College, this electronic learning aid, located at **www.mcgrawhill.ca/college/sayre**, offers a wealth of materials, including CBC Video Cases; Learning Objectives; Online Quizzing; Annotated Web Links; Internet Application Questions; Key Terms and Searchable Glossary; Electronic Lecture Notes; Econ Graph Kit; and a link to the E-STAT and CANSIM II database.

Answer Key

The Answer Key is available for download at the Student Centre. You have the option of viewing each chapter online in a PDF format, or downloading the entire Answer Key for off-line viewing.

GradeSummit [www.gradesummit.com]

GradeSummit is an Internet-based self-assessment service that offers a variety of ways for students to analyze what they know and don't know. By revealing subject strengths and weaknesses and by providing detailed feedback and direction, GradeSummit enables students to focus their study time on those areas where they are most in need of improvement. GradeSummit provides data about how much students know while they study for an exam—not after they take it. It helps the professor measure an individual student's progress and assess that progress relative to others in the class.

Supplements For Instructors

Your **Integrated i-Learning Sales Specialist** is a McGraw-Hill Ryerson representative who has the experience, product knowledge, training, and support to help you assess and integrate any of the below-noted products, technology, and services into your course for optimum teaching and learning performance. Whether it's using our test bank software, helping your students improve their grades, or putting your entire course online, your i-Learning Sales Specialist is there to help you do it. Contact your local i-Learning Sales Specialist today to learn how to maximize all McGraw-Hill Ryerson resources!

Instructor's Online Learning Centre

The OLC at **www.mcgrawhill.ca/college/sayre** includes a password-protected Web site for Instructors. The site offers downloadable supplements, including a new set of short answer problems, and **PageOut**, the McGraw-Hill Ryerson course Web site development centre.

Instructor's CD-ROM

This CD-ROM contains all the necessary Instructor Supplements, including:

Instructor's Manual

There are three parts to each chapter of the *Instructor's Manual.* First is a brief overview of the chapter, with some rationale for the topics included. Second is a description of how we think the material found in the chapter could be presented. Between the two of us, we have taught the macro principles course over two hundred times, and we pass on helpful hints gained from this extensive experience to instructors who may not have been at it so long. More experienced instructors who have found a comfortable groove will simply ignore these suggestions.

The third part contains the answers to the Chapter Self-Test questions and all questions and problems in the Unanswered Problems section.

Computerized Test Bank

Much effort went into writing the *Test Bank* in order to ensure that the questions cover all topics in the textbook, but *only* those topics. Questions are written in plain English and in true question form to minimize any misunderstanding by students as to what is being asked.

There are approximately one hundred questions per chapter. They come in the order of the topics covered in the chapter and include a mixture of both four- and five-answer questions. In addition, at the beginning of each Chapter, the true/false and multiple-choice questions from the Study Guide are repeated. This gives the instructor the option of including multiple-choice questions on an exam that students have, or have not, seen before.

PowerPoint® Presentations

Prepared by Anton Ljutic, this package includes dynamic slides of the important illustrations in the textbook, along with detailed, chapter-by-chapter reviews of the important ideas presented in the text.

CBC Video Cases

Available to users of the fourth edition is a series of video segments drawn from CBC broadcasts. These videos have been chosen to assist students in applying economic concepts to real-world events. A set of instructor notes accompanies each video segment and is available at the Instructor's Online Learning Centre. The video segments will be available in VHS format and through video-streaming from the Online Learning Centre, which is accessible to both instructors and students.

PageOut

This unique point-and-click course Website tool enables you to create a high-quality course Web site without knowing HTML coding. With PageOut you can post your syllabus online, assign McGraw-Hill Online Learning Centre or e-Book content, add links to important off-site resources, and maintain student results in the online gradebook. Visit **www.mhhe.com/pageout** or contact your i-Learning Sales Specialist for details.

In addition, content cartridges are also available for course management systems, such as *WebCT* and *Blackboard*, to expand the reach of your course and open up distance-learning options.

eServices

McGraw-Hill Ryerson offers a unique eServices package designed for Canadian faculty. This includes technical support, access to our educational technology conferences, and custom eCourses, to name just a few. Please speak to your i-Learning Sales Specialist for details.

Acknowledgements

We wish to thank the following economists who participated in the formal review process of the fourth edition:

Mian Ali, University of Prince Edward Island
George Archer, Marianopolis College
Jim Butko, Niagara College
John Cavaliere, Sault College
Eva Dabrowski, Seneca College
Barbara Gardner, Southern Alberta Institute of Technology
Geoff Malleck, Mohawk College
Pat Margeson, New Brunswick Community College
Ronald McDonald, Mohawk College
Dave McPherson, Humber College
Gyasi Nimarko, Vanier College
Stephen Rakoczy, Humber College
Duane Rockerbie, University of Lethbridge
Jim Sentance, University of Prince Edward Island
Martha Spence, Confederation College
Weiqiu Yu, University of New Brunswick

Our sincere thanks go to George Archer of Marianopolis College and Jim Sentance of the University of Prince Edward Island, who provided technical reviews of the manuscript.

We would like to acknowledge our colleagues in the Economics Department of Capilano College—Nigel Amon, Ken Moak, Mahak Yaseri, and C.S. Lum—for their encouragement and vigilance in spotting errors and omissions in earlier editions. Numerous colleagues in other departments also gave us encouragement, and sometimes praise, which is greatly appreciated.

Most particularly, we wish to acknowledge the help and support of Ron Doleman, our editorial consultant. Ron provided the original framework for revisions to the third edition and provided advice and support for our changes in this fourth edition.

Susan James' editing and Eugenia Canas's proofreading have been superb, while Maria Chu and Jaime Duffy at McGraw-Hill Ryerson offered excellent professional skills, and Lynn Fisher once again demonstrated her faith in our work, which is greatly appreciated.

In the end, of course, whatever errors or confusions remain are our responsibility.

Finally, we wish to acknowledge the continued love and support of our families and those close to us.

FOR THE INSTRUCTOR

- Want an easy way to test your students prior to an exam that ***doesn't*** create more work for you?
- Want to access your supplements ***without*** having to bring them all to class?
- Want an ***easy*** way to get your course on-line?
- Want to ***free up more time*** in your day to get more done?

Of course you do!

Then check out your
Online Learning Centre!

- Downloadable Supplements
- PageOut
- Online Resources
- eServices

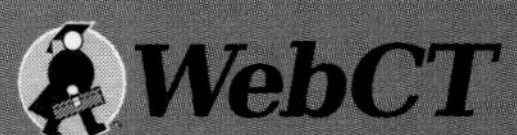

Higher Learning. Forward Thinking.™

Economics Toolkit

Some students take economics because it is a requirement for a program they have chosen or a degree that they are working toward. Some are interested in a career in business, and taking economics seems like a natural choice. Some even take it because they think that they might like it. Whatever might be the reason you chose to take it, we are glad you did and hope you will not be disappointed. Economics is a challenging discipline to learn, but it can also be one of the most rewarding courses you will ever take. The logic and analysis used in economics is very powerful, and successfully working your way through the principles of economics over the next term will do for your mind what a serious jogging program will do for your body. Bon voyage!

The Canadian Reality

The Land

Canada is a huge country—in fact, it is the second-largest country on this planet. It contains 7 percent of the world's land mass. It stretches 5600 kilometres from the Atlantic to the Pacific Ocean and encompasses six time zones. Ontario alone, which is the second-largest province (after Quebec), is larger than Pakistan, or Turkey, or Chile, or France, or the United Kingdom. Canada's ten provinces range in size from tiny Prince Edward Island to Quebec, which is nearly 240 times as large. In addition, its three territories—the Northwest Territories, the Yukon, and Nunavut—demand that we describe this country's reach as being from sea to sea *to sea*.

Within Canada there are at least six major mountain ranges: the Torngats, Appalachians, and Laurentians in the East, and the Mackenzie, Rocky, and Coast ranges in the West. Any one of these rivals the European Alps in size and grandeur. In addition, Canada has vast quantities of fresh water—9 percent of the world's total—in tens of thousands of lakes and numerous rivers, of which the St. Lawrence and the Mackenzie are the largest.

Canada is richly endowed in natural resources, including gas, oil, gold, silver, copper, iron, nickel, potash, uranium, zinc, fish, timber, and, as mentioned above, water—lots of fresh water. The conclusion is inescapable: Canada is a big, beautiful, and rich country.

The People

The word *Canada* comes from a Huron–Iroquois word meaning *village*. In a sense this is very appropriate, because big as the nation is geographically, it is small in terms of population. Its 30 million people make up only 0.5 percent of the world's population. In fact, there are more people in California or in greater Tokyo than there are in the whole of Canada. Interestingly,

Canada's population growth rate, at 1.1 percent, is the highest among the G8 countries, primarily because of Canada's high rate of immigration. Thirty-six percent of Canadians live in the province of Ontario, and 25 percent in Quebec. On the other hand, Prince Edward Island has a population of only 140 000, less than that of the cities of Sherbrooke, Quebec, or North Vancouver, B.C.

Despite the popular images of the small Maritime fishing village, the lonely Prairie grain farmer, or the remote B.C. logger, Canada is, in fact, an urban nation. Over three quarters of Canadians live in what Statistics Canada calls "urban" areas. There are four Canadian metropolitan areas with populations of over one million: Toronto, with 4.9 million; Montreal, 3.5 million; Vancouver, 2.1 million; and Ottawa–Hull, 1.1 million. It is also true that the vast majority of the 30 million Canadians live in a narrow band stretching along the border with the United States, which, incidentally, is the longest unguarded border in the world.

Approximately half of the Canadian population of 30 million is active in the labour force. The labour-force participation rate for males is 73 percent, and for females, 60 percent.

Multiculturalism

Within this vast, thinly populated country there is a truly diverse, multicultural mix of people. This reality was officially recognized in 1988 when Parliament passed the *Multiculturalism Act*.

There are two official languages in Canada, yet 18 percent of Canadians speak a language other than English or French. In fact, at least 60 languages are spoken in this country. In each year of the 1990s, more than 200 000 new immigrants arrived in Canada. Over 15 percent of all Canadians are first-generation immigrants. In both Toronto and Vancouver, over half the students in the public school system are from non–English-speaking homes. There are over 100 minority-language publications in Toronto, and Vancouver has three daily Chinese-language newspapers.

Canada's First Nations people number 533 000 (1.8 percent of the total population), and almost half of them live in Ontario.

Government

Canada is a constitutional monarchy with a democratic parliament made up of the House of Commons, with 301 elected members, and the Senate, with 104 appointed members. In addition to Parliament, the other two decision-making divisions of the federal government are the cabinet, composed of the prime minister and his or her twenty-five (or so) ministers and their departments, and the judiciary, which includes the Supreme, Federal, and Tax courts.

Just as there are two official languages in this country, Canada has two systems of civil law—one uncodified and based on common law in English Canada, and the other as codified civil law in Quebec. Canada's constitution, the *Canadian Charter of Rights and Freedoms*, came into being in 1982, a full 115 years after Confederation created the country in 1867.

The fact that Canada is a confederation of ten provinces results in the federal government sharing responsibilities with the provinces. For example, while the federal government has jurisdiction in national defence, international trade, immigration, banking, criminal law, fisheries, transportation, and communications, the provinces have responsibility for education, property rights, health, and natural resources. Inevitably, issues arise from time to time that do not fit neatly into any one of these categories, with the result that federal–provincial disputes are a continuous part of the Canadian reality.

Canada the Good

Most Canadians are well aware that they live in a good country. But perhaps many don't realize just how good. The average family income is currently over $64 000, which puts the Canadian living standard among the highest in the world.

The United Nations maintains a "Human Development Index" that uses other factors in addition to average income levels, including life spans, school enrollment, educational attainment, and the presence of human rights. This index ranks Canada as the number three nation in the world in which to live. One reason for this high ranking is that Canadian governments spend nearly 10 percent of the country's gross domestic product (GDP) on health care.

Nearly 65 percent of Canadians own their homes, well over 90 percent are literate, and over 50 percent of all Canadians have access to the Internet. All three of these statistics are among the highest in the world.

Canada the Odd

Canada *is* a good country in which to be born or to have emigrated to. However, it does have its oddities. In 1965, 98 years after its "birth," it was decided that Canada really should have a national flag. The Parliamentary selection committee set up to choose one received no less than two thousand designs, and the flag debate was acrimonious, to say the least. Today, however, most Canadians seem quite comfortable with the Maple Leaf. The English-language lyrics of Canada's national anthem, "O Canada," were formally approved only in 1975. Canada adopted the metric system of measurement in the 1970s, but the imperial system is still in wide use; for example, Statistics Canada still reports the breadth of this country in miles, we sell lengths of wood as "2 × 4s" (inches), and football fields are 110 yards long.

In this bilingual country, it is odd to note that there are more Manitobans who speak Cree than British Columbians who speak French. In this affluent country of ours, it also interesting to note that 4 percent of Canadian homes are heated exclusively by burning wood. Canada has an official animal—the beaver.

On a more serious note, it is a sad fact that the trade of many goods, and even some services, between any one province and the United States is freer than trade between provinces. There is an interesting history concerning trade patterns in North America. At the time of Confederation, trade patterns on this continent were mostly north–south. The Maritimes traded with the New England states, Quebec with New York, Ontario with the Great Lakes states to its south, and the West Coast traded with California. Canada's first prime minister, John A. Macdonald, was also elected as its third, after having lost his first re-election bid, on the basis of a campaign promise known as the National Policy. This policy had three aspects: a) to build a railway to the West Coast and coax British Columbia into joining Canada; b) to offer free land to new immigrants on the prairies in order to settle this area; and c) to force trade patterns into a east–west mode by erecting a tariff wall against U.S. imports. British Columbia did join Confederation; people did come to settle in Manitoba, Saskatchewan, and Alberta; and the pattern of trade did become more east–west.

So was the National Policy a success? Some would argue yes, pointing out that it built a nation and that, just possibly, Canada, as we know it, would not exist today without it. Others aren't so sure and would argue that it set back Canada's development by encouraging and protecting new, less efficient industries through the creation of a branch-plant economy. This occurred because American firms that had previously exported to Canada simply jumped over the tariff walls and established Canadian branch plants. Some believe that the National Policy also promoted Canadian regionalism and aggravated relations between regions because both the West and the Maritimes felt that most of its economic benefits favoured central Canada.

In any case, as a result of the North American Free Trade Agreement (NAFTA) of 1992, trade with the United States (and Mexico) is now mostly without tariffs and north–south trade patterns are re-emerging. Historically, Canadian policy has come full circle. However, the trade barriers between provinces, which were built piece by piece over a century, still remain.

The Economy

Canada is among the ten largest economies in the world, despite its small population. In 2001, Canada's GDP was $1 084 billion. This figure can be broken down as illustrated in **Table T.1**.

TABLE T.1

Category	Amount ($ billion)
Personal expenditures	620
Investment spending	184
Government spending	225
Exports	469
Less imports	(414)
Total GDP	1, 084

Source: Adapted from Statistics Canada, CANSIM II database <http://cansima.statcan.ca/cgi-win/CNSMCGI.EXE>, Table 380-0002.

The provincial breakdown of the 2001 GDP figure of $1 084 billion is shown in **Table T.2**.

TABLE T.2

Province	Population (millions)	GDP ($ billions)	GDP per capita ($ thousands)
Newfoundland (and Labrador)	0.53	13.9	26.2
Prince Edward Island	0.14	3.4	24.3
Nova Scotia	0.94	24.9	26.4
New Brunswick	0.76	20.2	26.5
Quebec	7.4	228.5	30.9
Ontario	11.8	440.0	37.2
Manitoba	1.1	35.0	31.8
Saskatchewan	1.0	33.0	33.0
Alberta	3.0	120.0	40.0
British Columbia	4.0	130.0	32.0
Yukon	0.3	1.1	34.2
Northwest Territories (pre-Nunavut)	0.4	29.0	22.5
Nunavut	0.2	0.9	20.0

Source: Adapted from Statistics Canada, CANSIM II database <http://cansima.statcan.ca/cgi-win/CNSMCGI.EXE>, Table 384-0002.

This table illustrates the wide disparity in average incomes between provinces, from a low of $24 300 per person in Prince Edward Island to a high of $40 000 in Alberta.

In most years, the economy grows and the GDP figure rises. To accurately compare growth in GDP, however, we need to use a common set of prices so that a simple rise in prices isn't confused with an actual increase in the output of goods and services. Using *real* GDP figures, which correct for any inflation, accomplishes this. **Table T.3** looks at some recent real GDP figures, using 1997 prices.

TABLE T.3

Year	Real GDP ($ billion)	Increase ($ billion)	% Increase
1997	885	—	—
1998	920	35	4.0
1999	966	46	5.0
2000	1009	43	4.5
2001	1024	15	1.5

Source: Adapted from Statistics Canada, CANSIM II database <http://cansima.statcan.ca/cgi-win/CNSMCGI.EXE>, Table 380-0002.

Next, let's look at a breakdown of Canada's GDP by industry in **Figure T.1**.

FIGURE T.1 Canada's GDP at Factor Costs, 2001

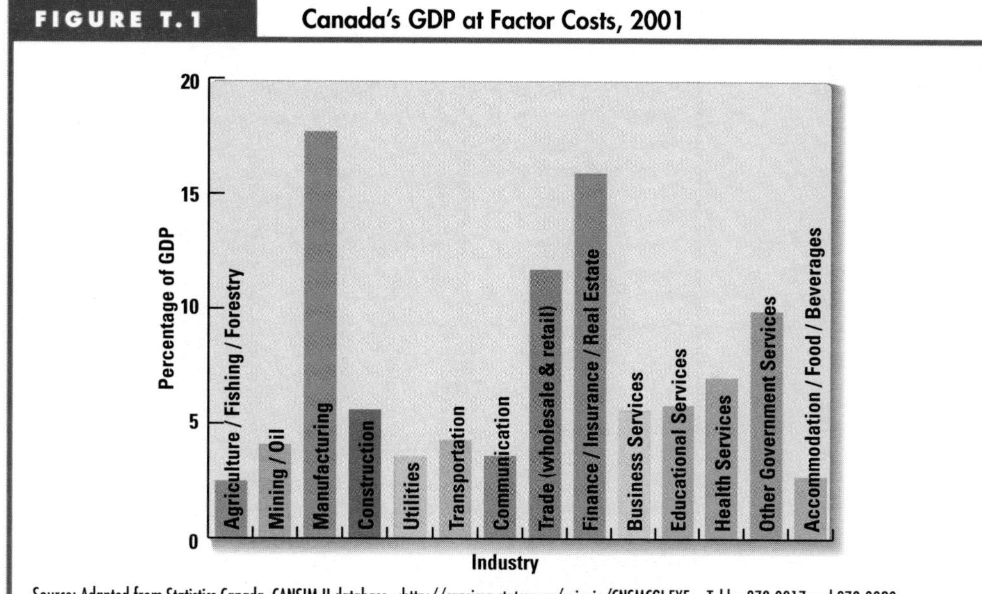

Source: Adapted from Statistics Canada, CANSIM II database <http://cansima.statcan.ca/cgi-win/CNSMCGI.EXE>, Tables 379-0017 and 379-0020.

This information is helpful in many ways. For example, it is certainly time to put to rest the idea that Canada is a resource-based economy and that Canadians are simply "hewers of wood and drawers of water," as many of us were taught in school. In fact, agriculture/fishing/forestry and mining/oil make up less than 7 percent of our economy's GDP. Another figure that makes the same point is that only 5 percent of working Canadians are employed in primary industries, down dramatically from 13 percent a quarter of a century ago.

In contrast, one can marshal an argument that Canada is a quite sophisticated and technologically advanced economy. For example, it is not generally recognized that Canada was the world's third nation to go into space, with the Alouette I satellite in 1962. Canadian industries pioneered long-distance pipeline technology, and Canada is a world leader in several areas of aviation, including turboprop, turbofan, and firefighting aircraft, not to mention the well-known Canadarm used on space shuttles. Canada is also a world leader in commercial submarine technology, and routinely maintains one of the world's longest and most efficient railway systems. One can also point to many outstanding Canadian companies that are truly world leaders in technology and performance, including Bombardier in transportation equipment, Ballard Power in fuel cell technology, SNC Lavalin in aluminum plant design, Nortel in cellular communications, Trizec Hahn in real estate development, and Magna International in automobile parts manufacturing.

Exports: The Engine that Drives the Economy

Exports are a fundamental part of the Canadian economy. Over 40 percent of its GDP is exported, which makes Canada one of the world's greatest trading nations. Exports to the United States alone directly support over 1.5 million Canadian jobs, and a $1 billion increase in exports translates into 11 000 new jobs. Again, contrary to historical wisdom, only 20 percent of Canadian exports are resources—the figure was 40 percent a quarter of a century ago.

Figure T.2 breaks down the $467 billion of Canadian exports in 2001 into nine categories.

FIGURE T.2 Canada's Exports by Category, 2001

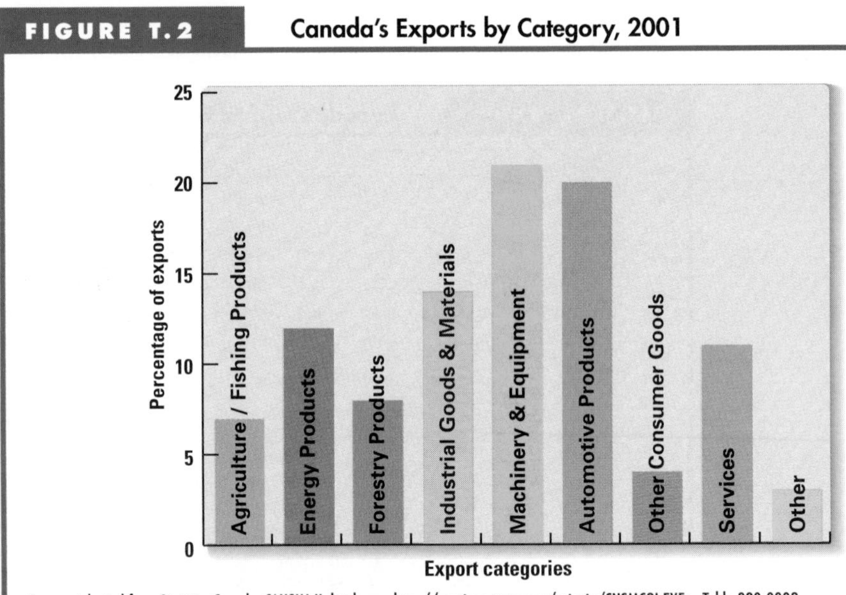

Source: Adapted from Statistics Canada, CANSIM II database <http://cansima.statcan.ca/cgi-win/CNSMCGI.EXE>, Table 380-0002.

A Mixed Economy

As we enter the twenty-first century, the market system dominates most of the world's economies, and Canada is no exception to this. Yet, government also plays a big role in our economy. For example, in the fiscal year 2000–2001, the three levels of government collected $437 billion in tax revenue, which represents over 42 percent of Canada's 2001 GDP. **Figure T.3** shows the sources of this revenue.

FIGURE T.3 Tax Revenue for All Canadian Governments, 2001

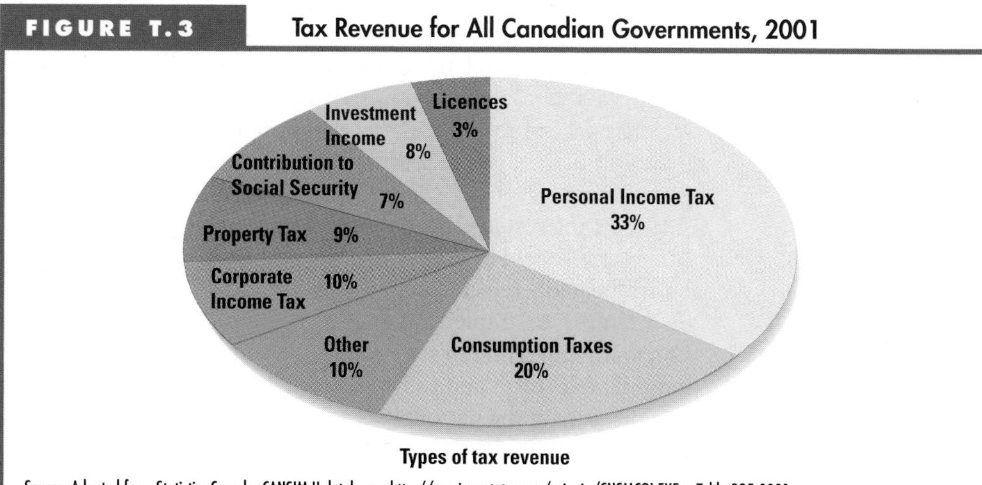

Source: Adapted from Statistics Canada, CANSIM II database <http://cansima.statcan.ca/cgi-win/CNSMCGI.EXE>, Table 385-0001.

The largest single source of the government's tax revenue, 33 percent, was personal income taxes. Consumption taxes include, most significantly, the GST (goods and services tax) and the PST (provincial sales tax) as well as gasoline, alcohol, and tobacco taxes, customs taxes, and gaming income. These indirect taxes accounted for 20 percent of total revenue. Thus we can see that the majority of the government's tax revenue comes from individual Canadians in the form of direct income taxes or consumption taxes.

And how does government spend these billions of dollars of tax revenue? **Figure T.4** shows us.

FIGURE T.4 Expenditures by All Canadian Governments, 2001

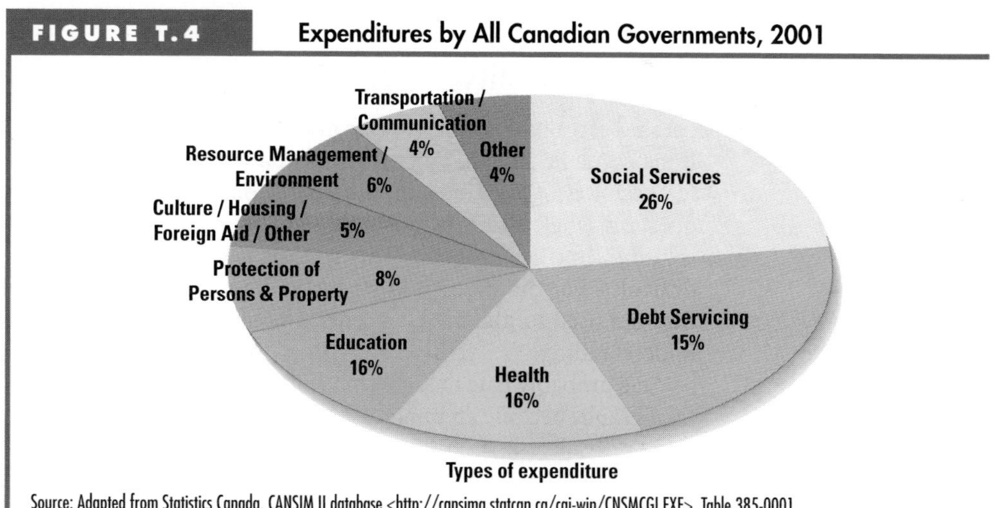

Source: Adapted from Statistics Canada, CANSIM II database <http://cansima.statcan.ca/cgi-win/CNSMCGI.EXE>, Table 385-0001.

Here we see that government's largest single category, which is 26 percent of spending, was on payments to individuals. The lion's share of this expenditure, (approximately two-thirds), was social assistance (welfare) payments. Thus we see that a large percentage of spending by government is an attempt to direct income to poorer Canadians. Since it is all Canadians who pay for most of these expenditures, we can see that the government is actively involved in *transferring* income from higher-income to lower-income families and individuals. This income distribution role is seen by many Canadians as an important function of government.

On the other hand, some Canadians take the view that government has gone too far in its interventionist role and yearn for less government involvement in the economy. They often point to the United States as an example of a economy in which both welfare, unemployment, and pension payments to individuals and direct government aid to poor regions of the country are lower. The difference in the general approach of the two governments may well lie in historical differences in the attitudes of Canadians and Americans toward government. Over the years, Canadians, by and large, have trusted governments to act in their best interest and been more tolerant of government attempts at income redistribution. Americans, on the other hand, have a history of being suspicious of big government and have repeatedly rejected attempts to expand its role. The recent rejection in the United States of attempts to implement a national health-care policy is an example. Another is the Canadian government's direct aid to cultural endeavours, including the funding of a national television and radio network, while no such efforts exist in the United States.

Interest on the national debt was the second-largest category of spending, at 20 percent. Over the years, government has borrowed about $550 billion to finance budget deficits, and the interest paid on this borrowing totalled $41 billion in 2001. Most Canadians believe that expenditures on health (the universal medical plan) and education make up government's largest spending categories. Though these two are large, so too are debt financing and expenditures on social services. The fifth category, protection of persons and property, includes expenditures on police, fire departments, the court system, and prisons. The sixth category includes a host of items such as culture (the Canada Council), housing, foreign affairs, immigration, labour, and research.

This completes our brief look at the Canadian economic reality. We hope that it has helped to fill in some gaps in your knowledge of the country. We are confident that you will come to know your country much better after a thorough grounding in the principles of economics, for, in a very real sense, economics is about understanding and improving on what we already know.

Graphing Reality

Let's face it: a lot of students hate graphs. For them a picture is not worth a thousand words. It may even be true that they seem to understand some economic concepts just fine until the instructor draws a graph on the board. All of a sudden, they lose confidence and start to question what they previously thought they knew. For these students, graphs are not the solution, but the problem. This section is designed to help those students overcome this difficulty. For those other, more fortunate, students who can handle graphs and know that they are used to illustrate concepts, a quick reading of this section will help reinforce their understanding.

It's probably true to say that if an idea can be expressed clearly and precisely with words, then graphs become an unnecessary luxury. The trouble is that from time to time, economists find themselves at a loss for words and see no way of getting a certain point across except with the use of a graph. On the other hand, by themselves, graphs cannot explain everything; they need to be accompanied by a verbal explanation. In other words, graphs are not a substitute for words, but a complement. The words accompanied by a picture can often give us a much richer understanding of economic concepts and happenings.

Graphing a Single Variable

The graphing of a single variable is reasonably straightforward. Often economists want to concentrate on a single economic variable, such as Canada's exports, or consumers' incomes, or the production of wine in Canada. In some cases they want to look at the composition of that variable, say, different categories of exports. In other cases they are interested in seeing how one variable changed over a period of time, say total exports for each of the years 1992 through 2002. In the first instance, we would be looking at a *cross-section*; in the second instance we are looking at a *time series*.

Cross-Sectional Graphs

One popular way of showing cross-sectional data is in the form of a **pie chart.** Figure T.5, for instance, shows the composition of Canada's exports for 2001 in terms of the type of goods or services that Canada sells abroad.

FIGURE T.5A Composition of Canadian Exports, 2001

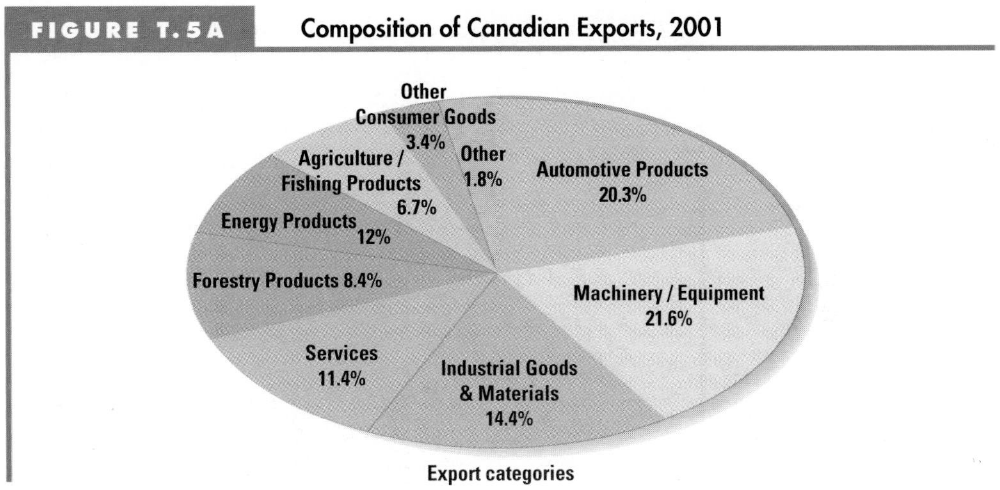

The size of each slice indicates the relative size of each category of exports. But the picture by itself is not always enough. We have added the percentage of total exports that each type represents. Notice, however, that there are no dollar amounts for the categories.

Alternatively, the same information could be presented in the form of a **bar graph**, as in Figure T.5B.

FIGURE T.5B Composition of Canadian Exports, 2001

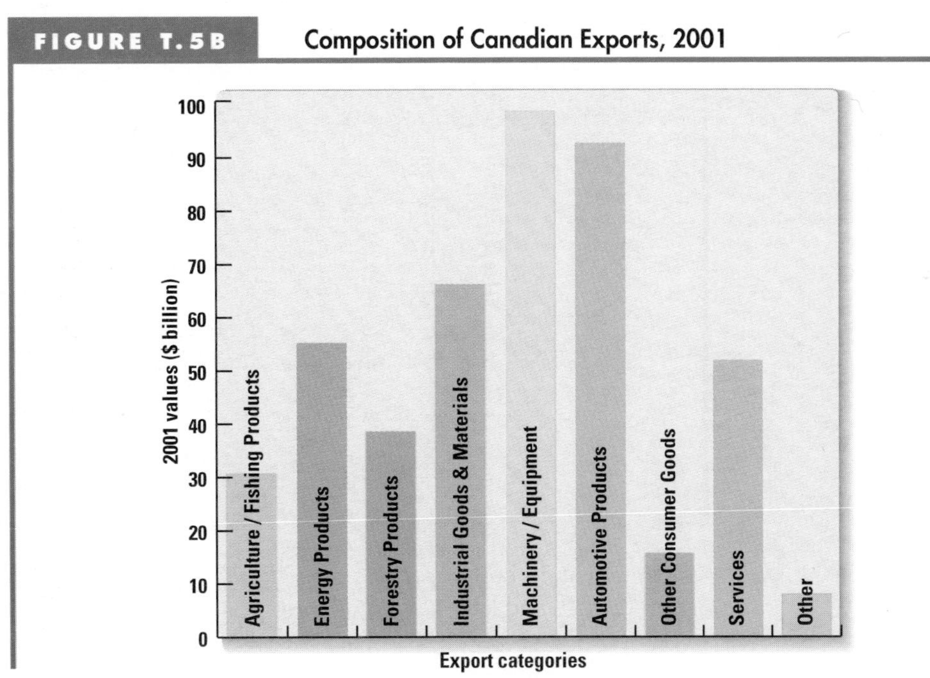

Looking at the bar graph, you'll notice that it's possible to estimate the dollar amounts, but it would be difficult to know the percentage share of the category without a lot of tedious calculations.

Time-Series Graphs

Time-series data can also be presented in the form of a bar graph. **Figure T.6A** shows a bar graph of how the dollar amount of Canada's total exports of goods (ignoring its composition) has changed over a five-year period.

FIGURE T.6A Total Canadian Exports of Goods, 1997–2001

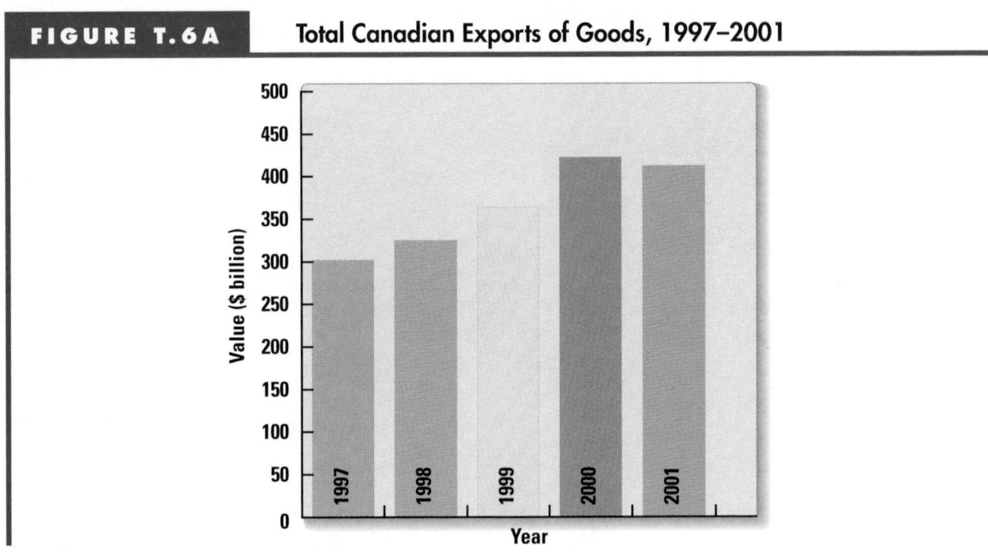

The same information can be presented in a **line graph**, as is done in **Figure T.6B**.

FIGURE T.6B Total Canadian Exports of Goods, 1997–2001

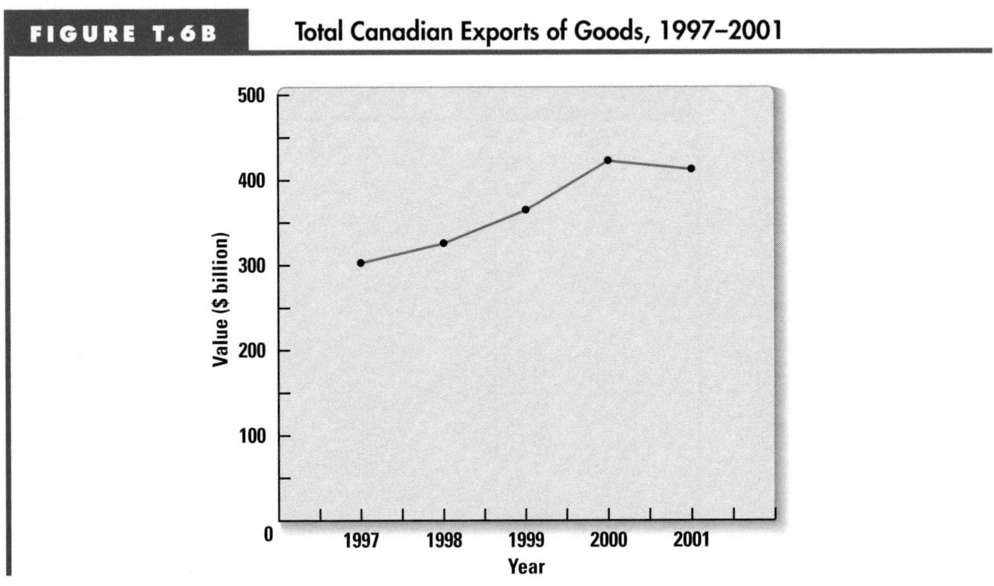

Note that, in both cases, the years (time) are shown on the horizontal axis; early years are on the left, and later years on the right. This is because graphs are always read from left to right.

Graphing Two Variables

Things get a little trickier when we want to deal with two variables at the same time. For instance, suppose we want to relate Canada's disposable income, which is the total take-home pay of all Canadians, and the amount spent on consumer goods (these numbers are in billions and are hypothetical). One obvious way to do this is with a table, as is done in **Table T.4**.

TABLE T.4

Year	Disposable Income	Spending on Consumer Goods
1	$100	$80
2	120	98
3	150	125
4	160	134
5	200	170

A time-series graph, using the same data, is presented in **Figure T.7**. You can see that the two lines in **Figure T.7** seem to be closely related, and that is useful information. However, to more clearly bring out the relationship we could plot them against one another. But if you look again at **Table T.4**, you will see that there are really three different variables involved: the time (five years), the values of disposable income, and the values of spending. However, it is very difficult to plot three variables, all three against each other, on a two-dimensional sheet of paper.

FIGURE T.7 Disposable Income and Spending on Consumer Goods (hypothetical numbers)

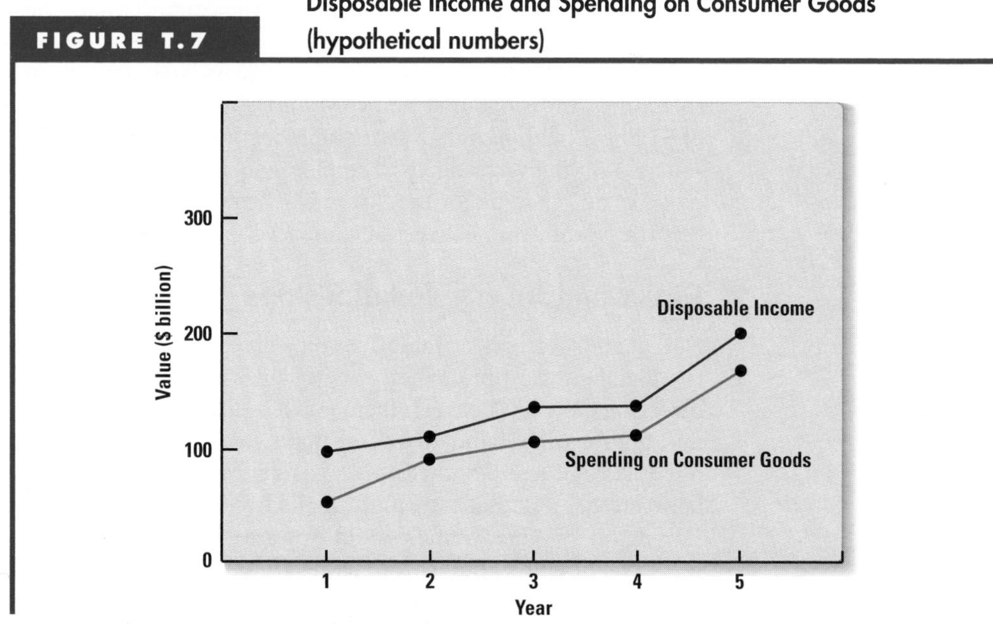

Instead, in **Figure T.8**, we will put disposable income on the horizontal axis (also called the X-axis), and consumer spending on the vertical axis (also called the Y-axis) and indicate time with written notation. There is a rule about which variable goes on which axis, but we will leave that for later chapters.

Next, we need to decide on a scale for each of the two axes. There is no particular rule about doing this, but just a little experience will enable you to develop good judgement about selecting these values. We have chosen to give each square on the axes the value of $20. This can be seen in **Figure T.8**.

FIGURE T.8 Spending on Consumer Goods

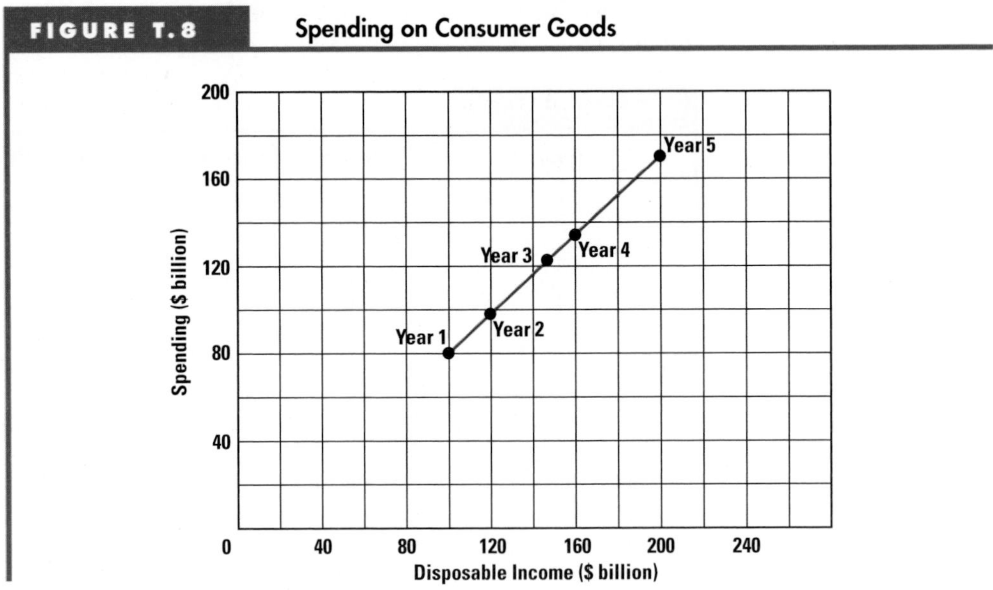

We started plotting our line using Year data. In Year 1, disposable income was $100 and consumer spending was $80. Starting at the origin (where the vertical and horizontal axes meet), which has an assigned value of zero, we move five squares to the right. Now from an income of $100, we move up vertically four squares, arriving at a value of $80 for consumer spending. This is our first plot (or point). We do the same for Year 2. First, we find a value of $120 on the horizontal (disposable income) axis and a value of $98 (just less than five squares) on the vertical axis. The place where these two meet gives us our second point to plot. We do the same for the three next years, and join up the five points with a line. Notice that the relationship between income levels and consumer spending plots as a straight line.

Direct and Inverse Relationships

Next, if you look back at **Table T.4**, you will see that disposable income and consumer spending rise together over time. When two variables move together in this way, we say that there is a **direct** relationship between them. Such a direct relationship appears as an upward-sloping line. On the other hand, if you see that two variables move in opposite directions, so that as one variable increases, the other variable decreases, we say there is an **inverse** relationship between them. In that case, plotting the two variables together would result in a downward-sloping line. (When we talk about upward-sloping and downward-sloping, remember that we are reading the graphs from left to right.)

One last point: the income–consumer-spending line in **Figure T.8** is a straight line. There is no reason that this has to always be the case. Some data might plot as a straight line, and other data might be non-linear when plotted (as in **Figure T.7**). Either, of course, could still be downward- or upward-sloping.

Measuring the Slope of a Straight Line

As you proceed with this course, you will find that you need to go a bit further than merely being able to plot a curve—in economics, by the way, all lines are described as curves, whether they are linear or non-linear. You will also need to know just how steep or how shallow the line is that you have plotted. That is, you will need to measure the slope of the curve. What the slope shows, in effect, is how much one variable changes in relation to the other variable as we move along a curve. In graphic terms, this means measuring the change in the variable shown on the vertical axis (known as the **rise**), divided by the change in the variable shown on the horizontal axis (known as the **run**). The rise and the run are illustrated, using our disposable income/consumer spending example, in **Figure T.9**.

FIGURE T.9 Rise Over Run

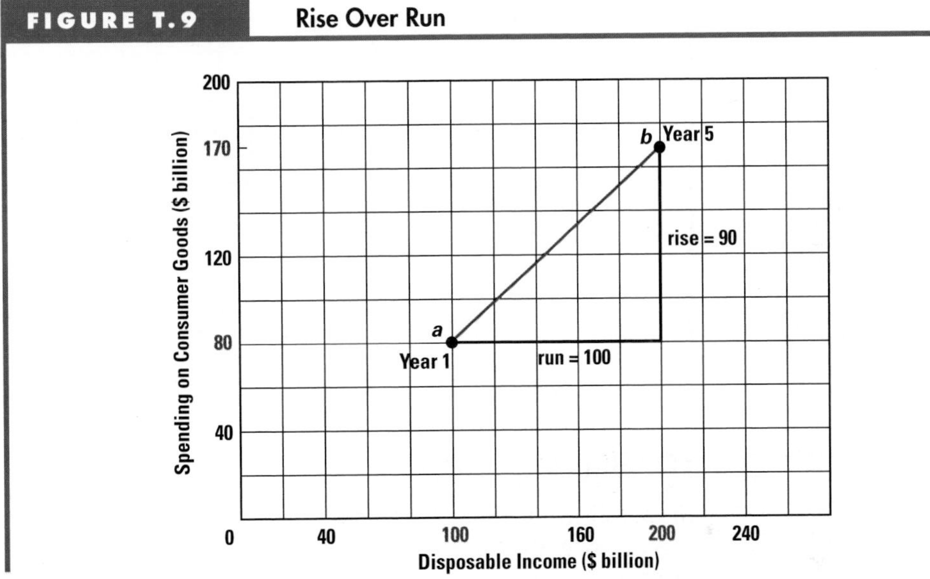

Notice that as we move from point a to point b, consumer spending increases by 90 (from 80 to 170). This is the amount of the rise. Looking along the horizontal axis, we see that disposable income increases by 100 (from 100 to 200). This is the amount of the run. In general, we can say:

$$\text{Slope} = \frac{\text{Rise}}{\text{Run}} = \frac{\text{Change in the value on the vertical axis}}{\text{Change in the value on the horizontal axis}}$$

Specifically, the slope of our line is therefore equal to:

$$\frac{+90}{+100} = +0.9$$

Figure T.10 shows four other curves, two upward-sloping and two downward-sloping, with an indication for each as to how to calculate the various slopes. In each case we measure the slope by moving from point a to point b.

FIGURE T.10 Four Different Slopes

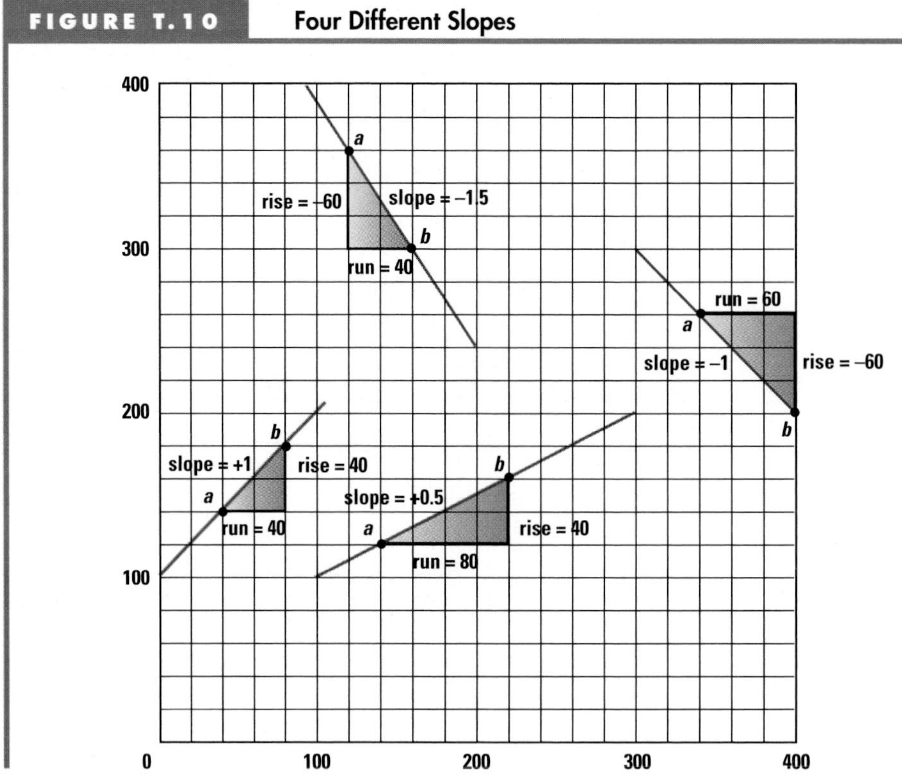

The Slopes of Curves

In measuring the slope of a straight line, it doesn't really matter where on the line we choose to measure it; the slope is constant throughout its length. But this is not true of a curve. The slope of a curve will have different values at every point along its length. However, it is possible to measure the slope at any point by drawing a straight line that touches the curve at that point. Such a line is called a tangent to the curve. **Figure T.11**, for instance, shows a curve that, at various points, has a positive slope (the upward-sloping portion), a zero slope (the top of the curve), and a negative slope (the downward-sloping portion). We have drawn in three tangents at different positions along the curve. From these straight-line tangents we can calculate the value of the slope at each of these points.

FIGURE T.11 The Slope of a Curve

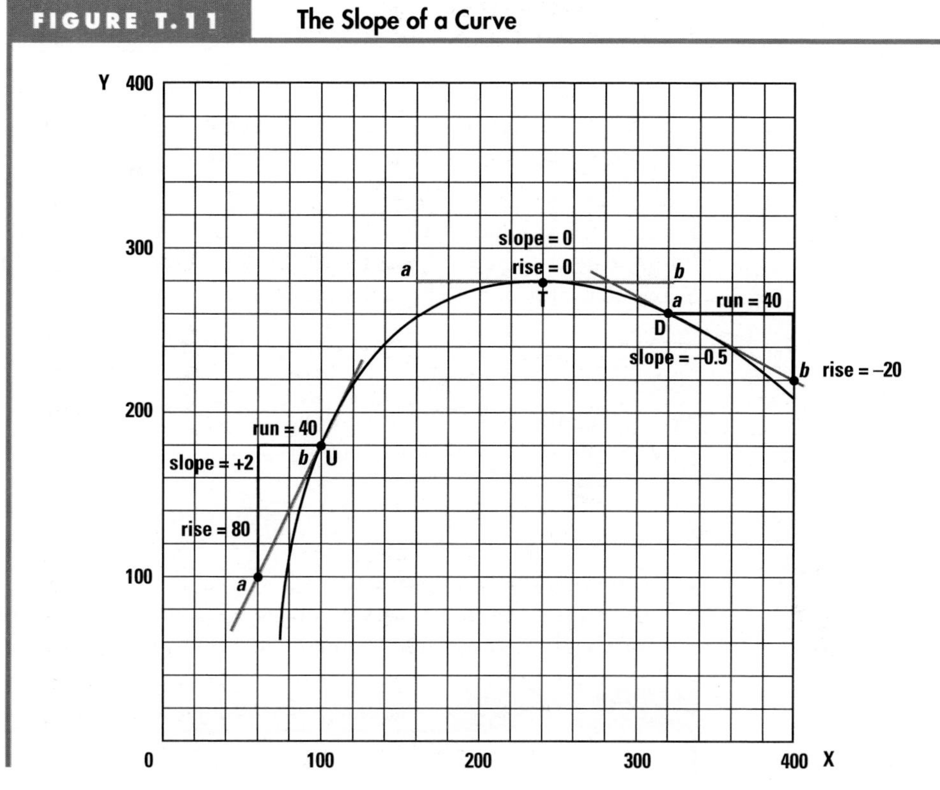

At point U, the curve is rising quite steeply. So what is its slope? Well, its slope at this point is the same as the value of the slope of the straight-line tangent. As we already know:

The slope of the straight line is: $\frac{\text{Rise}}{\text{Run}}$

At point U, this is equal to: $\frac{+80}{+40} = +2$

This is also the value of the slope of the curve at point U.

At point T, the tangent is a horizontal line, which, by definition, does not rise or fall. The rise/run at this point, therefore, is equal to 0. Finally, at point D, both the curve and the tangent are downward-sloping, indicating a negative slope. Its value is calculated, as before, as rise/run, which equals –20/40 or –0.5.

Equations for a Straight Line

In economics, graphs are a very important and useful way to present information. Thus you will find the pages of most economics books liberally sprinkled with graphs. But there are other, equally useful, ways of presenting the same data. One way is in the form of an algebraic equation. You will often find it very useful to be able to translate a graph into algebra. In this short section we will show you how to do this. Just to keep things simple, we will restrict our attention to straight-line graphs.

In order to find the equation for any straight line, you need only two pieces of information: the slope of the line and the value of the Y-intercept. You already know how to calculate the value of the slope. The value of the Y-intercept is simply the value at which the line crosses the vertical axis. In general, the algebraic expression for a straight line is given as:

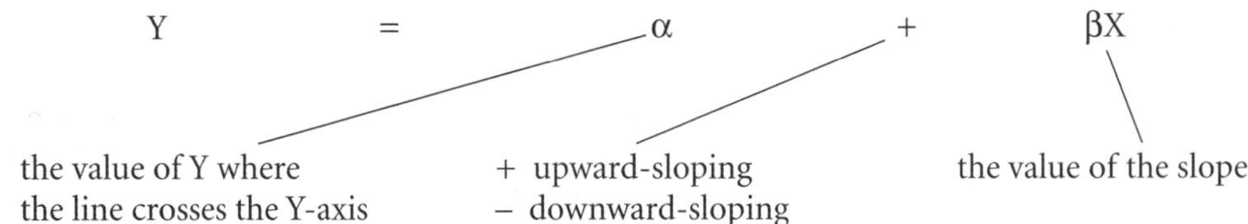

For instance, in **Figure T.12**, line 1 has a slope of +1 (the line is upward-sloping and therefore has a positive slope and rises by 10 units for every run of 10 units). The line crosses the Y-axis at a value of 50. The equation for line 1, therefore, is:

$$Y = 50 + (1)X$$

Armed with this equation, we could figure out the value of Y for any value of X. For example, when X (along the horizontal axis) has a value of 40, Y must be equal to:

$$Y = 50 + 40 = 90$$

You can verify this in **Figure T.12**.

In addition, we can work out values of X and Y that are not shown on the graph. For example, when X equals 200, Y equals: $50 + 200 = 250$.

FIGURE T.12 **Equations for Straight Lines**

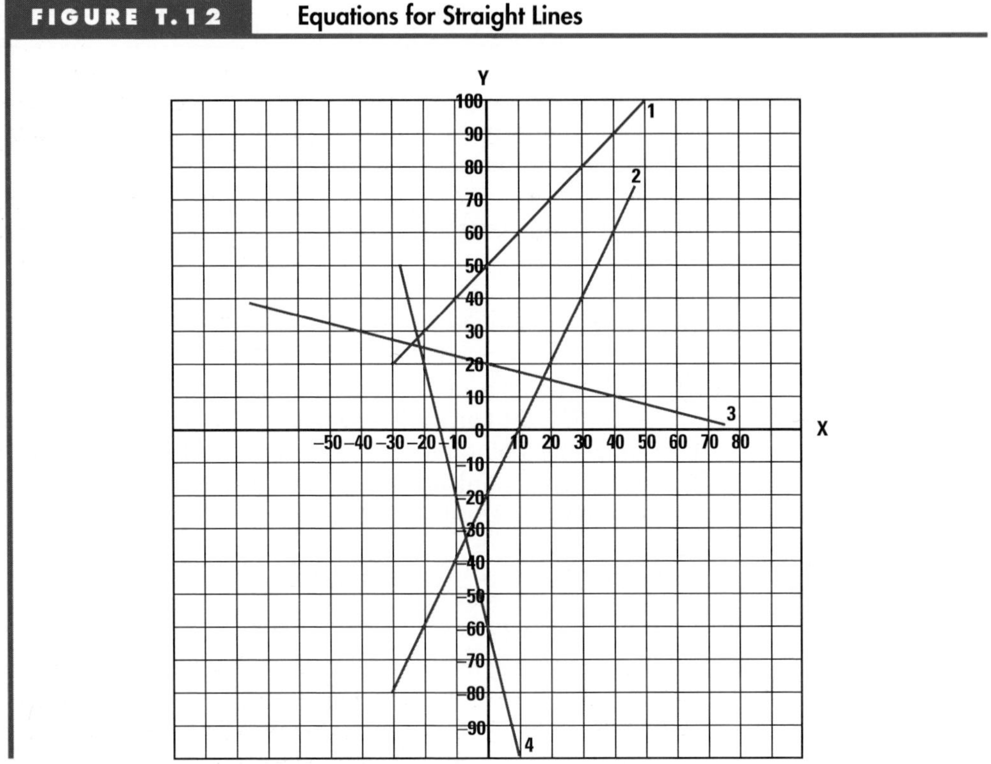

Let us work out the equations for the other lines shown in **Figure T.12**. Line 2 is also upward-sloping, but it is steeper than line 1 and has a slope of +2 (it rises by 20 for every run of 10). Its intercept, however, is in the negative area of the Y-axis and crosses at the value of –20. The equation for line 2 then is:

$$Y = -20 + 2X$$

Again, you can check that this is correct by putting in a value for X, finding the corresponding value of Y, and looking on the graph to see if it is correct. For instance, when X has a value of 40, the equation tells us that:

$$Y = -20 + 2(40) = 60$$

You can confirm in **Figure T.12** that this is indeed the case.

In contrast, line 3 has a negative slope of 0.25 and a Y-intercept at 20. Its equation therefore is:

$$Y = 20 - 0.25X$$

Finally, line 4 has the equation:

$$Y = -60 - 4X$$

Graphs and Logic

Now let's look at some potential problems in illustrating data with graphs. For example, the relationship between income and consumer spending in the earlier **Table T.4** is hypothetical, since we created it to plot well on a graph. However, any real-world relationship between two variables may not be as neat and simple. Data doesn't always plot into a nice straight line. Even more seriously, we can never be totally certain of the *nature* of the relationship between the variables being graphed. There's often a great danger of implying something that's not there. You need, therefore, to be on guard against a number of logical fallacies. Suppose, for instance, that you were doing a survey of women's clothing stores across the country. Reviewing the data you have collected, you notice that there seems to be a close relationship between two particular sets of numbers: the rent paid by the owners of the store and the average price of wool jackets sold. The data is shown in **Table T.5**.

TABLE T.5

Monthly Rent (per 100 m^2)	Average Jacket Price
$1500	$80
1600	90
1700	100
1800	110
1900	120
2000	130

The higher the monthly rent, the higher the price of jackets charged in that store. It seems clear, therefore, that the higher rent is the *cause* of the higher price, and the higher price is the *effect* of the higher rent. After all, the store owner must recoup these higher rent costs by charging her customers a higher price. If you think this, then you are guilty of the logical fallacy of **reverse causality**. As you will learn in economics, although the rent of premises and product prices are indeed related, the causality is the other way around. This is because stores in certain areas can charge higher product prices because of their trendy location, and landlords charge those stores higher rents for the same reason—it is a desirable location. Higher prices, therefore, are the *cause*, and high rents the *effect*. This is not obvious, and illustrates how using raw economic data without sound economic theory can lead to serious error.

A second logical fallacy is that of the **omitted variable**, which can also lead to confusion over cause and effect. **Table T.6** highlights this error. Here we see hypothetical data on rates of alcoholism and on annual income levels of individuals:

TABLE T.6

Average Income Levels ($)	Alcoholism (per thousand of population)
5 000	40
15 000	35
25 000	30
35 000	25
45 000	20
55 000	15

There certainly seems to be a very close relationship between these two variables. Presented in this form, without any commentary, one is left to wonder if low income causes alcoholism or if alcoholism is the cause of low income. Some people with low incomes may drink in order to try to escape the effects of poverty. Or is it that people who drink to excess have great difficulty in finding or keeping a good job? In truth, it is possible that neither of these views is true. Simply because two sets of data seem closely related doesn't necessarily imply that one is the cause of the other. In fact, it may well be the case that both are effects of an omitted variable. In the above example, it is possible, for instance, that both high alcoholism and low income levels are the result of low educational attainment.

A third fallacy can occur when people see a cause and effect relationship that doesn't really exist. This is known as the fallacy of **post hoc, ergo propter hoc**, which literally means *after this, therefore because of this*. That is to say, it is a fallacy to believe that just because one thing follows another, the one is the result of the other. For example, just because my favourite soccer team always loses whenever I go to see them, that doesn't mean I am the cause of their losing!

There is a final fallacy you should guard against, a fallacy, unfortunately, that even the best of economists commit from time to time. This is the **fallacy of composition**, which is the belief that because something is true for the part, it is true for the whole. You may have noticed, for instance, that fights occasionally break out in hockey games. These fights often occur in the corners, which makes them difficult to see. The best way for the individual to get a better view is by standing, and of course when everybody stands, then most people cannot see. Thus, what is true for a single fan—standing up to see better—is not true for the whole crowd. Similarly, a teacher who suggests that in order to get a good grade, a student should sit at the front of the class is also guilty of the same kind of logical fallacy!

We hope that this little primer on Canada and on graphing has been helpful. It is now time to move on to the study of economics.

STUDY GUIDE

Answered Questions

Indicate whether the following statements are true or false.

1. **T or F** Canada is the world's largest country in area and has 1 percent of the world's population.

2. **T or F** Ontario has the largest provincial economy and the largest provincial population; and it is Canada's largest province in area.

3. **T or F** Over 50 percent of Canada's exports are resources.

4. **T or F** The largest single source of government tax revenue is personal income taxes.

5. **T or F** Spending on social services is the largest category of spending by (all) governments in Canada.

SIMPLE CALCULATIONS

6. The following data shows the results of market research done on the latest Guns' n' Butter CD. The numbers indicate the total quantity of CDs that fans would purchase at the various prices.

TABLE T.7

Price per CD ($s)	Quantity (hundreds of thousands)
$20	20
19	30
18	40
17	50
16	60
15	70
14	80

   a) Graph the table (using a piece of graph paper) with the price on the vertical (y) axis and the quantity on the horizontal (x) axis.
   b) What is the slope of the line?
   c) What is the value of the Y-intercept?
   d) What is the equation for this line?

7. What are the values of the slopes of the four lines shown in **Figure T.13**?

8. What are the equations that correspond to the four lines shown in **Figure T.14**?

9. Graph the following equations, using the same scale for each axis:
   a) $Y = 5X$
   b) $Y = 20 + 2X$
   c) $Y = 30 - 3X$
   d) $Y = -10 + 4X$

FIGURE T.13

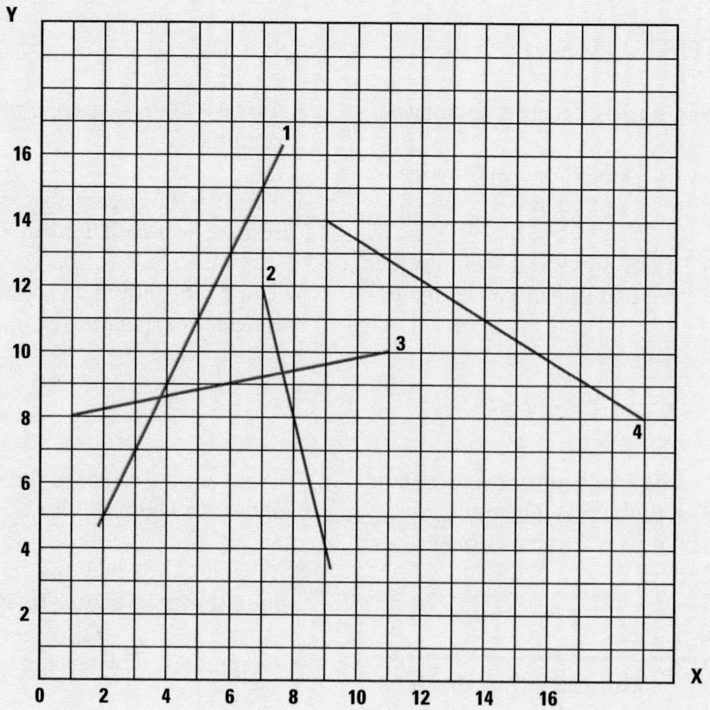

FIGURE T.14

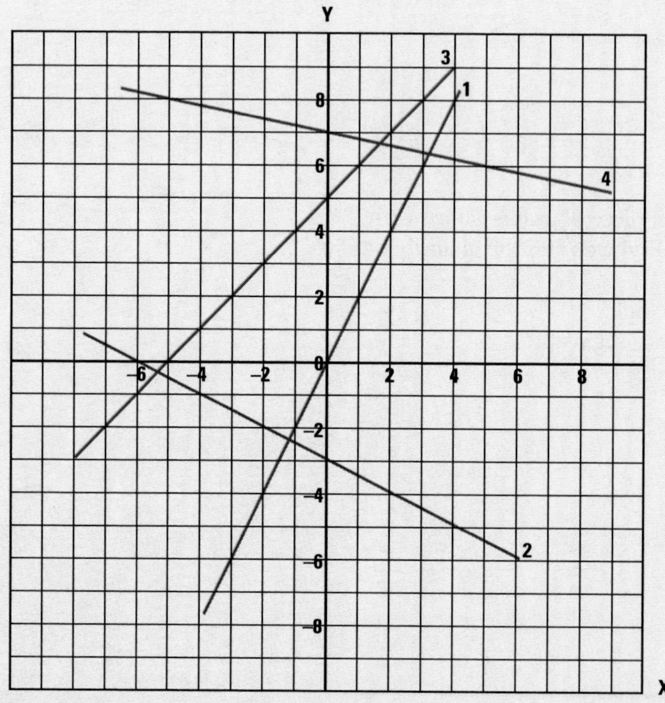

CHAPTER ONE

The Economic Problem

LEARNING OBJECTIVES

This chapter will enable you to:

LO1 **Realize that scarcity, choice, and cost are at the heart of economics.**

LO2 **Explain the three fundamental questions that all societies must address and understand the four major types of economies.**

LO3 **Discuss whether economics is an art or a science.**

LO4 **Understand the circular flow of income diagram.**

LO5 **Use the production possibilities model to illustrate opportunity costs, efficiency, and unemployment.**

LO6 **Define economics and understand why it is controversial but of great relevance.**

LO7 **List the economic goals of society and understand why they are often difficult to achieve.**

What's ahead...

In this first chapter we introduce you to the study of economics and hope to arouse your curiousity about this fascinating discipline. We will define economics, examine three fundamental economic questions, discuss the methodology and language of economics, and make the distinction between macro- and microeconomics. Next, we look at the production possibilities for a nation and, finally, focus on macroeconomics by discussing seven important macroeconomic goals and offering an overview of some important economic disputes.

A QUESTION OF RELEVANCE...

Jon and Ashok are both avid soccer fans and play for local teams. They both like old movies, chess, and *Star Trek*. They are both seventeen years of age, neither has a steady girlfriend, and both are vegetarians. The other thing they have in common is that their fathers are in banking. Jon's father is the executive vice-president of customer relations for the Royal Bank in Toronto. Ashok's father is a night janitor at a branch of the Bank of India in the dock area of Bombay. All of these points are relevant in forming a mental picture of a person, but you will probably agree that a person's economic circumstances are the most relevant of all. In truth, economics is one of the most relevant subjects you will study.

What might you expect from a course in economics? Well, it probably will not help you balance your chequebook and may not be directly helpful in your choice of the right stock to buy. But the study of economics will give you a broad understanding of how a modern market economy operates and what relationships are important within it. If you see yourself as a budding businessperson, the study of economics can offer some general insights that will be helpful. Yet you will not find specific tools or instructions here. Economics is an academic discipline, not a self-help or how-to course. The common conception that economics is about money is only partly true. We study money, but more in the sense of what it is and the effects of different central-bank money policies than in the sense of how to make it. The study of economics may not help you to function better in the world in any specific sense, but it will help you to understand better how the world functions.

1.1 Scarcity, Choice, and Opportunity Cost

LO1
Realize that scarcity, choice, and cost are at the heart of economics.

Economists put a great deal of emphasis on scarcity and the need to economize. Individual households face income limitations and therefore must allocate income among alternative uses. Most individuals also face a scarcity of time and must somehow decide where to spend time and where to conserve it. In the same sense, an economy as a whole has limited resources and must allocate those resources among competing uses.

Thus, economists see resources (the factors of production) as *scarce* in the sense that no economy has sufficient resources to be able to produce all the goods and services everyone wants. This is not to say that there aren't some people who would say that they have all that they want, but there are millions of people who possess a seemingly endless list of wants, and millions more like them waiting to be born. Since the economy cannot produce all that everyone wants, the resources available for production are scarce, and some kind of mechanism must be put into place to *choose* what will be produced and, by implication, what will not be produced. And this is why economics is sometimes called the *science of choice.*

In short:

In the face of people's unlimited wants and society's limited productive resources, choice becomes a forced necessity. Because of these choices, the decision to produce one thing means that some other thing will not be produced.

opportunity cost: the value of the next-best alternative that is given up as a result of making a particular choice.

This last point is so fundamental that economists have coined a special term to identify it: **opportunity cost**. For instance, suppose that the government is considering the purchase of 50 new helicopters with a price tag of $5 billion. In the conventional sense, that is their cost. However, economists would argue that it is more revealing to measure the cost of the helicopters in terms of the, say, 10 hospitals that won't be built because purchasing the helicopters was chosen. Opportunity costs can thus be defined as what must be given up as a result of making a particular choice; in this case, the hospitals instead of the helicopters. In addition we should recognize that the $5 billion could be spent on other things besides hospitals—say, schools, roads or mass-transit systems. At this point society would have to choose what it considers to be its *next-best* alternative: the hospitals, schools, roads, or mass transit. Understanding this concept allows us to make a formal definition of opportunity cost: the next-best alternative that is given up as a result of making a particular choice. Thus, the making of any decision always involves a trade off with the next-best alternative that is sacrificed.

Why is it better to think of costs in terms of opportunity cost rather than simply as money payments? Economists argue that using the concept of opportunity costs captures the true measure of any decision. If we use money payments as the measure, then we seemingly have unlimited means to produce goods, since governments can always print more money. But no matter what any government might wish, any society has only a limited amount of resources. When we realize this, we begin to realize that there is no such thing as a "free lunch"—any decision (to produce helicopters, for example) necessarily involves the use of scarce resources which could have alternatively been used to produce something else (hospitals). Recognizing that there are opportunity costs involved also forces us to rethink our idea of what we mean by "free." Simply because money does not change hands does not mean that a product is free. A free lunch is never free, because the provision of any meal involves the use of resources which could have been put to some other use.

The concept of opportunity cost can be applied not only at the level of the overall society, as we just saw, but also at the individual level. For the individual, the constraint is not the limited quantity of resources but, instead, a limited amount of income and time. For example, you could think of the cost of going to two movies on the weekend as the sacrifice of one new CD. If you want to think of both of these choices (two movies or one CD) as each costing about $16, that is fine. But thinking of the one as costing the other is often more effective. In general, your income will not allow you to have everything you may want, so you are forced to make choices about what you buy. And the cost of these choices can be measured in terms of what must be given up as a result of making the choice. We should also point out that there must be some benefit to be gained from the alternative that you do chose. Thus, if you chose the two movies, the benefit from that choice must in your view exceed (or at least equal) the opportunity cost of the CD. In the same sense, a society faces a similar set of choices imposed not by limited income but by a constraint on the quantity and quality of the factors of production available.

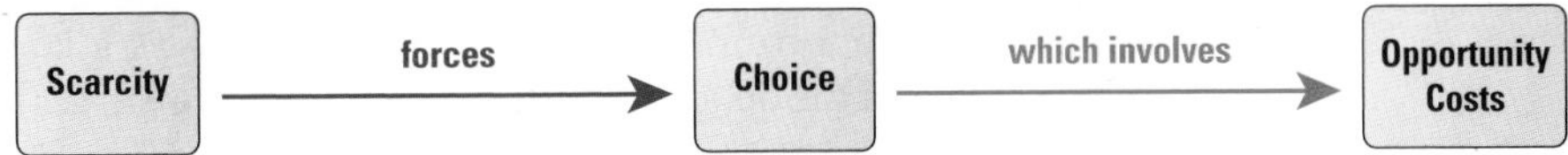

There is another aspect of choice that economists consider important: any society, much like an individual household, always has a choice between consumption now or consumption in the future. A household could choose to consume less now and save more, enabling it to consume more in the future. Societies that consume less now can use scarce productive resources to build more capital goods, such as machines and factories, with which to produce even more consumer goods and services *in the future*. We will return to this point later in this chapter.

Let us now look at the fact that in the last decade of the twentieth century it became clear that economies which use an economic system relying on individual choice and enterprise (for example, Canada, the United States, Japan, and Germany) continued to enjoy success while economies relying on centrally controlled systems (such as the former USSR, Poland, and Hungary) faltered.

Adam Smith, the father of economics, gave us a simple but elegant idea that goes a long way toward explaining why, throughout history, some economies have prospered while others have not. This is the recognition that *voluntary trade* always benefits both parties to the trade. If two peasants voluntarily trade a sack of rice for two bags of carrots, then we can assume that they both must feel that they have benefited, otherwise they would not have done it. If you buy a slice of pizza and a pop for lunch for $3.50, then we must assume that you feel you have gained by giving up the money and receiving the lunch—otherwise why did you do it? Likewise, the owner of the business that sold you the lunch must feel that she gained or she would not have been willing to offer the lunch for sale. There is a gain to both parties engaged in voluntary trade. It then follows that the more trade there is, the greater the overall benefits that accrue to those engaged in the trade. It comes as a surprise to many people that the same principle that applies to individuals in this regard also applies to nations. We can demonstrate that this is true by using the concept of opportunity costs to construct a simple example of two hypothetical countries—Athens and Sparta—each of which produces only two goods: bread (a consumer good) and plows (a capital good).

Suppose that the maximum quantities that can be produced of each product are (in thousands of units):

Athens	20 bread	or	10 plows
Sparta	10 bread	or	20 plows

If each country is self-sufficient (no trade between them) and each devotes half its resources to producing the two products, the output in each country would be:

Athens	10 bread	and	5 plows
Sparta	5 bread	and	10 plows

Clearly, the combined output of the two economies is 15 units of bread and 15 plows. It is also clear that Athens is far more productive at producing bread and Sparta is much better at producing plows. Thus, if the two countries could overcome their sense of rivalry, and if Athens concentrated on producing bread and Sparta on producing plows, then the total combined production of the two countries would be:

Athens	20 bread	(no plows)
Sparta	20 plows	(no bread)

With specialization and trade, the two countries can produce a combined total which is 5 more of each product (20 units of bread and 20 plows) than when each was self-sufficient. This is an illustration of why specialization is so important—countries enjoy more output when they do what they do best rather than trying to produce some of everything. For Athens, the opportunity cost of producing plows is a large sacrifice in bread production, while in Sparta the opportunity cost of producing bread is a large sacrifice in plow production. However, when they both specialize in what they do best, big benefits are gained.

This simple illustration helps us to understand that every economy faces important choices about what to produce. Let us expand on this point by turning to the three fundamental economic questions faced by every economy.

1.2 The Three Fundamental Questions of Economics and Four Types of Economies

LO2
Explain the three fundamental questions that all societies must address and understand the four major types of economies.

A broad perspective on the discipline of economics can be obtained by focusing on what can be called the three fundamental questions of economics: what, how, and for whom? That is, economics is about what and how much gets produced, how it is produced, and who gets it.

What to Produce?

As we have just seen, underlying the question of *what* should be produced is the reality of scarcity. Any society has only a fixed amount of resources at its disposal, and it must therefore have a system in place to make an endless number of decisions about production: from big decisions—like should the government buy more helicopters or build more hospitals?—down to more mundane decisions—like how many brands of breakfast cereal should be produced. If we decide to produce hospitals, should we produce ten without research facilities for the study of genetics, or eight without and one with such facilities? Should society exploit natural resources faster to create more jobs and more tax revenue, or slower to conserve these resources for the future? Should our resources be directed toward more preschool day-care facilities so that women are not so tied to the home? Or, instead, should those same

CP/Toronto Star

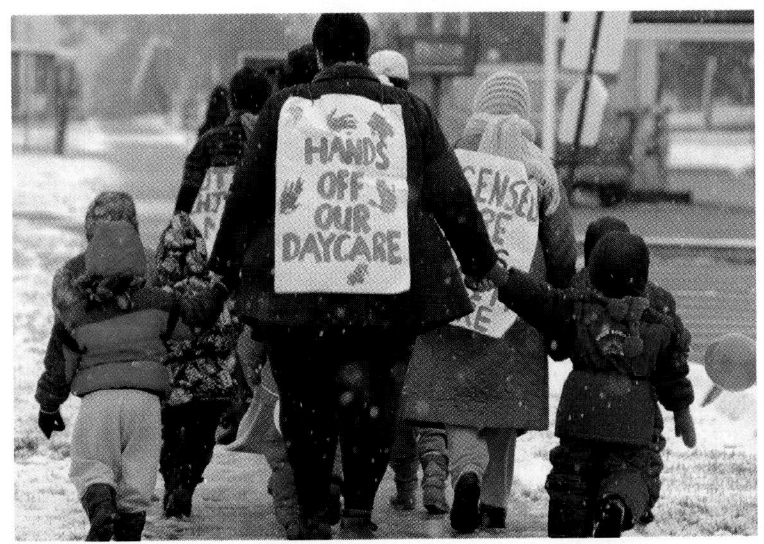

In this 1995 protest in Toronto, parents walked with children to protest day-care cuts proposed by the Ontario government.

resources be directed toward increasing the number of graduate students studying science and technology so that the Canadian economy can win the competitive international race in the twenty-first century?

No economist would claim to have the *right* answer to any of these questions. That is no more the role of an economist than it is of any other member of society. What the economist can do, however, is identify and measure both the benefits and the costs of any one answer—of any one choice.

How to Produce?

Let's move on to the second fundamental economic question that every society must somehow answer: what is the most appropriate technology to employ? We could reword this question by asking *how* we should produce what we choose to produce.

For example, there is a variety of ways to produce 10 kilometres of highway. At one extreme, a labour-intensive method of production could be used involving rock crushed with hammers, roadbed carved from the landscape with shovels, and material moved in wheelbarrows. The capital equipment used in this method is minimal. The labour used is enormous, and the time it will take is considerable. At the other extreme, a capital-intensive method could be used involving large earth-moving and tarmac-laying machines, surveying equipment, and relatively little but highly skilled labour. In between these two extremes is a large variety of capital–labour mixes that could also produce the new highway.

The answer to the question of how best to build the highway involves, among other things, knowing the costs of the various resources that might be used. Remember that technology means the way the various factors of production are combined to obtain output. The most appropriate technology for a society to use (the best way to combine resources) depends, in general, on the opportunity costs of these resources. Thus, in the example above, the best way to build a highway depends on the opportunity costs of labour and of capital as well as the productivity of each factor.

For Whom?

We are now ready to move to the third fundamental economic question that every society must somehow answer: *for whom*? Here we ask: how should the total output of any society's economy be shared among its people? Should it involve an equal share for all, or should it, perhaps, be based on people's needs? Alternatively, should it be based on the contribution of each member of society? If so, how should this contribution be measured—in numbers of hours, or in skill level, or in some other way? Further, how should we define what constitutes an important skill and which ones are less important?

Wrapped up in all this is the question of the ownership of resources and whether it is better that certain resources (like land and capital) be owned by society as a whole or by private individuals. In short, the *for whom* question (as well as the *what* and *how* questions) cannot be adequately addressed unless we look at the society's attitude toward the private ownership of resources and the question of who has the power to make crucial decisions.

You can see that in addressing the *for whom* question, other questions about the fairness of income distribution, incentives, and the ownership of resources all come into play. John Stuart Mill pointed out, nearly 150 years ago, that once an economy's goods are produced and the initial market distribution of income has occurred, society can intervene in any fashion it wishes to redistribute such income; that is, there are no laws of distribution other than the ones that society wants to impose. Whether this observation by Mill gives enough consideration to the incentive for productive effort remains an open question to this day.

The details of how these fundamental questions actually get answered depends, to a large extent, on the way that different societies organize themselves. Let's look now at the four types of economic organization.

ADDED DIMENSION

John Stuart Mill: Economist and Philosopher

John Stuart Mill (1806–73) is considered the last great economist of the classical school. His *Principles of Political Economy*, first published in England in 1848, was the leading textbook in economics for 40 years. Raised by a strict disciplinarian father (James), John Stuart began to learn Greek at the age of three, authored a history of Roman government by eleven, and studied calculus at twelve—but didn't take up economics until age thirteen. Not surprisingly, this unusual childhood later led to mental crisis. Mill credited his decision to put his analytical pursuits on hold and take up an appreciation of poetry as the primary reason for his recovery. He was a true humanitarian who held a great faith in human progress, had a love of liberty, and was an advocate of extended rights for women.

Types of Economies

Throughout history, humankind has coordinated its economies by using some blend of the four Cs: cooperation, custom, command, and competition. Thousands of years ago, members of small groups of hunter-gatherers undoubtedly relied on *cooperation* with one another in order to survive the dual threats of starvation and predators. They decided cooperatively what work needed to be done, how it was to be done, and who was to obtain what share of the produce. On the other hand, European feudal society in the Middle Ages was dominated by *custom*, which dictated who performed which task—sons followed the work of their fathers and daughters followed the roles of their mothers—and implied that traditional technology was superior to new ways of doing things. Also, serfs were required, by tradition, to share a portion of their produce with the feudal lord.

One need only think of an ancient civilization, such as Egypt 4000 years ago, as an example of how society answered the three fundamental questions by using *command*. There, most of the important economic questions were answered by the orders of those in power, such as the pharaohs and priests. In this century, command has been the prevailing coordinating mechanism in fascist and communist regimes, in which a central committee (or presidium) makes most of the fundamental economic decisions.

The fourth C, *competition*, is associated with market economies, such as we see in most of the industrialized countries around the globe today. Many people are surprised to learn how modern an invention this form of economic organization really is. Market economies did not begin to emerge until approximately *250 years ago*. That falls at about 11:59:45 on the "twelve-hour clock" of known human history, as illustrated in the following graphic:

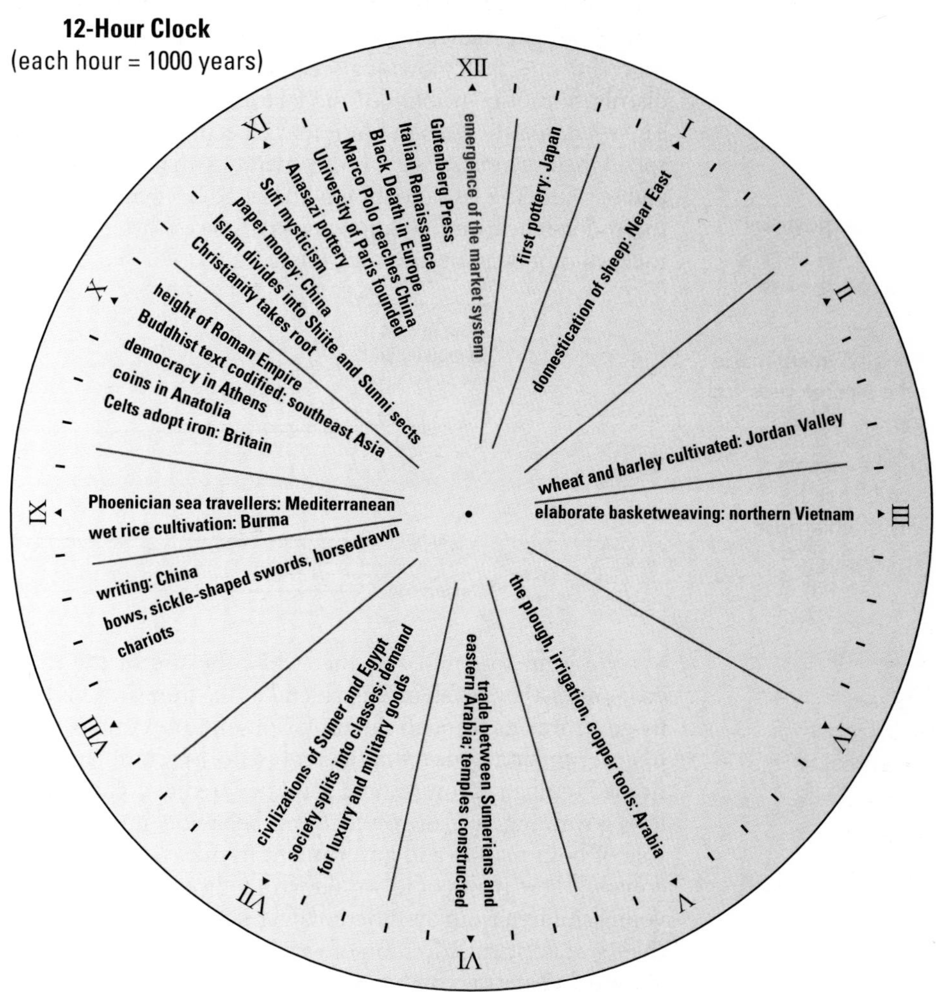

factors of production: the productive resources that are available to an economy, categorized as land, labour, capital, and enterprise.

land: any natural resource that can be used to produce goods and services.

labour: human physical and mental effort that can be used to produce goods and services.

To a large extent just what a market economy is and how it functions is the focus of any course (or textbook) in microeconomics. It is here that one looks at how supply and demand forces determine the prices of both consumer goods and resources, at the motivations of firms that produce these goods and the importance they place on the costs of production, at how the degree of competition shapes different industries, and at the important role of trade in the whole scheme of things. By the end of a course in microeconomics you will have a good feel for just what a market economy is, and how it plays a large part in determining what is produced, how it is produced, and who gets what share.

Perhaps one of the most significant characteristics of a market economy is found in the pattern of ownership and control of the economy's resources. The more formal term that economists use for resources is **factors of production** (or inputs) which are traditionally divided into four categories: land, labour, capital, and enterprise. **Land** is defined as anything natural, such as fertile soil, forestry, fisheries, or minerals in the ground. **Labour** refers to a broad spectrum of human effort, ranging from the work of a skilled naturopathic physician

capital: all human-made resources that can be used to produce goods and services.

enterprise: the human resource that innovates and takes risks.

wages: the payment made and the income received for the use of labour.

interest: the payment made and the income received for the use of capital.

rent: the payment made and the income received for the use of land.

profit: the income received from the activity of enterprise.

to that of a construction labourer. **Capital** is made up of the tools, equipment, factories, and buildings used in the production process. Finally, **enterprise** (some economists prefer the term entrepreneurship) is that very special human talent that is able to put abstract ideas into practical application.

In a market economy, incomes are earned through the payment of **wages**, **interest**, **rent**, and **profits** to the private owners of the factors of production: labour, capital, land, and enterprise. The higher the market value of the factor of production owned by a person, the more income that individual receives. Thus the *for whom* question is answered by the distribution of ownership of the factors of production that the market considers valuable. The *what* question in a modern market economy depends on the way that people choose to spend their income, since it is this spending that makes up the demand for the various goods and services. The *how* question is answered by firms finding the most appropriate technology to produce their output, knowing that success brings profits and that if they fail to do this they will not be in business for long.

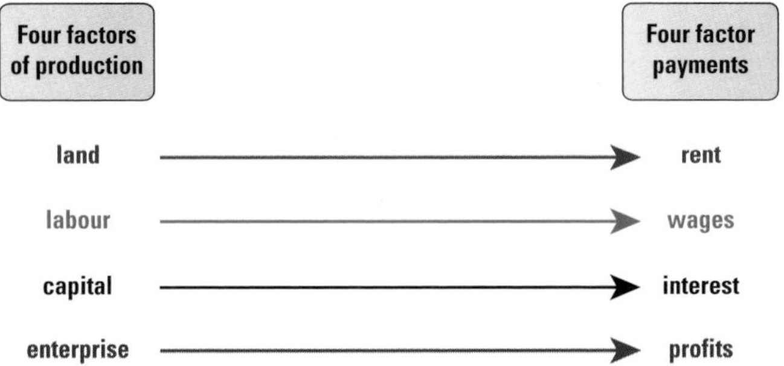

We want to emphasize that while the use of the market system is strong in today's economies, they are all in fact a blend of the four Cs. This blend includes the large role played by governments through the provision of, for example, health care and education. The role of government in our economy represents the command function in the sense that the taxes needed to finance government activities are not voluntary and in the same sense the various laws governing human conduct and behavior must be adhered to. The recognition of the role of both market and government in our society is what we mean by the term: *a mixed economy*. Few, if any, of us would wish to live in a pure market economy where, for example, young children from dysfunctional families with no income would be left to starve, or where there was no standardization of weights and measures and no "rules of the game" concerning the way business is conducted. On the other hand, few, if any, of us would want to live in a society where every decision about our lives was made by government. Some blend of the market, and the efficiencies achieved from its use, combined with the order and fairness imposed by government does seem to be the right way to go. On the other hand, exactly what constitutes the right amount of government intervention imposed upon the market is, of course, an issue of endless debate.

It is interesting to note that we can also still witness the role of custom in our society. Let's first look at a small but quite instructive example. There are probably as many people in a typical movie theater audience who use the restrooms as there are people who purchase soft drinks. Given this, surely it would be more profitable for the theatre to provide free soft drinks and charge for the use of restrooms rather than the other way around (as is now done). Yet, no theatre does it this way. Why? Because it is the custom in our society for theatres (and restaurants and large department stores, etc.) to provide the public with free restrooms. A much more significant example is the custom in our market economy of allowing people to pass wealth on to their children in the form of inheritance which sometimes has quite noticeable effects on the future distribution of income. Yet, notice that the government does step in and take a portion of this inter-generational transfer in the form of inheritance taxes. Thus we see a blend that recognizes the competitive accumulation of private wealth, the custom of keeping this wealth within the family, and the command that not all of it can be kept private.

And what about cooperation—do we see it in a modern society too? The answer is, of course, yes. The internal decision-making process in today's large corporations stresses the use of team play and group consensus, which is a form of cooperative behaviour. This same point can be made in reference to most family units within our society. Further, what, if not cooperative behaviour, would one call the fact that nearly half of all adults in our society engage (at some point in their life) in voluntary activities such as coaching soccer, or helping out at a local hospital or community centre?

Thus, we see that it is a blend of the four Cs that provides the organizational structure of all societies. This blend can take on many different shades—the foragers emphasized cooperation, ancient Rome used primarily command, feudal Europe was dominated by custom—and today's modern society emphasizes competition.

SELF-TEST

1. Below is a list of resources. Indicate whether the resource in question is land (N), labour (L), capital (K), or enterprise (E):

a) A bar-code scanner in a supermarket.

b) Fresh drinking water.

c) Copper deposits in a mine.

d) The work of a systems analyst.

e) The first application of CD-ROM technology to an economics textbook.

f) An office building.

You have no doubt heard the terms "capitalism" and "socialism" used in the media and in conversation. Just what do these terms mean to an economist? Basically they distinguish different degrees in the competition/command mix used by society to organize its economic affairs and answer the three fundamental questions. In "socialist" Sweden, for example, the state (government) plays a much larger role in the economy than in "capitalist" Hong Kong. While Sweden does *not* have central planning as found in the former Soviet Union and does have private property, it also has high taxes and high levels of social spending. Eighty percent of the work force is unionized; everyone receives a minimum of 37 days of paid vacation per year and unlimited sick leave benefits at nearly full pay. It has a generous unemployment insurance plan which also includes mandatory re-training. Until very recently, the Swedish government mandated an investment fund which required that corporations give a percentage of their profits to the central bank, which would then release these funds back to the companies in times of recession, with stipulations on how it was to be spent. By contrast, Hong Kong has almost none of this and relies instead on a policy of *laissez-faire*, which minimizes the role of government and emphasizes the role of the market in the economy. The United States leans towards the Hong Kong end of the spectrum and Canada towards the Swedish example.

1.3 Economics: Science or Art?

LO3
Discuss whether economics is an art or science.

It is often suggested that economics is a very difficult subject to study because it is so theoretical and uses a very specialized language. Well, as far as the language is concerned, every specialty—from sailing to lanscape painting, from pottery to chemistry—has its own language. Such specialized language is necessary because the development of complex ideas often requires a language that is either not in general use or requires a more precise definition than is generally understood. It's equally true that economics is all about theory (or principles or laws—the terms are used interchangeably) but that doesn't mean it is has to be boring or difficult to understand. For social scientists, theories are absolutely vital in order to make sense of the world. All of us ask questions to try to make sense of our existence: what? when? where? The answers to these questions are reasonably straightforward because they involve questions of fact. But the most important question of all, and often the most difficult to answer is: why? "Why" always involves cause and effect, and it addresses the relationship between facts. Few people believe that things occur at random in our world; rather, we recognize that actions are related. A road is covered in ice and a car crashes; a person smokes heavily for forty years and dies of lung cancer; an army of beetles bore into a tree-trunk and the tree falls. Explaining why these things happen is a matter of uncovering the links between phenomena. That is what theory is all about: explaining why things happen. But in order to begin an explanation, we first need to know what happened. In other words, theory must be based on solid facts. Theory is NOT just a matter of opinion; it is built on the solid foundation of facts, or of what are termed *positive statements*. Positive statements are assertions about the world that can be verified by using empirical data. "Mats Sundin scored 30 goals last year" or "The unemployment rate in Canada is presently 6.2 percent" are both positive statements in that their truth can be verified by finding the appropriate data. But "Mats Sundin should score more goals" or "The unemployment rate in Canada is far too high" are both what are termed *normative statements*, in that they are based on a person's beliefs or value systems and as such cannot be verified by appealing to the facts.

Economic theory is an attempt to relate positive statements. For instance, the price of apples decreases; people buy more apples. Economic theory looks at how the two things are related. In order to build a theory about, say, apple prices and apple purchases, we need to set up a simple *hypothesis*: for example, the lower the price of a product, the greater the quantity sold. But along with the hypothesis, we need to define the terms involved. For instance, what types of apples are we talking about—Granny Smiths, Galas, or all apples? And what price are we considering—wholesale? retail? Vancouver prices? Ottawa prices? Besides this, we need also spell out the assumptions (conditions) under which the hypothesis is true: people will buy more apples when the price falls *as long as the economy doesn't hit a recession* or *as long as the prices of other fruits remain the same*, and so on. The hypothesis is now ready for testing by gathering actual data and, as a result, accepting, rejecting, or possibly modifying, the theory.

This is what is termed the *scientific method*. It implies, among other things, that the results that the theory predicts should be valid regardless of who does the testing, and that different people should be able to repeat the tests and obtain the same results.

However, some people say that there is no way that economics can ever be considered a true science, even though the discipline does use the scientific method. In some senses this is true. Economics can never approach the pure sciences in terms of universality. For instance, it can never predict how every (or any one) consumer will react to the drop in the price of apples. But it can predict how the average consumer will react, i.e.: it deals in *generalities*. It is also true that the lag (delay) between the cause and the effect is often far longer in the social sciences than it is in the pure sciences, which makes the job of theorizing a lot more difficult. But to criticize economics because it is too abstract and unrealistic is not really fair. In fact, it could be suggested that the more realistic economic theory becomes, the less valuable it is. For example, no one would expect a map to be "realistic" because if it were, then every tree, house and road would have to be drawn to scale. And what would the scale be? 1:1! So while a map can capture a great deal of realism, trying to make it even more realistic can result in it becoming useless.

Economists try to explain the economic world in terms of models. Let's look at what we mean by this. Imagine walking into the sales office of a condominium project under construction. Part of the sales presentation is a model of the entire project sitting on a table. You would have no trouble recognizing the model as an *abstraction*, a representation, of what the building will eventually look like. This is true despite the fact that many of the details, such as the elevators, furniture, and appliances, are absent from the model. So, too, in making their models, economists abstract from reality only the features that are relevant, ignoring extraneous material that only adds clutter. Clearly, economists cannot construct a physical model of the economic world. Instead, the level of abstraction is greater, in that the model is all on paper and often in the form of numbers, equations, and graphs. But, for all that, the aim is not to make the simple and straightforward seem unnecessarily complicated, but just the opposite: to make the complexities of reality as clear and simple as possible. Let's now turn to two examples of how economic models can do this.

SELF-TEST

2. Identify each of the following statements as positive or normative:

a) The government should reduce its budget deficit by cutting its spending.

b) If the price of apples rises, then the quantity of oranges bought will increase.

c) Monopolies tend to set prices higher than would exist in competitive markets.

d) The economic cost of cleaning up the environment is too high.

e) Higher-income Canadians should be willing to share their wealth with lower-income Canadians.

1.4 Model Example One: The Circular Flow

LO4
Understand the circular flow of income diagram.

We can take even the little bit that we have learned so far and build a very simple model of the whole economy. We use **Figure 1.1** to help us.

FIGURE 1.1 **The Circular Flow**

Consumption spending and income flow in one direction between the two sectors, while goods and factors flow in the opposite direction.

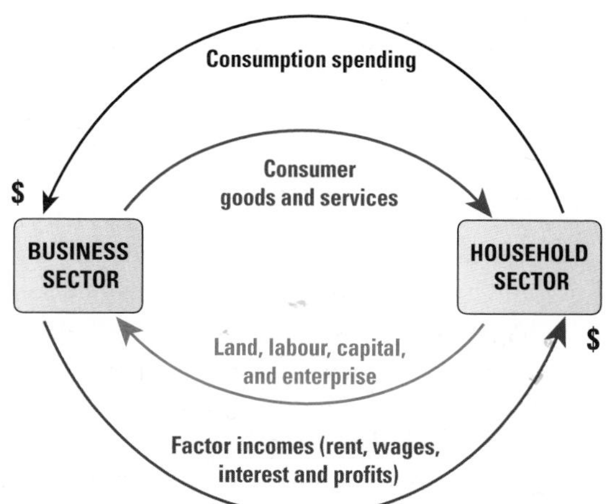

Figure 1.1 identifies two sectors in the economy: the business sector and the household sector. In a market economy like Canada's, the four factors of production, which we spoke of earlier, are owned by individuals who make up the household sector. These factors or

services flow to the business sector, as represented by the red line identifying land, labour, capital, and enterprise. The business sector uses these factors of production to produce goods and services which then flow to the household sector, as shown in green. Now, of course, the business sector must pay for the use of the factors of production. These factor payments, in the form of wages, interest, rents, and profits—shown in blue—represent expenditures to the firms, but become income to individuals in the household sector.

And what do people do with their income? They pay for the consumer goods and services that they receive from the business sector. This payment, shown in black, is called consumption spending. Again, expenditures by households become income for businesses. These expenditures are made with money and are thus referred to as financial flows.

Needless to say, our economy is far more complex than this. However, even a very simple model like this can help us to better understand how it works. Chapter 3 will take this circular flow model several steps further. What we need to remember is that every model is an abstraction from reality. It isn't meant to capture all possible relationships or details. In fact, it is often true that the more realistic we try to make our models, the more complex and thus the more confusing and distracting they become.

REVIEW

1. What is the discipline of economics sometimes called?
2. Define opportunity costs.
3. What are the three fundamental questions in economics?
4. What are the four Cs that humankind has used to organize its communities?
5. Identify the four factors of production.
6. Identify the four payments to the factors of production.
7. What is a positive statement?
8. Identify the financial flows in the circular flow model.

1.5 Model Example Two: Production Possibilities

LO5
Use the production possibilities model to illustrate opportunity costs, efficiency, and unemployment.

Let's now construct a second very simple model of a country's production possibilities. This allows us to return to a point that we made earlier, that every economy is faced with the constraint of limited resources. Imagine a society that produces only two products—cars and wheat. Let's then figure out what this economy is capable of producing if it works at maximum potential. This would mean that it is making use of all its resources: the labour force is fully employed, and all of its factories, machines, and farms are fully operational. But it means more than this. It also means that it is making use of the best technology known and is working as efficiently as possible. Given all of this and since it can produce either cars or wheat, the exact output of each depends on how much of its resources it devotes to the production of cars and wheat. **Table 1.1** shows six possible output combinations, as well as the percentage of the economy's resources used in producing each combination. These possible outputs are labelled A through F.

TABLE 1.1 Production of Cars and Tonnes of Wheat (millions of units)

	CARS		WHEAT	
Possible Outputs	% of Resources Used	Output	% of Resources Used	Output
A	0	0	100	20
B	20	10	80	19
C	40	18	60	17
D	60	24	40	13
E	80	28	20	8
F	100	30	0	0

The finite resources available to this economy allow it to produce up to a maximum of 20 tonnes of wheat per year, if 100 percent of its resources are used in wheat production. Notice that this can be done only if no cars are produced (combination A). At the other extreme, a maximum of 30 cars per year can be produced, if all available resources are used in car production. This, of course, would mean that no wheat is produced (combination F). There are many other possible combinations in between these two extremes, and **Table 1.1** identifies four of these (B, C, D, and E).

Since we want to focus on what is produced (the outputs) rather than on what resources are used to produce them (the inputs), we can present **Table 1.1** in the form of a production possibilities table, as is shown in **Table 1.2**:

TABLE 1.2 Production Possibilities for Cars and Wheat

	A	B	C	D	E	F
Cars	0	10	18	24	28	30
Wheat	20	19	17	13	8	0

production possibilities curve: a graphical representation of the various combinations of maximum output that can be produced from the available resources and technology.

Further, we can take the data from **Table 1.2** and use it to graph what is called a **production possibilities curve**, which is a visual representation of the various outputs that can be produced. What appears in **Figure 1.2** is simply another way of presenting the data in **Table 1.2**.

FIGURE 1.2 **Production Possibilities Curve I**

This society's limited resources allow for the production of a maximum of 20 tonnes of wheat if no cars are produced, as represented by point *a*. Moving down the curve from point *a*, we find other combinations of fewer tonnes of wheat and more cars until we reach point *f*, where 30 cars and no wheat are produced. Point *u* indicates either the underemployment of resources, inefficiency in resource use, or the use of inappropriate technology. Point *x* is unobtainable.

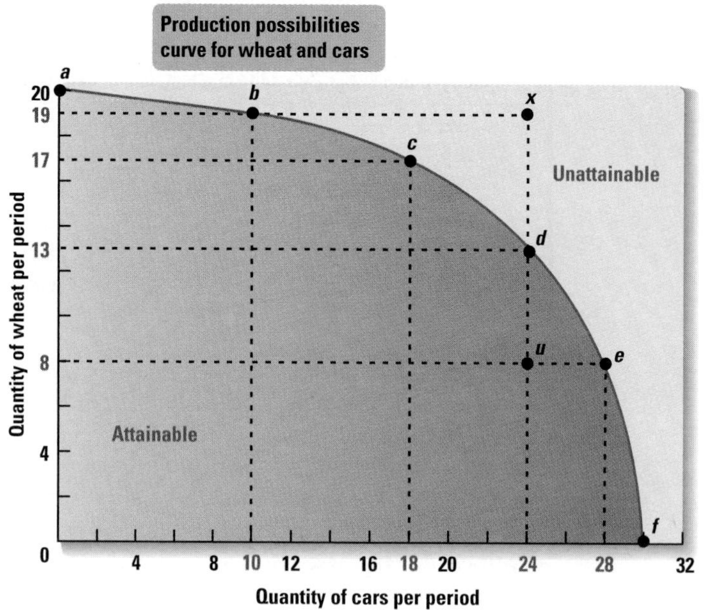

Now, recall that:

The three assumptions that lie behind the production possibilities curve are: full employment, the use of the best technology, and production efficiency.

If any one of these three assumptions does not hold, then the economy will be operating somewhere inside the production possibilities curve, as illustrated by point *u*, which is 24 cars and 8 tonnes of wheat. On the other hand, point *x* represents an output of 24 cars and 19 tonnes of wheat, which, given this economy's current resources and technology, is unobtainable.

Next, let's consider the actual shape of the curve. Why is it bowed out this way? We need to understand the implication of this particular shape. **Figure 1.3** will help.

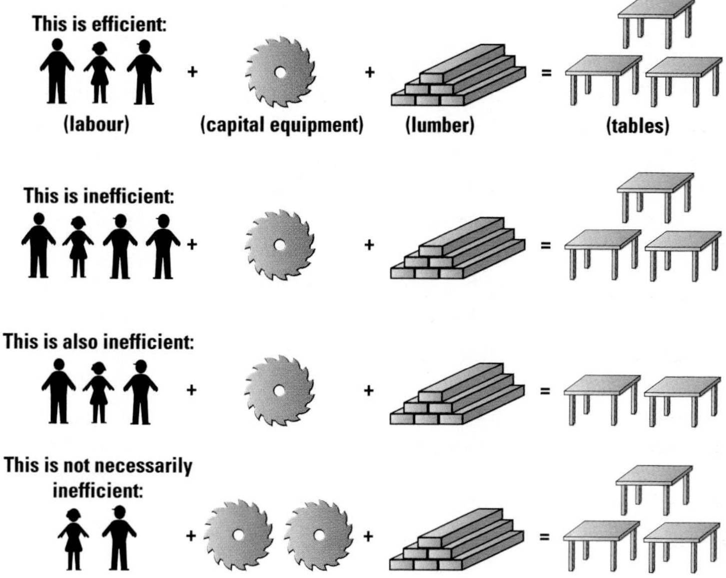

FIGURE 1.3 Production Possibilities Curve II

At point *b*, 19 tonnes of wheat and 10 cars are being produced. If this society decided that it wanted 8 more cars (point *c*), then 2 tonnes of wheat would have to be sacrificed. Thus, 1 more car would cost 0.25 tonnes of wheat. Moving from point *c* to *d* would increase car production by 6 (18 to 24) at a sacrifice of 4 tonnes of wheat (from 17 to 13). In this instance, one more car costs 0.67 tonnes of wheat. Moving from point *d* to *e* would increase car production by only 4 (from 24 to 28), while wheat production would drop by 5 (from 13 to 8). Thus, the cost of 1 more car rises to 1.25 tonnes of wheat.

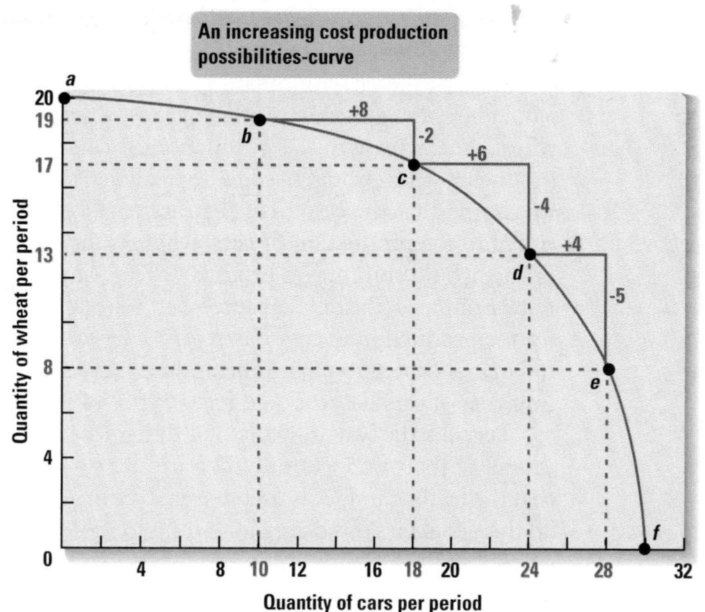

Assume that our hypothetical economy is currently producing 19 tonnes of wheat and 10 cars, as illustrated by point *b* on the production possibilities curve. Then let's assume that production decisions are made to reallocate 20 percent of the productive resources (labour, machines, materials) from wheat production to car production. This new output is illustrated by point *c*. Note that the opportunity cost of producing the additional 8 cars is *not* the additional 20 percent of resources that must be allocated to their production, *but* the decreased output of wheat that these resources could have produced. That is to say, the additional 8 cars could only be obtained by reducing the output of wheat from the original 19 tonnes to the new 17 tonnes. Thus, 8 more cars cost 2 tonnes of wheat. This can be restated as: 1 more car cost 0.25 tonnes of wheat (2 divided by 8). This seems clear enough, but we are not done.

Next, assume that society, still at point *c*, decides to produce even more cars, as illustrated by moving to point *d* (24 cars and 13 tonnes of wheat). This time an additional 20 percent of the resources produces only 6 more cars (18 to 24) at a cost of 4 units of wheat (17 to 13). This can be restated as: 0.67 tonnes of wheat for every additional car. This is considerably more than the previous cost of 0.25 units of wheat per car. Another shift of 20 percent of resources would move the economy from point *d* to *e*, with the result of an addition of only 4 more cars at a cost of 5 tonnes of wheat. Now, each additional car costs 1.25 (5 divided by 4) units of wheat.

law of increasing costs: as an economy's production level of any particular item increases, its *per unit* cost of production rises.

We have just identified what economists call the **law of increasing costs**. This law states that as the production of any single item increases, the per unit cost of producing additional units of that item will rise. Note that this law is developed in the context of a whole economy and, as we will see in later chapters, need not apply to the situation of an individual firm.

Thus, you can see that as the total production of cars is increased, the rising per unit cost of cars gives the production possibilities curve its bowed-out shape.

But why does the per unit cost of cars increase—what is the reason behind the law of increasing costs? The answer is that not all resources are equally suitable for the production of different products. Our hypothetical society has a fixed amount of resources that are used to produce different combinations of both wheat and cars. However, some of these resources would be better suited to producing cars, whereas others would be better suited to producing wheat. An increase in the production of cars requires that some of the resources currently producing wheat would need to be re-allocated to the production of cars. It is only reasonable to assume that the resources that are re-allocated first are the ones that are relatively well suited to the production of cars, whereas those resources less well suited to the production of cars would continue to produce wheat. After all this has taken place, if even *more* cars are to be produced, the only resources left to re-allocate will be ones that are not very well suited for the production of cars. Therefore, a larger quantity of less well suited resources will have to be re-allocated to obtain the desired increase in car production. This will increase the per unit cost of cars because a larger sacrifice of wheat production will be required.

Perhaps the way to really nail down this idea of increasing costs is to imagine another economy that produces only two products—leather shirts and leather moccasins. Assume that the leather and tools used to make both goods are exactly the same. Further, assume that all the people involved are clones of a long-deceased expert leatherworker and are therefore equally skilled. The production possibilities data for this economy are shown in **Table 1.3**. (This time the percentage of resources used to produce each combination is omitted.)

TABLE 1.3 Production Possibilities for Shirts and Pairs of Moccasins

	QUANTITIES PRODUCED PER DAY					
	A	B	C	D	E	F
Shirts	20	16	12	8	4	0
Moccasins	0	8	16	24	32	40

From the data in **Table 1.3**, we see that 8 additional pairs of moccasins can, in all instances, be obtained by giving up 4 shirts, which is a ratio of 2 pairs of moccasins for 1 shirt. This can also be stated as 1 additional shirt costing 2 pairs of moccasins. Taking this data and plotting it as a production possibilities curve yields a straight line, as can be seen in **Figure 1.4**.

FIGURE 1.4 Production Possibilities Curve III

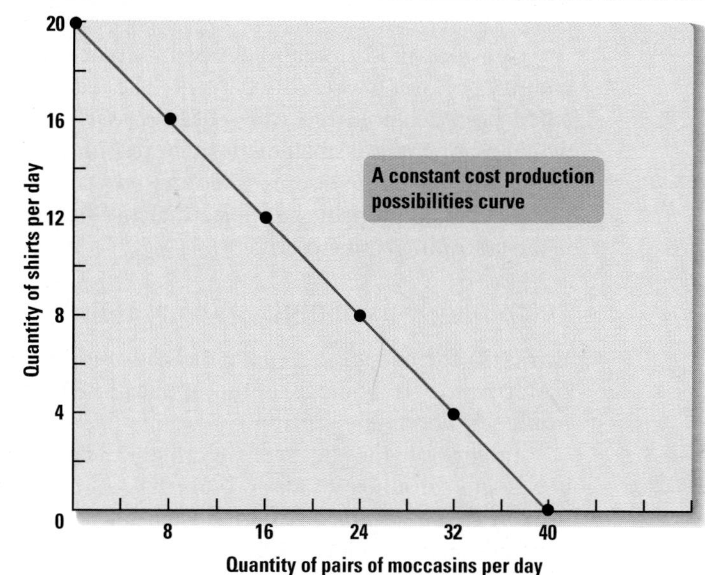

The opportunity cost of additional pairs of moccasins in terms of shirts sacrificed is constant; that is, 4 additional shirts always cost 8 pairs of moccasins. This yields a straight-line production possibilities curve.

Thus, we can see that a straight-line production possibilities curve is conceivable. The implications of a straight-line production possibilities curve is that the law of increasing costs does not apply. In fact, what we have above are constant costs—the cost of two pairs of moccasins is always one shirt.

Notice, however, what we had to assume in order to obtain such a result: homogeneous inputs to the production process—the same material (leather), identical tools, and labour that is equally skilled—and the very similar outputs of leather shirts and moccasins. If resource inputs are not homogeneous and if products are quite different, which is almost always the case, then we could not expect the production possibilities curve to be a straight line. Therefore, we would expect the law of increasing costs to prevail in the real world.

It is not difficult to find examples of this law. Thirty years ago, when there were very few air pollution controls in effect, the cost of obtaining a 10 percent reduction in air pollution was relatively cheap. Today, when air pollution levels have been substantially reduced in many industries, an additional reduction of 10 percent would be much more costly, because the most cost-effective reductions have already been made.

SELF-TEST

3. Given the accompanying figure:

a) If the society produces 1000 units of butter, how many guns can it produce?

b) Suppose that the society produces the combination shown as point *b* on the production possibilities curve; what is the cost of 1000 additional units of butter?

c) Would the cost of 1000 additional units of butter be greater, the same, or smaller as the society moves from point *c* to *d*, compared with a move from point *b* to *c*?

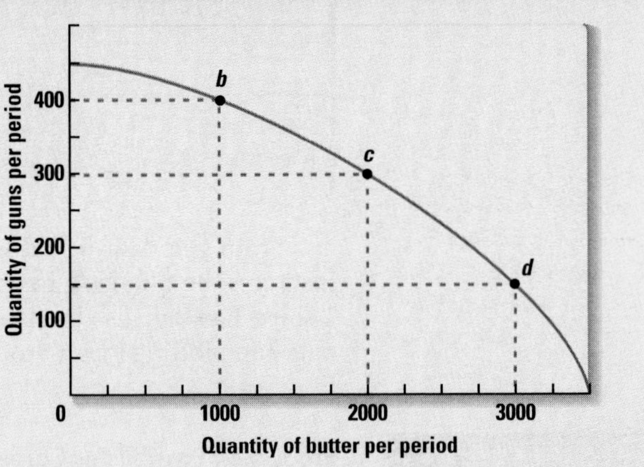

Consider another example. Assume that the infant mortality rate in a less-developed country is 55 out of every 1000 births. The reduction of this level by five (to 50 out of 1000), could been achieved relatively cheaply—say, with a smallpox vaccination campaign that would require only a small quantity of resources. However, once the rate dropped to, say, 25 out of 1000, then the resources required to gain an additional drop of five points, to 20 out of 1000, would probably be substantial and the costs involved would be much greater. This is the law of increasing costs.

Technological Change and Capital Accumulation

Earlier in the chapter we spoke of the important role that technology plays in economic performance. Technology is the application of human knowledge to lower the cost of producing goods and services.

consumer goods and services: products used by consumers to satisfy their wants and needs.

To illustrate the effects of technological change, imagine a society that produces capital goods and consumer goods and services. **Consumer goods and services** are those products used by consumers to satisfy their wants and needs.

Let's start, in **Figure 1.5**, with the economy operating efficiently on the production possibilities curve PP1 at point *a*. Now let's assume that a new technology becomes available that has application *only* in the consumer goods and services industry. This is represented by a shift outward in the curve, with the new production possibilities curve becoming PP2. There are three possible results. First, the same quantity of capital goods, but more consumer goods and services, can be produced as represented by *b*. Second, more of *both* goods can also be produced, as represented by point *c*. And third, this economy could now achieve an increase in the production of capital goods if the same number of consumer goods and services were produced (point *d*) *despite* the fact that this new technology could only be applied to the consumer goods and services industry. This emphasizes the important role of technological change. It widens the choices (there's that word again) available to society and is often seen in a positive light. Alas, technological change also carries costs, and this is another subject that will receive our attention later.

FIGURE 1.5 **The Effect of Technological Change on the Production Possibilities Curve**

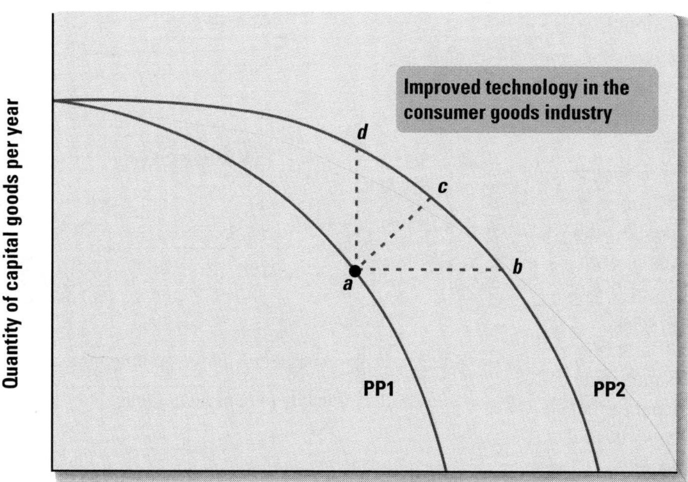

Start at point *a*, which is a point of efficient production on PP1. An improvement in technology in the consumer goods and services industry shifts the production possibilities curve to PP2. This creates three possible results. First, the same quantity of capital goods and services, and more consumer goods and services, can now be produced as represented by point *b*. Alternatively, more of *both* consumer goods and services and capital goods and services can be produced, as represented by point *c*. Point *d* represents the third possible result, which is more capital goods and services and the same quantity of consumer goods and services, despite the fact that the technological change was in the consumer goods and services industry.

Now, look at **Figure 1.5** and ask yourself the following question: which of the three new possible combinations is preferable? If the choice had been between two consumer goods and services, such as wheat and cars, then we could not give a definitive answer to this question without knowing something about the country's wants and needs. But the choices illustrated in this figure are between capital goods and consumer goods and services, and choosing combination *d*—more capital goods—leads to significantly different effects than choosing combination *b*.

This point is illustrated in **Figure 1.6**, in which we show two different economies. Atlantis places greater emphasis on the production of capital goods than does Mu. This can be seen by comparing point a_1 (40 units of capital goods) with point b_1 (20 units of capital goods). This emphasis on capital goods production also means a lower production of consumer goods (30 units in Atlantis, compared to 50 in Mu). The emphasis on capital goods production in Atlantis means that it will experience more economic growth in the future. This faster growth is illustrated by the production possibilities curve shifting more to the right in the case of Atlantis than in Mu. After the increase in production possibilities, Atlantis can continue producing 40 units of capital goods but now can produce 70 units of consumer goods (a_2). Mu, by contrast, can produce only 60 units of consumer goods and services while maintaining capital goods production at the original 20 units (b_2). All of this is a result of a different emphasis on the output choices by the two economies.

FIGURE 1.6 **Different Growth Rates for Two Economies**

We begin with Atlantis and Mu being the same size, as indicated by the same PP1 curves. However, since Atlantis chooses to emphasize the production of capital goods (point a_1) while Mu emphasizes the production of consumer goods and services (point b_1), Atlantis will grow faster. The result of this faster growth is that, over time, PP2 shifts out further in the case of Atlantis than it does in the case of Mu.

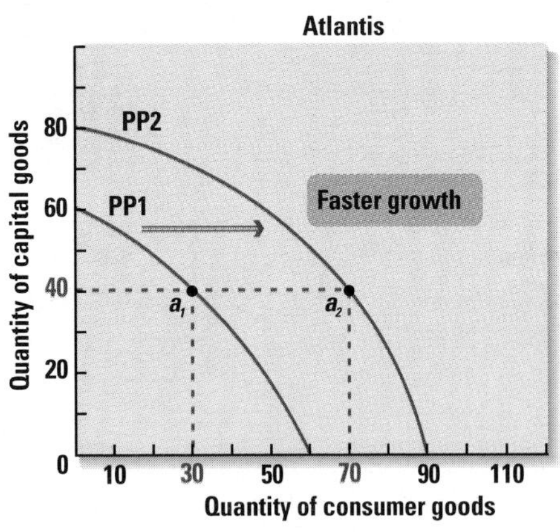

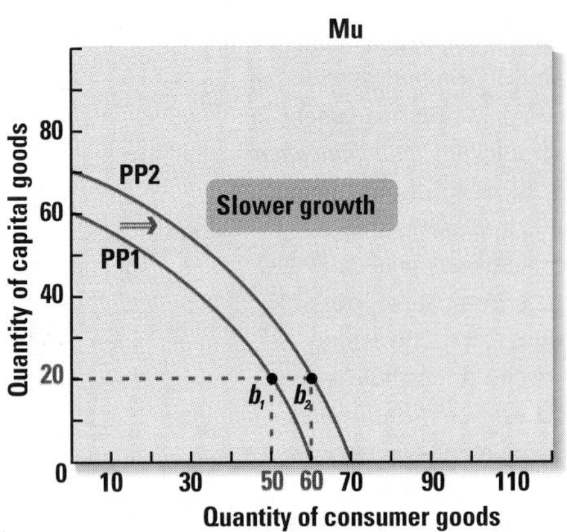

SELF-TEST

4. Below is a list of economic goods. You are to decide whether each is a consumer good (C), or a capital good (K), or possibly both, depending on the context in which it is used (D):
   - **a)** A jackhammer.
   - **b)** A carton of cigarettes.
   - **c)** An office building.
   - **d)** A toothbrush.
   - **e)** A hammer.
   - **f)** A farm tractor.
5. Assume that the economy of Finhorn faces the following production possibilities:

Quantities per Year

	A	B	C	D
Grain	50	40	25	0
Tools	0	4	8	12

   - **a)** Draw a production possibilities curve (PP1) with tools on the horizontal axis and grain on the vertical axis.
     Now assume new technology that can be used only in the tool industry is developed, which increases tool output by 50 percent.
   - **b)** Draw a new production possibilities (PP2) curve that reflects this new technology.
   - **c)** If Finhorn produced 12 units of tools per year, how many units of grain could be produced after the introduction of the new technology?

A sage of some bygone age said that there is no such thing as a free lunch. We can now make some sense out of this idea. Producing more of anything—a lunch, for example, since it involves the use of scarce resources—necessarily means producing less of something else. The lunch might be provided free to the people who eat it, but from the point of view of the society as a whole, it took scarce resources to produce it and therefore the lunch is not free.

1.6 A Definition, Potential Controversy and Relevance

LO6
Define economics and understand why it is controversial but of great relevance.

At Last: A Definition of Economics

In light of the discussion in this chapter we can now venture a definition of economics:

Economics is the study of the ways that humans organize themselves to make the necessary choices about how scarce resources are to be used to produce the goods and services necessary to satisfy human wants and needs.

All societies must somehow answer the questions of what is to be produced, how it is to be produced and who gets it once it is produced. Economists emphasize the role of specialization and trade in answering these questions, while relying on economic models to identify the crucial connections and important relationships between producers, consumers, and governments in whatever form of organization is chosen. All of this means that the discipline of economics is part science and part art, using rational deduction, good judgment and a general knowledge of human behaviour to mould a better understanding of the human condition. Economics is a discipline with magnificent scope and breadth and yet also one of very specific focus and attention to detail.

Courses in economics are traditionally divided into micro- and macroeconomics.

Many colleges and universities offer a separate course for each of these fields of study, but this is not always the case. **Macroeconomics** is the study of how the major components of the economy—such as consumer spending, investment spending, government policies, and exports—interact. It includes most of the topics a beginning student would expect to find in an economics course. These include unemployment, inflation, interest rates, taxation and spending policies of governments, and national income determination. **Microeconomics** studies the outcomes of decisions made by people and firms and includes topics like supply and demand, the study of costs, and the nature of market structures. This distinction can be described metaphorically as a comparison between the use of a wide-angle lens and a telephoto lens of a camera. In the first instance we see the big picture. In the second instance a very small part of that big picture appears in much more detail.

macroeconomics: the study of how the major components of an economy interact; it includes the topics of unemployment, inflation, interest rate policy, and the spending and taxation policies of government.

microeconomics: the study of the outcomes of decisions by people and firms through a focus on the supply and demand of goods, the costs of production, and market structures.

Agreements and Disagreements in Economics

At some point in the past, you may have heard jokes about economists, such as, "What do you get when you put five economists in the same room? Six opinions." Economists do often disagree with each other as is easily seen in the popular media. This is a natural by-product of a discipline that is part science and part art. An important reason for such disagreement is that economists, just like all other people, have a particular set of values that they have accumulated over a lifetime, and these values vary, sometimes radically, from person to person. Nonetheless, if each of us uses the scientific method in developing our arguments, then lively debate can be fruitful, despite the different value systems with which we started.

It is also true, however, that there is wide agreement among economists on many questions, and this is remarkable given that economists ask a wide variety of questions, many of which do not get asked in other disciplines. For example, why do firms produce some goods internally and buy others in the market? Why do nations sometimes both export and import similar goods? Why does society provide some things to children without charge (education) but not other things (food)?

ADDED DIMENSION

To illustrate the point that there is a great deal of agreement among economists, here are five examples of issues, with the percentage of economists who agree with the statement:

1. A ceiling on rents reduces the quantity and quality of housing available. (93%)
2. Tariffs and quotas generally reduce economic welfare. (93%)
3. A tax cut or an increase in government expenditure has a stimulative effect on a less than fully employed economy. (90%)
4. The government should restructure the social assistance system along the lines of a negative income tax. (79%)
5. Effluent taxes and marketable pollution permits represent a better approach to pollution control than the imposition of pollution ceilings. (78%)

Source: Richard M. Alston, J. R. Kearl, and Michael B. Vaughn, "Is There Consensus among Economists in the 1990s?" *American Economic Review,* May 1992, 230-239.

Is Economics Relevant?

Lastly, let's ask the question: how relevant is the study of economics? As we enter the twenty-first century, we find ourselves living in a society filled with a host of problems and a wide variety of issues that we are exposed to every day through the media and that dominate many of our conversations. Will Quebec separate from the rest of Canada? Will governments reduce spending on education, and will this drive up the cost of tuition? Are the threats to our environment too serious for us to adequately cope with them? What kinds of jobs will there be in the future, and will there be enough of them to meet the aspirations of our youth? Will Canada's health care system continue to meet people's expectations? Will this country's history of tolerance toward minorities continue, or will prejudice and hatred raise their ugly heads? Will a seemingly endless number of new special-interest groups begin to tear at the fabric of our stable and democratic system of governance? Will productivity in Canada grow rapidly enough for Canadian firms to thrive in an increasingly globalized marketplace?

Tragically, in light of the events of Sept 11, 2001, we must now ask: how high will be the price, in terms of resources and personal inconvenience, of re-establishing the security of person and property that we took for granted for so long?

These questions are broad and diverse. Yet there is an economic dimension to every one of them. In fact, economics is one of the *most relevant* subjects that a student might study. Strangely, however, not everyone shares this view. There are a variety of reasons for this. One is that people often see economics as being too theoretical. However, let's remember that the most effective way to say something intelligent about nearly all the issues of the day is to use theory and abstraction. Another observation that students often make about the discipline of economics is that it seems too narrow in its focus. Yet a precise focus is sometimes needed to identify cause and effect.

Trying to understand economic theory can be challenging and certainly does not come easily, but the rewards, in terms of a better understanding of the world we live in, are great. Economics is the study of ideas, and in a very real way this is the most important thing that a student can study. One of the most famous of twentieth-century economists, John Maynard Keynes, said:

> **The ideas of economists, both when they are right and when they are wrong, are more powerful than is commonly understood. Sooner or later, it is ideas, not vested interests, which are dangerous for good or evil.**[1]

[1]John Maynard Keynes, *The General Theory* (1936).

REVIEW

1. Define the term *capital good.*
2. Define the term *consumer good.*
3. What is a *production possibilities curve?*
4. Define the *law of increasing* costs.
5. What are two causes of a rightward shift in the production possibilities curve?

1.7 Macroeconomic Goals

LO7
List the economic goals of society and understand why they are often difficult to achieve.

The production possibilities model is very useful in highlighting a number of economic issues, including the costs of unemployment and the benefits of growth. But, more importantly, it graphically illustrates the important concepts of choice and cost. The dilemma facing policy makers in all governments is the same dilemma that faces all of us on a daily basis: how to satisfy conflicting goals. We know we cannot have everything in life, so we have to make choices. You have six hours available; you want to go for a walk, you want to visit friends, you want to study economics. What do you do? You could abandon two of your goals and wisely decide to study for the whole six hours. More probably, you might decide to divide up your time between the three activities. But do you allocate two hours to each activity or rank them in importance and spend more time on things you consider of greater importance? These are also the type of considerations that face policy makers who have to decide among a number of competing goals.

This raises the important question:

What would be a typical list of economic goals in a modern market economy like Canada?

Improved Standard of Living

Perhaps the most important goal for many of us is achieving and maintaining a decent standard of living. Each generation wants to improve on what the previous generation had and to leave the next generation even better off. Our standard of living is mostly determined by our income levels and Canada has been signally successful in producing comparatively high incomes for its citizens as **Figure 1.7** illustrates.

FIGURE 1.7 The Rise in Canada's Average Income, Decade by Decade

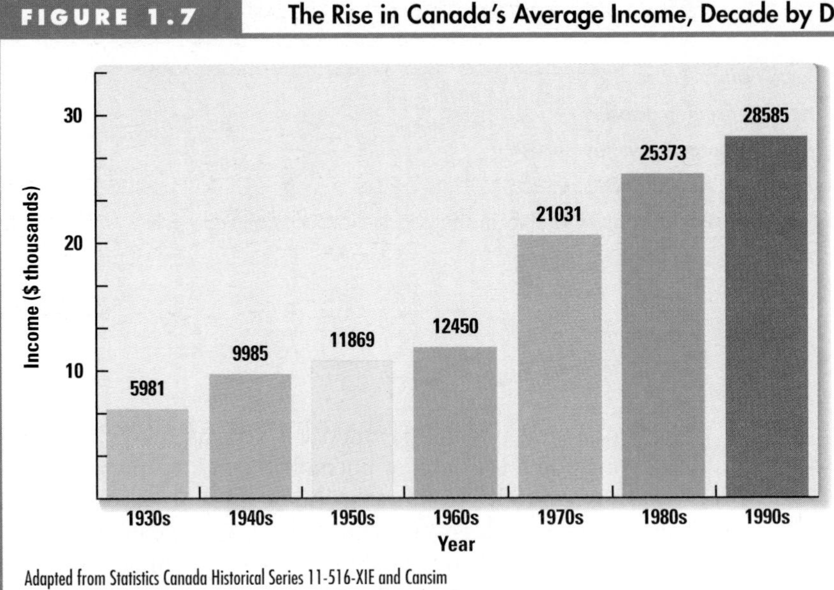

Adapted from Statistics Canada Historical Series 11-516-XIE and Cansim Tables 380-0002 (http://cansima.statcan.ca/cgi-win/CNSMCG1.EXE) and 051-0001.

Each decade has seen an improvement in real incomes (eliminating the effects of inflation) in Canada, from an average of just under $6000 in the 1930s to almost $30 000 per person in the past decade. But higher incomes don't just translate into bigger houses or more cars, for example, but more fundamentally, a richer country has the power to enrich the lives of its people in terms of better health and education. It can also allow them to enjoy a clean environment, open parklands and access to cultural pursuits. It is in this broad sense rather than simply in terms of the quantity of goods produced that people define the standard of living. If a country has a high national income, it doesn't necessarily guarantee that all of its citizens will enjoy a high standard of living. But it is equally true that the majority of citizens of poor countries are not doomed to low standards of living. A high and growing national income, though, is a necessary condition for a high standard of living for most citizens. This brings us to our second goal, that of achieving economic growth.

Economic Growth

Canada's present high standard of living is not just the result of what Canadians today are doing; it is as much the result of what Canadians did in the past. And what they did was to provide a social and economic climate that encouraged productivity and inventiveness. The growth of production (or real GDP as it is termed) is necessary in order to improve our standard of living and is essential in order to keep pace with the growth in Canada's population. As **Figure 1.8** shows, just a small change in growth rates can have a big impact on our incomes and standard of living.

FIGURE 1.8 The Growth of Canada's Average Income

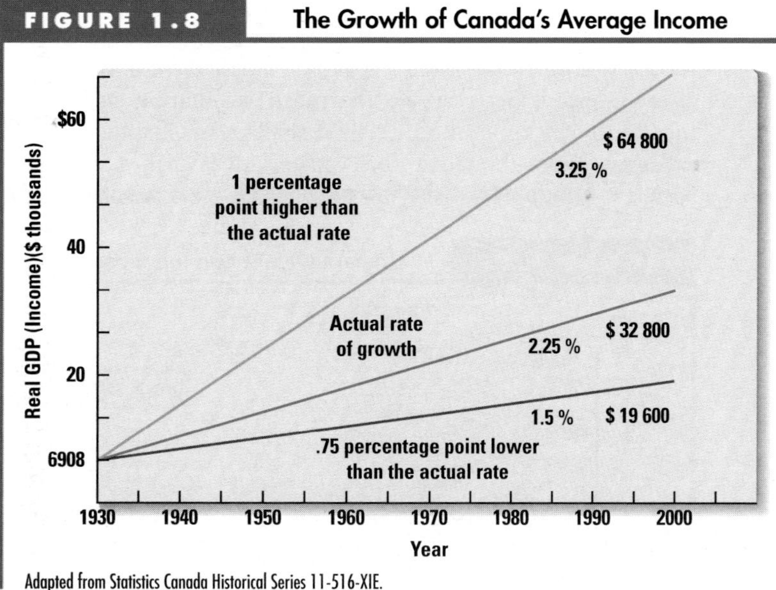

Adapted from Statistics Canada Historical Series 11-516-XIE.

Over the past 70 years the average income of Canadians has grown at a rate of 2.25 percent per year. While this rate doesn't sound like very much, it did result in incomes quadrupling over this period. And just a 1 percent point improvement on our actual performance would have left us with an average income per person of nearly $65 000, nearly double our present income. (On the contrary, a slightly lower rate of 1.5 percent per annum would have left the average Canadian with an income today of less than $20 000.) High growth rates do indeed increase our prosperity, but it should be borne in mind that economic growth can be a double-edged sword: it can improve our standard of living, but, unless the growth is handled sensibly, it can do exactly the opposite. This is because economic growth can often cause high rates of pollution, traffic congestion, noise, and stress. It can also lead to resource depletion and pressure on our natural environment, all of which can lower our quality of life despite leaving us with higher incomes.

Full employment

The goal of ensuring that all citizens who want to work have jobs appears to be a straightforward one. Since most people's income is derived from employment, few of us could survive for long without working. However, when we look at the question close up we discover that the goal of full employment may be difficult to achieve. For instance, does it mean that everyone should have a job (whether they want one or not) or does it apply only to those who are willing and able to work? If we believe that it is the latter, then should our goal be to ensure that such people have jobs, any jobs, or that they have jobs which are satisfying or stimulating, or jobs they've been trained or educated for, or jobs that are highly paid? If we grant that the goal of absolute full employment for all citizens all the time may be an impossibility, then what level of unemployment is acceptable: 2 percent? 5 percent? 10 percent? As **Figure 1. 9A** demonstrates, Canada's record with employment is a bit mixed. Although unemployment dropped steadily during the 1990s, it has not gone below 6 percent in the last 30 years.

Stable Prices

High rates of inflation can cause a great deal of damage to an economy and its people. But before we jump to the conclusion that a zero rate of inflation (no change in the overall price level) is desirable, remember that we are looking at things from a macroeconomic perspective. Thus, while higher prices may be looked on with alarm by buyers, they may be greatly welcomed by sellers. Perhaps some increase in prices is desirable. But how much—1, 3, or 5 percent per year? Furthermore, is inflation such a bad thing if wages are able to increase by the same amount? As we shall see in Chapter 4, the major problem is not so much inflation itself—though it does cause a great deal of suffering for a number of groups in society—but the fact that its unpredictability can be ruinous for an economy.

FIGURE 1.9 **Unemployment and Inflation Rates in Canada**

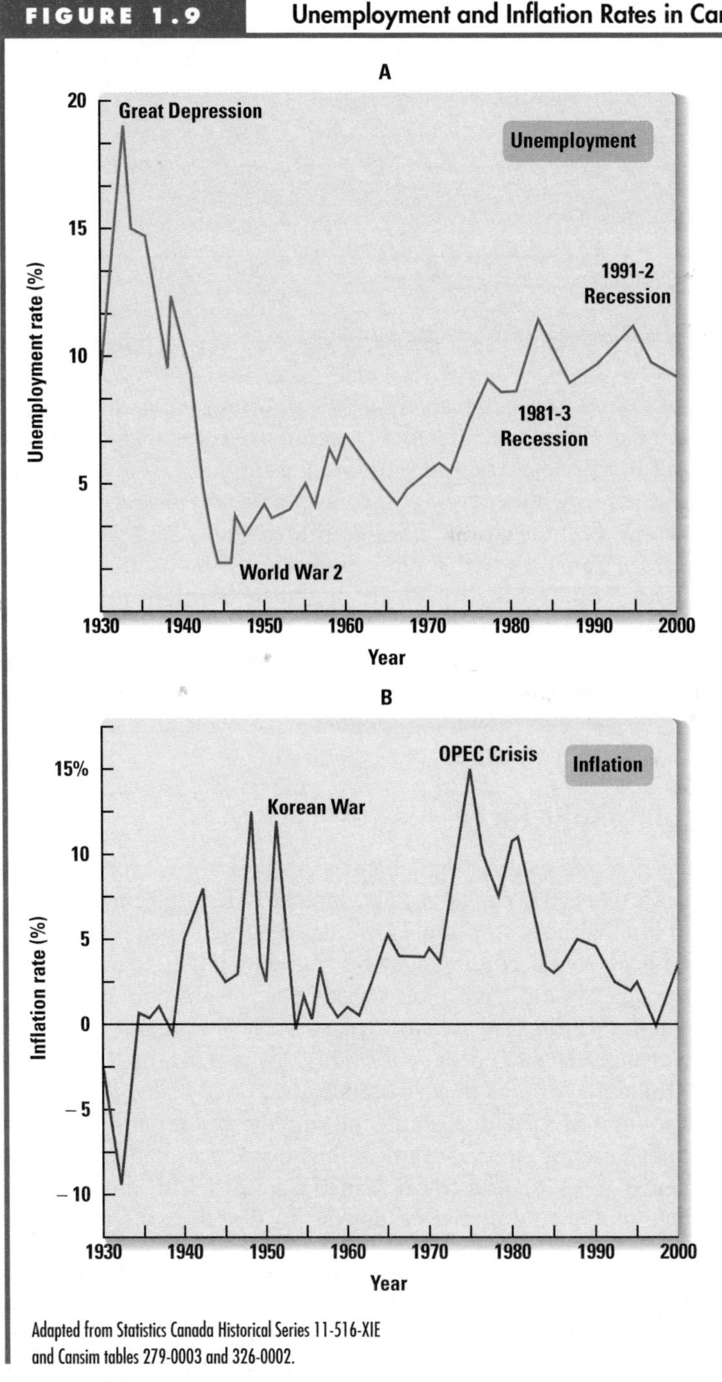

Adapted from Statistics Canada Historical Series 11-516-XIE and Cansim tables 279-0003 and 326-0002.

Figure 1.9B shows Canada's experience with inflation since the 1930s. Looked at in combination with the unemployment rates, some interesting features appear. We can see that the 1930s was a period of high unemployment and low inflation (in fact, a period of falling prices, or deflation, until 1933). The decade of the 1930s was the period of the Great Depression. The Second World War brought about an economic recovery, which saw unemployment rates dipping below 5 percent for the first time in over a decade and inflation rates starting to creep up. The 1950s and 1960s were periods of low unemployment and generally low inflation rates, although prices did take a sharp turn upward during the Korean War in the early 1950s. The mid-1960s to the mid-1980s saw both unemployment and inflation starting to rise, with an extra jump in the unemployment rate during the recession of the early 1980s. Following this recession, unemployment, along with inflation, generally fell throughout the rest of the 1980s. The beginning of the 1990s saw the Canadian economy head into another recession, with unemployment rising to over 11 percent by 1992. Thereafter, unemployment fell consistently in the 1990s and inflation was kept under 2 percent during most of the decade.

Before we take a look at other economic goals, one interesting point must be mentioned. Many economists believe that attaining *both* low unemployment and low inflation rates concurrently is virtually impossible in a modern economy. They would argue that the two goals are in conflict and one of these goals can be achieved only at the expense of the other. If this is true, **Figure 1.9** should indicate that low levels of unemployment are associated with high levels of inflation and high unemployment with low inflation. A cursory glance at the two curves doesn't show an obvious relationship of this nature, although until the mid-1960s there were a number of periods when the two did seem to move in opposite directions. However, since 1967 the two curves have, if anything, moved together more or less in tandem. In other words, when inflation rates were high, so too were unemployment rates. All of this raises interesting questions that we will try to answer in later chapters.

As a way of summarizing the first four of our goals, let's see how Canada has stacked up by international comparison. As you can see in **Table 1.4**, Canada compares very well with the rest of the world in terms of average income. Of the G8 countries (the world's biggest and most economically advanced nations) it is second only to the U.S. and has an average income almost four times as big as the world's average. It is the number one of the G8 nations in terms of growth and the second lowest when it comes to inflation. It is only when we come to unemployment rates that Canada's performance is distinctly mediocre, being fourth among the G8 countries but a lowly 42nd of the world's nations.

TABLE 1.4 **International Comparisons of Economic Performance 1**

Average Income per Person		Growth Rate per Person		Unemployment Rate		Inflation Rate	
Luxembourg (1)	45 410	Turkmenistan (1)	14.5%	Azerbaijan (1)	1.1%	Oman (1)	0.2%
1. USA (3)	34 260	Korea, Rep (2)	9.7	China (7)	3.1	1. Japan (2)	0.9
2. Canada (10)	27 330	China (7)	6.1	1. Japan (12)	4.1	2. Canada (8)	1.7
3. Japan (13)	26 460	1. Canada (24)	3.8	2.USA (17)	4.5	3. France (8)	1.7
4. Germany (21)	25 010	2. Russia (27)	3.6	3. UK (26)	6.1	4. Germany (19)	2.4
5. France (24)	24 470	3. France (52)	2.5	Korea, Rep (31)	6.8	5. USA (22)	2.7
6. UK (27)	23 550	4. USA (53)	2.4	4. Canada (42)	8.3	6. UK (23)	2.9
7. Italy (29)	23 370	5. UK (69)	1.7	5. Germany (48)	9.7	7. Italy (24)	3.9
Korea, Rep (46)	17 340	6. Germany (76)	1.4	6. France (58)	11.8	Korea, Rep (32)	5.3
8. Russia (80)	8030	7. Italy (78)	1.3	7. Italy (60)	12.3	China (63)	9.9
China (125)	3940	8. Japan (96)	0.1	8. Russia (61)	13.3	8. Russia (123)	116.1
World Average	7350	World Average	1.2	World Average	13.3	World Mode	10.0

Adapted from World Bank, World Development Indicators 2001 (the left-hand numbers indicate the ranking among the G8 nations, the numbers in parenthesis are world rankings).

Viable Balance of International Trade

Canada is truly one of the world's greatest trading nations and many would suggest that our high standard of living is a result of this. Economists would tend to agree that international trade is beneficial for all nations since it encourages specialization and promotes competition. It is better for a nation to concentrate its resources on producing goods and services which it can produce better and cheaper than others and, with the proceeds, buy those things that others can produce cheaper. The difference between what a nation exports and what it imports from abroad is known as the balance of trade. While it may not be possible to have a trade surplus (export more than one imports) every year; on the other hand, a country will experience a number of economic problems if it consistently has trade deficits. **Figure 1.10** shows the Canadian experience for the last seven decades.

FIGURE 1.10 **Canada's Balance of Trade 1930–2000**

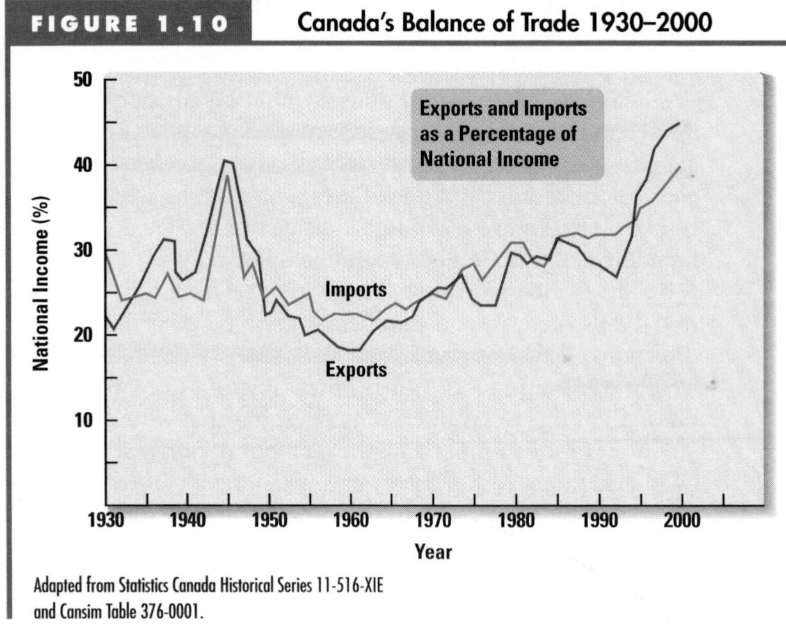

Adapted from Statistics Canada Historical Series 11-516-XIE and Cansim Table 376-0001.

As the graph illustrates, the 1990s have seen a dramatic upswing in international trade for Canada, mainly as a result of the North American Free Trade Agreement (NAFTA). In recent years Canada has been exporting and importing over 40 percent of its national income. But we should add a note of caution: it is not enough for a country to sell abroad as much or more than it buys. The types of things a country is selling can make a difference to its long-term welfare. For example, it is of some importance whether a country is selling manufactured and processed goods rather than selling off its raw materials, or whether it is selling goods and services rather than selling off its assets.

An Equitable Distribution of Income

Someone once said that the true test of a civilized country is how it treats its poorest members. After all, from a social and moral point of view, an increase in a nation's prosperity is not much use unless all of its citizens, rather than just a select few, get to enjoy and share in it. Large disparities in incomes can often lead to social unrest and high crime rates, so it is important that a country have a system in place to ensure that nobody literally dies for want of food or adequate medical services. But just how equal incomes should be is indeed a vexed question. If everyone was guaranteed the same income regardless of their efforts, this would obviously conflict with our desire to promote economic growth, since there would be little incentive for working harder or being innovative.

Figure 1.11 shows how Canada's economic pie was divided up in 1997. (It has hardly changed over the last 30 years.) The lowest quintile (the poorest 20 percent of the population) received just 3 percent of the national pie, whereas the top 20 percent received almost half: 47 percent. Clearly Canada's income is far from evenly distributed.

FIGURE 1.11 Distribution of Income (Share of Income by Quantities)

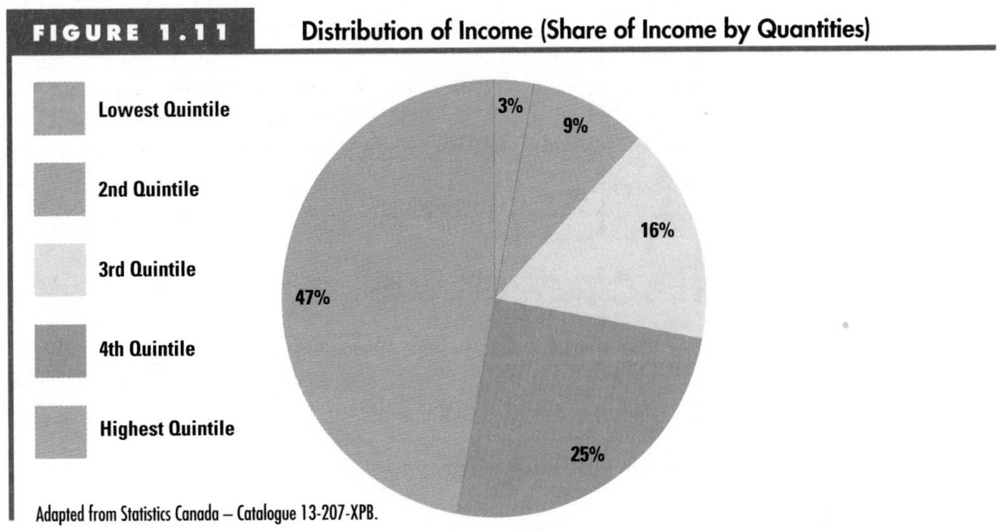

Adapted from Statistics Canada – Catalogue 13-207-XPB.

A Manageable Government Debt and Deficit

Most economists (unlike some politicians) feel that there is nothing intrinsically wrong with a government spending in any one year more than it earns in revenue, in other words running a budget deficit. It really depends on the state of the economy at the time. But if a government runs deficits regardless of the state of the economy, or runs deficits year in and year out, it is certainly going to cause grief for the nation, along with a higher public debt. It would be prudent, then, for a government to exercise a certain degree of fiscal responsibility. A look at **Figure 1.12** shows how the Canadian government has performed in the fiscal stakes over the past 70 years. As we shall see in later chapters, it is perhaps unavoidable that the government might overspend in a depression (because of falling tax revenues) or during wartime (with rising expenditures), but it would be difficult to justify the high deficits that Canada experienced in the 1980s and early 1990s. It is only in recent years that the Canadian government seems to have put its fiscal house in order.

FIGURE 1.12 Canada's Budget Deficits and Surpluses

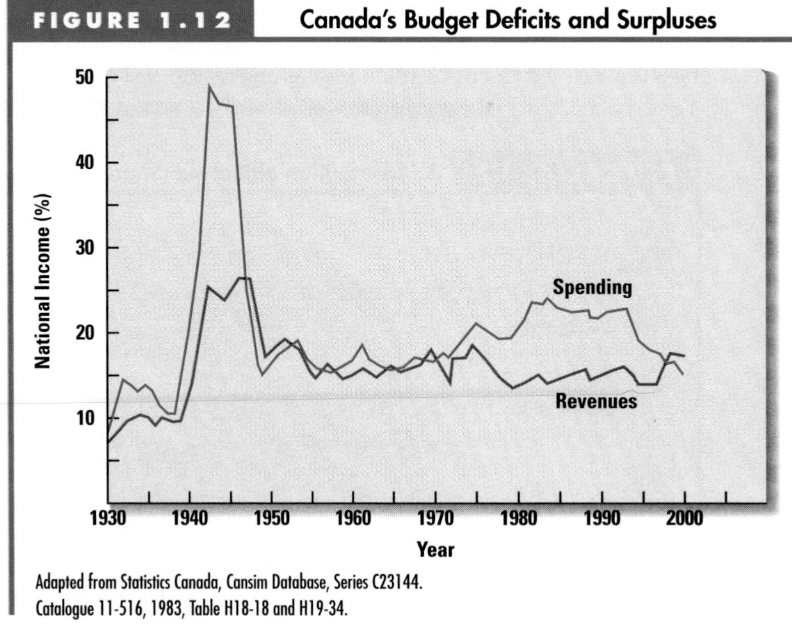

Adapted from Statistics Canada, Cansim Database, Series C23144.
Catalogue 11-516, 1983, Table H18-18 and H19-34.

Finally, **Table 1.5** shows the performance of the economy in achieving the final three goals in comparison with other countries. As we mentioned, despite being seventh of the G8 countries in terms of the volume of exports, we are first in terms of the percentage of our national income which is exported. As far as an equitable distribution is concerned, we perform worse than 25 other nations in the world, but are fourth among the G8 countries. As for our government's fiscal performance, its recent improvement is reflected in its reasonably high position of third of the G8 countries and 13th in the world.

TABLE 1.5 International Comparisons of Economic Performance 2

Exports	$	% National Income	Income Distribution (Top 20%/Bottom 20%)		Government Surplus/Deficit	% National Income
1. USA (1)	956	10.8%	Slovak Republic (1)	2.6	Singapore (1)	+3.4%
2. Germany (2)	626	29.8	1. Japan (4)	3.4	1. USA (8)	+0.8
3. Japan (3)	465	11.5	2. Italy (17)	4.2	2. UK (10)	+0.6
4. France (4)	382	26.3	3. Germany (23)	4.7	3. Canada (13)	+0.4
5. UK (5)	374	26.6	4. Canada (26)	5.2	4. Germany (29)	–0.9
6. Italy (6)	292	25.1	Korea (26)	5.2	Korea (36)	–1.3
7. Canada (7)	278	45.2	5. France (35)	5.6	China (50)	–2.2
China (9)	218	22.2	6. UK (53)	6.5	5. Italy (59)	–3.1
Korea, Rep (12)	172	43.2	China (69)	7.9	6. France (61)	–3.5
8. Russia (21)	85	25.8	7. USA (74)	8.9	7. Russia (77)	–5.3
			8. Russia (87)	12.2		
World Average	13.1		World Average	9.9	World Average	–1.5

Adapted from World Bank, World Development Indicators, 2001.

A final comment. Few people would disagree with the goals that we have briefly described, though they might argue about their order of importance. It's also clear that trying to achieve all seven goals simultaneously and consistently might be impossible. While some of these goals, economic growth and full employment, for example, are complementary, others are likely to be in conflict. We have already mentioned how trying to achieve full employment and stable prices at the same time may be very difficult. The same may also be true, for instance, if we try to stimulate economic growth by providing tax incentives for corporations and high income groups. While it might increase growth, it may well also lead to an increase in the government's budget deficit and also adversely affect an equitable distribution of income.

One of the major tasks of government then is to try to balance these goals in a way that secures the long-term well-being of all its citizens. To accomplish this difficult task the government has a number of tools at its disposal.

Tools for Achieving Macroeconomic Goals

Governments around the world pursue what economists call fiscal and monetary policies in an attempt to achieve the three macroeconomic goals that they have decided are at the top of the list, particularly full employment, stable prices, and economic growth. Fiscal policy is a term referring to the government's taxation and spending policies which we will study in detail in Chapter 11. Decreases in taxes or increases in spending will stimulate the economy towards more growth and less unemployment. Increased taxes and less spending will have the opposite effect, but may well reduce inflation. Monetary policy, on the other hand, refers to the central bank's (Bank of Canada) interest rate and money supply policies. We will look at this in detail in Chapter 12. Lower interest rates have a stimulative effect on the economy while higher rates are often used to control inflation.

There is also a category of policies that we call direct controls which run the gamut from tariffs and quotas on imports to minimum-wage laws to anti-pollution regulations. These are used to address more specific macroeconomic goals and will also be discussed in more detail in Chapter 12.

We have discussed a number of issues in this chapter and have introduced a number of terms, some of which may be unfamiliar to you. It is not vital for you to understand everything all at once, and for that reason we have avoided giving too many precise definitions at this stage. The topics discussed here, after all, are the subject matter of the whole book, and we will be returning to them throughout. It is hoped, however, that you can now at least taste the flavour of the various issues and debates.

REVIEW

1. List seven economic goals that might be considered when policy is being formulated.
2. What is meant by economic growth?
3. When was the last time Canada suffered double-digit inflation? When did it last experience deflation?
4. Since 1930, when did Canada experience major recessions and major booms?
5. With which other goal does full employment often come into conflict?
6. What is meant by a balance of trade surplus?

STUDY GUIDE

Review

CHAPTER SUMMARY

In this introductory chapter you gain an insight into the scope and depth of economics. You learn that economists are very focused on the choices, and the related costs of those choices that individuals, organizations, and governments face when making decisions. In the discussion on macroeconomic goals, you get a flavour of how the government's choice to emphasize any particular set of goals can have a profound effect on the performance of the economy.

1. Scarcity forces choice (for society, the government, and the individual) and choice involves an (opportunity) cost.

2. The three fundamental questions that all societies must somehow answer are:
- *What* is the right combination of consumer goods to produce and *what* is the right balance between consumer goods and capital goods?
- *How* should these various goods be produced?
- *Who* is to receive what share of these goods once they are produced?

3. The *economic organization* of all societies is based on one or more of the following:
- custom, cooperation, command, or competition;

and *modern (mixed) economies* use, primarily:
- competition along with a varying amount of command in the form of government intervention.

4. The factors of production are:
- land, labour, capital, and enterprise;

and the payments made to these factors are:
- rent, wages, interest, and profits.

5. The *production possibilities* model is an abstraction and simplification that helps to illustrate:
- the opportunity cost involved in making a choice;
- the necessity of choice in deciding what to produce;
- inefficient production and the consequences of unemployed resources;
- economic growth.

6. The discipline of economics is subdivided into:
- microeconomics, which studies the decisions made by people and firms and their outcomes;
- macroeconomics, which studies how the major components of the whole economy interact and how well an economy achieves economic goals such as full employment and economic growth.

7. The overall performance of an economy is measured by how well it achieves the *seven economic goals* of :
- improving the standard of living;
- maintaining economic growth;
- full employment;
- stable prices;
- a viable balance of payments;
- an equitable distribution of income;
- maintaining a manageable government debt and budget deficit.

NEW GLOSSARY TERMS

capital 8
consumer goods and services 18
enterprise 8
factors of production 7
interest 8
labour 7
land 7
law of increasing costs 16
macroeconomics 21
microeconomics 21
opportunity cost 2
production possibilities curve 13
profit 8
rent 8
wages 8

STUDY TIPS

1. Since this is the first chapter, do not be concerned if it seemed to contain so much new terminology that it was overwhelming. Mastering the principles of economics requires that you first learn the language of economics, and the best way to do this is to use it over and over. Let this Study Guide help you do this. Conscientiously work through all of the answered questions before proceeding to the next chapter.

2. Opportunity cost is one of the most important concepts in economics. As a start, make sure that you understand the basic idea that cost can be measured not just in dollars and cents but also in what has to be given up as a result of making a particular decision.

3. This chapter introduces you to the use of graphs with the production possibilities curve. If you have any difficulty understanding graphs, practice with the simple PP graphs until you become more comfortable using them, because graphs are an integral part of economics. The tool kit at the begining of the book provides a short primer on graphing.

4. For many of you, economics will be one of the more difficult courses that you will encounter in your undergraduate studies. Yet, it can be mastered, and doing so can be very rewarding. You will probably be much more successful if you work a little on economics several times a week, rather than have one long session a week. This way, you will gain mastery over the language more quickly through repetition, and thereby gain confidence. You might consider buying a pack of 3" x 5" index cards and writing two or three definitions or simple ideas on each card. Carry several cards around with you so that you can glance at them several times a day. The authors found this technique helpful when (oh, so many years ago) they started to learn the discipline.

Answered Questions

Indicate whether the following statements are true or false.

1. **T or F** An economy as a whole faces scarcity because of limited national income.

2. **T or F** The three fundamental questions in economics are what, how, and how many.

3. **T or F** Opportunity cost is the value of the next-best alternative that is given up as a result of making a particular choice.

4. **T or F** There are only three Cs that humankind has used to coordinate its economies: cooperation, custom, and competition.

5. **T or F** Wages, interest, rent, and profits are the four factors of production.

6. **T or F** A production possibility curve is a graphical representation of the various combinations of output that are wanted.

7. **T or F** Macroeconomics focuses on the outcomes of decisions by people and firms, whereas microeconomics is a study of how the major components of an economy interact.

8. **T or F** Technological improvement can be illustrated graphically by a rightward shift in the production possibilities curve.

9. **T or F** Tax policy, tariff policy, budget policy, monetary policy, and exchange rate policy are all examples of economic policies.

10. **T or F** Canada's highest unemployment rates were recorded in the 1930s.

Basic (Questions 11–23)

11. All of the following statements, except one, are valid examples of the way economists use the term scarcity. Which is the exception?
    a) Households face a scarcity of income.
    b) Individuals face a scarcity of time.
    c) Economies face a scarcity of resources.
    d) The world faces a scarcity of ideas.

12. What is the definition of opportunity cost?
    a) The amount of money spent on a good.
    b) The value of the next best alternative that is given up as a result of making a particular decision.
    c) The value of all the alternatives given up as a result of making a particular decision.
    d) The cost incurred in producing a good.

13. Meridith had only $16 to spend this last weekend. She was, at first, uncertain about whether to go to two movies she had been wanting to see or to buy a new CD she had recently heard. In the end she went to the movies. Which of the following statements is correct?
    a) The choice of the two movies and not the CD is an example of increasing costs.
    b) The opportunity cost of the two movies is one CD.
    c) The opportunity cost of the two movies is $16.
    d) The choice of two movies rather than one CD was a bad one.

14. In reference to voluntary trade, what was Adam Smith the first to recognize?
    a) It does not happen very often.
    b) It may or may not benefit one or both of the parties to the trade.
    c) It benefits one party to the trade but only at the expense of the other.
    d) It benefits both parties to the trade.

15. What are the three fundamental questions in economics?
    a) What to produce, how to produce it, and for whom to produce it.
    b) Is it necessary, is it right, and is it valuable?
    c) Who should produce, what is the right way to produce, and how should we decide?
    d) What to produce, how to produce it, and who should produce it.

16. What are the four basic ways that society can use to organize its economic affairs?
    a) With consumer goods, capital goods, models and positive statements.
    b) Using cooperation, command, custom, or competition.
    c) Using plentiful resources, opportunity costs, technology, and specialization.
    d) Using capitalism, communism, enterprise, and technology.

17. "Factors of production" is a term that can be used interchangeably with:
    a) Models.
    b) Consumer goods.
    c) Either resources or inputs.
    d) Technologies.

18. What are the factors of production?
    a) Land, labour, money, and enterprise.
    b) Land, labour, money, and capital.
    c) Land, labour, capital, and enterprise.
    d) Competition, command, custom, and cooperation.

19. What are the names of the factor payments?
    a) Consumption spending and investment spending.
    b) Wages and profits.
    c) Wages, interest, and profits.
    d) Wages, interest, rent, and profits.

20. What are two examples of economic models?
    a) Opportunity costs and comparative advantage.
    b) Scarcity of resources and unlimited wants.
    c) Positive statements and normative statements.
    d) The circular flow of income and the production possibilities curve.

21. All of the following, except one, are capital goods. Which is the exception?
    a) An office building.
    b) A boiler in a pulp mill.
    c) A garden shed.
    d) An airport runway.

22. Which of the following is not a macroeconomic goal?
    a) Improvements in the standard of living.
    b) Ensuring that the true needs of all people are met.
    c) Full employment.
    d) Stable prices.

23. Which of the following should be included in a definition of economics?
    a) Money, income, and wealth.
    b) The stock market.
    c) Ways that individuals can make money.
    d) The scarcity of resources, the necessity of choice, and human wants and needs.

Intermediate (Questions 24–30)

24. Which of the following refers to the concept of specialization?
    a) Different individuals value goods differently.
    b) Some individuals are richer than others.
    c) Different nations have different opportunity costs of producing goods.
    d) Some nations are richer than others.

25. A simple model of the circular flow includes reference to all but one of the following. Which is the exception?
   a) Spending on exports and imports.
   b) Both physical and financial flows.
   c) The factors of production.
   d) Both the business and the household sectors.

26. Which of the following is most valid with respect to macroeconomic goals?
   a) They tend to complement each other.
   b) They are always in conflict with each other.
   c) Some are complementary and some are in conflict.
   d) They are accepted as valid by everyone in society.

27. What is the distinction between a positive and a normative statement?
   a) Positive statements are assertions that can be tested with data, whereas normative statements are based on a value system of beliefs.
   b) Normative statements are assertions that can be tested with data, whereas positive statements are based on a value system of beliefs.
   c) The distinction depends on the context in which each statement is used.
   d) Positive statements are correct statements of fact, whereas normative statements are incorrect.

Figure 1.13 shows Mendork's production possibility curve for the only two goods that it produces—guns and butter. Refer to this figure to answer questions 28–32.

FIGURE 1.13

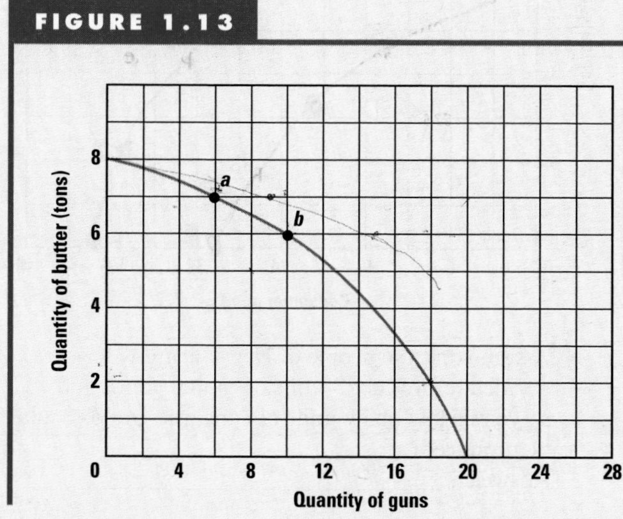

28. Refer to **Figure 1.13** to answer this question. If Mendork's production is currently that indicated by point *a*, what is the cost of producing four more guns?
   a) 1 ton of butter.
   b) 2 tons of butter.
   c) 6 tons of butter.
   d) 10 tons of butter.

29. Refer to **Figure 1.13** to answer this question. What is the opportunity cost of one more ton of butter as output changes from point *b* to *a*?
   a) 2 guns.
   b) 4 guns.
   c) 10 guns.
   d) 6 guns.

30. Refer to **Figure 1.13** to answer this question. Which of the following statements is correct if Mendork is currently producing 5 tons of butter and 8 guns?
   a) This society is using competition to coordinate its economic activities.
   b) This society is experiencing either unemployment or inefficiency.
   c) This economy is experiencing full employment.
   d) This society is not adequately answering the "for whom" question.
   e) This economy is growing quickly.

Advanced (Questions 31–35)

31. Refer to **Figure 1.13** to answer this question. What is the opportunity cost of producing 2 tons of butter?
   a) 2 guns.
   b) 18 guns.
   c) 20 guns.
   d) The answer cannot be determined from the information given.

32. Refer to **Figure 1.13** to answer this question. If new technology increased the output of guns by 50 percent, how many guns could be produced if 6 tons of butter were produced?
   a) 18 guns.
   b) 20 guns.
   c) 15 guns.
   d) 10 guns.
   e) 0 guns.

33. Which of the following statements is implied by a straight-line production possibilities curve?
   a) The law of increasing costs doesn't apply.
   b) The resources being used are homogeneous.
   c) The two goods being produced are very similar.
   d) The opportunity cost of both goods is constant.
   e) All of the above are correct.

34. Which of the following statements describes the law of increasing costs as it relates to the whole economy?

a) As the quantity produced of any particular item decreases, its per unit cost of production rises.
b) As the quantity produced of any particular item increases, its per unit cost of production rises.
c) The prices of consumer goods and services always rise and never fall.
d) If you wait to make a purchase, you will pay a higher price.
e) The total cost of production rises as output goes up.

35. Which of the following statements is correct for a society that emphasizes the production of capital goods over that of consumer goods?

a) The society could enjoy the same quantity of capital goods and a larger quantity of consumer goods in the future.
b) The society will have to save more now than a society that did not emphasize the production of capital goods.
c) The society could enjoy the same quantity of consumer goods and a larger quantity of capital goods in the future.
d) The society will grow faster than a society that emphasizes the production of consumer goods.
e) All of the above are correct.

Parallel Problems

ANSWERED PROBLEMS

36. Key Problem Table 1.6 contains the production possibilities data for capital goods and consumer goods in the economy of New Harmony.

TABLE 1.6

	A	B	C	D	E
Capital goods	12	9	6	3	0
Consumer goods	0	12	21	27	30

a) Use the grid in **Figure 1.14** to draw the production possibilities curve for New Harmony, and label it PPI. Label each of the five output combinations with the letters *a* through *e*.

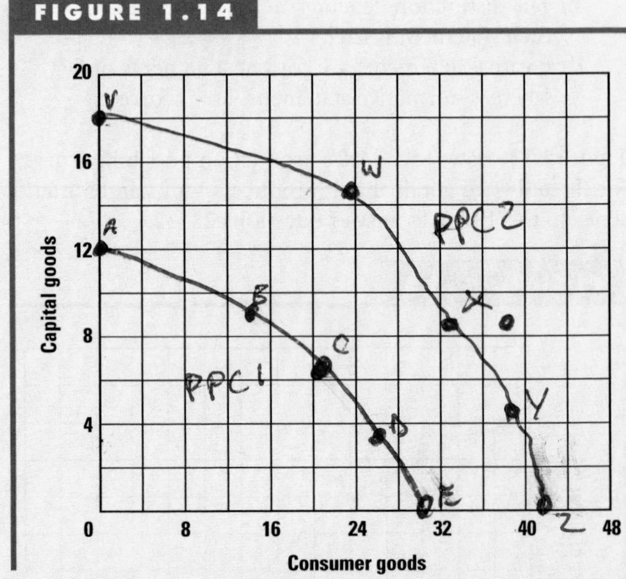

b) Assume that the people of New Harmony have decided to produce 3 units of capital goods and services. How many units of consumer goods could be produced?
Answer: ______________________.

c) Assuming the economy is producing combination C, what is the opportunity cost of 3 more units of capital goods?
Answer: ______________________.

d) Assuming the economy is producing combination B, what is the opportunity cost of 3 more units of capital goods?
Answer: ______________________.

e) What law is illustrated by your answers to c) and d)?
Answer: ______________________.

f) Fill in **Table 1.7** assuming that, 10 years later, the output potential of capital goods has increased 50 percent while the output potential for consumers goods has risen by 12 for each of combinations B through E.

TABLE 1.7

	V	W	X	Y	Z
Capital goods and services	___	___	___	___	___
Consumer goods and services	___	___	___	___	___

g) Using the data from this table, draw in PP2 in **Figure 1.14.**

h) Given **Table 1.7**, how many units of consumer goods could be produced if 9 units of capital goods were produced?
Answer: ______________________.

i) Given **Table 1.7**, what could you say about the economy of New Harmony if 8 units of capital goods and services, and 30 units of consumer goods and services were being produced?
Answer: ______________________
______________________.

j) What are three possible reasons that would explain the shift from PP1 to PP2?
Answer: ______________________
______________________.

Basic (Problems 37–40)

37. Match the letters on the left with the numbers on the right. Place the correct letter in the blank.

a) capital good
b) recession
c) exports and imports
d) labour
e) enterprise
f) factors of production
g) ways of coordinating an economy
h) the fundamental questions in economics

1. cooperation, custom, command, and competition ________
2. the service of a brain surgeon ________
3. high unemployment ________
4. a satellite ________
5. land, labour, capital, and enterprise ________
6. what, how, and for whom ________
7. balance of trade ________
8. the original marketing of a new power cell ________

38. Change the following two positive statements into normative statements.

a) The rate of savings in Canada is approximately 10 percent of national income.

____
____

b) Unemployment has increased by 2 percentage points over the last year.

____
____

39. Below is a list of resources. Indicate whether each is land (N), labour (L), capital (K), or enterprise (E).

a) An irrigation ditch in Manitoba. ________.
b) The work done by Jim Plum, a labourer who helped to dig the irrigation ditch.________.
c) A lake. ________.
d) The air we breathe. ________.
e) The efforts of the founder and primary innovator of a successful new software company. ________.

40. The data in **Table 1.8** below is for the small country of Xanadu. Assume that the economy is originally producing combination C and technological change occurs that enables it to produce 60 percent more capital goods.

TABLE 1.8

	A	B	C	D	E	F
Capital goods	0	25	40	50	55	58
Consumer goods	50	40	30	20	10	0

a) If the economy wants to continue with the same quantity of consumer goods, how many more capital goods can it now have as a result of the technological improvement? ________.

b) If instead the economy wants to continue with the same quantity of capital goods, how many more consumer goods can it now have as a result of the technological improvement? ________ .

c) Before the technological change, what was the opportunity cost of the first 40 consumer goods?

________ .

d) After the technological change, what was the opportunity cost of the first 40 consumer goods?

________ .

Intermediate (Problems 41–45)

41. Explain the analogy between the use of theory and the use of a map. ________________________________

____

________________________________ .

42. Shangri-La produces only two goods: bats and balls. Each worker comes with a fixed quantity of material and capital, and the economy's labour force is fixed at 50 workers. **Table 1.9** indicates the amounts of bats and balls that can be produced daily with various quantities of labour.

TABLE 1.9

Number of Workers	Daily Production of Balls	Number of Workers	Daily Production of Bats
0	0	0	0
10	150	10	20
20	250	20	36
30	325	30	46
40	375	40	52
50	400	50	55

a) What is the opportunity cost of increasing the output of bats from 46 to 52 units per day? ______ .

b) What is the opportunity cost of increasing the output of balls from 325 to 375 units per day? ___ .

c) Suppose that a central planning office dictates an output of 250 balls and 61 bats per day. Is this output combination possible? ________ .

d) Now assume that a new technology is introduced in the production of bats so *each worker* can produce 1/2 a bat more per day. Can the planning office's goal of 250 balls and 61 bats now be met? _______ .

43. Jennifer is planning how to spend a particularly rainy Sunday, and the choice is between watching video movies (each lasting 2 hours) or studying her economics textbook. She has 10 hours available to her. If she decides to study, she could read the following number of pages:

2 hours	80 pages
4 hours	130 pages
6 hours	160 pages
8 hours	175 pages
10 hours	180 pages

a) Given this information, draw Jennifer's production possibilities curve between movies watched and pages studied on the grid in **Figure 1.15**.

FIGURE 1.15

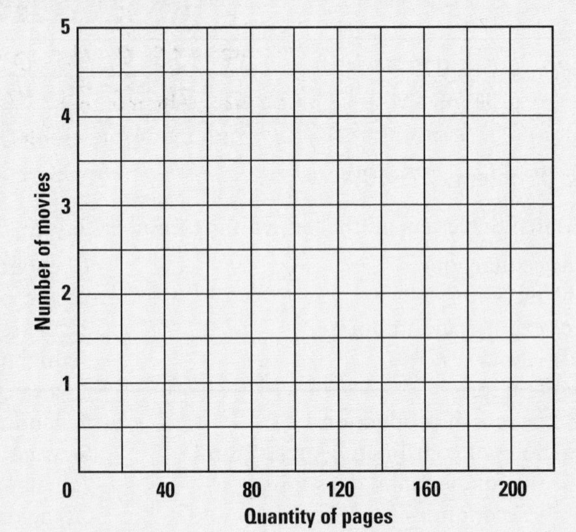

b) What is the opportunity cost of watching 2 movies?

________ .

c) Could Jennifer watch 3 movies and study 150 pages of her textbook? ________ .

d) If Jennifer has already watched 4 movies, what is the opportunity cost of watching the fifth movie?

________ .

44. The data below shows the total production (in millions) of the only two goods produced in Kitchener and Waterloo, two small planets in deep space.

Kitchener	16 kiwis	or	12 trucks
Waterloo	8 kiwis	or	14 trucks

a) What is the opportunity cost of a kiwi in Kitchener?

________________ .

b) What is the opportunity cost of a kiwi in Waterloo?

________________ .

c) What is the opportunity cost of a truck in Kitchener? ________________ .

d) What is the opportunity cost of a truck in Waterloo?

______________________.

e) Which planet is best at producing kiwis?

______________________.

f) Which planet is best at producing trucks?

______________________.

g) If, before trade, each planet was devoting half its resources to producing each product, what is the total amount that they were producing?

______________________.

h) If the two planets were to specialize in producing the product they do best, what would be the total amount they could produce?

______________________.

i) What are the total gains as a result of specialization?

______________________.

45. Match the letters on the left with the numbers on the right. Place the correct letter in the blank. (Data refers to Canada.)

a) $30 000 per person	**1.** inflation	______
b) 2.25 percent per year	**2.** unemployment	______
c) dropped steadily since 1993	**3.** economic growth	______
d) below 2 percent since 1993	**4.** standard of living	______

Advanced (Problems 46–47)

46. To what extent is the organization of family based on the four Cs? Give examples of how each of the four Cs is used to assign household chores to its members. What blend of the four Cs do you think is preferable, and why?

____

____

____

____.

47. Kant Skatte is a professional player in the National Hockey League. Beacause he loved the game so much, Kant dropped out of high school and worked very hard to develop his physical strength and overcome his limitations. Eventually he made it to the NHL. What data is needed to estimate Kant's annual opportunity costs, in dollars, of continuing to play in the NHL?

____

____

____.

UNANSWERED PROBLEMS

48. Key Problem Table 1.10 contains the production possibilities data for capital goods and consumer goods in the economy of Waldon.

TABLE 1.10

	A	B	C	D	E
Capital goods	8	6	4	2	0
Consumer goods	0	10	16	19	20

a) Draw a PPI for Waldon on **Figure 1.16.**

FIGURE 1.16

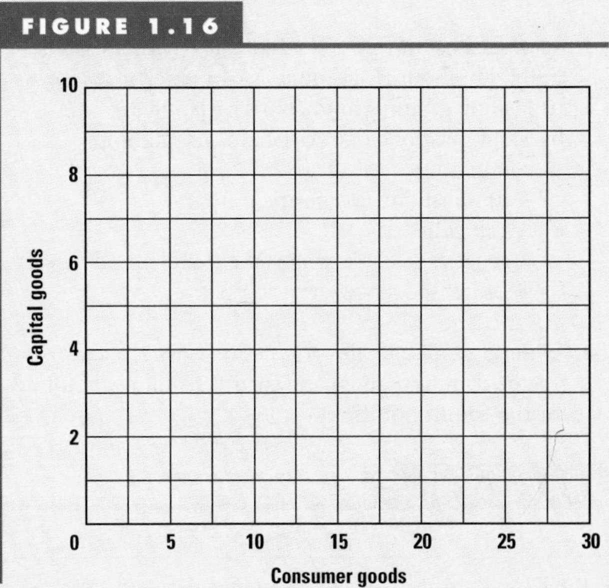

b) Assume that the people of Waldon have decided to produce 2 units of capital goods. How many units of consumer goods could be produced?
c) Assume that the economy is currently producing combination D. What is the opportunity cost of 2 more units of capital goods?
d) Again starting from combination D, what is the opportunity cost of 1 more unit of consumer goods?
e) What is the opportunity cost of the very first 2 units of capital goods? Of the last 2 units?
f) Make a table assuming that, 10 years later, the potential output of both capital and consumer goods increases by 25 percent.
g) Draw the data (from the table you constructed in f) above) on **Figure 1.16** as PP2.
h) Given PP2, how many units of consumer goods could be produced if 5 units of capital goods were produced?
i) Given the table you constructed in f), what could you say about the economy of Waldon if 5 units of capital goods and 18 units of consumer goods were being produced?
j) What are three possible reasons that would explain the shift from PP1 to PP2?

Basic (Problems 49–52)

49. Match the letters on the left with the blanks on the right.

a) scarcity	1. shifts the PP curve to the right	________
b) the 4 Cs	2. advantages to trade	________
c) specialization	3. forces choice	________
d) models	4. normative statement	________
e) circular flow	5. opportunity costs	________
f) technological improvement	6. financial and real flows	________
g) value judgment	7. ways of organizing society	________
h) next-best alternative	8. method of abstracting what is important	________

50. Change the following two normative statements into positive statements.
a) All students should take a course in economics.
b) Economic growth is a desirable goal for a country.

51. Below is a list of resources. Indicate whether each is land (N), labour (L), capital (K), or enterprise (E).
a) Fishing grounds in the north Atlantic.
b) The work done by Yves Gaton, a symphony conductor.
c) A fish farm in Nova Scotia.
d) A golf course.
e) A genetics scientist who is the founder and driving force behind a new drug company.

52. **Table 1.11** presents the production possibilities for tractors (in thousands) and carrots (millions of tonnes) for the country of Risa.

TABLE 1.11

	A	B	C	D	E	F
Tractors	200	180	150	110	60	0
Carrots	0	100	180	240	290	330

Assume that the economy is originally producing combination C and technological change occurs that enables it to produce 80% more carrots.
a) If the economy wants to continue with the same quantity of tractors, how many more carrots can it now produce as a result of the technological change?
b) If instead, the economy wants to continue to produce the same quantity of carrots, how many more tractors can it now produce?
c) Before the technological change, what was the opportunity cost of the first 60 tractors?
d) After the technological change, what was the opportunity cost of the first 60 tractors?

Intermediate (Problems 53–57)

53. Construct your own definition of economics.

54. Lost Horizon produces only two goods: stuffed elephants and stuffed donkeys. Each worker comes with a fixed quantity of material and capital, and the economy's labour force is fixed at 25 workers. **Table 1.12** indicates the amounts of elephants and donkeys that can be produced daily with various quantities of labour.

TABLE 1.12

Number of Workers	Daily Production of Elephants	Number of Workers	Daily Production of Donkeys
0	0	0	0
5	200	5	300
10	375	10	550
15	525	15	750
20	650	20	900
25	750	25	1000

a) What is the opportunity cost of increasing the output of elephants from 375 to 525?
b) What is the opportunity cost of increasing the output of donkeys from 750 to 900?
c) Suppose that the planning office dictates an output of 525 elephants and 750 donkeys. Is this output combination possible?
d) Now assume that new technology is introduced in the production of elephants so that each worker can produce 20 more donkeys a day. Can the planning office's dictate of 525 elephants and 750 donkeys now be met?

55. Gale is planning how to spend Sunday. She loves to cycle, but also needs to do some work editing pages for one of her publisher clients. She has eight hours available and can edit pages at the following rate:

2 hours	40 pages
4 hours	75 pages
6 hours	105 pages
8 hours	125 pages

a) Could Gale cycle for 6 hours and edit 105 pages?
b) If Gale has already cycled for 6 hours, what is the opportunity cost of 2 more hours of cycling?
c) What is the opportunity cost of cycling for the first two hours?

56. The data below shows the total production (in millions) of the only two goods produced in Amherst and New Glasgow, two small planets in deep space.

Amherst	40 haggis	or	8 carts
New Glasgow	10 haggis	or	20 carts

a) What is the opportunity cost of a haggis in Amherst?
b) What is the opportunity cost of a haggis in New Glasgow?
c) What is the opportunity cost of a cart in Amherst?
d) What is the opportunity cost of a cart in New Glasgow?
e) On which planet is haggis cheaper?
f) On which planet are carts cheaper?
g) If, before trade, each planet was devoting half its resources to producing each product, what is the total amount that they were producing?
h) If the two planets were to each specialize in producing the product they do best, what would be the total amount they could produce?
i) What are the total gains as a result of specialization?

57. Match the letters on the left with the numbers on the right. Place the correct letter in the blank.

a) high rates of unemployment	1) economic growth	______
b) consistently low inflation	2) Great Depression	______
c) both benefits and costs	3) 1990s	______
d) rising exports	4) NAFTA	______

Advanced (Problems 58–62)

58. Can you think of three examples in which contemporary Canadian society uses the element of command to help coordinate production?

59. Ken has just graduated from secondary school. His uncle has offered him a full-time job, for $20 000 per year, at his home improvement supply outlet. Ken, however, has his heart set on going to university for four years to get a degree in engineering, and unfortunately his uncle can't use him on a part-time basis. Tuition and books for the four years will cost Ken $14 000. What is Ken's opportunity cost of getting a degree?

60. Assume that a piece of land can produce either 600 bushels of corn and no soybeans, or 300 bushels of soybeans and no corn. You may further assume that this corn–beans ratio of 2:1 is constant.

Draw a production possibilities curve for this piece of land. Next, indicate with the letters *a* and *b* an increase in bean production. Finally, illustrate with a triangle the cost of these additional beans.

61. Comment on the following statement: "The 'for whom' question is the easiest of the three fundamental questions in economics to answer because it involves normative statements."

62. List three possible economic goals. For each goal, identify a conflicting goal and a complementary goal, and explain your reasoning.

Web-Based Activities

1. In order to get a grasp on an academic discipline such as economics, it is often important to know a little about the history and founders of that discipline. Go to **www.bizednet.bris.ac.uk/virtual/economy/library/economists** and briefly discuss each of the contributions made by the various economists to the main schools of thought: classical/neoclassical, Keynesian, and monetarist.

2. Read the following speech, given by the Honourable Paul Martin, then minister of finance, on November 2, 1999: **www.fin.gc.ca/update99/speeche.html**. What were the macroeconomic goals being followed by the federal government at that time? What do you think was the most important macroeconomic goal? Explain.

CHAPTER TWO

Demand and Supply: An Introduction

LEARNING OBJECTIVES

This chapter will enable you to:

LO1 Explain the concept of demand.

LO2 Explain the concept of supply.

LO3 Explain the term the market.

LO4 Understand the concept of (price and quantity) equilibrium.

LO5 Understand the causes and effects of a change in demand.

LO6 Understand the causes and effects of a change in supply.

LO7 Understand why demand and supply determine price and the quantity traded and not the reverse.

What's ahead...

This chapter introduces you to the fundamental economic ideas of demand and supply. It explains the distinction between individual and market demand and looks at the various reasons why the demand for products changes from time to time. We then take a look at things from the producers' point of view and explain what determines the amounts that they put on the market. Next we explain how markets are able to reconcile the wishes of the two groups, and we introduce the concept of equilibrium. Finally, we look at how the market price and the quantity traded adjust to various changes.

A QUESTION OF RELEVANCE...

Have you ever wondered why the prices of some products, like computers or CD players, tend to fall over time, while the prices of other products, such as cars or auto insurance, tend to rise? Or perhaps you wonder how the price of a house can fluctuate tens of thousands of dollars from year to year. Why does a poor orange harvest in Florida cause the price of apple juice made in Ontario to rise? And why do sales of typewriters continue to fall, despite their lower prices? This chapter will give you insights into questions like these.

If the average person were to think about the subject matter of economics, it is unlikely that she would immediately think of choice or opportunity costs, which was a principal topic of Chapter 1. More likely, she would think in terms of money or interest rates and, almost certainly, demand and supply. Most people realize, without studying the topic, that demand and supply are central to economics. In our own ways, and as a result of our experiences in life, most of us feel that we know quite a lot about the subject. After all, who are better experts on the reaction of consumers to changes in the market than consumers themselves? However, as we will see shortly, the way that economists define and use the terms "demand" and "supply" differs from the everyday usage. To make matters worse, there doesn't seem to be a consensus among non-economists about the meaning of either of these two words: there is a range of meaning. This is often the case with language, but it does lead to a great deal of confusion, which can be illustrated in the following exchange between two observers of the housing market:

> Isn't it shocking that house prices have increased so much in the past year? It makes it very difficult for first-time buyers to get into the market.
>
> Well, yes, but that's the law of demand. Presumably builders can get away with charging a higher price as long as people are willing to pay.
>
> Are you suggesting that the demand for new houses has increased, then?
>
> Yes, it must have.
>
> But surely, higher prices are going to lead to a lower demand. I thought that was the law of demand!
>
> Well, yes. But, don't you see, a lower demand will lead to lower prices.
>
> And lower prices to a higher demand…

What's happening here? There seems to be some confusion, but what is causing it? Is it because neither of the speakers know what they are talking about? Well, that's a possibility, of course. But more likely the root cause of the confusion surrounds that simple word "demand." As we shall see, demand is being used in two different ways, and neither speaker is aware of this. It's probably clear to you already that economists are very fussy about defining and using economic terms correctly, and this is particularly true in a discussion about demand and supply. Demand doesn't simply mean what people want to buy, nor is supply just the amount being produced. Besides the problem of definitions, another source of confusion in the above discussion is a misunderstanding of cause and effect: is the change in house prices the effect of changing demand, or is it the cause? This chapter will clear up some of the confusion and give us a basis upon which to analyze and clarify some real, practical problems. First, let us take a look at the concept of demand.

2.1 Demand

LO1
Explain the concept of demand.

demand: the quantities that consumers are willing and able to buy per period of time at various prices.

Individual Demand

There are several dimensions to the term **demand**. First, economists use the word not in the sense of commanding or ordering but in the sense of wanting something. However, this want also involves the ability to buy. In other words, demand refers to both *the desire and the ability to purchase* a good or service. This means that although I may well have a desire for a new top-of-the-line BMW, I unfortunately don't have the ability to buy one at current prices, and therefore my quantity demanded is zero.

Second, even though we know there are many factors that determine what products and what quantities a consumer purchases, economists would suggest that the price is usually the most important of these, and for this reason they look at how consumers might react to a change in the price assuming that all other factors remain unchanged. The Latin phrase for this perspective is **ceteris paribus**, which literally means "other things being equal." However, it is usually interpreted by economists to mean "other things remaining the same." In other words, demand is the relationship between the price of a product and the quantities demanded, *ceteris paribus.*

ceteris paribus: other things being equal, or other things remaining the same.

Third, demand is a hypothetical construct that expresses this desire and ability to purchase, not at a single price, but over *a range of* hypothetical prices. Finally, demand is also a flow concept, in that it measures quantities over a period of time. In summary, demand:

- involves both the consumers' desire and ability to purchase
- assumes that other things are held constant
- refers to a range of prices
- measures quantities over time

All of these aspects of demand are captured in **Table 2.1**, which shows the **demand schedule** for an enthusiastic beer drinker named Tomiko.

demand schedule: a table showing the various quantities demanded per period of time at different prices.

TABLE 2.1 **Individual Demand**

Price per Case	Quantity Demanded (Number of Cases per Week)
$12	6
13	5
14	4
15	3
16	2
17	1
18	0

Once again, what we mean by demand is the entire relationship between the various prices and the quantities that people are willing and able to purchase, and this relationship can be laid out in the form of a demand schedule. The above schedule shows the amounts per week that Tomiko is willing and able to purchase at the various prices shown. Note that there is an *inverse* relationship between the price and quantity. This simply means that at higher prices Tomiko would not be willing to buy as much as at lower prices. In other words:

The higher the price, the lower the quantity demanded; and the lower the price, the higher the quantity demanded.

Another, though less obvious, statement of this law of demand is to say that in order to induce Tomiko to buy a greater quantity of beer, the price must be lower. Tomiko's demand schedule is graphed in **Figure 2.1**.

In **Figure 2.1**, at a price of $15 per case, the quantity demanded by Tomiko is 3 cases per week, while at a lower price of $12 per case, she would be willing to buy 6 cases. The demand is therefore plotted as a downward-sloping curve. (To economists, curves include straight lines!) Once again, note that when we use the terms "demand," or "demand schedule," or "demand curve," we are referring to a whole array of different prices and quantities.

FIGURE 2.1 **Individual Demand Curve**

At a price of $12 per case, Tomiko is willing and able to buy 6 cases per week. At a higher price, $15 per case, the amount she is willing and able to buy falls to 3 cases. The higher the price, then, the lower the quantity demanded. (Note that the vertical axis contains a "broken" portion. In general, an axis is often broken in this manner whenever the information about, say, low prices, is unavailable or unimportant.)

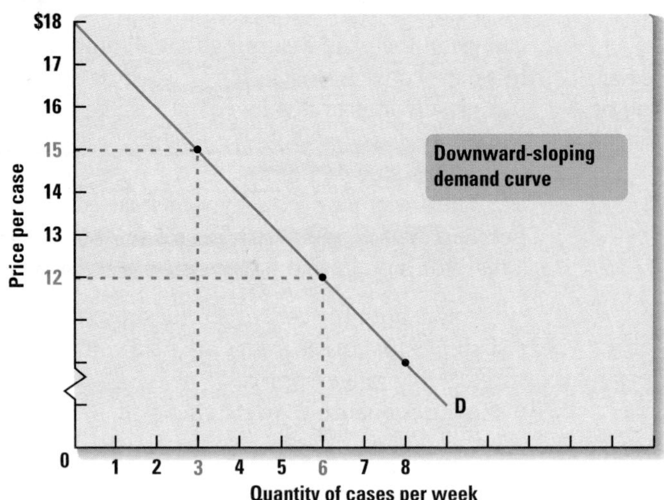

change in the quantity demanded: the change in quantity that results from a price change. It is illustrated by a movement along a demand curve.

It is very important for you to note that since the price of any product is part of what we call the "demand" for that product, a change in the price cannot change the demand. Certainly it can affect the *amounts* we are willing to purchase, and we express this by saying that:

A change in the price of a product results in a change in the quantity demanded for that product.

This is illustrated in **Figure 2.2**. Graphically, as we move down the demand curve, the quantity demanded increases; as we move up the demand curve, the quantity demanded decreases.

FIGURE 2.2 **Changes in the Quantity Demanded**

Whenever the price changes, there is a movement along the demand curve. An increase in the price from, say, P_1 to P_2, causes a decrease in the quantity demanded from Q_1 to Q_2. A decrease in the price from P_3 to P_4 leads to an increase in the quantity demanded from Q_3 to Q_4. Neither the demand nor the demand curve, however, changes.

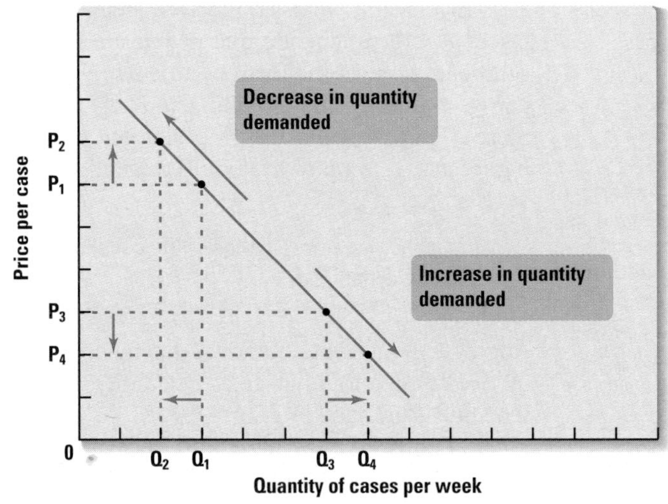

Why Is the Demand Curve Downward-Sloping?

There are a number of rationales for the proposition that people tend to buy more at lower rather than at higher prices. Most of us can confirm from our own experience that a lower price will induce us to buy more of a product or to buy something that we would or could not purchase before. Witness the big crowds that are attracted to nothing more than a sign saying,"SALE." In addition, most microeconomic research done over the years tends to confirm this law of demand, and theories of consumer behaviour (such as the marginal utility theory, which we will study in Chapter 5) lend additional support to the idea.

PhotoDisc

A SALE sign is often all it takes to attract consumers.

Let's begin our exploration of the question of why people tend to buy more at lower prices. Remember that our demand for products is a combination of our desire and our ability to purchase. A lower price affects both of these. The lower the price of a product, the more income a person has left to purchase additional products. Let's explain this by assuming, for instance, that the price of beer in **Table 2.1** was $14, and Tomiko was buying 4 cases per week, for a total expenditure of $56 per week. Next, let's say the price decreases to $12. Tomiko could, if she wished, buy the same quantity for an outlay of $48, thus saving a total of $8. It's almost as if Tomiko had received a pay raise of $8. In fact, in terms of its effect on Tomiko's pocketbook, it is exactly the same. Or, as economists would express it, her **real income** has increased. A decrease in price means that people can afford to buy more of a product (or more of other products) if they wish. This is referred to as the **income effect** of a price change, and it affects people's *ability* to purchase. This is because a lower price means a higher real income, and as a result people will tend to buy more of a product. (Conversely, an increase in the price would effectively reduce people's real income.)

real income: income measured in terms of the amount of goods and services that it will buy. Real income will increase if either actual income increases or prices fall.

In addition to this, a price change also affects people's *desire* to purchase. We are naturally driven to buy the cheaper of competing products, and a drop in the price of one of them increases our desire to substitute it for the now relatively more expensive product. For instance, if the price of wine were to drop (or for that matter, if the price of beer were to increase), then some beer drinkers might well switch to what they regard as a cheaper substitute. In general, there are substitutes for most products, and people will tend to substitute a relatively cheap product for a more expensive one. This is called the **substitution effect**. A higher price, on the other hand, tends to make the product less attractive to us than its substitutes, and so we buy less of it.

income effect: the effect that a price change has on real income, and therefore on the quantity demanded of a product.

When the price of a product drops, we will buy more of it because we are *more able* (the income effect) and because we are *more willing* (the substitution effect). Conversely, a price increase means we are less able and less willing to buy the product, and therefore we buy less. (There is a possible exception to this, which we will look at in the next chapter.)

substitution effect: the substitution of one product for another as a result of a change in their relative prices.

The close relationship that exists between the price and the quantity demanded is so pervasive that it is often referred to as the *law of demand*.

Market Demand

market demand: the total demand for a product by all consumers.

Up to this point, we have focused on individual demand. Now we want to move to **market demand** (or total demand). Conceptually, this is easy enough to do. By summing every individual's demand for a product, we are able to obtain the market demand. **Table 2.2** provides a simple example.

TABLE 2.2 Deriving the Market Demand

NUMBER OF CASES PER WEEK					
Price per Case	**Tomiko's Demand**	**Meridith's Demand**	**Abdi's Demand**	**Jan's Demand**	**Market Demand**
$12	6	3	4	9	22
13	5	2	4	7	18
14	4	2	4	6	16
15	3	0	3	3	9
16	2	0	3	1	6
17	1	0	2	0	3
18	0	0	2	0	2

Let's say we know not only Tomiko's demand but also the demands of three other friends in a small, four-person economy. The market demand then is the horizontal summation of individual demands, which simply means that to find the quantities demanded at $12 we add the quantities demanded by each individual, that is, 6 + 3 + 4 + 9 = 22. The same would be done for each price level. This particular market demand is graphed in **Figure 2.3**. Note that this demand curve, which is the summation of the specific numbers of the four people in **Table 2.2**, is not a straight line. Yet, it is still downward-sloping and so conforms to the law of demand. For the most part we will work with straight-line demand curves, although there is no reason to assume that all real-life demand curves plot as straight lines.

FIGURE 2.3 The Market Demand Curve

At a price of $12, the total or market quantity demanded equals 22 cases. As with individual demand, when the price increases to $16, then the quantity demanded will drop, in this case to 6. This is because at a higher price, each individual buys less, and in addition there are fewer people who can afford to or are willing to buy any at all. (Meridith has dropped out of the market.)

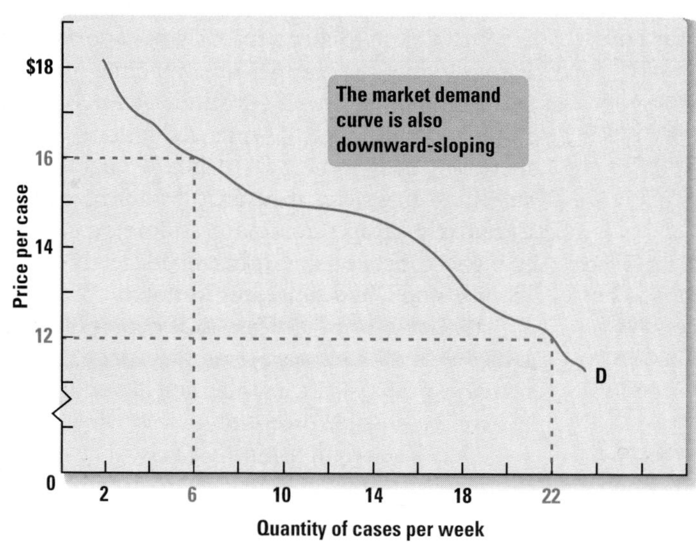

Note that, as with the individual demand curve, the market demand curve also slopes downward. This is because not only do people buy more as the price drops, but in addition more people buy. At a price of $18 in our example, only Abdi would buy any beer. As the price drops to $16, not only would Abdi buy beer, but so too would Tomiko and Jan. The price would need to drop to $14 to induce all four people to buy beer.

Finally, before we take a look at the supply side of the market, note again that our demand schedule tells us only what people *might* buy; it tells us nothing about what they are actually buying, because to know this we also need to know the actual price. And to find out what the actual price of beer is, we need to know...yes, the supply.

SELF-TEST

1. The data in the next table indicates the weekly demand for litres of soy milk by Al, Bo, and Cole (the only three people in a very small market).

a) Fill in the blanks in the table.

b) What is the basic shape of the demand curve in this market?

c) What is the total quantity demanded at a price of $2.50?

Price	Quantity Demanded: Al	Quantity Demanded: Bo	Quantity Demanded: Cole	Total (market) Quantity Demanded:
$4.00	1	0	0	______
3.50	1	1	0	______
3.00	1	1	1	______
2.50	2	1	1	______
2.00	2	2	1	______

2.2 Supply

LO2
Explain the concept of supply and demand.

Individual Supply

In many ways the formulation of supply is very similar to that of demand. Both measure hypothetical quantities at various prices, and both are flow concepts. However, we now need to look at things through the eyes of the producer, rather than the consumer. We will assume for the time being that the prime motive for the producer is to maximize profits, although we will examine this assumption in more detail in a later chapter. For now we can certainly agree with Adam Smith who, in *The Wealth of Nations*, noted that few producers are in business to please consumers, nor, of course, do consumers buy products to please producers. Both are motivated, instead, by self-interest.

The term **supply** refers to the quantities that suppliers are *willing and able* to make available to the market at various different prices. **Table 2.3** shows a hypothetical **supply schedule** for Bobbie the brewer.

supply: the quantities that producers are willing and able to sell per period of time at various prices.

supply schedule: a table showing the various quantities supplied per period of time at different prices.

ADDED DIMENSION

Adam Smith: The Father of Economics

Adam Smith (1723–90) is generally regarded as the founding father of economics. In his brilliant work, *The Wealth of Nations*, Smith posed so many interesting questions and provided such illuminating answers that later economists often felt that they merely were picking at the scraps he left behind. Smith was born and brought up in Scotland and educated at Glasgow and Oxford. He later held the Chair of Moral Philosophy at Glasgow College for many years. He was a lifelong bachelor and had a kind but absent-minded disposition.

Smith was the first scholar to analyze in a detailed and systematic manner the business of "getting and spending." In doing this, he gave useful social dignity to the professions of business and trading. Besides introducing the important idea of the *invisible hand*, which was his way of describing the coordinating mechanism of capitalism, he examined the division of labour, the role of government, the function of money, the advantages and disadvantages of free trade, what constitutes good and bad taxation, and a host of other ideas. For Smith, economic life was not merely a peripheral adventure for people but their central motivating force.

TABLE 2.3 The Supply Schedule for Bobbie the Brewer

Price per Case	Quantity Supplied (Number of Cases per Week)
$12	2
13	3
14	4
15	5
16	6
17	7
18	8

Note that there is a *direct* relationship between the price and the quantity supplied, which means that a higher price will induce Bobbie to produce more. Remember that Bobbie's reason for being in business is to make as much profit as possible. Suppose that Bobbie was asked how much she will, hypothetically, be prepared to supply if the beer could be sold at $12 per case. Knowing what her costs are likely to be, she figures that she could make the most profit if she produces 2 cases. At a higher price, there is a likelihood of greater profits, and therefore she is willing to produce more. Also, as we shall see in Chapter 6, as firms produce more, often the cost per unit tends to rise and therefore the producer needs the incentive of a higher price *in order to* increase production. For the time being, however, we can rely on the proposition that a higher price means higher profits and therefore will lead to higher quantities produced. This is illustrated in **Figure 2.4**.

Joining together the individual points from the supply schedule in **Table 2.3** gives us the upward-sloping supply curve shown in **Figure 2.4**. Again, we emphasize the fact that, as with the term "demand," the term "supply" does not refer to a single price and quantity, but to the whole array of hypothetical price and quantity combinations contained in the supply schedule and illustrated by the supply curve.

FIGURE 2.4 **Individual Supply Curve**

At a low price of $12, the most profitable output for Bobbie is 2 cases. If the price increased, she would be willing and able to produce more, since she would be able to make greater profits. At $18, for instance, the quantity she would produce increases to 8 cases.

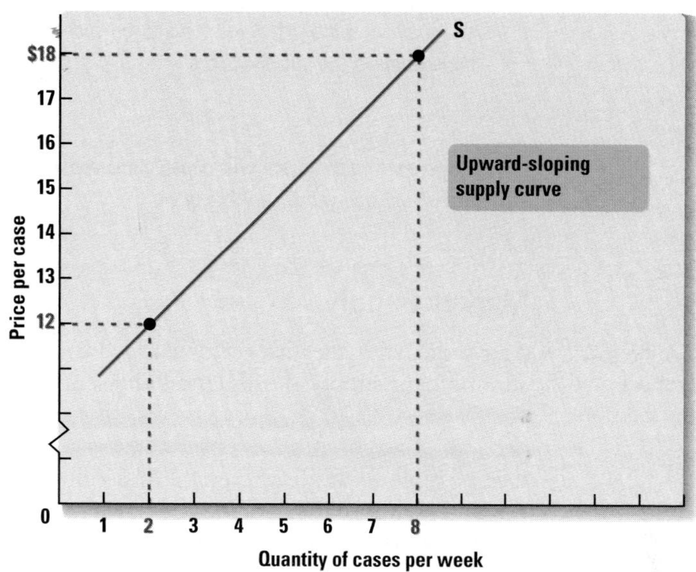

change in the quantity supplied: the change in the amounts that will be produced as a result of a price change. This is shown as a movement along a supply curve.

Since price is part of what we mean by the term supply, a change in the price level cannot change the supply. A change in price does of course lead to a change in the quantity that a producer is willing and able to make available. Thus, the effect of a change in price we call a **change in the quantity supplied.** This is illustrated in **Figure 2.5.**

FIGURE 2.5 **Changes in the Quantity Supplied**

If the price changes, it will lead to a movement along the supply curve. An increase in the price from, say, P_1 to P_2 will cause an increase in the quantity supplied from Q_1 to Q_2. A decrease in the price from P_3 to P_4 will lead to a decrease in the quantity supplied from Q_3 to Q_4. The supply curve itself, however, does not change.

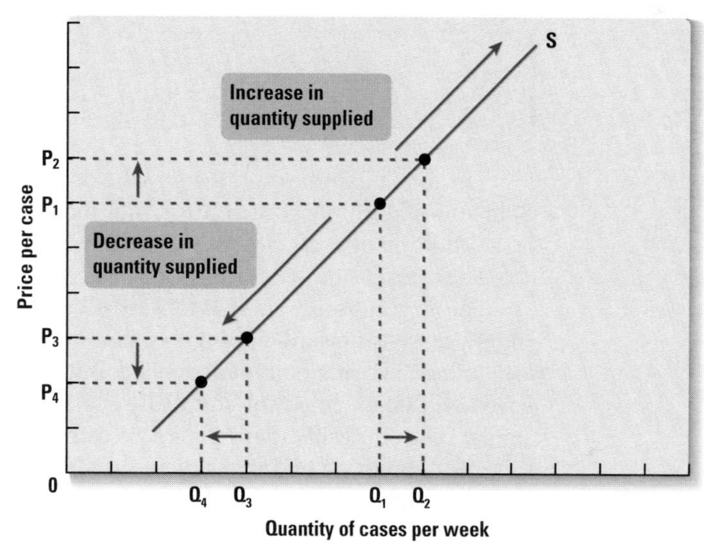

To summarize:

An increase in the price will lead to an *increase in the quantity supplied* and is illustrated as a movement up the supply curve.

A decrease in the price will cause a *decrease in the quantity supplied,* which is illustrated as a movement down the supply curve.

Market Supply

market supply: the total supply of a product offered by all producers.

As we did with the market demand, we can derive the **market supply** of a product by summing the supply of every individual supplier. A word of caution, however, is in order. We must make the necessary assumption that the producers are all producing a similar product and that consumers have no preference as to which supplier or product they use. Given this, it is possible to add together the individual supplies to derive the market supply. In our example, suppose that Bobbie the brewer is competing with three other brewers of similar size and with similar costs. The market supply of beer in this market would be as shown in **Table 2.4.**

TABLE 2.4 Deriving the Market Supply

	NUMBER OF CASES PER WEEK		
Price per Case	**Bobbie the Brewer's Supply**	**Supply of Other Brewers**	**Market Supply**
$12	2	6	8
13	3	9	12
14	4	12	16
15	5	15	20
16	6	18	24
17	7	21	28
18	8	24	32

The total quantities supplied by the three other brewers are equal to the quantities that Bobbie would supply at each price, multiplied by three. The fourth column, market supply, is the addition of every brewer's supply, that is, the second column plus the third column.

The market supply of beer is illustrated in **Figure 2.6.**

The *market* supply curve is upward-sloping primarily for the same reason the *individual* supply curve is upward-sloping: because higher prices imply higher profits and will therefore induce a greater quantity supplied. But there is an additional reason. In the example we have used, we assumed for simplicity's sake that the suppliers are of similar size and have similar costs. In reality that's unlikely: costs and size are likely to differ, so that a price which generates a profit for one firm may mean a loss for another. As the price of a product increases, however, some firms that were previously unable to produce will now find that they can successfully operate at a profit. Thus, as the price of the product increases, currently operating firms will produce more. In addition, other firms not previously producing will enter the market and start to produce.

FIGURE 2.6 **The Market Supply**

The market supply is the horizontal summation of each individual producer's supply curve. For instance, at a price of $15, Bobbie would supply 5 cases; the other brewers combined would produce 15 cases. The market supply therefore is the total quantity supplied of 20 cases. In short, to derive the market supply curve, we add the totals of each supplier at each price level.

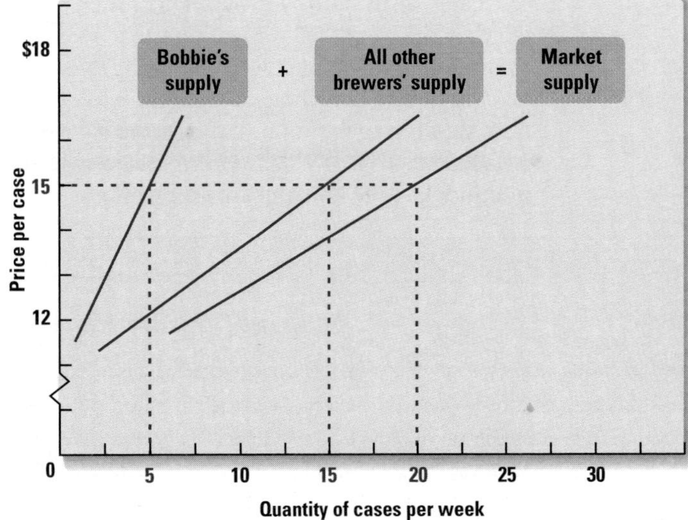

In summary, then, a higher price, which deters consumers from buying more, is an incentive for suppliers to produce more. Conversely, a lower price induces consumers to buy more but is a reason for suppliers to cut back their output.

The motives of consumers and producers are very divergent, the former wishing to obtain the lowest price possible, the latter wanting to sell at the highest. How can their wishes converge? How is trade possible in these circumstances? Well, if the question means: is it possible for *all* prospective consumers and suppliers to be satisfied, the answer must be no. If the question means: is it possible for *some* of these people to be satisfied, the answer will, almost always, be yes. Of course, this will require that they be able in some sense to meet and get together. A market enables them to do just that.

2.3 The Market

LO3
Explain the term the market.

market: a mechanism that brings buyers and sellers together and assists them in negotiating the exchange of products.

Most people are able to understand the terms market price and market demand, but many are not clear as to what constitutes a **market**. Certainly the term includes places that have a physical location, such as a local produce or fish market. But, in broader terms, a market really refers to any exchange mechanism that brings buyers and sellers of a product together. There may be times when we feel that we need to inspect or get further on-the-spot information about a product before we buy it, and this is the purpose of the retail market. But there are other times when we possess sufficient information about a product or a producer that it's not necessary to actually see either of them before we purchase. This applies, for instance, if you wish to buy stocks and bonds or make a purchase on the Internet. Increasingly, in these days of higher costs of personal service and greater availability of electronic communication, markets are becoming both wider and more accessible. The market for commodities such as copper, gold or rubber, for instance, is both worldwide and anonymous, in that the buyers and sellers seldom meet in person.

By a market, then, we mean any environment in which buyers and sellers can communicate, which is relatively open and operates without preference. When we talk of the market price, then, we mean the price available to *all* buyers and sellers of a product; by market demand we mean the total quantities demanded; and market supply refers to the quantity made available by all suppliers at each possible price.

Later in the text, you will encounter a variety of different types of markets, some of which work very well and others that work poorly, if at all. The analysis in this chapter assumes that the market we are looking at is very (economists call it "perfectly") competitive. We will devote the whole of Chapter 8 to examining this type of market in more detail. For now, we need to mention that a perfectly competitive market is, among other things, one in which there are many small producers, each selling an identical product. Keeping this caution in mind, let's see how this market works.

@-CONOMICS

Re-inventing the Market

Capitalism, as we know it today, first emerged and began to spread about 250 years ago as commerce moved out of the occasional village markets of Europe into the age of factory-centred manufacturing, which was then combined with widespread systems of wholesaling and retailing. However, this transformation also introduced a less predicable chain of supply and demand. While the seller in the village market was in direct contact with the buyer, the evolution of capitalism's mass markets and mass production techniques imposed vast gulfs in time and space between the two. Producers became much less sure of what the demand for their product was and buyers were never sure if there wasn't a better deal somewhere else. In response to this, sellers used the blunt tool of a fixed price list and adjusted output accordingly, while buyers just did the best they could. The phenomenon of the Internet is re-inventing commerce as the seller's market horizon expands, buyers have more information, real-time sales become routine, and the need to stockpile inventory diminishes. In short, supply-chain bottlenecks are being eradicated. What is emerging is far *more efficient markets* and the rise of dynamic pricing based on constantly fluctuating demand and supply.

2.4 Market Equilibrium

LO4
Understand the concept of (price and quantity) equilibrium.

We now examine the point at which the wishes of buyers and sellers coincide by combining the market demand and supply for beer in **Table 2.5**.

TABLE 2.5 Market Supply and Demand

NUMBER OF CASES PER WEEK			
Price per Case	**Market Demand**	**Market Supply**	**Surplus (+)/ Shortage (–)**
$12	22	8	–14
13	18	12	–6
14	**16**	**16**	**0**
15	9	20	+11
16	6	24	+18
17	3	28	+25
18	2	32	+30

You can see from this table that there is only one price, $14, at which the wishes of consumers and producers coincide. Only when the price is $14 will the quantities demanded

equilibrium price: the price at which the quantity demanded equals the quantity supplied such that there is neither a surplus nor a shortage.

and supplied be equal. This price level is referred to as the **equilibrium price**. Equilibrium, in general, means that there is balance between opposing forces; here, those opposing forces are demand and supply. The word equilibrium also implies a condition of stability, so that if this stability is disturbed, there will be a tendency to return automatically to equilibrium. To understand this point, refer to **Table 2.5** and notice that if the price were, say, $12, then the amount being demanded, 22, would exceed the amount being supplied, which is 8. At this price there is an excess demand or, more simply, a shortage of beer, to the tune of 14 cases. This amount is shown in the last column and marked with a minus sign. In this situation there would be a lot of unhappy beer drinkers. Faced with the prospect of going beerless, many of them will be prepared to pay a higher price for their suds and will therefore bid the price up. As the price of beer starts to rise, the reaction of consumers and producers will differ. Some beer drinkers will not be able to afford the higher prices, so the quantity demanded will drop. On the supply side, producers will be delighted with the higher price and will start to produce more—and the quantity supplied will increase. Both of these tendencies will combine to reduce the shortage as the price goes up. Eventually, when the price has reached the equilibrium price of $14, the shortage will have disappeared and the price will no longer increase. Part of the law of demand suggests, then, that:

Shortages cause prices to rise.

This is illustrated in **Figure 2.7**.

FIGURE 2.7 **How the Market Reacts to a Shortage**

At a price of $12, the quantity supplied of 8 is far below the quantity demanded of 22. The horizontal distance between the two shows the amount of the shortage, which is 14. As a result of the shortage, price bidding between consumers will force up the price. As the price increases, the quantity demanded will drop, but the quantity supplied will rise until these two are equal at a quantity of 16.

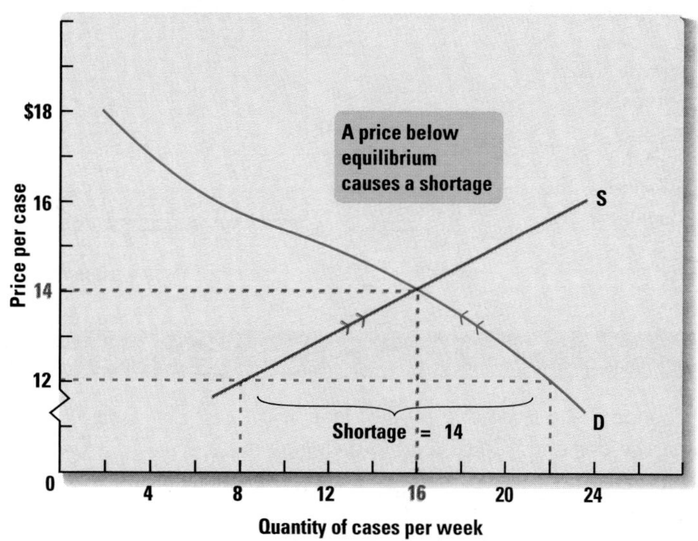

Now let's see, again using **Table 2.5**, what will happen if the price happens to be above equilibrium, at, say, $16 a case. At this price, the quantity demanded is 6 cases, and the quantity supplied is 24 cases. There is insufficient demand from the producers' point of view, or, more simply, there is a surplus (or excess supply) of 18 cases. This is shown in the last column of **Table 2.5** as +18. This is not a stable situation, because firms cannot continue producing a product that they cannot sell. They will be forced to lower the price in an attempt to sell more. As the price starts to drop, two things happen concurrently. Consumers will be happy to consume more, or, to use economic terms, there will be an increase in the quantity demanded. In **Figure 2.8**, note that as the price falls, the quantity demanded increases, and this increase is depicted as a movement down the demand curve. At the same time, faced with a falling price, producers will be forced to cut back production. This is what we have called a decrease in the quantity supplied. In the same figure, this is shown as a movement along (down) the supply curve. The net result of this will be the eventual elimination of the surplus as the price moves toward equilibrium. In other words:

Surpluses cause prices to fall.

equilibrium quantity: the quantity that prevails at the equilibrium price.

Only if the price is $14 will there be no surplus or shortage, and the quantity produced will be equal to the quantity demanded. This is the equilibrium price. The quantity prevailing at the equilibrium price is known as the **equilibrium quantity**, in this case 16 cases. This equilibrium quantity is the quantity both demanded and supplied (since they are equal).

FIGURE 2.8 **How the Market Reacts to a Surplus**

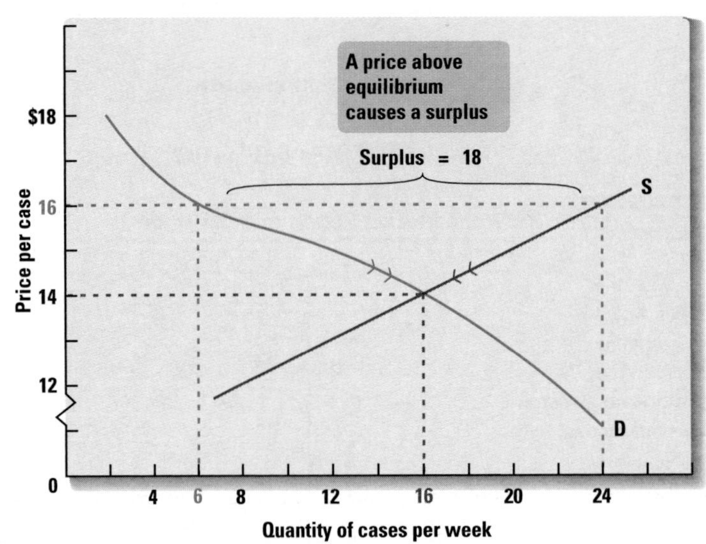

A price above equilibrium will produce a surplus. At $16, the quantity supplied of 24 exceeds the quantity demanded of 6. The horizontal distance of 18 represents the amount of the surplus. The surplus will result in producers dropping the price in an attempt to increase sales. As the price drops, the quantity demanded increases, while the quantity supplied falls. The equilibrium quantity is 16.

SELF-TEST

2. Can a change in the price of a product lead to a change in the demand? Can it lead to a change in supply? Explain.

3. The following table shows the demand and supply of eggs (in hundreds of thousands per day).

a) What is the equilibrium price and the equilibrium quantity?

b) Complete the surplus/shortage column. Using this column, explain why your answer to question A must be correct.

c) What would be the surplus/shortage at a price of $2.50? What would happen to the price and the quantity traded?

d) What would be the surplus/shortage at a price of $4.00? What would happen to the price and the quantity traded?

Price	Demand	Supply	Surplus/ Shortage
$2.00	60	30	______
2.25	58	33	______
2.50	56	36	______
2.75	54	39	______
3.00	52	42	______
3.25	50	45	______
3.50	48	48	______
3.75	46	51	______
4.00	44	54	______

REVIEW

1. Define and explain the difference between the terms *demand* and *quantity demanded.*
2. Why is the demand curve downward-sloping?
3. Explain the *income effect.*
4. Explain the *substitution effect.*
5. What is the distinction between the *supply* and the *quantity supplied*?
6. How will producers respond to a higher price for the product they sell?
7. What does the term *market supply* mean?
8. What is a *market*?
9. What do the terms *equilibrium price* and *equilibrium quantity* mean?
10. What will be the effect of a surplus on price? A shortage?

2.5 Change in Demand

LO5
Understand the causes and effects of a change in demand.

Recall from the definition of demand that the concept refers to the *relationship* between various prices and quantities. In other words, both price and quantity make up what is known as demand. Thus, a change in price cannot cause a change in demand but does cause a change in the quantity demanded. That said, we must now ask: what are the other determinants, besides the price, that would influence how much of any particular product consumers will buy? Another way of looking at this is to ask: once equilibrium price and quantity have been established, what might disturb that equilibrium? The general answer to this question is a **change in demand. Table 2.6** shows such a change in the demand for beer.

change in demand: a change in the quantities demanded at every price, caused by a change in the determinants of demand.

TABLE 2.6 An Increase in Demand

	NUMBER OF CASES PER WEEK	
Price per Case of Beer	**Quantity Demanded 1**	**Quantity Demanded 2**
$12	16	22
13	15	21
14	14	20
15	13	19
16	12	18
17	11	17
18	10	16

Here we will introduce new figures for demand in order to revert back to straight-line demand curves. Let's say that D_1 is the demand for beer that existed last month and D_2 is the demand this month. There has been an increase in demand of 6 cases per week at each price. Put another way, whatever the price, consumers are willing and able to consume an additional 6 cases. Thus, there has been an increase in the demand. **Figure 2.9** graphically illustrates an increase in demand.

An increase in demand, then, means an increase in the quantities demanded *at each price,* that is, a total increase in the demand schedule, which is illustrated by a rightward shift in the demand curve. Similarly, a decrease in demand means a reduction in the quantities demanded at each price—a decrease in the demand schedule—and this is illustrated by a leftward shift in the demand curve.

FIGURE 2.9 **An Increase in Demand**

At each price, the quantities demanded have increased. In this example, the increase is by a constant amount of 6, thus producing a parallel shift in the demand curve. For example, at $14, the quantity demanded has increased from 14 to 20 (by 6).

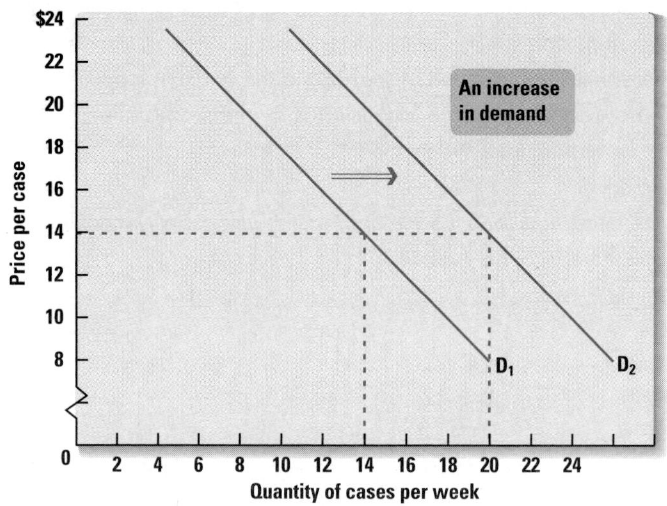

Determinants of a Change in Demand

Having illustrated what an increase in demand looks like, we now need to look at the factors that could bring about such a change. Some of these determinants of demand affect people's willingness to purchase, others affect their ability to purchase, and still others affect both. The first factor that affects our willingness to purchase a product is our own particular *preference*. An increase in demand as shown in **Table 2.6** could simply have been caused by a change in consumer preferences: consumers now prefer more beer.

A host of different things could affect our preferences. Tastes change over time and are influenced by the weather, advertising, articles and reports in books and magazines, opinions of friends, special events, and many other things. Specific examples would include decreased demand for steak as the summer barbeque season passes, increased demand for a book that Oprah featured on her TV show, or increased demand for security products following the tragedy of September 11, 2001. Such things can cause demand to either increase or decrease quite rapidly.

normal products: products whose demand will increase as a result of an increase in income and will decrease as a result of a decrease in income.

inferior products: products whose demands will decrease as a result of an increase in income and will increase as a result of a decrease in income.

The second factor affecting the demand for a product is the *income* of consumers. This will affect their ability to consume. Generally speaking, you would expect that an increase in income leads most people to increase their purchases of most products, and a decrease in income generally causes a drop in the demand, that is, there is a direct relationship between income and demand. This is true for most products that we buy, and these products are called **normal products.** But it is certainly not true for all people and products. For instance, as the incomes of most people increase, these consumers tend to buy less of such things as low-quality hamburger meats, packets of macaroni and cheese, cheap toilet-paper rolls, and so on. Instead, they start to substitute higher-quality and higher-priced articles that they could not previously afford. When income is low, we are forced to survive on lower-quality staple products that economists call **inferior products**. There is an inverse relationship between income and the demand for inferior products. As income levels go up, the demand goes down. It also means that as incomes fall, our demand for these inferior products will rise. In our beer example from **Table 2.6**, the increase in the market demand could have been caused by an *increase* in incomes, because beer is a normal product.

A third important determinant of demand is the *prices of related products.* A change in the price of related products will affect both people's willingness and their ability to purchase a particular good. Products are related if a change in the price of one causes a change in the demand for the other. For instance, if the price of Pepsi were to increase, a number of Pepsi drinkers might well switch over to Coke.

substitute products: any products whose demand varies directly with a change in the price of a similar product.

There are, in fact, two ways in which products may be related. They may be related as substitutes, or they may be related as complements. **Substitute** (or competitive) **products** are products that are sufficiently similar in the eyes of most consumers that price becomes the main distinguishing feature. Pepsi and Coke, therefore, are substitute products because an increase in the price of one will cause an increase in the demand for the other. The relationship between the price of a product and the demand for its substitute is, therefore, a direct one. It also means that if the price of a product falls, then the demand for its substitute will also fall, since many consumers are now buying the cheaper product.

complementary products: products that tend to be purchased jointly and whose demands therefore are related.

Complementary products tend to be purchased together, and their demands are interrelated. Skis and ski boots are complementary products, as are cars and gasoline, or beer and pretzels. If the price of one product increases, causing a decrease in the quantity demanded, then people will also purchase less of the complement. If the price of cameras were to increase so that people were buying fewer cameras, then we would also expect a decline in the demand for not only film but for other complementary products like lenses, tripods, carrying bags, and so on. There is, in this case, an inverse relationship between the price of a product and the demand for its complement, which means that an increase in price of the one product leads to a decline in the demand for the complementary product. Similarly, a decrease in the price of a product will lead to an increase in the demand for a complement.

SELF-TEST

4. The following table shows the initial weekly demand (D_1) and the new demand (D_2) for packets of pretzels (a bar snack).

Price	Demand (D_1)	Demand (D_2)
$2.00	10 000	11 000
2.50	9 800	10 800
3.00	9 600	10 600
3.50	9 400	10 400
4.00	9 200	10 200

To explain the change in demand from D_1 to D_2, what might have happened to the price of a complementary product, like beer? Alternatively, what might have happened to the price of a substitute product, like nuts?

A fourth determinant of demand is the *expectations of the future* on the part of consumers. There are many ways that our feelings about the future influence our present behaviour. Future expected prices and incomes can affect our present demand for a product, as does the prospect of a shortage. If consumers think that the price of their favourite beverage is likely to increase in the near future, they may well stock up in advance, just in case. The present demand for the product will therefore increase. Conversely, expected future price declines cause people to hold off their current purchases while awaiting the hoped-for lower prices.

In a similar fashion, an anticipated pay increase may cause some people to spend more now as they adjust to their expected higher standard of living. Similarly, it does seem likely that most people who fear a layoff or other cause of a drop in salary will cut down spending in advance of the fateful date. Finally, it should be added that the possibility of future shortages, caused for instance by an impending strike, often causes a mad rush to the stores by anxious customers trying to stock up in advance.

Canapress/Bill Becker

Statistics Canada reports that annual per capita beer sales fell to 81.4 litres in 2000 from 92 litres a decade earlier. The decline in beer drinking is probably due to the aging population, lifestyle changes, and higher taxes.

These four determinants of demand—preferences, income, prices of related products, and future expectations—affect people's individual demand in varying degrees. If we shift our attention to the market demand, these four factors still apply. In addition, a few other factors need to be mentioned. The *size of the market population* will affect the demand for all products. An increase in the size of the population, for example, will lead to an increase in the demand for most products in varying amounts. In addition, a *change in the distribution of incomes* will lead to an increase in the demand for some products and a decrease in the demand for others, even though the total income has not changed. The same will also be true for the *age composition of the population*. An aging population will increase the demand for products that largely appeal to older people (Anne Murray CDs), and decrease the demand for those that appeal only to the young (Tragically Hip CDs).

Notice that one factor is *not* included in this list of determinants of demand, and that is supply. Economists are scrupulous in their attempts to separate the forces of demand and supply. Remember that the demand formulation is a hypothetical construct based on the quantities that consumers are willing and able to purchase at various prices. There is an implied assumption that the consumer will be able to obtain these quantities; otherwise the demand schedule itself would not be relevant. In other words, when specifying the demand, we assume that the supply will be available, just as, when formulating supply, we make the assumption that there will be sufficient demand.

In summary, the determinants of demand are:

- consumer preferences
- consumer incomes
- prices of related goods
- expectations of future prices, incomes, or availability
- population size; or income and age distribution

The Effects of an Increase in Demand

We have just seen that the demand for any product is affected by many different factors. A change in any of these factors will cause a change in demand and lead to a change in price and production levels. Let us first consider the effects of an increase in the demand for a product. In summary, any one of the following could cause such an *increase* in the market demand:

- a change in preferences toward the product
- an increase in incomes if the product is a normal product, or a decrease in incomes if the product is an inferior product
- an increase in the price of a substitute product
- a decrease in the price of a complementary product
- the expectation that future prices or incomes will be higher or that there will be a future shortage of the product
- an increase in the population or a change in its income or age distribution

Any of these changes could cause people to buy more of a product, regardless of its price. As an example, let us combine supply and demand data in **Table 2.7**.

TABLE 2.7 The Effects on the Market of an Increase in Demand

	NUMBER OF CASES PER WEEK		
Price per Case	**Supply**	**Demand 1**	**Demand 2**
$12	10	16	22
13	12	15	21
14	14	14	20
15	16	13	19
16	18	12	18
17	20	11	17
18	22	10	16

You can see that at the old demand (Demand 1) and supply, the equilibrium price was $14 and the quantity traded was 14 cases. Assume now that the demand for beer increases (Demand 2 in **Table 2.7**). Since consumers do not usually signal their intentions to producers in advance, producers are not aware that the demand has changed until they have evidence. The evidence will probably take the form of unsatisfied customers. At a price of $14 a case, the producers in total have produced 14 cases. At this price, the new quantity demanded is 20 cases. There is a shortage of 6 cases, and some customers will go home disappointed because there is not sufficient beer, at a price of $14, to satisfy all customers. The important question is: will these brewers now increase production to satisfy the higher demand? The surprising answer is no—at least not at the present price. Brewers are not in the business of satisfying customers; they are in the business of making profits. As the dean of economics, Adam Smith, wrote over 200 years ago:

> It is not from the benevolence of the butcher, the brewer, or the baker that we expect our dinner but from regard to their own self-interest.[1]

You may object that unless firms are responsive to the demands of customers, they will soon go out of business. And you are right. But equally, a firm that is *solely* responsive to its

[1] Adam Smith, *Wealth of Nations* (Edwin Cannan edition, 1877), pp. 26–27.

customers will go out of business even faster. Look back at the supply schedule in **Table 2.7**. At a price of $14, the brewers said they are prepared to produce 14 cases. They are not prepared to produce 20 cases, the amount that consumers now want. Why is that? Because, presumably, they can make more profits from producing 14 cases than from producing 20 cases; otherwise they would have produced 20 in the first place. In fact, it may well be that if they produced 20 cases at the current price of $14, they would end up experiencing a loss. Does this mean that the shortage of beer will persist? No, because we have earlier seen that *shortages drive prices up* until the shortage disappears and the new quantity demanded is equal to the quantity supplied. This will occur at a price of $16, where the quantity demanded and the quantity supplied are equal at the equilibrium quantity of 18. This adjustment process can be seen in **Figure 2.10**.

FIGURE 2.10 **Adjustment to an Increase in Demand**

The increase in demand from D_1 to D_2 creates an immediate shortage of 6. This will cause an increase in the price of beer. The increase affects both producers, who will now increase the quantity supplied, and consumers, who will reduce the quantity demanded. Eventually, the price will reach a new equilibrium at $16, where the equilibrium quantity is 18, and there is no longer a shortage.

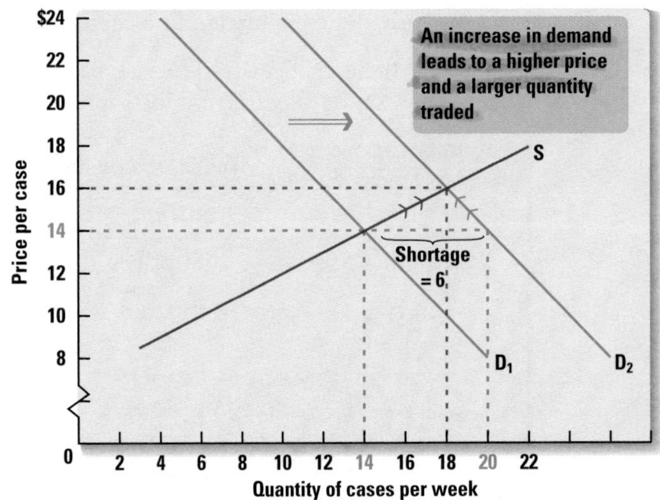

You can see in the graph that at the old price of $14, the new quantity demanded exceeds the quantity supplied. This shortage causes the price to rise. As it does so, notice that the quantity of beer that producers make also rises; that is, there will be an increase *in the quantity supplied*. Producers will produce more, *not* because there is a shortage, but because the shortage causes a rise in price. Note also that the increase in price causes some customers to reduce their purchases of beer; that is, there is a decrease *in the quantity demanded*. The price of beer will continue to increase as long as there is a shortage and will stop as soon as the shortage disappears. This occurs when the price has increased to $16. At the new equilibrium price, the quantity demanded will again equal the quantity supplied but at a higher quantity traded of 18 cases.

An increase in demand causes the price to increase and the quantity traded also to increase.

The Effects of a Decrease in Demand

Now let's see what happens when there is a decrease in demand. Remember that a decrease in demand cannot be caused by an increase in price but is caused by a change in any of the non-price determinants, such as:

- a decrease in the preferences for the product
- a decrease in incomes if the product is a normal product, or an increase in incomes if the product is an inferior product
- a decrease in the price of a substitute product
- an increase in the price of a complementary product
- the expectation that future prices or incomes will be lower
- a decrease in the population or a change in its income or age distribution

A decrease in demand is shown in **Table 2.8** and illustrated in **Figure 2.11**.

TABLE 2.8 **The Effects on the Market of a Decrease in Demand**

	NUMBER OF CASES PER WEEK		
Price per Case	**Supply**	**Demand 1**	**Demand 3**
$12	10	16	10
13	12	15	9
14	14	14	8
15	16	13	7
16	18	12	6
17	20	11	5
18	22	10	4

The initial equilibrium price is $14, and the quantity traded is 14. Assume that the demand now decreases to Demand 3 in the table and D_3 in **Figure 2.11**. At a price of $14, producers will continue to produce 14 cases; yet consumers now wish to purchase only 8 cases. A surplus is immediately created in the market. Mounting unsold inventories and more intensive competition between suppliers will eventually push down the price. Notice in **Figure 2.11** that as the price decreases, the quantity supplied also starts to decrease and the quantity demanded begins to increase. Both of these factors will cause the surplus to disappear. The price will eventually drop to a new equilibrium of $12 where the quantity demanded and the quantity supplied are equal at 10 cases. In short:

A decrease in demand will cause both the price and the quantity traded to fall.

FIGURE 2.11 **Adjustment to a Decrease in Demand**

The drop in demand from D_1 to D_3 will cause an immediate surplus of 6, since the quantity supplied remains at 14, but the quantity demanded drops to 8. This surplus will cause the price to fall, and, as it does, the quantity demanded will increase while the quantity supplied will fall. This process will continue until the surplus is eliminated. This occurs at a new equilibrium price of $12 and an equilibrium quantity of 10.

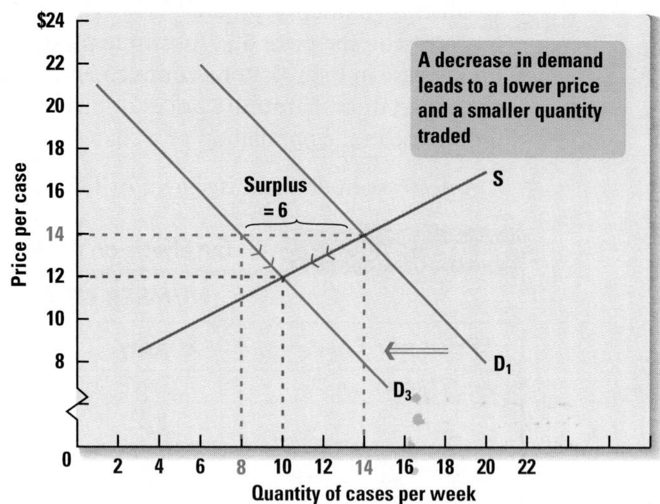

SELF-TEST

5. What effect will the following changes have upon (i) the demand for, (ii) the price, and (iii) the quantity traded of commercially brewed beer?
   a) A new medical report praising the healthy effects of drinking beer (in moderation, of course).
   b) A big decrease in the price of home-brewing kits.
   c) A rapid increase in population growth.
   d) Talk of a possible future strike of brewery workers.
   e) A possible future recession.

2.6 Change in Supply

LO6
Understand the causes and effects of a change in supply.

change in supply: a change in the quantities supplied at every price, caused by a change in the determinants of supply.

Let us again be clear about what we mean by supply: it is the relationship between the price of the product and the quantities producers are willing and able to supply. Price is part of what economists call supply. In other words, supply does not mean a single quantity. What we now need to figure out is what could cause a **change in supply**. What factors will cause producers to offer a different quantity on the market even though the price has not changed—what will cause a change in supply? We begin with **Table 2.9**, where an increase in supply is illustrated. For reasons we will soon investigate, suppliers are now willing to supply an extra 6 cases of beer at every possible price. This is illustrated in **Figure 2.12**.

An increase in supply causes the whole supply curve to shift right. (Be careful if you are tempted to describe it as a downward shift because then you would be saying that as the supply goes up, the supply curve goes down, which could make things very confusing! Better to talk about a rightward shift.) This means that at each and every price, producers are now willing to produce more.

TABLE 2.9 An Increase in Supply

	NUMBER OF CASES PER WEEK	
Price per Case of Beer	**Supply 1**	**Supply 2**
$12	10	16
13	12	18
14	14	20
15	16	22
16	18	24
17	20	26
18	22	28

FIGURE 2.12 An Increase in Supply

At each price, the quantities supplied have now increased, that is, the supply curve has shifted right, from S_1 to S_2. For example, at a price of $14, the original quantity was 14 and has now increased to 20. Similarly, at a price of $10, the quantity supplied has increased from 6 to 12. In this example, the quantities supplied have increased by 6 units at every price level, thus causing a parallel shift in the supply curve.

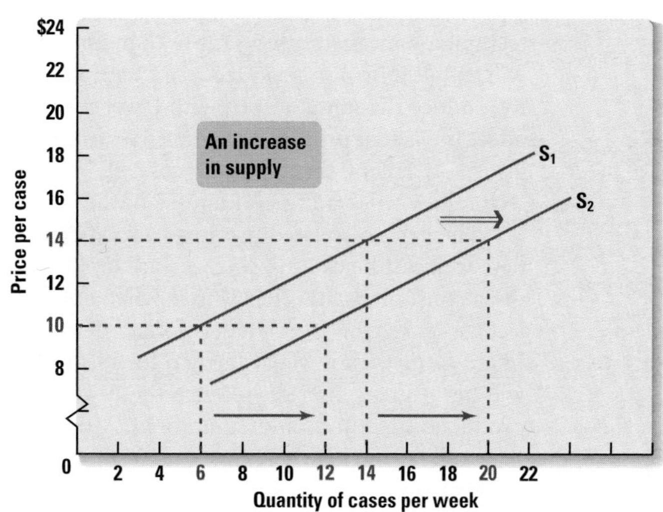

Determinants of a Change in Supply

What could have happened in the brewers' world to make them wish to produce more even though the price is unchanged? Since we are assuming that the prime motivation for the supplier is profit, then something must have happened to make brewing more profitable, which is inducing a higher supply. Profit is the difference between revenue and cost, and since the price (and therefore revenue) is unchanged, then something must have affected the cost of producing beer. The first factor we will look at which might have decreased costs is the *price of resources*. For the brewers this includes the price of yeast, hops, malt, and other ingredients, as well as the price that must be paid for the brewing vats, bottles, and so on. If any of these should drop in price, then the cost for the brewers will fall and profits will rise. Under these circumstances, since they are now making a bigger profit on each case of beer, they will be very willing to produce more. A fall in the price of resources will lead to an increase in supply. Conversely, an increase in the price of resources will cause a decrease in supply.

Another way of looking at the increase in supply, as shown in **Figure 2.12**, is to say that, rather than firms being willing to produce more at a given price, they are willing to accept lower prices to produce any given quantity. For instance, previously, in order to induce the brewers to supply a total of 20 cases per week, the price needed to be $17. Now that the costs of production have dropped, these same brewers are able to make the same profits by producing the 20 cases at a lower price of $14. This is the same thing as saying that the brewers are now willing to produce the same quantities as before at lower prices. Again, this would produce a rightward shift in the supply curve.

It is often suggested that the availability of resources is a major determinant of the supply of a product. A bad grape harvest—grapes being the key input in the making of wine—will obviously have an impact on the supply of wine. However, it's not really the difficulty in obtaining grapes that causes a decrease in the wine supply, since most things can be obtained *at a price*. But there's the rub. A bad grape harvest will cause the price of grapes to increase, and this increase will reduce the profitability and production of wine producers.

A second major determinant of supply is the *business taxes* levied by the various levels of government. They are similar to the other costs of doing business, and a decrease in them (or an increase in a subsidy) will lead firms to make higher profits and encourage them, therefore, to increase the supply; an increase in business taxes, on the other hand, will cause a decrease in supply.

A third determinant of supply is the *technology* used in production. An improvement in technology means nothing more than an improvement in the method of production. This will enable a firm to produce more with the same quantity of resources (or, for that matter, to produce the same output with fewer resources). An improvement in technology will not affect the actual price of the resources, but, because more can now be done with less, it will lead to a fall in the per unit cost of production. This means that an improvement in technology will lead to an increase in the supply.

The price of related products also affects the supply, just as it affected the demand. But here we must be careful, since we are looking at things from a producer's point of view and not a consumer's. In other words, what a producer regards as related will usually differ from a consumer's view of related. A fourth determinant of supply, then, is the *price of substitutes in production*. To a wheat farmer, for instance, the price of other grains like rye and barley will be of great interest because the production of all grain crops are related in terms of production methods and equipment. A significant increase in the price of rye, for example, may well tempt the wheat farmer to grow rye in the future. In other words, an increase in the price of one product will cause a drop in the supply of products that are substitutes in production. A decrease will have the opposite effect.

A fifth determinant of supply is the *future expectations of producers*. Again, this is analogous to the demand side of the market, but with a difference. While consumers will eagerly look forward to the drop in the price of products, producers view the same prospect with great anxiety. If a producer feels that the market is going to be depressed in the future and that prices are likely to be lower, she may be inclined to change production now, before the anticipated collapse. Lower expected future prices therefore tend to increase the present supply of a product. Higher expected future prices have the opposite effect and cause producers to hold off selling all of their present production in the hopes of making greater profits from the future higher prices.

Finally, the market supply will also be affected by the *number of suppliers*. An increase in the number of suppliers will cause an increase in the market supply, whereas a decrease in the number of suppliers will reduce the overall market supply.

Again, notice that one thing omitted from this list of supply determinants is any mention of demand. At the risk of repetition: firms are in business not to satisfy demand but to make profits. Simply because the demand for a product increases does not mean that producers will immediately increase production to satisfy the higher demand. However, the higher demand will cause the price to increase, and this increase induces firms to supply more, but this is an increase in the quantity supplied and *does not* imply an increase in the supply. That is, the supply curve remains unchanged.

In summary, the determinants of market supply are:

- prices of resources
- business taxes
- technology
- prices of substitutes in production
- future expectations of suppliers
- number of suppliers

The Effects of an Increase in Supply

We have just discussed six different factors that could affect the supply of a product. Let us be more specific and look at what can cause an *increase* in supply:

- a decrease in the price of productive resources
- a decrease in business taxes (or increase in subsidies)
- an improvement in technology
- a decrease in the price of a productively related product
- the expectation of a decline in the future price of the product
- an increase in the number of suppliers

Let us see the effects of an increase in supply by using the original demand for beer, and the increase in supply by using **Table 2.10**.

TABLE 2.10 The Effect on the Market of an Increase in Supply

	NUMBER OF CASES PER WEEK		
Price per Case of Beer	**Demand 1**	**Supply 1**	**Supply 2**
$12	16	10	16
13	15	12	18
14	14	14	20
15	13	16	22
16	12	18	24
17	11	20	26
18	10	22	28

At the original demand (Demand 1) and supply (Supply 1), the equilibrium price was $14 per case and the quantity traded was 16 cases. Assume that the supply now increases to Supply 2. At the present price of $14, there will be an immediate surplus of 6 cases. Before we look at the implications of this surplus, we ought to address a couple of possible qualms that some students might have. The first is this: won't customers take up this excess of beer? It is easy to see that, at this price, consumers have already given their response: they want to buy 14 cases, not 20 cases, or any other number. In other words, consumers are buying beer to satisfy their own tastes, not to satisfy the brewers. A second question is this: why would producers produce 20 cases, knowing that the demand at this price is only 14 cases? The answer is that they don't know. Each producer knows the circumstances in her own brewery and knows that, until now, she has been able to sell everything she has produced. With the prospect of higher profits coming from, let's say, a decrease in costs, the brewer wants to produce more. If all producers do the same, there will be a surplus of beer. **Figure 2.13** shows what will happen as a result of this surplus.

FIGURE 2.13 **Adjustment to an Increase in Supply**

The increase in the supply has the immediate effect of causing a surplus because the demand has remained unchanged. In this figure, at a price of $14, the quantity supplied has increased from 14 to 20, causing a surplus of 6. This will cause the price to drop, and as it does, the quantity demanded increases and the quantity supplied decreases, until a new equilibrium is reached at a new equilibrium price of $12 and quantity of 16.

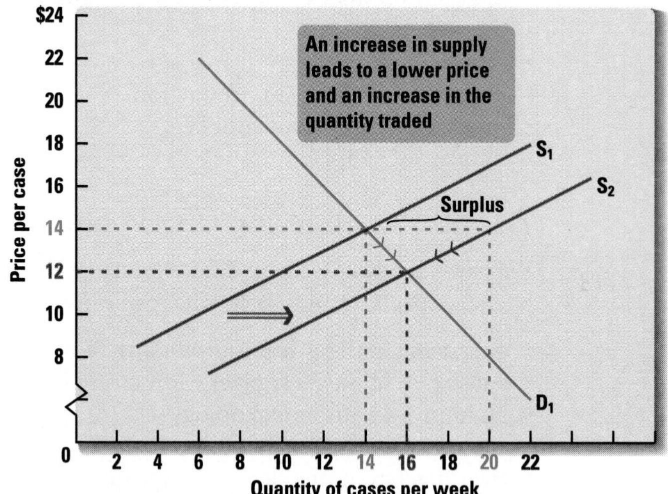

Faced with a surplus of beer, the market price will be forced down. As the price falls, the quantity demanded increases and the quantity supplied falls. Production increased initially, but because of the resulting drop in price, it is now dropping back slightly. The price will continue to drop until it reaches $12. **Table 2.10** shows that, at this price, the quantity demanded and the quantity supplied are now equal at 16 cases. The effect of the increase in supply, then, is a lower price and a higher quantity traded.

SELF-TEST

6. Suppose that the demand and supply for strawberries in Corona are as follows (the quantities are in thousands of kilos per week):

Price	Demand	Supply 1	Supply 2
$4.00	140	60	______
4.25	130	70	______
4.50	120	80	______
4.75	110	90	______
5.00	100	100	______
5.25	90	110	______
5.50	80	120	______

a) What are the present equilibrium price and equilibrium quantity? Graph the demand and supply curves, labelling them D_1 and S_1, and indicate equilibrium.

b) Suppose that the supply of strawberries were to increase by 50 percent. Show the new quantities in the Supply 2 column. What will be the new equilibrium price and quantity? Draw in S_2 on your graph and indicate the new equilibrium.

7. What effect will the following changes have on the supply, price, and quantity traded of wine?

a) A bad harvest in the grape industry results in a big decrease in the supply of grapes.

b) The number of wineries increases.

c) The sales tax on wine increases.

d) The introduction of a new fermentation method reduces the time needed for the wine to ferment.

e) The government introduces a subsidy for each bottle of wine produced domestically.

f) The government introduces a quota limiting the amount of foreign wine entering Canada.

g) There is a big increase in wages for the workers in the wine industry.

h) A big increase occurs in the prices of wine coolers (an industry that is similar in technology to the wine industry).

We leave it to the student to confirm that a decrease in supply will cause a shortage that will eventually raise the price of the product. The net result will be a higher price *but* a lower quantity traded.

2.7 Final Words

LO7
Understand why demand and supply determine price and the quantity traded and not the reverse.

To complete this introduction to demand and supply, let's use the following chart as a summary:

↑ Demand	→	shortage	→	↑ P	and	↑ Q traded
↓ Supply	→	shortage	→	↑ P	and	↓ Q traded
↓ Demand	→	surplus	→	↓ P	and	↓ Q traded
↑ Supply	→	surplus	→	↓ P	and	↑ Q traded

Note that when the demand changes, both the price and the quantity traded move in the same direction; when the supply changes, the quantity traded moves in the same direction, but the price moves in the opposite direction.

From this table you should confirm in your own mind that it is the supply of, and demand for, a product that determines its price, and not the price that determines supply and demand. A change in any of the factors that affects demand or supply will therefore lead to a change in the price. The price of a product *cannot* change *unless* there is a change in either the demand or the supply. It follows therefore that you cannot really analyze any problem that starts: "What happens if the price increases (decreases)…?" The reason for this, as the above chart makes clear, is that an increase in the price of a product might be caused by either the demand increasing or by the supply decreasing. But in the case of an increase in the demand, the quantity traded also increases, whereas in the case of a decrease in the supply, the quantity traded falls. In the first case, we are talking about an expanding industry; in the second, we are looking at a contracting industry.

ADDED DIMENSION

The Famous Scissors Analogy

Since the time of Adam Smith, economists have continually struggled to understand how prices are determined. Toward the end of the nineteenth century, they tended to group into one of two camps: those who believed that the cost of production was the main determinant; and those who believed that consumer demand was the main determinant. Demand, in turn, was determined by what the famous economist Alfred Marshall called the utility (or satisfaction) derived from consumption.

Marshall, writing at the end of that century, was the first to present a lucid synthesis of the two views and suggest that neither demand nor supply alone can provide the answer. His famous analogy of the scissors says, "We might as reasonably dispute whether it is the upper or the under blade of scissors that cuts a piece of paper, as whether value [price] is governed by utility or cost of production. It is true that when one blade is held still, and the cutting is effected by moving the other, we may say with careless brevity that the cutting is done by the second; but the statement is not strictly accurate, and is to be excused only so long as it claims to be merely a popular and not a strictly scientific account of what happens."[1]

Finally, make sure you understand clearly the distinction between changes in quantities demanded and supplied and changes in demand and supply as illustrated in **Figure 2.14**.

[1]Alfred Marshall, *Principles of Economics*, 8th ed., p. 348.

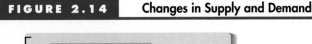

FIGURE 2.14 Changes in Supply and Demand

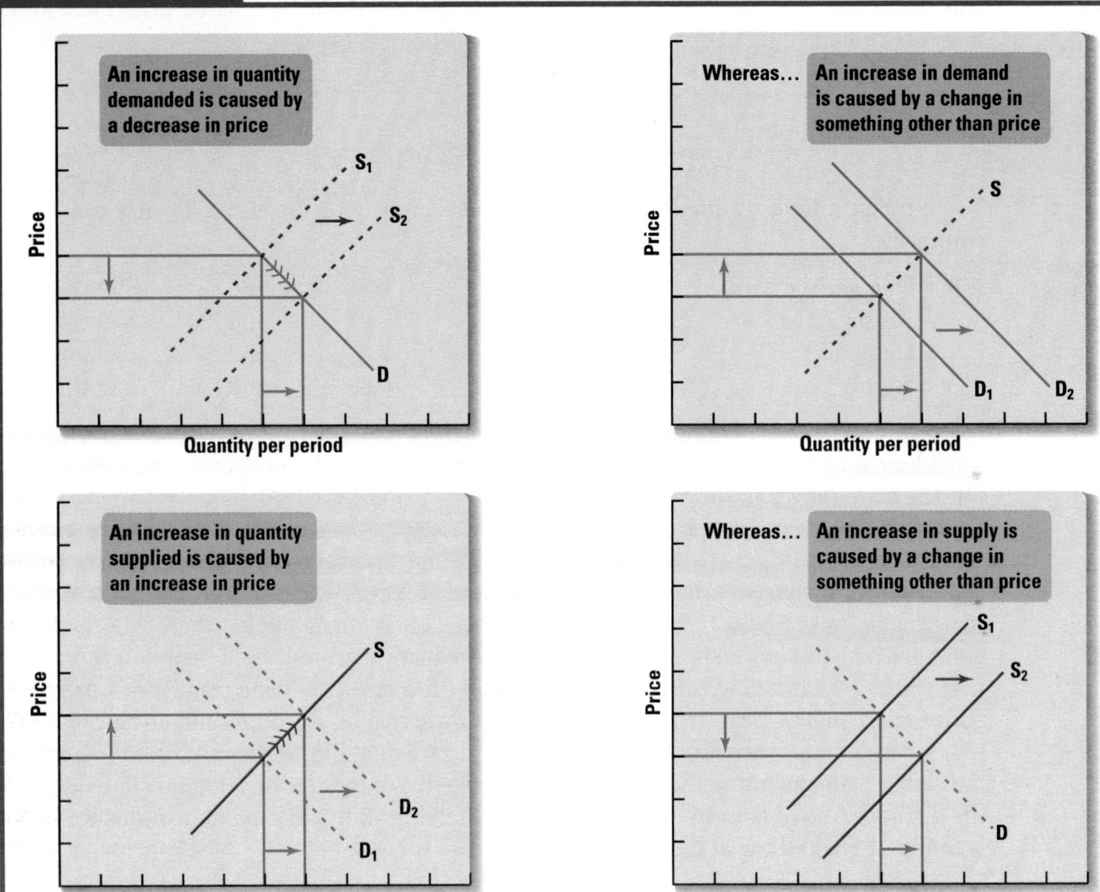

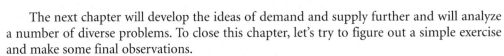

The next chapter will develop the ideas of demand and supply further and will analyze a number of diverse problems. To close this chapter, let's try to figure out a simple exercise and make some final observations.

Looking back over the past decade or so, what has happened to the prices of home computers? Generally speaking, even allowing for inflation, they have decreased. And what about the quantity of computers that are bought and sold now, compared with the situation a decade ago? Definitely, it has increased. So, according to our little chart above, what could have produced this result in the marketplace? Well, there is only one thing that could lead to a decrease in price and an increase in the quantity traded, and that is an increase in supply. And what in the computer world over the past years could have caused an increase in supply? The answer must be an improvement in technology that has significantly reduced the costs of producing computers.

As we shall see in Chapter 3, not only is the market system an efficient way of preventing persistent surpluses and shortages, but it also functions very well in rationing scarce goods, services, and resources.

SELF-TEST

8. The following are various changes that occur in different markets. Explain what will happen to either demand or supply and to the equilibrium price and quantity traded.

a) An increase in income upon the market for an *inferior product.*

b) A decrease in the price of steel on the *automobile industry.*

c) A government subsidy given to operators of *day-care centres.*

d) A government subsidy given to parents who want their children to attend *day-care centres.*

e) A medical report suggesting that *wine* is very fattening.

f) A big decrease in the amount of Middle East oil exports on the *refined-oil market.*

g) An increase in the popularity of *antique furniture.*

h) An increase in the price of coffee on the *tea market.*

However, we should mention a number of themes that we will take up in Chapter 8. In the modern world, competitive markets are few and far between, since many markets are dominated by big corporations, big trade unions, and consumer associations, and are affected by government intervention. In addition, even when they are competitive, markets do not provide any guarantee that there will not be future periods of recession or inflation. Further, competitive markets cannot ensure that the right type or quantities of products are produced or that the distribution of incomes and wealth in a country is fair.

Finally, let's look back at the discussion that started this chapter and see if we can make sense of it. The one speaker started by stating that the price of houses has increased. (We presume he is talking about the market for existing, as well as new, houses.) Well, there are two major causes for a price increase: either the demand has increased (caused perhaps by lower interest rates or high immigration into the area); or the supply has decreased (caused by higher building costs or perhaps the expectation by sellers that prices will be higher in the future). In this particular conversation we are given no indication of the cause. However, the effects are going to be different. If housing prices increased because of a higher demand, you would expect to see a higher number of housing sales than usual; if they increased because of a lower supply, then the number of sales would be smaller than usual. It would be an easy enough job to figure out which was the cause. The rest of the conversation on the effects of a higher price is merely an exercise in confusion. Assuming that the present price is the equilibrium price, then nothing further will happen—at least until there is another change in demand or supply. Hopefully, you now realize what an important and versatile tool supply and demand analysis can be—but, like all tools, you must use it properly (and clean it off after every use!).

ADDED DIMENSION

Sales Always Equal Purchases

It is important not to confuse the terms "demand" and "supply" with "purchases" and "sales." As we have seen in this chapter, the quantity demanded and the quantity supplied are not always equal. However, purchases and sales, since they are two sides of the same transaction, must always be equal. The accompanying graph explains the differences in the terms.

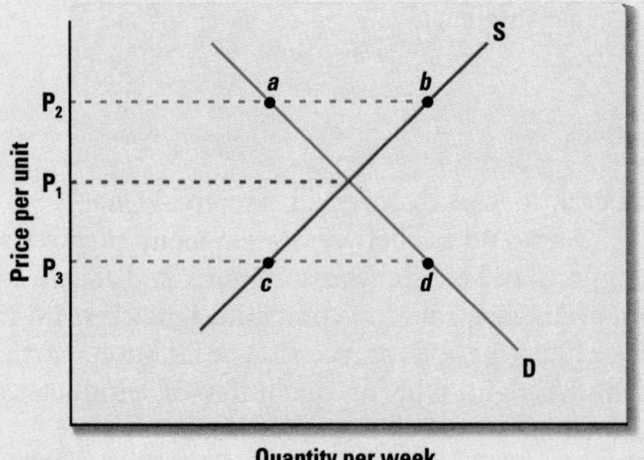

P_1 is the equilibrium price, and at this price the quantity demanded and supplied are equal—this is the amount traded and is the same thing as the amount sold and purchased. If the price happened to be above equilibrium, however, at a price, say, P_2, then the quantity demanded is denoted by *a*, and the quantity supplied by *b*. Clearly, the two quantities are not equal. But how much is bought and sold at this price? The answer is quantity *a*. It really doesn't matter how much is being produced since, at this price, this is the maximum amount that consumers are willing to buy. The difference *ab* represents the amount unsold, or the surplus.

On the other hand, what is the effect of the price being below equilibrium? Suppose the price is P_3, where the quantity supplied (*c*) is less than the quantity demanded (*d*)? This time, how much is being bought and sold? The answer must be quantity *c*. It doesn't matter how much consumers want to buy of this product if producers are only making quantity *c* available. In general, the amount bought and sold is always equal to the smaller of the quantity demanded or supplied.

REVIEW

1. What are the four major determinants of individual demand?
2. Explain the difference between an *inferior* and a *normal* product.
3. What will happen to the price of a product if:
   a) the price of its substitute decreases?
   b) the price of its complement decreases?
4. Explain, step by step, how an *increase* in demand eventually affects both the price and the quantity traded.
5. What are the six major determinants of the market supply?
6. Explain how the market adjusts to an increase in the supply of a product.
7. What can cause the price of a product to rise? What can cause it to fall?

STUDY GUIDE

Review

CHAPTER SUMMARY

In this chapter you learned that, in competitive markets, the price and quantity traded of any product depends on both the demand for, and the supply of, that product. Once equilibrium is achieved, price and quantity will not change unless either supply or demand changes first. In order to fully understand this lesson, you must also understand the following:

1. *Demand* is the price/quantity relationship of a product that consumers are willing and able to buy per period of time.

2. *Market demand* is simply the conceptual summation of each individual's demand within a given market.

3. The demand curve is *downward sloping* because of the:
   - substitution effect;
   - income effect.

4. Market demand *changes* if there is a change in:
   - consumers' preferences;
   - consumers' incomes;
   - the price of related products;
   - expectations of future prices, incomes, or availability;
   - the size of the market or income and age distribution.

5. Products can be *related* in two ways, as:
   - complements;
   - substitutes.

6. All products are *either*:
   - normal products;
   - inferior products.

7. *Supply* is the price/quantity relationship of a product that producers are willing and able to sell per period of time.

8. *Market supply* is simply the conceptual summation of each firm's supply within a given market.

9. Market supply *changes* if there is a change in:
   - the price of resources;
   - business taxes;
   - technology;
   - prices of substitutes in production;
   - future expectations of suppliers;
   - the number of suppliers.

10. An *increase in demand* will cause a shortage and result in both price and quantity traded rising.

11. A *decrease in demand* will cause a surplus and result in both price and quantity falling.

12. An *increase in supply* will cause a surplus and result in price falling and quantity traded rising.

13. A *decrease in supply* will cause a shortage and result in price rising and quantity falling.

NEW GLOSSARY TERMS

ceteris paribus 45
change in demand 57
change in supply 64
change in the quantity demanded 46
change in the quantity supplied 51
complementary products 59
demand 44
demand schedule 45
equilibrium price 55
equilibrium quantity 56
income effect 47
inferior products 58
market 53
market demand 48
market supply 52
normal products 58
real income 47
substitute products 59
substitution effect 47
supply 49
supply schedule 49

STUDY TIPS

1. It is with this chapter that you will learn to appreciate the need for precision in the use of economic terms. For instance, the terms *demand* and *supply* have very clear definitions. "Demand" does *not* mean the amount a person wishes to buy or the amount she is buying. Demand is not a single quantity but a combination of different prices and quantities. Similarly, you cannot use the term "supply" synonymously with output, production, or quantity supplied. It is *not* a single quantity but, again, a range of different quantities and prices.

2. If you have understood the first point, then this next one should make sense. A change in price cannot affect the demand, since price is already part of what we mean by demand. That doesn't mean that a change in price doesn't affect consumers; generally, people change the amounts they purchase as a result of a price change, but this is what we call a change in the quantity demanded and *not* a change in demand. Similarly, a change in price leaves the supply unaffected. But it definitely affects the *quantity supplied*. These points are illustrated in the way that the demand and supply curves are affected. A change in price causes no change in the demand or supply curves but results in a movement *along* the curves. Only changes in other determinants, besides price, will cause a shift in the curves.

3. It is important for you to keep the concepts of demand and supply separate in your mind. A change in demand does *not* have any effect on the supply. This means that the supply curve will not shift when the demand curve changes. Similarly, you must disconnect the demand from the supply. A change in the supply has no impact on demand.

4. There really is no alternative to learning the factors that do affect the demand and supply. Memorize the five determinants of market demand and the six determinants of market supply. Note that, with the exception of expectations of future price changes, the factors that affect demand have no impact on supply, and vice versa. If possible, try not to be too "cute" when trying to figure out the way in which various changes in determinants affect markets. It is possible to give a convoluted explanation of why, for example, a change in the number of suppliers can affect preferences and, therefore, the demand of customers of that product. While remotely possible, the effect would be of minor significance. Instead use common sense and focus on the main effects. Remember that usually a change in one determinant will affect *only* the demand or the supply, seldom both.

5. Don't skip the basics in this chapter even if, at times, they might seem a little simple. For example, don't try to work out the effects of changes in demand or supply until you first have a good grasp of equilibrium.

6. Finally, the most important lesson that you can get from this chapter is that the price of a product is determined by both demand and supply. Price is the effect and not the cause. This means that equilibrium price cannot change in a free market unless there has been a change in either the demand or the supply.

Answered Questions

Indicate whether the following statements are true or false.

1. **T or F** The term "demand" means the quantities that people would like to purchase at various different prices.

2. **T or F** A change in the price of a product has no effect on the demand for that product.

3. **T or F** An increase in the price of a product causes a decrease in the real income of consumers.

4. **T or F** An increase in the price of a product leads to an increase in the supply.

5. **T or F** Equilibrium price implies that everyone who would like to purchase a product is able to.

6. **T or F** Surpluses drive prices up; shortages drive prices down.

7. **T or F** An increase in incomes will lead to a decrease in the demand for an inferior product.

8. **T or F** A decrease in the demand for a product will lead to a decrease in both the price and the quantity traded.

9. **T or F** An increase in business taxes causes the supply curve to shift left.

10. **T or F** A decrease in supply causes the price to fall and the quantity traded to increase.

Basic (Questions 11–12)

11. What does the term "demand" refer to?
   a) The amounts that consumers are either willing or able to purchase at various prices.
   b) The amounts that consumers are both willing and able to purchase at various prices.
   c) The quantity purchased at the equilibrium price.
   d) The price consumers are willing to pay for a certain quantity of a product.

12. What will a surplus of a product lead to?
   a) A reduction in supply.
   b) A reduction in price.
   c) An increase in price.
   d) An increase in supply.

13. What is the effect of a decrease in the price of a product?
   a) It will increase consumers' real income while leaving their actual income unchanged.
   b) It will increase consumers' actual income while leaving their real income unchanged.
   c) It will decrease demand.
   d) It will have no effect on income.

14. What is the effect of an increase in the price of coffee?
   a) It will lead to an increase in the demand for tea.
   b) It will lead to a decrease in the demand for tea.
   c) It will have no effect on the tea market.
   d) It will decrease the demand for coffee.

15. What is the slope of the demand curve?
   a) It is downward-sloping because when the price of a product falls, consumers are willing and able to buy more.
   b) It is upward-sloping because when the price of a product falls, consumers are willing and able to buy more.
   c) It is upward-sloping because when the price of a product increases, consumers are willing and able to buy more.
   d) It is downward-sloping because higher prices are associated with larger quantities.

16. What is the effect of an increase in the price of a productive resource? a
   a) It will cause a decrease in the supply of the product.
   b) It will cause an increase in the supply of the product.
   c) It will cause a decrease in the demand for the product.
   d) It will cause an increase in the demand for the product.

17. In what way are Pepsi Cola and Coca Cola related?
   a) They are substitute products.
   b) They are complementary products.
   c) They are inferior products.
   d) They are unrelated products.

18. Which of the following could cause an increase in the supply of wheat?
   a) A decrease in the price of oats.
   b) An imposition of a sales tax on wheat.
   c) An increase in the price of fertilizer.
   d) A decrease in the price of wheat.

19. All of the following, except one, would cause an increase in demand for a normal product. Which is the exception?
   a) An increase in consumers' incomes.
   b) An increase in the price of a substitute product.
   c) An increase in the size of the market.
   d) Consumer expectations of a lower future price for the product.

20. Which of the following pairs of goods are complementary?
   a) Coffee and tea.
   b) Skis and ski boots.
   c) Bread and crackers.
   d) Popcorn and pretzels.

21. All of the following, except one, would cause a decrease in the supply of product A. Which is the exception?
   a) An increase in the price of resources used to make product A.
   b) An increase in business taxes.
   c) An improvement in technology.
   d) The expectation by suppliers that future prices of product A will be higher.

22. Which of the following best describes a normal product?
   a) A product that people both need and like.
   b) A product whose demand increases if income increases.
   c) A product whose demand increases if income decreases.
   d) A staple product that everyone needs.

Intermediate (Questions 23–32)

23. How will a change in income affect the demand for an inferior product?
  a) The demand will increase if the income of consumers increases.
  b) The demand will increase if the income of consumers decreases.
  c) The demand for an inferior product is not affected by consumer incomes.
  d) The demand will remain the same but the quantity demanded will increase if income decreases.

24. Which of the following factors will shift the demand curve left?
  a) An increase in the price of a substitute product.
  b) A decrease in the price of a complementary product.
  c) An increase in income if the product is an inferior product.
  d) The expectation that future prices of the product will be higher.

25. A rightward shift in the supply curve for a product could be caused by all of the following except one. Which is the exception?
  a) The expectation by suppliers that the future price of the product will be higher.
  b) A decrease in the price of a productive resource used in its manufacture.
  c) A decrease in the price of a product that is a substitute in production.
  d) A technological improvement in manufacturing methods.

26. What is the effect of a decrease in the supply of a product?
  a) It will cause an increase in both the price and the quantity traded.
  b) It will cause an increase in the price but a decrease in the quantity traded.
  c) It will cause a decrease in both the price and in the quantity traded.
  d) It will cause a decrease in the price but an increase in the quantity traded.

Table 2.11 depicts the market for mushrooms (in thousands of kilograms per month). Use this table to answer questions 27 and 28.

TABLE 2.11

Price ($)	2.50	3.00	3.50	4.00	4.50	5.00	5.50	6.00
Quantity demanded	64	62	60	58	56	54	52	50
Quantity supplied	40	44	48	52	56	60	64	68

27. Refer to **Table 2.11** to answer this question. What are the values of equilibrium price and quantity traded?
  a) $3 and 52.
  b) $3 and 62.
  c) $4 and 58.
  d) $4.50 and 56.
  e) They cannot be determined from the data.

28. Refer to **Table 2.11** to answer this question. What will happen if the price of the product is $3?
  a) There would be a surplus of 18, which would lead to a decrease in price.
  b) There would be a shortage of 18, which would lead to an increase in price.
  c) There would be a shortage of 18, which would lead to a decrease in price.
  d) There would be a surplus of 18, which would lead to an increase in price.
  e) There would be neither a surplus nor a shortage.

29. In what way are products A and B related if an increase in the price of product A leads to a decrease in the demand for product B?
  a) Product A must be a resource used in the manufacture of product B.
  b) Product B must be a resource used in the manufacture of product A.
  c) The two products must be complements.
  d) The two products must be substitutes.
  e) The two products must be inferior products.

30. What is the effect of a shortage?
  a) It will cause a decrease in the price, leading to an increase in the quantity supplied and a decrease in the quantity demanded.
  b) It will cause a decrease in the price, leading to a decrease in the quantity supplied and an increase in the quantity demanded.
  c) It will cause an increase in the price, leading to an increase in the quantity supplied and a decrease in the quantity demanded.
  d) It will cause an increase in the price, leading to a decrease in the quantity supplied and an increase in the quantity demanded.

31. What is the effect of an increase in demand for a product?
   a) Its price will rise and quantity traded will decrease.
   b) Its price will rise and quantity traded will increase.
   c) Its price will fall and quantity traded will decrease.
   d) Its price will fall and quantity traded will increase.

Refer to **Figure 2.15** to answer questions 32, 33, and 34.

FIGURE 2.15

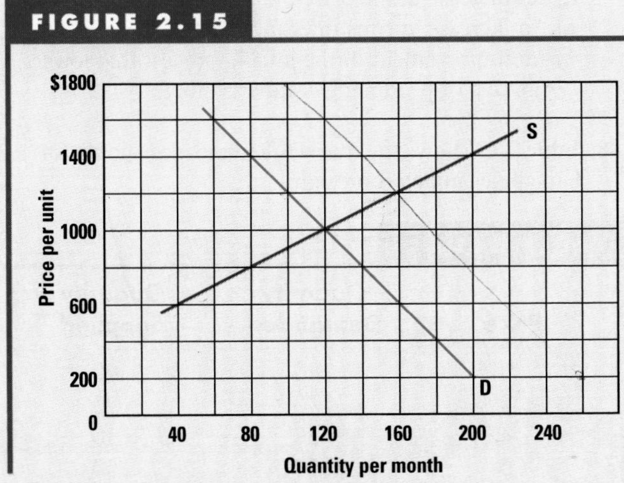

32. Refer to **Figure 2.15** to answer this question. What will be the effect if the price is now $1200?
   a) There would be a surplus of 30.
   b) There would be a shortage of 30.
   c) 160 would be purchased.
   d) There would be a surplus of 60.
   e) The price will increase.

Advanced (Questions 33–35)

33. Refer to **Figure 2.15** to answer this question. Assume that there is a shortage of 60 units. What does this mean?
   a) Purchasers would be willing to pay an additional $600 for the quantity they are now purchasing.
   b) The price must be above equilibrium.
   c) The price must be $1200.
   d) The price must be $600.
   e) None of the above are correct.

34. Refer to **Figure 2.15** to answer this question. Suppose that initially the market was in equilibrium and that demand increased by 60. What will be the new equilibrium as a result?
   a) A price of $1000 and quantity traded of 120.
   b) A price of $1000 and quantity traded of 160.
   c) A price of $1200 and quantity traded of 160.
   d) A price of $1400 and quantity traded of 160.
   e) A price of $1400 and quantity traded of 240.

35. How will the demand and supply of a product be affected if both producers and consumers expect the future price of a product will be higher than at present?
   a) It will cause an increase in demand but a decrease in supply.
   b) It will cause an increase in both the demand and supply.
   c) It will cause a decrease in both the demand and supply.
   d) It will cause an increase in supply but will have no effect on demand.
   e) It will cause an increase in supply but a decrease in demand.

Parallel Problems

ANSWERED PROBLEMS

36. **Key Problem Table 2.12** shows the market for wool in the economy of Odessa (the quantities are in tonnes per year).

TABLE 2.12

Price ($)	100	200	300	400	500	600	700
Quantity demanded	130	110	90	70	50	30	10
Quantity supplied	10	20	30	40	50	60	70

   a) Plot the demand and supply curves on **Figure 2.16** and label them D_1 and S_1. Mark the equilibrium as e_1 on the graph.

FIGURE 2.16

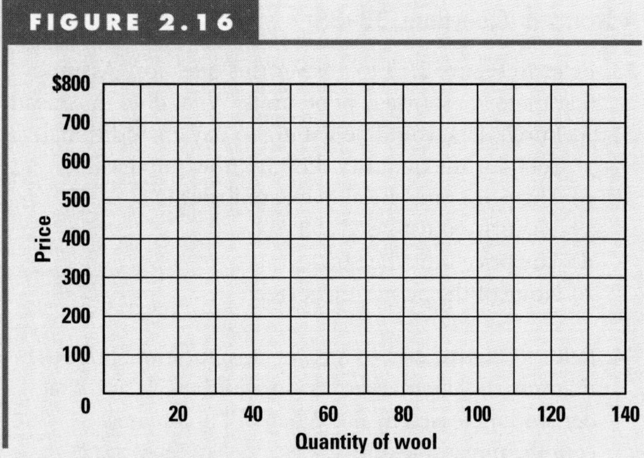

b) What are the values of equilibrium price and quantity?
equilibrium price: ________
equilibrium quantity: ________

c) If the price of wool was $600, would there be a surplus or shortage?
Surplus/shortage ____________ of ________.
Indicate the amount of the surplus or shortage on the graph.

d) Suppose that the demand were to increase by 60. Draw and label the new demand curve as D_2. What are the new values of equilibrium price and quantity?
equilibrium price: ________
equilibrium quantity: ________
Mark the new equilibrium as e_2 on the graph.

e) Following the change in d) suppose that the supply were to increase by 50 percent. Draw and label the new supply curve as S_2. Now what are the new values of equilibrium price and quantity?
equilibrium price: ________
equilibrium quantity: ________
Mark the new equilibrium as e_3 on the graph.

Basic (Problems 37–41)

37. Circle which of the following factors will lead to an increase in the demand for cranberry juice (which is a normal good).

a) A decrease in the price of cranberry juice.
b) A decrease in the price of cranberries.
c) The expectation by consumers that the price of cranberry juice is likely to increase.
d) An increase in the price of apple juice.
e) An increase in consumer incomes.
f) An improvement in the juicing process that lowers the cost of producing cranberry juice.

38. Table 2.13 shows the market demand and supply for Fuji apples in Peterborough.

TABLE 2.13

Price	Quantity Demanded	Quantity Supplied
0	180	90
2	170	110
4	160	130
6	150	150
8	140	170
10	130	190

a) What is the equilibrium price and quantity traded?
price: ________ quantity: ________

b) Suppose that the supply increases by 30. What would the price and quantity be at the new equilibrium?
price: ________ quantity: ________

c) After the increase in supply, what would the surplus/shortage be at a price of $8?
Surplus/shortage __________ of ________.

39. In each of the four graphs in Figure 2.17, explain the change in equilibrium from *a* to *b* in terms of (1) an increase or decrease in demand or supply; and (2) an increase or decrease in the quantity demanded or supplied.

FIGURE 2.17

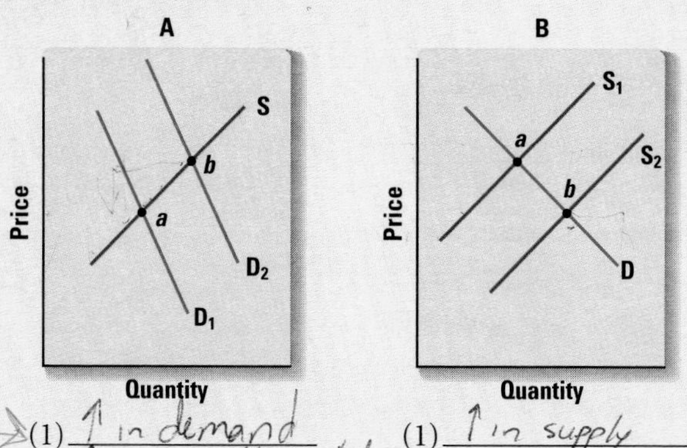

A: (1) ____________ (2) ____________

B: (1) ____________ (2) ____________

C: (1) ____________ (2) ____________

D: (1) ____________ (2) ____________

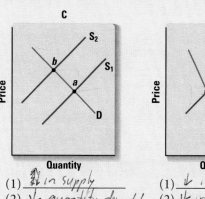

40. Suppose that new medical research strongly indicates that the consumption of coffee can cause cancer of the colon. What effect will this news have on either the demand or the supply, the equilibrium price, and quantity traded of the following products?

a) Coffee beans.
demand: ____________ price: ____________
quantity traded: ____________

b) Tea, a substitute for coffee.
demand: ____________ price: ____________
quantity traded: ____________

c) Danish pastries, a complement to coffee.
demand: ____________ price: ____________
quantity traded: ____________

d) Teapots, a complement to tea.
demand: ____________ price: ____________
quantity traded: ____________

41. What must have happened to demand or supply to cause the following changes?

a) The price of guitars falls, but the quantity traded increases.
Demand/supply __________ must have ________ .

b) The price and quantity traded of saxophones decrease.
Demand/supply __________ must have ________ .

c) The price of trombones increases, while the quantity traded falls.
Demand/supply __________ must have ________

d) The price and quantity traded of clarinets increases.
Demand/supply __________ must have ________ .

Intermediate (Problems 42–44)

42. Consider the effects of each of the events outlined in **Table 2.14** on the market indicated. Place a (↑), (↓) or (–) under the appropriate heading to indicate whether there will be an increase, decrease, or no change in demand (D), supply (S), equilibrium price (P), and quantity traded (Q).

43. Figure 2.18 shows the market for the new Guns and Butter compact disc, "Live at Saskatoon."

a) Suppose that the CD producers put the disc on sale for $8 each. How much will be the surplus or shortage? How many will be sold?
Surplus/shortage ____________ of ____________ .
quantity sold: ____________

b) What is the maximum price at which the quantity actually sold in a) could have been sold?
Maximum price: ____________

c) If the CD producers had actually put the CD on the market at the price mentioned in b), what would have been the resulting surplus/shortage?
Surplus/shortage ____________ of ____________ .

TABLE 2.14

Market	Event	D	S	P	Q
a) Compact discs	A technological improvement reduces the cost of producing compact disc players.				
b) Butter	New medical evidence suggests that margarine causes migraines.				
c) Newspapers	Because of worldwide shortages, the price of pulp and paper increases dramatically.				
d) Low-quality toilet paper	Consumer incomes rise significantly.				
e) Video rentals	Movie theatres halve their admission prices.				
f) Beef	World price of lamb increases.				

FIGURE 2.18

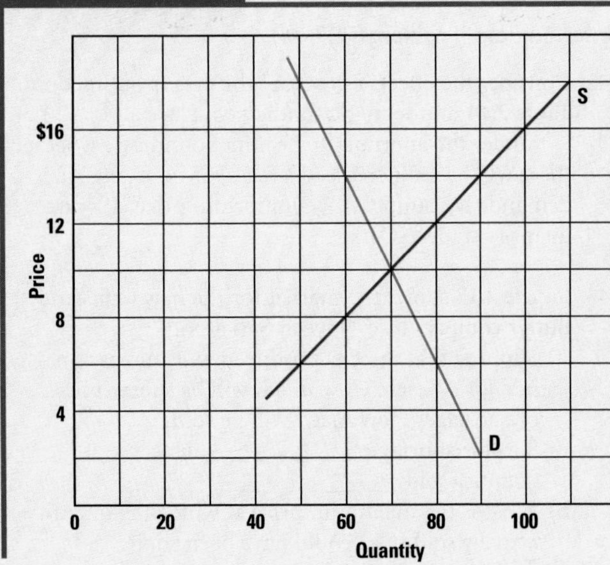

44. "The price of houses rises when the demand increases. The demand for houses decreases when the price increases." Change one of these statements so that the two are consistent with each other.

____

____.

Advanced (Problems 45–46)

45. In Kirin, at a market price of $1 per kilo, there is a shortage of 60 kilos of avocados. For each 50-cent increase in the price, the quantity demanded drops by 5 kilos, while the quantity supplied increases by 10 kilos.

a) What will be the equilibrium price? __________.

b) What will be the surplus/shortage at a price of $4.50? Surplus/shortage __________ of __________ kilos.

46. Identify any two possible causes and five specific effects involved in the movement from point *a* to *b* to *c* in **Figure 2.19**.

FIGURE 2.19

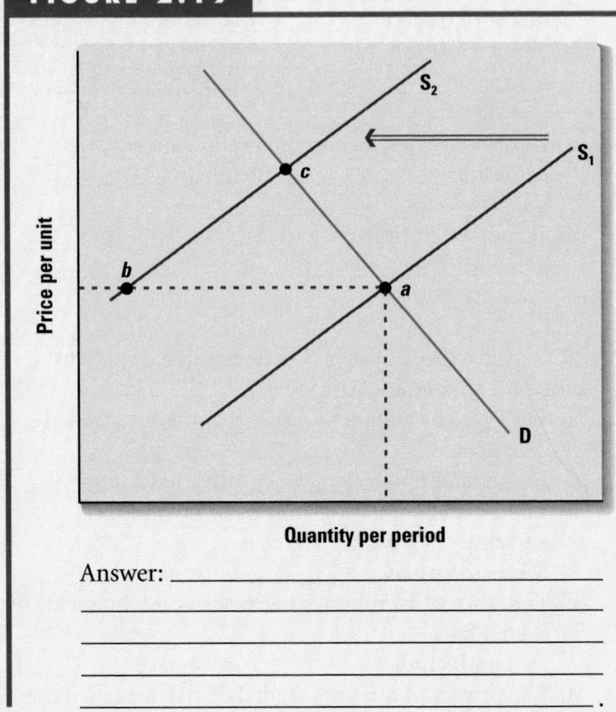

Answer: __________________________________

____

____

____

____.

UNANSWERED PROBLEMS

47. **Key Problem** Table 2.15 shows the market for olives in the economy of Sorel (the quantities are in thousands of kilos per year).

TABLE 2.15

Price ($)	2	4	6	8	10	12	14
Quantity demanded	700	600	500	400	300	200	100
Quantity supplied	100	200	300	400	500	600	700

a) Plot the demand and supply curves and label them D_1 and S_1. Mark the equilibrium as e_1 on the graph.
b) What are the values of equilibrium price and quantity?
c) If the price of olives were $10, would there be a surplus or shortage? How much? Indicate the amount of the surplus or shortage on the graph.
d) Suppose that the demand were to decrease by 200. Draw and label the new demand curve as D_2. What are the new values of equilibrium price and quantity? Mark the new equilibrium as e_2 on the graph.
e) Following the change in d) suppose that the supply were to decrease by 50%. Draw and label the new supply curve as S_2. Now what are the new values of equilibrium price and quantity? Mark the new as e_3 on the graph.

Basic (Problems 48–52)

48. What effect will each of the following have on the price of wine, which is a normal product regarded by many consumers as a substitute for beer and a complement to cheese.
a) A drop in the price of grapes.
b) An increase in the price of beer.
c) A drop in the wage costs in the wine industry.
d) A drop in the tax on wine.
e) A drop in the tax on beer but no change to the wine tax.

49. Table 2.16 shows the demand for and supply of packaged cookies in the economy of Hunter River.

TABLE 2.16

Price ($)	0	1	2	3	4	5	6	7	8	9	10
Demand	10	9	8	7	6	5	4	3	2	1	0
Supply	0	1	2	3	4	5	6	7	8	9	10

a) What is the equilibrium price and quantity?
b) Assume that the supply increases by 2 units at every price. What is the new equilibrium price and quantity?
c) Now assume that the demand increases by 2 units at every price. What is the new equilibrium price and quantity?

50. The two graphs in Figure 2.20 show the markets for orange juice and for apple juice, which are initially in equilibrium.

FIGURE 2.20

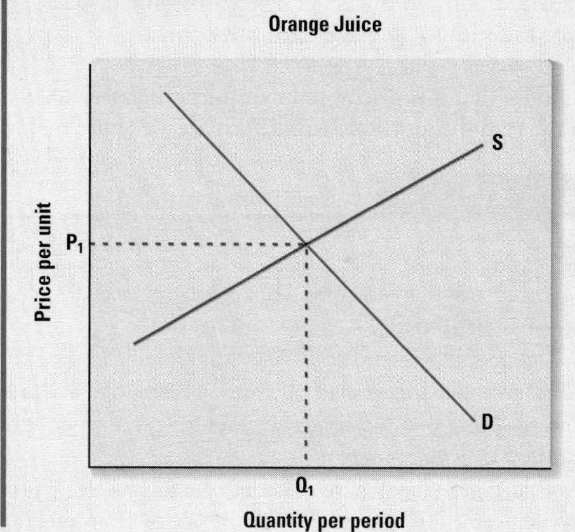

FIGURE 2.20 Continued

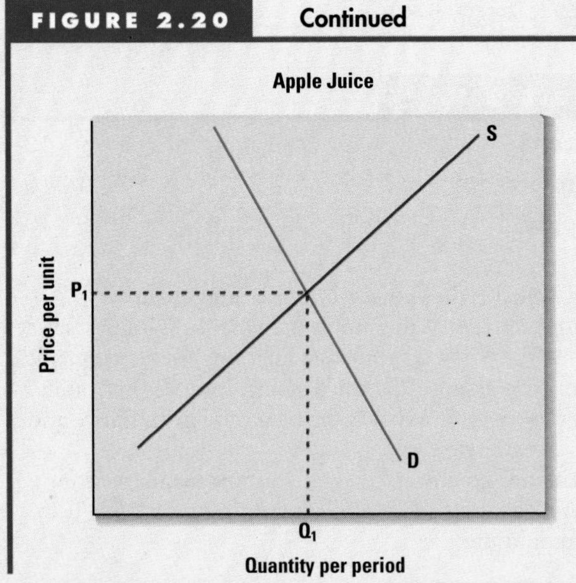

Show what will happen to the prices and quantities traded of both products if a severe frost in Florida were to seriously damage the orange crop.

51. Suppose that it is discovered that the herb anise, taken in the right proportions with chocolate, will cure male baldness. What effect will this have on the price and quantity traded of the following products?

a) Hair transplants.
b) Licorice candy, which is made with anise.
c) Hair-cutting scissors.
d) Chocolate.

52. How are each of the changes below explained in terms of changes in either supply or demand?

a) The price of golf clubs increases and the quantity traded increases.
b) The price of cigarettes increases and the quantity traded decreases.
c) The price of squash rackets decreases and the quantity traded decreases.
d) The price of computers decreases and the quantity traded increases.

Intermediate (Problems 53–55)

53. Consider the effects of each of the following events on the market *for beef* in Canada. Indicate, by placing a (↑), (↓), or (–) under the appropriate heading in **Table 2.17**, whether there will be an increase, decrease, or no change in demand, supply, equilibrium price, and quantity of beef traded.

TABLE 2.17

Event	Demand	Supply	Price	Quantity Traded
a) Medical research indicates that cholesterol in beef is a major cause of heart attacks.				
b) Improved cattle feeds reduce the cost of beef production.				
c) Chicken sales are banned after an outbreak of chicken cholera.				
d) The price of pork decreases because the government gives a subsidy to pork producers.				
e) A reduction in income taxes causes the incomes of Canadian consumers to rise sharply.				
f) The price of cattle feed rises during a drought.				

54. **Table 2.18** shows the demand for the upcoming concert to be given by the string quartet, Guns and Butter, at the new 3000-capacity Saskatoon Auditorium.

TABLE 2.18

Price	Quantity Demanded
$10	8000
15	7000
20	6000
25	5000
30	4000
35	3000
40	2000
45	1000

a) Over what price range would there be a shortage of seats? Over what range would there be a surplus?
b) Suppose the promoters of the concert set the price at $25 per ticket. What will be the result?
c) Suppose that, in response to the great demand for the first concert, the promoters decide to add a second show open *only* to those who were unable to attend the first concert. What is the maximum price they could charge for this concert and still fill the auditorium?

55. "The price of potatoes will increase if their supply decreases. When the price of potatoes increases their supply increases." Change one of these statements so that they are consistent with each other.

Advanced (Problems 56–58)

56. You are given **Figure 2.21**'s demand curves for Tomi, Tami, and Timi, citizens of Millerton.

FIGURE 2.21

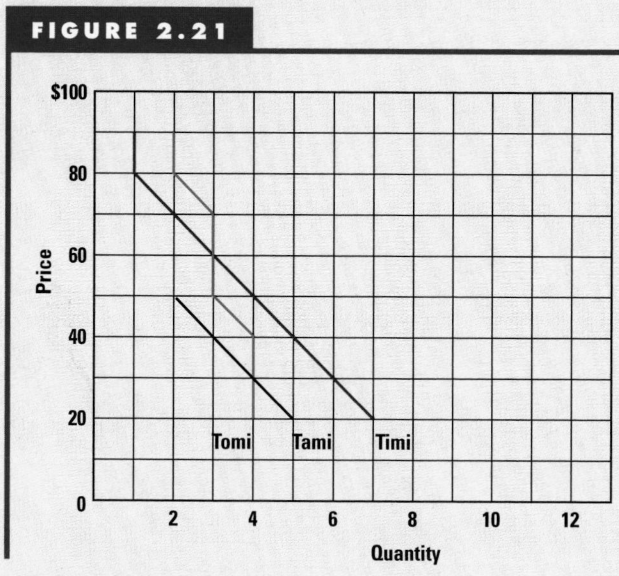

a) Draw in the total (market) demand curve. The market supply in Millerton is as shown in **Table 2.19**.
b) Draw in the market supply curve.
c) What is the equilibrium price and quantity traded?

TABLE 2.19

Price	Quantity
20	6
30	7
40	8
50	9
60	10
70	11
80	12
90	13
100	14

57. Given the graph of the market for starfruit shown in **Figure 2.22**, explain each change in terms of a shift in the appropriate curve, or movement along a curve; and for each change give an example of what might have caused the change:

FIGURE 2.22

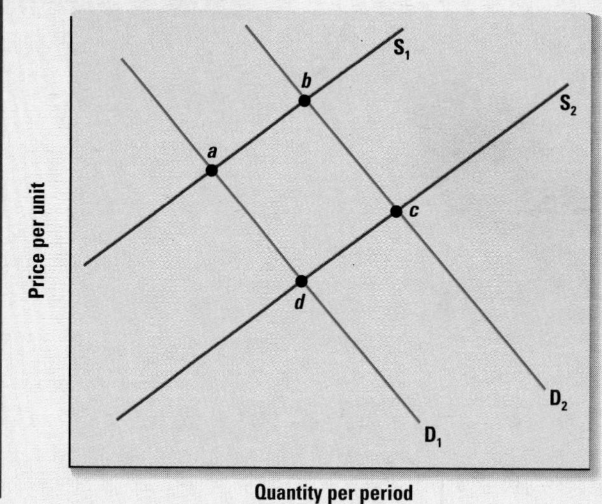

a) From point *a* to point *b*.
b) From point *a* to point *d*.
c) From point *c* to *d*.
d) From point *c* to *b*.

58. Suppose that in response to the high rent and low supply of affordable rental accommodation in the Vancouver market, the city decides to introduce a "rental chit" system. Low-income families will receive one chit per month with a value of $200, which can only be used to help pay their rent. Draw a supply and demand graph showing the effects on the rental market.

Web-Based Activities

Since this is the crucial introductory chapter to demand and supply analysis, rather than asking Web-based questions, we suggest that you spend some time doing the exercises in any one of the following three Web sites.

1. **http://ecedweb.unomaha.edu/Dem_sup/econqui2.htm**

2. **http://hadm.sph.sc.edu/COURSES/ECON/SD/SD.html**

3. **http://www.bized.ac.uk/stafsup/options/qbank/page2.htm**

APPENDIX TO CHAPTER TWO

The Algebra of Demand and Supply

The Algebra of the Market

We saw in the text how we can describe the market place in terms of both tables and graphs. In this appendix we will see how we can also analyze demand and supply algebraically. Suppose that **Figure A1**, the following graph and table, show the demand for soy milk in Canada:

FIGURE A1

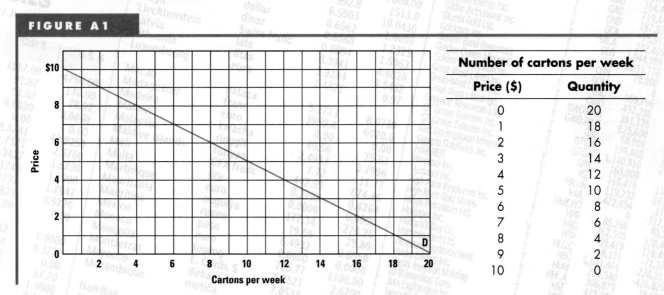

Number of cartons per week

Price ($)	Quantity
0	20
1	18
2	16
3	14
4	12
5	10
6	8
7	6
8	4
9	2
10	0

You will remember from the toolkit that, in general, the algebraic expression for a straight line is:

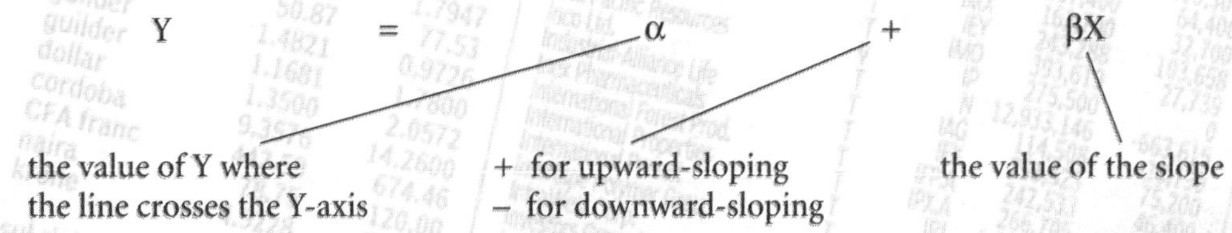

On our graph, price is shown on the vertical (Y) axis and quantity demanded on the horizontal (X) axis. Therefore the general expression for the demand curve is given as:

$$P = \alpha + \beta Q^d$$

Here, the value of α is equal to ($)10. This is where the demand curve crosses the price axis, i.e., it is the highest price payable. The value of the slope is the ratio of change or rise/run. In terms of the demand curve, the slope shows by how much the quantity changes as the price changes, in other words:

$$\text{the slope equals } \frac{\Delta \text{ (change in) P}}{\Delta \text{ (change in) Q}}$$

For our demand curve, that value equals:

$$\frac{1}{-2}$$

This means that each time the price changes by $1, quantity changes (in the opposite direction) by 2 units. The equation for this demand curve then is:

$$P = 10 - \frac{1}{2}Q^d$$

Though this is graphically the correct way to express it, in terms of economic logic, the quantity demanded is dependent on the price, rather than the other way about, so let us re-arrange the terms, as follows:

$$Q^d = 20 - 2P$$

Now let's look at the supply side of things. The following table and graph, in **Figure A2**, show the supply of soy milk in the market:

FIGURE A2

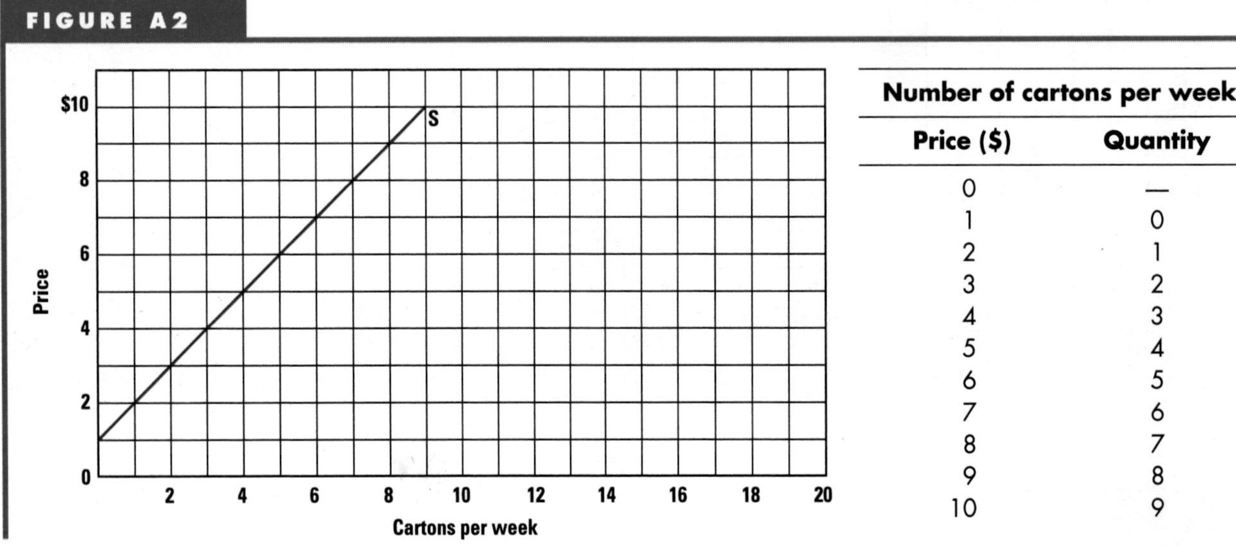

Number of cartons per week	
Price ($)	**Quantity**
0	—
1	0
2	1
3	2
4	3
5	4
6	5
7	6
8	7
9	8
10	9

The general equation for the supply curve is:

$$P = \alpha + \beta Q^s$$

As with the demand curve, α shows the value where the curve crosses the vertical (price) axis. This happens at a price of \$1. The value of the slope is, again, the same as for the demand curve:

$$\frac{\Delta\ (\text{change in})\ P}{\Delta\ (\text{change in})\ Q}$$

For this supply curve, it equals:

$$\frac{1}{+1}$$

A \$1 change in price causes a change of 1 unit in the quantity supplied. The equation for this supply curve, then is:

$$P = 1 + Q^s$$

As we did with the demand curve, let us rearrange this equation in terms of Q^s, thus:

$$Q^s = -1 + P$$

Bringing demand and supply together, in **Figure A3**, allows us to find the equilibrium values.

FIGURE A3

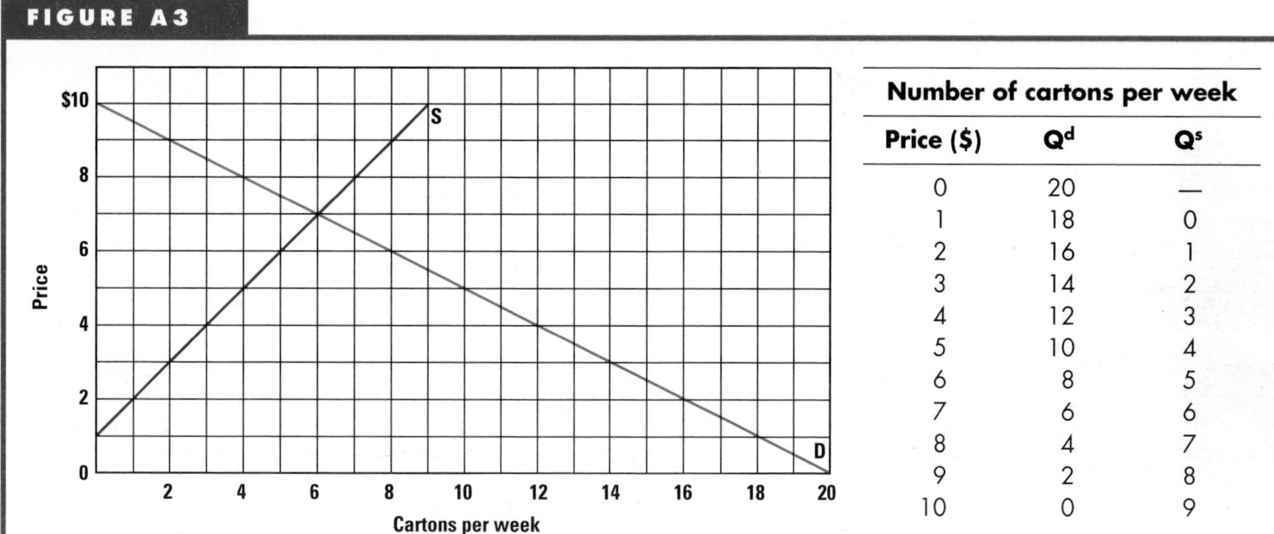

Number of cartons per week		
Price (\$)	**Q^d**	**Q^s**
0	20	—
1	18	0
2	16	1
3	14	2
4	12	3
5	10	4
6	8	5
7	6	6
8	4	7
9	2	8
10	0	9

From either the table or the graph, it is easy to see that the equilibrium price is equal to \$7. At this price, the quantity demanded and quantity supplied are both 6 units. Finding equilibrium algebraically is also straightforward. We want to find the price at which the quantity demanded equals the quantity supplied. We know the equations for each so we simply set them equal, as follows:

$$Q^d = Q^s$$

$$20 - 2P = -1 + P$$

This gives us:

$$3P = 21$$

Therefore, $$P = 7$$

Substituting P = 7 in either equation (and it's best to do both to make sure we are correct) gives us:

$$Q^d = 20 - 2(7) = 6$$

$$Q^s = -1 + (7) = 6$$

Doing things algebraically sometimes makes things easier. For instance, suppose the market demand increased by 3 units, i.e., the quantities demanded increased by 3 units at every price. What effect would this have on the equilibrium price and quantity? Algebraically, this is quite straightforward to calculate. The increase in demand means that the value of the (quantity) intercept increases by 3, and gives us a new demand equation as follows:

$$Q^d{}_2 = 23 - 2P$$

The supply has not changed, so we can calculate the new equilibrium as follows:

$$(Q^d{}_2 = Q_s) : 23 - 2P = -1 + P$$

This gives us:

$$3P = 24$$

Therefore, $$P = 8$$
and the new equilibrium quantity becomes 7.

STUDY GUIDE QUESTIONS FOR APPENDIX TO CHAPTER 2

1. If $Q^d = 40 - 2P$ and $Q^s = 10 + 3P$, what are the equilibrium values of price and quantity?

2. a) If $Q^d = 100 - 5P$ and $Q^s = 10 + P$, what are the equilibrium values of price and quantity?
   b) What will be the new equilibrium values of price and quantity if the demand increases by 30?

3. a) If $P = 11 - 0.25\,Q^d$, what is the algebraic expression for Q^d?
   b) If $P = -16 + 2\,Q^s$, what is the algebraic expression for Q^s?
   c) What are the equilibrium values of price and quantity?

CHAPTER THREE

Measuring National Income

LEARNING OBJECTIVES

This chapter will enable you to:

LO1 Understand the circular flow of national income.

LO2 Explain the concept of equilibrium and why national income can rise and fall.

LO3 Use StatsCan data to calculate various national income accounting statistics.

LO4 Understand some of the problems in determining official statistics.

What's ahead...

What determines the level of an economy's national income, and how that income relates to real output, is at the heart of macroeconomics. In this chapter we begin the explanation of this determination by using the circular flow of income approach. We then introduce the methods for measuring national income. Since we are just at the beginning of a long process, the introduction of many new terms here is unavoidable.

A QUESTION OF RELEVANCE...

Suppose that you heard on the TV news that tax rates were being cut by the government. It is easy for you to see immediately how this would affect you and other members of your family. Although people quickly recognize how some news items affect them directly, they fail to even notice other news items, sometimes just as important. For example, suppose that you read in the newspaper that Canadians were saving much less this year than last, that Canadian exports were higher this year than last, or that interest rates would likely remain unchanged for the foreseeable future. How would you react to these news items? Do you consider them as significant as the item on tax cuts? The fact is that they might be just as significant. This chapter will help to explain why.

In 2001, Canada's national income was $1,084 billion. What are the major determinants of a country's income? How is national income measured? How do decision makers in government and business influence the level of national income? How significant is international trade in determining this level? All these questions need reasonably well-thought-out answers. The first step in the process of finding these answers is to understand the way in which income flows within an economy. To do this, we will construct a simplified model of the economy.

3.1 Circular Flow of Income

LO1
Understand the circular flow of national income.

Flow of Factor Services

Imagine, to begin with, a simple economy with only two sectors: the household sector and the business sector. Clusters of individuals make up the household sector while businesses of various types and sizes, from small family-run proprietorships to large corporations, make up the business sector. Next, recall the definition of the factors of production. As mentioned in Chapter 1, the factors (think of them as production inputs, if that is helpful) are divided into four categories: land, labour, capital, and enterprise.

You may recall, also from Chapter 1, that economists consider land to be anything that is natural, such as minerals, all natural vegetation, natural harbours, supplies of water, and so on. The term labour is used in the broadest sense to describe a wide range of human endeavour, including that of a skilled surgeon, a construction worker, or a symphony musician. Capital is defined as the physical plant, tools, and equipment used to help produce other goods or services. Note that in conventional language, capital is often equated with money. In economics, however, capital refers to the tools, equipment, and machines that are used to produce other goods. Money can be used to purchase capital goods, but it is not, in itself, a factor of production. Finally, enterprise is the specialized human effort that organizes the other factors of production, innovates, and bears risks. These four factors of production are combined to produce the goods and services that individuals consume on a daily basis. In our private enterprise or market economy, the factors of production are, ultimately, owned by individuals. Individuals control the sale of their own labour; individuals own land and mineral rights; and individuals own the shares of a corporation's assets or (for our purposes) capital.

We can now begin to build our model with a series of diagrams. The factor services flow in **Figure 3.1** represents the provision of factor services from the household sector to the business sector. Businesses use these factor services, which are provided by the household sector in order to produce goods and services. This is illustrated by the upper-loop flow from the business sector to the household sector, which represents the provision of consumer goods and services from firms to households.

FIGURE 3.1 **The Flow of Goods and Services and Factor Services**

The two basic sectors of the economy are the Business sector and the Household sector.

The Financial Flows

Next, let's turn to the financial flows that move in the opposite direction. The business sector must pay for the factor services they receive. This payment goes to the household sector, becomes income, and is divided into the specific categories of rent, wages, interest, and profits. Remember that many of these terms differ from their conventional usage. Rent, for instance, is the income received from the use of the factor land, that is, the payment for the use of a natural resource, and is not the payment for the use of an apartment or other building. Wages means the income received for the use of labour services and includes commissions, tips, and all employee benefits. Interest means the income received for the use of the factor capital, which again differs from conventional usage. Finally, by profits economists mean income that is left over after the three factors of production have been paid, and it can be thought of as a reward for the fourth factor: enterprise. Thus, the basic lower-loop financial flow in **Figure 3.2** represents the flow of factor incomes (costs of production to the firm), wages (w), interest (i), rent (r), and profits (π) from the business sector to the household sector.

Individuals in the household sector earn income by receiving payment for the factors they sell or rent. And what do these same individuals do with their incomes? Primarily, they engage in **consumption**—paying for the consumer goods and services received from the business sector. This flow represents an expenditure for households but is an income (in the way of business receipts) for the firms. So, now we have two financial flows, as shown in **Figure 3.2**.

consumption: the expenditure by households on goods and services.

FIGURE 3.2 **The Financial Flows**

Households receive income from the sale of the factors of production and spend this income on consumption.

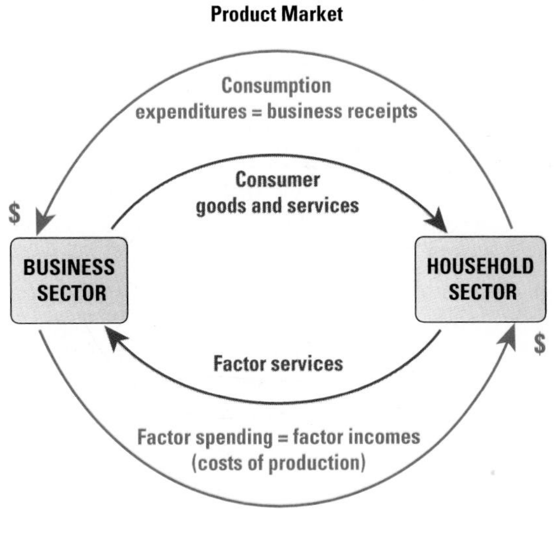

This is the basic circular flow:

Households sell factor services to the business sector and earn incomes. With this income, they pay for the goods and services received from the business sector.

Many complications are on the way, but each can be handled easily if you keep this basic circular flow clear in your mind.

ADDED DIMENSION

François Quesnay and the Circular Flow

The circular flow concept owes a big debt to François Quesnay (1694–1774), court physician to Louis XV and Madame de Pompadour of France, and the founder of a group of scholars called the Physiocrats, who were highly critical of the French government's interference in the economy. This interference had taken the form of a myriad of regulations and taxes. Quesnay published his *Tableau Economique* in 1758 to explain how income in an economy flows from one group in society to another. He believed that only nature was truly a creator of wealth, by generating what he called a surplus each year. Humans, he believed, merely "transformed" this surplus into various products. Further, this surplus eventually "flowed" to the landowners (the king, the aristocracy, and the church), and therefore only this group should be subject to taxation. He advocated that all other taxes should be abolished, leaving only a single tax on "wealth." Not surprisingly, his views were not well-received in the circles of power.

product market: the market for consumer goods and services.

factor market: the market for the factors of production.

We have now also identified what economists call the **product market**, which is the buying and selling of goods and services (the upper loops); and the **factor market**, which is the buying and selling of the factors of production (the lower loops).

Also notice that each buy–sell transaction in either market is income to one sector and spending to the other. Thus:

National income is the *sum of all incomes* earned from economic transactions or the *sum of all spending.*

The Flow of Income versus the Stock of Money

income: the earnings of factors of production expressed as an amount per period of time.

money: any medium of exchange that is widely accepted.

Before we move to some complications, there is a straightforward but very fundamental point that has to be understood. We are building a circular flow of **income** model, and it is important that we distinguish between the flow of income and the stock of **money**. An example will help. Imagine a simple economy made up of only three businesses: Bill owns and operates a bakery, Wick is the proprietor of a candle-making business, and Tammy has a tailor's shop. Within this economy there is only a single $10 bill, which is currently in the possession of Bill the baker. So we begin our story with three businesses (and three households), a stock of money equal to $10, and no income (yet). Let us assume that Wick has just produced some candles and that Bill the baker notices that his inventory of candles is getting low, so he goes to Wick and buys $10 worth of candles and pays cash. Wick, in receipt of $10, decides he needs to purchase a new pair of jeans, produced by Tammy the tailor, which just happen to cost $10. Tammy has spent all day producing these jeans and for her efforts receives $10 from Wick. After all this effort, Tammy requires sustenance and makes her way to Bill the baker to buy some freshly baked bread, which has a price of $10. Bill the baker receives the $10 bill for his efforts. Let us summarize today's activities in this mini-economy:

- Total production came to a value of $30.
- Total spending came to $30; and total income is $30.
- All of this activity was financed by a single $10 bill.

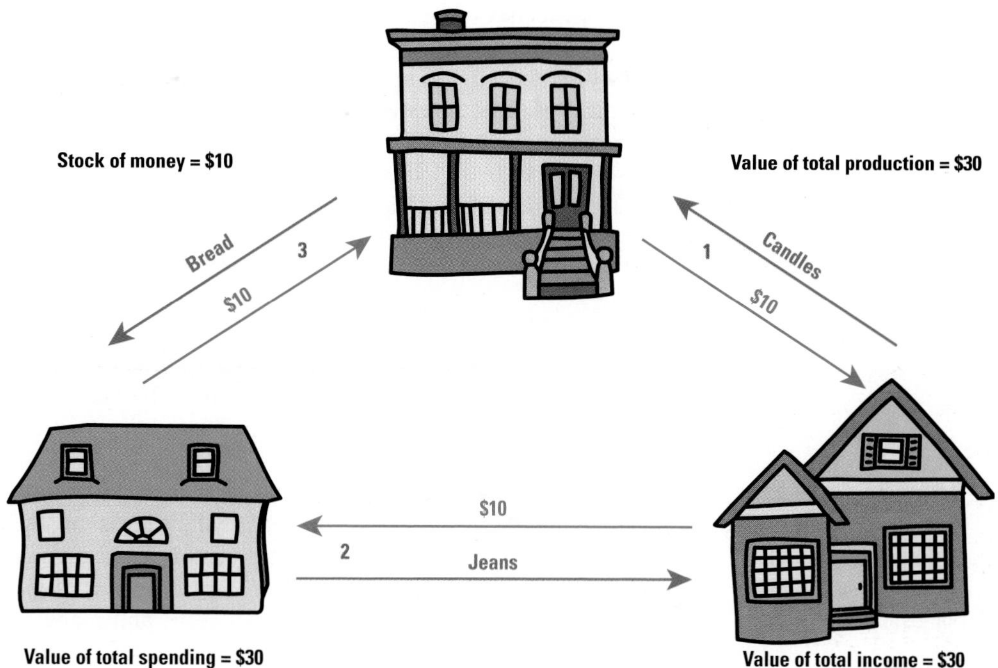

Clearly the stock of money and the flow of income are not the same thing! To cement this simple point, think of a retired couple with a lot of money—$200 000 in a bank account—but relatively little income—$16 000 a year in interest. Compare this with the young double-income professional couple just starting out, with an annual household income of $90 000 but almost no money, since all the income is going to mortgage and car payments and the expenses of a fast-lane lifestyle. Again, the fundamental point—distinguishing between the flow of income and the stock of money—is important. In 2001, Canada's stock of money was approximately $128 billion. The flow of income during the same year was approximately $1084 billion. These figures tell us that the velocity of money in Canada for that year was 8.5 (ie. $\frac{1084}{128}$). This means that each unit of currency in Canada was used (changed hands) approximately 8.5 times during that year.

The First Set of Leakages and Injections: Saving and Investment

Our simple economy described above seemed to demonstrate that: the value of a) total production ($10 worth of candles, of bread, and of jeans); b) total expenditure (the purchase of each of these three items); and c) total income (what Wick, Bill, and Tammy each receive) are equal. Does this equality always hold true, or is it merely a coincidence? We will answer this question soon, but for now you should realize that a good part of macroeconomics is concerned with the link between total spending and incomes.

saving: the portion of income that is not spent on consumption.

leakage: income received within the circular flow that does not flow directly back.

Keeping all this in mind, let's now return to the circular flow and introduce the first complication by asking the question: what else do individuals in the household sector do with their income besides spend on consumption? The answer is: they save. This activity of **saving** (S) can be defined as income (Y) received but not spent on consumption (*C*).

$$S = Y - C \qquad [3.1]$$

Saving thus becomes a **leakage** from the circular flow of income. This is shown in Figure 3.3.

Economists have developed a fairly standard set of abbreviations for often-used terminology. As you can see from the equation on page 93, C stands for consumption, *S* for saving, and Y for income. (If you are wondering why *I* is not used for income, the answer is quite simple—it is used for investment.)

The reasons that people want to save can be quite varied: for retirement; for a major purchase in the future, such as a house, car, or holiday; for a child's future education; or quite simply, for a rainy day. In this model, the primary determinant of how much people are able to save is their level of income, that is:

$$S = f(Y)$$

The above equation is read as: saving is a function of income. If you wish, you can replace the word "function" with "depends on." The fact that saving depends primarily on income is a point we'll want to keep in mind later, when we discuss the effect of changes in interest rates.

It should also be noted that a business can also save by not paying out *all* of its after-tax profits in dividends. Nonetheless, our focus will be on saving by households. People can hold both current-period saving (a flow), and accumulated savings held over from a previous period (a stock). People's **wealth** includes not only such savings, but also things like rare paintings, vintage wines, antique cars, real estate, and many other assets. Savings make up the portion of wealth that is held in the form of financial instruments, such as bonds, term deposits, savings accounts, and chequing accounts. Another way of looking at all this is that a portion of wealth makes up what we call **loanable funds**. Normally, these funds are deposited with various financial intermediaries, like banks, credit unions, and trust companies, and are available for loan. Loanable funds and financial intermediaries are also in **Figure 3.3**.

wealth: the sum of all valuable assets less liabilities.

loanable funds: the portion of wealth that is available for loan through financial intermediaries.

Let us pull together the main points made so far:

- Saving is both a function of income and a leakage from the circular flow of income.
- The reasons people want to save are varied.
- A large portion of saving flows to financial intermediaries.

Next we want to add the first injection. An **injection** is any expenditure received by firms in the business sector that does not come from the household sector in the form of consumption and thus does not depend on the level of income.

injection: any spending flow that is not dependent on the current level of income.

investment: spending on capital goods.

The first injection is **investment** spending. Investment is defined as spending that results in a physical increase in plant or equipment. Another way of thinking of investment is spending that increases the economy's stock of capital goods.

Why would a firm invest in new machinery or equipment, thereby expanding its production capacity? Quite simply, to increase potential profit in the future.

You will notice that the definition of investment differs from the conventional use of the term. If you overheard a fellow student say: "I invested in some General Corporation stock today," you would correctly understand him to mean that he had *bought* some General Corporation stock. Yet, he has technically misused the term "investment," at least from the economist's point of view! Let's get this sorted out. The person in our example was able to buy the stock through his broker only because someone else wanted to sell General Corporation stock. Someone sold the stock; someone bought it; brokers arranged the transactions and took a commission. From the point of view of the overall economy, what has changed? The answer is: very little. The portfolios of the two people in our example have changed, but the economy has not experienced any new investment. Investment, then, is an increase in the economy's capacity to produce goods and services and is done by business for profit.

To re-emphasize:

The reasons individuals save (for retirement, future purchases, and so on) differ from the reasons businesses invest. Saving (a leakage) and investment (an injection) are quite distinct actions.

Does this imply that there is no connection between saving and investment whatsoever? No, it doesn't mean that at all. Most of the time, investment by business is financed with borrowed funds, and it is the savings in the economy that provide the pool of loanable funds mentioned earlier. In short, the savings available in the economy, which become loanable funds, enable business investment to occur.

You may well ask: doesn't all saving become loanable funds? The answer is: most of it, but not all. Once again, saving is income received and not spent. If this saving is put into a bank, it does indeed become loanable funds, but if it ends up in the cookie jar or under the mattress, it does not add to the loanable funds available in the economy.

financial security: any claim on assets that usually takes the form of a bond or certificate of deposit or similar financial instrument.

Now we can finish things off. When households put their savings into financial intermediaries, they receive some sort of **financial security** in return, usually a certificate of deposit or a bond or equity stock. As a result, the households will receive interest payments or dividends in the future. These payments are an expense to the business that issues the financial instruments and income to the households that receive them. The investment injection is shown in **Figure 3.3**.

FIGURE 3.3 **The Saving Leakage and Investment Injection**

The financial intermediaries match the saving of the households with the desire of the business sector to borrow for investment.

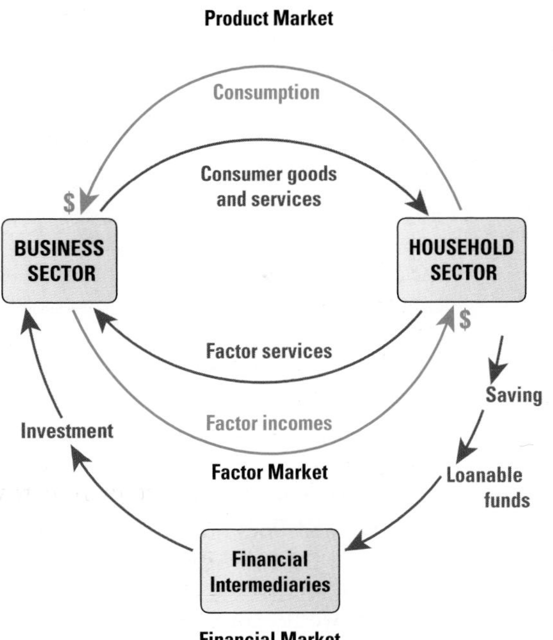

Let's now consider another aspect of this saving–investment link. Note that the mere existence of loanable funds is not sufficient to guarantee investment. For example, there were plenty of funds to borrow in the middle of the Great Depression of the 1930s, yet businesses simply were not borrowing much because of widespread pessimism about the economy's future.

Conversely, a country may suffer from a lack of loanable funds. This is the situation faced by some economically less developed countries today. Often, the total pools of savings within these economies are so small that loanable funds are very limited. The result is that many viable investment projects never come to fruition because the funds needed to finance them simply aren't available.

Even among the richer economies of the world, rates of saving can vary a great deal. What we can conclude from these points is the abstract but fundamental point that in an economy without government or international trade:

Saving is a *necessary but not sufficient* condition for investment.

ADDED DIMENSION

Investment during the Great Depression

Here are some actual data to illustrate the significant decrease in investment spending that occurred in Canada during the Great Depression:

Year	Investment ($ billions)
1929	1.41
1933	0.21
1937	0.76
1939	0.97

As you can see, investment decreased by more than 85 percent between 1929 and 1933 and, in fact, didn't return to the 1929 level until the early 1940s.

Source: Statistics Canada, National Income and Expenditure Accounts, Catalogue 13-001.

The Second Set of Leakages and Injections: Imports and Exports

Putting saving and investment aside for now, let's turn to the second pair of leakages–injections. First, the leakage. Some of the goods and services that households buy, as well as some of the investment goods purchased by business, are goods and services imported from outside the domestic economy. Such expenditure does not flow back to the domestic economy, but instead leaks out. We call this import spending, or just plain **imports** (IM). Although it is usually business that does the actual importing of goods, we will illustrate this leakage as coming from the household sector, reflecting the fact that the ultimate consumers of most imports are individuals.

imports: goods and services that are bought from other countries and constitute a leakage from the circular flow of income.

exports: goods and services produced in one country and sold to another country.

Conversely, the business sector receives payment for goods and services exported, and this payment is in addition to the consumption expenditure from (domestic) households. **Exports** (X) are, therefore, an injection into the circular flow of income. Note, then, that the value of exports does not depend on the level of income in this country, but on the level of income in the rest of the world. Both the import leakage and the export injection are illustrated in **Figure 3.4**.

FIGURE 3.4 **The Import Leakage and Export Injection**

Households spend on imports and the business sector exports to foreigners.

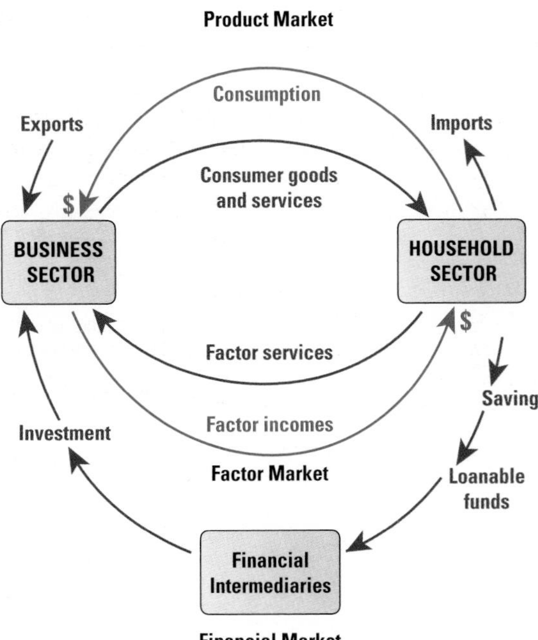

The Third Set of Leakages and Injections: Taxes and Government Spending

The third pair of leakages–injections that we will consider isn't so simply handled. First, we must add another sector to our analysis: government. The government sector taxes both the household sector and the business sector, so that taxes (T) are the third leakage. Also, the government sector purchases goods and services from the business sector, so that government spending (G) on goods and services is the third injection. In addition, government also disburses what are called **transfer payments** (TP). These are defined as payments made for which no goods or services are given in exchange (at the time of the payment). Examples of transfer payments would be Employment Insurance payments, Canada Pension Plan payments, and subsidies to businesses. We will treat all transfer payments as a flow from the government sector directly to individuals in the household sector. The addition of the government sector is illustrated in **Figure 3.5**.

transfer payments: one-way transactions in which payment is made, but no good or service flows back in return.

FIGURE 3.5 **The Addition of Government**

This Financial Market is an illustration of the circular flow of income with the three leakages:

- saving (S)
- import (IM)
- taxes (T)

and the three injections:

- investments (I)
- exports (X)
- government (G)

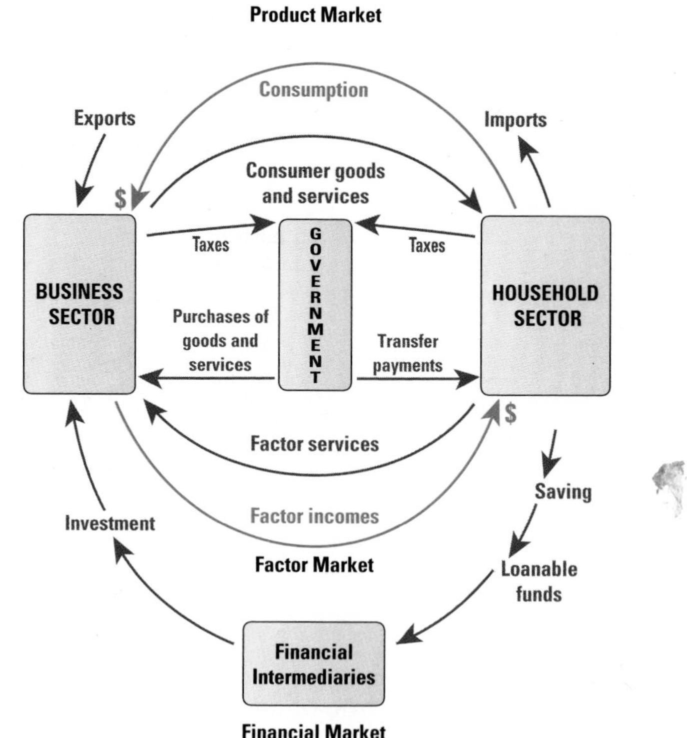

3.2 Equilibrium and the Level of National Income

LO2
Explain the rise and fall of national income.

equilibrium: a state of balance of equal forces resulting in no tendency to change.

We are now ready to take on the first of several views of **equilibrium** that we will encounter in our development of macro principles. The dictionary definition of this term is "a state of balance or equality between opposing forces." The opposing forces here are leakages on the one hand and injections on the other. If these two opposing forces are in balance, that is, if:

$$S + IM + T = I + X + G \qquad [3.2]$$

then the level of income will remain *unchanged* and can be said to be in equilibrium. On the other hand, if, say, investment spending were to rise, then injections would exceed leakages, creating disequilibrium. The higher injections would cause the level of income to continue to *rise* until the resulting increases in saving, imports, and taxes were enough to create a new equilibrium. Conversely, if, say, tax rates were to increase, then leakages would exceed injections and this would cause consumption spending to fall and income to continue to *fall,* until the resulting decreases in saving, imports, and (total) taxes were sufficient to bring injections and leakages back into equilibrium. A decrease in taxes would, of course, have the same effect as the increase in investment spending mentioned above. This gives an insight into a theme that we will be developing in subsequent chapters: changes in spending have a big impact on the level of income.

We could use an analogy here. Think of the income level as being the level of water in a bathtub. The injection could be thought of as the open tap that is adding water to the tub, and the leakage as the open drain letting water flow out. The level of water in the tub (the level of income) rises, falls, or remains unchanged, according to the flow of the leakage relative to the injection. Thus, our first formal definition of **national income equilibrium** is:

national income equilibrium: that level of income where total leakages from the circular flow equal total injections.

PhotoDisc

The level of income in the economy is analogous to the level of water in the tub.

The level of income where the total of all three leakages equals the total of all three injections.

value of production: the total receipts of all producers.

aggregate expenditures: total spending in the economy, divided into the four components: C, I, G, and (X – IM).

There is a second view of equilibrium, which introduces the concept of the **value of production** (or the value of total output). We measure the value of production by adding up what producers get when they sell their output; i.e., by summing the total receipts of producers. The amount that producers receive for their products is equal to the amount paid by those who buy the output and, in turn, this total spending by buyers is called **aggregate expenditures**. Thus, the aggregate expenditures of buyers and the total receipts of the business sector are the same thing. But we can also measure the value of production in terms of how much it costs to produce that output. Since the costs of production represent income to those who provide factor services, total costs of production must be equal to total income. In other words:

$$\text{Value of production} = \text{business receipts} = \text{aggregate expenditures} \quad [3.3]$$

and

$$\text{Value of production} = \text{cost of production} = \text{total income} \quad [3.4]$$

To emphasize, when an economy is in equilibrium, aggregate expenditures are equal to total incomes, and both are, in turn, equal to the value of production.

Let us use a simple example here. If, in a given period, aggregate expenditures (consumption spending, investment spending, government spending, and net exports) equal $100, then business receipts will, of course, also be $100. If we assume that inventories remain the same in this period, then it is also true that the value of production must have been $100, since this is the amount of goods that were bought. And how much income was generated in producing these goods? Exactly $100 worth—in the form of wages, interest, rents, and profits.

Once again, the fundamental point:

Equilibrium implies not only that total leakages equal total injections, but also that aggregate expenditures equal total income.

Now that this second definition of equilibrium is well in hand, we are ready to move on to the measurement of national income.

SELF-TEST

1. If the economy is in disequilibrium because total income exceeds aggregate expenditure, what must be happening to inventories?
2. Does the term "consumption" refer to spending by households on domestically produced goods and services only? Does the term "investment" include the purchase of stocks and bonds?

REVIEW

1. What are the four *factors of production*?
2. What is the payment to each factor of production?
3. Distinguish between the *product market* and the *factor market*.
4. Define the term *loanable funds*.
5. Distinguish between *savings* and *investment*.
6. List the three leakages and the three injections.
7. What does the word *equilibrium* mean?
8. Define the term *aggregate expenditure*.

3.3 Measuring National Income

LO3
Use StatsCan to calculate various national income accounting statistics.

The development of the circular flow of income model is complete. We now turn to the measurement of national income. Just as the circular flow diagram was helpful in conceptualizing equilibrium, it can also be helpful in recognizing that there are two different ways to measure income. The first is the *expenditures approach*. As the name implies, this approach adds up the four forms of expenditures, which, once again, are:

- C consumption
- I investment spending
- G government spending on goods and services
- X exports

and then subtracts spending on imports (IM).

In short, the basic expenditure—consumption—plus the three injections give us aggregate expenditures (AE). This gives us an equation you will become quite familiar with:

net exports: total exports minus total imports of goods and services which can be written as (X – IM) or as X_N.

$$AE = C + I + G + (X - IM) \quad [3.5]$$

Defining **net exports** (X_N) as X – IM, we could rewrite this as:

$$AE = C + I + G + X_N$$

The second conceptual approach to measuring national income—called the incomes approach—simply adds the four types of incomes that flow from the business sector to the household sector: wages, interest, rents, and profits.

Adding the total expenditures in the economy or adding the total incomes in the economy are both valid measurements of the value of production. When the economy is in equilibrium, these two sums will equal each other (after three technical adjustments which we will soon explain). So we have:

$$AE = C + I + G + X_N = \text{National Income} = w + i + r + \pi \quad [3.6]$$

Measuring National Income: The Mechanics

This section is filled with many terms that may seem a little tedious. Yet, every student of economics needs to have some understanding of how production is accounted for.

The most-used economic statistic is **gross domestic product (GDP)**, which is defined as the money value of all final goods and services produced in the whole economy within a given time period, usually a quarter or a year.[1]

gross domestic product (GDP): the value of all final goods and services produced in an economy in a certain period.

national income (Y): total earnings of all the factors of production in a certain period.

For our purposes, the other significant statistic is **national income (Y)**. (Government agencies use the symbol NI for national income, but we will use Y to be consistent with later chapters.) National income is defined as the total earnings of all factors of production within the economy in a given time period, usually in a quarter or a year.

There are two different ways to look at the value of any particular thing produced. The first, and most straightforward, is in terms of the price it finally sells for, for example, $3 for a tube of toothpaste off the retailer's shelf. Thus, one view is that the $3 is its price and thus will equal the amount spent on acquiring it. The other view, equally valid, is that there is $3 worth of income to distribute to all those factors that went into the activity of getting that tube of toothpaste to the retailer's shelf. So the value of the toothpaste is the $3 of total income generated, which is paid to the various factors of production. In short:

The value of output is determined by the income generated in getting it into the hands of the consumer and is equal to the amount that consumers have paid for it.

Conceptually then, at *equilibrium* GDP, the value of output must equal AE, which must equal Y.

$$GDP = AE = Y \quad [3.7]$$

Measuring GDP by the Expenditure Method

Let us next explain exactly what Statistics Canada includes in each item of expenditures. First, consumption includes spending on consumer goods and services and is subdivided into various components, such as: consumer durables (for example, cars and household appliances); semidurables (clothes); nondurables (food and beverages); and consumer services (educational, financial, health care, and legal).

The next item, investment, is composed of spending on machinery and equipment, changes in the value of inventories, and spending on all construction (including residential construction). The term *Ig* used below refers to gross investment—that is, before any depreciation (to be discussed later in this chapter) is taken into account. Government spending is

[1]All GDP figures and national income figures are adapted from Statistics Canada, Catalogue 30-001-X-PB.

made up of the total spending on goods and services at all levels of government (including investment spending by government). It does not, however, include transfer payments or subsidies. Finally, net exports is the total value of all exports (whether of consumer goods, capital goods, or government services) less the total value of all imports. The actual figures (in $ billions) for Canada in 2001 were as follows:

C	Ig	G	X_N
620	183	226	55

Summing these four figures gives us a GDP of $1084 billion.

Statistics Canada attempts to *measure* GDP, the value of production. If the economy is in equilibrium, GDP will equal aggregate expenditures. But what if the economy is not in equilibrium? For example, what happens if the total value of production exceeds aggregate expenditures? The result will be an increase in inventories (unsold goods) in the economy during that year. Conversely, if aggregate expenditures exceed the value of production, firms would find their inventories being depleted. Statistics Canada collects data on the change of inventories from one year to the next and can therefore quite easily calculate the value of production. For instance, suppose that the level of inventories in the economy at the beginning of the year is $100 billion. During the year total sales (equals aggregate expenditures) amounted to $500 billion, and the economy found itself with $120 billion in inventories at the end of the year. The value of total production during the year must therefore equal aggregate expenditure ($500 billion) plus or minus the change in the value of inventory. In this year, inventory changed by + $20 billion ($120 minus 100). Therefore, the value of production equals $520 billion. We can easily check that this is the correct answer:

Inventory at the beginning of the year:	$100 billion
Value of production:	$520 billion
Production available for sale:	$620 billion
Total sales (equals aggregate expenditures):	$500 billion
Inventory at the end of the year:	$120 billion

In summary, then,

value of production = aggregate expenditures plus or minus change in inventories

This adjustment for inventories is considered as a form of investment by Statistics Canada and is what economists term unplanned investment.

Note that the GDP measures the value (at market prices) of all goods and services produced *in Canada* in a year. Many of the other statistics we will be developing are concerned with production and incomes *by Canadians*. The term given to this latter statistic is the **gross national product (GNP)**. To calculate this measure, we need to add factor income (and production) by Canadians abroad, and subtract factor income (and production) earned by foreigners in Canada as follows:

gross national product (GNP): the total market value of all final goods and services produced by the citizens of a country regardless of the location of production.

GDP at market prices	1084
Plus/minus net foreign factor income	– 27
= GNP at market prices	1057

SELF-TEST

3. Identify the items in the statements below (from the point of view of the Canadian economy) according to the following code.

C consumption	S savings
I investment	IM imports
G government spending on goods and services	T taxes
N not applicable	X exports

a) A student gets her haircut from a self-employed hairdresser.

b) The hairdresser buys a pair of scissors from the Ace Beauty Supply Company.

c) Out of each day's revenue, the hairdresser puts $5 in her piggy bank.

d) Each time she has enough set aside, the hairdresser buys a share of GM stock.

e) GM expands its computer facilities in its head office.

f) American tourists go skiing in the Canadian Rockies.

g) Two Canadians go to Tokyo and stay at the Hilton Hotel.

h) Russia buys beef from Alberta cattle ranchers.

i) The Province of Saskatchewan pays for the building of a new highway.

Measuring GDP by the Income Method

Now, we turn to the income approach to measuring GDP. Statistics Canada uses five major groupings of income. The first is wages and salaries, which includes all benefits received and is expressed as gross earnings before taxes or deductions. Next is interest and investment income, which includes business interest only and not interest on consumer loans or on loans to government (the latter is regarded as a form of transfer payment). The third category is gross profits, the earnings of corporations before any distribution of dividends or payment of taxes. Farmers' incomes is a self-explanatory category, though you might wonder why Statistics Canada has decided to single out farmers for special treatment. The reason is simply that it is difficult to know what portion of their total income comes from wages, what portion is profits, and what portion is from crop-retention. (Yes, eating your own crops doesn't go unnoticed by the government.) The fifth category, the clumsily titled "net income of non-farm unincorporated business" (hereafter called self-employed income), includes the incomes of all businesses other than corporations (for example, sole proprietors and partners, and also includes some rent, as well as the profits of crown corporations). The amounts for these categories in 2001 (again in $ billions) were as follows:

Wages	Interest	Gross Profits	Farmers' Income	Self-employed Income
559	53	120	3	75

net domestic income: incomes earned in Canada (equals the sum of wages, profits, interest, farm, and self-employed income).

Therefore, total income or, using Statistic Canada's official term, **net domestic income** equals $810 billion.

This represents the total gross incomes in all forms received in Canada. As we did before, we need to make the same adjustment to find the total incomes received *by Canadians*, that is,

net domestic income	810
Plus/minus net foreign factor income	– 27
= national income (of Canadians)	783

Given what we learned about the circular flow of income earlier in this chapter, you may well be wondering why there is no separate category for rent. The absence of rent in the national income accounts is a practical problem rather than a conceptual one. Some profits are undoubtedly rent return, as are portions of farm income and even self-employed income. StatsCan, however, simply doesn't try to determine how much.

Therefore, what was "wages, interest, rents, and profits" in the circular flow analysis is "wages, interest, profits, farm income, and self-employed income" in the national accounts.

Reconciling GNP and National Income

Perceptive readers might have noticed that the GNP (the expenditures approach) and national income (the incomes approach) totals don't agree! Didn't we say earlier that they are conceptually the same thing? Yes, they are, but in national income accounting not all the receipts (the same as aggregate expenditures) of firms are paid out in the form of incomes. First, firms set up a fund for the replacement of worn-out capital. This is termed *depreciation* (or capital consumption allowance) and is not available for distribution, either to employees or to shareholders. If we subtract the amount of depreciation from the GNP, we have another statistic called **net national product (NNP)**. Thus, for 2001:

net national product (NNP): gross national product less capital consumption (or depreciation).

GNP at market prices	1057
less depreciation	142
= NNP at market prices	915

In addition to depreciation, there is another item of income that firms receive but do not pay out as income to anyone, and that is the amount of sales taxes (indirect taxes such as the GST) that firms are required to collect on behalf of the government. If this amount (net of subsidies) is taken into account, we get:

NNP at market prices	915
less indirect taxes (net of subsidies)	132
= NNP at factor costs	783

Thus, after the two technical adjustments (depreciation and indirect taxes), the expenditures approach and the incomes approach do balance at the figure $783 billion.

Table 3.1 illustrates that the flow of income and total expenditures are conceptually the same thing. As you can see on the left-hand side of the table, when we add up aggregate expenditures and then adjust for net foreign factor income, depreciation, and indirect taxes, we get NNP as factor costs, which is the figure $783. On the right-hand side of the table, if we add the five categories of income and then make the same adjustment for net foreign factor income, we get the same $783 figure for national income, which is the same thing as NNP at factor cost. In short, the conceptual point that the expenditures approach and the incomes approach are the same thing is verified.

TABLE 3.1

Expenditures			Incomes		
Consumption	$	620	Wages	$	559
Gross Investment	$	183	Interest	$	53
Government Spending	$	226	Gross Profits	$	120
Net Exports	$	+ 55	Farmers' Income	$	3
			Self-employed Income	$	75
Gross Domestic Product	**$**	**1084**	**Net Domestic Income**	**$**	**810**
+/– Net Foreign F. Income	$	– 27	+/– Net Foreign F. Income	$	– 27
Gross National Product	**$**	**1057**			
Less Depreciation	$	142			
Net National Product	**$**	**915**			
Less Indirect Taxes	$	132			
NNP at Factor Costs	**$**	**783**	**= National Income**	**$**	**783**

Figure 3.6 will help you understand the fundamental point that one person's spending is another person's income and that, at equilibrium, total spending (aggregate expenditures) is equal to total income, and both are equal to GDP (the value of production).

FIGURE 3.6

National income (after technical adjustments), aggregate expenditures and the value of production are equal in equilibrium.

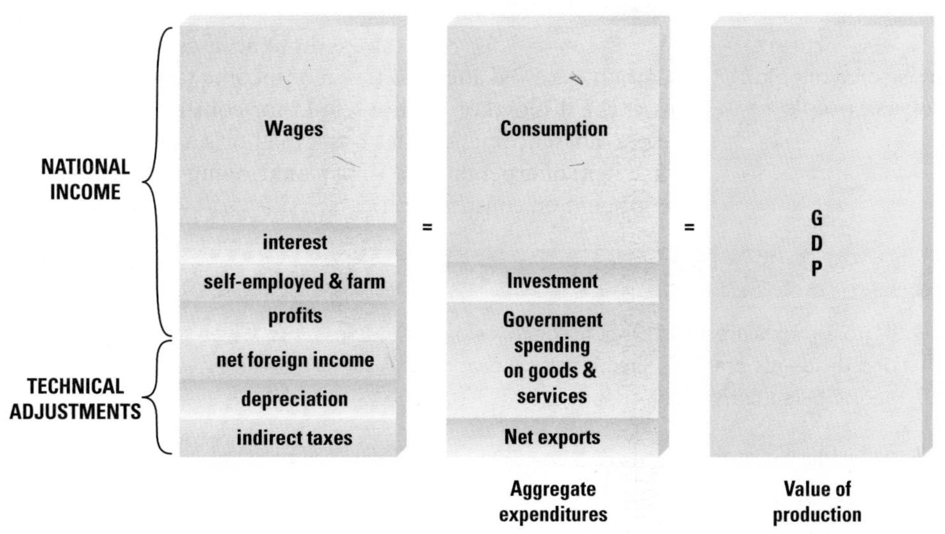

personal income: income paid to individuals before the deduction of personal income taxes.

So now you know that there is a technical difference between GDP and Y, and that is important. Even more important, you also know that conceptually the two terms—GDP and Y—can be used interchangeably. We will do so throughout the text.

Our next focus is on the term **personal income**, which can be thought of as people's gross income. Moving from national income to personal income in the national income accounting framework requires four adjustments (again we show the figures for 2001):

national income (or NNP at factor costs)	783
less undistributed corporate profits	55
less corporate profit taxes	41
plus government transfer payments	210
less other income not paid out	34
= personal income	863

Let's explain the top two subtractions first. A corporation does one of three things with the profits it earns:

- pays taxes
- retains (saves) them
- pays dividends to its shareholders

Obviously, only the portion paid in dividends actually goes to individuals and thus becomes part of personal income. Therefore, the portion that goes to taxes and the portion that is saved is not part of personal income and thus must be subtracted from national income to get personal income.

Transfer payments (the very same ones talked about in the circular flow discussion earlier in this chapter) have to be added because they do become part of people's gross income, but are not part of national income since they have nothing to do with the payment to the factors of production. The last adjustment, other income not paid out, includes quite technical items such as transfers from non-residents, and government investment income not paid out.

To complete our national income accounting framework, we need one final adjustment:

personal income	863
less personal income taxes	205
= disposable income	658

disposable income: the personal after-tax income of people.

Disposable income can be thought of as people's take-home or net income and is the amount received after deduction of income tax (and other payroll deductions). This is what is at the disposal of the household for consumption spending and saving. In other words, disposable income is either consumed or saved. In 2001, consumption was 620 (it was the first item of expenditures) so personal saving must have been 38 (658 disposable income less 620 spent on consumption).

SELF-TEST

4. If gross profits are $62, corporation taxes are $15, and dividends are $26, then what is the value of undistributed corporation profits?

5. Given the following data for the country of Hemlock:

net foreign factor income	–10
national income	600
government spending on goods and services	175
indirect taxes	50
gross investment	60
consumption	420
depreciation	20

determine the value of X_N.

6. Given the following data for the country of Seymour:

personal income	589
undistributed corporate profits	42
corporate profit taxes	41
other income not paid out	52
government transfer payments	172

determine the value of national income.

3.4 Problems in Measuring GDP

LO4
Understand some of the problems in determining official statistics.

Since many policy decisions are based on the level and growth of GDP (as we will see in later chapters), it is important for you to understand that there are some limitations in collecting and measuring the various statistics.

The real problem is in deciding what should and should not be measured. Let us spell out exactly what it is that we are trying to measure: the value of all final goods and services produced in an economy in a year. By and large, this will mean the market value of all items produced, plus government-provided services (which are included at cost). However, we do not want to include the market value of everything that has been produced. For instance, we don't want to include both the value of tires produced and the finished value of the car of which they are a part; the inclusion of these intermediate goods would represent double-counting. As the definition suggests, we want to include the value of final goods only. Another obvious exclusion would be the sale and purchase of financial transactions like stocks and shares. Although they are market activities, they do not represent real production but merely the transfer of asset ownership between people. (The value of the services of the stockbroker who made this transfer would be included.) For a similar reason, public transfer payments (CPP, EI, and so on) and private transfers (such as gifts and donations) are also excluded. Finally, because GDP is trying to measure current production only, second-hand sales would also be excluded since their value was included when they were first produced. In summary, economic transactions that are not included in the measurement of GDP are:

- the sale of intermediate goods
- sales that merely transfer ownership of assets
- both public and private transfer payments
- the sale of second-hand goods

Consider an additional thought: since the value of a good or service is measured by the amount that the consumer actually pays for it, it is clear that sales taxes are included. For this reason, many people suggest that national income (and not GDP) is a better measure of an economy's performance, since it excludes all indirect (sales) taxes.

Finally, we should mention a number of items that are excluded in the measurement of GDP even though they often do represent real productive effort. Some things are excluded because Statistics Canada does not hear of them. This includes all illegal activities and other activities that, though not illegal, are not reported to the tax collector (such as hairdressing or child care at home). The existence of this "underground economy" means that the GDP may be seriously understated. Also excluded are productive services such as the value of the activities of a homemaker, do-it-yourself work, and voluntary work. They are excluded because, again, they are non-market activities. A non-market activity is, quite simply, any economic activity that does not involve a payment (or the payment received is not reported to Revenue Canada). If this work were "paid for," then it would be included. This means, of course, that if one-half of the population were to do the housework of the other half and vice versa, and each paid the other, then the GDP would increase dramatically!

CP/Macleans/Phill Snel

Squeegee labour would be considered part of the "underground economy." Although not illegal, the income is not reported to tax collectors and is therefore not part of GDP measurement.

It means also that one must be very careful when making comparisons of GDP over a period of time. It is certainly true that the GDP of Canada has grown substantially over the years. But a part of the reason is that many of the services now provided commercially were once provided on a non-market voluntary basis. We now have commercial homemakers, day-care centres, interior decorators, gardeners, and so on, where once these services were mostly non-market activities. In summary, productive activities that are excluded from the measurement of GDP are:

- underground activities
  - illegal activities
  - unreported (but legal) activities
- non-market activities
  - services of homemakers
  - do-it-yourself production
  - volunteer services

ADDED DIMENSION

How Well is Canada Doing?

In terms of real GDP per capita Canada ranks well below many countries in the world. (Its ranking is something like 14th or 20th, depending on what exchange rate is used in the calculations.) Yet, when the United Nations "Human Development Index" (HDI) is used as a measure of the well being of a country's citizens, Canada's ranking is very high—sometimes even number one. The UN's HDI is an attempt to measure peoples' choices as indicated by the view that "the most critical of these wide-ranging choices are to live a long and healthy life, to be educated, and to have access to resources needed for a decent standard of living." The HDI therefore includes not only real GDP per capita but also life expectancy rates and levels of literacy. The UN recognizes that additional choices could include political freedom, guaranteed human rights, and personal self-respect, but that "a quantitative measure of these aspects has yet to be designed." One could also argue that any attempt at constructing this type of composite-index of well-being should include a measure of religious freedom, crime rates, levels of taxation, and an environmental index.

SELF-TEST

7. Forty years ago, few households employed a housekeeper and almost no one had a nanny. Today, more and more households employ part-time housekeepers, and nannies are not uncommon. What has this change in employment pattern done to GDP? Is more produced as a result of this change?

8. How could reported GDP remain constant while real production rose?

REVIEW

1. Define *net exports.*
2. Define *GDP.*
3. Define *NNP.*
4. What is the conceptual relationship between *GDP* and *Y*?
5. Distinguish between the *expenditures approach* and the *income approach* to the measurement of GDP.
6. What is another name for *depreciation*?
7. In Canada today, which is normally larger: *national income* or *personal income*?
8. Define *disposable income.*
9. What type of transactions are *not* included in GDP figures?
10. Are all productive activities that are *not* included in the measurement of GDP illegal activities?

STUDY GUIDE

Review

CHAPTER SUMMARY

In this chapter we use the circular flow of income model to give us a powerful overview of how a modern market economy works. The model shows how the level of income in an economy depends on the level of spending, and that equilibrium occurs when total spending = income = the value of production. Next, we look at how StatsCan measures economic activity to derive statistics like GDP, national income, and disposable income.

1. The circular flow model illustrates both the financial and the real flows between the *three sectors* of the economy: business, household, and government.
2. Within this model we find:
   - three *leakages*: savings, imports, and taxes;
   - three *injections*: investment, exports, and government spending on goods and services;
   - that if injections are greater than leakages then national income will rise, and if leakages exceed injections then national income will fall.
3. The *expenditures approach* to measuring national income involves adding up the four components of spending which are:
   - *consumption* spending by households;
   - *investment* spending by businesses;
   - spending by foreigners on *net exports*;
   - *government spending* on goods and services.
4. The *incomes approach* to measuring national income involves adding up the five types of income, which are *wages, interest, profits, self-employed income*, and *farmers' income*.
5. To *reconcile these two approaches* it is necessary to make adjustments for:
   - net foreign investment income;
   - depreciation;
   - indirect taxes.
6. For various reasons, national income statistics exclude the following:
   - intermediate goods;
   - transfers (both private and public);
   - second-hand sales;
   - sales taxes;
   - the value of productive non-market activities and illegal activity.

NEW GLOSSARY TERMS AND KEY EQUATIONS

aggregate expenditures 99
consumption 91
disposable income 106
equilibrium 98
exports 96
factor market 92
financial security 95
gross domestic product (GDP) 101
gross national product (GNP) 102
imports 96
income 92
injection 94
investment 94
leakage 93
loanable funds 94
money 92
national income (Y) 101
national income equilibrium 99
net domestic income 103
net exports 100
net national product (NNP) 104
personal income 105
product market 92
saving 93
transfer payments 97
value of production 99
wealth 94

Equations

[3.1] $S = Y - C$ page 93

[3.2] $S + IM + T = I + X + G$ page 98

[3.3] Value of production = business receipts = aggregate expenditures page 99

[3.4] Value of production = cost of production = total income page 99

[3.5] $AE = C + I + G + X_N$ page 100

[3.6] $AE = C + I + G + X_N$ = National Income $= w + i + r + \pi$ page 101

At equlibrium:

[3.7] $GDP = AE = Y$ page 101

STUDY TIPS

1. The circular flow diagram gives a very effective overview of the workings of the whole economy. While you do need to learn the details of the complete diagram, try not to, in the process, lose sight of the basic relationships that are contained within it. For example, if the flow of consumption spending from the household sector to the business sector decreases, then one of the leakages—imports, saving, or taxes—must have increased.

2. There are 27 new terms introduced in this chapter. Students who have studied microeconomics will recognize some of them. Students who are taking macroeconomics as a first course will simply have to "bite the bullet" and learn each of these as quickly as possible. Remember our point from Chapter 1's "Study Tips" that the language of economics must be learned before the concepts can be understood. Learn several new terms a day rather than attempting all 27 in one sitting.

3. When working through the circular flow presentation, you should recognize that the position of the household sector on the right and the business sector on the left or the product market at the top and the factor market on the bottom is arbitrary; that is, each could be put the other way around. It is customary, however, to put real flows as the inner loop and financial flows as the outer.

4. Almost all students need to be reminded often about the important distinction between money as a stock and income as a flow. A physical analogy may help. A lake is a stock in that the fixed amount of water, say 120 million litres, can be measured at any point in time. A river is a flow that can only be measured as a rate per unit of time, that is, 60 000 litres per minute.

5. There is no shortcut in learning the framework for national income accounting. It has to be memorized. You might try inventing your own "shorthand." For example, national income is equal to: farmers' income, interest, gross profits, self-employed income, and wages. This could be remembered as figs + wages (or the wages of figs, or as: "He was so cheap he paid wages in figs").

6. You will find the national income accounting framework (**Table 3.2**) helpful in doing several of the problems in the Study Guide. You may want to make a few photocopies.

TABLE 3.2

Expenditures			Incomes	
Consumption	$		Wages	$
Gross Investment	$		Interest	$
Government Spending	$		Gross Profits	$
Net Exports	$ ___________		Farmers' Income	$
			Self-employed Income	$ ___________
Gross Domestic Product	**$**		**Net Domestic Income**	**$**
+/– Net Foreign Factor Income	$ ___________		+/– Net Foreign F. Income	$ ___________
Gross National Product	**$**			
Less Depreciation	$ ___________			
Net National Product	**$**			
Less Indirect Taxes	$ ___________			
NNP at Factor Costs	**$**		**= National Income**	**$**
		Add Transfer Payments	$	
		Less Undistributed Profits	$	
		Less Corporate Profit Taxes	$	
		Less Other Inc. Not Paid	$ ___________	
		Personal Income	**$**	
		Less Personal Income Taxes	$ ___________	
		Disposable Income	**$**	
			Savings =	$
			Consumption =	$

Answered Questions

Indicate whether the following statements are true or false.

1. **T or F** Both the goods and services flow and the factors of production flow are money flows.

2. **T or F** Individuals in the household sector earn income by receiving payment for the goods and services that they sell.

3. **T or F** The amount of income in an economy is always equal to the amount of money in the economy.

4. **T or F** Savings is equal to consumption minus income.

5. **T or F** Transfer payments are a flow from the business sector to the government sector.

6. **T or F** At equilibrium, aggregate expenditures and income are equal.

7. **T or F** The two conceptual approaches used to measure GDP are the expenditures approach and the incomes approach.

8. **T or F** National income is the total earnings of all businesses.

9. **T or F** One definition of equilibrium income is the income at which total injections equals total leakages.

10. **T or F** National income may be a better measure of an economy's economic performance than GDP because it excludes, among other things sales taxes.

Basic (Questions 11–21)

11. What are the names of the factors of production?
    a) Competition, cooperation, command, and custom.
    b) Land, labour, capital, and enterprise.
    c) Land, labour, capital, and money.
    d) Wages, interest, rents, and profits.

12. What are net exports?
    a) Exports less imports.
    b) Exports plus imports.
    c) Exports plus consumption.
    d) Exports plus consumption less imports.

13. Which of the following fall under the category of enterprise?
    a) Adopting high-risk innovations.
    b) The organization and coordination of a business.
    c) The investigation and establishment of new markets.
    d) All of the above.

14. Which of the following is necessary for national income to be in equilibrium?
    a) $S + IM + T = I + X + G$.
    b) $S + IM + T = I + X_N + G$.
    c) $C + I + G - X_N = GNP$.
    d) $C + I + G + X = GDP$.

Refer to Figure 3.7 to answer questions 15 to 18.

FIGURE 3.7

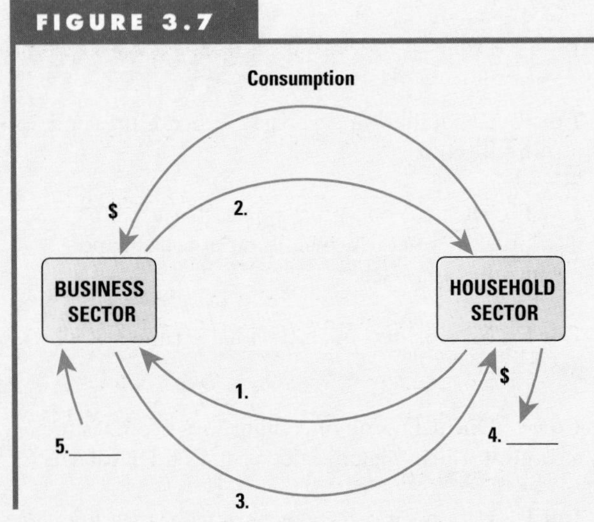

15. Refer to Figure 3.7 to answer this question. What is flow 1?
    a) Consumer goods and services.
    b) Factor services.
    c) Factor incomes.
    d) Investment.

16. Refer to Figure 3.7 to answer this question. What is flow 2?
    a) Consumer goods and services.
    b) Factor services.
    c) Factor incomes.
    d) Investment.

17. Refer to Figure 3.7 to answer this question. What is flow 3?
    a) Consumer goods and services.
    b) Factor services.
    c) Factor incomes.
    d) Investment.

18. Refer to Figure 3.7 to answer this question. What are flows 4 and 5 respectively?
    a) Exports and imports.
    b) Exports and taxes.
    c) Savings and investment.
    d) Investment and savings.

19. All of the following, except one, are examples of the factor "land". Which is the exception?
    a) Minerals.
    b) Natural harbours.
    c) Mortgages held on land.
    d) Supplies of fresh water.
    e) Fertile soil.

20. All of the following, except one, are components of aggregate expenditures. Which is the exception?
    a) Investment.
    b) Government spending on goods and services.
    c) Transfer payments.
    d) Consumption.
    e) Net exports.

21. What does the sum of national income, indirect taxes, and depreciation equal?
    a) Personal income.
    b) Disposable income.
    c) Gross domestic product.
    d) Gross national product.
    e) Net national product.

Intermediate (Questions 22–32)

22. Which of the following is included by Statistics Canada in investment?
    a) An increase in business inventories from one year to the next.
    b) The purchase of any durable good, such as a car or television.
    c) An increase in total saving in the economy.
    d) The change in the value of mutual funds from one year to the next.

23. Which of the following is regarded as real capital?
    a) A savings account.
    b) A share of Bank of Montreal stock.
    c) A dump truck.
    d) A stock certificate.

24. Which of the following leads to an understatement of total production?
    a) The exclusion of work done by homemakers.
    b) A decrease in the GST rate.
    c) Government spending on an oil-spill clean-up.
    d) The exclusion of intermediate goods.

25. Which of the following will result in an increase in the stock of capital goods?
    a) If net investment is negative.
    b) If net investment is positive.
    c) If gross investment is less than consumption.
    d) If gross investment is negative.

26. What is the level of savings in an economy with no government and no international trade, if total factor income is $600 and consumption spending is $480?
    a) –$120.
    b) $120.
    c) $1080.
    d) Cannot be determined from the information given.

27. What does the simple circular flow show?
    a) That households are both buyers and sellers of products and resources.
    b) That businesses are sellers of resources and buyers of products.
    c) That households are buyers of products and sellers of resources.
    d) That businesses are sellers and households are buyers of both products and resources.
    e) That businesses both buy and sell products and resources, whereas households only buy.

28. All of the following, except one, adjustments to national income are necessary to obtain personal income. Which is the exception?
    a) Subtract undistributed profits.
    b) Subtract corporate-profit taxes.
    c) Subtract indirect taxes.
    d) Subtract other income not paid out.
    e) Add government transfer payments.

29. What is true about aggregate expenditures?
    a) It always equals national income.
    b) At equilibrium it is equal to national income.
    c) It equals C + I + X.
    d) It depends on the rate of savings.
    e) It is determined by inventory changes.

30. If the three injections are added to consumption spending and then imports are subtracted, what is the result?
    a) Equilibrium national income.
    b) Aggregate expenditures.
    c) The total personal income of all households.
    d) The value of production.

31. What would be the effect if one half of the population did the housework for the other half of the population, and vice versa, and each group paid the other for these services?
    a) GDP would not be affected because the one set of transactions would cancel out the other.
    b) GDP would rise.
    c) GDP would fall.
    d) GDP would not be affected but the personal income of people would be.

32. What is included in consumption and investment spending respectively?
    a) Spending on domestically produced goods and services and on real capital.
    b) Spending on domestically produced and foreign-produced goods and services, and on real capital.
    c) Spending on domestically produced goods and services and on net foreign investment income.
    d) Spending on domestically produced goods and services and on the purchase of stocks and bonds.

Advanced (Questions 33–35)

33. How does government spending on goods and services differ from transfer payments?
    a) The former is done by the federal government and the latter by provincial governments.

b) The former does not include investment spending but the latter does.
c) The former represents payments for services performed but the latter does not.
d) They are the same thing and therefore there is no difference.

34. All of the following expect one are true in equilibrium. Which is the exception?
a) Total leakages equal total injections.
b) The value of production equals aggregate expenditures.
c) Y = AE.
d) The value of production equals consumer spending.

35. In equilibrium, the value of production is equal to all of the following, except one. Which is the exception?
a) The total receipts of all businesses.
b) Total income.
c) Output plus inventory accumulation.
d) Aggregate expenditures.

Parallel Problems

ANSWERED PROBLEMS

36. Key Problem Figure 3.8 is the circular flow diagram for the economy of Argos.
a) Place the numbers below in the appropriate blanks on the diagram in **Figure 3.8.**

Rent	$100	Savings	$100
Wages	400	Government spending	280
Profits	60	Exports	100
Interest	80	Imports	80
Taxes (HH's only)	360	Investment	40
Transfer payments	120		

What are the values of the following?
b) The costs of production?
Answer: ______________.
c) Total factor payments?
Answer: ______________.
d) Disposable income?
Answer: ______________.
e) Aggregate expenditures?
Answer: ______________.
f) The total receipts of all businesses?
Answer: ______________.
g) Total injections? Leakages? (*Hint*: Use net taxes, that is, taxes less transfer payments.)
Injections: ______________;
leakages ______________.
h) The balance of trade (net exports)?
Answer: ______________.
i) The government's budget surplus/deficit? (*Hint*: Use net taxes.)
Answer: ______________.

FIGURE 3.8

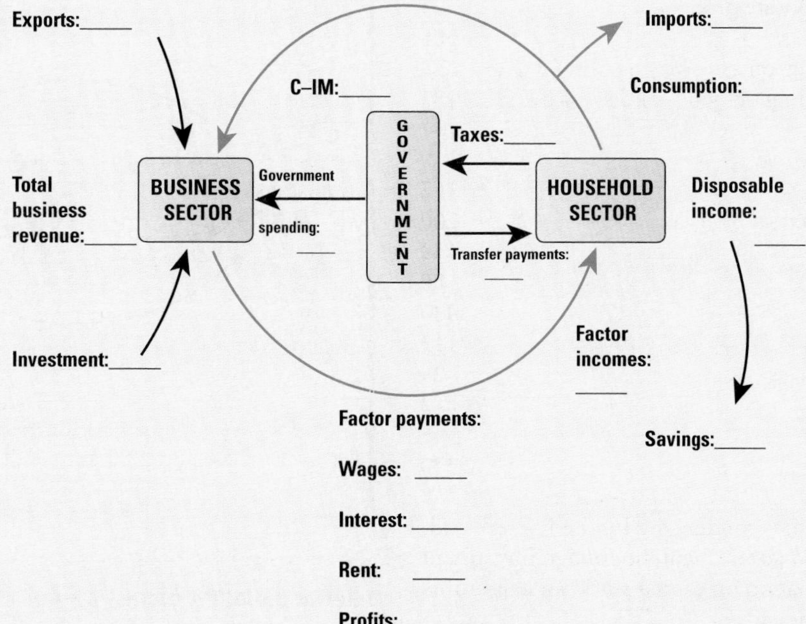

Basic (Problems 37–42)

37. You are given the following data for the country of Sequoia:

Exports	130	Government spending	198
Consumption	430	Imports	118
Gross investment	126	Net foreign factor income	–22
Depreciation	64	Indirect taxes	80

a) What is the value of GDP? ____________ .

b) What is the value of NNP? ____________ .

c) What is the value of national income (net national product at factor costs)? ____________ .

38. You are given the following data for the country of Hemlock:

National income	600
Personal income taxes	140
Other income not paid out	40
Corporate profit taxes	45
Undistributed profits	28
Transfer payments	90

a) What is the value of personal income? ____________ .

b) What is the value of disposable income? ____________ .

39. Use the circular flow model and the data below to answer the questions for the country of Tamarack. (*Hint*: you will need to calculate consumption using earned income, taxes, and saving.)

Saving	$80	Transfer payments	$90
Government spending	130	Taxes (households)	240
Exports	70	Interest	60
Imports	60	Profit	50
Investment	90	Wages	260
Rent	70		

What are the values of the following?

a) The costs of production: ____________ .

b) Total factor payments: ____________ .

c) Factor income: ____________ .

d) Disposable income: ____________ .

e) Aggregate expenditures: ____________ .

f) Total business receipts: ____________ .

g) Total injections/leakages: ________ and ________ .

h) Net exports: ____________ .

i) The government's budget surplus/deficit: ________ .

40. Below is actual 1997 data for Canada. From this data, calculate the value of (you will find **Table 3.2** to be helpful framework):

GDP at market prices: ____________ .

GNP at market prices: ____________ .

Net domestic income: ____________ .

National income: ____________ .

NNP at market prices: ____________ .

NNP at factor costs: ____________ .

Personal income: ____________ .

Disposal income: ____________ .

Self employed income	58
Other income not paid out	9
Undistributed corporate profits	25
Consumption	505
Net foreign factor income	–28
Government spending on goods and services	187
Interest	47
Depreciation	110
Transfer payments	182
Personal income taxes	200
Gross investment	149
Gross profits	80
Wages	446
Indirect taxes	113
Corporate profit taxes	29
Farmers' income	2
Exports	345
Imports	330

41. **Figure 3.9** depicts the economy of Hundred Acre Wood, in which there is no government, no foreign investment income, no depreciation on capital stock, and all profits are paid out in dividends.

What is Hundred Acre Wood's:

a) GDP? ________.

b) National income? ________.

c) Disposable income? ________.

d) Total injections? ________.

e) Total leakages? ________.

FIGURE 3.9

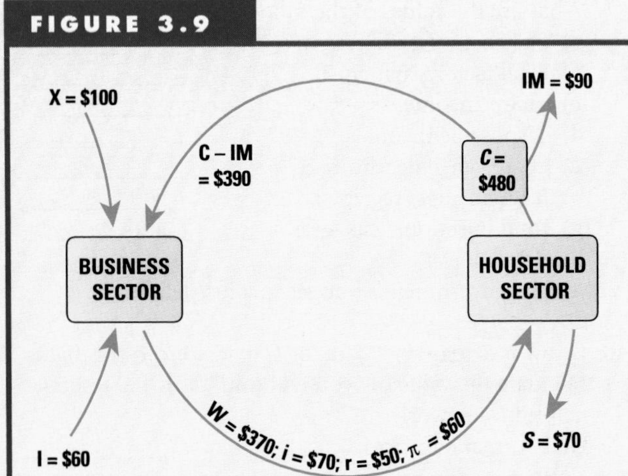

42. In **Figure 3.10**, replace each(∗) with the appropriate term(s).

FIGURE 3.10

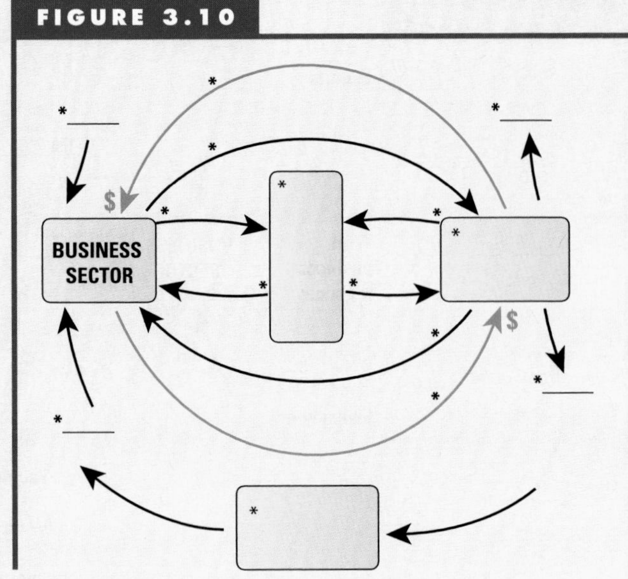

Intermediate (Problems 43–46)

43. Using the data below for the country of Magnolia, complete the national income accounting framework in **Table 3.2.**

Disposable income	920
Dividends paid out by corporations	80
Imports	240
Investment (net)	80
Corporate profit taxes	60
Other income not paid out	20
Personal savings	120
Wages	530
Net exports	–40
Depreciation	120
Personal income taxes	160
Net foreign factor income	–20
Gross profits	180
Indirect taxes	220
Transfer payments	200
Government spending on goods and services	400
Interest	160
Farmers' income	90

44. Fill in the blanks in the data below for the country of Baobob.

C	______
Ig	______
G	340
X_N	20

GDP	800
Net foreign factor income	____
GNP	780
Depreciation	70
NNP	____
Indirect tax	____
National income	550
Transfer payments	210
Undistributed corporate profits	30
Corporate profit taxes	80
Other income not paid out	20
Personal income	____
Personal income tax	230
Disposable income	____
Personal savings	50

45. Compare the expenditures approach of GDP measurement to the incomes approach.

____

____

______________________________.

46. Explain the difference between the stock of money and the flow of income.

____

____

______________________________.

Advanced (Problems 47–48)

47. Suppose that new automobile purchases were treated like new housing purchases in national income accounts. How would that affect savings, consumption, investment, GDP, and DI? (*Hint*: This question is about reclassification, not about cause and effect.)

____

____

______________________________.

48. Explain why transfer payments are excluded from the measurement of GDP.

____

____

______________________________.

UNANSWERED PROBLEMS

49. Key Problem Figure 3.11 is the circular flow diagram of the economy of Naxos.

a) Place the numbers below in the appropriate blanks on the diagram in Figure 3.11.

FIGURE 3.11

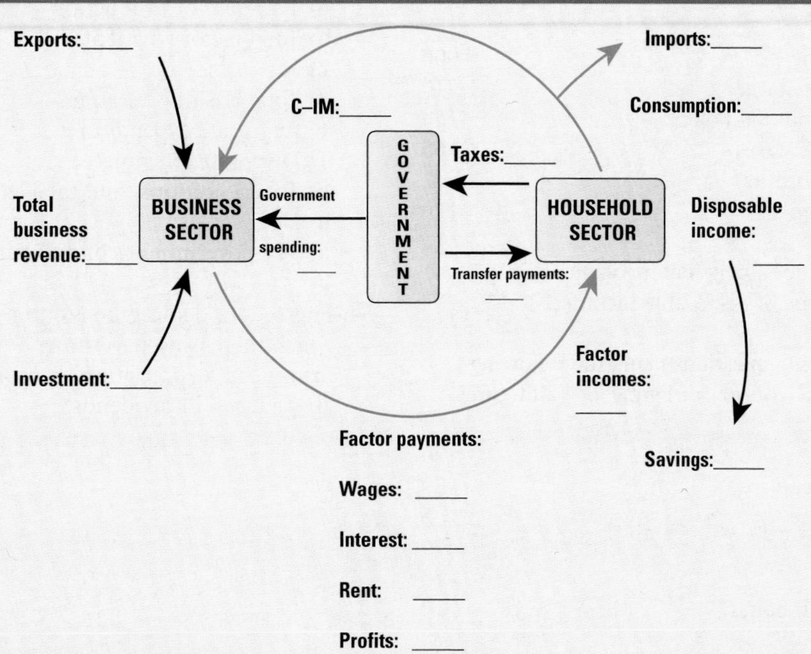

Rent	$150	Savings	$200
Wages	600	Government spending	220
Profits	90	Exports	150
Interest	120	Imports	120
Taxes (HH's only)	340	Investment	110
Transfer payments	180		

What are the values of the following?

b) The costs of production?
c) Total factor payment?
d) Disposable income?
e) Aggregate expenditures?
f) Total revenue of all business?
g) Total injections (and leakages)?
h) The balance of trade (net exports)?
i) The government's budget surplus/deficit?

Basic (Problems 50–55)

50. You are given the following data for the country of Chestnut:

Exports	100	Government spending	160
Consumption	350	Imports	80
Gross Investment	90	Net foreign factor income	–10
Depreciation	40	Indirect taxes	50

a) What is the value of GNP?
b) What is the value of NNP?
c) What is the value of national income?

51. You are given the following data for the country of Poplar:

National income	900
Personal income taxes	210
Other income not paid out	60
Corporate profit taxes	65
Undistributed profits	42
Transfer payments	120

a) What is the value of personal income?
b) What is the value of disposable income?

52. Answer the following questions using the following information for the country of Dogwood (all figures are in $ billions).

Consumption	120
Transfer payments	29
Farmers' income	5
Depreciation	20
Interest	10
Self-employed income	12
Exports	30
Gross corporate profits	34
Wages	113
Indirect taxes	21
Undistributed corporate profits	8
Personal savings	17
Imports	25
Personal income taxes	30
Corporate profit taxes	9
Government spending on goods and services	40
Investment (gross)	50
Other earnings not paid out	9
Net foreign factor income	–10

a) GDP
b) National income
c) Personal income
d) Disposable income
e) Net investment
f) Dividends

53. Use the circular flow model and the following data to answer the questions below, for the country of Arbutus.

Rent	$50	Saving	$50
Wages	200	Government spending	90
Profit	30	Exports	60
Interest	40	Imports	40
Taxes (households)	180	Investment	60
Transfer payments	60		

What are the values of the following?

a) The costs of production
b) Total factor payments
c) Factor income
d) Total business receipts
e) Aggregate expenditures
f) Disposable income
g) Total injections (and total leakages)
h) Net exports
i) The government's budget surplus or deficit

54. Figure 3.12 depicts the economy of Willow Tree, in which there is no government, no foreign investment income, no depreciation on capital stock, and all profits are paid out in dividends.

FIGURE 3.12

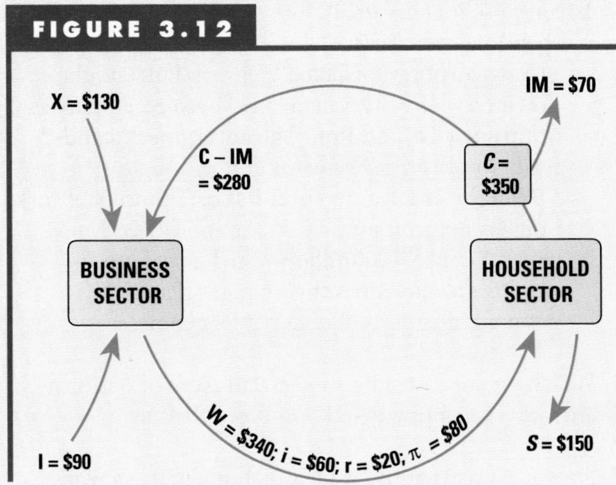

What is the value of Willow Tree's:

a) GDP
b) National income
c) Disposable income
d) Total leakages
e) Total injections

55. In Figure 3.13 replace each asterisk (*) with the appropriate terms(s).

FIGURE 3.13

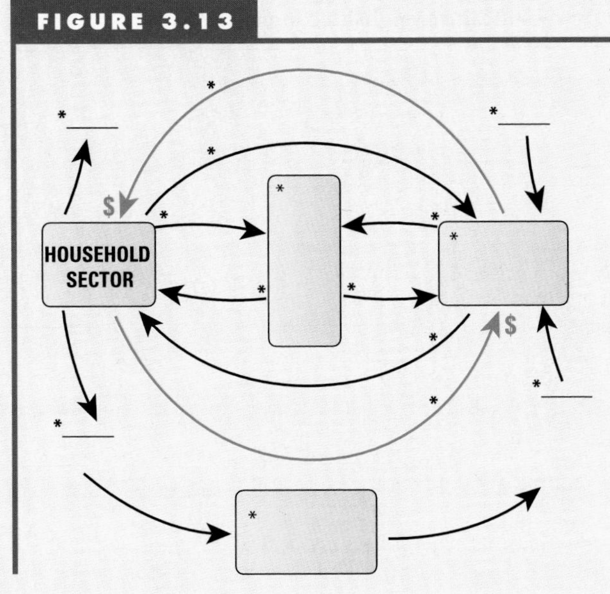

Intermediate (Problems 56–59)

56. The following are *some* of the national income accounts for the economy of Willow Place (all figures are in $ billions).

Investment (net)	40
Wages	350
Net foreign factor income	–10
Imports	120
Gross corporate profits	90
Personal savings	60
Transfer payments	100
Disposable income	460
Depreciation	60
Government spending on goods and services	200
Dividends paid out by corporations	40
Net exports	–20
Indirect taxes	110
Corporate profit taxes	30
Other income not paid out	10
Personal income tax	80

From this information, calculate the value of:

a) Consumption.
b) GDP.
c) GNP.
d) National income.
e) Personal income.

57. Fill in the blanks below for data from the country of Alder.

C	380
Ig	120
G	360
X_N	____
GDP	900
Net foreign factor income	–20
GNP	____
Depreciation	80
NNP	____
Indirect Tax	60
National income	____
Transfer payments	70
Undistributed corporate profits	30
Corporate profit taxes	20
Other income not paid out	10
Personal income	____
Personal income tax	____
Disposable income	420
Personal saving	____

58. While there is a technical difference between the level of national income and the level of GDP, they are conceptually the same. Explain.

59. Equilibrium occurs when the level of aggregate expenditures equals the value of total production, but not necessarily when the value of total production equals the level of income. Explain.

Advanced (Problems 60–62)

60. a) As part of its drive to replace welfare with "welwork," the government decides to reclassify all welfare recipients as government employees. The welfare benefits of $100 million become government wages. How does this change affect GDP, national income, and disposable income?

b) Suppose that, in an attempt to reduce government spending even further, the government sets up a private corporation called Welwork Ltd. and the previous welfare recipients now become employees of this new corporation. The government stands ready to subsidize Welwork Ltd. with up to $100 million a year to cover its costs. Since Welwork Ltd. has no products to sell, the subsidy ends up being the full $100 million, which is paid to its employees. How does this change affect GDP, national income, and disposable income?

61. Which do you consider the best measure of performance of an economy: GDP, GNP, or NI? Why?

62. Do you think that the value of a homemaker's work should be included in the GDP? What would be the biggest difficulty in trying to include it?

Web-Based Activities

1. Draw a picture of the circular flow of income. Now, go to **www.statcan.ca/english/econoind/gdpexp.htm** and fill in the dollar amounts for consumption, investment, government, and net exports in your diagram.

2. From the data found on the following Web pages, do leakages equal injections? Illustrate and explain.
www.statcan.ca/english/econoind/gdprev.htm
www.statcan.ca/english/econoind/gdpexp.htm
www.statcan.ca/english/econoind/indic.htm

CHAPTER FOUR

Growth, Unemployment, and Inflation

LEARNING OBJECTIVES

This chapter will enable you to:

LO1 **Understand the meaning and benefits of economic growth.**

LO2 **Explain what is meant by unemployment and employment.**

LO3 **Understand what inflation is and why it is costly to any economy.**

What's ahead...

This is a mostly descriptive chapter, because its focus is on issues rather than on explaining specific principles or model building. We discuss the issues of growth, unemployment, and inflation. These are eternal issues, because it is a political reality that all governments have to, in some way, develop policies to address them. First, we describe how economic growth is measured and look at both the benefits and costs of growth. Next, we describe how unemployment and inflation are each measured, give a brief explanation of their causes, and discuss their costs.

A QUESTION OF RELEVANCE...

In the second half of the twentieth century, market economies have shown a remarkable tendency to grow over time. Canada's real GDP per capita more than tripled between 1960 and 1995. Do we want economic growth to continue at this rapid pace? Will you be able to avoid being an unemployment statistic during your working life? Does the rate of inflation really affect you personally? These are questions that begin to take on more urgency as you approach the transition from student to active participant in the labour force with career aspirations. This chapter will help you think more deeply about these issues.

There are three macroeconomic issues that seem to always be with us, in the sense that one or another, (or sometimes a combination of two), seems always to be making headlines in the media. The first is the issue of economic growth—is the economy growing fast enough, or maybe too fast? The second is unemployment—what can be done to lower this rate in Canada, and why is the rate different in other countries? The third issue is inflation—what are the costs of containing it, and are these costs too high? We will look at these three issues one at a time.

4.1 Economic Growth

LO1
Understand the meaning and benefits of economic growth.

economic growth: an increase in an economy's real GDP per capita or an increase in the economy's capacity to produce.

The discussion in Chapter 1 about growth as an economic goal established that growth has both positive and negative aspects. Before we discuss this in more depth, we need to define **economic growth**. While the media often refer to any increase in GDP as economic growth, economists prefer to define it as an increase in an economy's *real* GDP (we explain the term "real" below). Often, this is extended to include an increase in real GDP per capita, which is real GDP divided by total population. This recognizes the fact that the population as a whole will not experience the benefits of growth unless real GDP grows faster than population.

Let's look first at how modern economies measure economic growth and later we will see exactly why growth presents difficult challenges that all economies have to face. Economic growth undoubtedly improves the welfare of people today and also gives society opportunities to address social needs to an extent that was undreamed of by previous generations. But we need to recognize that growth is a double-edged sword which can also inflict costs on society.

Measuring Growth

You will recall from Chapter 3 that Statistics Canada measures the GDP of Canada by taking the market value of all final goods and services produced in the country in a year. It's possible, then, for GDP to increase from one year to the next simply because market prices rose. The economy may not have, in fact, produced more. Thus, we need to make the important distinction between nominal GDP and real GDP. To see if an economy is growing, we need to know if it did actually produce more goods and services. In other words, we need to eliminate the effect of rising prices. StatsCan does this by measuring each year's output in terms of constant prices. This distinction between nominal and real GDP is so important that we need to go through a detailed example to really nail it down. In **Table 4.1**, we use four different goods—machines (a capital good), kilometres of road construction (a government good), bread and cars (consumer goods)—and three different years.

TABLE 4.1 Calculating Real GDP, Using Hypothetical Data

1	2	3	4	5	6	7	8	9	10	11	12	13	14
	Year 1			Year 2					Year 3				
Item	Qty	Prices Year 1	Nominal GDP	Qty	Prices Year 2	Nominal GDP	Prices Year 1	Real GDP	Qty	Prices Year 3	Nominal GDP	Prices Year 1	Real GDP
Machines	100	$100	**$10 000**	120	$120	**$14 400**	$100	**$12 000**	130	$125	**$16 250**	$100	**$13 000**
Km of Road	50	300	**15 000**	40	320	**12 800**	300	**12 000**	50	350	**17 500**	300	**15 000**
Bread	500	2	**1000**	600	2.50	**1500**	2	**1200**	650	3	**1950**	2	**1300**
Cars	20	800	**16 000**	25	820	**20 500**	800	**20 000**	26	840	**21 840**	800	**20 800**
Totals			**42 000**			**49 200**		**45 200**			**57 540**		**50 100**

If you compare columns 2 and 5, you will notice that the output of machines, bread and cars increased in Year 2, compared to Year 1, but the output of roads declined. In comparing columns 3 and 6 you can see that the prices of all four products increased in Year 2 compared to Year 1.

With this information, we can begin the calculation of nominal GDP by simply taking the quantities produced of each good and multiplying by the price of each good. This is done in column 4 for Year 1 and in column 7 for Year 2. If we then add up the four figures in each of these columns, we get a nominal GDP in Year 1 of $42 000, and, in Year 2, of $49 200.

Next, if we slide our focus over to column 10, we see that in Year 3, the production of all four goods increased over Year 2. In column 11 we see that the prices of all four goods also increased over what they were in Year 2. By taking the quantities of goods produced in column 10 times their prices in column 11, we get the four figures in column 12, and then by adding these numbers, we arrive at a nominal GDP in Year 3 of $57 540.

nominal GDP: the value of GDP in terms of prices prevailing at the time of measurement.

Thus, using *current market prices* in each year we see that nominal GDP rose from $42 000 in Year 1 to $49 200 in Year 2 to $57 540 in Year 3. This is the meaning of **nominal GDP**—total output of all goods produced times current market prices.

real GDP: the value of GDP measured in terms of prices prevailing in a given base year.

As we can see from the table, some of the increase in nominal GDP was because the output produced increased, but some of it was simply a result of higher prices. If we could take out the effect of higher prices, then we would be left with only increases in production and that would give us **real GDP**.

In fact, doing this is not hard. All we need to do is measure the output produced in each of the three years, using only Year 1 prices. This has, of course, already been done for Year 1. In Year 2 we take column 8—prices in Year 1—times the output produced in Year 2 (column 5) and get the four figures in column 9, and then add these four figures to get a real GDP in Year 2 of $45 200. We are now able to see that while nominal GDP rose in Year 2 compared to Year 1 by $7200, real GDP rose only by $3200.

In a similar fashion, if we multiply column 13 by column 10 and then add the resulting figures (in column 14), we get a real GDP in Year 3 of $50 100. Again this real GDP figure is found by using Year 1 prices. Now the GDP for all three years is calculated using the same (Year 1) prices and, again, this is what we mean by real GDP.

GDP deflator: a measure of the price level of goods included in the GDP. It is calculated by dividing the nominal GDP by the real GDP and multiplying by 100.

Besides calculating real GDP in this manner, Statistics Canada is also able to extract a very useful statistic known as the **GDP deflator**. This statistic measures the change in the average level of prices from one period to the next. In doing so, we are able to find out how much of the increase in nominal GDP is solely the result of price changes.

The GDP deflator is calculated as follows:

$$\text{GDP deflator} = \frac{\text{nominal GDP}}{\text{real GDP}} \times 100 \quad [4.1]$$

For instance, we can calculate the value of the GDP deflator for Year 2 from **Table 4.1** as follows:

$$\text{GDP deflator}_{\text{year 2}} = \frac{49\ 200}{45\ 200} \times 100 = 109$$

Since the GDP deflator rose from 100 in Year 1 to 109 in Year 2, we know that the price level increased by 9 percent. (You might want to confirm that the value of the GDP deflator in Year 3 was 114.9.)

Table 4.2 shows the value of Canada's nominal GDP, real GDP, and the GDP deflator in recent years.

TABLE 4.2 Canada's Real GDP, 1996–2001 (Base Year prices = 1997)

Year	Nominal GDP (billions)	Real GDP (billions)	GDP Deflator
1996	$839	$849	98.8
1997	885	885	100.0
1998	916	920	99.6
1999	976	966	101.1
2000	1056	1009	104.6
2001	1084	1024	105.9

Source: Adapted from Statistics Canada, CANSIM Database, Matrices 6547 and 6544.

Over the whole period, we can see that nominal GDP rose from $839 billion in 1996 to $1084 billion in 2001, or a total increase of $245 billion. However, the fourth column shows that the GDP deflator also increased over this period from 98.8 to 105.9, or an increase of 7.1 percent. In real terms, then, real GDP as shown in column 3 shows an increase of only $175 billion.

While we have made allowance for the fact that inflation increases the GDP figures, we may want to also consider the fact that while real GDP may have risen, population may have increased as well. If that were the case, then the average person may not be any better off. To calculate real GDP per capita (per head), we simply divide real GDP by the population,

$$\text{Real GDP per capita} = \frac{\text{real GDP}}{\text{population}} \qquad [4.2]$$

For example, using the real GDP figure from **Table 4.2** and knowing that Canada's population was 30.5 million, we can calculate the figure for 1999 as follows:

$$\text{Real GDP per capita} = \frac{966\ 000\ 000\ 000}{30\ 500\ 000} = \$31\ 672$$

Table 4.3 shows real GDP per capita in Canada for recent years.

TABLE 4.3 Canada's Real GDP per Capita, 1996–2001

Year	Real GDP (billions)	Population (millions)	Real GDP per Capita	Annual Growth Rate (%)
1996	$849	29.7	$28 586	—
1997	885	30.0	29 500	3.2
1998	920	30.2	30 463	3.3
1999	966	30.5	31 672	4.0
2000	1009	30.8	32 759	3.4
2001	1024	31.0	33 032	0.8

We can see then that in say, 1999 the real GDP per capita rose by an average of $1209 (31 672 minus 30 463) over the 1998 figure for every man, woman, and child in Canada. We can express this increase as a percentage; in other words we can calculate the amount of economic growth as a percentage, as follows:

$$\text{(Economic) growth rate} = \frac{\text{increase in real GDP per capita}}{\text{real GDP per capita (previous year)}} \times 100 \qquad [4.3]$$

$$\text{The economic growth in 1999 was: } \frac{+1209}{30\ 463} \times 100 = 4\%$$

The last column of **Table 4.3** shows the annual growth rate in real GDP per capita for Canada for the years 1996 to 2001.

Note that over the whole six-year period, Canada's real GDP per capita rose by $4446—an increase of 15.6 percent, or approximately 2.6 percent per year.

SELF-TEST

1. Fill in the blanks (to one decimal place) in the following table of Etruria's GDP statistics:

	1999	2000	2001
Nominal GDP ($billion)	443	474	507
Real GDP ($billion)	374	389	402
GDP deflator (1997 = 100)	____	____	____
Population (millions)	26.1	26.4	27
Real GDP per capita	____	____	____

To appreciate the benefits of economic growth, it is both sobering and instructive to ask, from time to time, what would our condition in life most likely have been if we had lived just 300 or 400 years ago? For almost all of us, the answer would probably have meant eking out a subsistence existence in a potato field somewhere in Europe or a rice paddy in Asia. By contrast, all of us today have an incredible wealth of material well-being—from central heating and clean water to cheap air travel and VCRs. All this is the more visible benefit of economic growth. Not so apparent, but just as important, is the fact that economic growth enables society to better meet the social needs of its population. An economy that has just experienced 20 years of robust growth can provide more freeways, seats in colleges and universities, exercise rooms in community centres, and state-of-the-art medical care. In sum, all of us have far more opportunities and are far richer materially than our ancestors were, thanks to economic growth.

Despite all of this, students are often unimpressed with the concern that economists show over growth rates. What difference does it make, many wonder, if the annual growth rate of an economy is only 3 percent rather than 4 percent? Considering that Canada's nominal GDP was, in 2000, $1056 billion (in current prices), a 1 percent difference in growth translates into $10.6 billion. If we divide the $10.6 billion by the approximately 10 million families in Canada, we get $1060. Could your family use an extra $1060 per year *every year* from now on? As you can see, even small differences in the growth rate can be significant over time.

ADDED DIMENSION

Asian Tigers

The effects of a high growth rate, especially in an economy that starts off with a relatively low per capita GDP, can be very dramatic, even over a short period. Let's take a hypothetical example of a developing Asian nation in the 1990s whose per capita income starts at only one-half of that of a typical developed nation. Let's assume a growth rate in the Asian "tiger" of 8 percent (*below* the actual rates experienced by some of the fast-growing Asian economies in the early 1990s, by the way). We will assume a growth rate of 1 percent in the developed economy. You can see what would be the results, in only twelve years, in **Table 4.4**. With the higher growth rate, in just over a decade, the tiger has not only caught up with the developed nation but surpassed it! And all of this is a result of growth rates that aren't that wildly different—8 percent compared with 1 percent. Thus you can see the power of high growth rates.

TABLE 4.4 The Effect of Different Growth Rates on Real GDP per Capita

Year	Asian Tiger: Real GDP per Capita	Developed Economy: Real GDP per Capita
1989	$7 500	$15 000
1990	8 100	15 150
1991	8 748	15 300
1992	9 448	15 455
1993	10 203	15 610
1994	11 020	15 765
1995	11 902	15 923
1996	12 854	16 082
1997	13 882	16 243
1998	14 993	16 405
1999	16 192	16 570
2000	17 487	16 736

Table 4.5 illustrates a fact that seems to come as a surprise to many Canadians. Canada's growth in real GDP has been good over the last few years. For example, it was the highest of the G8 nations (Canada, United States, Britain, France, Germany, Italy, Japan, and Russia) in terms of real GDP between 1995 and 1999. The real GDP per capita figures are a little lower, however, reflecting Canada's relatively rapid population growth. The table below shows the growth rates of real GDP and of real GDP per capita in the G8 countries.

TABLE 4.5 Growth rates of Real GDP and Real GDP Per Capita

Country	Change in real GDP 1995–1999 (%)	Change in real GDP per Capita 1995–1999 (%)
Canada	3.3	2.3
France	2.8	2.4
Germany	1.9	1.7
Italy	1.4	1.2
Japan	0.8	0.6
Russian Federation	–2.1	–1.8
United Kingdom	2.7	2.4
United States	3.1	2.0

Source: *World Development Report,* World Bank 1998–2002.

Growth and Economic Welfare

Despite the many benefits that flow from economic growth, we do need to add a word of caution to this discussion. "More" doesn't always mean "better." It is true that economic growth is seen by many people as an indicator of the comparative "wellness" of an economy.

After all, most people would feel that we are all better off if our economy grows, since most people view growth in a positive way. Although there is truth in this proposition, we should realize that GDP figures are *not designed to measure welfare*; they simply measure market activity of produced goods and services. In this context, we cannot simply assume that higher GDP is necessarily better. As we saw in the previous chapter, there are many services—such as child care and housework—which are now paid for, whereas previously they were done by family and friends. This means that it is possible for measured GDP to grow year after year, even though we are not actually producing more. Conversely, the reported GDP may be constant, whereas in reality production is actually increasing.

There are other problems with equating the level of GDP with the well-being of a population. GDP figures give no indication of the quality of goods produced, nor do they tell us what types of goods are being produced: a gun and an economics textbook are rated equally if they are priced the same. Nor can we assume that anyone is better off if population grows faster than GDP. For this reason, as we saw, it is better to express GDP in terms of GDP per capita. We could also mention that if people begin to value leisure time more and choose to work less, then GDP would grow more slowly but people would consider themselves better off despite the slower growth. Finally, the social and environmental costs of growth may well exceed the benefits. Simply producing more and more each year may not be a desirable goal if it means more pollution, more garbage dumps, more stress, and more crime. In summary, higher GDP doesn't necessarily mean that citizens are better off, because:

- higher GDP may be the result of including the value of some services that were previously excluded
- the quality or desirability of the goods produced is ignored
- per capita GDP will fall if population growth exceeds the growth of GDP
- the social and environmental costs of higher GDP are ignored

In trying to better address the question of how to measure a society's well-being, the United Nations compiles a list of the more desirable countries to live in. Things like the level of pollution, crime rates, and the availability of health care, as well as the level of GDP, are considered. Canada has consistently ranked high on this list.

In conclusion, we should recognize that, while an increase in GDP, even real GDP, is likely a positive thing, it doesn't automatically mean an increase in the well-being of the population. The way that GDP gets measured should caution us from automatically equating the value of an economy's GDP with the well-being of its population.

REVIEW

1. Define *economic growth.*
2. Why is an increase in real GDP per capita a better indicator of economic growth than real GDP?
3. How is the GDP deflator measured?
4. Is a 3 percent growth in GDP significantly different from a 4 percent growth rate?
5. Why might economic growth not mean an increase in economic welfare?

4.2 Unemployment

LO2
Explain what is meant by unemployment and employment.

unemployment: the situation in which persons 15 years old and over are actively seeking work but do not have employment.

frictional unemployment: that part of total unemployment caused by the fact that it takes time for people to find their first job or to move between jobs.

Unemployment, as a concept, can apply to any of the three factor markets—land, labour, or capital. If the economy is not producing at full capacity, then some of the factors of production must be idle—or unemployed (assuming efficient methods of production). For our purposes, however, we will focus only on the labour market. **Unemployment** can be defined as the number of persons 15 years of age and older who are not in gainful employment but who are actively seeking employment. First, we will examine three types of unemployment: frictional, structural, and cyclical.

Frictional Unemployment

In a free society, where employees have the right to quit a job and employers have the right to dismiss their employees, **frictional unemployment** is inevitable. This is simply a reflection of the fact that seldom does anyone who leaves, is laid off, or dismissed from a job on, say, Friday, start a new job on the following Monday. In more general terms, unemployment and unfilled job vacancies can exist simultaneously because it takes time for a match to be found between vacant jobs and people seeking employment.

In addition to this matching process, there are other aspects to frictional unemployment. The first involves the growing phenomenon of people searching for the right job rather than for just any job. A growing percentage of households have more than one wage earner. Thus, if one partner earns a good income, the unemployed partner can take longer in the job-search process to increase the chances of finding job satisfaction. There is a benefit to society if more people have jobs closely matched to their interests and skills. Prolonging the job search would, of course, result in the level of frictional unemployment rising.

Furthermore, many feel that Canada has, by world standards, generous employment insurance benefits that allow for people, in some circumstances, to accept periodic layoffs without actually searching energetically for other work. Examples would be a racetrack employee in the winter or a contract college instructor in the summer. Some economists call this phenomenon insurance-induced unemployment.

Finally, we should mention that there is a continuous inflow of new people into the labour market. This includes students who leave school and begin looking for a job as well as homemakers who enter (or re-enter) the labour market after their children are older. These people often do not find work immediately and are, therefore, frictionally unemployed until they do.

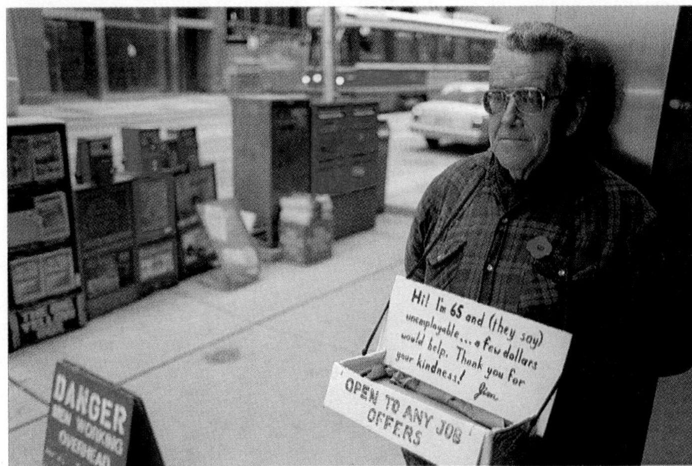

CP/John Lehmann

Unemployment can affect all ages.

Frictional unemployment is a part of a modern market economy. It will never be eliminated and, in fact, we don't want to try to eliminate it. We need to recognize that it takes time to match people and jobs, and that some people take extra time in searching for the right job. In addition, there are some on layoff who are not actively searching for alternative employment. We can therefore conclude that frictional unemployment in Canada is a significant portion of the official unemployment rate reported monthly in the popular press.

Structural Unemployment

structural unemployment: the part of total unemployment that results from structural changes in an economy's industries.

Next, we want to examine **structural unemployment**. Some have called this "long-term frictional," but such a description doesn't capture the sense of the major shifts that take place in the economy that result in structural unemployment. A natural spinoff of a dynamic, growing economy is the fact that new industries are continually emerging and entering the expansionary stage—think of computer software, underwater submersibles, and cardboard packaging for the fast-food industry. Meanwhile, others are "sunset" industries, which have experienced declining employment for years—the East Coast fishery, for example. Some industries might even suddenly die, as was the case with the slide rule, carbon paper, and typewriter industries.

People working in the sunset industries may require both a geographical and an occupational move in order to transfer into one of the newly created jobs in the growth industries. Whether retraining is required or not, this undoubtedly takes some time. In short, continuous structural changes within the economy lead to a certain amount of structural unemployment being always present. In addition, some economic observers argue that the forces of globalization in the world today have increased the rate at which businesses, and even whole industries, leave Canada in order to set up in some other, lower-wage, country. To the extent that this is true, structural unemployment becomes a bigger problem.

Cyclical Unemployment

In the next chapter we will look at fluctuations in the economy called business cycles. These fluctuations are reflected in changes in the level of employment and unemployment. A complete cycle consists of an expansion followed by a recession or contraction and then, once again, a recovery or expansion. This sequence of change is recurrent, but not regular in length or duration.

full employment: the situation in which there is only frictional and structural unemployment, that is, where cyclical unemployment is zero.

cyclical unemployment: unemployment that occurs as a result of the recessionary phase of the business cycle.

natural rate of unemployment: the unemployment rate at full employment.

When the business cycle is at its expansionary peak, the economy will likely be at what is called **full employment**. Another way of looking at this is to realize that "full employment" refers to the situation in which any unemployment in the economy is a result of only frictional and structural causes. In other words, full employment is the situation of no **cyclical unemployment**.

It is from the concept of zero cyclical unemployment that economists get the **natural rate of unemployment**. This exists when there is only frictional and structural unemployment and no cyclical unemployment. When an economy is in a recession, the total amount of unemployment is greater than the sum of frictional and structural unemployment and is therefore above the natural rate.

Thus we could say that full employment exists when the economy is experiencing *only* the natural rate of unemployment. This natural rate is considered to be the lowest unemployment rate an economy can achieve without accelerating inflation. This means that it is possible to achieve a lower rate of unemployment, but only at the cost of higher prices. In addition, the natural rate of unemployment can vary from country to country and from time to time within the same country, as social and economic conditions change. For example, Japan, where the practice of changing jobs frequently is thought to show a lack of loyalty (and loyalty is a highly regarded virtue), is likely to have a much lower natural rate of unemployment than is found in North America, where people frequently change jobs. As another example, some economists argue that Canada's natural rate of unemployment increased in the 1970s following an overhaul of the unemployment insurance plan that increased coverage and benefits, as well as an increase in two-income families. Today, it appears that Canada's natural rate of unemployment is in the range of 5 to 7 percent.

We should re-emphasize the point that regardless of the phase of the business cycle there is always unemployment in the economy, while at the same time there are always job vacancies. The labour market is dynamic: the type and place of the vacancies are constantly in flux and the people who are unemployed may or may not have the particular skills or experience to fill those vacancies. Furthermore, even if they do, the jobs and those unemployed may not be in the same area. Thus, regardless of the level of performance in the economy, there will be thousands of unfilled job vacancies. In fact, the number of vacancies might well equal the number of unemployed people. This phenomenon serves to emphasize the notion that the natural rate of unemployment is the result of unavoidable mismatching in the labour market. When an economy is suffering from cyclical unemployment, not only is there this mismatching problem, but in addition, there simply aren't enough jobs to go around; the number of unemployed people often greatly exceeds the number of available jobs.

If the natural unemployment rate in Canada today is 5–7 percent, it is surely higher than it was just 25 or 30 years ago. There are three possible explanations for this increase in the natural rate of unemployment. First, changes in employment insurance (EI) legislation in the early 1970s significantly increased benefits. Second, a longer job-search time is being taken by job seekers, who are now more affluent than they used to be and therefore can afford to extend the time spent looking for a satisfying job. Third, an increase in the female participation rate has contributed to a rapid increase in the number of people looking for employment. If these explanations are correct, the reductions in EI coverage and benefits in the mid-90s and the levelling out in the growth of the female participation rate may well result in a decrease in the natural rate of unemployment in Canada in the first few years of the millennium. In summary, the natural rate of unemployment could change if:

- employment insurance benefits change
- the average job search time changes
- labour-force participation rates change

SELF-TEST

2. Categorize each of the following set of circumstances as frictional, structural, or cyclical unemployment.

a) Sanjit, a pulp-mill worker, is laid off because the mill's inventories are at an all-time high.

b) Five weeks ago, Alison left a job she didn't like and is still looking for another job.

c) Ian was a fisher on the East Coast but sold his boat after years of hard work with little return. He hasn't been employed now for almost a year.

Measuring Unemployment

To get us started on the actual measurement of Canada's unemployment rate, we turn to **Table 4.6** for some 2001 data.

TABLE 4.6 **Population and Employment, Canada 2001 (millions)**

Total population	31.1
Working age population	24.6
Labour force	16.2
Employed	15.1
Unemployed	1.1

Source: Adapted from Statistics Canada, CANSIM Database, Table 282-0002.

working age population: the total population in a country, excluding those under 15 years of age, those in the armed forces, and residents of aboriginal reserves or the territories.

labour force: members of the working age population, either employed or unemployed.

The term **working age population** is defined as the country's total population, *excluding*:

- those under 15 years of age
- those living in the three territories or on aboriginal reserves
- full-time members of institutions such as schools or hospitals, and those in the armed forces

As can be seen in the table, 6.5 million (31.1 minus 24.6) people fell into one of these three categories. Next, Statistics Canada takes all those in the working age population and subtracts those considered to be "not in the labour force." The result gives us the category entitled the **labour force**. Those not in the labour force include retired people, those who are financially independent, and those who choose not to participate in the labour market for reasons such as devoting full attention to child rearing. As can be seen in **Table 4.6**, those in the category called the labour force totalled 16.2 million while those not in the labour force totalled 8.4 million (24.6–16.2).

The information from **Table 4.6** is illustrated in the following visual:

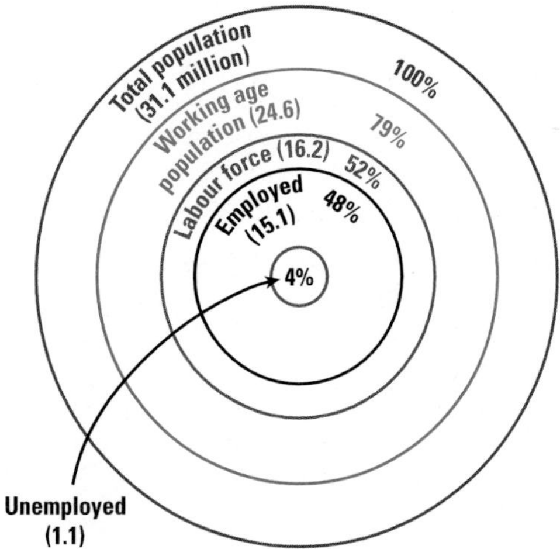

The actual mechanics of computing this data involves a random survey of 58 000 Canadian households done each month. Questions are asked of each member 15 years of age and older in each household. The questions used to determine if an individual is in the labour force are as follows:

1. Is he or she currently gainfully employed for at least one hour per week, or self-employed?
2. Is he or she employed but not on the job due to illness, vacation, or industrial dispute?
3. Is he or she laid off (within the last 26 weeks) but expecting to be recalled?
4. Is he or she not employed but starting a new job within 30 days?
5. Is he or she not employed, nor laid off, but actively seeking employment?

employed: those who are in the labour force and hold paid employment.

unemployed: those who are in the labour force and are actively seeking employment, but do not hold paid employment.

participation rate: the percentage of those in the working age population who are actually in the labour force.

If none of the above five categories apply, then that person is categorized as not in the labour force.

Having identified those who are in the labour force (employed and unemployed), the next distinction is between those who have gainful employment of at least one hour per week—those who are **employed** (categories 1 and 2 above)—and those who are **unemployed** (categories 3, 4, and 5), since they do not currently hold paid employment. It is important to note that the fact that a person does not have a job does not mean that he or she is unemployed. To be unemployed, the person must be available for work and actively seeking employment.

Out of these various categories come two important rates: first, the **participation rate**, which is the percentage of the working age population who are in the labour force:

$$\text{Labour force participation rate} = \frac{\text{labour force}}{\text{working age population}} \times 100 \qquad [4.4]$$

In Canada for 2001, this rate was:

$$\text{Labour force participation rate} = \frac{16.2}{24.6} \times 100 = 65.9\%$$

Table 4.7 shows this rate as a total, and for both genders over a 17-year period.

TABLE 4.7 Labour-Force Participation Rates, Canada, 1985–2001

Year	Total (%)	Male (%)	Female (%)
1985	65.3	76.6	54.6
1986	65.7	76.6	55.3
1987	66.2	76.6	56.4
1988	66.7	76.6	57.4
1989	67.0	76.7	57.9
1990	67.3	76.3	58.7
1991	66.7	75.1	58.5
1992	65.9	74.0	58.0
1993	65.5	73.5	57.9
1994	65.3	73.5	57.6
1995	64.8	72.5	57.4
1996	64.9	72.4	57.6
1997	64.8	72.2	57.8
1998	65.1	72.1	58.4
1999	65.6	72.5	58.9
2000	65.9	72.5	59.5
2001	65.9	72.5	59.7

Source: Adapted from Statistics Canada, CANSIM Database, Table 282-0002.

Over these 17 years, the female participation rate in Canada rose, while the male rate fell by approximately the same amount. This is a significant change in the make-up of the labour force. In addition, Canada's overall labour force (labour supply) also grew.

unemployment rate: the percentage of those in the labour force who do not hold paid employment.

The second important employment statistic is the **unemployment rate**, which is the percentage of the labour force actually unemployed. The equation for the unemployment rate is:

$$\text{Unemployment rate} = \frac{\text{number of unemployed}}{\text{labour force}} \times 100 \qquad [4.5]$$

We can use 2001 data to illustrate:

$$\text{Unemployment rate} = \frac{1.15}{16.25} \times 100 = 7.1\%$$

Table 4.8 below shows Canada's unemployment rates for the last 12 years.

TABLE 4.8 Unemployment Rates, Canada, 1990–2001

Year	Total (%)
1990	8.1
1991	10.3
1992	11.3
1993	11.2
1994	10.4
1995	9.5
1996	9.7
1997	9.2
1998	8.3
1999	7.5
2000	6.8
2001	7.1

Source: Adapted from Statistics Canada, CANSIM Database, Table 282-0002.

Table 4.8 illustrates an important feature of the economy. The unemployment rate rises in periods of economic slowdown (1990–93) and falls in periods of expansion, such as occurred in 1997–2001. Also, it is quite clear that the fluctuation is not between zero and say, 4 or 5 percent, but instead moves between a low of about 6.8–7.5 percent and up to 10–11 percent, and back down.

ADDED DIMENSION

Economic Growth and Recessions

A recession is defined by StatsCan as a decline in real GDP in two consecutive quarters. We know that a drop in real GDP will lead to layoffs in the economy and therefore a rise in unemployment. Therefore, the average person is more likely to define a recession as an increase in the unemployment rate rather than a decrease in the growth rate. Are these two perspectives one and the same?

Although it is true that a negative or low growth rate is usually associated with high unemployment and that a high growth rate implies low unemployment rates, this relationship is not exact. For example, in the early years of the Great Depression of the 1930s, the Canadian economy experienced negative growth rates and high unemployment. Then from 1934 onwards the economy actually experienced positive growth in real GDP at an average annual rate of 7.1 percent yet the unemployment rate remained at an annual average rate of 12.3 percent. That is, an economy in the recovery stage of a recession can expect to record positive growth rates but may not experience lower unemployment for some time. Thus, while there may be some truth in regarding negative growth as heralding a recession, it would be a mistake to assume that positive growth rates always mean an economic boom.

As a final note on the measurement of unemployment, we should point out that the figures in **Table 4.8**, as well as those often reported in the media, are actually what StatsCan calls "seasonally adjusted" unemployment rates. What this means is that increases and decreases in the unemployment rate that are *purely* the result of seasonal influences are removed. The rationale behind all this is that the seasonally adjusted rate is a better indicator of the economy's current performance than an unadjusted rate, which would always rise in the winter and fall in the summer.

SELF-TEST

3. a) If a person is categorized as retired, would that person be included in the category called the working age population?

b) What types of people are in the category of "not in the labour force"?

c) Is it possible for the total number of people employed and the total number of people unemployed to rise at the same time?

Criticism of the Official Rate

There are four grounds on which one could criticize the official unemployment rate, despite the fact that the interview and statistical techniques used to measure it are quite legitimate. The first two criticisms discussed below cause the official rate to be *understated.*

First, we must realize that a person who responds that she worked only part time (and it may be as little as one hour a week) in the previous week will be classified as employed. However, if this part-time status is not what the person was hoping for, then some real unemployment is being covered over in the reported statistics.

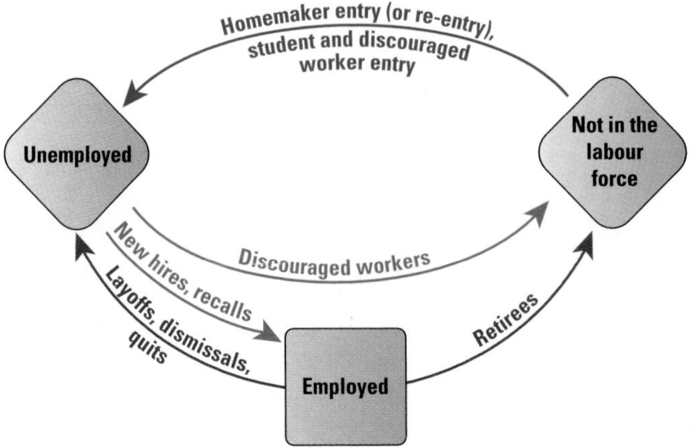

discouraged worker: an individual who wants work but is no longer actively seeking it because of the belief that no opportunities exist.

The second point involves what critics refer to as the **discouraged worker** phenomenon. According to the official definitions used by StatsCan, a person who is not actively seeking work is not in the labour force and thus would not be counted as unemployed. Yet, some argue, many individuals have become so discouraged in their attempts to secure employment that they have stopped looking. To exclude these discouraged workers is to understate the magnitude of the unemployment problem.

SELF-TEST

4. What would happen to the size of the labour force if 100 000 unemployed people became discouraged workers? What effect, if any, would this have on the unemployment rate?

The third common criticism of unemployment statistics is one that may cause the official rate to be *overstated*. When people who are collecting EI or welfare payments are asked if they are actively seeking work, the response is very likely to be "yes." Yet, at least some of these individuals are not involuntarily unemployed but are, instead, simply waiting for benefits to expire (or their claim to be challenged) before returning to active participation in the job market.

The fourth cause of unreliability is due to the fact that there is a whole group in the underground economy who are working in illegal occupations and, for obvious reasons, are going to declare themselves unemployed. The same may well be true for people with legal jobs who are not declaring their incomes. They too would probably declare themselves unemployed.

We will make no attempt to judge whether reasons one and two, which tip the scale one way, outweigh reasons three and four, which tip it the other way. What is probably more important to note is that measuring the unemployment rate *consistently* is crucial if we are to make sense out of time comparisons. Measured consistently, the official rate allows valid conclusions about the economy's performance in one year compared to another, and that's useful. In summary, the reported unemployment rates can be:

- understated because part-timers are included as full-timers
- understated because they exclude discouraged workers
- overstated because of false information from some EI recipients
- overstated because of false information from those working in the underground economy

The Costs of Unemployment

How serious a problem is unemployment? Should we really be concerned with it? Certainly, there are some obvious personal economic costs associated with unemployment. In addition, there are serious social costs that can affect all of us. Therefore, the true costs of unemployment cannot be measured simply in terms of EI or welfare payments going to those not working. In a sense, you might regard them as costs for the taxpayer, but obviously, from the recipient's point of view, they definitely represent a benefit. Overall, to an economist they are not true economic costs at all, but merely transfer payments. The true economic costs come from the fact that unemployment in an economy means that the quantity of goods and services being produced is less than it could be. (Like time, this lost production is gone forever.) This means that a country is producing below its potential, or in terms of Chapter 1's model, the economy is operating inside its production possibilities boundary. The amount of "lost" goods and services that did not get produced because the economy was operating at less than full employment is what economists refer to as the **GDP gap**. In the form of an equation, it is shown as:

GDP gap: the difference between potential GDP and actual GDP.

$$\text{GDP gap} = \text{potential GDP} - \text{actual GDP} \qquad [4.6]$$

An American economist named Okun established a relationship between the amount of cyclical unemployment in the economy and the size of the GDP gap. **Okun's law** observes that for every 1 percent of cyclical unemployment, the economy's level of GDP falls 2.5 percent short of its potential:

Okun's law: the observation that for every 1 percent of cyclical unemployment an economy's GDP would be 2.5 percent below its potential.

$$\text{GDP gap} = 2.5 \times \text{cyclical unemployment (\%)} \times \text{actual GDP}$$

For example, in 2001, the unemployment rate was 7.1 percent (see **Table 4.8**). If one assumes 6 percent as the natural rate of unemployment, then Canada was experiencing cyclical unemployment of 1.2 percent. In that year its nominal GDP was $1084 billion. Given this information, we are able to calculate the size of its GDP gap as follows:

$$\text{GDP gap} = 2.5 \times 1.2\% \times \$1084 = \$33 \text{ billion}$$

This is a measurement of the economic cost of unemployment and is a significant figure. If Canada could have eliminated this cyclical unemployment, its potential GDP would have been $33 billion higher at $1117 billion, and each person in Canada would have earned on average an additional $1065 in that year ($33 billion/31 million).

As important as these dollar amounts are, the social costs to the individual and to society can represent an even greater waste. Cyclical unemployment of 1.2 percent translates into approximately 195 000 people being involuntarily unemployed. In those 195 000 stories, one would find a lot of bitterness, disappointment, anger, loss of self-esteem, and a sense of failure. In addition, people who are unemployed for a significant period of time often lose some of the job skills that they had learned. Such feelings are not a recipe for social harmony. Alcoholism, accidents, claims on the healthcare system, violence, and crime will all rise as a result. Furthermore, these social costs do not fall evenly across society. Young people and those with less education are hit hardest, as are those who live in the Maritime provinces and in Quebec.

Whether we try to categorize these costs as social, psychological, economic, or political, the fact remains that by whatever measure, unemployment is expensive.

SELF-TEST

5. Given a natural rate of unemployment of 8 percent, an actual rate of 10 percent, and actual GDP of $800 billion, calculate potential GDP gap.

REVIEW

1. Distinguish between *frictional* and *structural unemployment.*
2. Define the *natural rate of unemployment.*
3. Define *cyclical unemployment.*
4. Define the terms *employed, unemployed,* and the *labour force.*
5. How are the *participation rate* and the *unemployment rate* measured?
6. What has been the general trend of the *participation rate* over the past 20 years?
7. What is meant by *GDP gap*?

4.3 Inflation

LO3
Understand what inflation is and why it is costly to the economy.

inflation: a persistent rise in the general level of prices.

Let's now turn to inflation. Public-opinion polls consistently show that people consider inflation, or the threat of inflation, to be a major problem facing society. In fact, people's concern about inflation usually ranks above their concern about unemployment. The reason for this is probably the simple fact that while unemployment in the economy touches only the unemployed and others close to them, inflation touches everyone daily. For our purposes, **inflation** can be defined as an increase in the general level of prices that is sustained over a period of time in an economy.

Measurement of Inflation

consumer price index: a measurement of the average level of prices of the goods and services that a typical Canadian family consumes.

The measurement of inflation with which most people are familiar uses the monthly **consumer price index** (CPI). This index is similiar to the GDP deflator that we looked at earlier, except that the CPI includes only consumer goods (both domestic and imported) while ignoring capital goods and government goods and services. StatsCan derives this index by first defining a representative basket of goods and services and then collecting prices, monthly, on each item. The basket reflects the spending habits of a household of four, and the prices are weighted to reflect a typical consumption pattern.

The cost of this basket is then converted to an index, based upon a chosen (base) year. Currently, StatsCan uses 1992 as the base year. That is to say, the prices of the defined basket that prevailed in 1992 are given the value 100. The CPI for the next nine years is shown in **Table 4.9**.

TABLE 4.9 **Consumer Price Index, 1992–2001**

1992	100.0
1993	101.8
1994	102.0
1995	104.2
1996	105.9
1997	107.6
1998	108.6
1999	110.5
2000	113.5
2001	116.4

Source: Adapted from Statistics Canada, CANSIM Database, Table 326-0002.

Thus, Canada's CPI grew by 16.4 percent in this nine-year period. One has to be careful when interpreting CPI data. For example, the *inflation rate* for 1995 is not simply the CPI for 1995 (104.2) less that for 1994 (102.0), which is 2.2. In fact, to get the inflation rate for any one year, we would use the following equation:

$$\text{Inflation rate} = \frac{\text{change in price index}}{\text{price index for previous year}} \times 100 \qquad [4.7]$$

In the case of 1995 this would be:

$$\text{Inflation rate} = \frac{2.2}{102.0} \times 100 = 2.16\%$$

Actual data for Canada's inflation rates in recent years are presented in **Table 4.10**.

TABLE 4.10 Inflation Rates, Canada, 1992–2001

Year	Rate
1992	1.5%
1993	1.8
1994	0.2
1995	2.2
1996	1.6
1997	1.6
1998	0.9
1999	1.7
2000	2.7
2001	2.6

These inflation rates are low compared to those experienced in the 1970s and 1980s, when Canada's inflation went as high as 12.4%.

One interesting use of the CPI is that it allows us to compare the actual price of a product in the past in terms of today's prices. For example, the actual price of a movie in 1959 was (about) $2, while today it is, say, $9 (it varies from city to city). On the other hand, we know that people's wages and incomes are also much higher in 2001 than they were in 1959. So did the real price of a movie increase or not? We can answer this question using the following equation:

$$\begin{array}{c}\text{Price of a 1959 movie}\\\text{(in 2001 dollars)}\end{array} = \begin{array}{c}\text{Price of a 1959 movie}\\\text{(in 1959 dollars)}\end{array} \times \frac{\text{price level in 2001}}{\text{price level in 1959}}$$

We then look up the price level for 1959, which was 30, and have:

$$\begin{array}{c}\text{Price of 1959 movie}\\\text{(in 2001 dollars)}\end{array} = 2 \times \frac{116.4}{30} = \$7.76$$

It does appear that the real price of a movie has gone up a little.

Along the same lines, what do you think is Hollywood's biggest box office hit? Might it be *Titanic* from the 90s, *ET: The Extra Terrestrial* from the 80s, *Star Wars* from the 70s, or, perhaps, *Gone With the Wind* from 1939? Well, the actual dollars taken in for each of these movies are:

Titanic	$601 million
Star Wars	461
ET	400
Gone With the Wind	199

But, look at the result of converting these numbers to constant (2001) dollars:

Gone With the Wind	$923 million
Star Wars	674
Titanic	634
ET	594

Interesting, isn't it? The old classic *Gone With the Wind* is still number one in box office revenues after all these years, while *Star Wars* nudges out *Titanic* for second place.

We have not included the two big hits of 2001–2002—*Harry Potter* and *Lord of the Rings*—since final figures were not available at the time of writing. However, both will probably make the list by the next edition.

The Rule of 70—A Helpful Tool

We have all heard how a few years of rapid inflation can ravage an economy or how compound interest can dramatically increase a given sum of money over time. The "rule of 70" is useful in estimating the time it will take for a figure to double in value given a certain percentage growth rate. The formula is:

$$\text{Number of years to double} = \frac{70}{\text{\% growth rate}} \qquad [4.8]$$

For example, if inflation is 5 percent per year, the CPI will double in:

$$\frac{70}{5} = 14 \text{ years}$$

Or, $1000 in a savings account earning 10 percent will double in:

$$\frac{70}{10} = 7 \text{ years}$$

The Costs of Inflation

nominal income: the present dollar-value of a person's income.

real income: the purchasing power of income, that is, nominal income divided by the price level.

Like unemployment, inflation involves some very heavy costs. Economists often categorize such costs as the *redistributive* effects on the one hand and the *output* effects on the other. We will analyze each of these, starting with the redistributive effects. To do this we need to distinguish between a person's **nominal income**—the actual amount printed on the paycheque—and his or her **real income**, which is the purchasing power of the paycheque's amount. If, one year from now, your take-home pay—nominal income—is 8 percent higher and prices have increased by 5 percent during the year, would you be any better or worse off? The answer is that your real income has increased by 3 percent and you would be better off.

Real income can be expressed in terms of an equation:

$$\text{Real income} = \frac{\text{nominal income}}{\text{price level}} \qquad [4.9]$$

and a change in real income is:

$$\text{\% change in real income} = \text{\% change in nominal income} - \text{the inflation rate}$$

With this definition in hand we can go on to say that the inflationary effects on the real income of different groups is quite uneven. The classic contrast is between an elderly couple living primarily on a private pension and a yuppie couple who are both in sales and receive, as income, a percentage of total sales volume. The real income of the elderly couple is eroded annually by inflation—in fact, during the high inflation years between 1972 and 1981, for example, it was cut in half! Meanwhile it is quite possible that the yuppie couple gained from inflation, because their sales volume grew faster than the overall rate of inflation. In short, inflation can be unfair in that it at times hurts the economically weak and often leaves the strong unaffected or, perhaps, even benefits them. In general, those whose nominal income increases less than the rate of inflation will suffer because their real income decreases.

A second example of the effects of inflation is on those employees who have weak bargaining power in the market place. This may be the result of being non-unionized or working in a declining industry. In contrast, employees who are members of a big powerful trade union or are working in a growing industry may well have little difficulty keeping up with inflation.

Inflation can also redistribute wealth, particularly if the inflation rate was unexpected. The easiest way to see this is to imagine yourself borrowing $1000 today, assuming a current inflation rate of, say, 5 percent. This means that what costs you $1000 today will cost you $1050 a year from now. Anyone lending you $1000 now will definitely want to ensure they get the equivalent amount back. But in addition, they will want to earn a return on the money they lend, if for no other reason than the risk that the loan may never be re-paid. Let's say that they want to earn a real return of 7 percent. They would therefore charge you 5% to cover anticipated inflation + 7% = 12%. In other words:

real interest rate: the rate of interest measured in constant dollars.

$$\text{Real interest rate} = \text{nominal interest rate} - \text{inflation rate} \quad [4.10]$$

So, let's say that you agree to the nominal rate of 12 percent and therefore the repayment of $1120 in a year's time. If the actual inflation rate turns out to be 5 percent, then your friend will receive in real terms exactly what he expected to receive. But what would happen if the actual inflation rate turned out to be 10 percent? You will still pay back $1120 to your friend. But how much is this worth to him in purchasing power compared with the $1000 he lent to you a year ago? The answer is only approximately $1020, because of the increase in prices. He earned, in real terms, therefore, only $20 on $1000, or 2 percent. In other words:

$$\text{Real interest rate} = \text{nominal rate } (12\%) - \text{the inflation rate } (10\%) = 2\% \quad [4.11]$$

This clearly hurts the lender of the $1000, while you are not hurt. If your real income rises because of the higher inflation, then you, the borrower, will actually gain. In general, an unexpected rise in inflation hurts lenders and can benefit borrowers, with the result being an unpredictable redistribution of wealth. On the other hand, an unexpected drop in the inflation rate will hurt borrowers and help lenders.

While these redistribution costs hurt some people, they help others. On the other hand, inflation can have another cost that really does hurt everyone. These are what are termed the output costs.

Let's start this discussion by pointing out that long-term investment is an uncertain business at the best of times. Consider the example of a company that anticipates it will have to spend $10 million to produce and market a new product. The financial viability of such a decision depends on many variables—from expected sales to production costs. If estimating these unknowns also requires that uncertain inflation rates—which will affect both revenue and production costs—must be factored in, then the risks may become just too large to accept, and as a result the company may shelve the launching of the new product. All the investment spending and new hiring that would have otherwise gone ahead is foregone.

The key phrase in the above paragraph is "unknown inflation rate." Any rate—zero, 10 percent, 20 percent—is not a problem in the sense that we are discussing, as long as it remains unchanged and therefore predictable. It's the *uncertainty* associated with inflation that generates concern, making investment decision-makers nervous. If such hesitancy reduces the amount of investment in the economy, then the rate of economic growth slows and total output will be lower than it would have been.

Before leaving this discussion of the costs of inflation, it's worth taking a minute to look at the problems of the opposite situation—falling prices—which is called deflation. Japan, for example, is currently facing just this situation. One of the effects of deflation is a reduction in both consumer and investment spending, because when prices are falling it pays people to put off purchases till the future in order to take advantage of the lower prices. In addition, investment spending is likely to be further affected because of the effects of deflation on the real interest rate. A number of studies have concluded that, over the last three hundred years or so, the real rate of interest has gravitated around the 4 percent level. **Table 4.11** shows what the nominal rate needs to be in order to achieve a real rate of 4 percent.

TABLE 4.11 Hypothetical Real Rates of Inflation

Real Rate of Interest	Inflation Rate	(Needed) Nominal Interest Rate
4%	2%	6%
4%	12%	16%
4%	–4%	0%

For instance, if the inflation rate is 2 percent, then a nominal rate of 6 percent is needed in order to ensure a real rate of 4 percent, which will satisfy both lenders and borrowers. However, if the inflation rate rises to say, 12 percent, then a nominal interest rate of 16 percent is needed to yield a real rate of 4 percent. But it is hard for borrowers to accept nominal rates this high and borrowing might be greatly reduced, with the resulting loss in output because of the reduced spending by both consumers and businesses. Now consider the effects of deflation. If the *deflation* rate is 4 percent, then those who have money to lend can gain a real rate of interest of 4 percent by simply doing nothing but holding on to their money. Therefore, they will not be willing to lend and, since nominal interest rates cannot become negative, there is nothing that will change to correct this situation. In short, deflation freezes credit markets and this also reduces output.

There are other examples of the output costs of inflation. The first is termed the *menu costs of inflation*. This refers to the business costs involved in changing prices, which is something that obviously has to be done more often in times of higher inflation. Let's take the case of Colonial Music, a small wholesaler of musical instruments which it imports from Asia and sells to school boards across North America. Colonial Music produces three separate printed catalogues that it mails out—one for English Canada, one for French Canada, and one for the U.S.—as well as a Web site which has the same three categories. Since the company offers literally hundreds of instruments, the production of the catalogues and the updating of the Web site involves a lot of time and expense—literally tens of thousands of dollars. Any increase in the inflation rate may necessitate the production of new catalogues sooner than the regularly scheduled time and this clearly adds to the costs of doing business.

In addition, we know that inflation in Canada has a negative effect on the levels of Canadian exports. Higher inflation pushes up the prices of Canadian goods and reduces Canadian exports, unless the countries that we compete with also experience similarly high inflation. Furthermore, Canadian consumers will begin to substitute imports for the now higher-priced Canadian products. The result is less production in Canada and this means less national income and fewer jobs.

ADDED DIMENSION

Galloping Inflation

In the twentieth century some unfortunate countries have experienced the ravages of extreme rates of inflation that economists term galloping or hyper-inflation. The experience of Germany following the First World War is both instructive and well-documented. As a result of the Versailles Peace Treaty at the end of the war, Germany was presented, by the victorious nations, with a staggering reparations bill of 132 billion gold marks, which was an estimate of the war damage "caused" by Germany. Although the German government was (kindly?) allowed to pay this reparation in annual installments, the amount was far in excess of what it could reasonably raise through taxation or by borrowing. It therefore resorted to a method used by despotic kings, emperors, and corrupt governments throughout history—it simply printed more money in order to pay its bills. The result of "too much money chasing too few goods" was that prices rose by 5470 percent in 1922 alone. In 1923, things got even worse and prices rose an astonishing 1 300 000 000 000 times! One egg cost 600 000 marks, butter cost 1.5 million marks, and a pound of meat cost 2 million marks. (If you put a dollar sign in front of these figures you will sense the seriousness of the situation.)

Prices rose so rapidly at one point that waiters changed the amount charged for menu items throughout the meal. Workers demanded to be paid daily, and then, later, twice a day. And immediately upon being paid, people would rush to buy almost anything that was available for sale—especially non-perishable goods. Eventually, money was literally not worth the paper it was printed on. It was used by people to light the fire in stoves or by children to make building blocks. At this point, the economy collapsed and unemployment and violence rose quickly. All of this contributed to one of the darkest chapters in human history—the rise of Hitler and the Nazi Party.

Causes of Inflation: Two Classifications

In a very real sense, the entire study of macroeconomic principles is necessary to understand what causes inflation. Nevertheless, it is useful to briefly identify two classifications of causes at this point.

demand–pull inflation: inflation that occurs when total demand for goods and services exceeds the economy's capacity to produce those goods.

cost–push inflation: inflation caused by an increase in the costs of production or in profit levels, with the effect being on the supply side.

The first is referred to by economists as **demand–pull inflation**, which occurs when the total demand for goods and services in the whole economy exceeds its capacity to produce those same goods. That is to say, people are trying to buy more goods and services than the economy is capable of producing, even at full employment. This excessive demand will pull up prices and cause demand–pull inflation.

You may well ask at this point: but don't we also experience inflation at times when unemployment is high and, thus, when there is no demand–pull inflation? The answer is yes, and thus we have the second classification of inflation, called **cost–push inflation**. This occurs on the supply side of the economy, whereas demand–pull inflation is a demand-side phenomenon. Cost–push inflation has three variations.

The first of these is *wage–push inflation*. For example, if a union succeeds at the bargaining table in pushing the nominal wage rate up more than any recent increase in labour productivity would justify, then the employer's real cost will rise. If we assume that this increase was not simply a catch-up in response to inflation from some other cause, then we have the makings of further inflation. If the employer who agreed to the increased nominal wage did so thinking that by increasing the price of the products she sells she can recoup the increased costs, and if the employer has sufficient market power, then we have a completed picture of wage–push inflation: increased wages pushing up costs, which push up prices. Needless to say, the impact of one union and one employer probably isn't noticeable, but if the above scenario is typical of a general pattern, then the impact will become very apparent.

The second variation of cost–push inflation, called *profit–push inflation*, can occur if firms have enough market power to enhance profits by simply increasing the prices of what is sold. This is more likely to occur in industries in which competition is weak and aggregate demand is strong.

The name of the third variation, *import–push inflation*, is almost self-explanatory. The classic example here is the OPEC oil price increases of the 1970s, which affected every economy in the world, particularly those that imported a significant percentage of the oil they consumed. Here, the cost of imported oil triggered price increases in all industries that were heavily dependent on oil. This had a snowballing effect throughout the economy.

What this brief little glimpse does for us at this point is emphasize that the cause of inflation can be either a demand-side or a supply-side phenomenon. We will go much deeper into this distinction in a later chapter.

SELF-TEST

6. a) If you borrowed a sum of money for one year at a nominal rate of interest of 11 percent and during that same year the inflation rate was 4 percent, what real rate of interest did you pay?

b) Assume that you retire with a pension fixed at $12 000 per year and that, in each of the two years following retirement, the inflation rate is 5 percent. At the end of those two years, what will be the amount of your real income?

REVIEW

1. Define *inflation*.
2. Distinguish between *nominal* and *real GDP*.
3. What is the *GDP deflator*?
4. What is the *rule of 70*?
5. Distinguish between the *nominal* and the *real interest rate*.
6. Give an example of the *distributional* effect of inflation.
7. What is *demand–pull inflation*?
8. What is *cost–push inflation*?

STUDY GUIDE

Review

CHAPTER SUMMARY

In this chapter we first define economic growth and discuss how economists measure economic growth. Next, we look at two of the ongoing economic issues of the day—unemployment and inflation. We will return to all three of these topics later in the book.

1. *Measuring* the economy's output includes:
- *nominal* GDP, which is the economy's current year's output of goods and services measured in current year's prices;
- *real* GDP, which is the current year's output measured in the prices of a chosen base year;
- the GDP *deflator,* which is a ratio of these two statistics.

2. The benefits of economic growth include:
- an increase in material well-being;
- improved social infrastructure, such as better health and educational facilities.

3. Economic growth doesn't always mean improved welfare, because:
- it may simply be the result of previous non-market activities becoming market activities;
- the quality of goods may have decreased;
- population growth may exceed economic growth;
- it might have occurred at great social or environmental cost.

4. The three *types of unemployment* are:
- frictional, which is the movement of people between jobs;
- structural, which results from structural changes in the economy's major industries;
- cyclical, which is caused by fluctuations in the economy's growth rate.

5. StatsCan divides the total population into four sub-sets:
- working age population: which excludes those in the total population who are under 15 years of age, in the military, and others;
- labour force: members in the working age population who are either employed or unemployed;
- employed;
- unemployed.

6. Labour force data is used to show that:
- the *unemployment rate* is the number of people unemployed as a percentage of the labour force;
- the *participation rate* is the number of people both employed and unemployed as a percentage of the working age population.

7. Criticisms of the official unemployment rates include:
- part-time employees are regarded as fully employed;
- discouraged workers are excluded;
- some employment insurance recipients give false information;
- those working in the underground economy are not counted.

8. One way to measure the *costs of unemployment* is:
- Okun's law, which relates cyclical unemployment to the GDP gap.

9. The costs of inflation are subdivided into *distributional effects*, such as shifting income:
- from the economically weak to the strong;
- from lenders to borrowers;

and the *output effect*, which:
- reduces the level of investment and thus economic growth.
- increases the costs of changing catalogues, Web sites, menus, etc.
- reduces exports and increases imports.

10. The two causes of inflation are *demand–pull* and *cost–push*. Cost-push is subdivided into:
- wage–push;
- profit–push;
- import–push.

NEW GLOSSARY TERMS AND KEY EQUATIONS

consumer price index (CPI) 137
cost–push inflation 142
cyclical unemployment 129
demand–pull inflation 142
discouraged worker 134
economic growth 122
employed 132
frictional unemployment 128
full employment 129
GDP deflator 123
GDP gap 135
inflation 136
labour force 131
natural rate of unemployment 129
nominal GDP 123
nominal income 139
Okun's law 135
participation rate 132
real GDP 123
real income 139
real interest rate 140
structural unemployment 129
unemployed 132
unemployment 128
unemployment rate 132
working age population 131

Equations:

[4.1] $\text{GDP deflator} = \dfrac{\text{nominal GDP}}{\text{real GDP}} \times 100$ page 123

[4.2] $\text{Real GDP per capita} = \dfrac{\text{real GDP}}{\text{population}}$ page 124

[4.3] $\text{(Economic) growth rate} = \dfrac{\text{increase in real GDP per capita}}{\text{real GDP per capita (previous year)}} \times 100$ page 124

[4.4] $\text{(Labour force) Participation rate} = \dfrac{\text{labour force}}{\text{working age population}} \times 100$ page 132

[4.5] $\text{Unemployment rate} = \dfrac{\text{number of unemployed}}{\text{labour force}} \times 100$ page 132

[4.6] $\text{GDP gap} = \text{potential GDP} - \text{actual GDP}$ page 135

[4.7] $\text{Inflation rate} = \dfrac{\text{change in price index}}{\text{price index for previous year}} \times 100$ page 137

[4.8] $\begin{matrix}\text{Rule of 70} \\ \text{(\# years to double)}\end{matrix} = \dfrac{70}{\text{\% growth rate}}$ page 139

[4.9] $\text{Real income} = \dfrac{\text{nominal income}}{\text{price level}} \text{ or } = \dfrac{\text{nominal income}}{\text{price index}} \times 100$ page 139

[4.10] $\text{\% change in real income} = \text{\% change in nominal income} - \text{the inflation rate}$ page 140

[4.11] $\text{Real interest rate} = \text{nominal interest rate} - \text{inflation rate}$ page 140

STUDY TIPS

1. The material covered in this chapter contains very little theory; the chapter is mostly descriptive or institutional. This does not mean that it is unimportant, but it probably does mean that you don't need to study it quite as much as some of the other chapters. If you have gained a sense of the limitations of the measurements, this is very good.

2. In a very real sense, growth, unemployment, and inflation are subjects of the entire course that we call macroeconomics. This chapter is meant to be an introduction to these topics and not the final word. Therefore, you should not be concerned at this point if you are still unclear about questions like what is the cause of unemployment and what are the solutions to inflation. We still have a long way to go.

3. The concept of full employment and the definition of the natural rate of unemployment both play an important role in later chapters. Make sure that you understand that full employment does not mean zero unemployment.

4. Statistics Canada releases unemployment and inflation rates around the middle of each month. Often, upon their release, the media coverage is extensive. You might start listening and looking for this coverage and thus become a little more attuned to the significance of what you are studying.

5. Many students have a tendency to assume that a person who is not working is, therefore, unemployed. You should recognize that many people who are not working are doing so either because they don't have to work (for example, they have accumulated enough money to live happily without a regular source of employment income) or because they choose not to work (such as a parent who chooses to stay home with young children). In short, people are unemployed only if they are actively seeking, but do not have paid employment.

Answered Questions

Indicate whether the following statements are true or false.

1. **T or F** Frictional unemployment is likely to be greatest in sunset industries.

2. **T or F** The natural rate of unemployment is the unemployment rate at full employment.

3. **T or F** If the number of job vacancies in an economy is equal to the number of people unemployed, then cyclical unemployment is zero.

4. **T or F** Both male and female participation rates in Canada have been steadily rising for the past 20 years.

5. **T or F** The higher the rate of inflation, the lower the redistribution effect of inflation.

6. **T or F** Cost–push inflation is caused by the total demand for goods and services exceeding the economy's capacity to produce those goods.

7. **T or F** The real interest rate is equal to the nominal interest rate plus the expected inflation rate.

8. **T or F** Real GDP is the value of nominal GDP measured in base year prices.

9. **T or F** If the annual inflation rate is 7 percent, then the price level will double in ten years.

10. **T or F** An increase in the quality of goods produced would increase the well-being of people, but this will not be captured in real GDP figures.

Basic (Questions 11–21)

11. What is the real rate of interest if the nominal rate of interest is 10 percent and the rate of inflation is 4 percent?
   a) 6 percent.
   b) 14 percent.
   c) 10 percent.
   d) 40 percent.

12. Which of the following is a variation of cost–push inflation?
   a) Import–push inflation.
   b) Demand–deficient inflation.
   c) Galloping inflation.
   d) National inflation.

13. What can be said about Canada's real GDP growth rate between 1995 and 1999?
   a) It was the highest of the G-8 countries.
   b) It was the third highest of the G-8 countries.
   c) It was the lowest of the G-8 countries.
   d) It was the same as that in the U.S.A.

14. What is the type of unemployment that is associated with recessions?
   a) Structural.
   b) Cyclical.
   c) Frictional.
   d) Real.

15. Which of the following does inflation affect?
   a) Both the level and the distribution of income.
   b) The distribution but not the level of income.
   c) The level but not the distribution of income.
   d) Neither the level nor the distribution of income.

16. All of the following, except one, are economic issues that seem to persist over time. Which is the exception?
   a) Budget deficits.
   b) Inflation.
   c) Unemployment.
   d) Low or negative economic growth rates.

17. According to the official StatsCan definition, what is the minimum amount of time a person must have worked in the previous week in order to be counted as employed?
   a) 5 hours.
   b) 36 hours.
   c) 40 hours.
   d) 60 minutes.

18. Which of the following statements is correct if we apply the "rule of 70" to a known rate of inflation?
   a) We would be able to calculate the corresponding rate of unemployment.
   b) We could determine when the value of a real asset will approach zero.
   c) We could calculate the number of years it will take for the price level to double.
   d) We could calculate the size of the GDP gap.

19. Which of the following is a valid description of economic growth?
   a) It is an increase in an economy's real GDP per capita.
   b) It is an increase in an economy's total output of goods and services.
   c) It can be represented by a shift out in the production possibilities curve.
   d) All of the above.

20. How is real income calculated?
   a) By dividing the price level by nominal income.
   b) By dividing nominal income by a price index and multiplying the result by 100.
   c) By multiplying nominal income by the rate of inflation.
   d) By adding the rate of inflation to the rate of increase in nominal income.

21. What is the cause of cyclical unemployment?
   a) A downward fluctuation in the business cycle.
   b) The declining importance of goods production and the growing importance of service production in our economy.
   c) The normal dynamics of a free-market economy.
   d) Technological change.
   e) The changing nature of demand from one product to another.

Intermediate (Questions 22–31)

22. What would be the effect on the unemployment rate if all the part-time workers were to become full-time workers?
   a) It would decrease.
   b) It would increase.
   c) It would remain unchanged.
   d) It depends on the size of the labour force.

23. Which of the following statements supports the contention that larger real GDP per capita figures may not mean a better life for the population?
   a) Work such as housecleaning, which used to be entirely a non-market activity, is becoming more and more a market activity.
   b) Higher production has negative side-effects, such as more pollution.
   c) In the measurement of GDP, no distinction is made as to the type of goods produced.
   d) All of the above.

24. When is the Canadian economy considered to be at full employment?
   a) When 12 percent of the labour force is unemployed.
   b) When 90 percent of the working age population is employed.
   c) When 90 percent of the labour force is employed.
   d) When approximately 5 to 7 percent of the labour force is unemployed.
   e) When everyone who wants a job has one.

25. Which of the following statements concerning the natural rate of unemployment is correct?
   a) It is made up of both frictional and structural unemployment.
   b) It is the rate of unemployment at full employment.
   c) It is when the total number of job vacancies equals the number of people unemployed.
   d) It is probably about 5 percent to 7 percent in Canada today.
   e) All of the above.

26. What does Okun's law refer to?
   a) The relationship between job vacancies and unemployment.
   b) The seemingly constant ratio between those in the labour force and the total population.

c) The relationship between the level of cyclical unemployment and the difference between potential and actual GDP.
d) The difference between an economy's real and nominal GDP.
e) The time it takes a number to double given a certain percentage growth rate.

27. All of the following statements, except one, are correct concerning unanticipated increases in inflation. Which is the exception?
a) It redistributes wealth and income in unpredictable ways.
b) It increases the real value of savings.
c) It decreases the purchasing power of money.
d) It benefits debtors at the expense of creditors.
e) It affects some individuals much more than others.

28. What could cause an increase in nominal GDP?
a) An increase in the output of goods and services but no change in prices.
b) An increase in the prices of goods and services but no change in their output.
c) An increase in both the output and the prices of goods and services.
d) All of the above.

29. Which two pieces of information would allow us to calculate a GDP deflator?
a) Prices and interest rates.
b) Nominal GDP and real GDP figures.
c) Unemployment rates and Okun's Law
d) Prices and the Rule of 70.
e) GDP rates and the Rule of 70.

30. Which of the following categories would a thirty-five-year-old, healthy male who does not work because he has inherited a large fortune most likely fall into?
a) In the labour force.
b) In the working age population.
c) Employed.
d) Unemployed.

31. Under what condition could the employment and unemployment rates both increase?
a) If the economy entered a severe recession.
b) If the number of people in the labour force increased more than the number of people employed.
c) If the total number of discouraged workers increased.
d) If the total population decreased.
e) If the number of people in the labour force grew slower than the increase in the number of people employed.

Advanced (Questions 32–35)

32. How is real GDP calculated?
a) By dividing nominal GDP by the GDP deflator and multiplying by 100.
b) By multiplying nominal GDP by the GDP deflator and dividing by 100.
c) By multiplying nominal GDP by the CPI and dividing by 100.
d) By dividing the GDP deflator by nominal GDP and multiplying by 100.

33. What would be the effect of 100 000 unemployed people becoming discouraged workers?
a) The unemployment rate would remain unchanged, and the size of the labour force would decline.
b) Both the unemployment rate and the size of the labour force would decline.
c) The unemployment rate would decline, and the size of the labour force would remain unchanged.
d) Both the unemployment rate and the size of the labour force would rise.

34. How does StatsCan define a recession?
a) A decline in real GDP during one quarter.
b) A decline in real GDP over two consecutive quarters.
c) An unemployment rate in excess of 8% along with a decline in GDP.
d) A decline in nominal GDP over one quarter.
e) An unemployment rate in excess of 8%.

35. Why are economists concerned about deflation?
a) Because it is associated with high rates of unemployment.
b) Because it could lead to very rapid and uncontrollable rates of growth.
c) Because it could drive the nominal interest rate to very high levels.
d) Because it could cause credit markets to freeze up and in turn cause economic growth to stop.

Parallel Problems

ANSWERED PROBLEMS

36. Key Problem The data in Table 4.11 shows the total output (a mixture of consumer, capital, and government services) and the prices of each product for the distant country of Vindaloo. (All figures are in billions and the base year is 2000.) Complete the table and answer the questions which follow (to one decimal place):

TABLE 4.11

1	2	3	4	5	6	7	8	9	10	11	12	13	14
	2000			2001					2002				
Item	Qty	Prices Year 2000	Nominal GDP	Qty	Prices Year 2001	Nominal GDP	Prices Year 2000	Real GDP	Qty	Prices Year 2002	Nominal GDP	Prices Year 2000	Real GDP
Hot dogs	50	2	100	55	2.40				58	2.50			
CDs	10	12	120	12	13				14	13.50			
Farm tractors	3	100	300	4	95				4	110			
Parking meters	4	50	200	4	60				5	70			
Totals			720										

a) What is the value of nominal GDP in:
2001: $ ____________; 2002: $ ____________.

b) What is the value of real GDP in:
2001: $ ____________; 2002: $ ____________.

c) What is the value of the GDP deflator in:
2001: $ ____________; 2002: $ ____________.

d) What is the inflation rate (using the GDP deflator) in:
2001: $ ____________; 2002: $ ____________.

Suppose that the population in Vindaloo is as follows in Table 4.12:

TABLE 4.12

2000	2001	2002
23 million	24 million	25 million

e) What is the real GDP per capita in:
2000: $ ____________; 2001: $ ____________;
2002: $ ____________.

f) What is the growth rate in real GDP per capita:
2001: $ ____________% 2002: $ ____________%.

g) Suppose that the representative consumer in Vindaloo buys 5 units of each consumer good. What is the cost of each bundle in:
2000: $ ____________; 2001: $ ____________;
2002: $ ____________.

h) Converting the cost of each bundle into a consumer price index, what is the value of each bundle using 2000 as the base year:
2000: $ ____________; 2001: $ ____________;
2002: $ ____________.

i) What is the inflation rate using this price index?
2001: $ ____________% 2002: $ ____________%

Basic (Problems 37–42)

37. The following data in Table 4.13 is for the country of Eturia:

TABLE 4.13

	2000	2001	2002
Nominal GDP ($billions)	420	456	500
Real GDP ($billions)	400	422	447
Population (millions)	16	16.56	17.14

Give your answers to one decimal place.

a) Calculate the GDP deflator for years 2000, 2001, and 2002. ____________; ____________ and ____________.

b) Calculate real GDP per capita for the three years. ____________; ____________ and ____________.

c) Calculate the growth rate of real GDP per capita for years 2001 and 2002. __________ and __________ .

38. The labour force data for Eturia (all in millions) is as follows in **Table 4.14**:

TABLE 4.14

	2000	2001	2002
Working age population	12	12.5	12.8
Labour force	8.4	9	9.2
Unemployed	0.7	0.8	0.85

a) What are the (labour force) participation rates in each year? __________ ; __________ and __________ .

b) What are the unemployment rates in each year? __________ ; __________ and __________ .

39. The CPI in Eturia is as follows in **Table 4.15**:

TABLE 4.15

	2000	2001	2002
CPI (1996 = 100)	116	121	128

What are the inflation rates in years 2001 and 2002? __________ and __________ .

40. The population of Eturia is as follows in **Table 4.16**:

TABLE 4.16

	2000	2001	2002
Population (millions)	16	16.56	17.14

a) What is the percentage growth in population in both 2001 and 2002? __________ and __________ .

b) If the population continues to increase at this rate, how long will it take for the population of Eturia to double? __________ .

41. The average nominal income earned in Eturia and the CPI are as shown in **Table 4.17**:

TABLE 4.17

	2000	2001	2002
Nominal income	$28 000	$29 600	$32 000
CPI (1996 = 100)	116	121	128

a) Calculate real incomes for each year. __________ ; __________ and __________ .

b) By what percent did real incomes rise in Years 2001 and 2002? __________ and __________ .

42. Interest rates in Eturia are as follows in **Table 4.18**:

TABLE 4.18

	2000	2001	2002
Nominal interest rate	8%	6%	5.2%
Inflation rate	6.8%	4.3%	5.9%

Calculate the real interest rate in each year. __________ ; __________ and __________ .

Intermediate (Problems 43–46)

43. The information in **Table 4.19** is for the economy of Mensk:

TABLE 4.19

Working-age population	20.0
Number of people in full-time employment	11.5
Number of people in part-time employment	2.0
Number of people unemployed	1.5
Number of discouraged workers	1.5
CPI	117

a) What is the unemployment rate? 10% __________ .

b) What is the participation rate? 75% __________ .

c) How much inflation has occurred since the base year? __________ .

44. **Table 4.20** shows national data (in billions) for the economy of Westfall. (Round your answers to the nearest one decimal point.)

TABLE 4.20

	2000	2001	2002
Nominal GDP	$850	$958	______
GDP deflator (1992 = 100)	______	115	118
Real GDP	780	______	______
Population (in millions)	______	30.5	31
Real GDP per capita	$26 000	______	$28 390

a) Fill in the blanks in the table.
b) What is the inflation rate in 2001? ________ .
c) What is the growth rate of real GDP per capita in the year 2002? ________ .

45. If the inflation rate unexpectedly rises from 2 to 5 percent, would each of the following individuals gain or lose as a result?
a) Nigel, who borrowed $20 000 last year, repayable over three years, to buy a new boat. __________ .
b) Lars, who is an elderly man living on a fixed company pension. ____________________ .
c) Yoko, who keeps her savings in a credit union that pays a fixed 4 percent on customers' deposits. ____________________ .
d) Joan, who is an assembly-line worker whose employment is covered by a two-year union contract. The contract calls for an annual wage increase of 5 percent. ______________ .
e) Robert, who owns shares in the company where Joan works. ____________________ .

46. The data in **Table 4.21** is for the economy of Merton, which has a natural rate of unemployment of 5 percent.

TABLE 4.21

	2001	2002	2003
Real GDP	$600	$600	$630
Unemployment rate	8%	6%	6%

What is the size of the GDP gap for each of the three years?
2001: ____________ ; 2002: ____________ ;
2003: ____________ .

Advanced (Problems 47–48)

47. Explain how an increase in the rate of unemployment might suggest an improvement in economic conditions.
____
______________________________________ .

48. Suppose that the labour force is currently 5 million and the unemployment rate is 11 percent. Then, on August 1st the government announces that it will create 40 000 new jobs to be filled over the next three months. Only those people who were without employment on August 1st will be hired. As a result, 120 000 people immediately apply for the jobs; half of these people had previously not been actively seeking work.
a) Has the labour force changed as a result of this announcement? Explain. ______________
______________________________ .
b) What will be the unemployment rate before the jobs are filled? ____________________ .
c) Once all the jobs are filled, what will the unemployment rate be? ________________ .

UNANSWERED PROBLEMS

49. Key Problem The data in **Table 4.22** shows the total output (a mixture of consumer, capital, and government services) and prices of each product for the distant country of Harappa. (All figures are in billions and the base year is 2000.) Complete the table and answer the following questions (to one decimal place):

TABLE 4.22

1	2	3	4	5	6	7	8	9	10	11	12	13	14
	2000			2001					2002				
Item	Qty	Prices Year 2000	Nominal GDP	Qty	Prices Year 2001	Nominal GDP	Prices Year 2000	Real GDP	Qty	Prices Year 2002	Nominal GDP	Prices Year 2000	Real GDP
Hot dogs	30	3	90	40	3.25				40	3.50			
CDs	10	15	150	15	18				15	20			
Farm tractors	4	150	600	4	160				4	170			
Parking meters	5	90	450	5	100				5	110			
Totals			**1290**										

a) What is the value of nominal GDP in 2001 and 2002?
b) What is the value of real GDP in 2001 and 2002?
c) What is the value of the GDP deflator in 2001 and 2002?
d) What is the inflation rate (using the GDP deflator) in 2001 and 2002?

Suppose that the population in Harappa is as follows in Table 4.23:

TABLE 4.23

2000	2001	2002
80 million	81 million	82 million

e) What is the real GDP per capita in 2000, 2001, and 2002?
f) What is the real GDP per capita growth rate in: 2001 and 2002.
g) Suppose that the representative consumer in Harappa buys 10 units of each consumer good. What is the cost of each bundle in 2000, 2001, and 2002?
h) Converting the cost of each bundle into a consumer price index, what is the value of each bundle (using 2000 as the base year)in 2000, 2001, and 2002?
i) What is the inflation rate using this price index in 2000, 2001, and 2002?

Basic (Problems 50–52)

50. The following data, in Table 4.24, is for the country of Gendor:

TABLE 4.24

	2000	2001	2002
Nominal GDP ($billions)	800	840	900
Real GDP ($billions)	760	805	845
Population (millions)	29	29.2	29.5

a) Calculate the GDP deflator for years 2000, 2001, and 2002.
b) Calculate real GDP per capita for the three years.
c) Calculate the growth rate of real GDP per capita for years 2001 and 2002.

51. Below, in Table 4.25, is additional data for the economy of Gendor:

TABLE 4.25

	2000	2001	2002
Population (millions)	31.25	32.5	33.8
Working age population	16	16.5	16.8
Labour force	11.6	11.9	12.4
Unemployed	0.5	0.7	0.6
CPI (1992 = 100)	112	113.5	116

a) What are the (labour force) participation rates in each year?
b) What are the unemployment rates in each year?
c) What are the inflation rates in years 2001 and 2002?

d) What was the percentage increase in population in 2001 and 2002?
e) If the population continues to increase at this rate, how long will it take for the population to double?

52. Below, in **Table 4.26**, is more data for the economy of Gendor:

TABLE 4.26

	2000	2001	2002
Average Nominal income	$14 000	$15 000	$16 000
CPI (1992 = 100)	112	113.5	115
Nominal interest rate	6.5%	6%	5.5%
Inflation rate.	1.0%	1.3%	2.2%

a) Calculate real incomes for each year.
b) By what percentage did real income rise in Years 2001 and 2002?
c) Calculate the real interest rate in each year.

Intermediate (Problems 53–56)

53. The information in **Table 4.27** is for the economy of Ziduk.

TABLE 4.27

Working age population	500
Number of people in full-time employment	160
Number of people in part-time employment	65
Number of people unemployed	25
Number of discouraged workers	15
CPI	140

a) What is the unemployment rate?
b) What is the participation rate?
c) How much inflation has occurred since the base year?

54. **Table 4.28** shows national data for the economy of Darian.

TABLE 4.28

	2000	2001	2002
Nominal GDP (in billions)	$480	$520	______
GDP deflator (1991 = 100)	______	125	128
Real GDP	$400	______	______
Population (in millions)	______	20.2	21
Real GDP per capita	$20 000	______	$21 429

a) Fill in the blanks in the table (to the nearest whole number).
b) What is the inflation rate in 2002?
c) What is the growth rate of real GDP per capita in 2001?

55. Suppose that an economy unexpectedly experiences a *deflation* rate of 4 percent. Would each of the following individuals gain or lose as a result?
a) Ken, who borrowed $30 000 last year to renovate his house.
b) Sharon, who is a retired schoolteacher living on a fixed pension.
c) Myra, who keeps her savings in a bank account that pays a fixed rate of 3 percent on all deposits.
d) Jeri, a retail clerk whose employment is covered by a union contract which calls for an annual wage increase of 3 percent.
e) Bob, who owns shares of Ajax Finance, which earns its income from lending money.

56. The data in **Table 4.29** below is for the economy of Crestal, which has a natural rate of unemployment of 4 percent.

TABLE 4.29

	2000	2001	2002
Real GDP ($billions)	$200	$204	$210
Unemployment rate	5.5%	6%	5.8%

What is the size of the GDP gap for each of the three years?

Advanced (Problems 57–61)

57. Could a decrease in the unemployment rate ever imply that economic conditions are worsening?

58. Suppose that on January 1 the government creates 100 000 new jobs. Only those people currently without employment may apply for these jobs. The advertisement attracts 300 000 applicants, half of whom would not normally be looking for work in January.
   a) Has the labour force in January changed from what it would otherwise have been without the new jobs? Why?
   b) Suppose that without the new jobs, the labour force would have been 10 million and the unemployment rate 7 percent. What will be the unemployment rate for January before the jobs are filled?
   c) What will be the unemployment rate after the jobs have been filled?

59. In this chapter, we mentioned some of the criticisms of the definition of unemployed and employed. Can you devise a definition that overcomes the problem of including part-time workers and excluding discouraged workers?

60. Suppose that Ingrid's income in year 1 was $40 000. Over the next five years her income increases by 5 percent per year. At the same time, the economy experiences an inflation rate of 3 percent per year. At the end of five years, what will be Ingrid's real income?

61. Suppose that an economy were to experience zero economic growth, but the amount of cyclical unemployment dropped by 2 percent. Comment on the change in the GDP gap.

Web-Based Activities

1. Economists spend a great deal of time researching the costs and benefits of inflation. Go to **www.bank-banque-canada.ca/english/res/tr83-e.htm** and download the report. Skim over and summarize what the author believes the costs and benefits of inflation to be.

2. Canada's unemployment rate has persistently been higher than that of the United States. Go to **www.csls.ca/new/cpp.html** and read the article written by W. Craig Riddell and Andrew Sharpe. Explain why our unemployment rate is higher than the U.S. rate.

CHAPTER FIVE

Aggregate Demand and Supply

LEARNING OBJECTIVES

This chapter will enable you to:

- **LO1** **Understand the concept of potential GDP.**
- **LO2** **Explain what is aggregate supply.**
- **LO3** **Understand the concept of aggregate demand.**
- **LO4** **Explain the concept of macroeconomic equilibrium.**
- **LO5** **Understand the causes of recessions and inflationary booms.**

What's ahead...

This is an important chapter in which we develop the AD/AS model and look at the factors which explain changes in the level of GDP. In later chapters, we will use this model extensively to examine various economic policies and problems. In this chapter we look separately at how aggregate demand and aggregate supply are determined and then explain the factors that cause them to change and how this will affect the economy. Finally, through the eyes of two opposing schools of thoughts, we look at the question of whether the economy is self-adjusting or needs the active intervention of government.

A QUESTION OF RELEVANCE...

Which of the following acts do you think will improve economic conditions more: you buy a new CD player for $300, or you increase your work productivity effort by 20 percent? Aside from your obvious objection that neither act will have much impact on the whole economy, you probably would opt for the second one, since it seems to involve real production. After all, if we all became 20 percent more productive at our work, then the economy would surely be more wealthy than if people simply bought more things. Surprisingly, in the short run, the two acts will have about the same effect on the economy. In the longer run, however, a sustained productivity increase will make for a healthier economy.

In Chapter 4, we looked at how economic growth, unemployment, and inflation are measured and briefly discussed some of the problems related to these issues. In this chapter, we want to get a bit more analytical and develop a model that will help us understand the causes of these problems. As we shall see, economic growth, inflation, and unemployment are all inter-related and in order to understand one we need to understand all three. Our model of aggregate demand/aggregate supply will do that for us.

As we are all aware, the level of production and real GDP in Canada has risen over time. The reasons for this are not complicated. The size of the labour force grows, the amount of capital stock in the economy grows and, most importantly, there are continuous advances in the level of technological knowledge. However, it would be a mistake to assume that production and real GDP rise at a steady rate or even that they rise each and every year. In fact, in some years firms find that their sales fall off and they need to cut their level of production. This leads to lay-offs, rising rates of unemployment, and falling levels of incomes. When this happens we say that the economy is in a recession. In other years, firms might well experience exactly the opposite set of circumstances with rising levels of sales, increased production, and additional hiring, which lead to falling rates of unemployment, and rising levels of income. We can recognize, then, that there is underlying trend which is pushing up production and incomes but at the same time there are short term fluctuations which sometimes push the economy beyond this trend (an economic boom) and sometimes below this trend (an economic recession). We shall begin developing our model by looking at this long-term upward trend.

5.1 Potential GDP

LO1
Understand the concept of potential GDP.

In the last chapter, we defined economic growth as an increase in an economy's real GDP per capita. Although this is the definition used by Statscan to measure economic growth, many economists prefer to define economic growth as an increase in the economy's *capacity* to produce. This refers to the maximum level of production the country is capable of producing, assuming that it is at full employment. In other words, it is the amount of GDP that would be produced if all of its labour and all other resources were fully employed (at normal levels of utilisation). This is what is meant by **potential GDP**. It could also be called full-employment GDP or economic capacity. (Some economists refer to it as the long-run aggregate supply or LAS.) In this sense, potential GDP can be looked at as the amount of GDP when the economy is at its natural rate of unemployment, i.e., when there is no cyclical unemployment.

potential GDP: the total amount that an economy is capable of producing when all of its resources are being fully utilized.

In emphasizing potential rather than actual GDP, economists are making the point that without increases in potential GDP, the prospects for sustained growth in the future are limited. In a sense, economists are making a distinction between actual growth in the present and sustainable growth in the future. This distinction can be illustrated by way of the following production possibilities diagram. In **Figure 5.1A**, production possibilities curve PP1 shows the maximum quantities of capital and consumer goods that this economy is presently capable of producing.

FIGURE 5.1 **Economic Growth and Production Possiblilities**

Figure A shows the economy growing from point A to point B. But this growth may not be sustained, since its potential level (the PP curve) has not changed. Figure B shows similar economic growth from point A to point B. But in this case the growth is more likely to be sustained, since its potential has similarly increased (from PP1 to PP2).

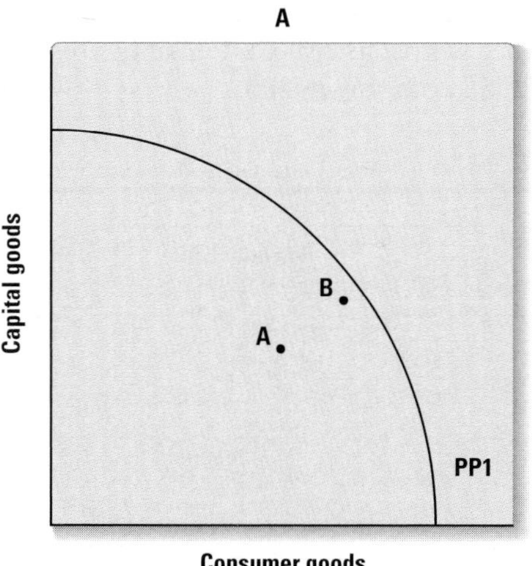

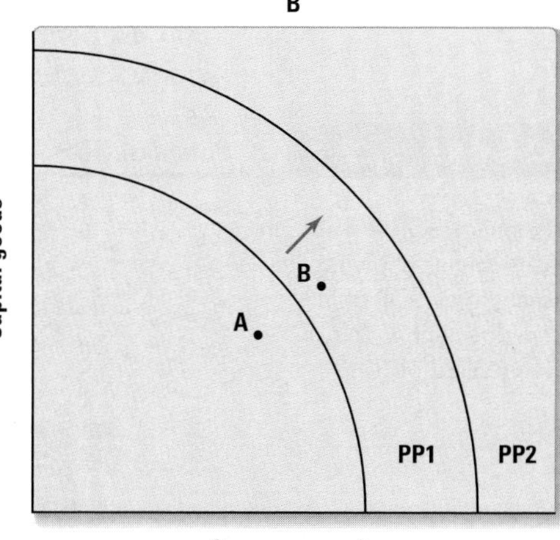

You will recall that the curve itself does not show what the economy is actually producing nor what it would like to produce (there is no indication of demand), it merely shows what it is capable of producing, i.e., its potential levels of production. Let's assume that initially this economy is producing at point A in **Figure 5.1A**, and since this is inside the curve, it is producing less than it is capable of. In the following year, let us suppose that the economy increases its output of both capital and consumer goods, as depicted in the movement to point B. The economy has experienced economic growth and is now close to its potential output. Since an economy cannot (permanently) go beyond its production possibilities boundary, the amount by which it can increase production past point B is very small. Now contrast this to the situation in **Figure 5.1B**. Here, point A is the same starting point shown in **Figure 5.1A** and the movement to point B is also the same. However, we also see that the production possibilities curve has shifted from PP1 to PP2, which indicates an increase in the economy's potential GDP. Obviously, the prospects for future growth in this case are much brighter. Economists would be more impressed by the growth depicted in **Figure 5.1B**, since not only is the economy producing more, it is also *capable* of sustaining this level of production in the future.

ADDED DIMENSION

Economic Capacity

To economists, the idea of capacity can only be understood with reference to costs. Capacity does not literally mean the absolute maximum that can be produced in the short run. Firms can and do produce at a level of literal full physical capacity from time to time, but it is a very expensive proposition in terms of overtime pay, high maintenance costs, and so on. Such high costs could not be sustained in the long run. Capacity, then, means the output level at which the firm can produce at the lowest per unit cost, and this level may well be at only 70, or 80, or 90 percent of the physical capacity of the plant.

The ideas we have just presented can easily be shown in terms of a demand/supply diagram. On the vertical axis of **Figure 5.2**, we show the price level for the economy in terms of a GDP deflator. The horizontal axis shows the total output of all finished goods and services in the economy, in other words, its real GDP. The figures shown here are the approximate numbers for the Canadian economy in 2001.

FIGURE 5.2 **Potential GDP**

Potential GDP is a straight vertical line showing the amount of GDP at full employment. In 2001, it equalled 1030.

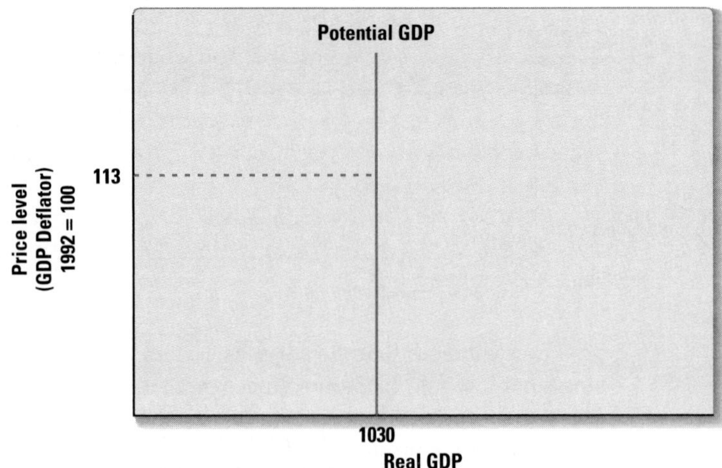

In this year, Canada's potential real GDP was approximately $1030 billion and this figure is unaffected by the price level (which was, in 2001, equal to 113). The vertical nature of the potential GDP curve illustrates the fact that while a higher price level would raise nominal GDP, it would leave potential real GDP unaffected. Put another way, what an economy is physically capable of producing is not affected by the prices those goods and services happen to be sold at. Bear in mind that potential GDP is merely a benchmark—albeit an important one—and doesn't tell us what the economy is actually producing or even what policy makers might want it to produce. We will look at actual production a little later.

Next, we want to address the question of what makes an economy grow, i.e. what will cause an increase in an economy's potential real GDP? Graphically, this is a rightward shift in potential GDP and is, in many ways, analogous to asking: what factors will enhance (shift out) a country's production possibilities?

Sources of Economic Growth

Let us start with the most obvious source of economic growth—people themselves. Since labour is one of the most important resources, then an increase in the size of the labour force, caused by either a higher population or a higher participation rate, will enable a country to produce more. But we must not get carried away with the idea that an increase in working population will by itself guarantee economic growth. If that were so, then the world's most populous countries, China and India, would also be its most economically developed.

In reality, there is a growing consensus among economists that the *quality of an economy's labour resources* is the prime source of economic growth. A highly educated population results in a labour force that is both mobile and adaptable. As the world moves into the twenty-first century, these traits of mobility and adaptability are becoming more and more important. We are witnessing a shift in the paradigm (that is, the fundamental pattern) of what is important for an economy to be successful.

Between 100 and 200 years ago, today's successful economies shifted internally from an emphasis on agriculture to one on manufacturing. Tomorrow's successful economies are already in the process of a shift from a manufacturing base to an information–communications base, in which the whole world is "the market." The areas in which new jobs are being created are changing—in fact, the definition and nature of work is also experiencing a paradigm shift. Gone are the days when a high-school graduate could step into a job at the local mill and earn, for a lifetime, an above-average income. Young people today will probably change careers three or four times in their working life, and training and education, both formal and self-taught, will be essential. Thus, the need to educate, and not just train, young people becomes increasingly important. And what of the older workers who have been laid off from the mills, which are now moving to other parts of the world? Here, we see the need for some form of retraining and encouragement to relocate. The old words to describe a high-quality labour force might have been "hard-working and dedicated." The new words are likely to be "smart, mobile, and adaptable."

labour productivity: a measure of the amount of output produced per unit of labour input (per unit of time).

human capital: the accumulated skills and knowledge of human beings.

What we are driving at in this discussion is a very important concept that economists call productivity. **Labour productivity** is the output per unit of labour input during a specific time period:

$$\text{Labour productivity} = \frac{\text{output per period}}{\text{units of labour}}$$

As an example, assume that 100 workers produce 6000 tonnes of paper in a week. Here, labour productivity would be 60 tonnes per unit of labour or per worker. If, in three years, that figure rises from 60 to 70 tonnes per worker, there has been an increase in labour productivity. To a large extent, economic growth is about just such increases in productivity. But as the nature of work changes, just what is regarded as productive, and what isn't, also changes. Within the already industrialized countries of the world, output per unit of the mill worker is becoming less important, compared with the creativity of computer programmers, product designers, and organizational managers. All this brings a whole new meaning to the term "labour quality." This last point emphasizes the importance of what economists call **human capital**, which is defined as the accumulated skills and knowledge of human beings. An economy with a government that encourages human capital investment with well-funded and innovative education and training efforts, combined with a population that embraces the desire to improve its accumulated skills and knowledge, will be an economy with bright growth prospects.

CP/Ryan Remiorz

Chief executive James Nininger and chief economist Jim Frank from the Conference Board of Canada discuss the economic outlook of Canada on October 15, 1998. The report called for increased productivity if Canadians were to maintain their standard of living.

A second fundamental source of economic growth is the amount of physical capital available within the economy. A worker with a mechanical backhoe will move more earth in a day's work than a worker with a hand shovel could in a week. Thus, an economy with a *higher capital–labour ratio* will be an economy with higher labour productivity.

Increasing the amount of capital stock in an economy is a direct result of more investment spending, which can be defined as a physical increase in the economy's plant and equipment. Canada has one of the highest capital–labour ratios in the world, and this, along with our rich endowment of natural resources, has resulted in relatively high labour productivity in past years. However, again, things are now changing so fast that we cannot continue to rely on huge machines or natural resources to provide us with continued economic growth.

The third source of economic growth is *technological change*. Here, we are referring not just to more machines (capital) but better machines, not just to finding more natural resources but finding and extracting them more efficiently. Technological change often involves better machines and equipment and always involves better methods of production, better ways of organizing work, and better ways of solving problems—in short, becoming more productive. A society that fosters and embraces technological change will soon be far ahead of one that does not. To some extent, this involves the attitudes of people as much as it does the brainpower that a society has at its disposal. Technological change can also be stimulated by spending, in both the public and the private sectors, on research and development—something that the Japanese have done more than any other society.

Finally, it is important to mention that the amount and quality of an economy's *natural resources* can be a source of growth. Canada is richly endowed in this area, and that does make growth easier. This was particularly true in the early development of this country, in which beaver, fish, lumber, grain, and minerals played a significant role in growth. But we should not assume that a rich endowment of natural resources by itself ensures economic growth—think of Brazil with its rich endowment and poor growth record. Nor should we assume that a poor endowment means no growth—witness Japan, which has practically no natural resources but a fantastic growth record.

In summary, the sources of economic growth for an economy are:

- the quality of its labour resources (the level of human capital)
- the amount of capital available
- the rate of technological change
- the amount and quality of its natural resources

What causes economic growth is a fascinating topic that can extend to almost all aspects of economics. We have given you just a bare outline of what is involved. We hope that it is enough to leave you with a sense of its importance.

ADDED DIMENSION

Robinson Crusoe and Economic Growth

Let's assume that Robinson Crusoe, the celebrated fictional castaway, is troubled by the prospects of making it on his own for an indefinite period of time on his new-found, uninhabited island. He obviously needs to catch a lot of fish to do more than just survive. He has a crude fishing pole and has been catching the odd fish recently, but he wonders if there isn't a better way to catch more and thus improve his standard of living. Perhaps there is another location on the island, where the fish are more plentiful, bigger, and easier to catch. But spending time looking for another place would leave less time for his current fishing efforts. Alternatively, he could stay where he is and hope that his fishing skills improve with experience and persistence (he curses the day he chose a course in Chinese cooking rather than a fishing class at night school). Finally, there is the possibility of fashioning a crude net or even building a boat, but, again, either of these activities would take time away from actual fishing. He has three choices in trying to improve his economic well-being:

- increase the resources available to him (find a better fishing spot)
- improve his productivity (become a better fisher through experience)
- increase his physical capital (a net or a boat rather than just a pole)

Each of these choices requires that he sacrifice time and the fish that would be caught during this time (consumption), but in return promises a richer harvest of fish in the future. In effect, every economy faces the same choices and sacrifices, because economic growth involves more effort, less leisure, and less *present* consumption. The rewards, however, can be great and continue to pay off long into the future.

SELF-TEST

1. Given the following information:

Year	Output	Labour Input
2000	12 600 tonnes	1000 units
2001	13 860 tonnes	1050 units

Calculate labour productivity (to one decimal place) per unit in both years. Approximately what percentage increase in labour productivity has occurred?

Figure 5.3 illustrates the growth in potential GDP graphically.

FIGURE 5.3 **Economic Growth and Potential GDP**

A positive change in any of the determinants of economic growth will result in a rightward shift of the potential GDP curve.

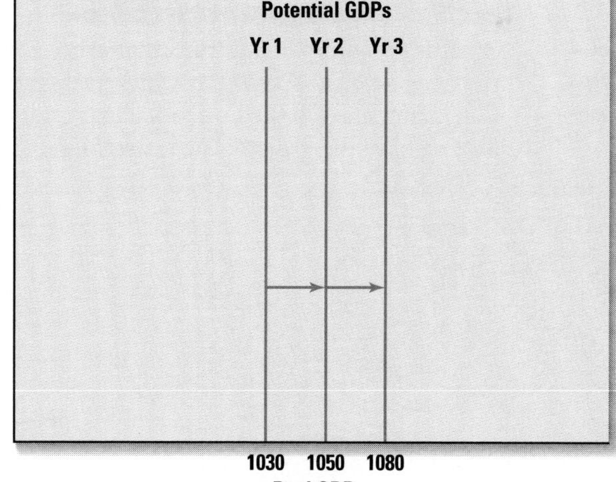

The result of a change in any one of the factors just discussed would increase the economy's potential to produce. In **Figure 5.3**, potential GDP has increased from $1030 in Year 1 to $1050 in Year 2 to $1080 in Year 3. This is illustrated by a rightward shift in the Potential GDP levels.

Economic Growth and the Business Cycle

Although Statscan does not measure or record potential GDP on a regular basis, evidence suggests that it tends to increase by small, regular amounts each year. Research indicates that for Canada, potential GDP grew by about 3 percent each year in the 1990s.

On the other hand actual economic growth is seldom so smooth and steady. **Table 5.1** shows the annual growth in actual real GDP for Canada for 1988 to 2001.

TABLE 5.1 Canada's Rate of Growth in Real GDP

Year	% Growth Rate of Real GDP
1988	5.0
1989	2.4
1990	–0.2
1991	–1.8
1992	0.6
1993	3.8
1994	4.5
1995	2.8
1996	1.7
1997	4.0
1998	3.1
1999	4.2
2000	4.5
2001	1.5

Source: Adapted from Statistics Canada, CANSIM Database, Matrices 6547 and 6544.

The average annual rate of growth for the period is 2.6 percent. As you can see from the data, however, the actual growth rate was nowhere near a steady 2.6 percent *each* year. This is true for most periods and most economies. In any period such as this, some years will have high growth rates, say 5 or 6 percent, while other years will have rates below average or negative. While the *average* long-run growth *rate* is positive for most economies, the year-to-year fluctuations can be quite unstable. In short, all economies experience **business cycles**. What is meant by this term is that every economy goes through expansionary and contractionary phases in the rate at which real GDP changes. **Figure 5.4** illustrates this point using Canadian data. On the horizontal axis we have time, starting with 1988, while on the vertical axis we have the growth rate (in real GDP).

business cycle: the expansionary and contractionary phases in the growth rate of real GDP.

FIGURE 5.4 The Business Cycle

The rate of growth in real GDP reflects two contractionary phases (in red) and two expansionary phases (in blue). The average annual growth rate for the period is 2.7 percent.

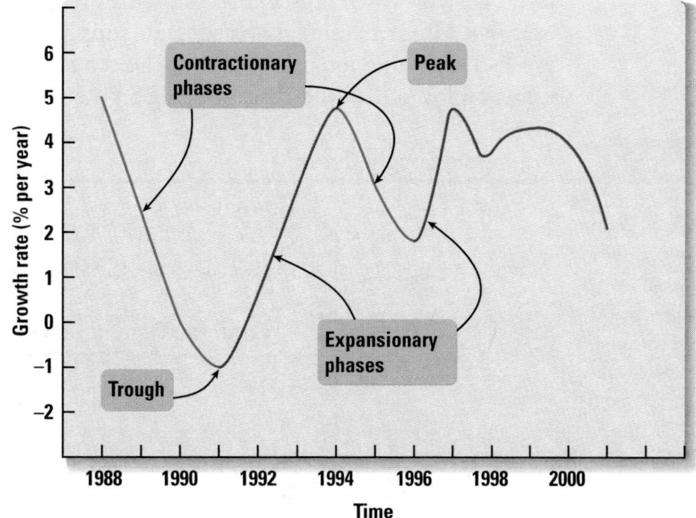

You can see that the growth rate declined in the first three years of this period (1989–91). We call this a contractionary phase. The growth rate then rose in the next three years (1992–94), an expansionary phase. Next, we have another contractionary phase, this time of two years (1995 and 1996). Finally, the growth rate again rose in 1997, which signalled the beginning of another expansionary phase. These expansionary and contractionary phases in the growth of real GDP form the business cycle—what goes up comes down, and vice versa.

In order to better understand the business cycle and explain why there are these periodic fluctuations in the economy—in all economies, not just the Canadian economy—we need to look at the forces of supply and demand that lie behind them.

5.2 Aggregate Supply

LO2
Explain what is aggregate supply.

aggregate supply: the aggregate quantity of goods and services produced by all sellers at various price levels.

Aggregate supply refers to the total quantity of goods and services that firms in the economy would be willing and able to produce at various prices. While most firms have little control over the market demand for their products, they can and do try to exercise as much control over their own supply as they can and this certainly includes their own costs, both present and future costs. They also address future costs by entering into contracts with their suppliers and with their employees (or their unions) to achieve some certainty of future resource prices and wage rates. Because of these contracts, a firm is able to increase production (and therefore demand and employ more factor services) without experiencing an increase in the costs of those resources. Therefore, what this implies is that if firms find that, as a result of increased demand, they can sell their products at a higher price, they will be only too willing to produce more (and employ more resources) since with resource costs that remain constant (at least for a while), their total profits will rise. On the other hand, lower prices represent lower profits and will cause the firm to reduce production (and employment). In other words:

The higher the price levels, the greater the aggregate quantity supplied (up to some maximum); the lower the price level, the smaller will be the aggregate quantity supplied.

The aggregate supply curve therefore is upward-sloping. However, it's unlikely to be a straight line. Or put another way, the amount by which production increases in response to an increase in the price level depends on the condition of the economy in general. For example, **Figure 5.5** shows an aggregate supply curve for the Canadian economy, labelled AS. We also show the potential GDP for the economy which indicates that if this economy were fully employed it would be producing a potential real GDP of $1050.

FIGURE 5.5 **Aggregate Supply Curve**

The shape of the AS curve depends on the condition of the economy. At low income levels, like $600 or $650, the curve is quite flat. But at income levels closer to full employment, such as at $1000, the curve becomes almost vertical.

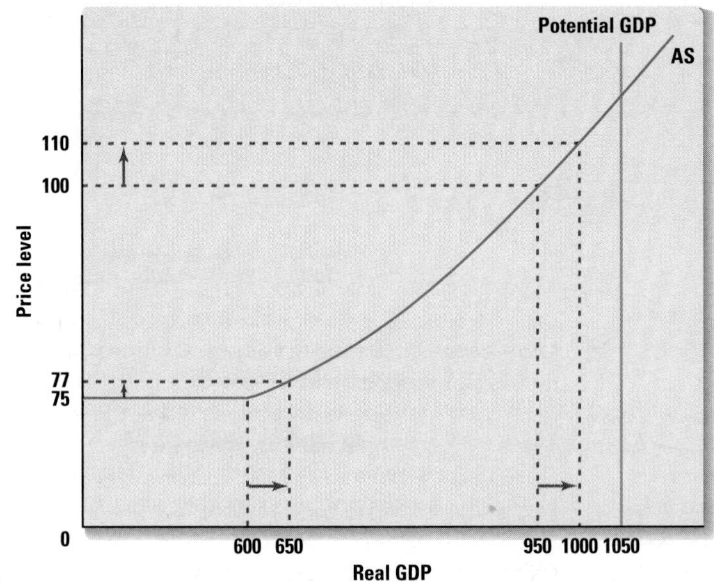

Suppose that the economy were initially in a recession, with its GDP of $600 sitting far below its potential level. In this situation, most firms do not need much of an inducement to produce more, since they are operating well below capacity and have idle equipment and machines and a portion of their labour force is probably laid off but can quickly be recalled. Thus, an increase in production can be done with little impact on the per unit cost of production, since firms are currently using the best of their inputs and, therefore, increased orders will be eagerly accepted, even if they were to receive little or no price increase. In our graph, production could be increased to $650 with only an increase in the price level of 2 points (from 75 to 77). This results in the AS curve being almost horizontal.

But what happens if the economy has recovered from the recession and is now producing a GDP of $950, not far below its potential, full-employment level of $1050? Here, productivity per worker will probably be less than when it was in a recession, because it has had to hire less experienced labour and is using older, less efficient machines. This results in the per unit cost of production rising as output is increased. Thus, firms will be willing to produce more only if the price that they receive for their output is considerably higher. In our graph, if production increases from $950 to $1000, the price level would increase by 10 points (from 100 to 110) as a result. In short, the closer the economy is to potential GDP, and the closer firms are to capacity output, the steeper the AS curve. In fact, some economists see the AS curve eventually becoming nearly vertical as the economy reaches its potential GDP.

@-CONOMICS

Is the AS Becoming Flatter?

A recent report in *The Economist* magazine suggests that there is growing opinion that the shape of the aggregate supply curve is becoming flatter as the economy approaches full employment. If true, this would be good news indeed, because it would mean that there would be less inflationary pressure as the full-employment level of output was approached. The main reason for this optimism involves the globalization of the world's economies and the rise of e-commerce. The increased competition that results from these two revolutionary trends is thought to severely restrain the ability of companies to raise prices. As a result, there is a growing recognition by business that they must generate profit by boosting efficiencies rather than prices.

5.3 Aggregate Demand

LO3
Understand the concept of aggregate demand.

aggregate demand: the total quantity of final goods and services that consumers, businesses, government, and those living outside the country would buy at various price levels.

Let us now turn our focus to **aggregate demand**, which is the total quantity of goods and services that people are willing to buy at different price levels. Its components are already familiar to you: consumption expenditures, investment spending, government purchases of goods and services, and net exports.

Figure 5.6 shows an aggregate demand curve which illustrates the output of goods and services that people will buy at various price levels. We have labelled the horizontal axis real GDP and indicated the particular level at different prices as Y_1, Y_2, etc. This reflects the fact that the value of production (real GDP) and the level of real income are always equal, as you learned in Chapter 3. The vertical axis is labelled price level and you can think of this as the value of the GDP deflator—the weighed composite of prices for all goods and services. At price level P_1, real GDP is Y_1. At a lower price level, P_2, real GDP is higher, as seen in Y_2. Similarly, at price level P_3, real GDP is Y_3.

FIGURE 5.6 **The Aggregate Demand Curve**

As the price level drops from P_1 to P_2 and to P_3, the quantity of goods and services that buyers are willing and able to purchase increases from Y_1 to Y_2 and to Y_3.

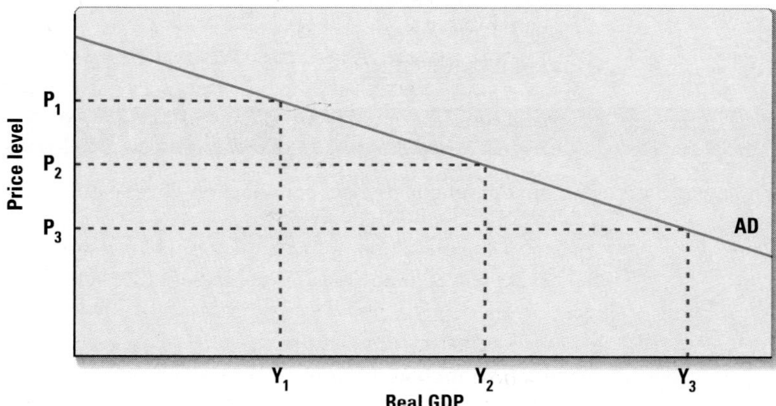

Now, we need to understand why aggregate spending is lower when the price level is higher, i.e., why the AD curve is downward-sloping. To most people, whether or not they have studied economics, one possible explanation seems fairly straightforward: if the price level goes up, people will simply buy less. But we need to be very careful here since microeconomics suggests that one of the reasons for this is that people would substitute other products for the now more expensive ones. However, here we are looking at the average price level of *all* goods and services, and there are no substitutes for *all goods*. The other reason for the downward slope that we remember from microeconomics is that with higher prices, people simply cannot afford as much. However, this explanation is equally invalid because higher prices also means that total incomes must also rise, since someone must be receiving the benefit of the higher prices.

The centre of our focus needs to be on the level of real GDP. If the price level were to go up, then the measured value of nominal expenditures, and *nominal* GDP, would increase proportionately. However, the values of both *real* GDP and real consumption would remain unchanged. Therefore, what we need to work out is the effect on spending if both the price level and nominal incomes rise by the same proportion, so that real income remains the same. You might suggest that under these circumstances, expenditures may well remain unchanged. However, one portion of wealth which is affected by a price change is the real value of savings, which will decline as the price level rises. This is called the **real-balances effect**. Lower real wealth will cause people to cut down on spending. So a higher price level leads to lower real wealth, lower consumption, and lower aggregate expenditures and, therefore, will produce a lower level of real GDP. In **Figure 5.6**, therefore, a higher price level like P, will lead to a lower real GDP, Y_1. A lower price level will produce the opposite results: it will cause real balances and consumption spending to increase, as we can see in the combination of P_3 and Y_3.

real-balances effect: the effect that a change in the value of real balances has on consumption spending.

interest-rate effect: the effect that a change in prices, and therefore interest rates, has upon investment; for example, higher prices cause higher interest rates, which leads to lower investment.

foreign-trade effect: the effect that a change in prices has upon exports and imports.

We have now established that the aggregate demand curve is downward-sloping because consumption expenditures are inversely related to the price level. There are two other additional explanations for the downward-sloping aggregate demand curve. First, a higher price level tends to push up interest rates, which in turn causes a reduction in investment spending and, therefore, aggregate expenditures. This is known as the **interest-rate effect**. In addition, higher Canadian prices make our exports less attractive while at the same time making imports more appealing to Canadians. This is called the **foreign-trade effect**. We will examine both of these effects in detail in later chapters. So, in addition to lower levels of consumption, higher prices cause a drop in investment spending and in net exports. Lower prices will, of course, have the opposite effect. In summary, the aggregate demand curve is downward-sloping because of the:

- real-balances effect
- interest-rate effect
- foreign-trade effect

SELF-TEST

2. Explain how a drop in the price level could affect consumption, investment, and net exports.

5.4 Macroeconomic Equilibrium

LO4
Explain the concept of macroeconomic equilibrium.

Macroeconomic equilibrium exists when the quantity of aggregate demand equals the quantity of aggregate supply. Only at one price level will the total that people want to buy equal the total that is produced. This is illustrated in **Figure 5.7A**, where P_1 and Y_1 are the equilibrium values for the price level and real GDP.

FIGURE 5.7 **Macroeconomic Equilibrium**

Equilibrium exists where the aggregate demand and the aggregate supply curves intersect. This determines the equilibrium price level P_1 and the equilibrium real GDP level Y_1, as seen in Figure 5.7A. In Figure 5.7B, P_2 is a price level above equilibrium, and there is a surplus of goods and services. In this circumstance, firms will be forced to cut prices. At prices below equilibrium, as seen by P_3 in Figure 5.7C, there is a shortage, which will force the price level up.

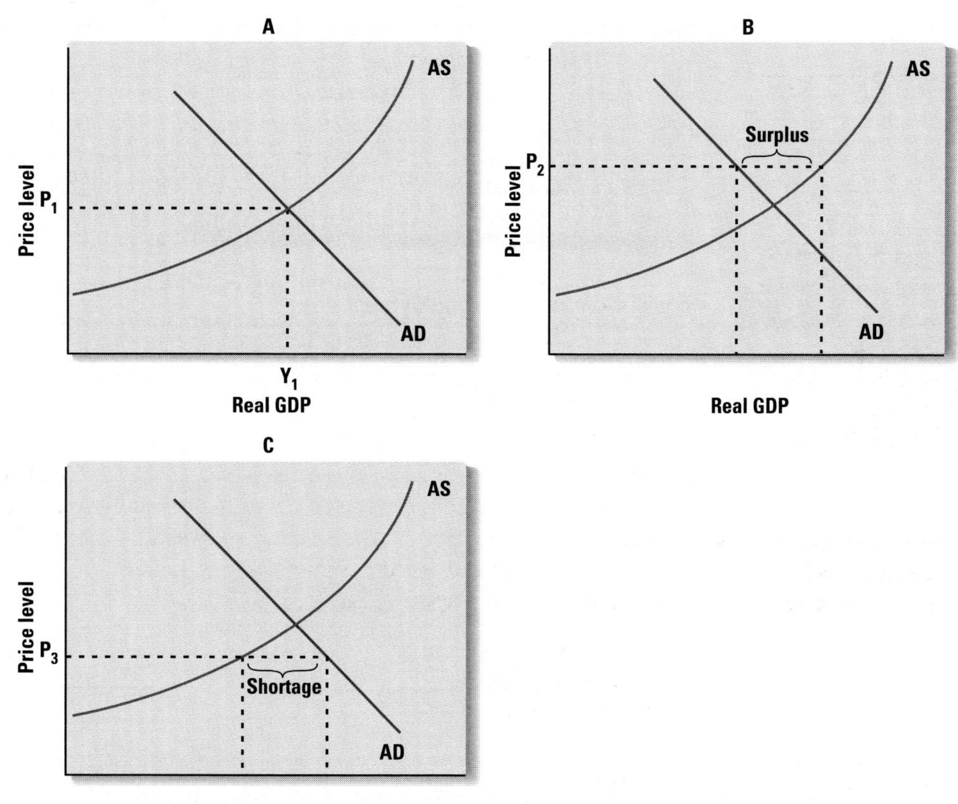

macroeconomic equilibrium: a situation in which the quantity of real GDP demanded equals the quantity of real GDP supplied.

Only at price level P_1 are the quantity demanded and quantity supplied equal. It is possible that the price level, temporarily, may not be at equilibrium, but if this is the case it is an unstable situation. This is illustrated in **Figure 5.7B**, where the price level is above equilibrium at P_2. At this higher price level there is a surplus of goods and services, because the quantity supplied exceeds the quantity demanded. To rid themselves of such surpluses, firms will be forced to cut prices and will continue to do so until the price level is back to equilibrium. In contrast, a lower price level of P_3, as seen in **Figure 5.7C**, would result in a shortage of goods and services, and prices would be pushed up until the economy is back at equilibrium, with neither surpluses nor shortages.

SELF-TEST

3. Following are the aggregate demand and supply schedules for the economy of Tagara:

Price Index	Aggregate Quantity Demanded	Aggregate Quantity Supplied
90	$1200	$950
95	1150	1025
100	1100	1100
105	1050	1150
110	1000	1190
115	950	1220

a) What is the equilibrium level of prices and real GDP?

b) If the price level were 95, would there be a shortage or surplus? How much? What if the price level was 115?

It is important to point out that there's no guarantee that equilibrium also means that the economy is operating at its potential (capacity) full-employment level of GDP. In fact, equilibrium could exist at any level of real GDP, as **Figure 5.8A**, **B**, and **C** illustrates.

FIGURE 5.8 **Equilibrium and Full Employment**

Figure 5.8A shows an economy in equilibrium, and this equilibrium is also at full employment. In other words, the AD and AS curves intersect at potential GDP. Figure 5.8B shows equilibrium occurring below full employment; that is, there is a recessionary gap. In Figure 5.8C, equilibrium occurs above full employment; that is, there is an inflationary gap.

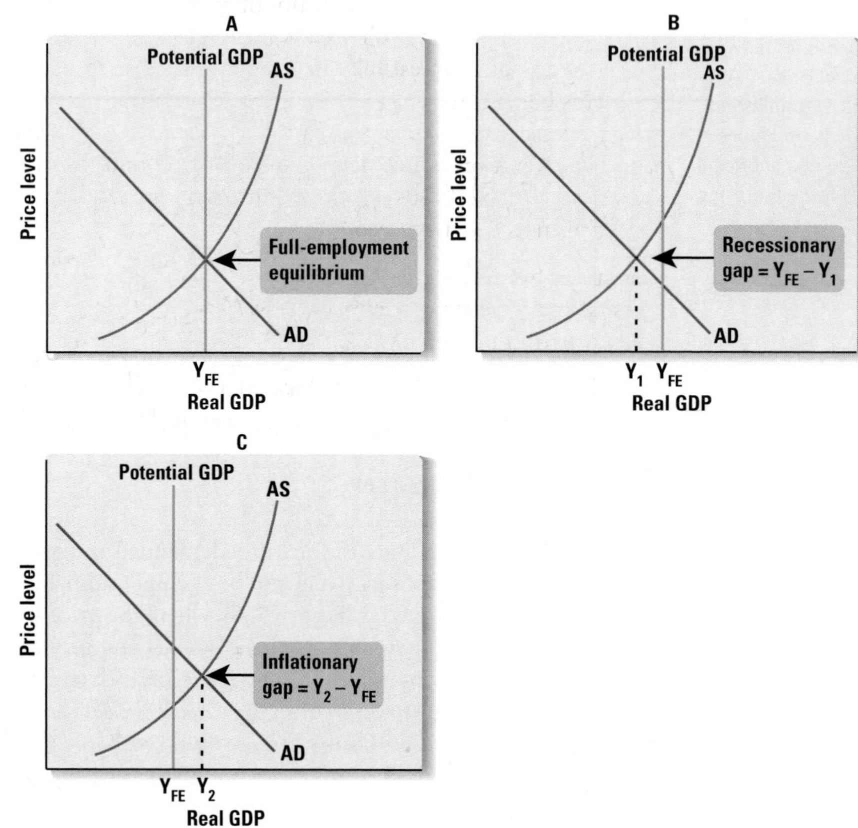

This figure shows three possible positions for an economy. In **Figure 5.8A**, the economy is in equilibrium because the quantity of aggregate demand is equal to the quantity of aggregate supply. In addition, this economy is also at potential GDP. In **Figure 5.8B**, the economy is suffering a **recessionary gap** because, while it too is in equilibrium (the AD curve intersects the AS curve at the level of real GDP, Y_1), this equilibrium is below potential GDP, Y_{FE}. A recessionary gap implies that some of the factors of production are unemployed. In most people's minds, therefore, recession and unemployment are synonymous. Keynes felt that this was the type of situation in which many economies found themselves in the 1930s. The economies of North America were in a sense caught in a low-level trap. Unemployment was high and production was low, but there was no incentive for firms to produce more because they were barely selling what they produced. Despite this recessionary gap, the economy was stable because there was no tendency, and no incentive, to change.

recessionary gap: the difference between actual real GDP and potential real GDP when the economy is producing below its potential.

Figure 5.8C shows the opposite situation. Here again the economy is in equilibrium at a real GDP level of Y_2, but the equilibrium occurs above the full-employment potential GDP. In this situation, unemployment is below its natural rate, which means that labour is scarce relative to the demand for it. This is the situation of an **inflationary gap**. People are trying to buy more goods and services than the economy can produce on a sustainable basis. The level of aggregate demand, indicated by Y_2, exceeds the level of sustainable potential output. The result is a situation that could be termed "too much spending chasing too few goods" but is often erroneously described as "too much money chasing too few goods." We, however, know that money is a stock and spending is a flow, and we must be careful how we state things. Certainly, in such a situation, prices and wages will start to increase, but it may not have anything to do with the amount of money in the economy. What is certainly true is that the amount of spending is in excess of the economy's present ability to produce goods. Such a situation is going to result in buyers bidding up prices in an effort to secure what they want and firms being forced to pay higher wages to attract labour, which is in high demand. Such price increases are, of course, inflationary, and the gap between Y_2 and Y_{FE} is the inflationary gap. This situation is not stable, since the economy simply cannot continue to produce a level of real GDP above its full-employment level on a sustained basis. In summary, equilibrium in the macroeconomy might:

inflationary gap: the difference between actual real GDP and potential real GDP when the economy is temporarily producing an output above full employment.

- occur at full employment
- result in a recessionary gap
- result in an inflationary gap

What we need to do now is look at how these various situations come about and what will happen as a result. In other words, we need to look at the dynamics of the model.

5.5 Determinants of Aggregate Demand

Let us now consider the factors that will cause aggregate demand to change, and, therefore, the aggregate demand curve to shift. Remember that aggregate demand is simply the amount of total expenditure at various price levels. You will recall from Chapter 3 that the components of aggregate expenditures are consumption, investment, government spending on goods and services, and net exports. Anything that changes any one of these components will also change aggregate demand. We need to be very clear about the fact that we are talking about the aggregate demand curve *shifting* so we need to isolate the factors *other than a change in the levels of prices or real GDP* that change aggregate demand.

Let's start with consumption spending. How might you react if a stock that you had bought a couple of months ago suddenly doubled in value? Would you go out and buy yourself something special? If you would, your consumption level will go up despite the fact that your income and the price level have not changed. We have just isolated the first factor that can change consumption: *changes in wealth*. An increase in the nation's wealth, therefore, will cause an increase in aggregate demand, reflected in a rightward shift of the AD curve. It's interesting to note that one factor which can significantly impact on the wealth of a big segment of the population is the state of the stock market. A sudden and serious drop in stock prices can have a big impact on the real wealth of investors and as a result might cause them to curtail some of their planned consumer spending. The second factor is the age of consumer durables. For most of us, when our car gets older and begins to wear out we somehow find the means to either spend more on car repairs or maybe even buy a new car. This means that the greater the *age of consumer durables* in the economy, the more likely it is that they will be replaced, causing an increase in consumer spending. A third factor involves *consumer expectations*. As confidence in the economy's future improves, people tend to loosen the purse strings and increase their consumption.

Turning to investment spending, a primary determinant of a change in investment spending is the *rate of interest*. The reason for this is straightforward—most major investment projects are funded with borrowed money and if the cost of borrowing falls because of a decrease in the interest rate, then investment spending will increase. Once again, notice that this is true even though the level of national income or the price level has not changed. Secondly, the *purchase price and the installation, operating, and maintenance costs of the capital asset* might well be determining factors for a firm trying to decide whether or not to go ahead with a particular investment. If there is a sudden decrease in the purchase price of a new piece of equipment, many firms will be encouraged to go out and buy, thus increasing the amount of investment spending. This is especially true if their present equipment is fairly old or has been in constant use. Thus, the third determinant of investment is the *age and amount of spare capacity of the present capital stock*. A firm which already has new machinery that often sits idle is unlikely to embark on any new investment any time soon. Additionally, a firm may well be encouraged to invest if the future of the industry or the economy as whole looks bright, and will be disinclined if the future looks gloomy. Since investment spending is always postponable—unlike much of consumer spending—*business expectations* have an important role to play in determining the level of investment. Finally, *government policies and regulations*, by increasing the amount of "red tape," can often add considerably to the cost of doing business and might affect the potential profitability of investing.

An increase in investment as a result of a change in any of these factors will cause an increase in aggregate demand, reflecting a higher level of spending whatever the price level.

Three factors combine to determine the level of Canadian net exports. First is the *value of the exchange rate*. A lower Canadian dollar means that Canadian goods, in the eyes of foreigners, are cheaper and may result in more Canadian goods being sold abroad. In addition, a lower Canadian dollar will mean that Canadians will buy fewer imports because they are now more expensive. Higher exports and lower imports mean an increase in *net* exports and an increase in aggregate demand. Similarly, an *increase in the level of incomes* abroad will have the same positive effect on Canadian exports. If Americans are enjoying higher levels of income, they will spend more on consumption, including buying more Canadian goods. Third is the *price level of competitive (foreign) goods*. If the Brazilians raise the price of their short-range jet aircraft, then Bombardier Corporation will sell more of their Canadian-made aircraft.

As far as the role of the government in the economy is concerned, this is affected by a number of factors, ranging from the social and cultural standards of the people and their expectations to the political philosophy of the governing party and the amount of time left in its mandate. Its specific role in directing the economy will be reflected in changes in the government's revenue (through taxation), or in its spending, or both. As we shall see when we look at fiscal policy in Chapter 11, these changes are designed to have an impact on the amount of spending in the economy. Aggregate demand will increase as a result of a decrease in taxes (whether it is a decrease in sales taxes, income taxes, or corporate profit taxes) or an increase in spending by the government (whether on government-provided services like health or education, or on transfer payments like pensions or welfare.) In addition, as Chapter 12 will show, a change in the money supply can also affect aggregate demand, because it tends to affect interest rates. An increase in the money supply will increase aggregate demand, causing a rightward shift of the AD curve.

If any of the determinants of aggregate demand were to change, it would mean that at any given price level buyers would be willing to buy more or less goods and services than before. This is illustrated in Figure 5.9.

FIGURE 5.9 **Shifts in the Aggregate Demand Curve**

An increase in aggregate demand shifts the AD curve to the right, from AD_1 to AD_2. This means that at every price level, the quantity of goods and services demanded has increased. In contrast, a decrease in aggregate demand will shift the AD curve to the left, in this case from AD_1 to AD_3.

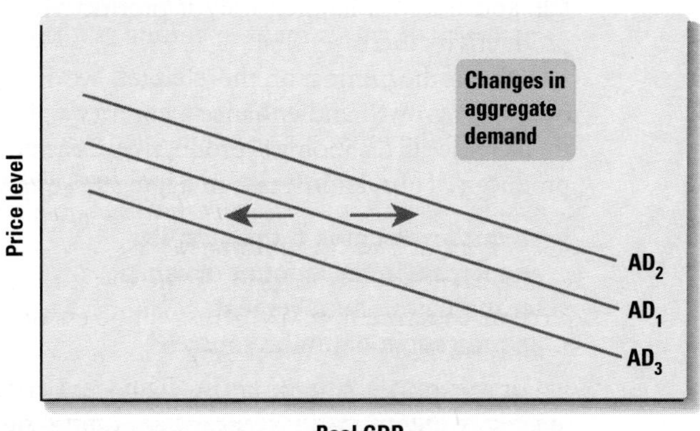

SELF-TEST

4. Which of the following factors will lead to an increase or decrease in aggregate demand (and a shift in the AD curve)?

a) A decrease in the stock market index.

b) An increase in interest rates.

c) A decrease in government spending.

d) An increase in foreign incomes.

e) A drop in the price of capital goods.

In summary, the determinants of aggregate demand are:

Consumption
- wealth
- age of consumer durables
- consumer expectations

Investment
- interest rates
- purchase price, installation and maintenance costs of capital goods
- age of capital goods and amount of spare capacity
- business expectations
- government regulations

Net Exports
- value of exchange rate
- income levels abroad
- price of competitive (foreign) goods

Government Spending and Tax Rates

Money Supply

5.6 Determinants of Aggregate Supply

We now need to work out the circumstances that would lead to an increase in aggregate supply. What factors, for instance, could lead firms to be willing and able to produce more than at present *even though the price level remains the same*? Now since firms are in business to make profits, it's clear that they will produce more at the same price only if their costs of production fall, and this will happen only if productivity increases or factor prices fall. Let us look at productivity increases first.

At the beginning of the chapter, we investigated those factors that would result in economic growth and enhance a country's potential GDP. Since each of these factors tends to increase an economy's productivity, each will in turn improve the profitability of its producers. Thus, an increase in aggregate supply will result from:

- an improvement in human capital
- an increase in the amount of capital
- technological improvement
- an increase in natural resources

Each of these factors will increase the productivity of producers. As a result, they will be able to produce at lower per unit costs and thus make greater per unit profits. Since profits are now higher, firms will be willing and able to produce more without the incentive of higher prices. In other words, if any of these four factors were to occur, it will increase aggregate supply, which means graphically, a rightward shift in the AS curve.

In summary then, if potential GDP increases, so too does aggregate supply. This is illustrated in Figure 5.10.

FIGURE 5.10 **An Increase in Aggregate Supply**

An increase in the size or the quality of the labour force, or in the amount of capital stock and natural resources, or an improvement in technology shifts the aggregate supply curve to the right. (It also equally shifts potential GDP.)

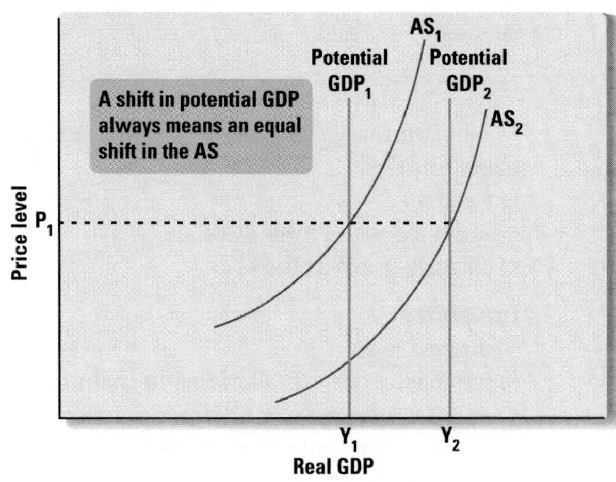

Figure 5.10 shows how, for instance, a technological improvement will increase an economy's potential GDP, shifting it from Y_1 to Y_2. In addition, technological improvements will also cut production costs and increase profits. This will cause an increase in the aggregate supply from AS_1 to AS_2.

In addition to these productivity factors, there is one other thing that will affect the aggregate supply and this is a drop in wage rates or in the prices of factor services. Lower wage rates will increase a firm's profits and lead to an increase in aggregate supply. So too will a fall in the prices of resources like oil, steel, wood—raw materials in general. This too will lead to an increase in aggregate supply. The same would be true of a fall in other costs like business taxes. On the other hand, an increase in resource prices (including wage rates) will cause profits to fall and lead to a reduction in aggregate supply. However, it is important to remember that a change in factor prices does not affect an economy's potential GDP.

SELF-TEST

5. Suppose the potential GDP for the country of Taymar is $1100 and the aggregate supply is as follows:

Price Index	Aggregate Quantity Supplied
90	$950
95	1025
100	1100
105	1150
110	1190
115	1220
120	1240

a) Plot the aggregate supply curves and show potential GDP.

b) Assume that the aggregate supply changed by $100 as a result of increased productivity. Plot the new AS curves and show potential GDP.

A change in factor prices is shown in **Figure 5.11**. This figure shows the effect of, say, a significant reduction in the prices of imported inputs such as oil. This will cause a drop in production costs in Canada and will encourage firms to produce more at the present price level. This implies a rightward shift in the aggregate supply curve from AS_1 to AS_2. Once again, since a change in factor costs has no effect on the productive capacity of the economy, there is no change in potential GDP.

FIGURE 5.11 **Change in Factor Prices**

A decrease in factor prices, such as lower prices of imported oil, for instance, will lower the costs of production and therefore shift the aggregate supply curve from AS_1 to AS_2 while leaving potential GDP unaffected.

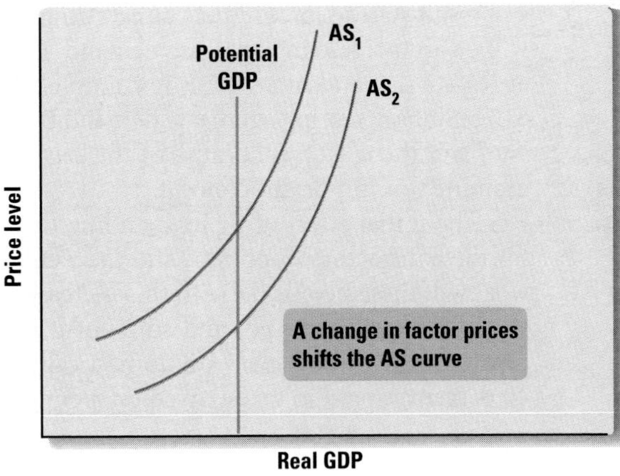

SELF-TEST

6. What effect will the following changes have on aggregate supply and on potential GDP?
   a) An increase in the price of imported crude oil.
   b) An increase in the number of immigrants entering Canada.
   c) The discovery of extensive oil deposits in northern Canada.
   d) A substantial increase in wage settlements.
   e) The introduction of a microchip that reduces computer processing time by 80 percent.

REVIEW

1. What does the term *potential GDP* mean?
2. What are the main sources of economic growth?
3. What are the main features of the business cycle?
4. What does the term *aggregate supply* mean?
5. Explain the shape of the aggregate supply curve.
6. What does the term *aggregate demand* mean?
7. What are the three reasons for the downward slope of the aggregate demand curve?
8. What does *macroeconomic equilibrium* mean?
9. Explain the three types of macroeconomic equilibria.
10. What factors will cause a change in aggregate demand?
11. What factors will cause a change in aggregate supply?

5.7 Determinants of Real GDP and the Price Level

It's now time to put this model to work and see how it explains various changes in the economy. It is clear that changes in the aggregate demand and aggregate supply can bring about changes in the price level and in real GDP, so let us take each one in turn.

A Change in Aggregate Demand

multiplier: the effect on income of a change in autonomous spending, such as I, G, X, or autonomous C.

Suppose that firms become more optimistic about future economic conditions in Canada and as a result start to loosen their purse strings and spend more on investment. The effect of this will be an increase in aggregate demand. But the important question here is: how much will aggregate demand increase? Is it a simple case of an increase in investment spending of, say, $10 billion increasing aggregate demand by the same $10 billion? The answer is, surprisingly, "no" and the reason is because of the existence of what economists call the **multiplier**. Let's examine this important concept.

The initial effect of firms spending this additional $10 billion is an increase in income for the contractors, suppliers, and their employees who provide the investment goods. And what will these people do with this increase in income? Well, some of it will be paid in taxes, some of it will be saved, and some of it will be spent on imports. However, a significant portion of it will be spent on domestically produced goods and services. Let's assume that 40 percent is paid in taxes, saved or spent on imports and 60 percent, or $6 billion, is spent on the consumption of Canadian goods and services. When this $6 billion gets spent there is a further increase in income of the same $6 billion which generates another round of tax payments, savings, import purchases, and the buying of more Canadian goods and services. This process continues, so that we get a series of income increases.

Using Figure 5.12, we can track the total increase in income which results from the initial increase in investment spending of $10 billion.

FIGURE 5.12

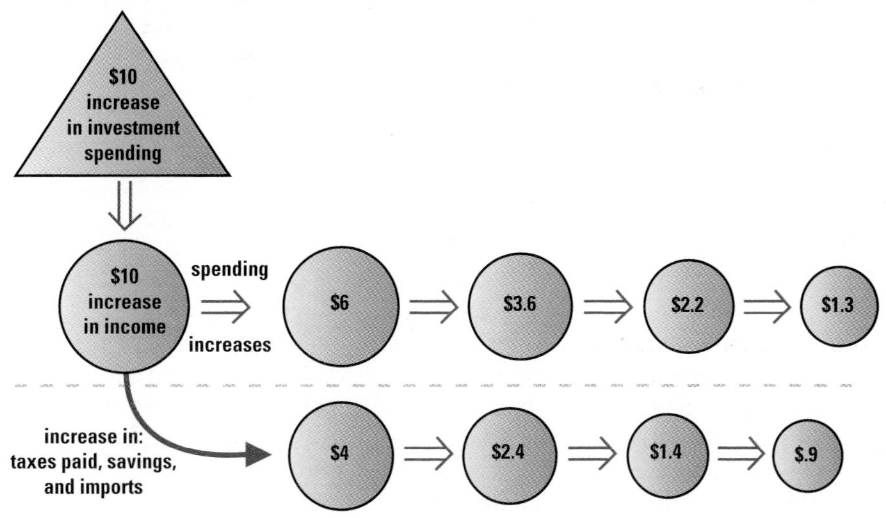

Initial round	$10.0 billion
Second round	6.0
Third round	3.6
Fourth round	2.2
Fifth round	1.3
All subsequent rounds	1.9
Total increase in income	25.0

In this example, an increase in investment spending of $10 billion will result in an increase in income of $25 billion which means a multiplier of 2.5. If the portion spent on domestic production was higher, then the value of the multiplier would be larger. On the other hand, if taxes, savings, and imports were higher, then the value of the multiplier would be smaller. Also, we should point out that while our example illustrates the effect of an increase in investment spending, increases in other types of spending, such as exports, government spending, or autonomous consumption, would have the same effect.

The concept of the multiplier can also be illustrated graphically, as is done in Figure 5.13.

FIGURE 5.13 **The Effect of an Increase in Aggregate Demand on Real GDP**

An increase in aggregate demand from AD_1 to AD_2 would result in an increase in real GDP from $800 to $825 (point *a* to *b*) if the price level did not change from its original level of P_1. However, since the equilibrium price level does rise to P_2, the increase in real GDP is smaller as seen by point *a* to *c*.

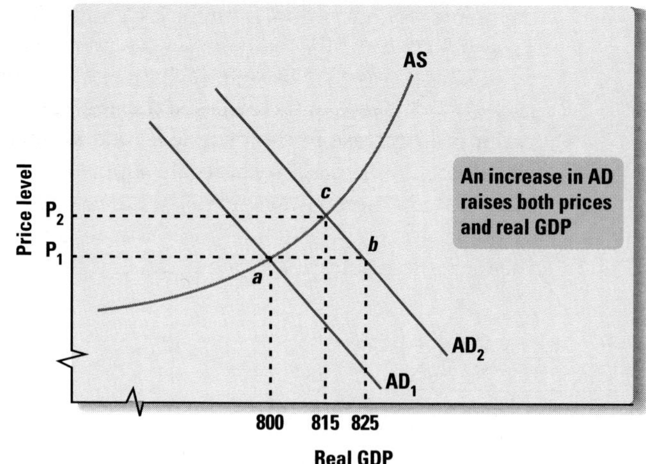

In Figure 5.13, the aggregate demand curve shifts to the right, from AD_1 to AD_2, as a result of the increase in investment spending of $10 billion. If the price level (and for that matter, interest rates) were to remain unchanged, at P_1, then a multiplier of 2.5 would result in the level of real GDP increasing from $800 to $825, as seen by the movement from point *a* to *b*. However, since the AS curve is upward-sloping, the increase in *equilibrium* real GDP will be only the movement of *a* to *c* which is from $800 to, say, $815. What we are saying here is that the multiplier will have its full effect only if the AS curve is horizontal. As we discussed earlier, this would be the case only if the economy was in an extreme recession. Normally, some of the effect of the multiplier would be cancelled out by an increase in the price level associated with any increase in demand.

SELF-TEST

7. The following table shows the aggregate demand and aggregate supply schedules for the economy of Zee:

Aggregate Quantity Demanded	Price Index	Aggregate Quantity Supplied
$1950	90	$1670
1900	95	1700
1850	100	1740
1800	105	1800
1750	110	1890
1700	115	2000

a) What are the equilibrium values of price and real GDP?

b) Assume that aggregate demand decreases by $200 at every price level. What will be the new equilibrium values of price and real GDP?

A Change in Aggregate Supply

As we have seen, a number of factors influence aggregate supply, but we want to focus on factor prices since, as mentioned, they do not affect the potential GDP. Assume for instance that the price of imported oil were to fall. **Figure 5.14** illustrates the effect of such a change. When there is a decrease in factor costs, the aggregate supply curve will shift to the right, and the result is a decrease in the price level and an increase in real GDP. Other factors that might also cause an increase in aggregate supply include a decrease in the prices of raw materials, a decrease in money wage levels, or a decrease in business taxes. If any of these factors were to move in the opposite direction, this would produce a leftward shift and, of course, have the opposite result on the price level and the real GDP. We can generalize this to say that:

Any change in the price of any of the factors of production will shift the aggregate supply curve.

FIGURE 5.14 **An Increase in Aggregate Supply**

A decrease in the price of imported oil will improve profitability, causing the aggregate supply curve to shift to the right from AS_1 to AS_2. This change will cause the price level to drop from P_1 to P_2 and the level of real GDP to increase from Y_1 to Y_2.

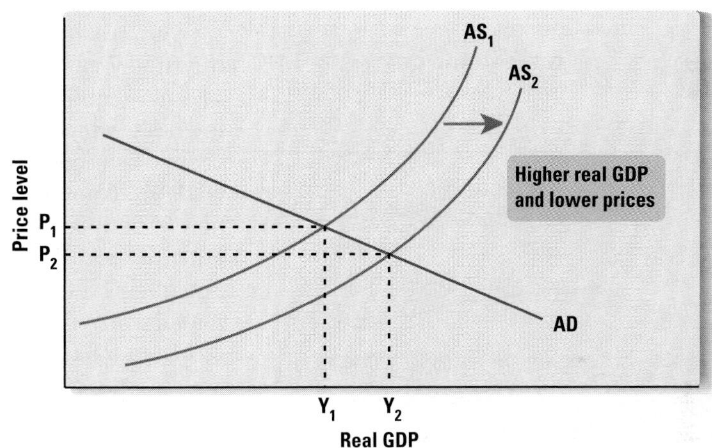

As we mentioned, a change in productivity will also lead to a change in aggregate supply. In addition, it will cause a change in potential GDP. Assume for instance that the labour-force participation rate increases, which effectively means that the size of the labour force increases. Let us examine the effect of such a change on an economy. (We assume that the economy is initially at full-employment real GDP). We know that, in this case, both the aggregate supply and potential GDP will increase simultaneously, as illustrated in **Figure 5.15**.

FIGURE 5.15 **An Increase in Aggregate Supply and Potential GDP**

An increase in the size of the labour force will shift the aggregate supply curve to the right (from AS_1 to AS_2) and also increase potential GDP. This change causes a reduction of the price level from P_1 to P_2 and an increase in real GDP from Y_1 to Y_2. The economy is now experiencing a recessionary gap; that is, the GDP is at Y_2, which is below the new potential GDP_2.

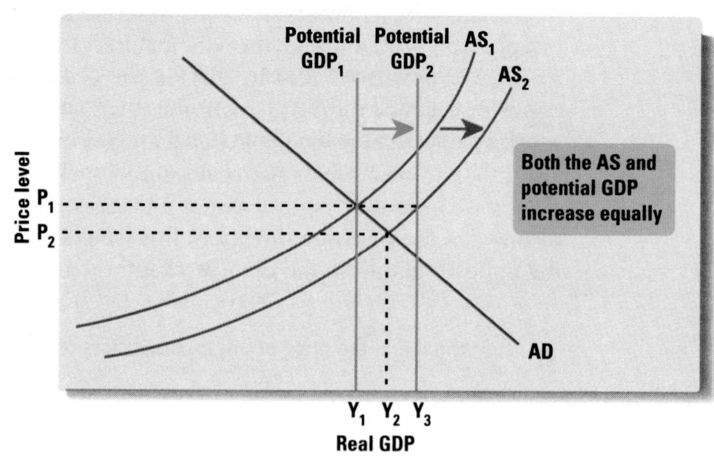

Corel

What impact would a decrease in the price of imported oil have on the aggregate supply?

As a result of the increase in the size of the labour force, the supply curve shifts to the right as does potential GDP. The new equilibrium is where the AD_1 and the AS_2 curves intersect, which is at real GDP level Y_2. The result of the change is a lower price level, P_2, and a higher level of real GDP, Y_2. Note that a recessionary gap now exists, since the new level of equilibrium real GDP is below the new level of potential real GDP, Y_3. As can be seen in **Figure 5.15**, the potential real GDP is now greater than the new output level. Actual real GDP has grown, but potential real GDP has grown more, resulting in a recessionary gap.

SELF-TEST

8. Potential GDP for the economy of Ithica is $1500. The aggregate demand and aggregate supply schedules are shown below:

Price Index	Aggregate Quantity Demanded	Aggregate Quantity Supplied
90	$1700	$1200
95	1650	1240
100	1600	1300
105	1550	1380
110	1500	1500
115	1450	1630

a) What are the equilibrium values of price and real GDP? What type of equilibrium is this?

b) Assume that an increase in productivity increases aggregate supply by $300. What will be the new equilibrium values of price and real GDP? Is there now a recessionary or inflationary gap? How much is the gap?

Is the Economy Self-Adjusting?

We have now seen what happens when there is a shift in both aggregate demand and aggregate supply. In doing this, we have seen that the economy may experience a recessionary gap as a result. We now need to ask whether the economy is doomed to remain in this situation unless it is bailed out by government intervention (as Keynes believed), or on the contrary, whether it is capable of curing itself. The answer to this depends on how well or how quickly wages and prices adjust to changing demand and supply. If they do adjust quickly—if they are totally flexible—an economy is likely to move to a full-employment situation very rapidly. At the other extreme, if prices and wages do not change at all in the short run, then a recessionary (or, for that matter an inflationary) gap is likely to last indefinitely. The view of most economists these days is that neither extreme view is valid. Although prices and wages are often inflexible in the short run, eventually they do adjust to the changing conditions of the economy. Let us explain exactly how this adjustment process works. Assume, as in **Figure 5.16**, that the economy finds itself in a recessionary-gap situation, with actual real GDP below potenital real GDP.

FIGURE 5.16 **Adjustment from a Recessionary Gap**

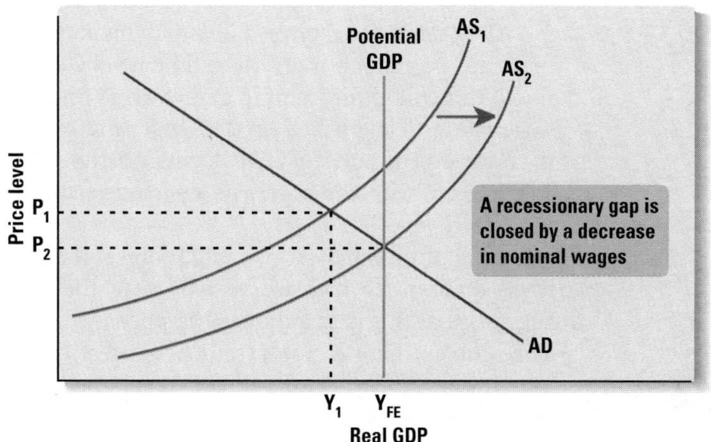

Initially, the economy is at price level P_1 and real GDP level Y_1, below the full-employment level Y_{FE}. This situation will put downward pressure on wages. As nominal wages fall, the aggregate supply curve shifts to the right until it is at AS_2. The net result will be a lower price level, P_2, and a full-employment real GDP, Y_{FE}.

The economy is currently in equilibrium at real GDP level Y_1, where the aggregate quantity demanded is equal to the aggregate quantity supplied. However, the potential level of real GDP is at Y_{FE}. In this recessionary gap situation, unemployment is above its natural rate. Firms find it easy to hire labour, and workers find it difficult to get jobs. Eventually, nominal wage levels will be forced down. Remember that aggregate supply is based on a particular unchanging level of nominal wages; that is, the wage rate is constant along the AS curve. If the nominal wage level drops, this means that the aggregate supply curve will shift rightward. As this happens, firms hire more workers, production (real GDP) increases from Y_1 to Y_{FE}, and the price level falls from P_1 to P_2. As a result of this process, the economy finds equilibrium at Y_{FE}, where the new aggregate supply curve, AS_2, intersects the aggregate demand curve. This new equilibrium is at full employment.

Let's turn to the opposite situation and work out how the economy adjusts to an inflationary-gap situation. Assume that the economy finds itself in equilibrium at real GDP level Y_3 in **Figure 5.17**.

FIGURE 5.17 **Adjustment from an Inflationary Gap**

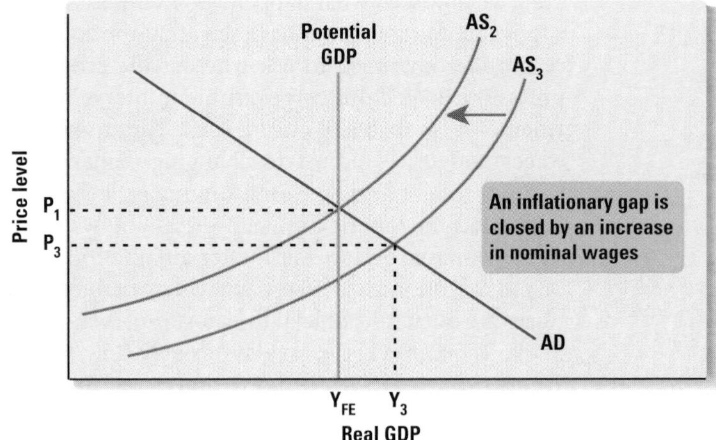

The economy is initially at equilibrium, with the AD curve intersecting AS_3 at real GDP level Y_3. With real GDP above its potential level, the unemployment rate is below the natural rate. The high demand for labour will push up nominal wage rates, causing aggregate supply to decrease and pushing the AS curve back to AS_2. The new equilibrium level of real GDP is now lower and the price level is higher than initially—price increases from P_3 to P_1.

The economy is above full employment, which means that, faced with a high demand, firms are producing more than they would consider their normal capacity output. Firms find it difficult to hire labour, and workers find it easy to get jobs. In this situation, nominal wage rates will be pushed up. This will cause the aggregate supply curve to shift left, pushing the price level up and real GDP down until the economy is back at potential (full-employment) equilibrium, with the aggregate demand curve, AD, intersecting the new aggregate supply curve, AS_2.

In all of this analysis you might object that, in the modern world, while price and wage levels do seem to increase year by year, they very seldom decrease. And yet this model suggests that this is exactly what happens when there is a surplus of production or labour. The problem here is not so much a defect of the model, but the limitation of picturing changes in terms of a two-dimensional graph. In reality, all economies are in a perpetual state of flux, with both the aggregate demand and supply constantly changing. If we could, it would be better to depict *rates of change* rather than actual changes, but then the analysis becomes unnecessarily complicated. In actuality, rather than the nominal wage level dropping, it rises, but at a slower pace than the price level.

This completes our discussion of the aggregate demand–supply model, which is the model that we will use to look at various issues in later chapters. However, it may be helpful in understanding this model to highlight in a bit more detail the disagreement between the two major schools of thought regarding the flexibility of prices and wages, which we have touched on in this chapter.

5.8 Keynesians versus the Neoclassical School

The opposing camps were the neoclassical school and the Keynesians. Although the heat has died down a little since the sometimes acrimonious debates that raged between the two in the decades following the publication of Keynes's *General Theory* in 1936, occasional flare-ups still break out. The neoclassicists generally believed that the marketplace was competitive and efficient and would adjust rapidly whenever there was a general shortage or surplus. By adjustment, they meant that prices and wages would move up or down quickly and easily to ensure full employment. In addition, the economy would always remain at its potential, full-employment level. This is illustrated in **Figure 5.18**.

FIGURE 5.18 **Neoclassical Aggregate Demand-Supply**

The neoclassical AS is synonymous with potential GDP. This means that the price level has no effect on the quantity supplied. The aggregate supply curve will always be at the full-employment level of real GDP, labelled Y_{FE}. Changes in aggregate demand, therefore, have no effect upon real GDP and affect *only* the price level. An increase in aggregate demand from AD_1 to AD_2, for instance, will increase the price level from P_1 to P_2 but will leave real GDP unaffected at Y_{FE}.

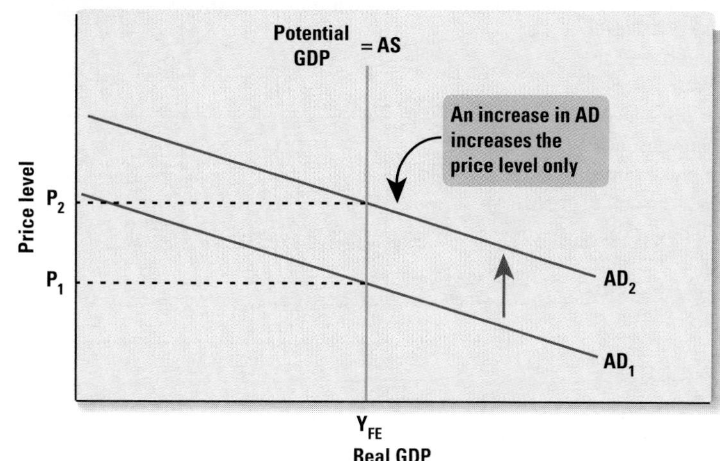

The neoclassical school believed that the aggregate supply curve is a vertical straight line at the full-employment level of real GDP, Y_{FE}; i.e., it is the same as potential GDP. The position of the curve is determined by the real variables that we discussed in reference to economic growth. The neoclassicists saw the aggregate demand curve as the normal downward-sloping demand curve. (To most neoclassical economists, the only factor that could really affect aggregate demand was the money supply.) In addition, a change in aggregate demand would leave real GDP unaffected but would most definitely cause a change in the price level. Furthermore, it is the only thing that could produce such a change. This means that neoclassical economists believed that demand–pull was the only cause of inflation. Moreover, they felt that the economy can only grow if there is a growth in the factors of production or in labour productivity. Of course, in their model, a major depression or recession is impossible.

In contrast, Keynesian economists believed that the marketplace is not very competitive because of the existence of big corporations and unions. They felt that prices and wages are, as a result, inflexible. Changes in aggregate demand, therefore, have little impact on the price level. This is shown in **Figure 5.19**.

FIGURE 5.19 **The Keynesian View of Aggregate Demand–Supply**

The aggregate supply curve, according to Keynesians, is horizontal at the prevailing price level. Changes in aggregate demand, therefore, have no effect on the price level but do cause changes in real GDP. An increase in aggregate demand from AD_1 to AD_2 will cause an increase in real GDP from Y_1 to Y_2 but leave the price level unchanged at P_1.

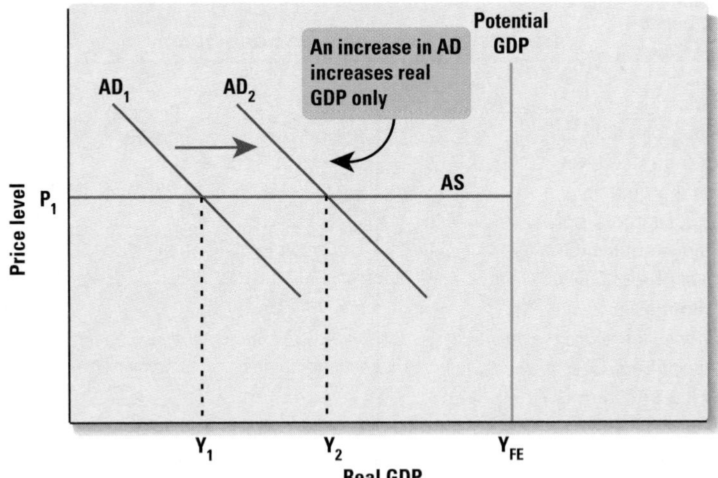

The aggregate supply curve is horizontal at the prevailing price level, P_1. Shifts in the aggregate demand can and will lead to changes in real GDP, but the price level will change little, if at all. In addition, Keynesians believe that if there is a recessionary gap, wage levels would not drop and therefore the aggregate supply curve would remain unchanged. Only if the economy were at its potential, full-employment GDP level, would changes in aggregate demand affect the price level. However, without government intervention, there is nothing to guarantee that the economy will ever be at full employment.

Looking back on this historical debate, what can we say now? In a very real sense both the neoclassical and the Keynesian positions have been vindicated by the fact that modern analysis recognizes that the AS curve can be horizontal in times of recession and becomes almost vertical at the full-employment GDP level. Thus, the essence of the debate today is the one over the self-adjustment process. If the economy can quickly adjust to recessionary and inflationary gaps, then the argument for needed government policy intervention is weakened. On the other hand, if government intervention can quicken the adjustment process, then there remains a strong argument in its favour.

SELF-TEST

9. Explain what will happen to nominal GDP and real GDP if there is an increase in aggregate demand according to:

   a) Keynesians (if the economy is below full employment);

   b) Neoclassicists.

REVIEW

1. What effect will a decrease in aggregate demand have on price and real GDP?
2. What effect will a decrease in aggregate supply have on price and real GDP?
3. Will an increase in aggregate supply produce a recessionary or inflationary gap?
4. How does the economy adjust if there is a recessionary gap? If there is an inflationary gap?
5. What is the shape of the aggregate supply curve, according to neoclassicists? According to Keynesians?

STUDY GUIDE

Review

CHAPTER SUMMARY

This chapter introduced you to the aggregate demand aggregate supply model, which is a powerful tool that can be used to better understand the causes of unemployment and inflation as well as the effects of economic growth. You have learned to use the aggregate demand curve and the aggregate supply curve to illustrate and help understand real-world events.

1. Potential GDP is the total amount that the economy is capable of producing at full employment (at the natural rate of unemployment). An increase in potential GDP is analogous to a rightward shift in the production possibilities curve.

2. Economic growth implies an increase in an economy's potential GDP and is illustrated by a rightward shift in its potential GDP line. The four sources of economic growth are:
   - improved levels of human capital (an increase in the quantity or quality of labour employed);
   - increases in capital stock;
   - technological change;
   - additional quantities of natural resources.

3. Economic growth rates are not steady, which means that economies are subject to business cycles, which refer to the periodic economic expansions and contractions that they all experience.

4. The aggregate quantity of goods and services demanded varies inversely with the price level because of the:
   - real-balances effect;
   - interest rate effect;
   - foreign-trade effect.

5. Aggregate demand will change, causing the AD curve to shift, if the money supply changes or if there are changes in any of the four components of total spending:
   - consumption spending as a result of changes in wealth, the age of consumer durables, or expectations;
   - investment spending as a result of changes in interest rate, purchase price, the age of capital goods, or expectations;
   - net exports as a result of changes in the exchange rate, income levels abroad, or the price of competitive (foreign) goods;
   - government spending on goods and services or taxes.

6. The aggregate quantity supplied varies directly with the price level because:
   - factor prices are constant and increases in the price level will raise profits resulting in producers increasing output;
   - supply will change, causing the AS curve to shift, if factor prices or any of the determinants of economic growth change;
   - the slope of the AS curve gets steeper as GDP levels approach potential GDP.

7. Equilibrium real GDP occurs when:
   - the aggregate quantity of goods and services demanded equals the aggregate quantity supplied (the AD curve intersects the AS curve).

8. Equilibrium real GDP at a level other than full employment will mean one of the following:
   - a recessionary gap which means an output level below potential GDP;
   - an inflationary gap which means an output level greater than potential GDP.

9. Modern economists say that:
   - recessionary gaps are eliminated by factor prices eventually falling and the AS curve shifting to the right;
   - inflationary gaps are eliminated by factor prices eventually rising and the AS curve shifting to the left.

10. At the heart of the historical debate between the Keynesians and neoclassicists is the question of whether the economy is capable of self-adjusting.
    - neoclassicists said the economy can adjust and any gaps will immediately disappear;
    - Keynesians said that such gaps occur often and can last indefinitely.

NEW GLOSSARY TERMS

aggregate demand 165
aggregate supply 163
business cycle 162
foreign-trade effect 166
human capital 159
inflationary gap 169
interest-rate effect 166
labour productivity 159
macroeconomic equilibrium 167
multiplier 174
potential GDP 156
real-balances effect 166
recessionary gap 169

STUDY TIPS

1. When you think about what a supply curve means, remember that it doesn't refer to the amounts that firms are actually producing *now*, but hypothetically what they would produce under certain circumstances. In particular, aggregate supply is based on what firms are *willing and able* to produce at various prices if nominal wages and other resources prices don't change. On the other hand, potential GDP has nothing to do with this willingness, but is tied totally to an economy's ability to produce. It's rather like a production possibilities curve, which shows physical amounts a country is capable of producing. It tells you nothing about what a country is actually producing. Nor does it tell you how long it will take to get there nor, for that matter, if it ever will.

2. Think of aggregate supply as having to do with profitability, and anything that affects profitability will affect it. Think of potential GDP as having to do with productivity, and anything that affects productivity will affect it. Imagine, in other words, that there is a $ sign above the supply curve. A change in nominal wages or in the price of imported resources will definitely affect profitability and therefore aggregate supply. These factors do not, however, affect a country's productive potential; that is, potential GDP.

3. A number of students will have difficulty at times disentangling those things that affect the demand side of things and those that affect the supply. As in microeconomics, it's a good idea not to get too "cute" by thinking of ways in which a change in one thing can have an impact on other factors, however remote they may be. By some esoteric reasoning it's possible to link pretty well all factors in life; in economics it is better to stick to the more obvious. Learn the things that determine aggregate demand and aggregate supply and remember that these factors affect only the demand or the supply, and not both.

Answered Questions

Indicate whether the following statements are true or false.

1. **T or F** Aggregate demand is the total quantity of final goods and services that consumers, businesses, government, and those living outside the country would buy at various different price levels.

2. **T or F** The foreign-trade effect is the effect that a change in exports and imports has on the price level.

3. **T or F** The aggregate supply curve is upward-sloping.

4. **T or F** Macroeconomic equilibrium occurs where the aggregate demand is equal to potential GDP.

5. **T or F** A change in resource prices will shift both the aggregate supply and the potential GDP curves.

6. **T or F** An increase in potential GDP has no effect on macroeconomic equilibrium.

7. **T or F** An increase in aggregate demand will cause an increase in both real GDP and the price level.

8. **T or F** An increase in wage rates will cause an increase in both real GDP and the price level.

9. **T or F** According to Keynes, the aggregate supply curve is vertical.

10. **T or F** According to neoclassicists, an increase in aggregate demand will have no effect upon real GDP but will cause the price level to increase.

Basic (Questions 11–24)

11. Why is the AD curve downward-sloping?
    a) Because production costs decline as real GDP increases.
    b) Because higher prices cause an increase in wealth which increases spending.
    c) Because lower prices cause an increase in real balances which increases spending.
    d) Because lower prices cause interest rates to increase which increases spending.

12. Why is the AS curve upward-sloping?
    a) Because firms will produce more if prices are higher, despite a lack of increase in profits.
    b) Because firms will experience higher profits at higher prices and will therefore produce more.
    c) Because aggregate demand rises with higher prices.
    d) Because the potential GDP curve is also upward-sloping.

13. Which of the following will cause the aggregate demand curve to shift to the right?
    a) A decrease in the money supply.
    b) A decrease in the interest rate.
    c) An increase in the exchange rate.
    d) A decrease in government spending.

14. When does macroeconomic equilibrium occur?
    a) When aggregate supply equals potential GDP.
    b) When the aggregate demand curve intersects the aggregate supply curve.
    c) When the aggregate demand curve intersects the potential GDP curve.
    d) When full employment occurs.

15. What could cause the level of real GDP to rise but the price level to fall?
    a) A rightward shift in the aggregate demand curve.
    b) A leftward shift in the aggregate demand curve.
    c) A rightward shift in the aggregate supply curve.
    d) A leftward shift in the aggregate supply curve.

16. What can cause an increase in potential GDP?
    a) An increase in nominal wage rates.
    b) A decrease in taxes.
    c) Technological improvement.
    d) A leftward shift in the AS curve.

17. What does the real-balances effect mean?
    a) A higher price level will lead to an increase in the rate of interest, thereby causing a decrease in consumption.
    b) A lower price level will lead to an increase in the rate of interest, thereby causing a decrease in consumption.
    c) A higher price will increase the real value of financial assets, thereby causing an increase in consumption.
    d) A higher price will decrease the real value of financial assets, thereby causing an increase in consumption.
    e) A higher price will decrease the real value of financial assets, thereby causing a decrease in consumption.

Refer to Figure 5.20 to answer question 18.

FIGURE 5.20

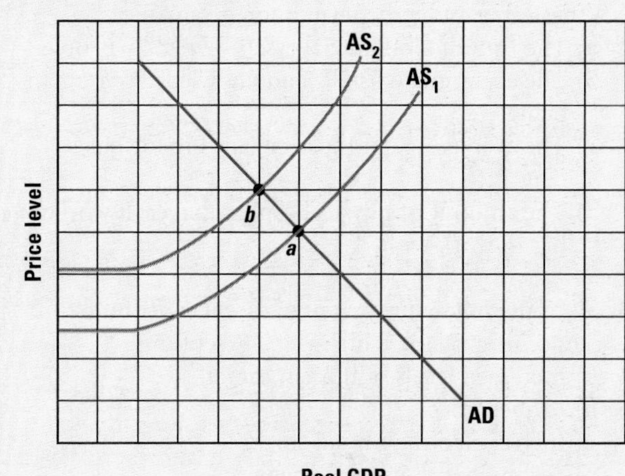

18. Refer to Figure 5.20 to answer this question. What could cause a movement from point *a* to point *b*?
    a) An increase in government spending.
    b) A decrease in labour productivity.
    c) The discovery of new oil fields.
    d) A decrease in taxes.
    e) A decrease in the prevailing nominal wage.

19. What effect will a decrease in aggregate demand have if the economy is in a recession?
    a) The price level will drop a great deal, but real GDP will fall only a little.
    b) The price level will drop a little, but real GDP will fall a great deal.
    c) The price level will drop a little, but real GDP will increase a great deal.
    d) The price level will drop a little, and real GDP will increase a little.
    e) Both the price level and real GDP will increase by the same amount.

20. If 120 workers could produce 600 widgets in a day, what is the daily productivity per worker?
a) 120.
b) 5.
c) 72 000.
d) 600.

21. What is the business cycle?
a) The periodic cycles of profits and losses that all firms experience.
b) The natural evolution of new firms growing quickly at first, then slowing and fading into obsolescence.
c) The fact that real GDP falls as often as it rises.
d) The expansionary and contractionary phases in the growth rate of real GDP.

22. What is meant by the term human capital?
a) The sum of all financial assets owned by people.
b) The accumulated skills and knowledge of human beings.
c) The average age of those engaged in formal education.
d) The amount of physical capital that each worker has to work with.

23. All of the following, except one, will contribute to economic growth. Which is the exception?
a) Increased levels of human capital.
b) Higher prices.
c) Increases in the capital stock.
d) Technological improvement.
e) Increased quantities of natural resources.

24. What are the four components of aggregate demand?
a) Consumption, investment, government spending, and net exports.
b) Consumption, investment, productivity, and net exports.
c) Consumption, investment, productivity, and human capital.
d) Potential GDP, AD, AS, and the GDP deflator.

Intermediate (Questions 25–30)

25. What effect will an increase in the Canadian price level have on trade?
a) It will increase the volume of both Canadian exports and imports.
b) It will decrease the volume of both Canadian exports and imports.
c) It will increase the volume of Canadian exports but decrease the volume of imports.
d) It will decrease the volume of Canadian exports but increase the volume of imports.

26. What is the domestic effect of an increase in the incomes of a country's major international trading partners?
a) The aggregate demand curve will shift to the right.
b) The aggregate demand curve will shift to the left.
c) The aggregate supply curve will shift to the right.
d) The aggregate supply curve will shift to the left.

Refer to **Figure 5.21** to answer questions 27 and 28.

FIGURE 5.21

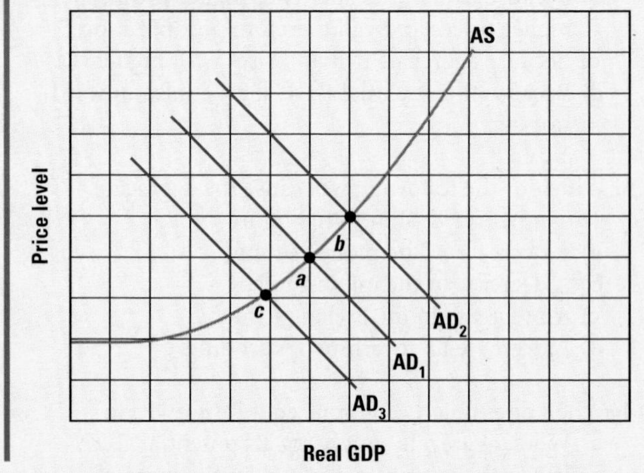

27. Refer to **Figure 5.21** to answer this question. All of the following, except one, would cause a movement from *a* to *b*. Which is the exception?
a) An increase in the price level.
b) An increase in wealth holdings.
c) An increase in government spending.
d) A decrease in the interest rate.
e) An increase in foreign incomes.

28. Refer to **Figure 5.21** to answer this question. Which of the following would cause a movement from point *a* to point *c*?
a) A decrease in the price level.
b) An increase in wealth holdings.
c) An increase in government spending.
d) An increase in the interest rate.
e) An increase in foreign incomes.

Table 5.2 shows the aggregate demand and supply schedules for the economy of Adana.

TABLE 5.2

Aggregate Quantity Demanded	Price Index	Aggregate Quantity Supplied
$800	100	$550
750	105	650
700	110	700
650	115	740
600	120	770

29. Refer to **Table 5.2** to answer this question. What are the implications if the price level is 100?
a) The price level is above equilibrium.
b) There is a shortage of real output of $250.
c) There is a surplus of real output of $250.
d) There is a surplus of real output of $150.

30. Refer to **Table 5.2** to answer this question. If the aggregate quantity demanded falls by $100 at every price level, what will be the new equilibrium price level and real output, respectively?
a) 100 and $550.
b) 105 and $650.
c) 110 and $650.
d) 115 and $500.

Advanced (Questions 31–35)

31. Refer to **Table 5.2** to answer this question. At what level of real output will full-employment occur in this economy?
a) $600.
b) $650.
c) $700.
d) Cannot be determined from the information.

32. What is the slope of the aggregate supply curve, according to neoclassical economists?
a) Vertical, because prices tend to be inflexible.
b) Vertical at the capacity level of output in the economy.
c) Horizontal, because wages are flexible.
d) Horizontal, because prices are flexible.

Refer to **Figure 5.22** to answer questions 33 and 34.

FIGURE 5.22

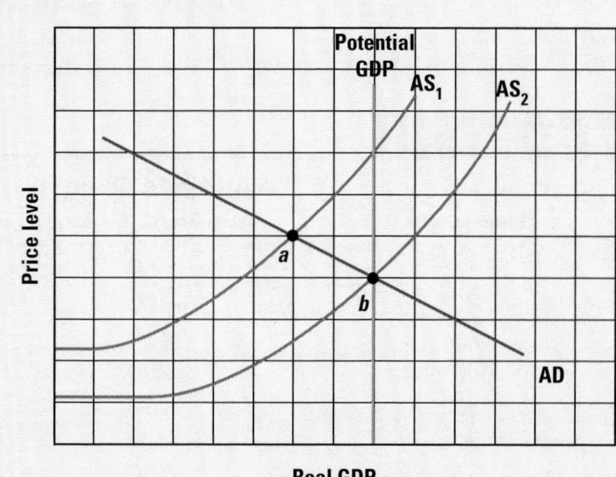

33. Refer to **Figure 5.22** to answer this question. Which of the following statements is true if the economy is at point *a*?
a) Firms will find it hard to hire labour, and people will find it easy to find jobs.
b) Wages will eventually be forced down.
c) An inflationary gap exists.
d) Unemployment is at its natural rate.
e) The achievement of full employment must await a decrease in aggregate demand.

34. Refer to **Figure 5.22** to answer this question. If the economy was initially at point *a*, then what would a movement to point *b* suggest?
a) The movement could be the result of an increase in aggregate demand.
b) The movement could be the result of a decrease in prices.
c) The movement could be the result of a decrease in wages.
d) It is a movement from one full-employment level of real GDP to another.
e) The movement could be the result of expansionary monetary policy.

35. What is the slope of the AS curve according to Keynesians?
a) Vertical, because prices tend to be inflexible.
b) Vertical, at the level of potential GDP.
c) Horizontal, because wages are inflexible.
d) Downward-sloping, because wages are inflexible.

Parallel Problems

ANSWERED PROBLEMS

36. Key Problem Table 5.3 shows AD and AS for the economy of Everton. Potential GDP is currently 200.

TABLE 5.3

Price Level	Aggregate Quantity Supplied 1 (AS_1)	Aggregate Quantity Demanded 1 (AD_1)	Aggregate Quantity Supplied 2 (AS_2)
65*	$0	$260	$100
70*	100	240	180
75	160	220	220
80	200	200	245
85	230	180	260
90	250	160	270
95	260	140	274
100	270	120	275

(*The price level is inflexible downwards at $70 for AS_1 and at $65 for AS_2)

a) On **Figure 5.23** draw in and label curves AS_1 and AD_1.

FIGURE 5.23

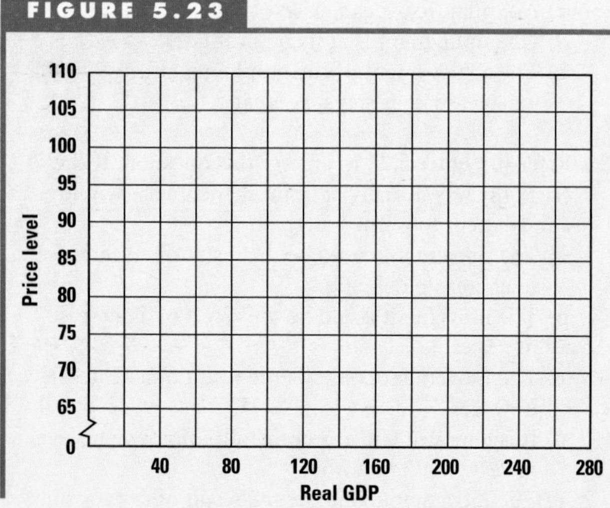

b) What are the equilibrium values for the price level and real GDP?
Price: ___________; Real GDP: ___________.

c) Suppose that aggregate demand in Everton decreased by 60. Draw a new AD_2 curve on **Figure 5.23** to show this change. What are the new equilibrium values for the price level and real GDP?
Price: ___________; Real GDP: ___________.

d) Is there now a recessionary or an inflationary gap? What is the amount of this gap?
There is a(n) ___________ gap of ___________.

e) Put an "X" next to each of the following factors that could have caused the decrease in demand that you illustrated in c):
increased exports ______
higher taxes ______
higher interest rates ______
lower government spending ______

f) Assuming the original AD_1, suppose that aggregate supply changed as a result of a dramatic decrease in the price of oil as shown by AS_2 in **Table 5.3**. Draw in the new AS_2 in **Figure 5.23**. What are the equilibrium values for the price level and real GDP now?
Price: ___________; Real GDP: ___________.

g) Is there now a recessionary or inflationary gap? What is the amount of this gap?
There is a(n) ___________ gap of ___________.

Basic (Problems 37–42)

37. What are the four sources of economic growth?
a) ___________________________.
b) ___________________________.
c) ___________________________.
d) ___________________________.

38. The following shows labour data for Eturia:

TABLE 5.4

Price	2000	2001	2002
Output (in millions of cases per week)	120	126	130
Labour input (in millions of workers per week)	8	8.07	8.55

a) Calculate the productivity rates for each year. __________; __________ and __________.
b) In which year was labour productivity highest? __________.

39. Indicate whether each of the following factors will affect aggregate demand (AD) or aggregate supply (AS) and whether the effect would be an increase or a decrease. Then indicate what will happen to the price level and the level of real GDP.
a) A decrease in interest rates: __________; price level: __________; real GDP: __________.
b) An improvement in technology: __________; price level: __________; real GDP: __________.
c) An increase in the exchange rate: __________; price level: __________; real GDP: __________.
d) A decrease in government spending: __________; price level: __________; real GDP: __________.
e) An increase in the money supply: __________; price level: __________; real GDP: __________.
f) An increase in the nominal wage rate:__________; price level: __________; real GDP: __________.

40. Starting from equilibrium, explain in terms of changes in either AD or in AS (not both) how each of the following results could have occurred.
a) Real GDP increases and the price level increases.
__________.
b) Real GDP decreases and the price level increases.
__________.
c) Real GDP increases and the price level decreases.
__________.
d) Real GDP decreases and the price level decreases.
__________.

41. Explain, in terms of a graph, how an increase in aggregate demand could have no effect on the price level.
____
____
__________.

42. Assume that the potential GDP of the economy of Arion is $1000 and that the aggregate demand and the aggregate supply are as shown in Table 5.5.

TABLE 5.5

Aggregate Quantity Demanded	Price Level	Aggregate Quantity Supplied
$1080	96	$880
1060	97	940
1040	98	965
1020	99	985
1000	100	1000
980	101	1015
960	102	1025
940	103	1033
920	104	1040
900	105	1045

a) What is the value of equilibrium real GDP and the price level? Is there a recessionary or inflationary gap?
Real GDP: __________; Price level: __________.
There is __________ gap of $ __________.
b) If firms become more optimistic and aggregate demand increases by $65, what will be the new values of equilibrium real GDP and the price level? Is there a recessionary or inflationary gap? What is the size of the gap?
Real GDP: __________; Price level: __________.
There is __________ gap of $ __________.

Intermediate (Problems 43–45)

43. Use the graph in Figure 5.24 to illustrate the effect on the Canadian economy during the Great Depression of the 1930's, when prices, production, and employment all decreased dramatically. (Assume the economy was originally at full-employment equilibrium.)

FIGURE 5.24

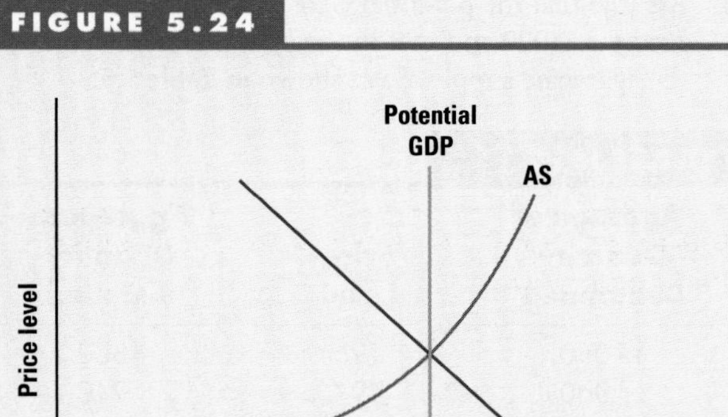

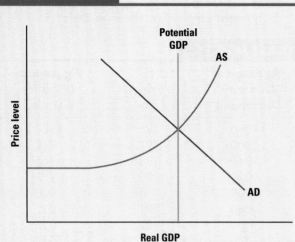

FIGURE 5.25

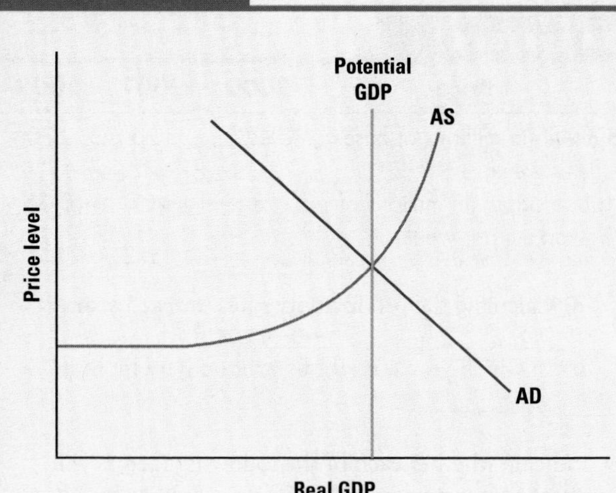

44. In **Figure 5.25**, show a new equilibrium on the graph illustrating demand-pull inflation, and then give three reasons that could have caused the change.

a) ______________________________.
b) ______________________________.
c) ______________________________.

45. Assume that the size of the labour force in the economy of Mersin remained unchanged in the year 2002, while labour productivity increased. If real GDP also reminded unchanged, what change in the labour market must have occurred? ______________________________
______________________________.

Advanced (Problems 46–47)

46. Why does an increase in potential GDP leave the economy in a recessionary gap? ______________________________
____
____
______________________________.

47. Explain how an economy eventually recovers from a recessionary gap. How does it recover from an inflationary gap? ______________________________
____
____
____
______________________________.

UNANSWERED PROBLEMS

48. Key Problem Table 5.6 shows AD and AS for the economy of Ajax. Potential GDP is currently 880.

TABLE 5.6

Price Level	Aggregate Quantity Supplied 1 (AS_1)	Aggregate Quantity Demanded 1 (AD_1)	Aggregate Quantity Supplied 2 (AS_2)
98*	$0	$900	$800
100*	800	880	880
102	860	860	920
104	900	840	965
106	930	820	980
108	950	800	990
110	960	780	996
112	968	760	999

(*The price level is inflexible downwards at $100 for AS_1 and at $98 for AS_2)

a) On graph paper, with real GDP starting at 800 and rising by 40s and the price level starting at 98 and rising by 2s, draw in and label curves AS_1 and AD_1.
b) What are the equilibrium values for the price level and real GDP?
c) Suppose that aggregate demand in Ajax decreased by 80. Draw a new AD_2 curve on your graph to show this change. What are the new equilibrium values for the price level and real GDP?
d) Is there now a recessionary or an inflationary gap? What is the amount of this gap?
e) Which of the following factors could have caused the decrease in demand that you illustrated in c): decreased exports; a lower exchange rate; technological change; lower consumer expectations?
f) Draw the data for AS_2 on your graph. Assuming the original AD_1, what are the equilibrium values for the price level and real GDP now?
g) Is there now a recessionary or inflationary gap? What is the amount of this gap?

Basic (Problems 49–52)

49. What will be the effect on the economy of an increase in the level of human capital, or an increase in physical capital, or a significant technological change?

50. Given the information in Table 5.7:

TABLE 5.7

Year	Output per Year	Labour Input
2000	80	5
2001	90	5
2002	99	5.5

Calculate labour productivity for each year. What is the percentage increase in productivity for 2001 and for 2002?

51. Indicate whether each of the following factors will affect aggregate demand (AD) or aggregate supply (AS) and whether the effect would be an increase or a decrease. Then indicate what will happen to the price level and the level of real GDP.
a) A rise in the nominal wage rate.
b) A decrease in the money supply.
c) An increase in income taxes.
d) A large rise in the value of stocks.
e) A drop in the price of imported oil.
f) An increase in exports.

52. Starting from equilibrium, explain in terms of changes in either AD or in AS (not both) how each of the following results could have occurred.
a) Real GDP decreases and the price level decreases.
b) Real GDP increases and the price level increases.
c) Real GDP decreases and the price level increases.
d) Real GDP increases and the price level decreases.

53. Explain, in terms of a graph, how an increase in aggregate demand might have no effect on real GDP.

54. Assume that the potential GDP of the economy of Arion is $1000, and that the aggregate supply and aggregate demand are as shown in **Table 5.8**. If the prices of imported resources increase and the aggregate supply decreases by $120, what will be the new values of equilibrium real GDP and the price level? Is there a recessionary or inflationary gap? What is the size of the gap?

TABLE 5.8

Aggregate Quantity Demanded	Price Level	Aggregate Quantity Supplied
$1080	96	$880
1060	97	940
1040	98	965
1020	99	985
1000	100	1000
980	101	1015
960	102	1025
940	103	1033
920	104	1040
900	105	1045

Intermediate (Problems 55–57)

55. Use an AD/AS graph to illustrate the effect on the Canadian economy during the mid-1970s, when, as a result of a large increase in the price of oil coming from OPEC countries, both the price level and unemployment increased. (Assume that the economy started from full-employment equilibrium.)

56. Draw an AD/AS graph that illustrates full-employment equilibrium GDP. Then shift one of the curves so as to illustrate cost-push inflation.

57. Assume that the numbers of workers employed in the economy of Ramad remained unchanged in the year 2002, while labour productivity increased 3 percent. If prices remained unchanged, by how much would real GDP increase?

Advanced (Problems 58–63)

58. Why does a decrease in potential GDP leave an economy with an inflationary gap?

59. Explain how the economy eventually adjusts itself from an inflationary gap back to full-employment equilibrium GDP.

60. **Table 5.9** shows the aggregate demand for the economy of Mandu.

TABLE 5.9

Price Level	Aggregate Quantity Demanded
97	$1150
98	1100
99	1050
100	1000
101	950
102	900
103	850
104	800

Table 5.10 below shows two aggregate supplies for the same economy.

TABLE 5.10

Price Level	Aggregate Quantity Supplied (1)	Price Level	Aggregate Quantity Supplied (2)
97	$1000	100	$850
98	1000	100	900
99	1000	100	950
100	1000	100	1000
101	1000	100	1050
102	1000	100	1100
103	1000	100	1150
104	1000	100	1200

a) Which of the two aggregate supply schedules, (1) or (2), is the neoclassical aggregate supply? Which is the Keynesian aggregate supply? According to each, what would be the equilibrium levels of price and real GDP?

b) Assume that the aggregate demand increased by $100. What would be the new equilibrium values of price and real GDP, according to neoclassicists? According to Keynesians?

61. Suppose that the economy of Wunderland is initially at full-employment equilibrium. Explain, in terms of shifts in AD or AS, how the following results could occur:

a) Real GDP increases; the price level increases; the economy is experiencing an inflationary gap.
b) Real GDP increases; the price level decreases; the economy is experiencing an inflationary gap.
c) Real GDP decreases; the price level increases; the economy is experiencing an inflationary gap.
d) Real GDP decreases; the price level increases; the economy is experiencing a recessionary gap.
e) Real GDP decreases; the price level decreases; the economy is experiencing a recessionary gap.
f) Real GDP increases; the price level decreases; the economy is experiencing a recessionary gap.

62. Suppose that the economy of Punderland in Figure 5.26 is at full-employment equilibrium and the present nominal wage rate is $910 per week.
a) What is the real wage rate (in base year prices)?
b) Suppose that aggregate demand increases by $60. At the new equilibrium real GDP level, what will be the value of the real wage rate?
c) As a result of the change in prices in b), suppose that nominal wages increase, causing aggregate supply to change by $120. At the new equilibrium, what will be the value of real wages?
d) At the new equilibrium in c), what is the value of nominal wages?

FIGURE 5.26

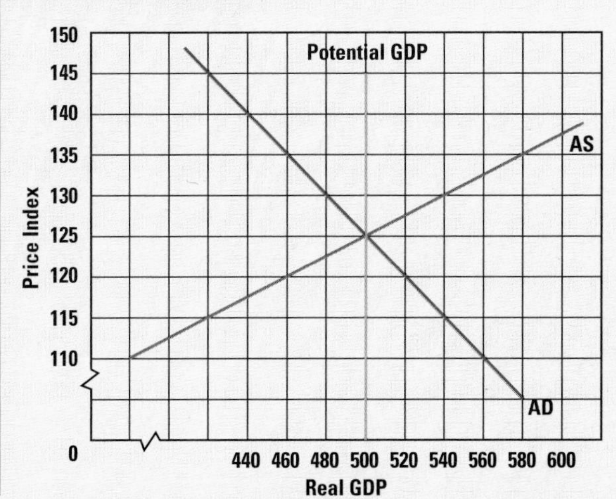

63. Albion's nominal GDP increased from $720 billion to $802 billion last year. During the year its economy experienced 5 percent inflation (its price index increased from 100 to 105), while the number of employed persons increased by 4 percent (from 30 million to 31.2 million). By what percentage did its labour productivity increase during the year?

Web-Based Activities

1. For each of the articles found below, illustrate and explain how the event described in the article will affect the aggregate demand/aggregate supply model. Be sure to explain what happens to the price level and the level of real GDP.
a) **www.cnnfn.com/1998/07/28/economy/confidence/**
b) **www.cnnfn.com/1998/10/21/economy/ifo__survey/**
c) **www.cnnfn.com/1998/11/10/economy/sanctions**

2. In this chapter you learned about some of the factors that affect aggregate demand and supply. One of these factors is interest rates.
Read:
www.techweb.com/wire/story/TWB19990824S0022
and answer the following questions:
a) Illustrate and explain how an increase in interest rates will affect the aggregate demand/supply model. Be sure to explain what happens to the price level and the level of real GDP.
b) According to the article, what effect does an interest rate hike have? Why is the Internet sector more adversely affected by an increase than other sectors?

CHAPTER SIX

Aggregate Expenditures

LEARNING OBJECTIVES

This chapter will enable you to:

LO1 **Distinguish between autonomous and induced expenditures.**

LO2 **Understand the concept of expenditures equilibrium.**

LO3 **Explain what factors can affect spending and how they can affect income.**

LO4 **Describe how small changes in spending have a large effect on national income.**

LO5 **See the significance of the Keynesian revolution.**

What's ahead...

In this chapter we present the expenditures model of national income determination. You will see that the basic tenet of this model is that the level of national income depends on the level of spending in the economy. The discussion of the model, which is done in tabular, graphical, and algebraic forms, will increase your awareness of how the various parts of the economy are interrelated. It is important that you understand the concept of equilibrium first presented early in this chapter and then discussed in detail later. Understanding the concept of equilibrium is the key to your understanding of how national income is determined.

A QUESTION OF RELEVANCE...

You are probably aware that Canada is one of the best countries in the world to live in. One reason for this is this country's relatively high level of national income, which, of course, means a high level of per capita income. But have you wondered what determines this level of national income? And why does it grow quickly at times and not at all at other times? What role does consumer spending play in all this? And what about business investment and exports? This chapter will help you answer questions like these.

In the last chapter we saw how changes in both aggregate demand and supply can produce changes in production (and therefore income and employment), and in the price level (and therefore inflation). While changes in aggregate supply can bring about more long-term and radical changes to an economy, their short-term effect can often go unnoticed. As well, such changes are difficult to instigate by government and policy makers. On the other hand, changes in spending (demand) are likely to have a more obvious short-term effect and in addition are more easily effected by governments. For this reason, changes in spending lay at the heart of Keynes's *General Theory*. Keynes realized that it was inadequate spending which was the root cause of the Great Depression and that an increase in spending was necessary to cure it. In this chapter we will look at total spending (aggregate expenditures) and examine what determines aggregate expenditures and how the economy is affected by changes in them.

The circular flow model in Chapter 3 gave us an overview of the macroeconomy by highlighting the role of the four elements of spending—consumption, investment, exports, and government—and three leakages: savings, imports, and taxes. This same model also revealed a fundamental aspect of how an economy works. The production of goods and services (GDP) generates income (national income). In fact, income can be generated *only* from real production, and the value of that production (at whatever level it might be) is the amount of income generated as a result. It is important for you to remember that:

GDP and national income (Y) are conceptually the same thing—two sides of the same coin—and thus always equal to each other.

National income ends up in the hands of individuals. And what do people do with this income? Well, they spend it on the consumption of both domestically produced goods and services and imports, pay taxes with some of it, and save some of it. Thus we have our three leakages and the first of the four components of aggregate expenditures: consumption. Taxes paid are the source of the government's spending on goods and services, and savings are the source of investment spending. Add exports, which originate from outside the economy, and we have all four components of spending, or aggregate expenditures.

Production of goods and services creates:

The central question of this chapter is: do aggregate expenditures always equal national income? The clear and simple answer is no. Is it possible for aggregate expenditures to equal national income? Yes it is, and this is the condition economists call expenditure equilibrium. But it is *only* at equilibrium that aggregate expenditures equal national income. And, as we shall see, when these two are not equal (and most of the time, they are not) the economy will change as income rises or falls, and when income rises or falls all the other components will change as well. This is one of the conclusions of John Maynard Keynes, who published his *General Theory* in 1936. The expenditures model presented in this chapter is in many respects a brief summary of some of the essential ideas of the *General Theory*.

6.1 The Expenditures Model

LO1
Distinguish between autonomous and induced expenditures.

Let us start our investigation with **Table 6.1**, which shows data for the hypothetical country of Karinia (all figures are in billions of Karinian dollars), and then explore, one by one, each of the relationships between the various components in the table. We will be using the term "(national) income" throughout this discussion, but keep in mind that we could have just as easily used the term GDP.

TABLE 6.1 **National income and aggregate expenditures**

Y	T	Y_D	C	S	I	G	X	IM	X_N	AE $(C + I + G + X_N)$
0	160	−160	50	−210	250	400	150	50	100	800
200	200	0	170	−170	250	400	150	70	80	900
400	240	160	290	−130	250	400	150	90	60	1000
600	280	320	410	−90	250	400	150	110	40	1100
800	320	480	530	−50	250	400	150	130	20	1200
1000	360	640	650	−10	250	400	150	150	0	1300
1200	400	800	770	30	250	400	150	170	−20	1400
1400	440	960	890	70	250	400	150	190	−40	1500
1600	480	1120	1010	110	250	400	150	210	−60	1600
1800	520	1280	1130	150	250	400	150	230	−80	1700
2000	560	1440	1250	190	250	400	150	250	−100	1800

The levels of expenditures shown in the blue shaded columns indicate what the level of spending *would be* at various levels of income (Y). You can see right away that the first column (income) and the last column, AE, (aggregate expenditures) are quite different. The AE column is derived by adding together the amounts of consumption (C), investment (I), government spending (G) and net exports (X_N). Once again:

$$AE = C + I + G + X_N$$

At low incomes, for instance, aggregate expenditures exceed income, whereas at high incomes it is the other way around. Furthermore, the table suggests that even if income in Karinia were zero, aggregate expenditures would not be zero.

autonomous spending: the portion of total spending that is independent of the level of income.

We have a term for spending that does not depend on the level of income: **autonomous spending** (autonomous simply means "independent of"). Spending that occurs when income is zero is autonomous. You will notice in **Table 6.1** that we have autonomous consumption spending of \$50, autonomous investment spending of \$250, autonomous government spending of \$400, and autonomous net exports of \$100. This gives us a total of \$800 in autonomous aggregate expenditures.

Next, notice how income and aggregate expenditures are directly related. Clearly the two increase and decrease together. Furthermore, this relationship is constant in that for every \$200 increase in income, aggregate expenditures increase by \$100. This illustrates the point that higher incomes *induce* higher levels of spending. In other words, some spending is autonomous spending and some is **induced spending**. Note therefore that:

induced spending: the portion of spending that depends on the level of income.

$$\text{Aggregate expenditures} = \text{autonomous expenditures} + \text{induced expenditures}.$$

Now, you may well ask how any economy could experience any spending at all if income were zero. Or how is it possible for the country to spend more than it earns in income? The answer is that people, businesses, or the government (or all three) must be borrowing. And who would they be borrowing from? From anyone who has built up a fund of past savings, which includes lenders in their own country and lenders from outside the economy. In short, the source of autonomous spending is past savings, and it really doesn't matter who or where those past savings come from.

marginal propensity to expend: the ratio of the change in expenditures that results from a change in income.

On the other hand, the source of induced spending is current income. Again, this is seen by the fact that aggregate expenditures increase as income increases. The relationship between changes in income and the corresponding changes in spending is termed the **marginal propensity to expend** (MPE). The term propensity is similar to the concept of demand and includes the idea of both willingness and ability to spend. The formula for the MPE is:

$$\text{MPE} = \frac{\Delta \text{ aggregate expenditures}}{\Delta \text{ income}} \qquad [6.1]$$

marginal leakage rate: the ratio of change in leakages that results from a change in income.

Given the data in **Table 6.1**, the value of the MPE in Karinia is 100/200, or 0.5. What this means is that every *additional* dollar of income earned in Karinia results in an *additional* 50 cents of induced spending. If you are wondering what happens to the other 50 cents, the answer is that it "leaks" into taxes, savings, or imports. The amount of each extra dollar not spent on *domestic* products is referred to as the **marginal leakage rate** (MLR). Thus,

$$\text{MLR} = \frac{\Delta \text{ total leakages}}{\Delta \text{ income}} \qquad [6.2]$$

Since all income is either spent or is part of a leakage, we know that:

$$\text{MLR} = (1 - \text{MPE}) \qquad [6.3]$$

We now have the necessary information to derive the equation for the AE function for our model, which is:

$$\text{AE} = 800 + 0.5\text{Y}$$

$$\text{AE} = (\text{autonomous expenditures}) + (\text{induced expenditures}) \qquad [6.4]$$

With this equation, we can calculate the value of aggregate expenditures for any value of income. For instance, when $\text{Y} = 1000$, $\text{AE} = 800 + (0.5) \times 1000 = 1300$. This can be confirmed by looking back at **Table 6.1**.

expenditure equilibrium: the income at which the value of production and aggregate expenditures are equal.

Before we go any further, you should note that incomes equal aggregate expenditures in Karinia only at *one* income level. This occurs at $1600 and is referred to as **expenditure equilibrium.** Again, we ask the question: does this mean that the economy of Karinia will always be at this income level of $1600? Again, the answer is no, not necessarily. But, as we shall soon see, there are forces at work that will drive the economy toward equilibrium.

We will return to this idea of equilibrium soon, but first we need to take a closer look at the various categories of expenditure and leakages. Let's take each element of **Table 6.1** (which is duplicated in the Answer Key for easy download and reference) in turn, beginning with the tax function.

The Tax Function and Disposable Income

Notice that in Karinia taxes are $160 even when income is zero. This is the level of autonomous taxes. There are several examples of autonomous taxes, including highway tolls, user fees, property taxes, and so on. These taxes do not depend on the level of income.

However, the majority of the Karinian government's tax revenue comes from induced taxes. These are taxes whose amount depends on, or is related to, income levels. Examples would be personal income taxes, corporate taxes, and sales taxes. Some of the tax revenue that goes to the government is given back in the form of transfer payments. These payments take the form of unemployment insurance, pensions, and welfare payments. The balance of the government's revenue is spent on the purchase of goods and services.

Total taxes are made up of autonomous taxes and induced taxes:

$$\text{Total taxes} = \text{autonomous taxes} + \text{induced taxes} \quad [6.5]$$

We can deal with the third column very quickly. It shows the disposable income of Karinian householders. Disposable income (the third column, labelled Y_D) is simply income minus tax, or:

$$Y_D = Y - T \quad [6.6]$$

Disposable income increases with income but at a slower rate: for every $200 increase in income, disposable income increases by $160, reflecting the tax bite.

The Consumption Function

Consumption spending is the first of the four components of aggregate expenditures and, as you can see in column 4 (blue-shaded) in **Table 6.1**, it rises as income rises. This indicates a direct relationship between income and consumption spending. In addition, you should note that there is an amount of consumption spending even at zero income. In other words, consumption is made up of both an induced and an autonomous element:

$$\text{Total consumption} = \text{autonomous consumption} + \text{induced consumption} \quad [6.7]$$

autonomous consumption: the portion of consumer spending that is independent of the level of income.

induced consumption: the portion of consumer spending that is dependent on the level of income.

marginal propensity to consume: the ratio of the change in consumption to the corresponding change in income.

The amount of **autonomous consumption** is the value of consumption when income is zero. A glance at **Table 6.1** shows that in this example it has a value of $50.

Induced consumption is the amount of consumption that results from higher levels of income. The relationship between the increase in consumption and the increase in income is known as the **marginal propensity to consume** (MPC). Thus,

$$\text{Marginal propensity to consume (MPC)} = \frac{\Delta \text{ consumption}}{\Delta \text{ income}} \quad [6.8]$$

In our example, the MPC has a value of: $\frac{120}{200}$ or 0.6.

In other words, we see in our table that whenever income increases by $200, this induces increased consumption of $120. Given this, and with our knowledge that autonomous consumption is $50, we can write the complete formula for the consumption function in our example:

$$C = 50 + 0.6Y$$

This equation then allows us to calculate the value of consumption for any level of income. For example, at an income of $2000:

$$C = 50 + 0.6(2000) = 50 + 1200 = 1250.$$

You can confirm this by looking back at the table.

The Saving Function

We now come to the second leakage, saving (taxes was the first). Saving is defined quite simply as that portion of disposable income (Y_D) which is not consumed. This is indicated by:

$$S = Y_D - C \quad [6.9]$$

$$\text{or } Y_D = C + S$$

Table 6.1 shows us that when disposable income is, say, \$1280, consumption equals \$1130. Saving is therefore the difference of \$150. Notice that at low levels of disposable income, saving is negative. This is called dissaving. In other words, when income is zero, dissaving is \$210. This is because at zero income, Karinians still pay \$160 in autonomous taxes and \$50 in autonomous consumption. Doing this is possible only by borrowing. This means that Karinians must make use of their accumulated past savings, and the total amount of these accumulated savings will therefore fall. This is what is meant by dissaving. At incomes above \$1200 (in reality, above \$1050), saving is positive, and Karinians are therefore adding to their accumulated savings.

marginal propensity to save: the ratio of the change in saving to the corresponding change in income.

The **marginal propensity to save** (MPS) defines the *relationship* between a change in income and a corresponding change in saving. The formula for the MPS is:

$$\text{MPS} = \frac{\Delta \text{ saving}}{\Delta \text{ income}} \quad [6.10]$$

Note that saving increases at a constant rate, just as consumption did. For every \$200 increase in income, saving increases by \$40. Therefore, the value of the marginal propensity to save in Karinia is 40/200, or 0.2. The equation for the saving function in our model, then, is:

$$S = -210 + 0.2Y$$

The consumption and saving functions are both graphed in **Figure 6.1** below:

FIGURE 6.1 **The Consumption and Saving Functions**

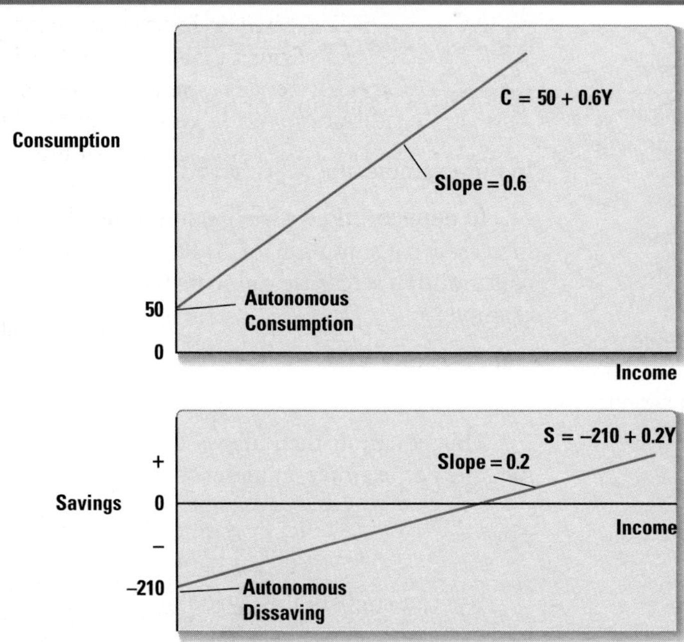

Both the consumption and saving functions are upward-sloping, showing that both consumption *and* saving increase with incomes. The slope of the consumption function is equal to the MPC and the slope of the saving function is equal to the MPS. The points at which the curves cross the vertical axis show the amounts of autonomous consumption and autonomous saving.

Figure 6.1 shows the consumption and saving functions for our model. Both are upward-sloping, indicating that consumption and saving increase as real GDP increases. The slope of the consumption function is equal to the marginal propensity to consume (MPC). The higher the value of the MPC, the steeper the line will be. Similarly, the slope of the saving function indicates the marginal propensity to save (MPS). A higher MPC will indicate a *lower* MPS since, assuming taxes don't change, the more that is consumed of every additional dollar earned, the less will be saved.

@-CONOMICS

A Big Boost to Investment Spending

The U.S. Commerce Department recently made changes to some of the definitions and methods used in measuring income. One of these was reclassifying all software purchases (over a certain minimum price) as investment spending. Previously these purchases were treated as costs of production and, therefore, not counted in income, just as the production of steel for automobiles is not counted (just the autos are counted). As a result of this reclassification, investment spending in the U.S. economy for the year 1999 was revised upwards and the level of income increased by $250 billion over the previous official level. Since investment was revised upwards, so was the rate of saving, since the one is a mirror image of the other. As one commentator noted, the real significance of these changes is that government statistics now better reflect the high-growth, high-productivity, low-inflation *New Economy.*

The Investment Function

Again, looking at **Table 6.1**, our model regards investment spending as wholly autonomous in the amount of $250. That is to say, there is no direct relationship between investment spending and income levels. The equation for the investment function, therefore, is straightforward:

$$I = 250.$$

It is possible to argue that there is a natural link between the level of income and the level of investment spending, since an increase in income *may* increase corporate profits, which in turn *may* encourage firms to invest more. But, in reality, the link between them is, at best, weak. In our model, therefore, we will regard investment spending as entirely autonomous. This also has the advantage of keeping things a little simpler.

Do not get the impression that "autonomous" means unchanging. Certainly, the amount of investment spending can change from time to time. There are many factors that can cause this to happen, and we will look at some of these factors a little later.

The Government Spending Function

As with investment spending, government spending is also treated as wholly autonomous and its function is:

$$G = 400.$$

Now, you might object to this and believe that the amount that a government is able to spend is, in turn, determined by the amount of tax and other revenue it receives. Since this tax revenue is dependent on income, wouldn't this mean that the amounts the government spends are also dependent on the level of income? While there is some truth in this, it would be a gross simplification. In fact, governments can and do spend whatever they feel is necessary, irrespective of the tax revenues they receive. Therefore, we will regard government spending as autonomous. Making this assumption again offers the advantage of simplicity. We will return to this point later.

The investment and government functions are both graphed in Figure 6.2.

FIGURE 6.2 **The Investment and Government Functions**

Both investment and government spending are constant and remain unchanged whatever the level of income. They therefore plot as horizontal straight lines.

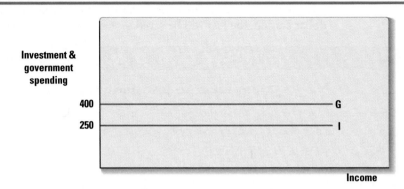

Since both investment and government spending are wholly autonomous, they plot as horizontal straight lines. Irrespective of the value of real GDP, their values remain constant.

Exports, Imports, and the Net Export Function

Table 6.1 indicates that exports, just like government spending on goods and services, are solely autonomous. That is to say, Karinia's exports have nothing to do with its own income but everything to do with the income levels of the countries that buy Karinian exports. We have assumed exports to be an autonomous \$200, but, again, you should realize that this level can change from one period to the next.

Imports are a different story. As we saw earlier, an increase in Karinian income will cause an increase in consumption spending. But that spending will not be just on domestically produced goods and services; some of it will be on imports. Therefore, the level of imports is directly related to the level of income. The relationship between imports and the level of income is known as the **marginal propensity to import** (MPM). Formally, this is:

marginal propensity to import: the ratio of the change in imports that results from a change in income.

$$MPM = \frac{\Delta \text{ imports (IM)}}{\Delta \text{ income (Y)}} \qquad [6.11]$$

For Karinia, the value of the MPM is currently 0.1, since for every \$200 increase in national income, imports increase by 20, that is, 20/200 = 0.1.

You will notice that there is an autonomous component to imports also, since the level of imports is \$100 when income is zero. Presumably, since Karinia does not possess certain products and resources, it will need to import them from abroad, regardless of its income level. That is to say, import spending is both autonomous (the \$100) and induced (the MPM), just as we saw when we looked at the consumption function.

The equation for the import function, therefore, is:

$$IM = 50 + 0.1Y$$

SELF-TEST

1. What exactly does it mean to suggest that some amount of imports may be autonomous? Explain the phrase and give examples to illustrate your answer.

balance of trade: the value of a country's export of goods and services less the value of imports.

Let's turn now to net exports, which is, quite simply, the difference between exports and imports. It is also referred to as the **balance of trade**, and this balance might be positive or negative. Notice in **Table 6.1** that net exports are positive and highest when income is lowest. This is a result of autonomous exports being a constant \$200, whereas imports are mainly induced and thus rise as income rises. In fact, at income levels above \$1000, imports have risen sufficiently so as to exceed exports. As a result, net exports become negative. This means that as Karinia enjoys a higher income, it also starts to see a reduction in its trade surplus and then an increase in its trade deficit. This is illustrated in **Figure 6.3**.

We see in **Figure 6.3** that since exports are an autonomous \$200, the export function is a horizontal line at that level. Since imports are partly autonomous, the import function starts at \$100. However, it is also related to incomes so that the import function rises from that point. The slope of the import function is equal to the value of the MPM, which, you recall, has a value of 0.1 in Karinia.

FIGURE 6.3 **The Net Export Function**

Imports increase as income levels increase, so that the import function is upward-sloping. Exports are autonomous of income levels, and therefore its function is a horizontal line. At low income levels, exports exceed imports, which results in a trade surplus. At higher income levels, however, imports exceed exports, which implies a trade deficit. At income level of \$1000, the trade balance is zero.

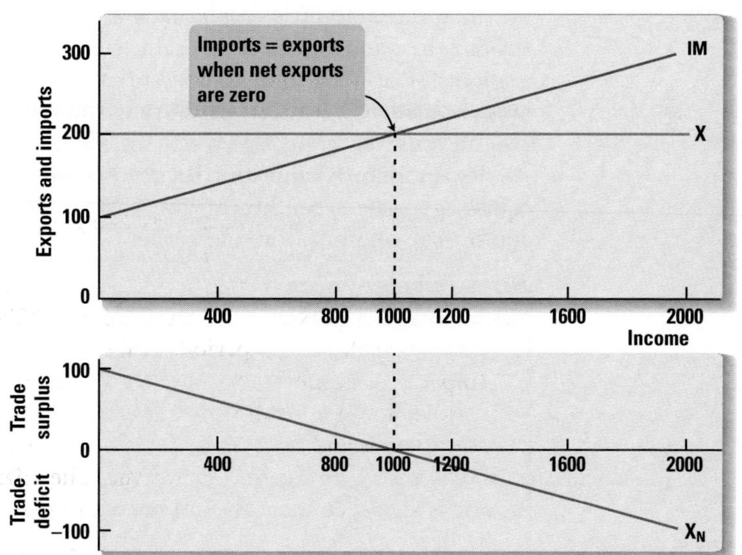

Figure 6.3 also shows that the net export function begins at a surplus of \$100 since this is the amount of the difference between autonomous exports and autonomous imports. As income rises, imports also rise. However, exports do not change with income levels, so that *net* exports (or the trade surplus) declines. At an income level of \$1000, exports are equal to imports, which means that net exports are zero; that is, there is a zero balance of trade. This is indicated by the net export function crossing the horizontal line. In algebraic terms:

$$X_N = X - IM$$

Therefore for our model, it is equal to:

$$X_N = 150 - (50 + 0.1Y), \text{ or}$$

$$X_N = 100 - 0.1Y$$

In bringing our discussion of **Table 6.1** to a close, you are reminded that if we add the four components of spending, $C + I + G + X_N$ (the shaded columns), we get aggregate expenditures. It is this interplay between aggregate expenditures and national income to which we now turn.

SELF-TEST

2. If autonomous imports = 40, autonomous exports = 200, and MPM = 1/5, what is X_N at Y = 650?

6.2 Expenditure Equilibrium

LO2
Understand the concept of expenditures equilibrium.

Before we can fully grasp all the details of the expenditure model, we need to return to our discussion of what equilibrium means. Try this. Imagine throwing a stone into a pond and watching the concentric ripples fade as they widen. In response to the shock of the stone striking the water's surface, that same surface immediately begins returning to normal or to a smooth state—returning to equilibrium. Thus, equilibrium can be thought of as a state of rest, or a state of normalcy, which can, from time to time, be disrupted by various shocks. It also suggests, as we shall see, a state of equality and balance between opposing forces.

Expenditure equilibrium occurs in our model at $1600, since this is where income equals aggregate expenditures. To clearly understand *why* that is so, we have extracted the appropriate columns from our earlier table and added an additional one to create **Table 6.2**.

TABLE 6.2 Income and Aggregate Expenditures

Y	AE $(C + I + X_N + G)$	Unplanned Investment
$0	800	–800
200	900	–700
400	1000	–600
600	1100	–500
800	1200	–400
1000	1300	–300
1200	1400	–200
1400	1500	–100
1600	1600	0
1800	1700	+100
2000	1800	+200

unplanned investment: the amount of *unintended* investment by firms in the form of a build-up or run-down of inventories; that is, the difference between production (Y) and aggregate expenditures (AE).

Recall that the level of income always equals the value of production. However, these two may or may not equal aggregate expenditures. In fact, you can see that for levels of income less than $1600, aggregate expenditures are greater than the value of production. This means that at these income levels there would be shortages, since people want to buy more goods and services than are currently being produced. The last column, unplanned investment, could also have been labelled shortages (–)/surpluses (+). **Unplanned investment**, therefore, is simply the difference between the value of production and the level of spending. At incomes greater than $1600, aggregate expenditures are less than production, which would cause surpluses, as is shown in the last column. Another way of looking at equilibrium income is that:

Equilibrium income is that level of income (and production) at which there is neither a surplus nor a shortage of goods.

Let's make sure that we understand this last point. Suppose that the level of income was $1200. Here, aggregate expenditures are $1400. So where is this additional $200 of goods and services coming from? The answer is that since spending in the economy is greater than current levels of production, firms must be depleting their levels of inventory below the desired level. After all, they are not going to refuse to fill orders. On the other hand, there is a definite shortage of products. This situation cannot last. In the next period, firms will increase the level of production in order to replenish those inventories to the desired level and to meet the higher demand for products. The result will be a higher level of production, and if production rises, so too will income. How high will production and income rise? **Table 6.2** has already provided us the answer: it will eventually increase to the point where there are no shortages, and that will be at the $1600 level of income.

Now let us look at the opposite scenario. Suppose that the level of GDP and income in Karinia happened to be above the equilibrium level, say at $2000. In this case **Table 6.2** tells us that aggregate expenditures, at $1800, are lower than income of $2000. Firms are producing, in total, more products than people are buying. The result is a surplus of goods and services produced. Firms will find that they have an unwanted build-up of inventories. You can imagine that in the next period, producers are not likely to produce another $2000 worth of goods. Instead, their response will be to produce less. This process will continue with production and incomes both falling and unemployment rising, until the economy is at the equilibrium level of national income of $1600.

We have uncovered something significant here:

Production, income and employment will adjust to the level of aggregate expenditures in the economy.

There is another way of looking at the concept of equilibrium. If you think back to Chapter 3, the circular flow model defined expenditure equilibrium as a situation in which total injections and total leakages are equal. Let us see if this is the case in Karinia. In **Table 6.3**, we have brought forward the appropriate information (from **Table 6.1**) and have added columns for total leakages and injections.

TABLE 6.3 Income and Aggregate Expenditures

Y	T	S	IM	Total Leakages	I	G	X	Total Injections	AE $(C + I + X_N + G)$
$0	160	−210	50	0	250	400	150	800	800
200	200	−170	70	100	250	400	150	800	900
400	240	−130	90	200	250	400	150	800	1000
600	280	−90	110	300	250	400	150	800	1100
800	320	−50	130	400	250	400	150	800	1200
1000	360	−10	150	500	250	400	150	800	1300
1200	400	30	170	600	250	400	150	800	1400
1400	440	70	190	700	250	400	150	800	1500
1600	480	110	210	**800**	250	400	150	**800**	**1600**
1800	520	150	230	900	250	400	150	800	1700
2000	560	190	250	1000	250	400	150	800	1800

As we pointed out earlier, the three injections—investment spending, government spending, and exports—are all autonomous. The reason that the injections in the circular flow model are autonomous is the same reason they are autonomous in the expenditures model: they do not depend on the level of Karinia's income. The total for these three autonomous expenditures is $800 and remains constant. On the other hand, each of the three leakages—taxes, savings, and imports—are (mainly) induced, and therefore the total value of leakages depends on the level of income. Total leakages increase as the levels of income increase. Thus, there is only one level of income where total injections and leakages are equal, and that is at $1600. This is expenditure equilibrium. Below $1600, injections exceed leakages, which will serve to increase income. Above $1600, leakages exceed injections, which will serve to reduce income. In summary, expenditure equilibrium implies all three of the following:

- the income level at which the value of production and aggregate expenditures are equal
- the income level at which there is neither a surplus nor a shortage of goods produced
- the income level at which total injections equal total leakages

SELF-TEST

3. If injections exceed leakages, is there a surplus or shortage? Which is greater, Y or AE?

The Expenditures Model Algebraically

Calculating the value of expenditures equilibrium algebraically is not difficult since we have already derived an equation for the aggregate expenditures function, which in our example is:

$$AE = 800 + 0.5Y$$

We could also have derived this equation by summing up the individual elements of aggregate expenditures, each of which we have now derived. Thus,

$$\begin{aligned} C &= 50 + 0.6Y \\ I &= 250 \\ G &= 400 \\ \underline{X_N} &\underline{= 100 - 0.1Y} \\ AE &= 800 + 0.5Y \end{aligned}$$

Looking at it this way confirms again that autonomous aggregate expenditures are equal to $800 and the value of the MPE is 0.5. This latter parameter tells us that 0.5 or 50 percent of all extra income earned in the economy is spent on domestically produced goods. In fact 0.6 or 60 percent of extra income is spent on consumer goods (the MPC is 0.6) but of this, 10 percent of income is spent on imports (MPM = 0.1). In other words:

$$MPE = MPC - MPM \text{ or, for this model:} \qquad [6.12]$$

$$MPE = 0.6 - 0.1 = 0.5$$

To find the value of expenditures equilibrium we need to recall that equilibrium is the value of income (Y) at which aggregate expenditures equals income, i.e. equilibrium occurs where:

$$Y = AE$$

If we substitute Y for AE in our first equation we get:

$$Y = 800 + 0.5Y$$

Gathering together the Y terms gives us:

$$Y - 0.5Y = 800$$

Or 0.5Y = 800 and dividing both sides by 0.5, we get:

$$Y = \frac{800}{0.5} = 1600$$

This confirms what we have already discovered, i.e., that expenditures equilibrium occurs at a income level of 1600.

The Expenditures Model Graphically

We have already drawn graphs for the consumption, investment, government spending, and net exports functions. To draw the aggregate expenditures function, we could "add" together the four curves like a layer-cake to derive the AE curve. This is shown in Figure 6.4.

FIGURE 6.4 **Aggregate Expenditures**

Both investment and government spending are wholly autonomous and therefore plot as straight lines parallel to the horizontal axis. The consumption function is upward-sloping and the net export function is downward-sloping, but the consumption function increases faster than the net export function decreases. The result is an upward-sloping AE function that has a slope of 0.5.

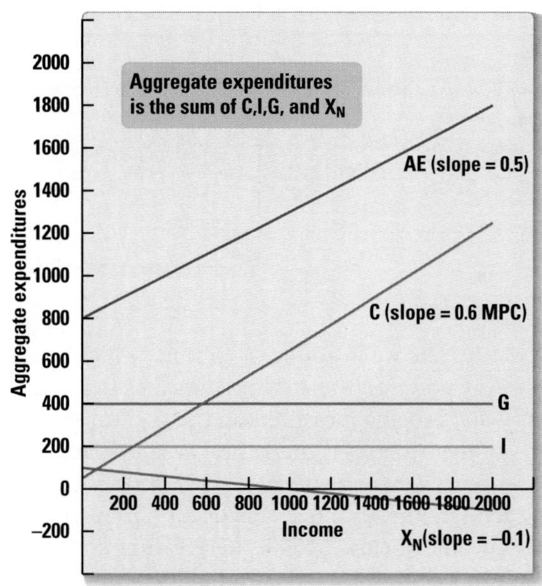

The value of the AE intercept (where the AE line crosses the vertical axis) is the amount of autonomous aggregate expenditures and is equal to \$800. (It is equal to the sum of autonomous consumption, investment, government, and net exports). The slope of the AE function is the value of the MPE (in this case it is equal to 0.5). It is equal to the slope of the consumption function (the MPC) minus the value of the net export function (the MPM), i.e., 0.6 – 0.1. Note therefore that the consumption and aggregate expenditure functions are not parallel lines—the consumption function is always steeper.

Having derived the AE curve, let us show expenditures equilibrium in Figure 6.5.

FIGURE 6.5 **Expenditures Equilibrium**

Autonomous aggregate expenditures are $800. The slope of the aggregate expenditures function is 0.5, so that expenditures increase by $100 for each increase of $200 in income. When income reaches $1600, aggregate expenditures will have increased by $800 and will now equal income. This is expenditure equilibrium and is graphically indicated by the AE function crossing the 45° line.

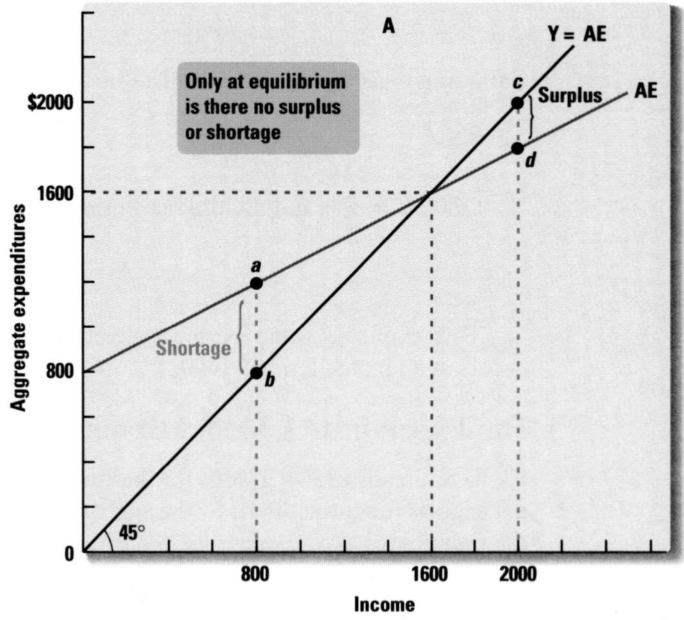

Total injections are an autonomous $800. Total leakages increase with income and are equal to injections at the equilibrium income of $1600.

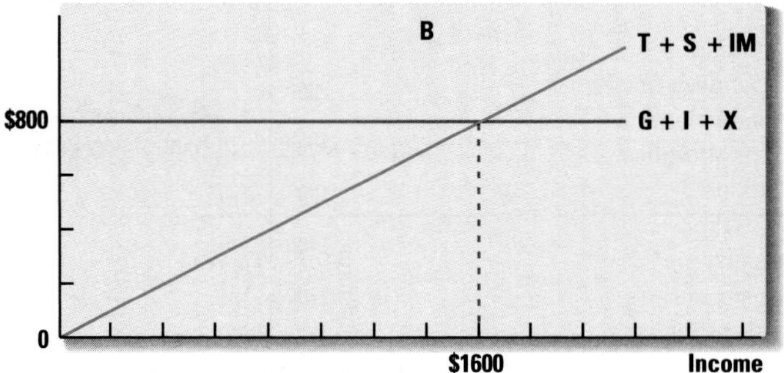

Here we introduce a 45° line, which enables us to easily locate expenditure equilibrium. Any point on the 45° line indicates that what is being measured on the horizontal axis and what is being measured on the vertical axis are equal. (Of course, this assumes that the scale of the two axes is the same.) We have labelled the 45° line Y = AE. Expenditure equilibrium occurs where aggregate expenditures equals income, and this is where the AE function crosses the 45° line. This occurs in our model at the $1600 level of income. Notice that at incomes below $1600, the AE function is above the 45° line. This means that aggregate expenditures exceed national income. Any gap between the two curves, say the distance *ab*, represents the amount of shortage (unplanned disinvestment) that exists at that income level (the shortage equals $400 at the $800 income level in this case). At incomes greater than $1600, the AE function is below the 45° line, which illustrates the fact that income (and production) exceeds aggregate expenditures, thus resulting in a surplus (unplanned increase in investment). For example, at an income level of $2000, the distance *cd* (equal to $200) is the amount of the surplus. Figure 6.5B shows that at the equilibrium income of $1600, total injections are equal to total leakages of $800.

SELF-TEST

4. If autonomous aggregate expenditures equal 200 and the value of the MPE is 0.6, draw both the AE function and a 45° line on a graph and indicate equilibrium income.

REVIEW

1. What is meant by *autonomous expenditures*?
2. What are *induced expenditures*?
3. What is the *marginal propensity to expend*?
4. How are people able to consume at a *zero level of income*?
5. Explain the *marginal propensity to import.*
6. What happens to the value of *net exports* as *national income* increases? Why?
7. What is meant by the term *expenditure equilibrium*? What are the three equivalent ways of expressing it?

6.3 From Income to Disposable Income

LO3
Explain what factors can affect spending and how they can affect income.

We need just a little more algebra to help us fully understand the relationships between income and expenditures. We know that disposable income is simply income minus taxes, or

$$Y_D = Y - T$$

We can easily work out the tax function for our model since it is similar to our other functions:

$$\text{Total taxes} = \text{autonomous taxes} + \text{induced taxes}$$

The autonomous taxes are the amount of tax when income is zero. A glance at **Table 6.1** shows this to be $160. Induced taxes are those taxes, like income taxes, which are related to income and rise and fall as income rises and falls. In the table we see that as income rises by $200, taxes rise by $40. The value of the **marginal tax rate** (MTR) then is:

marginal tax rate: the ratio of the change in taxation as a result of a change in income.

$$\text{Marginal tax rate (MTR)} = \frac{\Delta \text{ taxes}}{\Delta \text{ income}} = \frac{40}{200} = 0.2 \quad [6.13]$$

ADDED DIMENSION

Average and Marginal Tax Rates

The average tax rates paid by individuals on earned income vary a great deal from country to country. The first reason for this is that the amount of tax-free income that an individual enjoys ranges from $10 000 of income in Canada to $18 000 in the United States, $28 000 in Hong Kong, and an incredible $35 800 in Luxembourg. Second, taxes on additional income above the tax-free level (the marginal tax rate) vary a great deal. Nonetheless, we can get some sense of the differences from the table below. The average rate shown here is for a married couple with two children making an income of $60 000. The other two columns give the lowest and highest marginal tax rates that apply to income above this tax-free amount.

Country	Average Tax Rate (%)	Lowest MTR (%)	Highest MTR (%)
Canada	27	30	53
United States	19	22	53
Japan	15	15	65
United Kingdom	26	22	42
Germany	29	28	55
France	25	12	58
Hong Kong	1	3	20
Singapore	22	3	28

The tax function in our model therefore is:

$$T = 160 + 0.2Y$$

Noting that $Y_D = Y - T$, we can express things as:

$$Y_D = Y - (160 + 0.2Y) \text{ or,}$$

$$Y_D = Y - 160 - 0.2Y$$

$$Y_D = 0.8Y - 160$$

SELF-TEST

5. If autonomous taxes are equal to $300 and the marginal tax rate is 0.25, write an equation for disposable income.

Finally, we need to relate consumption not just to income but also to disposable income. First we find the value of autonomous consumption, but here we are looking at consumption which is autonomous to *disposable income*. **Table 6.1** shows us that this value is equal to 170 (second row of the table). Next we need to know the value of the marginal propensity to consume *out of disposable income*. We already know its value with respect to income, but here we are trying to discover what happens to consumption as disposable income changes. The marginal propensity to consume out of disposable income, or

$$MPC_D = \frac{\Delta \text{ consumption}}{\Delta \text{ disposable income}} = \frac{120}{160} = 0.75 \qquad [6.14]$$

You can check this in the table by noting, for example, that as disposable income increases by 160 from one row to the next (say from 160 to 320), consumption increases by 120 (from 290 to 410).

Remembering that autonomous consumption is 170 when disposable income is zero, the equation for the consumption function out of disposable income is:

$$C = 170 + 0.75Y_D$$

Substituting our equation for disposable income ($Y_D = 0.8Y - 160$), gives us:

$$C = 170 + 0.75(0.8Y - 160) \text{ or,}$$

$$C = 170 + 0.6Y - 120$$

$$C = 50 + 0.6Y$$

This confirms the value of the consumption function which we initially derived straight from **Table 6.1**. In other words, we can derive an algebraic expression for the consumption function directly from a table (if we have one) or indirectly if we know the tax function and the consumption function out of disposable income.

SELF-TEST

6. Suppose that the tax function for an economy is: $T = 50 + 0.3Y$ and the consumption function out of disposable income is: $C = 200 + 0.9Y_D$. Write an algebraic equation relating consumption to *income*.

We are now in a position to pull things together and explain the relationships in this table. A glance at the table shows us that as income increases, so do taxes, disposable income, saving, imports, and aggregate expenditures, while the value of net exports declines. But we need to concentrate on the relationship between income and aggregate expenditures. This is a vital relationship because spending on domestically-produced goods is what determines employment and our own economic well-being.

So let us look in some detail at exactly what happens to every additional dollar—in this case, every additional \$200—that is earned in Karinia. We note that with a MTR of 0.2, the government takes \$40 in taxes, leaving income earners with \$160 (or 80 percent). Of this extra \$160, they consume \$120, or 75 percent (the MPC_D is 0.75), and save \$40, or 25 percent (the MPS_D is 0.25). Of the \$120 spent on consumption, \$20 (the MPM is 0.1, i.e., $0.1 \times \$200$) is spent on imported goods. This leaves \$100 being spent on domestically produced goods and services, the other \$100 leaking into taxes, saving, and imports.

Figure 6.6 will help to explain the relationships:

FIGURE 6.6 Where the Income Goes

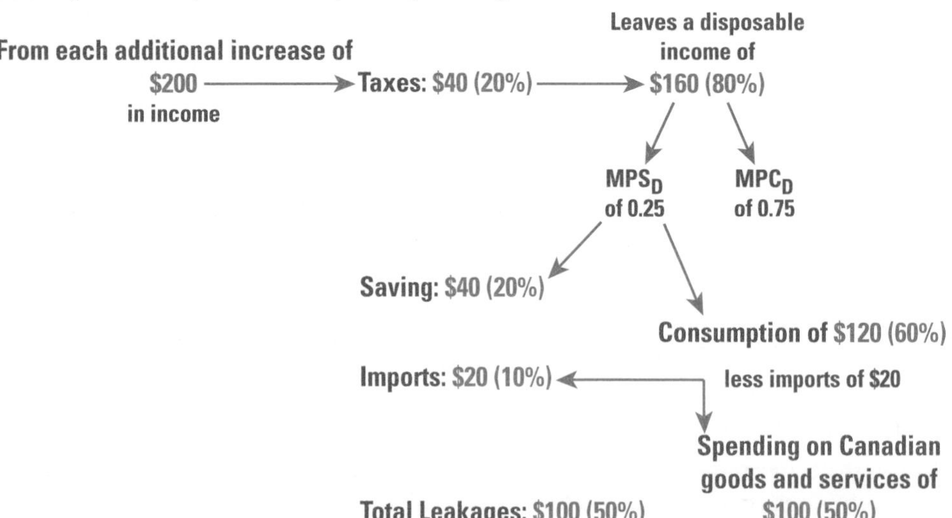

We can now relate the MPC_D to the MPC as follows:

$$MPC = (1 - MTR) \times MPC_D \quad [6.15]$$

In our model, consumers spend 75 percent (0.75) of every after-tax dollar they earn. Since they pay a 20 percent tax rate (MTR is 0.2), they spend 75 percent of 80 percent (1 – 0.2) or 60 percent of every dollar earned. In other words,

$$MPC = (1 - 0.2) \times 0.75 = 0.6$$

And finally, in our model, imports account for 10 percent (MPM = 0.1) of every dollar earned, so that:

$$MPE = MPC - MPM \text{ or } = 0.6 - 0.1 = 0.5$$

We can now see that the amount spent on domestically-produced goods (the MPE) depends on the tax rate, the marginal propensity to consume (and therefore the marginal propensity to save), and the marginal propensity to import. The greater these three marginal leakages are—i.e., the greater portion of our incomes we pay in taxes, we save or we import—the smaller the value of the MPE will be. In contrast, the smaller these amounts are, the greater the value of the MPE will be.

SELF-TEST

7. Suppose that the marginal tax rate is 0.25 and the marginal propensity to consume out of disposable income is 0.9. What is the value of the marginal propensity to consume out of income? What would be its value if the marginal tax rate were to increase to 0.3?

Let us work through a simple example of these relationships. Suppose that in another economy, the marginal tax rate is only 0.1, the MPC_D is equal to 0.8 (it spends 80 percent of after-tax dollars, and saves 20 percent), and the MPM is 0.12. We can easily calculate the value of the MPC and the MPE as follows:

$$MPC = (1 - 0.1) \times 0.8 = 0.72 \text{ and,}$$

$$MPE = 0.72 - 0.12 = 0.6$$

Therefore 60 percent of its earned income is spent on domestically produced goods, and 40 percent leaks (the marginal leakage rate, MLR, is $1 - 0.6 = 0.4$) into taxes, savings, and imports.

SELF-TEST

8. If the MPC equals 0.75 and the MPM equals 0.1, what is the value of the MPE and of the MLR? What are their values if the MPM increases to 0.15?

6.4 Autonomous and Induced Spending Graphically

LO4
Describe how small changes in spending have a large effect on national income.

We have spent some time with the expenditure model. Hopefully, you can now appreciate how interrelated the variables are and how important spending is in determining the level of income. Since a rise or fall in income will also mean a rise or fall in total employment, the expenditures model is also a model that indicates the level of employment, and unemployment, in the economy. In fact, Keynes regarded the role of expenditures in an economy as pivotal in determining income and employment. Thus, it is important for us to understand what can cause expenditures to *change* and what the effect of these changes will be.

We now know that some spending is induced by income. Therefore, aggregate expenditures will increase if the level of income increases. This happens because a higher income will induce more consumption spending. This is illustrated in Figure 6.7A, which shows how an increase in aggregate expenditures, from \$1600 to \$1700, is the *result* of an increase in the level of income from \$1600 to \$1800. That is, aggregate expenditures rises because income rises.

FIGURE 6.7 **An Increase in Spending and an Increase in the Level of Spending**

Figure 6.7A illustrates how a \$200 increase in income can increase aggregate expenditures by \$100. This is an increase in induced expenditures, causing a movement along the AE curve. Figure 6.7B shows a similar increase in aggregate expenditures of \$100. However, this is caused by an increase in autonomous expenditures, causing a shift in the AE function from AE_1 to AE_2.

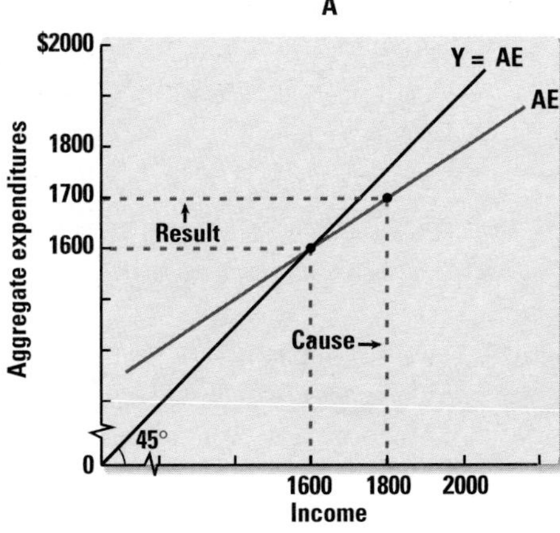

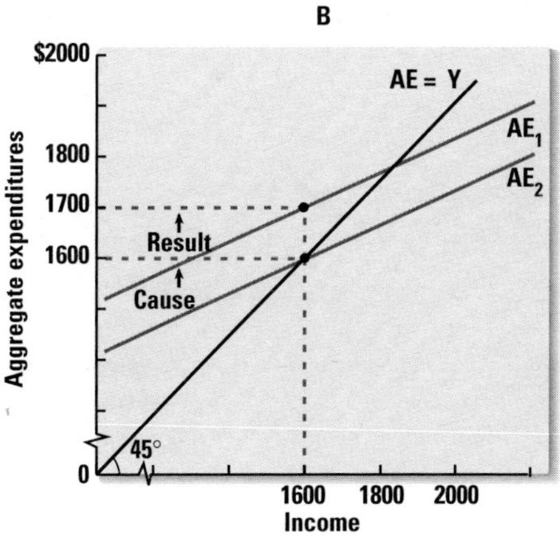

In contrast, **Figure 6.7B** shows a quite different source of change, reflecting the fact that some expenditures are autonomous. Here, aggregate expenditures have also increased from $1600 to $1700 *at the same* $1600 level of income. This increase in aggregate expenditures must be the result of a change in something other than the level of income. In fact, what this reflects is the result of a change in autonomous expenditures.

In graphical terms, a change in income will produce a movement *along* the AE curve, whereas a change in autonomous expenditures will cause a *shift* in the AE curve. We now turn to what causes these shifts.

6.5 Changes in Autonomous Expenditures

LO5
See the significance of the Keynesian revolution.

We have just seen that a change in autonomous spending will, graphically, shift the aggregate expenditures function and this will lead to a new equilibrium level of income. In the last chapter we discussed the various factors that can change aggregate demand. The same factors also affect autonomous expenditures, so this section should be something of a recap. Recall that all four sectors of spending can be affected by autonomous changes, some partially, and some wholly. Let us take each in turn and see what factors might affect each of them.

PhotoDisc

These days, it seems the majority of household spending takes place in a mall.

wealth effect: the effect of a change in wealth on consumption spending (a direct relationship between the two).

A Change in Autonomous Consumption

First, let's look at what will cause a change in autonomous consumption. Economists know that the wealth held by people can influence consumption spending. This is called the **wealth effect**. To use a micro-level example, imagine a middle-aged professional computer programmer driving home from work, reflecting on how well her life seems to be unfolding—good job, kids well on their way to growing up, spouse working at something he likes, and a mortgage that is now quite manageable. She then hears the day's closing stock quotations, which prompt her to do quick calculations after dinner on the current value of the $5000 she put into stocks a couple of years back. She is pleasantly surprised to realize that the stock is now worth over $8000—at least on paper. Her thought is to surprise the family with a proposal for a spontaneous holiday, or perhaps announce that the hot tub they had been discussing will indeed be purchased. The point is that the rise in wealth might well lead to increased consumption, even though income is unchanged.

Stockholders' wealth went up on this particular day.

TSE	Dow	London	FPX Gth.	C$
+48.33	**-36.05**	**+113.00**	**+4.87**	**-0.09**
5822.66	7897.20	5103.30	1320.37	US65.38¢
ME	**S&P 500**	**Tokyo**	**FPX Bal.**	**Gold**
+21.81	**+5.91**	**+192.51**	**+3.38**	**-1.00**
3000.42	1029.80	13789.81	1330.07	US$287.50
VSE	**Nasdaq**	**Hong Kong**	**FPX Inc.**	**Crude oil**
-3.94	**+17.37**	**+203.28**	**+3.16**	**+0.18**
397.17	1697.80	7373.51	1320.51	US$15.67

Source: *The Financial Post*, September 21, 1998.

Next, let us recognize, as we did in Chapter 5, that the level of consumption also depends on the price level. A change in the price level will cause consumption spending to change. The reason for this may seem obvious. However, it is not simply a case of higher prices causing spending to drop because people can afford less and lower prices causing them to spend more because they can afford to. The proper explanation has to do with the real value of assets. Suppose, for instance, that both prices *and* your own money income were to increase by 10 percent, so that your real income remained constant. Would this change have any real effect on your consumption? Well, even though your real income is unchanged, there is one portion of your wealth that is adversely affected by the price increase, and that is the value of your financial assets. Your wealth now has a lower purchasing power and has, in fact, declined in value. Under these conditions you may well cut your consumption and save more to replenish your real wealth. Similarly, a drop in prices will increase the real value of your wealth and lead to an increase in consumption. The effect of a change in the price level on the level of real wealth, and therefore on consumption, is known as the **real-balances effect**.

real-balances effect: the effect that a change in the value of real balances has on consumption spending (the value of real balances is affected by changing price levels).

A third aspect that can affect the level of autonomous expenditures is the fact that most households today possess a number of durable goods, ranging from kitchen appliances to VCRs, from autos to furniture. These things get replaced for two reasons. First, people get tired of them and can afford to replace them. Such action is obviously dependent on income. Second, durables get replaced simply because they wear out and must be replaced regardless (within reason) of the current state of the householder's income flow. When the water heater quits, most of us just shrug, mumble that we will have to manage somehow, and arrange for a replacement. Thus, as the stock of consumer durables gets older, the likelihood of increased consumption spending grows as the need for replacement increases.

Finally, at any given time there is a prevailing mood among an economy's consumers concerning the future state of the economy, particularly in the area of job availability, salary and wage rate trends, and expected changes in future prices. If this mood changes from, say, pessimistic to optimistic, then an autonomous increase in consumption spending is very likely to occur as well. In short, a change in consumer expectations can cause an autonomous change in consumption spending. In summary, the major determinants of autonomous consumption spending are:

- changes in wealth (wealth effect)
- changes in the price level (real balances effect)
- changes in the age of consumer durables
- changes in consumer expectations

SELF-TEST

9. Explain how each of the following affects the level of consumption and saving:

a) A sharp decrease in stock prices.

b) Rising fears of political uncertainty concerning the possible break-up of the country.

c) A dramatic decrease in the prices of most consumer goods.

d) A decrease in income tax rates.

e) A significant increase in the Goods and Services Tax (GST).

ADDED DIMENSION

Are Interest Rates Important?

You may have noticed a possible important omission from this list of the major determinants of consumption: interest rates. It is certainly true that increases in interest rates may cause some people to think twice before taking out consumer loans or buying a new car. (Remember that new house purchases are regarded—at least by StatsCan—as a form of investment and will, as we shall see in the next section, definitely be affected by changes in interest rates.) Then why are most economists reluctant to include interest rates as a determinant of consumption? The reason is that research on the topic is inconclusive.

It could well be that for some people higher interest rates mean that they cut down on consumer loans and instead start saving more because of the higher return they can now expect. But other people may see the higher interest rates as a reason to cut back on their monthly saving, since they can now earn as much as they did before, given the higher interest rates.

Keynes himself felt that interest rates are not important determinants of consumption and saving. Most of us, he felt, are creatures of habit, and it is a fairly painful exercise to readjust our spending patterns, which of course is what we would have to do if we adjusted our level of saving each time there was a change in interest rates. Income levels, and the other factors we have mentioned, are far more significant when it comes to figuring out our spending levels.

A Change in Investment

You will recall that our model regards investment spending as totally autonomous of income. So what determines the level of investment spending in the economy? For most businesses, most of the time, investment spending is financed with borrowed money. That is, corporations don't just write a cheque for several million dollars to refit some of their production equipment. Instead, they borrow the money from a bank, or perhaps from some other financial intermediary via a bond issue. Given this, it is important to recognize the impact of an interest-rate change on the total interest cost of borrowing. As an example, look at the difference in interest costs when $10 million is borrowed at 10 percent for a 20-year period and when it is borrowed at 12 percent:

$$\$10 \text{ million @ } 10\% \text{ for 20 years} = \$20 \text{ million}$$

$$\$10 \text{ million @ } 12\% \text{ for 20 years} = \$24 \text{ million}$$

It is clear that a particular investment possibility may be judged to be "worth it" at, say, 10 percent interest but not at 12 percent because of the additional $4 million that must be paid in interest.

In short, whether an investment project appears profitable or not depends on the interest costs of the money that must be borrowed to finance it. Note also that even if the investment is self-financed by a company, the rate of interest is still a determining factor in deciding whether or not to invest, since the alternative to investing is simply to leave the money in some form of savings certificate, or in a savings account, and earn a guaranteed return.

In all of this it is important to realize, as we mentioned in Chapter 4, that the real, not the nominal, rate of interest is the important determinant of investment spending. A firm that must pay a nominal rate of interest of 10 percent per annum over the next three years will be less inclined to borrow if it believes the rate of inflation is going to be 2 percent per annum over that period (making the real rate of interest it has to pay equal to 8 percent) rather than if it believes that inflation will be 7 percent (which would make the real rate equal to only 3 percent).

Besides the interest rate, the initial price that must be paid for equipment or building has a clear impact on whether that purchase will be profitable or not. Similarly, the maintenance and operating costs involved over the life of the new machine, equipment, or building must also be considered in calculating potential profitability.

Sometimes new investment must be undertaken simply because equipment has worn out or a building is in a serious state of disrepair. Thus, as the age of an economy's capital stock increases, this sort of thing occurs with greater frequency, and investment spending is higher than it would otherwise have been. In addition, investment spending may well increase when businesspeople turn optimistic about the future, and decrease as pessimism sets in. These psychological factors have an important bearing on investment decisions. Finally, bureaucracy or "red-tape requirements" add to costs and thus have an impact on the potential profitability of any proposed investment project. If red tape was cut, one would also expect that investment spending would increase.

In summary, the major determinants of investment spending are:

- interest rates
- purchase price, installation, maintenance, and operating costs of capital goods
- the age of capital goods
- business expectations
- government regulations

SELF-TEST

10. Explain how each of the following affects the level of investment:

a) A sharp increase in the world price of oil.

b) A decline in interest rates.

c) Rising fears of political uncertainty concerning the possible break-up of the country.

d) The prospect of a big increase in corporate taxes over the next few years.

e) An increase in the level of saving in the country.

A Change in Government Spending

Although our model assumes that the amount spent on goods and services by a government is autonomous, this spending component can change at any time as a result of a change in government policy. We asked earlier whether the amount of government spending is determined by tax revenues, which in turn are partly determined by the level of income. The truth is that the amount that a government spends on the purchase of goods and services in any one period has little, if any, relation to the current level of income. In the short run, the level of government spending is not constrained by the level of tax and other revenues. Governments can and often do spend in excess of revenues. In addition, other factors play their part in determining the government's spending policies. These factors include the level of interest rates, social and cultural standards, voters' expectations, budget philosophies, and political considerations. Government spending therefore can change for many reasons.

A Change in Autonomous Net Exports

We have established that exports are wholly autonomous, whereas imports are partially autonomous and partly induced by income. If you recall, there are two major factors affecting net exports. First, net exports will be affected by the level of prices in the country compared with prices abroad. If the prices of goods and services were to fall in Karinia, then foreigners would be more likely to buy Karinian exports and Karinians would be less likely to buy as many foreign imports. Second, the value of a country's currency in relation to foreign currencies will also affect net exports. A decrease in the Karinian dollar (in terms of foreign currencies) has the same effect as a decrease in the price of Karinian goods and services. Finally, Karinian exports (but not imports) are affected by the level of income in the countries that import Karinian products. A change in any of these three factors will cause a change in net exports. In summary, the factors that determine net exports are:

- comparative price levels
- the value of the exchange rate
- income levels abroad

6.6 The Multiplier

As you can now see, many factors influence the level of autonomous spending in a country, and we need to be able to work out the effect of these changes. For instance, let's start with the assumption that businesses in Karinia become more optimistic about the future. As a result they decide to increase their spending on new investment projects. Instead of spending $250 billion on investment, as they did last year, let's suppose their investment spending increases to $350 billion. Karinian businesses place additional orders for new construction, equipment, computers, and other capital projects. This will, of course, increase production by $100 billion above that of the previous year and thus boost income by a similar amount. But is that the end of the story? Is it simply the case that an extra $100 billion in spending translates into $100 billion of extra income? The answer is, in fact, no. As we shall soon see, income will increase by *more* than $100 billion. **Figure 6.8** will help to provide an explanation.

FIGURE 6.8 **The Multiplier**

The increase in autonomous spending of $100 has an immediate effect of increasing aggregate expenditures by $100. This results in a shortage. This will lead to an increase in production and, thus, income. The economy will eventually move to a new equilibrium, where the new AE function (AE_2) crosses the Y = AE curve. As a result, income here increases by a total of $200, twice as much as the initial increase in spending.

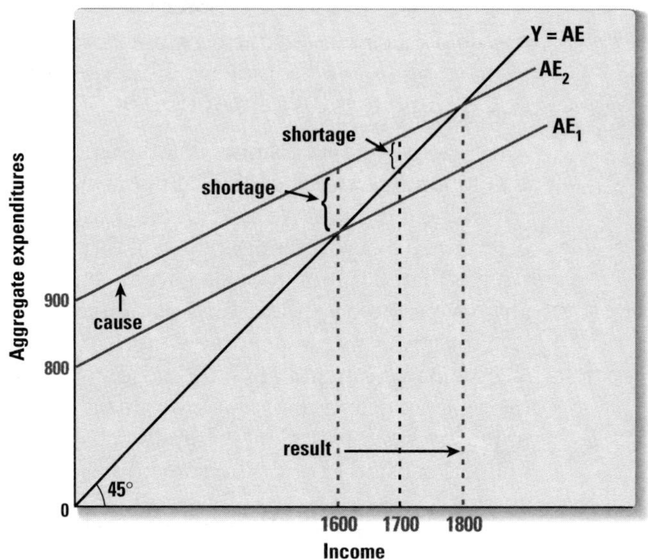

The increase in investment spending increases aggregate expenditures by $100 at every level of income, so that there is a parallel shift up in the AE function from AE_1 to AE_2. After the shift, there would be a shortage of goods and services of $100 *at the original level of income of $1600*. The result of the shortage is that production will increase. Even if income rises by \$100 (the same amount as the increase in spending) to \$1700, there would still be a shortage of goods and services, since at this income level AE_2 is still above the Y = AE line. The new equilibrium, in fact, occurs at the \$1800 level of income. In other words, income will increase by *twice* the amount of the increase in aggregate expenditures. The reason for this phenomenon is termed the *multiplier*, and it is one of the more intriguing aspects of macroeconomics. Let us work through a simple example of the multiplier at work.

The Multiplier Derived

Suppose that a new bicycle plant was built in a small community in Central Karinia. The cost of the investment is \$10 million. The immediate effect of this increase in spending is a rise in income for the contractors, suppliers, and their employees, who set up the plant. But this is not the end of the story. Presumably, these income recipients will do something with their extra income: they will spend it, or at least part of it. In other words:

An increase in investment will lead to an increase in income, which will in turn lead to an increase in consumption.

But by how much will consumption in Karinia increase? The answer depends on the value of the marginal propensity to expend. Recall that in Karinia, the MPE is equal to 0.5. That is to say, consumption will not initially increase by the full \$10 million because the government will take away taxes, some will be saved, and some of it will be spent on imports. In fact, we know that 50 percent leaks out, since the marginal leakage rate (MLR) in Karinia is also 0.5. This means that spending on goods and services produced in Karinia will initially increase by \$5 million.

We know that this \$5 million in spending becomes additional income for other producers and their employees in Karinia. And what will this second group of people do with this additional income? The answer is: spend 50 percent of it. This second round of spending becomes income for a third group of people; 50 percent of this third round of income is spent … and so on. Arithmetically we would have the following series of income increases:

Initial round		\$10 million
(assuming that the MPE is 0.5)		
Second round	(10×0.5)	5.00
Third round	(5×0.5)	2.50
Fourth round	(2.5×0.5)	1.25
Fifth round	(1.25×0.5)	0.625
Sixth round	(0.625×0.5)	0.3125
	Total	\$20 million

Therefore, given an MPE of 0.5, a \$10 million rise in autonomous investment will generate a \$20 million rise in national income. Another view of exactly the same phenomenon is that the eventual increase in income is twice the original increase in autonomous spending. This is what is meant by the **multiplier**. In terms of an equation the multiplier is equal to:

multiplier: the effect on income of a change in autonomous expenditures.

$$\text{Multiplier} = \frac{\Delta \text{ income}}{\Delta \text{ autonomous expenditures}} \qquad [6.16]$$

This is a very important conclusion. It says that if autonomous spending in Karinia could be increased by \$1 million, it would increase incomes and production by \$2 million, which would lead, accordingly, to a decrease in unemployment.

On the surface, this seems to provide a dramatic solution to any recession and a simple formula for growth. We just need to encourage people to spend more! We will do more with this idea later in the chapter. But first, it is important for you to be able to calculate the multiplier. The formula is:

$$\text{Multiplier} = \frac{1}{(1 - \text{MPE})} \quad \text{or} \quad \frac{1}{\text{MLR}} \tag{6.17}$$

So Karina's multiplier is equal to:

$$\text{Multiplier} = \frac{1}{0.5} = 2$$

If we remember that:

$$\text{MPE} = \text{MPC} - \text{MPM} \quad \text{or} \quad = (1 - \text{MTR})\text{MPC}_\text{D} - \text{MPM} \tag{6.18}$$

we could express the multiplier, in terms of the individual elements, as:

$$\text{Multiplier} = \frac{1}{\text{MPC} - \text{MPM}} \quad \text{or} \quad \frac{1}{(1 - \text{MTR})\text{MPC}_\text{D} - \text{MPM}} \tag{6.19}$$

$$\text{Multiplier} = \frac{1}{0.6 - 0.1} \quad \text{or} \quad \frac{1}{(1 - 0.2) \times 0.75 - 0.1} = 2$$

This means then that an increase in investment of $10 million would lead to an increase in income of 2 × $10 million, or $20 million.

Suppose that the MPE in Karinia were to increase to 0.6. That would mean that each round of extra income creates a greater amount of additional spending and less would go into leakages. Consequently, the MLR would be lower and have a value of 0.4. The result is a bigger multiplier. Its value is: 1/0.4, or 2.5. This leads us to the conclusion that:

A country with a high MPE will have a bigger multiplier than will a country with a low MPE.

Working with fractions can often make the job of calculating multipliers easier. For instance, if the MPE is $\frac{3}{4}$, then the MLR is $\frac{1}{4}$. To find the multiplier, simply flip (or invert) the MLR to 4. A MPE of $\frac{2}{3}$ gives and MLR of $\frac{1}{3}$ and a multiplier of 3.

SELF-TEST

11. What is the value of the multiplier in the case of the following values of the MPE?

a) 0.75; **b)** 0.9; **c)** 1; **d)** 0.5; **e)** 0.

12. Suppose that the MPC is 0.7 and the MPM is 0.1. What are the values of the MPE, the MLR, and the multiplier?

13. Suppose that the MPC_D is 0.8, the MTR is 0.15, and the MPM is 0.08. What is the value of the MPE and the multiplier?

Finally, let us examine the effects of the changes brought about by the multiplier. Let's look in a bit more detail at the effects of Karinian businesses increasing their investment spending from $250 billion to $350 billion. We have already seen the effects graphically in **Figure 6.8**. We know that, with a multiplier of 2 in Karinia, income will increase by $200. Let us confirm that the new level of equilibrium income in Karinia is indeed $1800 and, also, see how this affects the other parts of the economy:

Y	T	Y_D	C	S	I	G	X	IM	X_N	AE $(C+I+X_N+G)$
1600	480	1120	1010	110	250	400	200	260	–60	1600
1800	520	1280	1130	150	350	400	200	280	–80	1800

You can see that the additional $100 of investment spending leads to an increase in aggregate expenditures of $200. But why did it increase by this amount? The reason is that the extra income also increased consumption, which went up by $120 (from $1010 to $1130).

However, $20 of this extra consumption went on foreign products (imports rose from $260 to $280). Therefore, spending on Karinian-made consumer products rose by $100, which, with the additional $100 spending on investment products, makes up the extra $200 of aggregate expenditures.

The other changes that occurred were in the other two leakages: taxes went up by $40 and savings also went up by $40. If we add these amounts to the extra $20 in imports, we can see that total leakages went up by $100. Therefore, the increase in investment of $100 not only increased the equilibrium level of income, but in doing so, induced additional leakages of $100.

6.7 A Summing Up

The level of national income is determined by the level of aggregate expenditures. An *increase* in any of the following will cause the level of income to *increase*:

- autonomous consumption
- investment
- exports
- government spending

The size of the increase is determined by the value of the multiplier.

Of course, a decrease in any of the above items will cause a multiple decrease in income. Furthermore, an *increase* in either of the following will cause a *decrease* in national income:

- autonomous taxes
- autonomous imports

Finally, the value of the multiplier will *increase* if any of the following were to *decrease*:

- marginal propensity to save (either MPS_D or MPS since they move together)
- marginal tax rate
- marginal propensity to import

The above summary brings out the essence of the expenditures model. Income depends on the level of autonomous spending, and if this spending changes, then income will change by some multiplied amount. That is to say, small changes can have a larger effect on the level of income.

Also, we realize that the model demonstrates that the macroeconomy is always driving income to its equilibrium level. But we should add a cautionary note by asking: is it a desirable level of income? The answer unfortunately is: not necessarily. Simply because an economy is at an expenditure equilibrium tells us nothing about how well it is performing. The economy could well be in a low-level trap: it is at equilibrium, but that equilibrium is well below the full-employment level. This is the message of Keynesian economics: though competitive markets have a natural tendency to move toward equilibrium, they do not necessarily have the same tendency to move toward full employment. In fact, according to Keynes, the only way to move toward full employment is by achieving the *right level* of aggregate expenditures. This is a topic we will explore in detail in Chapters 11 and 12.

6.8 A Look at the Keynesian Revolution

What happened to the industrial economies of the world in the Great Depression of the 1930s is that they all got stuck in low-level traps: national incomes fell alarmingly in the early years of the decade and showed no signs of ever recovering. Once this occurs, the only way back to recovery is for spending to increase. But this was much easier said than done in the 1930s. Let's do more with this idea.

Getting consumers to spend more requires people to increase their autonomous spending on consumption goods, that is, to spend more even when they have not experienced a rise in income. In the 1930s, unemployed people without steady incomes simply were not able to do this. Households headed by someone who was still employed could, but wouldn't, because most were terrified that tomorrow or next week, or next month, it would be their turn to be laid off. In short, frightened people spend as little as possible. As the decade wore on, little occurred that might have changed this fear.

You might well ask, at this point: couldn't government have lowered taxes to raise consumption spending? The answer is yes, and it would have helped. Such an option was not, however, as clear-cut then as it appears to us now, simply because, for the average income earner, taxes were already very low—there just wasn't much to cut! More importantly, most governments were wedded to the idea of balancing their budgets, and seeing their own taxes revenues decline dramatically as the depression worsened would have caused them to reject any suggestion of cutting tax rates. An increase in autonomous investment spending would have done the trick, but there was little prospect of this occurring, given that a large proportion of the existing stock was underemployed or just plain unemployed. In short, who was going to build new factories when many existing ones were idle?

Well, what about export spending? Wouldn't an increase in exports mean an increase in spending? The answer, in the abstract, is yes. However, with the outbreak of the Great Depression and the collapse of the world's gold standard, international trade also collapsed as each individual nation tried, fruitlessly, to protect domestic jobs with higher and higher tariffs (taxes) on imports.

The conclusion we are approaching here is that there was very little prospect of consumption spending, investment, or exports rising. If this was valid, then the only way out of the Great Depression was to increase the fourth component of aggregate expenditure—government spending on goods and services.

Paradoxically, it appeared that governments needed to spend their way out of the Great Depression. This idea of spending our way to prosperity was and (to a lesser extent) still is a difficult concept for most to accept. In the 1930s it ran counter to the prevailing ideology of *laissez-faire*, which implied that a government was supposed to remain small and in the background and, above all, to balance its budget annually. The depression had caused tax revenues to fall, and thus the only appropriate response, according to the thinking of the day, was for governments to cut spending, not increase it. With little fiscal stimuli from governments, the depression wore on.

So, how did it finally end? The answer is simple: with the outbreak of the Second World War. Government spending for the war effort rose dramatically and rapidly. The expenditures model of Keynes would predict, given such an increase in aggregate expenditures, a prompt return to full-employment equilibrium. This is exactly what happened.

The Keynesian perspective seemed validated, and more and more people within the economics profession began calling themselves "Keynesians." Equally significant, the public mood changed, and with the end of the Second World War, governments around the world passed legislation that we could roughly tag "Full Employment Acts." In these pieces of legislation, governments committed themselves, at least in principle, to pursuing economic policies that would result in full employment. For our purposes, the significant point here is that it was recognized that government policy could be used to achieve the goal of full employment and, further, that governments had some *responsibility* in this matter. Laissez-faire economics was dead. The Keynesian revolution was complete. At least for the time being.

SELF-TEST

14. Explain how a government could spend more in the face of reduced tax revenues. In other words, where would it obtain the funds?

ADDED DIMENSION

John Maynard Keynes

John Maynard Keynes (1883–1946) (the pronunciation rhymes with "rains") was an extraordinary man who in 1936 published a revolutionary work titled *The General Theory of Employment, Interest and Money*. Keynes was a man of many talents—not only was he an economist but also a mathematician, philosopher, civil servant, corporate executive, editor, sponsor of the arts, and gambler. He exhibited a true "love of life" in all of these pursuits. The *General Theory* will certainly live on as a classic in economics and is, despite its age, quite relevant today as a starting point in a serious student's study of macroeconomics. It is a classic because it revolutionized the way economists understood the workings of the economy, particularly in the area of the causes and cures of unemployment.

6.9 Deriving Aggregate Demand

As a final wrap-up to this chapter, let us show that the aggregate demand that we looked at in the last chapter is merely an extension of, and is derived from, aggregate expenditures.

We have already discussed two ways that a change in the price level can have an impact on total expenditures. We saw how, by affecting real value of money balances, an increase in the price level reduces the level of real consumption. In addition, we know that a change in domestic prices affects net exports: a higher domestic price reduces exports and increases imports. We now want to show explicitly how a price change affects aggregate demand. Since aggregate demand means the same thing as the amount of aggregate expenditures at various price levels, what we want to do is to find the quantity of aggregate expenditures at price levels P_1, P_2, P_3 and so on. **Figure 6.9** shows how we can derive an aggregate demand curve directly from the expenditures equilibrium diagram.

FIGURE 6.9 **The Aggregate Demand Curve**

The price level P_2 is paired with a lower level of GDP, Y_2. If the price were to decrease to P_3, then the aggregate quantity demanded would increase and real GDP would rise to Y_3. Joining these points together produces a downward-sloping aggregate demand curve.

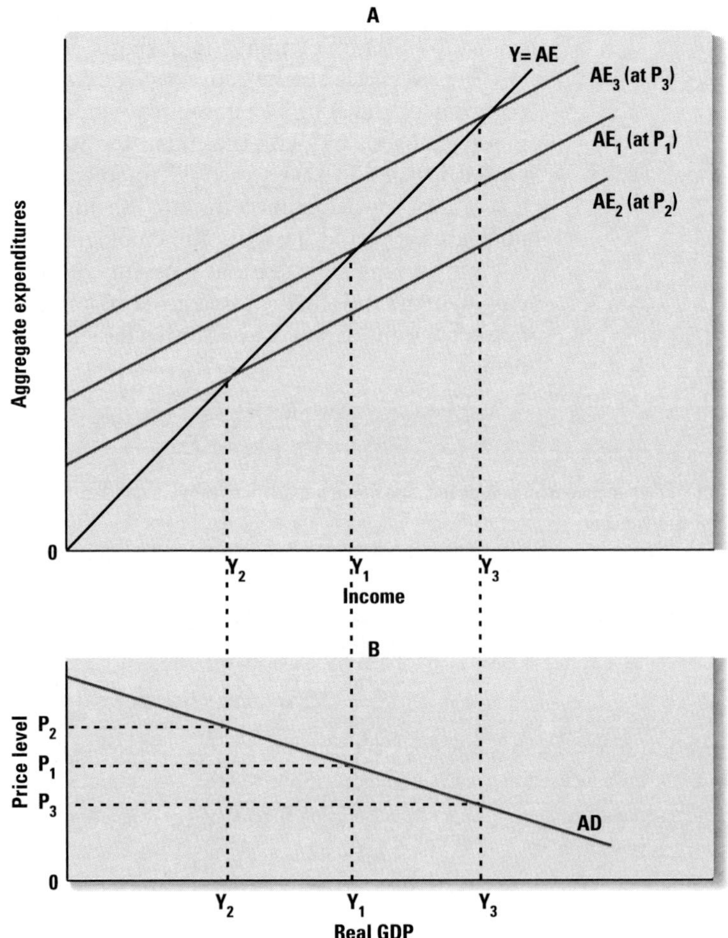

In **Figure 6.9A**, the initial expenditure equilibrium is at Y_1 where AE_1 crosses the 45° line (Y = AE). This spending is done at a particular price level. Let's call this price level P_1 and show in the bottom **Figure 6.9B** that when the price level is P_1, equilibrium real GDP is at Y_1. You should note that we have made a change in the way we label the horizontal axes. When we use aggregate expenditures on the Keynesian 45° graph, the horizontal axis is labelled income. When we use the aggregate demand graph, we label the horizontal axis real GDP. Of course, real GDP and real income are conceptually the same, but this change is to help you keep the two graphs distinct.

Now we want to figure out the effect on aggregate expenditures if the price level is higher. We just mentioned that a higher price reduces the real value of money balances (as well as other assets denominated in money). Earlier in the chapter we called this the real balances effect and suggested that the result of people holding assets with reduced values will be a reduction in their consumption spending. In addition, higher domestic prices also make our products less competitive in international markets, so that the value of exports will fall and domestic consumers will be encouraged to buy comparatively cheaper foreign goods.

As a result, net exports will decline. Lower consumption and lower net exports will mean a lower level of aggregate expenditures at each level of income. This implies a downward shift in the aggregate expenditure curve, as shown in **Figure 6.9A**: from AE_1 to AE_2. This, in turn, results in a lower level of real income: from Y_1 to Y_2. Therefore, we see in **Figure 6.9B**, a higher price level, P_2, is matched with a corresponding lower real GDP of Y_2. A lower price level will produce the opposite results: it will cause real balances, consumption spending, and net exports to increase in value. A lower price level will therefore shift the AE curve up from the original AE_1 to AE_3. This leads to a higher equilibrium income level, Y_3. In **Figure 6.9B**, therefore, a lower price level (P_3) means a higher level of real GDP (Y_3). As you can now see, every point on the aggregate demand curve is a point of equilibrium between aggregate expenditures and income. Simply put, the aggregate demand curve is downward-sloping because consumption and net exports are inversely related to the price level. This completes our look at the aggregate expenditures model.

REVIEW

1. What four factors will cause a change in *autonomous consumption*?
2. What five factors will cause a change in *autonomous investment*?
3. What three factors will cause a change in the *net export function*?
4. Define the *multiplier* and write it out in the form of a ratio.
5. What can cause a change in the *value* of the multiplier?
6. What will happen to income if *exports* fall? If *autonomous taxes* increase?
7. What is the difference between *equilibrium income* and *full-employment equilibrium*?
8. Why was it necessary for a government to spend its way out of the Great Depression of the 1930s?

STUDY GUIDE

Review

CHAPTER SUMMARY

In this chapter we use the *aggregate expenditures model* to determine the level of equilibrium income. We begin with a table of data (**Table 6.1**) which immediately exposes the *seven key variables*—all of which are familiar to you from the circular flow model in Chapter 3. We then identify the important relationships between these key variables by taking the table apart, piece by piece. In the process, we learn how to express these relationships in words, from data in tables, graphically, and using algebra.

1. Production generates income which goes to households. Individuals use this income to:
   - buy domestically produced goods and services and *imports*;
   - *save*;
   - pay *taxes*.
2. In addition to the *consumption* spending by households we have:
   - *investment* spending;
   - *government* spending on goods and services;
   - *exports*.
3. *Taxes* are both autonomous (independent of income) and induced (dependent on income). When taxes are subtracted from income we get:
   - $Y_D = Y - T$
4. *Consumption* spending (C) also has an autonomous portion and an induced portion, and can be expressed:
   - in terms of national income using the MPC; or
   - in terms of disposable income using the MPC_D.
5. *Investment* spending (I), government spending (G), and exports (X) are all autonomous spending.
6. *Saving* (S) can be expressed:
   - in terms of income using the MPS; or
   - in terms of disposable income using the MPS_D.
7. Imports (IM) have both an autonomous component and an induced component. The MPM shows the fraction of increased income that is spent on imports.
8. The *relationship* between aggregate expenditures ($C + I + G + X_N$) and income is
   - if AE is greater than Y, then a shortage exists and Y will rise;
   - if AE is less than Y, then a surplus exists and Y will fall;
   - if AE is equal to Y, then equilibrium exists.
9. Changes in *autonomous consumption* are a result of:
   - the wealth effect;
   - the real balances effect;
   - changes in the age of consumer durables;
   - changes in consumer expectations.
10. Changes in *autonomous investment* are a result of:
    - changes in the interest rate;
    - changes in the purchase price of capital goods;
    - changes in the age of capital goods;
    - changes in business expectations;
    - changes in government regulations.
11. Changes in *autonomous government* spending are a result of changes in government policies.
12. Changes in *exports* are a result of:
    - comparable price levels;
    - the value of the exchange rate;
    - income levels abroad.
13. The *multiplier* refers to the fact that an increase in autonomous spending leads to a multiplied increase in income and can be expressed in several ways:
    $$\frac{1}{1 - MPE}; \frac{1}{MLR}; \frac{1}{MPC - MPM};$$
    $$\frac{1}{(1 - MTR)MPC_D - MPM}$$

14. The way that economists look at the workings of the macroeconomy was revolutionized by the experience of the Great Depression and *Keynes's* analysis of its causes and cures.

15. We can derive the *aggregate demand curve* used in the previous chapter from the aggregate expenditures graph.

NEW GLOSSARY TERMS AND KEY EQUATIONS

autonomous consumption 199
autonomous spending 197
balance of trade 203
expenditure equilibrium 198
induced consumption 199
induced spending 197
marginal leakage rate 198
marginal propensity to consume 199
marginal propensity to expend 198
marginal propensity to import 202
marginal propensity to save 200
marginal tax rate 209
multiplier 219
real-balances effect 215
unplanned investment 204
wealth effect 214

[6.1] $MPE = \dfrac{\Delta \text{ aggregate expenditures}}{\Delta \text{ income}}$ page 198

[6.2] $MLR = \dfrac{\Delta \text{ total leakages}}{\Delta \text{ income}}$ page 198

[6.3] $MLR = (1 - MPE)$ page 198

[6.4] AE = autonomous expenditures + induced expenditures page 198

[6.5] Total taxes = autonomous taxes + induced taxes page 199

[6.6] $Y_D = Y - T$ page 199

[6.7] Total consumption = autonomous consumption + induced consumption page 199

[6.8] $MPC_D = \dfrac{\Delta \text{ consumption}}{\Delta \text{ disposable income}}$ or $MPC_D = \dfrac{\Delta C}{\Delta Y_D}$ page 199

[6.9] $S = Y_D - C$ (or $Y_D = C + S$) page 200

[6.10] $MPS = \dfrac{\Delta \text{ savings}}{\Delta \text{ income}}$ or $MPS = \dfrac{\Delta S}{\Delta Y}$ page 200

[6.11] $MPM = \dfrac{\Delta \text{ imports}}{\Delta \text{ income}}$ or $MPM = \dfrac{\Delta IM}{\Delta Y}$ page 202

[6.12] $MPE = MPC - MPM$ page 206

[6.13] $MTR = \dfrac{\Delta \text{ taxes}}{\Delta \text{ income}}$ page 209

[6.14] $MPC = \dfrac{\Delta \text{ consumption}}{\Delta \text{ disposable income}}$ page 210

[6.15] $MPC = (1 - MTR) \times MPC_D$ page 212

[6.16] $\text{multiplier} = \dfrac{\Delta \text{ income}}{\Delta \text{ autonomous expenditures}}$ page 219

[6.17] $\text{multiplier} = \dfrac{1}{1 - MPE}$ or $\dfrac{1}{MLR}$ page 220

[6.18] multiplier = $MPC - MPM$ or $(1 - MTR)MDC_D - MPM$ page 220

[6.19] $\text{multiplier} = \dfrac{1}{MPC - MPM}$ or $\dfrac{1}{(1 - MTR)MPC_D - MPM}$ page 220

STUDY TIPS

1. It is essential for you to be clear about the distinction between autonomous spending, which does *not* depend on the level of income, and induced spending, which does.

2. Be careful when you draw your diagrams that the vertical and horizontal axes are drawn to the same scale. If they are not, your line will not be 45°, and your graph will be misleading. When constructing graphs in this chapter, it is important that you construct reasonably large, accurate graphs. It's worth the extra effort.

3. Another aspect of graphing deserves mention. The vertical axis in math is often referred to as the Y-axis, and the horizontal is called the X-axis. This might occasionally be confusing, since economists use the letter Y to stand for income. In macroeconomics, income (or Y) is placed on the X-axis.

4. Probably the area of this chapter that causes most confusion for the student is the distinction between national income (GDP) and disposable income. If it helps, think back to Chapter 3 and remember all the additions and subtractions that had to be made to GDP to arrive at a figure for disposable income. In this model, all of those adjustments have been lumped together into a single heading: tax. Again, remember from GDP accounting that the amounts people consume and save are determined by *disposable* income and not by *national* income.

5. Some students have difficulty appreciating the fact that Y stands for not just the concept of income, but also the *value* of income. When the letter Y occurs in an equation like Y = 100 + 0.6Y, for instance, the Y is short for 1Y.

6. Be careful in your derivation of disposable income that taxes are deducted and not added to income. For example, if autonomous taxes are $100 and induced taxes are 20 percent of national income, then total taxes are (100 + 0.2Y). This *whole term* is subtracted from national income to give disposable income:

$$\underset{\text{(disposable income)}}{Y_D} = \underset{\text{(national income)}}{Y} - \underset{\text{(taxes)}}{(100 + 0.2Y)}$$

When you remove the brackets from the tax function, the plus sign becomes a minus:

$$Y_D = Y - 100 - 0.2Y$$

Answered Questions

Indicate whether the following statements are true or false.

1. **T or F** Autonomous spending depends on the level of income, whereas induced spending does not.

2. **T or F** Equilibrium income occurs where the value of production is equal to aggregate expenditures.

3. **T or F** Induced taxes do not change with income, but autonomous taxes do.

4. **T or F** It is possible for the economy to be in equilibrium but not at full employment.

5. **T or F** The real-balances effect refers to the effect that a change in interest rates has on the real value of wealth.

6. **T or F** A decrease in the interest rate will cause an increase in investment spending.

7. **T or F** The value of the multiplier is equal to the inverse of the marginal leakage rate.

8. **T or F** Growth in an economy's GDP (if not caused by a change in exports) results in a larger trade deficit or in a reduction of a previous trade surplus.

9. **T or F** If taxes increase, disposable income will fall but consumption will remain the same.

10. **T or F** If the marginal tax rate increases, then the marginal propensity to expend will be smaller and the marginal leakage rate will be larger.

Basic (Questions 11–22)

11. What does the multiplier effect indicate?
    a) That a small increase in income will generate a large decrease in aggregate expenditures.
    b) That a change in autonomous expenditures will cause income to change by a larger amount.

c) That a small increase in income will generate a large increase in aggregate expenditures.
d) That a change in induced expenditures will cause income to change by a larger amount.

12. What does the marginal propensity to expend mean?
a) It is the fraction of income that is not spent.
b) It is the ratio of change in income that results from a change in expenditures.
c) It is the ratio of change in expenditures that results from a change in income.
d) It is the fraction of income that is taxed.

13. What is the effect of a decrease in government spending?
a) It leads to an even larger increase in income.
b) It leads to an even larger decrease in income.
c) It leads to a smaller increase in income.
d) It leads to a smaller decrease in income.

14. What effect does an increase in exports have?
a) It leads to an even larger increase in income.
b) It leads to an even larger decrease in income.
c) It leads to a smaller increase in income.
d) It leads to a smaller decrease in income.

15. What is the effect of a decrease in the MTR?
a) The MLR will increase and the multiplier will increase.
b) The MLR will decrease and the multiplier will increase.
c) The MLR will increase and the multiplier will decrease.
d) The MLR will decrease and the multiplier will decrease.

16. What is the most important determinant of the level of consumption?
a) The level of prices.
b) Consumer expectations.
c) The stock of wealth.
d) The level of income.

17. What circumstance will lead to a smaller multiplier?
a) If the MPS becomes bigger.
b) If the MPC becomes bigger.
c) If the MPM becomes smaller.
d) If the MLR becomes smaller.

18. All, except one, of the following statements concerning the equilibrium level of income are correct. Which is incorrect?
a) There will be no tendency for firms to increase or decrease production.
b) The economy is operating at full employment.
c) Unplanned investment in inventories will not occur.
d) Leakages equal injections.
e) Aggregate expenditures equal income.

Refer to **Figure 6.10** to answer questions 19 and 20.

FIGURE 6.10

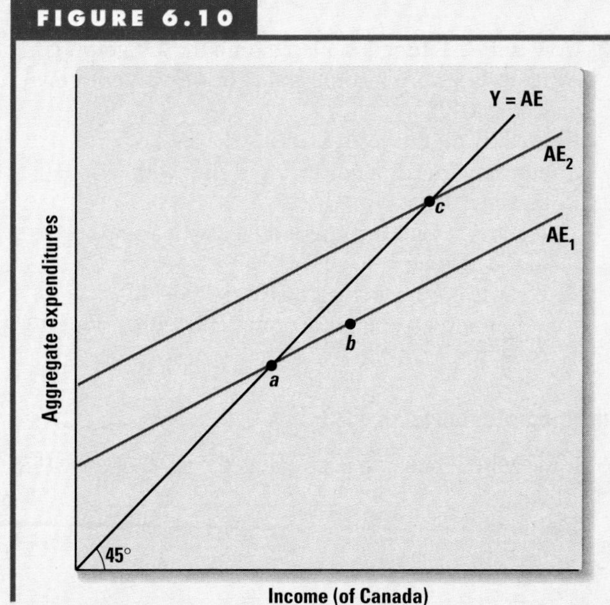

19. Refer to **Figure 6.10** to answer this question. What could cause a change from *a* to *b*?
a) An increase in U.S. income.
b) An increase in government spending.
c) A decrease in interest rates.
d) An increase in Canadian income.
e) A decrease in autonomous taxes.

20. Refer to **Figure 6.10** to answer this question. All of the following, except one, could cause a change from *a* to *c*. Which is the exception?
a) An increase in Canadian income.
b) A decrease in interest rates.
c) A decrease in the Canadian exchange rate.
d) A decrease in autonomous taxes.
e) An increase in U.S. income.

21. What are induced consumption and the marginal propensity to consume, respectively?
a) The amount of income that results from higher levels of consumption and the change in income divided by the change in consumption.

b) The amount of consumption that results from higher levels of income and the change in consumption divided by the change in income.
c) The amount of consumption that occurs at zero income and the change in consumption divided by the change in income.
d) The amount of consumption that occurs at zero income and the change in income divided by the change in consumption.

22. How is the AE function placed onto the 45° graph ?
a) It starts at zero income and rises with a slope equal to the MPE.
b) It starts on the vertical axis at the level of autonomous expenditures and rises with a slope equal to the MPE.
c) It starts at zero income and falls with a slope equal to the MPE.
d) It starts on the vertical axis at the level of autonomous expenditures and falls with a slope equal to the MPE.

Intermediate (Questions 23–30)

23. If the MPE is equal to 0.4, what is the value of the MLR?
a) 0.6.
b) 2.5.
c) 0.4.
d) 40.

24. If the MPE is equal to 0.4, what is the value of the multiplier?
a) 1.67.
b) 2.5.
c) 0.25.
d) 0.167.

25. If X_N is an autonomous $90 and the MPM is 0.2, what is the value of X_N at an income of $500?
a) +$10.
b) −$10.
c) +$90.
d) +$590.

26. What does the real-balances effect refer to?
a) The effect that a change in savings has on the real rate of interest.
b) The level of income where it is exactly equal to the level of consumption.
c) The effect that a change in interest rates has on the real value of savings.
d) The effect that a change in the price level has on the real value of wealth.
e) The effect of a change in consumption on the real value of wealth.

27. Which of the following variables in the expenditure model are wholly autonomous and which are partly induced?
a) I, G, and X_N are autonomous; S, IM, and C are partly induced.
b) I, G, and C are autonomous; S, IM, and X are partly induced.
c) I, G, and X are autonomous; S, IM, and C are partly induced.
d) G, X, and IM are autonomous; S, C, and I are partly induced.

28. Which two of the four components of the aggregate expenditures are wholly autonomous?
a) C and I.
b) C and G.
c) I and G.
d) I and X_N.
e) C and X_N.

29. What happens to income earned in Canada?
a) It is spent on exports, imports, and investment and saved.
b) It is spent on consumption, imports, and taxes and saved.
c) It is spent on consumption, exports, and taxes and saved.
d) It is spent on consumption, imports, taxes, and investment.
e) It is spent on imports, taxes, and government spending.

30. Graphically, when is the balance of trade equal to zero?
a) When the rising IM line intersects the horizontal X line.
b) When the rising X line intersects the horizontal IM line.
c) When the rising IM line intersects the horizontal axis.
d) When the rising X line intersects the horizontal axis.

Advanced (Questions 31–35)

Refer to **Table 6.4** to answer questions 31 and 32.

TABLE 6.4

Y	T	Y_D	C
100	40	60	50
200	60	140	90
300	80	220	130
400	100	300	170
500	120	380	210

31. Refer to **Table 6.4** to answer this question. What is the algebraic expression for consumption?
- **a)** C = 100 + 0.4Y.
- **b)** C = 10 + 0.4Y.
- **c)** C = 100 + 0.6Y.
- **d)** C = 0 + 0.5Y.

32. Refer to **Table 6.4** to answer this question. What is the algebraic expression for the consumption function (out of Y_D)?
- **a)** C = 20 + 0.5Y_D.
- **b)** C = 20 + 0.4Y_D.
- **c)** C = 50 + 0.4Y_D.
- **d)** C = 10 + 0.4Y_D.

Answer questions 33–35 on the basis of the parameters for an economy shown in **Table 6.5**. (All figures are in $billion.)

TABLE 6.5

G = 1200
I = 400
C = 100 + 0.6Y
X_N = 700 – 0.2Y

33. Refer to **Table 6.5** to answer this question. What is the value of the multiplier in this economy?
- **a)** 1.
- **b)** 1.54.
- **c)** 1.67.
- **d)** 2.
- **e)** 5.

AE = 2400 + 0.4Y
autonomous agg. expenditures — mpe (induced expend)

34. Refer to **Table 6.5** to answer this question. What is the value of equilibrium income in this economy?
- **a)** $3840.
- **b)** $3967.
- **c)** $4000.
- **d)** $4133.
- **e)** $5000.

AE = Y
Y = 2400 + 0.4Y

35. Refer to **Table 6.5** to answer this question. At equilibrium, what is the balance of trade?
- **a)** A surplus of $100.
- **b)** A deficit of $100.
- **c)** A surplus of $300.
- **d)** A deficit of $300.
- **e)** A zero balance of trade.

Parallel Problems

ANSWERED PROBLEMS

36. Key Problem Table 6.6 shows some of the expenditure amounts in the economy of Arkinia.

TABLE 6.6

Y	T	Y_D	C	S	I	G	X	IM	X_N	AE $(C+I+X_N+G)$
$0	____	____	____	____	60	150	50	____	____	____
100	____	50	____	–10	____	____	____	____	30	____
200	75	____	120	5	____	____	____	____	____	____
300	100	____	180	____	____	____	____	40	____	____
400	125	____	____	35	____	____	____	50	____	____
500	____	____	300	____	____	____	____	60	____	____
600	____	425	____	____	____	____	____	____	____	____
700	____	____	420	____	____	____	____	____	____	____
800	____	575	____	95	____	____	____	____	–40	____

The MPC, the MTR, and the MPM are all constant, as are the values of the three injections.

a) Complete **Table 6.6**, and in **Figure 6.11** graph a 45° line and the aggregate expenditure function, labelled AE_1. Identify expenditure equilibrium with the letter e.

FIGURE 6.11

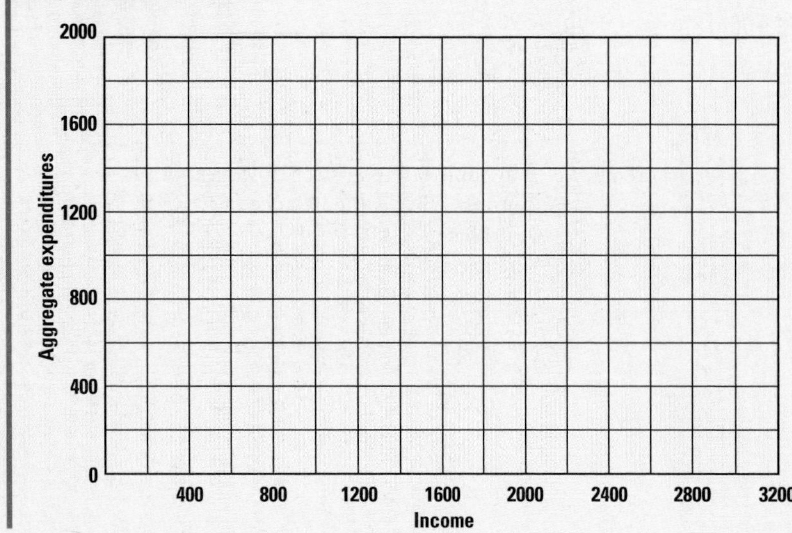

b) What is the value of equilibrium income?
Income: $ ________________ .

c) What is the value of total injections and total leakages at equilibrium?
Total injections: ________________ ;
total leakages: ________________ .

d) What is the value of the MPE in Arkinia?
MPE: ________________ .

e) What is the value of the multiplier in Arkinia?
Multiplier: ________________ .

f) Suppose that exports from Arkinia were to increase by $150. Draw the new aggregate expenditure function on **Figure 6.11** and label it AE_2. Identify the new expenditure equilibrium.

g) What is the value of the new equilibrium income, and at equilibrium, what is the value of net exports?
Income: ________________ ;
net exports: ________________ .

Basic (Problems 37–42)

37. The economy of Irinika has the following parameters:
Autonomous exports = $400 million;
Autonomous imports = $100 million; MPM = 0.25

a) What is the balance of trade at an income of $800?

________ .

b) What is the balance of trade at an income of $2000? ________.

c) At what income level is there a zero balance of trade? ________.

38. In Irinika, income rose by $75 million over the past year. During the same period, its aggregate expenditures increased by $48 million. What are the values of its MPE, MLR, and multiplier?

________; ________; ________.

39. In Arkania, income rose by $200 million over the past year. During the same period, tax revenue increased by $40 million, savings rose by $16 million, and imports rose by $24 million. What are the values of its MPE, MLR, and multiplier?

________; ________; ________.

40. The data in Table 6.7 is for the economy of Anariki.

TABLE 6.7

Y	AE	Unplanned Investment
$1600	______	–$400
1800	______	–300
2000	______	–200
2200	______	–100
2400	______	0
2600	______	+100
2800	______	+200

a) Fill in the AE column.

b) What is the value of equilibrium income? Equilibrium income: $ ________.

c) At income $2000, will inventories be increasing or decreasing?

________.

41. Irkania's aggregate expenditures function is shown in Figure 6.12.

FIGURE 6.12

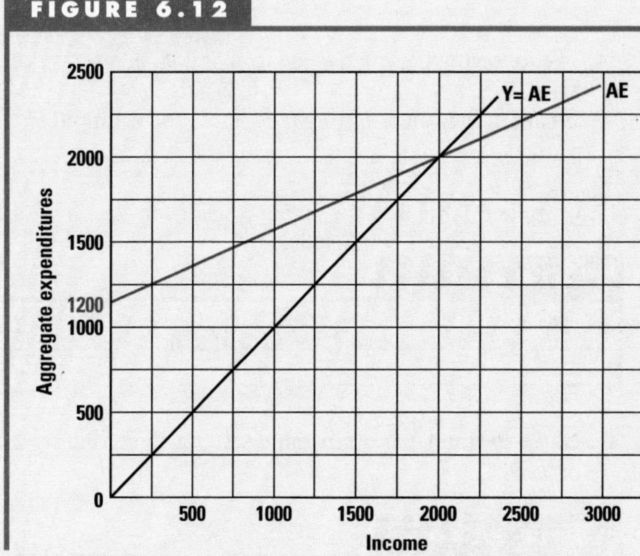

a) What is the value of MPE and the multiplier in Irkania?
MPE: ________;
multiplier: ________.

b) What is the value of equilibrium income? ________.

c) If investment in Irkania were to decrease by $450, what would be the new level of equilibrium income?

________.

42. The partial data in Table 6.8 are for the economy of Arinaka. Planned investment, government spending, and *all* taxes are autonomous. Furthermore, you may assume that the MPC, MPS, and MPM are constant.

a) Fill in the blanks in Table 6.8.

b) What is the value of equilibrium income? ________.

c) If planned investment decreases by 20, what is the new value of equilibrium income? ________.

TABLE 6.8

Y	T	Y_D	C	S	I	G	X_N	AE	Unplanned Investment
$400	$40	____	$320	$40	$60	$50	+ $10	____	________
450	____	____	____	45	____	____	–5	____	________
500	____	____	____	____	____	____	____	____	________
550	____	____	____	____	____	____	____	____	________

Intermediate (Problems 43–47)

43. If Kaniria's MTR is 0.3, and its MPC_D is 0.6, what is the value of its MPS_D, its MPC, and MPS?

__________; __________; __________.

44. The following parameters are for Nirakia:

$MPC_D = 0.9$; MTR = 0.25 MPM = 0.175

What are the values of its MPE, MLR, and multiplier?

__________; __________; __________.

45. Complete **Table 6.9**'s balancing row for the economy of Kaniria, which is in equilibrium:

TABLE 6.9

Y	T	Y_D	C	S	I	G	X	IM	X_N	AE
____	____	____	____	110	80	180	____	80	10	800

46. Given the information in **Table 6.10** for the economy of Zawi:

TABLE 6.10

$C = 42 + 0.65Y$	$X_N = 18 - 0.15Y$
$I = 120$	$G = 220$

a) What is the value of equilibrium income?

__________.

b) Set up a balancing row to verify your calculations (the tax equation is: T = 60 + 0.2Y and X = 200).

Y										AE

c) If exports decrease by 50, what would be the new equilibrium income? __________.

47. You are given the following parameters for the economy of Patria in **Table 6.11**:

TABLE 6.11

$C = 32 + 0.9Y_D$	$T = 30 + 0.1Y$
$I = 110$	$IM = 42 + 0.06Y$
$G = 170$	
$X = 57$	

a) What is the value of expenditures equilibrium?

__________.

b) What is the value of total leakages and injections at expenditures equilibrium? __________.

c) What is the value of the multiplier? __________.

Advanced (Problems 48–50)

48. **Figure 6.13** shows the economy of Itassuna.

FIGURE 6.13

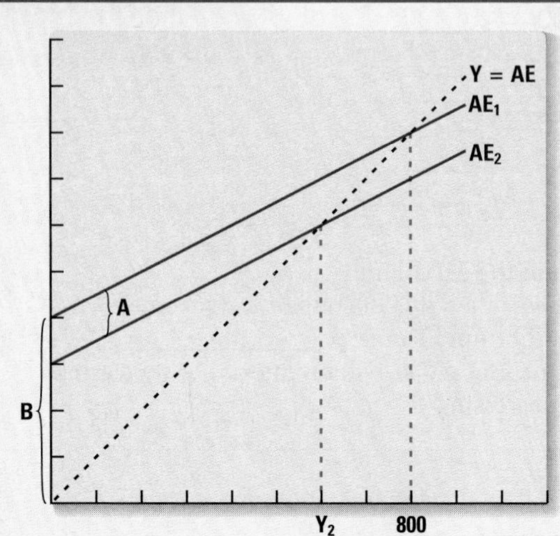

a) If the value of A is 50 and the multiplier is 4, what is the value of Y_2? __________.

b) If the value of Y_2 is 700 and the value of A is 60, what is the value of the multiplier? __________.

c) Given AE_1, if the value of the multiplier is 2, what is the value of B? __________.

49. **Table 6.12** shows the parameters for the economy of Hutu.

TABLE 6.12

C = 80 + 0.6Y	X_N = 140 – 0.1Y
I = 200	G = 300

a) What is the value of equilibrium income? ________ .

b) If exports were to increase by 30, what would be the new value of equilibrium income? ____________ .

c) Given your answer in b), what is the new value for X_N? ____________ .

d) Given the equilibrium income in a), if full employment income is 1350, what change in government spending is necessary to move the economy to this level? ____________________ .

50. The following data provide information on Akinira's economy in a particular year.
Y = \$500; savings = \$120;
investment spending = \$100;
government spending = \$200; taxes = \$180; and
the balance of trade = +\$70.

a) Explain which variables depend on others. ________________________________ .

b) Is the economy in equilibrium, and what has happened to the country's level of inventories in this particular year? ________________________________ .

c) Comment on what implications this might have for the following year's GDP. ________________________________ .

UNANSWERED PROBLEMS

51. **Key Problem Table 6.13** shows some of the expenditure amounts in the economy of Nakarini. The MPC, the MTR, and the MPM are all constant, as are the values of the three injections.

TABLE 6.13

Y	T	Y_D	C	S	I	G	X	IM	X_N	AE (C + I + X_N + G)
\$0					135	320	150			
200		100		–35					110	
400	140			5						
600	180		375					80		
800	220		495	85				100		
1000			615					120		
1200		900								
1400			855							
1600		1220		245					–30	

a) Complete **Table 6.13**, and in **Figure 6.14** graph a 45° line and the aggregate expenditure function, labelled AE_1. Identify expenditure equilibrium.

b) What is the value of equilibrium income?

c) What is the value of total injections and total leakages at equilibrium?

d) What is the value of the MPE in Nakarini?

e) What is the value of the multiplier in Nakarini?

f) Suppose that government spending from Nakarini were to decrease by \$200. Draw the new aggregate expenditure function on **Figure 6.14**, and label it AE_2. Identify the new expenditure equilibrium.

g) What is the value of the new equilibrium income, and at equilibrium, what is the value of net exports?

FIGURE 6.14

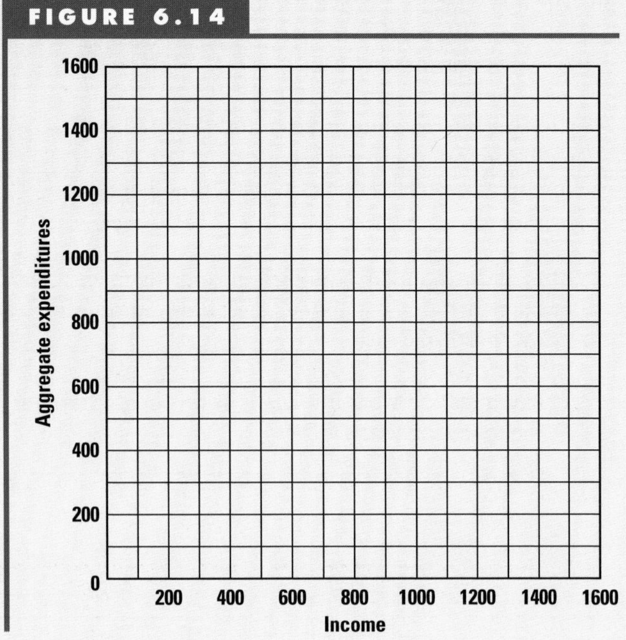

Basic (Problems 52–57)

52. The net export function for the economy of Yarim is: $X_N = 480 - 0.1Y$.
   a) What is the balance of trade at an income of $4200?
   b) What is the balance of trade at an income of $5000?
   c) At what income level is there a zero balance of trade?

53. In Lefaat, income fell by $20 billion in the past year. During the same period, its aggregate expenditures fell by $12 billion. What are the values of its MPE, MLR, and multiplier?

54. In Nina, income decreased by $9 billion over the past year. During the same period tax revenue, savings, and imports all decreased by $1 billion each. What are the values of Nina's MPE, MLR, and multiplier?

55. The data in **Table 6.14** is for the economy of Choga.

TABLE 6.14

Y	AE	Unplanned Investment
$900	______	–$75
1000	______	–50
1100	______	–25
1200	______	0
1300	______	+25

   a) Fill in the AE column.
   b) What is the value of equilibrium income?
   c) At an income level of $1300, are inventories increasing or decreasing?

56. **Figure 6.15** shows the aggregate expenditure function for the economy of Arianki.

FIGURE 6.15

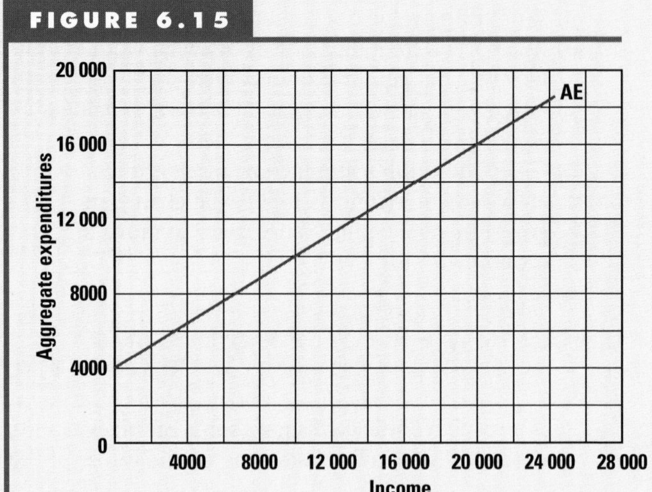

   a) What is the value of equilibrium national income in Arianki?
   b) What is the value of the multiplier?
   c) If government spending were to increase by 4000, what would be the new value of equilibrium income?
   d) If, instead, autonomous imports were to increase by 2000, what would be the new value of equilibrium income?

57. The partial data in **Table 6.15** is for the economy of Mari. Planned investment, government spending, and *all* taxes are autonomous. Furthermore, you may assume that the MPC, MPS, and MPM are constant.
   a) Fill in the blanks in **Table 6.15**.
   b) What is the value of equilibrium income?
   c) If government spending increases by $3 billion, what is the new value for equilibrium income?

TABLE 6.15

Y	T	Y_D	C	S	I	G	X_N	AE	Unplanned I
$80	____	____	____	____	____	____	____	____	____
90	____	80	59	____	____	____	____	____	____
100	10	____	65	25	____	30	0	____	____
110	____	____	____	____	10	____	–1	____	____

Intermediate (Problems 58–62)

58. If Girsu's MTR is 0.2 and its MPC_D is 0.8, what is the value of its MPS_D, MPC, and MPS?

59. The following parameters are for the economy of Jarmo.
$MPC_D = 0.9$ MTR = 0.1
MPM = 0.06
What are the values of Jarmo's MPE, MLR, and multiplier?

60. Table 6.16 shows partial data for the economy of Nikaria, which is in equilibrium. Fill in the blanks in the balancing row.

TABLE 6.16

Y	T	Y_D	C	S	I	G	X	IM	X_N	AE
____	____	480	____	____	110	300	90	105	____	800

61. Given the information in Table 6.17 for the economy of Zawi:

TABLE 6.17

$C = 20 + 0.6Y$	$I = 70$
$X_N = 50 - 0.2Y$	$G = 160$

a) What is the value of equilibrium income?
b) Set up a balancing row to verify your calculations (the tax equation is: $T = 30 + 0.25Y$ and $X = 120$)

Y										AE

c) If exports increase by 30, what would be the new equilibrium income?

62. You are given the following parameters for the economy of Matria in Table 6.18:

TABLE 6.18

$C = 18 + 0.8Y_D$	$T = 20 + 0.15Y$
$I = 90$	$IM = 20 + 0.08Y$
$G = 120$	
$X = 48$	

a) What is the value of expenditures equilibrium?
b) What is the value of total leakages and injections at expenditures equilibrium?
c) What is the value of the multiplier?

Advanced (Problems 63–67)

63. Figure 6.16 shows the economy of Kinaria.

FIGURE 6.16

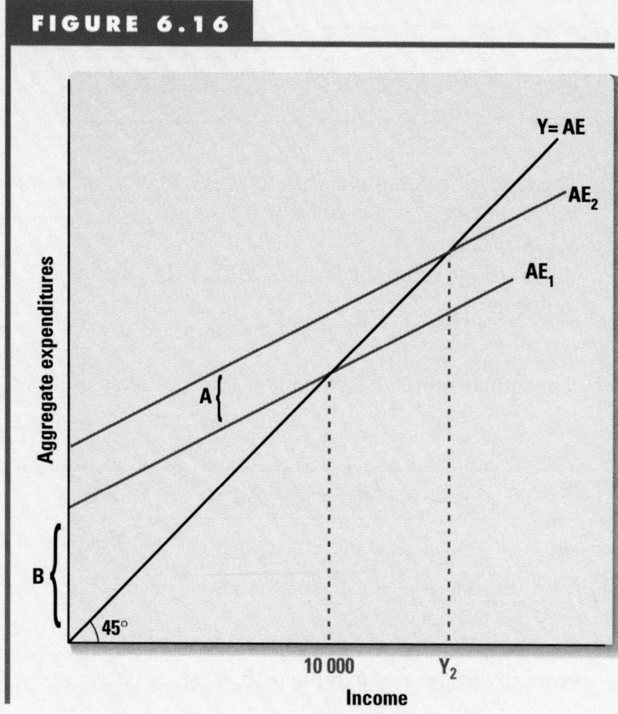

a) If the value of A is 3000 and the multiplier is 2, what is the value of Y_2?
b) If the value of Y_2 is 14 000 and the value of A is 2000, what is the value of the multiplier?
c) Given AE_1, if the value of the multiplier is 4, what is the value of B?

64. Table 6.19 shows the parameters for the economy of Irakian.

TABLE 6.19

$C = 40 + 0.5Y$	$I = 150$
$X_N = 90 - 0.1Y$	$G = 350$

a) What is the value of equilibrium income?
b) If exports were to decrease by 30, what would be the new value of equilibrium income?
c) Given your answer in b), what is the new value for X_N?
d) Given the equilibrium income in a), if full employment income is $900, what change in government spending is necessary to move the economy to this level?

65. The following data provides information on Susa's economy.
Y = $160; savings = $30; investment spending = $20; government spending = $30; taxes = $30; and the balance of trade = –$10.
a) Explain which variables depend on others.
b) Is the economy in equilibrium and what has happened to the level of inventories in this particular year?
c) Comment on what implications this might have for the following year's level of income.

66. Sometimes spending increases because income increases, and sometimes spending increases without a change in income. Explain.

67. If, initially, injections were equal to leakages and injections were to increase, this would cause an increase in leakages until the two are again equal. Explain what this means and which leakages are affected.

Web-Based Activities

1. Go to **www.statcan.ca/english/Pgdb?Economy/econom.htm#nat** and click on "National accounts" and then click on "Private and public capital expenditures." What has happened to capital expenditures in Canada in the last five years? What implications does this have for Canada's real GDP?

2. Go to **www.statcan.ca/english/Pgdb?Economy/econom.htm#nat** and click on "National accounts" and then click on "Canada's balance of international payments." Calculate Canada's net exports for the last five years (goods and services receipts less goods and services payments). Do net exports contribute to Canada's economic growth?

CHAPTER SEVEN

Money and Banking

LEARNING OBJECTIVES

This chapter will enable you to:

LO1 **Understand the functions and characteristics of money.**

LO2 **Recognize the various kinds of money.**

LO3 **Explain what is included in the money supply.**

LO4 **Explain what is and is not money.**

LO5 **Describe the main function of modern banks as money lenders.**

LO6 **Explain how a small amount of cash can support many loans and create more money.**

What's ahead...

In this chapter we look at the definition and functions of money. We look at its origins and at how the concept of money has changed over the centuries. We then briefly examine the development of banks and explore the process through which the banking system is able to create money.

A QUESTION OF RELEVANCE…

You and four friends decide to go out for a fancy meal to celebrate another successful year at college. When the bill arrives, you split it into five shares. Frederick pays by cheque. Sian pays by credit card. Althea digs deep into her pocket and comes up with 20 loonies. Bosie gives an IOU to the manager (a friend of his). Finding that you have none of the above means, you have to pay by "volunteering" to wash up (for yourself and 200 other diners). You all paid in different ways. But who used money? Some of you? All of you? So what does constitute money in our modern economy?

Money has been called humanity's greatest invention and its greatest curse. People fret for it, and they sweat for it. For some it's the root of all evil and for others it is the source of all joy. Economists, however, being less fanciful and poetic, refer to it merely as a medium of exchange. The reason economists don't wax quite so lyrical when they discuss money is that they regard it as merely one form of holding wealth. After all, it is possible to be extremely wealthy but literally have no money. In fact, there is a problem with wealth holding in the form of money, because money generally doesn't accumulate. That is, you cannot earn a return from money alone. This is not the case with other forms of wealth, such as stocks and bonds, real estate, or a term deposit in a bank. The other reason why economists remain subdued on the topic of money is because they do not focus on the effect of money on the individual (in that respect, most economists revere money as much as the next person), but on the role of money in the whole economy.

CP/Toronto Star/Bernard Weil

A group of young students in Toronto take turns playing the "My Money" game. The former stockbroker who designed the game for the Bank of Montreal hopes it will help children learn to invest wisely once they get some money of their own.

As for this latter aspect, economists over the centuries have held differing views. Adam Smith suggested that money was merely a veil that often conceals the phenomenon of real production that lies behind it. He used the analogy of money being like a river that helps to bring goods to the market but does not affect the actual volume of goods. Today, we know that money can have a determining influence over the "real" variables, such as production and employment. For example, we saw in the previous chapter that an increase in the money supply can result in an increase in real GDP. It is these and other aspects of money that we will be looking at in these two chapters. We'll conclude these opening remarks by mentioning one obvious aspect of money: it has an important role in determining prices.

SELF-TEST

1. What do you think Adam Smith might have meant by the phrase, "money is a veil"?

As the market economy was emerging in the sixteenth and seventeenth centuries, many people had personal experience of how the amount of money (and, more specifically, changes in the amount of money) in a society could affect prices. The huge influx of gold from the new colonies into Europe produced a persistent and pernicious increase in prices in most European countries. Gold meant money, and if the amount of money quickly increases while the volume of production changes slowly, then you get the makings of what we previously called demand–pull inflation. This is sometimes characterized as too much money chasing too few goods. In the same vein, consider one of the possibly apocryphal stories coming out of the Second World War, which relates a devious scheme by the Germans to disrupt the Allied war effort. This plan involved the dispatch of bombers over Britain, equipped not with bombs but with millions of counterfeit pound notes. These were to be scattered all over British towns and cities. The effects would have been obvious. The British people, as the heirs to this sudden windfall, would do the predictable: they would spend it.

Thus the demand for the limited quantity of consumer goods would rise dramatically, and since production could not increase immediately, the only effect would be the bidding up of prices. Britain would have been faced with the same devastating phenomenon that the Germans themselves had experienced in the early 1920s: galloping or hyper-inflation. This story is used to illustrate the very strong link between changes in the supply of money and the level of prices. More on this later.

7.1 The Functions and Characteristics of Money

LO1
Understand the functions and characteristics of money.

medium of exchange: something that is accepted as payment for goods and services.

So far we have discussed some aspects of money without actually defining it. Let's continue to skirt around the definition for now by asking the question: what is money good for? Well, of course the answer is: to spend. In fact, it has been suggested that money imparts value only in parting. The first, and prime, function of money is that it acts as a **medium of exchange**. Without money, people would be forced to barter goods and services directly. However, barter requires what is called the double coincidence of wants. This simply means that if I am to trade with you, you must have what I want, and I must have what you want. If this is not the case, then we must try to find a third, fourth, or fifth party to act as intermediaries. This would mean that to obtain a bare minimum of goods and services through barter, a person would spend far more time and effort in exchanging than in producing. Thus, economists describe the barter system as having high transactions costs.

ADDED DIMENSION

Money Increases Wealth

A society possessing no money would be very simple and materially very poor. Since exchange would be difficult and time-consuming, almost everybody would be forced to produce most of the necessities of survival for themselves. Few could earn a livelihood by specializing in producing just one product and then trading it for other products. This lack of specialization, along with the high cost of exchange, would ensure an existence in which a minimal quantity of goods and services were exchanged. Thus, the use of money increases a nation's wealth.

The use of money reduces the wasted effort associated with barter as long as people will readily accept money as a medium of exchange. Money, as we will see, can be almost anything, but its most important characteristic is that it should be widely acceptable. In addition, if we are going to carry it around with us, it should be reasonably portable.

store of wealth: the function of money that allows people to hold and accumulate wealth.

Money, however, is not just used for exchange. Some of us like to keep it. In other words, money can be used as a **store of wealth**. This is its second function. As we mentioned, wealth can be stored in other forms—from stocks and bonds to real estate, or from savings accounts to art collections—but these other forms are not as convenient as money and often involve more risk. If it is to act as a store of wealth, money should obviously possess other desirable characteristics. Besides portability, it should also be reasonably durable and of such a nature that people are willing to hold it.

unit of account: the function of money that allows us to determine easily the relative value of goods.

Finally, money is used as a **unit of account** (or measure of value). Think of the problems in trying to value a commodity in a moneyless community. Assume, for instance, that a suit of clothes is worth 10 flagons of beer, that a flagon of beer is worth 2 loaves of bread, and that you need 100 loaves of bread to buy a table—how many suits of clothes does it take to buy a table? The answer is 5 suits, but the answer doesn't come quickly. By providing a single uniform measure of values, money simplifies comparisons of prices, wages, and incomes.

In summary, the functions of money are:

- a medium of exchange
- a store of value
- a unit of account

SELF-TEST

2. Given the clothes–table example above, how many suits of clothes will it cost to buy a table if a flagon of beer is worth only one loaf of bread?

In a money-using society, each product and service can be valued in terms of a single commodity, money. If we measure everything in money terms, that is, in dollar-and-cents, we might ask the question: what is money itself worth? The answer must be in relative terms—what we can get in exchange for it. And what we can get is determined by prices: the lower the price, the more we can obtain, and therefore the higher the value of money. The *value of money* is therefore inversely related to the price level. If prices were to increase, then the value of a unit of money would decrease.

While anything can be, and most things have been, used as money, some things are definitely better than others. For instance, let us imagine a (particularly silly) society that hit upon the idea of using stones as a form of money. Well, certainly stones are durable, portable, divisible (big stones and little stones), and easily recognized, which are characteristics that all money needs. The trouble is that without very much trouble at all, everybody would think they had become fabulously rich overnight. It would make sense, therefore, that money should also have the characteristic of being reasonably scarce. On the other hand, it should not be so scarce and limited in supply that it couldn't be increased as trade and circumstances dictate. In short, money needs to be:

- acceptable
- durable
- portable
- divisible
- easily recognized
- relatively scarce

7.2 Different Kinds of Money

LO2
Recognize the various kinds of money.

commodity money: a type of money that can also function, and is useful, as a commodity.

When such things as beads, whales' teeth, salt, or shells are used as money, they have intrinsic value in themselves as well as having value as money. This type of money is called **commodity money**. Even today, in situations like jails and prisoner-of-war camps, where people have no access to the outside community, things such as cigarettes or playing cards act as forms of commodity money.

One particularly important commodity that has been used as money over the ages is gold (and, less often, other precious metals). Gold certainly fits the bill in terms of portability, durability, and scarcity. However, there is one serious drawback: precious metals don't come in standardized units; the metal needs to be weighed out each time a transaction is made. To overcome this problem, since the dawn of civilization metals have been produced in the standardized form of coins of specific size and weight. The trouble with *coins* made of gold is that they are open to abuse. Gold is a particularly soft metal, so that in earlier times it was possible for some people to make money out of money. They did this by such practices as sweating the currency (shaking the coins up in a bag so as to produce a residue of gold dust in the bottom) or by clipping the currency (shaving a thin sliver from the outside of unmilled coins). Perhaps the worst offenders were the sovereigns whose portrait on the coins was supposedly a mark of trust and integrity. An important event like a coronation or royal wedding was the occasion for the sovereign to call in the old coin and replace it with newly minted coins. However, in the process of melting down the old coins, a base metal like lead was often added to the vat of gold. Over time, the currency became more and more debased, so that it became worth only its own weight in lead.

In addition, gold has another serious defect as a form of money: it is very heavy. Because of this, and because of the dangers of carrying about large sums of money, people in Europe in the Middle Ages started to deposit their money in the goldsmith's vault. In return for making a deposit (for which they were required to pay a fee), they received a certificate from the goldsmith acknowledging the deposit. In time, these certificates were considered as reliable as gold and could be easily transferred from one person to another as a form of payment. In other words, *paper money* was introduced. (It is interesting to note that paper currency appeared in China even earlier). With the formation of commercial banks in the early eighteenth century, many of the functions of the goldsmiths were taken over by these banks—including that of issuing paper money. Since 1935 in Canada, the only bank with the power to issue currency—sometimes called fiat money in that it is declared legal tender by law—is the Bank of Canada. As we will see later, Canada's central bank no longer acts as a commercial bank, as it once did, but now acts solely as an agent of the government.

PhotoDisc

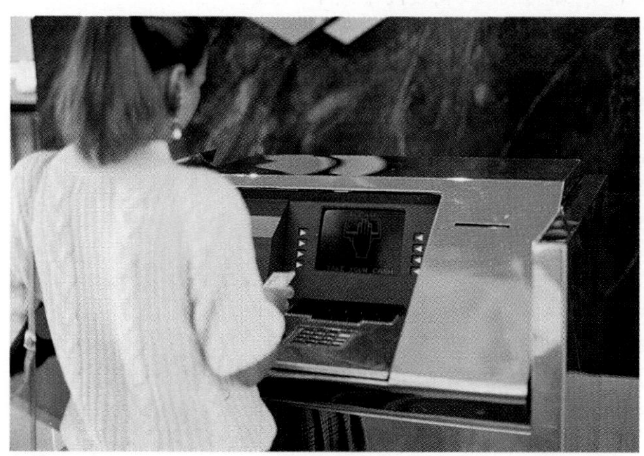

Many transfers that were once carried out using cheques are now completed using electronic banking machines.

As the commercial banks became more prominent, so too bank notes became more acceptable. But just as people, in earlier times, were wary of carrying large sums of gold and coins, they also preferred to deposit their bank notes in the banks. Thus, the nineteenth century saw the development of the last form of modern money: *chequebook money*. In return for depositing notes and coins with the bank, the customer could now receive a chequebook from the bank. A cheque is nothing more than a standardized form of instruction by a customer to the bank, telling it to transfer a sum of money from the customer's account to the person specified on the cheque. Generally speaking, this order from one of its customers presents the bank with no great problem. The average bank certainly has enough cash. However, banks do not act simply as big safety deposit boxes, guarding your money until you require it. This means that if all of the bank's customers were to descend *en masse* demanding their money, any bank in the modern banking world would find itself acutely embarrassed. It simply wouldn't have that amount of cash on hand. So what happened to the cash that you and all the other customers deposited in the past? The answer is that the bank lent it out. Banks only keep a small fraction of the amounts of cash that have been deposited, and thus they may be vulnerable to a run on the bank, i.e.: more money being withdrawn than deposited. So how did such a state of affairs come to be? Before answering this question, let's summarize the different kinds of money:

- commodity money
- gold and other precious metals
- coins
- paper money
- chequebook money (deposits)

@-CONOMICS

Electronic Money

Cash has a number of advantages, including the fact that the transactions costs of using it are low. If I want to buy something, I just hand over the cash. I don't need to register the transfer, and the seller need not record that she received the cash from me. Also, in the case of cash, possession implies ownership. But this is also one of its great disadvantages. Cash is easy to steal and it is difficult to recover once gone. For this reason, many people look forward to the day when we can dispense with cash.

Well, the day has already arrived. In many cities around the world, experiments with using "electronic money" are taking place. Small plastic cards embedded with computer chips have been introduced that will record the value of each transaction and the remaining balance on the card. For instance, you could buy a $30 card (say, from a bank) that enables you to spend up to that amount using only your card. You could use the card to pay for items like transit fares, parking meters, telephone calls, and so on.

Could this idea be extended to chequing accounts too? Some observers are predicting chequebook money may also disappear as people shift from paper currency and chequebooks to electronic cash (e-cash). This vision sees smart-cards becoming the customary circulating medium along with *privately* supplied digital cash which is stored in computer hard drives and used over the Internet to facilitate e-commerce. Obviously, for all this to happen, people will have to trust and feel comfortable with the new e-money as well as with e-commerce itself. However, there are potential drawbacks to this idea. What would happen, for instance, if the private company that issued the card went out of business? Who is going to honour the e-money then? Furthermore, there are many people in society who would be concerned about leaving an electronic trail of their purchases. This includes not only members of the underworld, but also ordinary consumers who may not want merchants and card issuers to obtain detailed information about their spending habits.

7.3 Fractional Reserve Banking

LO3
Explain what is included in the money supply.

Now let's go back to the goldsmiths. Goldsmiths discovered, very early on in the game, that most of the time the gold and coins sitting in the vaults did just that: they sat there. Most unproductively! Certainly, customers came in from time to time to withdraw some of their cash, but that same cash usually got redeposited with the goldsmith rather soon. Certainly, money was turning over. But the goldsmiths realized that, on any one day of the week, about as much gold was deposited as was withdrawn.

fractional reserve system: a banking system in which banks keep only a small fraction of their total deposits on reserve in the form of cash.

So what would be the harm in the goldsmiths lending out the gold that wasn't needed? Unless all of the customers arrived on the doorstep at the same time—a very remote possibility—there would be no harm done. So, lend it they did. In fact, the goldsmiths also learned that when they started offering loans, most people didn't particularly want to receive gold but preferred to receive one of the goldsmiths' certificates of deposit. The goldsmiths could simply make loans by giving customers a piece of paper. Thus was born the basis of modern banking: the **fractional reserve system.** In a similar manner, with the rise of commercial banking, bankers discovered that they too only needed to keep a small fraction of their customers' deposits in the form of cash reserves. Today, banks in Canada keep only a very small percentage of their customers' deposits in the form of cash. As long as people don't hoard it, any cash that any one bank issues to its customers generally finds its way back to another bank, that is, back into the banking system. So the average bank is safe as long as its depositors do not all demand their cash on the same day. The fact that modern banks operate on a fractional reserve basis has important implications for the monetary system and for monetary policy, as we shall see later.

7.4 And at Last a Definition

LO4
Explain what is and is not money.

money: anything that is widely accepted as a medium of exchange and therefore can be used to buy goods or to settle debts.

M1: currency in circulation plus demand deposits.

M2: M1 plus all notice and personal term deposits.

M3: M2 plus non-personal term deposits known as certificates of deposits.

The following definition of **money** encompasses the vital elements: money is any item that is widely accepted as a medium of exchange and is used to buy goods and services and to settle debts.

In the next chapter we will see that changes in the amount of money in an economy can have significant consequences. It is of some importance therefore that economists and policy makers be able to define clearly what constitutes money in a modern economy. Let us start with the simplest, most basic definition, called the **M1** definition, which includes currency in circulation (coins and paper bank notes) plus demand deposits in the chequing accounts of all commercial banks. The word *demand* in demand deposits refers to the fact that depositors can demand their deposits in cash at any time.

The money supply (in $ billions) in Canada in August 2002 was:

M1 =	currency	plus	demand deposits
135 =	40	+	95
	(30%)		(70%)

Some have suggested, however, that this definition is too narrow. They argue that if chequing accounts are included as part of the money supply, then why not also include savings accounts and other types of notice deposits? Notice deposits, as the name suggests, requires the depositor to give notice to the bank before making a withdrawal. Surely, these accounts, in practice, are no different from chequing accounts, since banks seldom enforce the requirement of giving notice before withdrawal. So, we have a wider definition of money, called **M2**, which includes all of M1 plus all notice deposits (savings accounts on deposit for an undefined length of time) and what are called personal term deposits, which are on deposit for a specific term such as six months. The amounts in August 2002 were:

M2 =	M1	plus	notice deposits and personal term deposits
551 =	124	+	416
	(25%)		(75%)

Finally, an even broader measurement, **M3**, includes M2 but adds to it term deposits of businesses (known as certificates of deposits), which are easily convertible into chequable deposits. The M3 measurement, then, includes all of M2 plus certificates of deposits. Again, for August 2002, the amounts were:

M3 =	M2	plus	certificate of deposits
751 =	551	+	200
	(73%)		(27%)

Money Supply in Canada as of August 2002 (in billions)

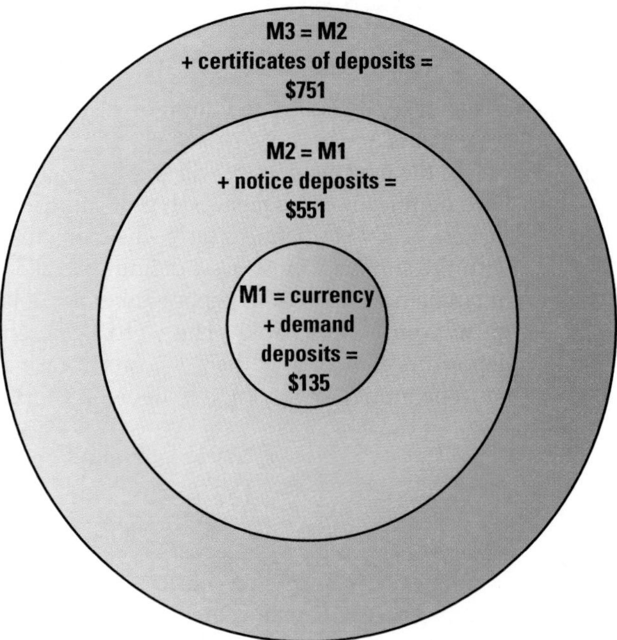

For reasons of expediency we will confine our discussion and analysis of money to the simplest definition, M1: currency in circulation plus demand deposits (chequing accounts). This helps to keep things simple and recognizes the essential characteristic of money: the direct and immediate control over goods and services.

What Is Not Money?

Not all currency issued by the Bank of Canada is included as money, only the portion that is in circulation. In other words, the currency in the vaults or tills of banks is not included in any definition of money.

The reason for this is that when you or I deposit currency in a bank, the balance of our bank account increases, and since the amount of deposits in our accounts is part of the money supply, it would be double-counting to count both the increase in our accounts and the increase in the bank's tills. In other words, when people deposit currency in a bank, the amount of currency *in circulation* goes down, and the amount in deposit accounts goes up. You should note that:

A new bank deposit of currency changes the composition of the money supply but does not change its total.

Another exclusion from the money supply is gold. (Try paying for your designer jeans with a bar of gold.) Similarly, such financial securities as stocks and bonds are also excluded. So too is peoples' available credit on their credit cards. That is, credit cards, as well as the more recent debit cards, are merely a means of accessing money but are not money in themselves. You might argue that in many instances credit cards are more acceptable than personal cheques, and that's true. However, credit cards merely represent a loan that you have negotiated with a finance company. More importantly, you cannot pay off a debt with a credit card. Certainly you can obtain cash with a credit card, but that's the clue: you can use a credit card to get money; it is not itself money. Similarly, cheques are not money but merely give you access to the money in your chequing account. The final exclusion from the modern definition of money is chequing accounts at **near-banks**. These near-banks include credit unions, trust companies, and mortgage and loan associations. In other words, all of our three alternative definitions of money—M1, M2, M3—refer to accounts only at commercial banks. Canada's central bank, the Bank of Canada, exercises a degree of control over the commercial banks but has a lesser degree of power over near-banks (also termed non-bank financial intermediaries). The central bank prefers to count as money only that which it can control directly; hence the exclusion of accounts at near-banks. Nonetheless, the Bank of Canada does also measure what it calls M2+, which includes demand and notice deposits at near-banks.

near-banks: financial institutions, like credit unions or trust companies, which share many of the functions of commercial banks but are not defined as banks under the Bank Act (they are also known as non-bank financial intermediaries).

The term *chartered banks* includes the six major commercial banks in Canada (all of which received a charter under the *Bank Act*) and a few dozen much smaller banks.

ADDED DIMENSION

Canada's Big Banks

The six largest chartered banks in Canada, in order of size, are: Royal Bank, Bank of Montreal, Canadian Imperial Bank of Commerce, Bank of Nova Scotia, TD Canada Trust, and the National Bank of Canada. Credit unions, which are regulated provincially, are major players in British Columbia and in Quebec, where they are called *caisses populaires*.

Recently, the world has seen a trend of mergers of large banks. It appears, however, that this trend will not include Canada, since the attempted merger a few years ago of the Bank of Montreal and the Royal Bank of Canada was blocked by the federal government.

7.5 A Word on Modern Banks

LO5
Describe the main function of modern banks as money lenders.

Banks, like other corporations, are in business to make profits. Their major source of profits comes from using any excess deposits productively by lending them out. Their profit comes from the **spread**, the difference between the interest rate a bank charges to borrowers and the interest rate it pays to depositors. There's not much difference in the spread among Canada's major banks. The total profits of a bank come more from the total volume of its transactions rather than from a difference in the spread. Like any other business, banks do not like to carry excess inventories. In the case of banks, their inventory is money. They do not earn a return on idle money balances. They will always try to ensure that the amount of reserves they retain is kept to a minimum, consistent with security. Until recently, the *Bank Act* laid down exactly how much commercial banks had to keep in reserves. Such a required reserve ratio is no longer applicable, but banks still hold reserves. What we will call the **target reserve ratio** is the proportion of demand deposits that a bank wants to hold in the form of cash in its vaults or with the Bank of Canada. These target reserves provide a small degree of security for the bank's customers. However, the main security for depositors comes from insurance. All banks are required by law to take out insurance on customers' deposits. The deposits are insured with the Canada Deposit Insurance Corporation up to a maximum of $60 000 per depositor per bank.

spread: the difference between the rate of interest a bank charges borrowers and the rate it pays savers.

target reserve ratio: the portion of deposits that a bank wants to hold in cash.

The Canadian banking system is remarkably secure. (There were only three bank failures in all of the twentieth century, although two were within the last 20 years.) What economists call a branch banking system accounts for this stability. This is a system dominated by a few large banks, each of which has many branches operating across the entire country. For example,

Canada's big six banks each have several hundred branches coast to coast. The sheer size and geographical diversity of this type of structure minimizes the possibility of bank failure.

Contrast this with a unit banking system, which, though currently in transition, is still the basic system in the United States. This system is made up of thousands of relatively small banks that either have only one branch or multiple branches that are confined to a single state. Such a system is less secure. For example, the First National Bank of Dalton (Nebraska) is small compared with the average branch of any one of Canada's big six banks. Furthermore, most of the loans by First National would be to local wheat farmers for equipment, seed, and so on. If a bad hailstorm wipes out the local wheat crop and most of the farmers go bankrupt, then the bank could face the same fate.

PhotoDisc

Chances are that your bank branch doesn't look like this. Canada's six major banks have several hundred branches across the country.

Does this mean that the Canadian banking system is superior? From a security sense, yes. But the source of this security is a system dominated by only six big banks, and this means that competition within the system is weak. There are several consequences of this lack of competition. First, the merely irritable: long line-ups for routine transactions, short operating hours (closed on Saturdays and Sundays), and the inability of customers to deal face-to-face with the decision makers. More significantly, the spread in the Canadian banking system is, historically, wider than that in the American system. Finally, there is the issue of the banks' loan policies. From time to time throughout history, one can find references to a recurring complaint by small businesses in Canada: large banks don't recognize the unique circumstances of a small business, and they don't make loans to unproven companies or ideas. Although one can understand the position of the large banks on this issue, it is also obvious that the whole economy does, from time to time, fail to benefit from the potential success of a new business or product because of the lack of loans needed to get started. In summary, the Canadian branch banking system is very secure and stable, but it is also very conservative.

Some of this may be changing. Foreign banks have recently been allowed to operate in Canada, although there are constraints on their size. This should, at least to some extent, increase competition in this industry.

disadv. of branch system:

1) competition is weak → line-ups, short hours, no face to face,
2) higher spread than other countries' unit system
3) loan policies aren't sympathetic to small bus

ADDED DIMENSION

Financial Markets

The financial market consists of different types of financial institutions. All of these institutions have one thing in common: they are intermediaries and act as agents between households, businesses, and governments that have funds available for lending and others who want to borrow those funds. Canadian banks are the biggest borrowers and lenders. Other institutions came into existence because banks were originally forbidden to provide certain types of loans. Mortgage companies specialized in giving long-term loans (mortgages) for people wishing to purchase real estate like houses or apartments. Trust companies looked after pensions and trust accounts of both firms and individuals. Credit unions (*caisses populaires* in Quebec) sprang up because many small firms were unable to obtain loans from the banks.

The financial market can be divided into the money market and the capital market. Money markets usually deal in loans with terms of less than three years, whereas capital markets are for longer-term loans. Long-term loans take the form of bonds, which are nothing more than a type of IOU. Suppose that you are a big firm interested in obtaining funds to finance a major expansion. You could, of course, apply for a loan from one of the various financial institutions. But why bother? Why not cut out the agent and go directly to the public? Consequently, many corporations, as well as the federal, provincial, and municipal governments, sell bonds directly to the public. These bonds are for a fixed term and pay a fixed rate of interest. Generally speaking, shorter-term bonds pay a lower interest rate than longer-term bonds. As well, bonds issued by governments and larger corporations pay a lower interest rate than those of smaller or newer firms.

The capital market deals not only in bonds but also in stocks. A corporation could issue either bonds or stocks, and both bring new funds into the firm. These instruments are easily negotiable, which means holders can freely sell them in the market. The main differences between these two financial instuments is that the holder of a bond is a creditor of the corporation, whereas the holder of stock (the shareholder) is a part-owner of the firm. If the corporation is successful, the shareholder will share in that success and get part of the profits, in the form of dividends, but may get no return at all if the firm struggles. The bondholder, on the other hand, will simply receive a fixed amount of interest, regardless of the performance of the firm.

REVIEW

1. What are the three functions of money?
2. What will happen to the value of money if the general price level rises?
3. Historically, how did those in power debase the money supply?
4. Distinguish between *M1*, *M2*, and *M3*.
5. Define the term *target reserve ratio*.
6. Define the term *spread*.
7. What is the role of the Canada Deposit Insurance Corporation?

7.6 Creation of Money by the Banks

LO6
Explain how a small amount of cash can support many loans and create more money.

We now know that money includes demand deposits as well as currency. The only institution that can actually create currency is the Bank of Canada. The public can decide what fraction of this currency is held outside the banks and what fraction it deposits with banks and other financial institutions. However, it is the banks, given the amount of currency they hold, that decide how much they wish to hold as reserves and how much they want to lend.

To understand how just a small amount of reserves can support a multiple amount of loans and deposits, we need first to understand a few very basic accounting terms.

Assets, Liabilities, and Balance Sheets

assets: the part of a company's balance sheet that represents what it owns or what is owed to it.

liabilities: the part of a company's balance sheet that represents what it owes.

net worth: the total assets less total liabilities of a company—also called equity.

Actually, all we need to understand are the basic features of a balance sheet. (The profit and loss statement is of no concern here.) A balance sheet presents the financial condition of an institution at a particular moment in time. On one side, we list all the assets, and on the other side, the liabilities. The **assets** represent what a company owns or what others owe it. **Liabilities** represent what a company owes to others. The difference between the two is the **net worth** of the company, otherwise known as the equity. The equity is the book value of the company to its shareholders. (The company's market value may be more or less than its book value.) The following is a simplified balance sheet of the Saymor Bank Limited:

Balance Sheet of Saymor Bank Ltd.
as of December 31, 2002

Assets		Liabilities and Equity	
Reserves	$ 10 000	Demand deposits	$100 000
Loans to customers	60 000	Shareholders' equity	20 000
Securities	30 000		
Fixed assets	20 000		
	$120 000		$120 000

The assets are all listed in terms of liquidity (closeness to cash), with the most liquid at the top. Remember that reserves are the currency held by the bank as cash on hand (vault cash) and with the Bank of Canada. Loans to customers represent one of the income-earning assets of the bank and are their most important and most lucrative assets. Securities are stocks (gilt-edged, i.e., very secure—"as good as gold") or bonds (usually government bonds and treasury bills). Fixed assets include the buildings, equipment, and furniture of the bank. The major liability, and the only one shown here, is demand deposits, which represents the total amount of depositors' accounts owed by the bank to its customers. (We will ignore notice or savings deposits.) The equity figure shows that the book value of this bank is $20 000 (in $ million, of course).

Let's practise a few simple transactions to familiarize ourselves with bookkeeping entries. Standard accounting procedures require that every transaction involve two entries. In addition, after making any entries, the balance sheet should remain in balance. (The totals may change, but the assets should still equal liabilities plus equity.)

Transaction 1: Fred, a customer of the bank, deposits $200 cash in the bank. The reserves of the bank would therefore increase by $200. The other entry? Fred's bank balance will increase by $200. (An asset for Fred, of course, but a liability for the bank since it now owes Fred $200 more.) So demand deposits increase by $200. In sum, both assets and liabilities have increased.

Transaction 2: Penny withdraws $500 cash from her account. This is straightforward, since it is just the reverse of transaction 1. The bank's reserves are reduced by $500 and the demand deposits go down by $500. So, both assets and liabilities are reduced accordingly.

Transaction 3: The bank buys some securities for $200 cash. In this case, reserves decrease by $200 and securities increase by $200. Therefore, one asset decreases and another increases; the net effect on total assets is zero.

The next transaction is of more significance since it is the foundation for the commercial banks' ability to create money.

Transaction 4: Suppose that the bank grants you a loan. What exactly does this imply? Generally speaking, it does not mean that the bank gives you cash. Instead, in exchange for your written acceptance of the terms and conditions for repayment of the loan, the bank will give you immediate credit in your chequing account for the amount of the loan. Now, whether you actually draw out cash or instead write a cheque for the whole or part of the amount is up to you. But what the bank has given you is "direct and immediate access to goods and services" and the ability to settle a debt. It has, in other words, by a single bookkeeping entry, created money for you. The two accounts affected, therefore, are: an increase in loans (an asset) and an increase in demand deposits (a liability). Cash reserves are unaffected.

Each time that a bank issues a loan, it creates money.

Now, having been granted the loan you might do one of three things:

Transaction 4a: You decide that you are going to withdraw some or all of it in cash. In which case, the bank's reserves decrease by the amount of the withdrawal and the demand deposits are decreased by the same amount.

Transaction 4b: You decide to write a cheque to buy an airline ticket. Suppose that the airline company also does its banking at the same bank. In that case, your demand deposit balance is reduced by the amount of the cheque and that of the airline company is increased by the same amount. Here, the total amount of demand deposits remains unchanged. In addition, note that the bank's reserves were unaffected.

Transaction 4c: You write a cheque to buy a new sofa from the Sogood Sofa company. Sogood Sofa deposits your cheque at their bank, which is a different bank from yours. At the end of the day, their bank will come to yours for payment of the cheque. The cheque is then *cleared against* your bank, whose reserves will drop as a result. Therefore, your bank's reserves and demand deposits will be reduced, while the other bank's reserves and demand deposits will increase.

SELF-TEST

3. Give the necessary bookkeeping entries for each set of circumstances below.

a) The bank makes a $2000 loan to Fadia.

b) Fadia writes a $2000 cheque to Middle East Travel, which has its accounts at a different bank.

The Money Multiplier

That's enough bookkeeping for the present. Now, what we want to figure out are the implications for a bank and for the banking system when a bank holds more than its targeted reserves. Let's start off the analysis by assuming that the Saymor Bank and all other banks are just meeting their target reserves of 10 percent. Remember that this means that each bank wants to hold a minimum of 10 percent of its demand deposits in the form of cash reserves, i.e.,

$$\text{target reserves} = \text{target reserve ratio} \times \text{demand deposits}. \quad [7.1]$$

For instance, assume that Saymor starts from this position:

Balance Sheet of Saymor Bank Ltd.
as of December 31, 2002

Assets		Liabilities and Equity	
Reserves	$ 10 000	Demand deposits	$100 000
Loans to customers	60 000	Shareholders' equity	20 000
Securities	30 000		
Fixed assets	20 000		
	$120 000		$120 000

Now, assume that Tom, rummaging about under his bed one morning, comes across $1000 in currency. Not knowing what to do with it, he decides to deposit it in the bank. The bank credits the $1000 to his account. Its reserves now equal $11 000, and its demand deposits are $101 000. The bank now finds that it has *excess reserves*, since it wants to hold only 10% × $101 000, or $10 100. It is over-reserved to the tune of $900, i.e.,

$$\text{Excess reserves} = \text{Actual reserves minus target reserves} \quad [7.2]$$
$$900 = 11\ 000 - 10\ 100(10\% \times 101\ 000)$$

Or, look at it another way: of the $1000 that Tom deposited, the bank aims to keep only 10 percent in the form of cash reserves and therefore has $900 more than it considers necessary to hold. As we mentioned before, banks do not like to have such idle cash; they want to earn some return on it. They will be very happy to lend it out. Now let's assume Wing Kee happens to come into the bank the next day in need of a $900 loan. The loan is happily granted, and he walks out having $900 more in his chequing account. Within a few hours Wing Kee purchases a used Volkswagen from the New Star Car Company. A New Star employee deposits his cheque in the J.M.K. Bank. Recall our assumption that this bank, prior to the deposit by New Star, had no reserves in excess of its targeted amount. After J.M.K. Bank clears Wing Kee's cheque against the Saymor Bank, the following accounts at J.M.K. Bank will be affected:

Reserves	+ $900	Demand deposits	+ $900

J.M.K. also wants to keep 10 percent of the increased demand deposits, that is, 10% × $900, or $90. It therefore has $810 in **excess reserves**. It too is anxious to lend these reserves out. Now let's assume that Sue is in need of $810 to pay off a debt to her friend Sarbjit and manages to negotiate an $810 loan, in the form of an increased credit balance to her chequing account, from J.M.K. She immediately pays Sarbjit by cheque. Sarbjit deposits the cheque at his bank, the M.P.C. Bank. After this deposit, and Sue's cheque clearing, the balance sheet of the M.P.C. Bank changes as follows:

excess reserves: reserves in excess of what the bank wants to hold as its target reserves.

Reserves	+ $810	Demand deposits	+ $810

M.P.C. Bank now finds itself with excess reserves (over its targeted amount). It wants to keep back only 10 percent of the $810, or $81, as cash reserves. Therefore, it has $810 minus $81, or $729 in excess reserves. Let's assume that this amount is lent out. Regardless of whom it is lent to, and regardless of how the loan is spent (assuming that recipients of the cheque deposit it back into a bank), sooner or later one of the banks in the banking system will find itself again with excess reserves and be ready and able to lend. Although the cash moves from bank to bank, the banking *system* seems unable to get rid of this additional cash. A bank lends it out, but each time it returns to some other bank. However, each time it returns, the bank decides to retain 10 percent of that new deposit in additional reserves. Let's follow the trail resulting from Tom's initial deposit of $1000:

Reserves	Loans	Deposits
+1000		+1000 (Tom)
	+900 (to Wing Kee)	+900 (New Star)
	+810 (to Sue)	+810 (Sarbjit)
	+729	+729
	. . .	. . .
	. . .	. . .
	. . .	. . .

You can see that both the loans and deposits columns above follow a geometric pattern. What we are interested in finding out is the total of the deposits column. Why would we be interested in this figure? Because *it is money*. Think back to the definition of money (M1): currency in circulation plus demand deposits. The banks' cash reserves are not part of the money supply, but the total amount in peoples' chequing accounts certainly is. As we said before:

Each time a bank issues a loan, it creates money.

We will do more with this idea in a moment.

So what will be the total of all demand deposits that result from Tom's initial deposit of $1000? The answer is 1000 + 900 + 810 + 729 + . . . It's reasonably easy to solve if you remember the formula for summing a geometric progression. But let's tackle the problem from a different perspective by looking at part of the balance sheet of the *entire banking system*. Assume it looked like the following prior to Tom's deposit:

Reserves	$100 000	Demand deposits	$1 000 000
Loans	$900 000		

Staying with our assumption that banks want to keep a 10 percent reserve ratio, the banking system illustrated above is neither over- nor underreserved. If the target reserves must equal 10 percent of deposits, it means that demand deposits will equal ten times the amount of reserves. Now Tom deposits $1000 in one of the banks, so that reserves equal $101 000. Demand deposits can potentially rise to a maximum of 10 × $101 000, or $1 010 000. As a result of the lending process we described, the new combined balance sheet would look like this:

money multiplier: the increase in total deposits that would occur in the whole banking system as a result of a new deposit in a single bank.

Reserves	$101 000	Demand deposits	$1 010 000
Loans	$909 000		

In other words, if the target reserve ratio is 10 percent, a new deposit of $X will lead to an increase in total deposits throughout the *whole* banking system of ten times $X. As you probably recognize, what we have here is another multiplier; this time, the **money multiplier**, which is determined in the following way:

$$\text{Money Multiplier} = \frac{\Delta \text{ deposits}}{\Delta \text{ reserves}} \tag{7.3}$$

or

$$\text{Money Multiplier} = \frac{1}{\text{target reserve ratio}} \tag{7.4}$$

In our example, the target reserve ratio is 10 percent, or 0.1, so the money multiplier is 1/0.1, or 10. If the target reserve ratio was 5 percent, or 0.05, it would mean that banks want to keep a smaller amount of reserves and therefore would have more to lend out. In this case, the money multiplier would be 1/0.05, or 20.

The principle of the money multiplier is based on the fact that banks only keep a small fraction of deposits in the form of cash reserves. Excess reserves allow banks to increase loans and therefore increase deposits by a multiple of the excess reserves. The money multiplier shows what will happen in the whole banking system over a period of time.

SELF-TEST

4. The following is the balance sheet for the Islanders' Bank:

Reserves	5 000	Demand Deposits	60 000
Loans	41 000		
Securities	18 000	Shareholder's Equity	10 000
Fixed Assets	6 000		
	70 000		70 000

a) If the target reserve ratio is 8 percent, what is the amount of its target reserves?

b) If the target reserve ratio is 5 percent, what is the amount of its target reserves?

5. a) Given the Islanders' Bank balance sheet in Self-Test 4, how much does it have in excess reserves if the target reserve ratio is 8 percent?

b) How much does it have in excess reserves if the target reserve ratio is 5 percent?

Be careful not to confuse the effect of the money multiplier working through the *whole* banking system with the circumstances facing a single bank. Simply because a *single* bank happens to find itself with excess reserves does not mean that it could increase loans by a multiple of those excess reserves. For instance, look at the following circumstances for the Saymor Bank:

Reserves	\$100	Demand deposits	\$1000

The target reserve ratio is 10 percent. Someone now deposits cash of \$50. Excess reserves would then equal \$45 (90 percent of \$50), and this is all Saymor wants to lend. It could not lend out \$450, since the bank would be in a very embarrassing situation if the borrower immediately asked for cash. In short:

A single bank has to tread carefully and limit its loans to the amount of its excess reserves.

SELF-TEST

6. What will be the increase in total deposits in the whole banking system of a new deposit of $2000 into the XYZ bank in each of the following circumstances?

a) a target reserve ratio of 20 percent;

b) a target reserve ratio of 5 percent.

7. The J.M.K. Bank has demand deposits of $60 000 and reserves of $6000. By how much can it increase its loans if:

a) the target reserve ratio is 8 percent?

b) the target reserve ratio is 5 percent?

c) Assume the same $60 000 and $6000 applied to the entire banking system. What are your new answers to a) and b)?

Can Banks Ever Be Short of Reserves?

bank rate: the rate of interest that the Bank of Canada charges a commercial bank for a loan.

It can certainly happen that at the end of a day's business, a bank might find that it has less reserves than it targeted. In that case what can it do? It would need to borrow. The Bank of Canada will lend money to a commercial bank, but the bank must pay interest equal to the **bank rate** to the Bank of Canada. However, since the bank rate is regarded by the banks as a penalty rate (since they can borrow from the public at a much lower rate), banks will try to ensure that they pay off any loans from the Bank of Canada as quickly as possible. As a result, such loans tend to be very short-term.

The Money Multiplier Also Works in Reverse

Are there other consequences if a single bank—Saymor, for instance—finds itself underreserved? Well, after receiving a loan from the Bank of Canada, Saymor will have to increase its reserves in some more permanent way. While it is not difficult for a single bank to increase its reserves, doing so will be at the expense of some other bank's reserves. Let's explain this by assuming that Saymor calls in an outstanding loan that was made earlier to the New Star Car Company. New Star will be forced to quickly sell off some of its inventory. The buyers involved in this selloff will be reducing their deposits in other banks as they pay for their purchases. This will result in other banks finding themselves underreserved and thus forced to call in some of their loans. Soon, we will find the total loans in the whole banking system decreasing and, as a result, deposits also being reduced by an amount determined by the money multiplier. As an example, look at the following combined balance sheet of a banking system:

Reserves	$ 95	Demand deposits	$1000
Loans	$905		

If the target reserve ratio is 10 percent, the banking system is underreserved in the amount of $5. How can the whole banking system produce another $5 worth of reserves? The answer is it cannot. What will happen, in fact, is that the banking system, over a period of time, will be forced to call in outstanding loans. In this case, the money multiplier is 10, so the banks in total will have to call in 10 × $5, or $50, to get their reserves back in line with the deposits. After this contraction, the balance sheet will look like this:

Reserves	$ 95	Demand deposits	$950
Loans	$855		

We emphasize that banks can neither create nor destroy *currency*. What they can do is create or destroy loans and demand deposits, and this is what they do whenever they are over- or underreserved. It is in this sense that we mean that banks can create and destroy *money* (demand deposits). However, as we will see in the next chapter, it is the Bank of Canada that ultimately controls the money supply by determining the amount of currency held by the commercial banks.

A Smaller Money Multiplier?

There are certain instances, when the size of the money multiplier will be diminished. As we have already seen, if a bank were to increase its target reserves, it would be lending out less and the money multiplier would be reduced. However, in a modern banking system, banks are likely to keep their targets as low as is safely possible, since they earn no return on idle cash. Second, it is possible that people may decide to keep a larger portion of their assets in the form of cash. This increase in cash holdings will mean fewer deposits into the banking system and would reduce the size of the multipler. (This is referred to as *currency drain.*) Thirdly, simply because a bank has excess reserves does not mean that it will make more loans. It is possible that the banks may find, in their judgement, that there are not enough creditworthy applicants for loans and their excess reserves would persist. Finally, it should be noted that in a recession, banks often find it difficult to make loans because many people simply do not want to go deeper into debt when times are tough. Here, again, the banks' excess reserves would persist and reduce the size of the multiplier. In summary, the four factors that may reduce the size of the multiplier are:

- an increase in the banks' target reserves;
- an increase in amount of cash that people hold;
- an insufficient number of creditworthy applicants for loans.
- a reduced demand for loans by people in times of recession.

REVIEW

1. What is included in a list of a bank's *assets*?
2. What is included in a list of a bank's *liabilities*?
3. Define the *money multiplier*.
4. What is the *bank rate*?
5. What does it mean for a bank to be *overreserved*?
6. How does the banking system create money?

STUDY GUIDE

Review

CHAPTER SUMMARY

In this chapter you examined the functions and characteristics of money and came to understand that there is more than one measurement of money. The central idea in this chapter is the process of money creation which occurs as a result of banks making loans and thereby increasing the amount of deposits, via the money multiplier, in the whole banking system.

1. The functions of money are as a:
   - medium of exchange;
   - store of value;
   - unit of account.
2. The various types of money are:
   - commodity money;
   - gold and other precious metals;
   - paper money;
   - chequebook money.
3. The modern definition of money includes:
   - M1, which is currency plus demand deposits;
   - M2, which is M1 plus notice deposits and personal term deposits;
   - M3, which is M2 plus certificates of deposits.
4. Modern banks keep only a small fraction of their deposits on reserve and loan out the balance. This fact allows the whole banking system to create money, since the new demand deposits of any one bank get spent and re-deposited into other banks and then loaned out again. This is the important money multiplier process. The money multiplier varies inversely with the target reserve ratio; i.e., if the reserve ratio falls, the multiplier gets larger.

NEW GLOSSARY TERMS AND KEY EQUATIONS

assets 250
bank rate 255
commodity money 242
excess reserves 252
fractional reserve system 244
liabilities 250
M1 245
M2 245
M3 245
medium of exchange 241
money 245
money multiplier 253
near-banks 247
net worth 250
store of wealth 241
spread 247
target reserve ratio 247
unit of account 241

Equations:

[7.1] target reserves = target reserve ratio × demand deposits page 251

[7.2] excess reserves = actual reserves – target reserves page 252

[7.3] $$\text{money multiplier} = \frac{\Delta \text{ deposits}}{\Delta \text{ reserves}}$$ page 254

[7.4] $$\text{money multiplier} = \frac{1}{\text{target reserve ratio}}$$ page 254

STUDY TIPS

1. Many students have a lot of trouble with the material in this chapter. For a long time, we had difficulty in understanding this, because the concepts involved are not complicated. We have now come to believe that the source of the difficulty is, yet again, the mistake of equating money with income. The chapter is about how the banking system can create money. Students who (consciously or unconsciously) confuse this with creating income seem to "freeze up" at this prospect and never really understand much that follows. Only by combining resources in production can we create wealth and real income. On the other hand, a banking system is quite capable of creating more money, even though no more real income has been created. Obviously, if this is done in excess, prices will be driven up because more money will be chasing the same quantity of goods. There really isn't anything mysterious going on here. Don't let yourself get spooked into thinking that there is.

2. When working with the many balance statements in this chapter, remember that the key entry is the amount of demand deposits. This is the bank's (or the system's) primary liability, and reserves must be large enough to cover expected net withdrawals (new withdrawals less new deposits in the future). The target reserve ratio is always a percentage of demand deposits.

3. Students sometimes have difficulty in understanding what might happen if a bank becomes underreserved. The bank might be able to get a loan and thus increase its reserves by the amount that it borrows; that is easy to comprehend. Not quite so easy is the idea that the only other way out of being underreserved is for the bank to decrease its demand deposits. The way a bank does this is to call in loans that it has previously made. A bank cannot call in, say, a fixed-term mortgage that it made to you (or your parents) a year or two ago. However, many loans to businesses are what are called demand loans and are subject to being called in "on demand" if necessary.

Answered Questions

Indicate whether the following statements are true or false.

1. **T or F** Money acts as a medium of exchange, a store of wealth, and a unit of account.

2. **T or F** Individuals in a society that had no medium of exchange would be forced to use barter to exchange goods.

3. **T or F** The most important characteristic of money is that it be portable.

4. **T or F** Canada's largest commercial bank is the Bank of Canada.

5. **T or F** M1 is defined as currency in circulation plus notice deposits in commercial banks.

6. **T or F** The target reserve ratio is that portion of a bank's deposits that it wishes to loan out.

7. **T or F** The spread is the difference between the interest rate that a bank pays to borrowers and the interest rate it charges depositors.

8. **T or F** A bank will try to lend out all of its excess reserves.

9. **T or F** The bank rate is the rate of interest that the Bank of Canada charges a commercial bank for a loan.

10. **T or F** If some of the recipients of bank loans keep a portion of the loan in the form of cash, the money expansion process would expand.

Basic (Questions 11–25)

11. What is the basis of the modern banking system?
    a) Fractional reserves.
    b) Commodity money.
    c) A medium of exchange.
    d) Gold.

12. What is the value of the money multiplier?
    a) 1 divided by the target reserve ratio.
    b) The reciprocal of the MPC.
    c) M1 divided by the multiplier.
    d) It is always 2.

13. What kind of banking system does Canada have?
 a) A unit banking system.
 b) A branch banking system.
 c) A money banking system.
 d) A provincial banking system.

14. If you were working out the cost of attending school next year, which function of money would you be using?
 a) A medium of exchange.
 b) A unit of account.
 c) A store of wealth.
 d) The commercial function.

15. If you wrote out a cheque to make a purchase of textbooks, which function of money would you be using?
 a) A medium of exchange.
 b) A unit of account.
 c) A store of wealth.
 d) The commercial function.

16. What is the spread?
 a) The difference between a bank's actual reserves and its target reserves.
 b) The interest rate difference between what a bank charges borrowers and what it pays savers.
 c) The difference between a bank's demand deposits and its total loans to customers.
 d) The geographical distribution of banks across the country.

17. Why is the banking system able to increase loans and demand deposits by a multiple of its excess reserves?
 a) Because reserves lost by one bank are gained by another.
 b) Because the MPC of borrowers is positive.
 c) Because one person's debt becomes another person's income.
 d) Because the target reserve ratio is greater than 1.

18. What is the definition of M1?
 a) Currency in circulation only.
 b) Currency in circulation plus demand deposits and savings accounts.
 c) Currency in circulation plus demand deposits and Canada Savings Bonds.
 d) Currency in circulation plus demand deposits.

19. Which of the following statements about the value of money is correct?
 a) It varies inversely with the price level.
 b) It varies directly with the interest rate.
 c) It varies directly with the price level.
 d) It varies directly with the quantity of money.

20. Which of the following are assets to a bank?
 a) Demand deposits, equity, and reserves.
 b) Reserves, loans to customers, and securities.
 c) Reserves, property, and equity.
 d) Equity, property, and demand deposits.

21. Suppose that the Canucks Bank has excess reserves of $6000 and demand deposits of $100 000. If its targeted reserve ratio is 10 percent, what is the size of the bank's actual reserves?
 a) $4000.
 b) $16 000.
 c) $10 000.
 d) $14 000.

22. All of the following, except one, are characteristics that money should possess. Which is the exception?
 a) It should have general acceptability.
 b) It should be divisible.
 c) It should be convertible into gold or other precious metals.
 d) It should be portable.
 e) It should be durable.

23. Suppose that a banking system has $10 000 000 in demand deposits and actual reserves of $1 200 000. If the target reserve ratio for all banks is 10 percent, what is the maximum possible expansion of the money supply?
 a) $2 200 000.
 b) $115 000.
 c) $200 000.
 d) $12 000 000.
 e) $2 000 000.

24. What is the difference between M1 and M2?
 a) M1 includes currency in circulation and M2 does not.
 b) M2 includes certificates of deposit and M1 does not.
 c) M2 includes notice deposits and personal term deposits and M1 does not.
 d) M2 is always smaller than M1.

25. How is the money multiplier calculated?
 a) By dividing the target reserve ratio by 1.
 b) By dividing the change in deposits by the change in reserves.
 c) By multiplying the target reserve ratio by M1.
 d) By multiplying the target reserve ratio by 1.

Intermediate (Questions 26–31)

26. Historically, why were goldsmiths able to create money?
- **a)** Because consumers and merchants preferred to use gold rather than currency for transactions.
- **b)** Because they always kept 100 percent reserves.
- **c)** Because only a few of their customers would redeem their notes for gold at any one time.
- **d)** Because they held the right to print money.

27. Suppose that Adam Ricardo deposits $1000 of cash into the Penguins Bank. On the same day, David Smith negotiates a loan for $4000. By how much has the money supply changed?
- **a)** It has increased by $3000.
- **b)** It has decreased by $3000.
- **c)** It has increased by $4000.
- **d)** It has increased by $5000.

28. The currency held by banks is considered to be part of what definition of money?
- **a)** M1.
- **b)** M2.
- **c)** M3.
- **d)** Part of all three—M1, M2, and M3.
- **e)** Not part of any definition of money.

29. If Guy and Laraine both have chequing accounts at the same bank and Guy writes a cheque for $1000, payable to Laraine, what will happen to the bank's accounts?
- **a)** They will not be affected.
- **b)** Assets and liabilities will both decrease by $1000.
- **c)** Liabilities will decline and the bank's equity will increase by $1000.
- **d)** Reserves and demand deposits will both decrease by $1000.
- **e)** Demand deposits will increase and loans to customers will decrease by $1000.

30. Which of the following statements is correct if a bank is holding excess reserves?
- **a)** It is in a position to make additional loans.
- **b)** Its reserves exceed its loans.
- **c)** It is making above-normal profits.
- **d)** Its actual reserves are less than its targeted reserves.
- **e)** Its loans to customers exceed its required loans.

31. Suppose that the Just Right Coffee Company negotiates a $100 000 loan from the Blackhawks Bank and takes $40 000 in the form of cash, leaving the remainder in its account. What has happened to the supply of money?
- **a)** It has increased by $100 000.
- **b)** It has decreased by $100 000.
- **c)** It has increased by $40 000.
- **d)** It has increased by $60 000.
- **e)** It has not changed.

Advanced (Questions 32–35)

32. All of the following statements, except one, are correct. Which is the exception?
- **a)** A bank's total reserves are equal to its excess reserves plus its target reserves.
- **b)** A bank's assets plus its net worth equals its liabilities.
- **c)** When a bank makes a loan, it creates demand deposits.
- **d)** A single bank can safely lend out only an amount up to the value of its excess reserves.
- **e)** If a bank transaction decreases the value of one of its assets, then either some other asset must increase in value or one of its liabilities must decrease in value.

33. What is true about deposits in near-banks such as credit unions?
- **a)** They are part of M1 but not M2.
- **b)** They are part of M1 and M2 but not M3.
- **c)** They are part of M3 only.
- **d)** They are not part of the money supply at all.

34. What is true if a bank's balance sheet has $1.2 million in assets and $1 million in liabilities?
- **a)** The bank must have been profitable this year.
- **b)** The bank has shareholders' equity of $0.2 million.
- **c)** Demand deposits must be $0.2 million.
- **d)** Cash reserves must be $0.2 million.

35. Suppose that Bank Apollo has a target reserve ratio of 5 percent, $10 000 in demand deposits, and $1000 in reserves. Assume that the bank makes a loan equal to its excess reserves and the borrower spends this amount at a business that does not use Bank Apollo. What is the net effect on Bank Apollo?
- **a)** It will be neither under- or overreserved.
- **b)** It will be overreserved by $500.
- **c)** It will be underreserved by $500.
- **d)** It will be underreserved by $25.
- **e)** Its reserve status will be unaffected.

Parallel Problems

ANSWERED PROBLEMS

36. Key Problem Table 7.1 is the current balance sheet for the Maple Leafs Bank. Answer the following questions, assuming that the bank's target reserve ratio is 5 percent.

TABLE 7.1 Maple Leafs Bank Balance Sheet as of the Current Date

Assets		Liabilities/Equity	
Reserves	$ 100 000	Demand deposits	$1 000 000
Loans	650 000		
Securities	300 000	Shareholders' equity	250 000
Fixed assets	200 000		
	1 250 000		1 250 000

a) Is this bank over- or underreserved, and what is the amount?
Answer: Over, by 50000.

b) Suppose that a loan, in the amount of the excess reserves found in a), is made to Sats Mundin. What effect does this transaction have on the bank's balance sheet?
Answer: Loans ↑ by 50000, demand deposits ↑ by 50000

c) Suppose that Sats immediately spends all of his loan by writing a cheque to his psychologist, Freda Freud. She deposits it in her bank account, which happens to also be at the Maple Leafs Bank. What effect do these transactions have on the bank's balance sheet?
Answer: no effect.

d) Is the Maple Leafs Bank now over- or underreserved? If so, by how much?
Reserved? over; amount? 47500.

e) Suppose instead that the bank makes a loan for the amount of your answer in a), which then clears against the Maple Leafs Bank. How much excess reserves does the bank have now?
None.

Suppose that the balance sheet for the whole banking system just happens to be exactly ten times that of the Maple Leafs Bank's statement in **Table 7.1**. The balance sheet for the whole system is presented in **Table 7.2**. You can assume that each of the other banks also has a target reserve ratio of 5 percent.

TABLE 7.2 Whole Banking System Balance Sheet

Assets			Liabilities/Equity		
Reserves	$1 000 000	________	Demand deposits	$10 000 000	________
Loans	6 500 000	________	Shareholders' equity	2 500 000	________
Securities	3 000 000	________			
Fixed assets	2 000 000	________			
	$12 500 000	________		$12 500 000	________

f) In **Table 7.2**, show the balance sheet of the banking system when it is fully loaned up.

g) What is the increase in the money supply as a result of all the banks becoming fully loaned up?
Answer: ________________.

h) Finally, returning to the balance sheet in **Table 7.2**, what would be the consequence of the economy's central bank imposing a 12.5 percent required reserve ratio on all banks? What amount of loans would have to be called in?
Answer: ________________.

Basic (Problems 37–42)

37. Identify the necessary bookkeeping entries in the accounts of the Friedman Bank to record the following transactions.

a) The Friedman Bank sells some of its old computers for $20 000 in cash. ________________.

b) The bank buys $50 000 worth of government bonds from one of its customers and pays by cheque.
________________.

c) The Friedman Bank calls in the $5000 loan of Kim's, who pays in cash. ________________.

d) The bank grants a loan of $10 000 to Radim.
________________.

e) Radim, a customer of the Friedman Bank, writes a cheque for $10 000 payable to his father, who deposits it in his own account at the same bank.

______________________________ .

38. Table 7.3 shows the balance sheet of the Bruins Bank.

TABLE 7.3 **Bruins Bank Balance Sheet**

Assets		Liabilities/Equity	
Reserves	$ 24	Demand deposits	$400
Loans	280	Shareholders' equity	20
Securities	80		
Fixed assets	36		
Totals	$420		$420

By how much is the Bruins Bank over- or underreserved, if the target reserve ratio is as follows:

a) 2% __________ ; b) 5% __________ ;
c) 8% __________ ; d) 12% __________ .

39. What is the value of the money multiplier if the target reserve ratios of the banking system are as follows:

a) 2% __________ ; b) 5% __________ ;
c) 8% __________ ; d) 12% __________ .

40. Table 7.4 is the balance sheet for the Oilers Bank, which has a target reserve ratio of 5 percent.

TABLE 7.4 **Oilers Bank Balance Sheet as of the Current Date**

Assets		Liabilities/Equity	
Reserves	$ 6 000	Demand deposits	$80 000
Loans	68 000		
Securities	17 000	Shareholders' equity	20 000
Fixed assets	9 000		
Totals	$100 000		$100 000

a) By how much is the Oilers Bank over- or underreserved?
Answer: 2000 over .

b) If the bank makes a loan equal to the excess reserves and the borrower writes a cheque (for the full amount of the loan) to another customer of the bank, who then deposits it, what will be the new amount of excess reserves?
Answer: ______________________________ .

c) If, instead, the cheque written by the borrower is cleared against the Oilers Bank (the cheque was written to a customer of another bank), what will be the amount of excess reserves held by Oilers Bank?
Answer: 1900 .

41. Table 7.5 is the balance sheet for all banks combined in the banking system. All banks have a target reserve ratio of 8 percent.

TABLE 7.5 **Whole Banking System Balance Sheet**

Assets		Liabilities/Equity	
Reserves	$ 78 000	Demand deposits	$900 000
Loans	720 000		
Securities	102 000	Shareholders' equity	100 000
Fixed assets	100 000		
Totals	$1 000 000		$1 000 000

a) What is the amount of excess reserves?
Answer: 6000 .

b) What is the maximum amount that loans and deposits can be increased?
Answer: 75000 .

c) If the system becomes fully loaned up, by how much will the money supply have increased?
Answer: ______________________________ .

42. In which of the following circumstances has the money supply changed?

a) Mario deposits $1000 at his bank.
Yes ______ No ✓

b) Mario withdraws $1000 from his bank.
Yes ______ No ✓

c) Mario lends Luigi $1000.
Yes ______ No ✓

d) The bank lends Mario $1000.
Yes ✓ No ______

e) Mario lends the bank $1000.
Yes ______ No ✓

Intermediate (Problems 43–46)

43. Answer the questions below from the data in **Table 7.6**. (All figures are in $ billions.)

TABLE 7.6

Total currency issued by the Bank of Canada	$ 20
Total personal savings deposits	192
Total demand deposits	23
Deposits of the federal government at the Bank of Canada	2
Currency held by commercial banks	2
Government bonds owned by public	100
Non-personal fixed-term deposits (certificates of deposit)	46

a) What is the total currency in circulation?
Answer: ________________ .

b) How much larger is M1 than total currency in circulation?
Answer: ________________ .

c) How much larger is M2 than M1?
Answer: ________________ .

d) How much larger is M3 than M2?
Answer: ________________ .

44. Fill in the blanks in the balance sheet of the Flames Bank in **Table 7.7**, assuming that the value of fixed assets is the same as shareholders' equity and that the bank is fully loaned up. The target reserve ratio is 5 percent.

TABLE 7.7 Flames Bank Balance Sheet

Assets		Liabilities/Equity	
Reserves	$ ______	Demand deposits	$100 000
Loans	______	Shareholders' equity	______
Securities	10 000		
Fixed assets	______		
Totals			$120 000

TABLE 7.8 Senators Bank Balance Sheet

Assets			Liabilities/Equity		
Reserves	$ 60 000	______	Deposits	$400 000	______
Securities	80 000	______	Shareholders' equity	60 000	______
Loans	260 000	______			
Fixed assets	60 000	______			
Totals	$460 000	______		$460 000	______

45. **Table 7.8** is the balance sheet for the Senators Bank. The target reserve ratio is 10 percent.

a) What is the size of the bank's excess reserves?

________________ .

b) Change the balance sheet to show the effect of the bank loaning out all of its excess reserves.

c) Now change the balance sheet to show the effect of a cheque for the amount of the loan in b) clearing against the bank.

d) Suppose, instead, that the target reserve ratio is 20 percent. What is the bank's reserve situation, and what action will it take? ________________

________________ .

46. Many students think that the government (or the Bank of Canada) still has a pile of gold somewhere that "backs" our money. Since this is not true, what does back Canadian money? ________________

________________ .

Advanced (Problem 47)

47. The central bank of Muldovia has issued $100 000 in Muldovian dollars. What is the size of the Muldovian money supply if:

a) Muldovians have deposited none of the currency in its banks?

________________ .

b) Muldovians have deposited all of the currency in its banks, and the banks have a 100 percent target reserve ratio?

________________ .

c) Muldovians have deposited 50 percent of the currency in its banks, and the banks have a 100 percent target reserve ratio?

________________ .

d) Muldovians have deposited 50 percent of the currency in its banks, and the banks have a 10 percent target reserve ratio and are fully loaned up?

________________ .

UNANSWERED PROBLEMS

48. Key Problem **Table 7.9** shows the current balance sheet for the Canadiens Bank. Answer the questions below assuming that the bank's target reserve ratio is 10 percent.

TABLE 7.9 Canadiens Bank Balance Sheet as of Current Date

Assets		Liabilities/Equity	
Reserves	$ 120 000	Demand deposits	$900 000
Loans	680 000		
Securities	250 000	Shareholders' equity	500 000
Fixed assets	350 000		
Totals	$1 400 000		$1 400 000

a) Is this bank over- or underreserved, and by what amount?
b) Suppose that a loan, in the amount of the excess reserves found in a), is made to Panic Yerreault. What effect does this transaction have on the bank's balance sheet?
c) Suppose that Panic immediately spends all of his loan by writing a cheque to his astrologer, Misty Starship, who deposits it in her account at the Canadiens Bank. What effect do these trans-actions have on the bank's balance sheet?
d) Is the Canadiens Bank now over- or under-reserved? If so, by how much?
e) Suppose *instead* that the bank makes a loan for the amount in your answer in a), which then clears against the Canadiens Bank. How much excess reserves does the bank now have?

Suppose that there are a total of nine other banks in the economy and that the balance sheet for the whole banking system is presented in **Table 7.10**. You can assume that each of the other banks also has a target reserve ratio of 10 percent.

TABLE 7.10 Whole Banking System Balance Sheet

Assets		Liabilities/Equity	
Reserves	$1 200 000	Demand deposits	$9 000 000
Loans	6 800 000		
Securities	2 500 000	Shareholders' equity	5 000 000
Fixed assets	3 500 000		
Totals	14 000 000		14 000 000

f) Write out a balance sheet of the banking system if it were fully loaned up.
g) What is the increase in the money supply as a result of all the banks becoming fully loaned up?
h) What would be the consequence of the economy's central bank imposing a 15 percent required reserve ratio on all banks? What amount of loans would have to be called in?

Basic (Problems 49–54)

49. Identify the necessary bookkeeping entries in the accounts of the Thurow Bank to record the following transactions.
a) The Thurow Bank sells some of its office furniture for $10 000 in cash.
b) The bank buys $20 000 worth of government bonds from one of its customers and pays by cheque.
c) The bank calls in a $10 000 loan of Sean's, who pays in cash.
d) The bank grants a loan of $1000 to Steffany.
e) Steffany writes a cheque for $1000 to her brother, who deposits it in his own account at the Thurow Bank.

50. **Table 7.11** shows the balance sheet of the Rangers Bank.

TABLE 7.11 Rangers Bank Balance Sheet

Assets		Liabilities/Equity	
Reserves	$100	Demand deposits	$900
Loans	800	Shareholders' equity	100
Securities	60		
Fixed assets	40		
Totals	1000		1000

By how much is the Rangers Bank over- or underreserved if the target reserve ratio is:
a) 2% b) 5%
c) 8% d) 12%

51. What is the value of the money multiplier if the target reserve ratio of the banking system is:
a) 4% b) 8%
c) 10% d) 20%

52. **Table 7.12** is the balance sheet for the Kings Bank, which has a target reserve ratio of 10 percent.

TABLE 7.12 Kings Bank Balance Sheet

Assets		Liabilities/Equity	
Reserves	$20 000	Demand deposits	$160 000
Loans	120 000	Shareholders' equity	60 000
Securities	62 000		
Fixed assets	18 000		
Totals	220 000		220 000

a) By how much is the Kings Bank over- or underreserved?
b) If the bank makes a loan equal to the excess reserves and the borrower writes a cheque (for the full amount of the loan) to another customer of the bank who then deposits it, what will be the new amount of excess reserves?
c) If, instead, the cheque written by the borrower is cleared against the Kings Bank, what will be the amount of the excess reserves?

53. **Table 7.13** is the balance sheet for the whole banking system. All banks have a target reserve ratio of 10 percent.

TABLE 7.13 Whole Banking System Balance Sheet

Assets		Liabilities/Equity	
Reserves	$ 200 000	Demand deposits	$1 600 000
Loans	800 000	Shareholders' equity	600 000
Securities	880 000		
Fixed assets	320 000		
Totals	2 200 000		2 200 000

a) What is the amount of excess reserves?
b) What is the maximum amount that loans and deposits can be increased?
c) If the system becomes fully loaned up, by how much will the money supply have increased?

54. In which of the following circumstances has the money supply changed?
a) Mary deposits $500 into her bank account.
b) Mary withdraws $200 from her account through a cash machine.
c) Mary lends her friend Lynn $600.
d) Mary negotiates a $1000 loan from her bank.
e) Mary lends the bank $1000.

Intermediate (Problems 55–58)

55. Answer the questions below from the data in **Table 7.14** (all figures are in $ billions).

TABLE 7.14

Total currency issued by the Bank of Canada	$ 32
Total personal savings deposits	220
Total demand deposits	38
Deposits of the government at the Bank of Canada	3
Currency held by commercial banks	4
Government bonds owned by the public	120
Non-personal term deposits (certificates of deposit)	50

a) What is the total currency in circulation?
b) How larger is M1 than total currency in circulation?
c) How much larger is M2 than M1?
d) How much larger is M3 than M2?

56. Given **Table 7.15**:

TABLE 7.15

Fixed assets	$180 000
Demand deposits	$800 000
Reserves	$ 50 000
Loans	$500 000
Securities	$170 000

a) Arrange the data in the form of a balance sheet.
b) What is the value of equity for this bank?
c) If the bank has a 5 percent target reserve ratio, what is the value of excess reserves?

57. **Table 7.16** is the balance sheet for the Blues Bank. The target reserve ratio is 12 percent.

TABLE 7.16 Blues Bank Balance Sheet

Assets		Liabilities/Equity	
Reserves	$30 000	Demand deposits	$200 000
Loans	40 000	Shareholders' equity	20 000
Securities	120 000		
Fixed assets	30 000		
Totals	220 000		220 000

a) What is the size of the bank's excess reserves?
b) Change the balance sheet to show the effect of the bank loaning out all of its excess reserves.
c) Now change the balance sheet to show the effect of a cheque for the amount of the loan in b) clearing against the bank.

58. What gives the Canadian dollar its value?

Advanced (Problems 59–64)

59. The central bank of Malawi has issued $200 000 in Malawian dollars. What is the size of the money supply if:
    a) Malawians have deposited none of the currency in its banks?
    b) Malawians have deposited all of the currency in its banks and the banks have a 100 percent target reserve ratio?
    c) Malawians have deposited 50 percent of the currency in its banks and the banks have a 50 percent reserve ratio and are fully loaned up.
    d) Malawians have deposited 50 percent of the currency in its banks and the banks have a 12.5 percent reserve ratio and are fully loaned up?

60. **Table 7.17** is the balance sheet for all the banks combined in the banking system.

TABLE 7.17 Whole Banking System Balance Sheet

Assets		Liabilities/Equity	
Reserves	$ 900 000	Demand deposits	$900 000
Loans	—		
Securities	50 000	Shareholders' equity	100 000
Fixed assets	50 000		
Totals	$1 000 000		$1 000 000

a) Which one of the above figures is part of the money supply?
b) If all banks maintain 100 percent reserves, what happens to the money supply if $1000 cash is deposited into one of the banks in the system?
c) If none of the banks maintain reserves, what happens to the money supply if $1000 cash is deposited into one of the banks in the system?

61. **Table 7.18** is the combined balance sheet for all the banks in a banking system. Each bank has a target reserve ratio of 5 percent.

TABLE 7.18 Whole Banking System Balance Sheet

Assets		Liabilities/Equity	
Reserves	$ 80	Demand deposits	$800
Loans	300		
Securities	690	Shareholders' equity	40
Fixed assets	40		
Totals	$840		$840

a) Write out a new balance sheet that reflects the complete effect of all excess reserves being loaned out.
b) What is the maximum possible increase in the money supply?
c) Given **Table 7.18**, if the target reserve ratio changes to 12.5 percent, what quantity of loans will the system be forced to call in? Write in the figures that show this process completed.

62. Rearrange in correct position the items in the balance sheet shown in **Table 7.19**. Change one figure only to reflect the bank achieving a 10 percent target reserve ratio.

TABLE 7.19 Balance Sheet of Canucks Bank Ltd., December 31, 2000

Assets		Liabilities/Equity	
Reserves	$100 000	Demand deposits	$500 000
Loans	330 000		
Shareholders' equity	80 000	Securities	120 000
Fixed assets	80 000		

63. Many people believe that the ability to buy goods with credit cards makes such cards "money." Explain why a credit card is *not* money. Do you think debit cards are money?

64. Why can't a single bank increase its loans by a multiple of its excess reserves? Can you imagine a situation in which it could?

Web-Based Activities

1. Go to **www.bank-banque-canada.ca/publications/review/atab-002.pdf** and select Table A2. Notice the annual percentage increase in both M1 and M2 over the last several years. Can you explain why M1 grew in 1998 while M2 actually decreased?

2. How will the transition from a paper-based monetary system to an electronic payments system affect the process of money creation? Go to **www.cato.org/pubs/books/money/tableof.htm** and read the introduction written by J. Dorn to answer this question. Do you think that electronic money will be beneficial to the economy? Why or why not?

3. The Canada Deposit Insurance Corporation (CDIC) was created to insure deposits in Canadian financial intermediaries. Go to **www.cdic.ca** and find out how many of its member institutions have failed since CDIC was set up. What are the four major players in the financial system?

CHAPTER EIGHT

The Money Market

LEARNING OBJECTIVES

This chapter will enable you to:

LO1 Recognize that demand for money is not the same as desire for income.

LO2 Distinguish two types of money demand.

LO3 Explain the downward-sloping money demand curve.

LO4 Explain and illustrate graphically how the money supply and demand affect the equilibrium interest rate.

LO5 Describe two views of how the money market affects the level of real GDP and inflation.

What's ahead...

This chapter has two main objectives: to explain how interest rates are determined, and to show how changes in the money supply can bring about important changes in the economy. To begin with, we explain how the money supply is determined and then we examine the factors that influence the demand for money. We then look at how this equilibrium can be disturbed and at how the money market reacts to such disturbances. Finally, we look at two contrasting views of the way that changes in the supply of money can produce real changes in the market.

A QUESTION OF RELEVANCE...

How much money do you have at the moment? Remember, this includes coin and currency in your pocket, and at home, plus the current balance in your chequing account. Is it $20? $200? $1000? Does your holding of money vary from week to week or month to month, or is it some constant amount? What is the minimum you hold? What is the maximum you would hold before you started to look for something to "do with" your money? Have you thought about what determines the amount of money that you hold? Even people with the same level of income sometimes hold quite different amounts of money. Why is that? In this chapter we look at these questions and their implications.

Few people would dispute the usefulness of money to both individuals and society. In fact, most economists consider it one of the fundamental elements of a wealthy society, even though they do not consider money itself to be a form of wealth for a nation. However, as we shall see, economists do most definitely disagree on the role of money in producing real change in the economy. In order to see just how money can affect things like production and employment, we need to understand the workings of the money market. To begin with, we look at the supply side of the money market.

8.1 The Supply of Money

LO1
Recognize that the demand for money is not the same as desire for income.

For simplicity's sake we will use the narrow definition of the money supply, M1, in our discussion. The supply of money, if you remember, is composed of currency in circulation and the total of all demand deposits at chartered banks. The Bank of Canada can determine exactly how much currency is issued, but it is the public that decides what portion of this it wishes to keep in circulation (in our pockets, in the tills of shops, in office safes, and so on) and what portion is deposited with banks. The portion that is deposited constitutes the banks' reserves, which in turn will determine the amount of loans and demand deposits they are able to support. We will leave until Chapter 12 the discussion of the way in which the Bank of Canada is able to affect the amount of money in the economy. The important point we wish to make at this stage is that, to all intents and purposes:

The supply of money is determined by the Bank of Canada, which, can change the supply as it sees fit.

interest rate: the annual rate at which payment is made for the use of money (or borrowed funds); a percentage of the borrowed amount.

In other words, the money supply is autonomous with respect to its price—and the price of money, as we shall see, is the same thing as the **interest rate**. Graphically, then, the money supply plots as a straight vertical line, as shown in **Figure 8.1**.

FIGURE 8.1 **The Money Supply**

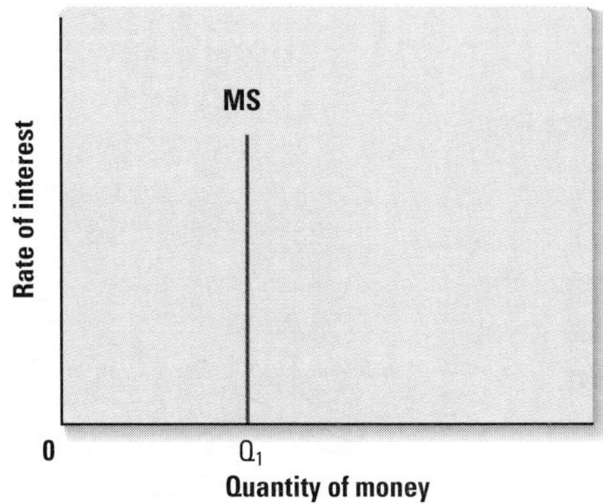

Since the Bank of Canada can set the money supply (MS) independently of the rate of interest, it plots as a perfectly inelastic (vertical) supply curve at the present quantity, Q_1.

Let us now look at the other side of the equation: the demand for money.

8.2 The Demand for Money

LO2
Distinguish two types of money demand.

Before you start thinking that the average person's demand for money is unlimited, bear in mind that money is a stock and is only one of many possible forms of wealth that people might hold. The average person's demand for *income* might well be unlimited, but we are speaking about (the stock of) money. Like any other form of wealth-holding, money has certain advantages and disadvantages. Except in times of high inflation, money maintains a resonably stable value unlike such things as land or stocks and bonds, whose value can vary greatly. From this point of view it involves less risk. The other advantage is that money is highly liquid. Balanced against that is the fact that holding money does not produce a return, whereas most other forms of wealth can provide a source of income. In general, the safer the "investment," the lower the return; the greater the risk, the higher the return. So why bother holding money at all; why not, on receipt of income, immediately transfer it into some sort of financial investment? The reason is obvious: we need to keep a portion of our wealth in the form of a balance in a chequing account or as currency simply because other forms of wealth are unacceptable as a means of payment. It is certainly true that over the years, the introduction of credit cards, debit cards, and chequing–savings accounts has meant that we need only keep a smaller proportion of our wealth in the form of money; nevertheless most of our transactions still require that we pay for them with money. One reason to hold money, therefore, is what economists call the **transactions demand for money**. And what is it that determines this transactions demand? The answer is the value of transactions we make. And what determines the value of our transactions? The level of our income. The higher the income level of an individual, the more she will spend, and the higher will be the transactions demand for money. This is similarly true for the whole economy. The higher the level of GDP, the higher will be the transactions demand for money. Note here that we are speaking of nominal GDP. This means that a higher demand for money can come about either because real GDP increases or because prices increase. The major determinants of the transactions demand for money, then, are the level of real income and the level of prices; a change in either can cause a change in the transactions demand for money.

transactions demand for money: the desire of people to hold money as a medium of exchange, that is, to effect transactions.

asset demand for money: the desire by people to use money as a store of wealth, that is, to hold money as an asset.

Another way of looking at the transactions demand is that it is related to money functioning as a medium of exchange. But, as we have already noted, money is often used as a store of wealth. Under what circumstances will it be a popular form of wealth holding? Presumably, when other forms of wealth holding are not attractive. If for instance, the return on bonds was a piddling 1 percent, and the value of stock markets and real estate was declining, then most people would start to regard money as a very secure "investment." When the return on other assets is low, therefore, people's demand for money tends to be high. This motive for holding money is termed the **asset demand for money**. On the other hand, when the average return on other types of financial investment is high, people will tend to economize on their money balances and try to ensure that they keep as little as possible beyond their transactions needs. In general, the best indicator of the return on bonds is the rate of interest. Rates of return tend to move in concert with the rate of interest. There is, therefore, an *inverse* relationship between rates of interest and the asset demand for money. When interest rates are high, asset demand is low; when rates are low, asset demand is high. This idea is illustrated in **Figure 8.2**.

Courtesy of the Bank of Canada.

The Bank of Canada building in Ottawa.

FIGURE 8.2 Transactions, Asset, and Total Demand for Money

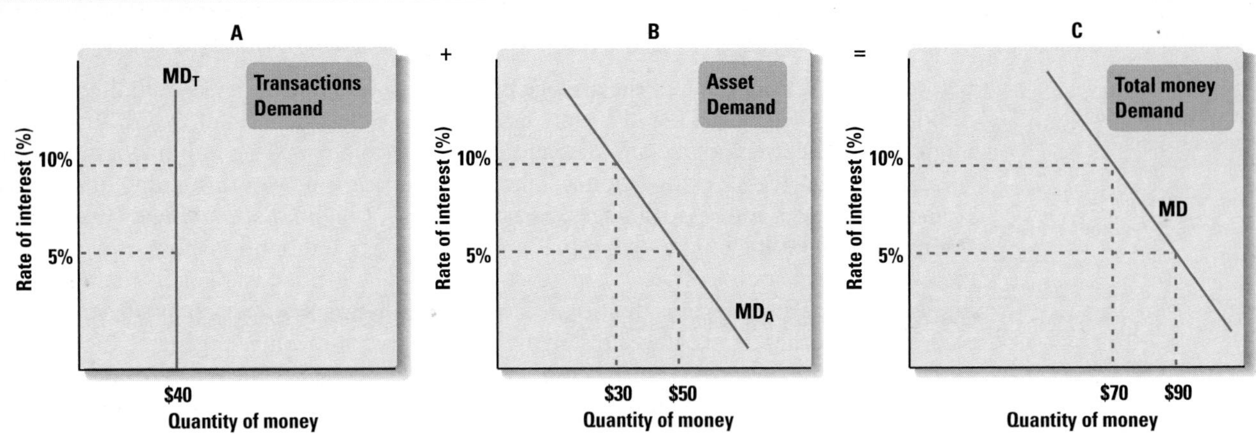

Graph A shows the transactions demand for money, which is equal to $40. Graph B shows the asset demand for money. When the rate of interest is 10%, the quantity of money demanded for asset purposes is $30, and at an interest rate of 5%, it is $50. The final graph, C, shows the total demand for money, which is obtained by summing the first two graphs horizontally.

Figure 8.2A simply states that the transactions demand for money is unrelated to the rate of interest. We need a certain amount of money—in this example, $40 billion—irrespective of how high or low the rate of interest is. Of course, this demand would increase with a rise in real incomes or prices, and decrease with a fall in either.

Figure 8.2B shows the inverse relationship between the asset demand for money and the rate of interest. At an interest rate of 10 percent, the asset demand will be relatively low at $30 billion. At this high rate of interest, people will economize as much as possible in their holdings of money (which earns no interest); they will try to put any excess cash into some form of income-earning asset. At an interest rate of 5 percent, on the other hand, the asset demand at $50 billion is high. At this low rate of interest, people are fairly indifferent about holding other financial investments and would just as soon hold onto money.

Figure 8.2C shows the total demand for money, which is simply the addition of the transactions and asset demands. (The two curves are just summed together horizontally.) It shows that when the rate of interest is at 10 percent, the total demand for money is $70 billion. This total is composed of $40 billion transactions demand plus $30 billion, the amount of idle money or asset demand. When the rate of interest is 5 percent, the total demand for money is $90 billion, composed of transactions demand $40 billion and asset demand of $50 billion.

What we have, then, is that people will hold enough money to finance their daily transactions, but will often possess an additional amount of "idle balances," which is what we have called the asset demand. There is controversy among economists regarding such idle balances. Keynes, for example, gave other explanations of why people might rationally hold such additional balances of money. He suggested it is perfectly rational to hold idle balances in situations where holding bonds is risky. This might happen if the interest rate is low (and bond prices are high) and peoiple expect it to rise. In this case they will hold onto money and, if the interest rate does go up, they will then be able to purchase bonds more cheaply.

(Keynes called this the speculative motive for holding money.) Besides offering this explanation, Keynes felt that many people might hold cash as a form of security, or insurance, for the future (what he termed the precautionary motive). Even allowing for the fact that the value of money erodes through inflation, many people may still want to hold on to money because of its immediate accessibility in an emergency. In summary, the demand for money in the economy is determined by:

- the level of transactions (real GDP)
- the average value of transactions (the price level)
- the rate of interest

SELF-TEST

1. Assume you are given the following asset demand for an economy:

Interest Rate (%)	Asset Demand ($ billions)
12	50
11	55
10	60
9	65
8	70
7	75
6	80

You may assume that the transaction demand for money is equal to 10 percent of nominal GDP.

a) If the level of GDP in this economy is $800 and the interest rate is 10 percent, what is the total demand for money?

b) If the money supply is $150 billion, will there be a surplus or shortage of money? How much?

8.3 Equilibrium in the Money Market

LO3
Explain the downward-sloping money demand curve.

We have now looked at both the supply of money and the demand for money in an economy. Hopefully, you know what's coming next. To find out under what circumstances the public will be happy to hold the amount of money that the Bank of Canada has supplied, we need to put the two together. **Figure 8.3** does this.

FIGURE 8.3 **Surplus and Shortage of Money**

This figure shows that at interest rates above equilibrium (such as at r_2), there is a surplus of money. People will rid themselves of this surplus by buying bonds, which will increase the price of bonds, thus reducing the interest rate. Conversely, at interest rates below equilibrium (such as at r_3), there will be a shortage, causing people to sell off bonds. The effect of this will be to push down bond prices, causing the rate of interest to rise. Only at equilibrium interest rate r_1 will people be happy to hold the amount of money that is supplied by the Bank of Canada.

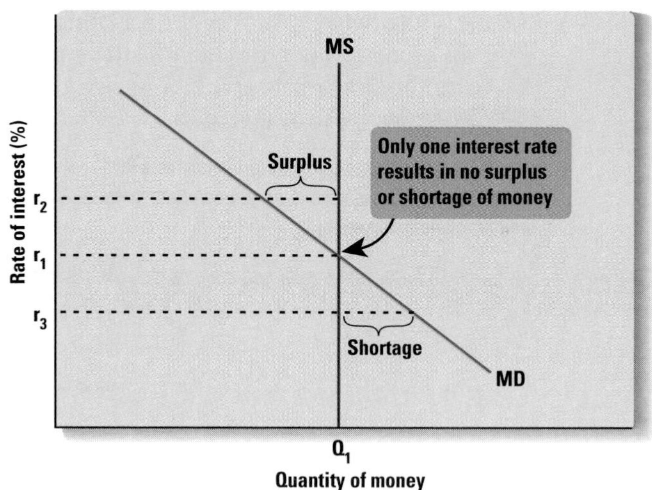

bond: a promise to pay the principle and interest on a loan by a specified date.

The supply of money, as mentioned before, is determined by the Bank of Canada, and we will regard it as independent of the rate of interest. It is simply a fixed autonomous amount equal to Q_1. The demand for money curve is merely a repeat of **Figure 8.2C**. The graph shows that only at interest rate r_1 will the quantities of money supplied and demanded be equal. At interest r_1, then, we have equilibrium in the money market. But what will happen if the money market is not in equilibrium? For instance, what will happen if the interest rate happens to be above the equilibrium, at say, r_2? At this rate of interest, there is obviously a surplus of money; that is, the quantity supplied exceeds the quantity demanded. The quantity demanded is lower because at higher rates of interest, people are going to reduce their money holdings; they will want to keep their money balances to a minimum and will want to buy some other financial instruments such as a **bond**. Now bonds are nothing more than loans which are issued for a set period—one year, five years and so on—and have a nominal face value, such as \$100 or \$1000, and pay a fixed rate of interest to the holder of the bond. They are issued by corporations, by banks, and by various level of government: municipal, provincial, and federal. The essence of a bond is that it can easily be bought and sold in the market. This means that the return you earn on a bond depends not just on the interest that you earn on it but also from the profit (or loss) on its sale. Suppose, for instance, that a new one-year \$100 bond was issued which pays an interest rate of 5 percent. Suppose also that you can earn 10 percent return on most other financial investments. You can imagine that not many people are going to buy the bond for this price. As a result, soon after its issue the price will quickly drop. How low will the price drop? The answer is: until it earns the same return, 10 percent, that is being offered on other financial investments. In other words, the price will drop to approximately \$95. Buyers will now earn \$5 from when the bond is redeemed a year later and will earn \$5 from the interest paid to it, for a total of \$10.

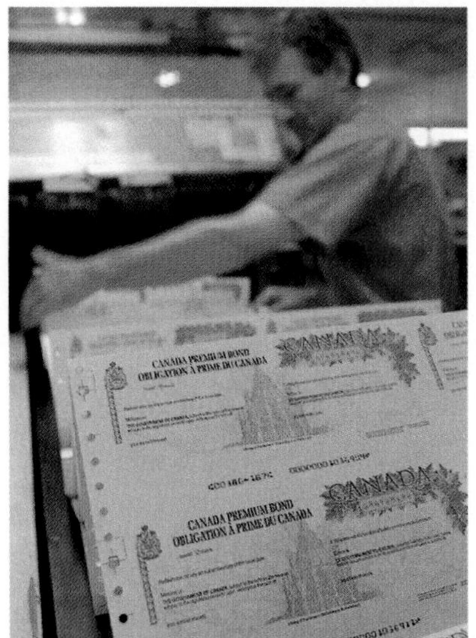

CP/Tom Hanson

A pressman stacks some of the new Canada Premium Bonds as they come off the presses at the Canada Bank Note Company in Ottawa.

In other words, as the price of bonds drop, the return that you earn (the rate of interest) goes up. It also means that the higher the price of bonds, the lower the yields (rates of return). In effect, this will mean a lower rate of interest. In short:

The lower price of bonds, the higher the rate of return; the higher the price of bonds, the lower the rate of return.

Like the demand and supply for any product, a surplus tends to cause prices to fall (and the rate of interest is the price of money). On the other hand, a shortage will cause the price (the interest rate) to increase. Perhaps this will become clearer when we look at what happens if the demand or supply of money changes. **Figure 8.4** shows the effect of an expansion of the money supply.

FIGURE 8.4 **A Shift in the Supply of Money**

An increase in the supply of money from MS_1 to MS_2 will initially cause a surplus of money at the prevailing interest rate r_1. People will want to rid themselves of the surplus by buying bonds, thus causing bond prices to rise and the interest rate to fall to r_2.

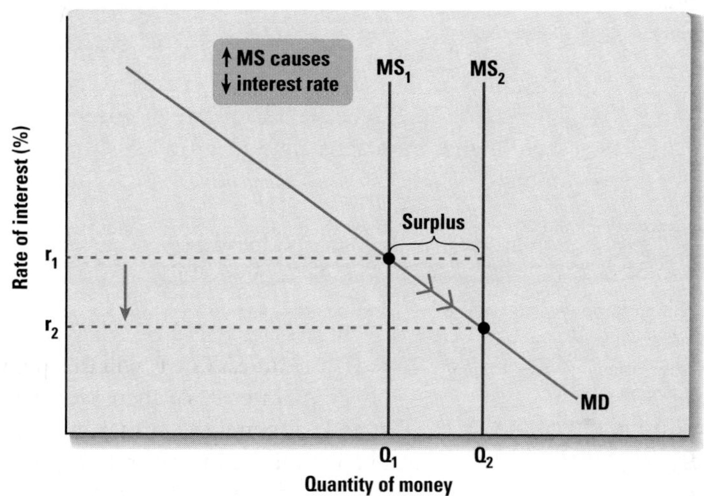

Suppose the money supply increases, which is illustrated by a rightward shift in the money supply curve from MS_1 to MS_2. Given the present interest rate, an increase in the supply of money will lead to an immediate surplus. People simply do not wish to hold this extra quantity supplied at this rate of interest. What they will do is get rid of any surplus by buying stocks, bonds, or other types of income-earning assets. This increase in the demand for bonds will cause bond prices to increase and, therefore, the rate of interest to fall, in **Figure 8.4**, from r_1 to r_2. Only when the rate of interest has fallen to r_2 will people be happy to hold the additional supply. In summary:

An increase in the supply of money will cause interest rates to fall; a decrease in the supply of money will cause interest rates to rise.

From this, one can appreciate that it is impossible for the Bank of Canada to change the money supply without also affecting interest rates.

SELF-TEST

2. Assume that the money demand for a particular economy is as follows (all money figures in $ billions):

Rate of Interest (%)	Asset Demand ($)	Transactions Demand ($)	Total Demand ($)
12	50	80	______
11	55	80	______
10	60	80	______
9	65	80	______
8	70	80	______
7	75	80	______
6	80	80	______

Complete the table and answer these questions:

a) If the money supply equals $150, what must the equilibrium interest rate be?

b) If the money supply equals $140, what must the equilibrium interest rate be?

c) If the rate of interest is 11 percent and the money supply is $150, what are the implications?

Let's now look at the effect of a change in the demand for money on the rate of interest. Assume, for instance, that the demand for money increased because nominal GDP increased. At a higher GDP, the value of transactions will increase and people will want to hold higher money balances. **Figure 8.5** shows the effect of an increase in the demand for money.

FIGURE 8.5 **An Increase in the Demand for Money**

The total demand for money will change if nominal GDP changes. A higher price level or a higher GDP will shift the demand for money curve to the right. Such an increase will initially result in a shortage of money, causing people to sell some of their bonds. As a result, bond prices will drop, which means that interest rates will rise (from r_1 to r_2).

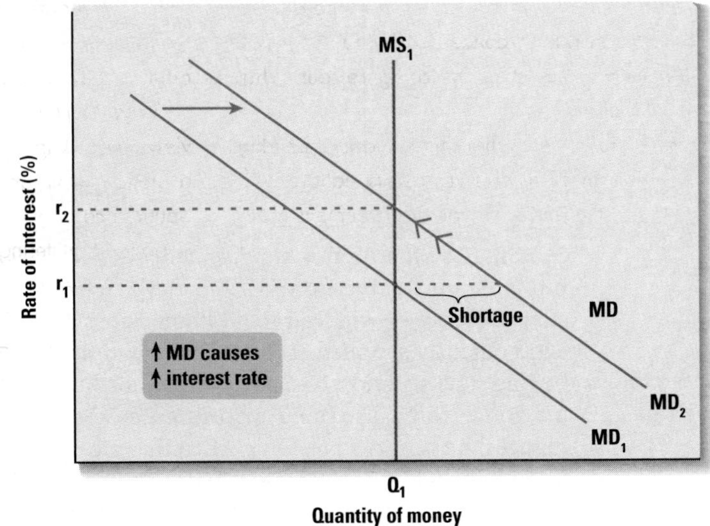

Here we see that the money demand curve has shifted right from MD_1 to MD_2 as a result of an increase in either real income or the price level. At interest rate r_1, this increased demand will produce a shortage of money. (After all, we cannot assume that the Bank of Canada will automatically increase the supply of money just because the demand increases.) To obtain this extra money, people will be forced to sell off some of their income-earning investments. (For instance, they may have to transfer money from a savings account to a chequing account, sell off bonds or other financial instruments.) The effect of this action will be to increase the supply of these types of instruments as people cash them in. This causes their price to fall and the rate of interest to rise, as it does in **Figure 8.5**, from r_1 to r_2. Similarly, a decrease in the demand of money will cause interest rates to fall. In summary:

An increase in the demand for money causes interest rates to rise; a decrease in the demand for money will cause interest rates to fall.

This whole discussion (in fact, this whole book) has spoken of *the* interest rate as if there were one single rate. In fact, what we have in any economy is an interest-rate structure made up of many rates: the rate paid by banks on savings accounts, the rate charged by banks for loans of different types (mortgages, personal loans, or credit card charges), as well as the bank rate, which we will look at in more detail in Chapter 12. For convenience, however, we will continue to speak of "the interest rate," and the reader can use the context of the discussion to determine whether it would be for saving or for borrowing.

ADDED DIMENSION

Gold and Wealth

One of the reasons that Adam Smith's *The Wealth of Nations* became the seminal work in economics is because it attempted to look beyond the economic fears and aspirations of the individual and shift the focus to a study of the whole economy. The title of Smith's opus is, after all, *The Wealth of Nations*, not *The Wealth of People*. It would have been a very simple task for Smith to have defined what constitutes wealth as far as the individual is concerned. What is far less obvious and far more interesting is to figure out what comprises the wealth of nations.

At first glance, it would seem that this is made up of the total wealth of all the individuals plus any assets that are held in common. However, there was major disagreement as to whether or not money should be included as a form of wealth. Although gold could certainly be used as an international medium of exchange, did it mean that the more gold a country had, the richer it was? What if a country's stock of gold were to increase appreciably—would the country be any richer? Well, by and large, people in possession of gold are able to buy more foreign goods. However, they probably want to buy more domestic goods, too. Since there is no reason for the amount of goods produced to change, the only thing that is likely to happen is an increase in prices. What will happen eventually is that prices will increase in line with the amount of gold. The net result is that people are no better off than they were before.

What Smith tried to do in his book was to redirect people's views regarding wealth. Being wealthy for Smith meant that a nation was able to produce and had produced an abundance of goods and services—not that it merely owned a stock of glittering pieces of metal like gold. Gold is not wealth in the same way that labour and capital goods are forms of wealth. The latter are regenerative, in that they can recreate themselves; gold, in contrast, is totally sterile.

REVIEW

1. What are the two determinants of the transactions demand for money?
2. Is the transactions demand for money related to the rate of interest?
3. The asset demand for money is inversely related to what?
4. It is helpful to think of the interest rate as the price of what?
5. What does the term *equilibrium in the money market* mean?
6. How does a surplus of money disappear?
7. What effect will a decrease in the money supply have on interest rates?
8. What effect will a decrease in real income have on interest rates?

8.4 How Changes in the Money Market Affect the Economy

LO4
Explain and illustrate graphically how the money supply and demand affect the equilibrium interest rate.

So far we have been concerned with the mechanics of how changes in the money supply and demand affect interest rates. But by itself this is of no great interest (if you'll forgive the pun). We need to go one step further and show how this change in interest rates can bring about other changes in the economy.

A Change in the Price Level

transmission process: the Keynesian view of how changes in money affect (transmit to) the real variables in the economy.

As we shall discover, the money market and the product market are intrinsically linked: changes in the one will bring about changes in the other. For instance, let's work through the effects of a change in the price level. In working through this **transmission process**, we will see that the interest rate is the link between the two markets. You may recall from Chapter 5 that one of the reasons that aggregate quantity demanded increases when the price level decreases is because it causes the level of investment spending in the economy to increase. We called this the *interest-rate effect*, and it is one of the causes of the downward slope of the aggregate demand curve. Let us work through this process, illustrated in **Figure 8.6**.

Suppose, for instance, that the price level drops, caused perhaps by an increase in aggregate supply, as shown in **Figure 8.6A**. This drop in price means that we would be able to finance the same number of transactions as before, but with less money. The demand for money therefore falls. This is shown in **Figure 8.6B**.

The decrease in the demand for money from MD_1 to MD_2 causes a drop in the rate of interest from r_1 to r_2. We saw earlier that the type of spending most affected by changes in the interest rate is investment. A lower rate of interest will cause firms to invest more and a higher rate would result in a lower level of investment. Thus, there is an inverse relationship between the two.

FIGURE 8.6 **Equilibrium in the Money and Product Markets**

This figure shows the effect of a decrease in the price level in both the money market and the product market. In 8.6A we see a decrease in the price level as a result of an increase in AS. The lower price level results in a decrease in the demand for money, from MD_1 to MD_2, and a decrease in the interest rate from r_1 to r_2, as seen in 8.6B. Figure C shows how this lower interest rate will lead to an increase in investment spending from I_1 to I_2. Figure A shows that the effect on the product market is an increase in real GDP, from Y_1 to Y_2.

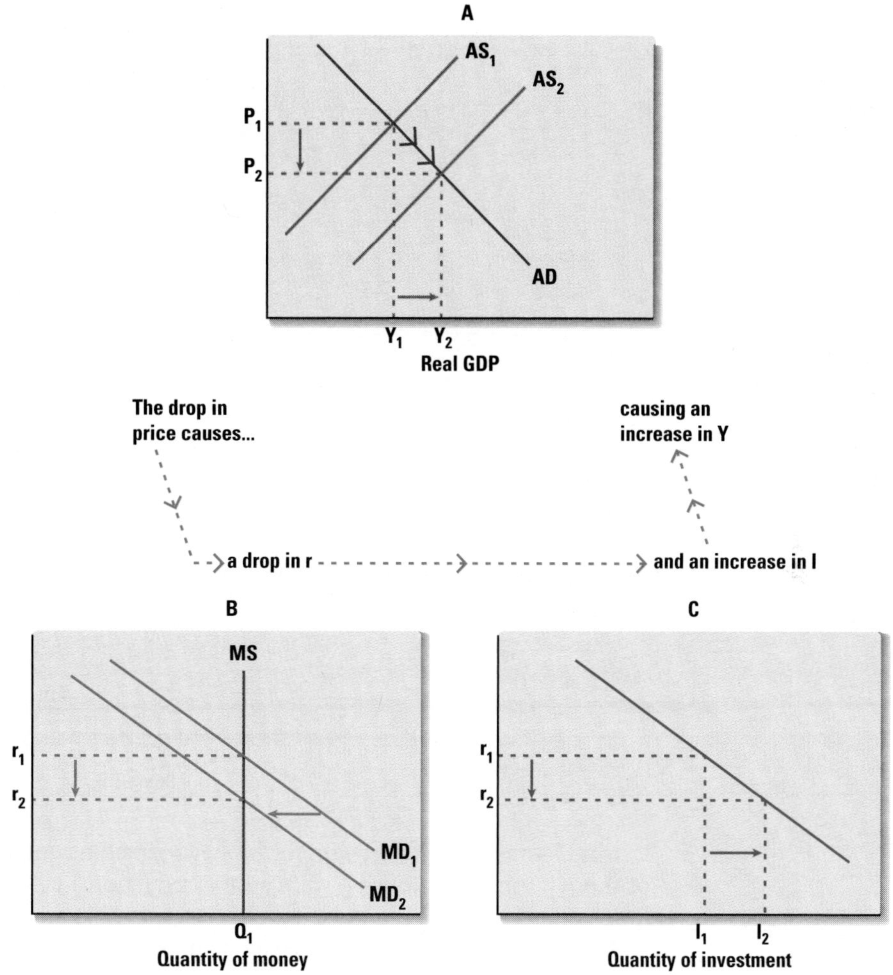

investment demand: the inverse relationship between investment spending and interest rates.

This relationship is referred to as the **investment demand** and is illustrated in **Figure 8.6C**. The fall in the rate of interest from r_1 to r_2 will reduce the cost of borrowing for firms which will be encouraged to increase investment spending from I_1 to I_2.

Finally, **Figure 8.6A** illustrates the effects on the product market of the original increase in aggregate supply, which involves a movement down the aggregate demand curve—i.e., an increase in aggregate quantity demanded—and an increase in income from Y_1 to Y_2.

In summary:

A lower price level causes a lower demand for money, reducing the interest rate and increasing both investment and real GDP.

Changes in the Money Supply: The Keynesian View

Figure 8.7 illustrates how the transmission process explains the effects of a direct change in the money supply.

FIGURE 8.7 **The Effects of an Increase in the Money Supply**

Figure A illustrates an increase in the money supply, MS_1 to MS_2, which results in a decrease in the interest rate from r_1 to r_2. B shows that this decrease in the interest rate increases the level of investment spending from I_1 to I_2. Since the price level has not changed, the increase in investment spending results in the AD curve shifting to the right: AD_1 to AD_2, as illustrated in Figure C.

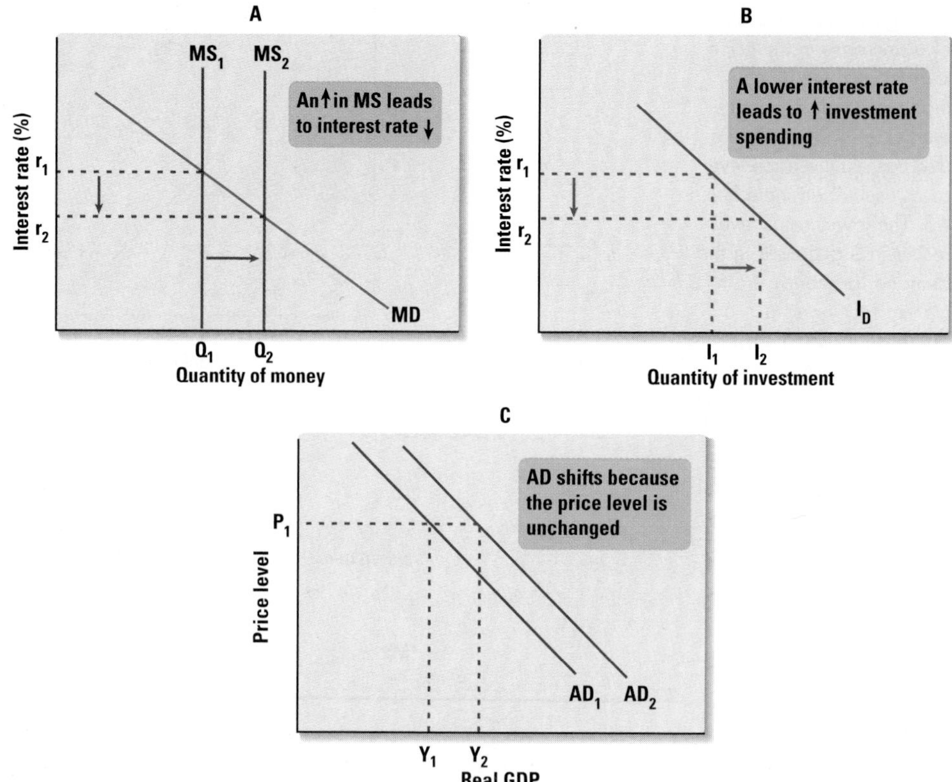

In **Figure 8.7A** we start with the money market in equilibrium. The increase in the supply of money from MS_1 to MS_2 will cause a reduction in the interest rate from r_1 to r_2. This lower interest rate will increase investment spending from I_1 to I_2, as illustrated in **Figure 8.7B**, which means a higher aggregate demand. We now have higher aggregate demand, but no change in the price level, which means that the AD curve must have shifted to the right from AD_1 to AD_2, as illustrated in **Figure 8.7C**. In short, increases in the money supply will shift the AD curve to the right. It is important for you to realize that the shift from AD_1 to AD_2 is larger than the increase in investment spending from I_1 to I_2. The existence of the multiplier is the reason for this. As we saw in earlier chapters, the increase in investment spending will trigger a series of increases in income and spending. In short, the multiplier ensures that the increase in income from Y_1 to Y_2 will be greater than the investment increase from I_1 to I_2.

In Chapter 12 we will look in more detail at how the Bank of Canada is able to fight recessions by increasing the supply of money, and how it combats inflation by decreasing the supply of money.

Money Market Changes	Transmit into	Product Market Changes
$P\downarrow \Rightarrow MD\downarrow \Rightarrow$ Surplus of Money $\Rightarrow$ Purchase of Bonds $\Rightarrow$ Bond Prices $\uparrow$	$\Rightarrow r\downarrow \Rightarrow$	$I\uparrow \rightarrow Y\uparrow$ (Movement along AD curve)
$M_S\uparrow \Rightarrow$ Surplus of Money $\Rightarrow$ Purchase of Bonds $\Rightarrow$ Bond Prices $\uparrow$	$\Rightarrow r\downarrow \Rightarrow$	$I\uparrow \rightarrow Y\uparrow$ (Shift in AD curve)

SELF-TEST

3. If the price level increases, what effect will this have on interest rates, investment, and the aggregate quantity demanded?

4. What would be the effect on the level of investment and real income if the money supply were reduced?

You can appreciate from our analysis that the transmission process is somewhat indirect. We will see in a later chapter that Keynesians feel that the effect of a change in the money supply on the economy may not be very powerful. In contrast, monetarists feel that the effect of changes in the money market are far more direct and certainly more powerful. Let's take a look at this view.

The Monetarist View

monetarism: an economic school of thought that believes that cyclical fluctuations of GDP and inflation are usually caused by changes in the money supply.

equation of exchange: a formula that states that the quantity of money times the velocity of money is equal to nominal GDP (price times real GDP).

velocity of money (or circulation): the number of times per year that the average unit of currency is spent (or turns over) buying final goods or services.

Monetarism refers to a school of thought popularized by the economist Milton Friedman. From the monetarist perspective, GDP determination can be summarized in a single equation referred to as the **equation of exchange**:

$$MV = PQ \quad [8.1]$$

The M is the supply of money that we have been discussing in this chapter. The V refers to the **velocity of money** (also called "velocity of circulation") and needs some explanation. If, for example, the GDP in a given year was \$800 billion and the supply of money was \$80 billion, the velocity would be ten. What this means is that every loonie, every \$5 bill, every \$10 bill, and so on, changes hands, from person to person, an average of ten times during the year. The velocity of money, therefore, is the rate at which the money supply turns over in generating income.

The Q refers to the quantity of goods and services sold (real GDP), whereas the P is a composite (or index) of their prices.

Given this equation of exchange, we can see that:

$$\text{nominal GDP} = M \times V \quad [8.2]$$

We also know that nominal GDP is equal to real GDP, which is Q, times the price level P. Thus:

$$\text{nominal GDP} = P \times Q \quad [8.3]$$

It therefore follows that MV equals PQ, in that they both equal nominal GDP. In short, the two terms equal each other *by definition*.

ADDED DIMENSION

Milton Friedman: Mr. Monetarist

The 1976 Nobel Prize winner in economics, Milton Friedman, has had an enormous influence on modern economic thinking. As a lifetime professor at the University of Chicago, he is most famous for his work in the field of monetary policy. However, he has been influential in many other areas too, including his seminal work on the consumption function, the role of expectations, the idea of a negative income tax, and the concept of the natural rate of unemployment. Also, he has gained fame outside economics as a journalist for *Newsweek*, in a television documentary series, and as adviser to then presidential candidates Barry Goldwater and Richard Nixon. His book *Capitalism and Freedom* is an elegant presentation of his laissez faire views.

ADDED DIMENSION

The Velocity of Money

The velocity of money can also be used to describe the number of times that money is actually used each year. In this case we are looking at money used to finance all sorts of expenditures, including stock market transactions, second-hand sales, and all those other transactions that we do not include in GDP. Defining V this way results in the equation of exchange being

$$MV = PT$$

where V relates to the number of times money is used to finance *all transactions* and T is the number of transactions (not just those on GDP items).

We are usually more interested in looking at the effect of money changes on GDP rather than its effects on all transactions in an economy during a year. However, it is only a short step from one formulation to the other, since the level of GDP is usually closely related to the total of all transactions that take place.

In terms of what the actual size of V in Canada is, it very much depends on which definition of money is used. This is because the actual velocity cannot be directly measured but is obtained by dividing nominal GDP ($P \times Q$) by the size of the money supply (M). If we use the narrow (M1) definition, empirical data shows that the value of V has increased steadily from approximately 7.5 in the early 1960s to over 17 in the early 1990s. Using the broader (M2) definition of money yields a value of V which has remained a fairly constant 3 over the last 30 years.

Now that this basic equation has been established, we can explore some of its implications. A fundamental assumption of the monetarists is that one can treat V (the velocity of money) as a constant. Thus:

$$M\overline{V} \equiv PQ$$

(The line above V indicates that the term is a constant; the triple equality symbol means that this is an identity rather than just an equality.)

If velocity is indeed constant, then this immediately establishes the fact that any change in M will have an impact on the right side of the equation: on prices or on the quantity of goods, that, combined, we just saw, is the same thing as nominal GDP. That is, if M were to rise by 10 percent, then either the price level or quantity of goods and services produced, or a combination of the two, would also rise by 10 percent.

If we were to assume that the economy is currently at full-employment output, then Q would not be able to rise (at least not permanently), and any increase in M would have a direct and proportional impact on P—the price level. That is, if both V and Q are constant, then increases in M translate into inflation—pure and simple. Thus the phrase: "inflation is a monetary phenomenon."

We should also point out that monetarists believe that V is constant because they feel that individuals only demand money for transaction purposes; that is, there is no asset demand for money. For monetarists, it is irrational for anybody to hold "idle balances" of money for any purpose. They point out that there are a whole variety of financial instruments (bonds, term deposits, and so on) that are as safe and convenient as money but also provide the individual with an income. Therefore, if people find themselves with excess cash balances—because, for example, of a recent increase in the supply of money—they will divest themselves of these excess balances by purchasing either financial instruments or goods and services, rather than hold those balances. According to the monetarist position, an increase in the money supply would cause a big drop in interest rates and a significant increase in investment spending. It will *also* cause an increase in consumption of major consumer goods, such as autos, as people try to rid themselves of what they see as excess cash balances. If the economy is experiencing a recessionary gap, then this additional demand will raise the *real* GDP. If, however, the economy is already at full-employment equilibrium, then the increase will directly raise only *nominal* GDP, by pushing up prices.

This is a wider view of how changes in the money market affect real GDP and brings the role of money more to centre stage, which can be helpful in our attempt to better understand inflation. As an example of this latter point, consider this true story, which is now more than 30 years old. This macroeconomics course was being taught by one of the authors in the soon-to-be-independent country of Malawi, in south-central Africa. In the class was the nation's designated minister of finance, who, one day, stated that the people of Malawi were poor (which was quite true then and continues to be so today) because they didn't "have enough money." The answer to this poverty, it seemed to him, was for the new government, once it took power, to increase the supply of money by some significant amount—say, double it.

You will undoubtedly see the fallacy in this argument. This very small, very underdeveloped economy would not be able to significantly increase the output of goods and services simply as a result of doubling the money supply. It is also unlikely that the average Malawian would hold cash as an asset. Much more likely, any increase in the supply of money would be quickly spent.

So what would the end result of a doubling of the money supply be in these circumstances? You're right—a doubling of prices! The fastest, easiest way of explaining this end result is with the equation of exchange:

$$MV = PQ$$

In sum, monetarists argue that "money does count" when it comes to understanding macroeconomic phenomena.

To wrap things up, let's point out that both the Keynesians and monetarists agree that changes in the supply of money do have an effect on spending and therefore on aggregate demand. However, they disagree on how such changes come about and the extent to which interest rates are affected.

SELF-TEST

5. **a)** If M is $100, P is $2, and Q is 500, what is the value of the velocity of money?

b) Given the same parameters as in a), if the velocity of money stays constant, and assuming the economy is at full employment, what will be the level of P if M increases to $120?

REVIEW

1. Explain how a decrease in the price level causes an increase in the aggregate quantity demanded.
2. In the Keynesian transmission process, what is the result of an increase in the money supply?
3. What effect does a decrease in the money supply have on interest rates, investment, and income?
4. Write out the *equation of exchange* and identify each of its terms.
5. What do monetarists say about the *asset demand for money*?
6. What effect does an increase in the money supply have on aggregate demand, the price level, and real GDP?

STUDY GUIDE

Review

CHAPTER SUMMARY

In this chapter you learned that the interest rate is the price of money and, like other prices, it is determined by the forces of supply and demand. The two main points of focus in this chapter are what lies behind the demand for money and how changes in either money demand or supply (the money market) affect the level of real GDP.

1. The economy's *money supply* is largely in the hands of the Bank of Canada.
2. *Money demand* can be subdivided into:
   - the transactions demand, which depends on the level of nominal GDP;
   - the asset demand, which varies inversely with the rate of interest.
3. The *interest rate* is the price of money and, like other prices, it is determined by the interaction of supply and demand.
4. A *change in the price level* will change money demand and, thus, change the equilibrium interest rate. This will, in turn, change the level of investment spending and real GDP. Because the price level has changed, the increase in real GDP is illustrated by a *movement* along the AD curve.
5. A *change in money supply* will change the equilibrium interest rate and, thus, the level of investment spending. Since this can occur without a change in the price level, the resulting change in real GDP is illustrated by a *shift* in AD curve.

NEW GLOSSARY TERMS AND KEY EQUATIONS

asset demand for money 271
bond 274
equation of exchange 281
interest rate 270
investment demand 279
monetarism 281
transactions demand for money 271
transmission process 278
velocity of money 281

Equations:

[8.1] $MV = PQ$ page 281

[8.2] $\text{Nominal GDP} = M \times V$ page 281

[8.3] $\text{Nominal GDP} = P \times Q$ page 281

STUDY TIPS

1. Once again, as in other chapters, it is very important not to confuse the concepts of money and income. Money is a commodity, and like all commodities, there are substitutes for it and there is a price attached to its ownership. The price of money, as we point out in this chapter, is the rate of interest. When we talk about the demand for (the stock of) money, we are not thinking of (the flow of) income. So try to think of money as something that can be bought and sold like any other commodity.
2. Perhaps you can get a good handle on the idea of what drives the transactions demand for money by realizing how it changes over the years. Thirty-five years ago, when one of the authors was still at school, he needed only $100 in cash to make normal day-to-day purchases for the whole month. These days, he finds himself having to take out twice that amount just to last through a single week. Although he is somewhat richer, the main reason for his increased demand for money is the increase in prices of goods and services that has

occurred over the years. Inflation, by itself, will cause the demand for money to increase. In addition, the transactions demand for money will also increase as both individuals and countries get richer in real terms.

3. At this stage don't be overly concerned about how the Bank of Canada controls the money supply and how it is able to increase or decrease it. This will come in Chapter 12. For now, just concentrate on the effects of such changes.

4. The relationship between interest rates and bond prices is not particularly complicated. Allowing for differences in risks and term lengths, the rates of return (the interest rate) on various bonds tend to be very similar. Let's say you earn $5 a year on a bond that sells for $50. This is the same return (10 percent) as earning $2 on a bond selling for $20. What if it were possible to earn $5 on some other bond worth $20? Now, that is a return of 25 percent a year. Everyone would be clamouring to purchase these higher-yielding bonds. And what would happen to their price? It would increase and continue to increase until its return is the same as on all other similar securities. When it got to a price of $50, it is no more or less attractive than other bonds. As the price of a bond rises, the interest earned by the bond holder declines.

Answered Questions

Indicate whether the following statements are true or false.

1. T or F The transactions demand for money is determined by how much money people need.

2. T or F The quantity of asset demand for money that people wish to hold increases as the rate of interest falls.

3. T or F The interest rate is determined by savings and investment.

4. T or F An interest rate above equilibrium will lead to a surplus of money.

5. T or F If there is a shortage of money in the economy, the Bank of Canada will increase the amount supplied.

6. T or F An increase in real GDP will cause an increase in interest rates.

7. T or F The Keynesian transmission process refers to the way in which changes in interest rates affect the demand for bonds and their prices.

8. T or F An increase in the money supply, according to Keynes, will cause investment and real GDP to increase.

9. T or F The velocity of money refers to the number of times a particular product is bought and sold in the period of a year.

10. T or F The equation of exchange is: MV = PQ.

Basic (Questions 11–23)

11. The supply of money is determined by:
a) The Bank of Canada.
b) The interest rate.
c) Commercial banks.
d) The level of nominal GDP.

12. What is the demand for money?
a) The same as the demand for income.
b) It is made up of the transactions demand plus asset demand.
c) It is made up of the transactions demand minus asset demand.
d) Whatever the Bank of Canada determines it to be.

13. What is the effect of an increase in the money supply?
a) It will lower the interest rate.
b) It will increase the interest rate.
c) It will decrease the demand for money.
d) It will decrease the quantity of investment spending.

14. The transactions demand is most closely related to which function of money?
a) Unit of account.
b) Medium of exchange.
c) Store of wealth.
d) Asset demand.

15. What is true about the quantity of asset money demanded?
a) It varies directly with nominal GDP.
b) It varies inversely with nominal GDP.
c) It varies inversely with the interest rate.
d) It varies directly with real GDP.

16. What is the effect of an increase in the money supply?
  a) It causes the aggregate demand curve to shift right.
  b) It causes the aggregate demand curve to shift left.
  c) It causes a movement down the aggregate demand curve.
  d) It causes a movement up the aggregate demand curve.

17. When does the demand for money curve shift to the left?
  a) If nominal GDP increases.
  b) If the interest rate increases.
  c) If the price level decreases.
  d) If real GDP increases.

Table 8.1 contains data relating to the money market.

TABLE 8.1

Rate of Interest (%)	Asset Demand for Money ($)	Transactions Demand for Money ($)	Total Demand for Money ($)
4	100	70	____
5	90	70	____
6	80	70	____
7	70	70	____
8	60	70	____

18. Refer to **Table 8.1** to answer this question. If the supply of money is $150, what is the value of the equilibrium interest rate?
  a) 4 percent.
  b) 5 percent.
  c) 6 percent.
  d) 7 percent.

19. Refer to **Table 8.1** to answer this question. What are the implications if the current supply of money is $160 and the interest rate is 7 percent?
  a) The interest rate will fall.
  b) The interest rate will rise.
  c) The asset demand will fall.
  d) The transactions demand will fall.

20. In the equation MV = PQ, what does the Q stand for?
  a) The quantity of goods and services sold.
  b) The quantity of investment.
  c) The quantity of money in circulation.
  d) The quantity of aggregate demand.

21. Suppose that in a particular economy, M = 200, P = 2, Q = 500, and V = 5. What is the value of nominal GDP?
  a) 200.
  b) 400.
  c) 500.
  d) 1000.

22. According to the Keynesian transmission process, what effect will an increase in the money supply have?
  a) An increase in the interest rate, an increase in investment spending, and an increase in GDP.
  b) An increase in the interest rate, an increase in investment spending, and a decrease in GDP.
  c) An increase in the interest rate, a decrease in investment spending, and a decrease in GDP.
  d) A decrease in the interest rate, an increase in investment spending, and an increase in GDP.
  e) A decrease in the interest rate, a decrease in investment spending, and a decrease in GDP.

Refer to **Figure 8.8** to answer questions 23, 24, and 25.

FIGURE 8.8

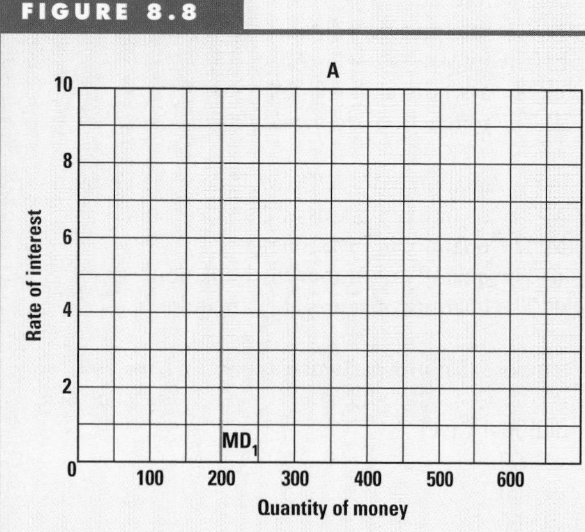

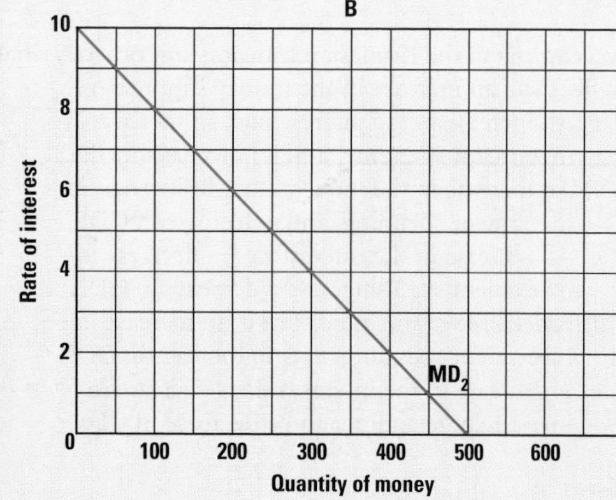

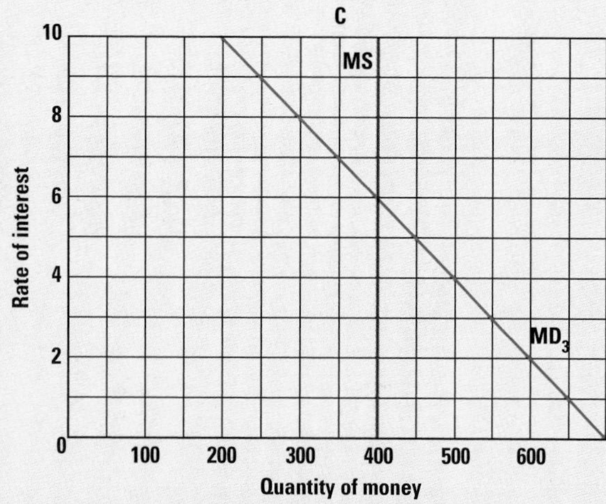

23. In **Figure 8.8**, what does curve MD_2 represent?
   a) The asset demand for money.
   b) The transactions demand for money.
   c) The investment demand.
   d) The stock of money.
   e) The total demand for money.

Intermediate (Questions 24–31)

24. Refer to **Figure 8.8**. How would people react if the interest rate was 3 percent?
   a) They would sell bonds, which would cause bond prices to fall and the interest rate to rise.
   b) They would buy bonds, which would cause bond prices to fall and the interest rate to rise.
   c) They would sell bonds, which would cause bond prices to rise and the interest rate to rise.
   d) They would buy bonds, which would cause bond prices to rise but have an uncertain effect on the interest rate.

25. Refer to **Figure 8.8** to answer this question. Suppose that the economy is in equilibrium and each dollar held for transaction purposes is spent, on average, five times per year. What can we infer from this?
   a) That nominal GDP is $1000.
   b) That real GDP is $1200.
   c) That the money supply is $1000.
   d) That nominal GDP is $400.
   e) None of the above can be inferred.

26. In which of the following cases would the quantity of money demanded be the greatest?
   a) When nominal GDP is $200 billion and the interest rate is 6 percent.
   b) When nominal GDP is $100 billion and the interest rate is 6 percent.
   c) When nominal GDP is $100 billion and the interest rate is 8 percent.
   d) When nominal GDP is $200 billion and the interest rate is 8 percent.

27. What effect will a lower price of bonds have on interest rates?
   a) It will raise interest rates.
   b) It will lower interest rates.
   c) It could either raise or lower interest rates.
   d) There is no connection between the price of bonds and interest rates.

28. According to Adam Smith, what is the wealth of a nation?
- **a)** The sum of its money, gold, and stocks and bonds.
- **b)** Its nominal GDP.
- **c)** Its real GDP.
- **d)** The quantity of gold it possesses.

29. How is a decrease in product prices illustrated graphically?
- **a)** By a shift to the right in the AD curve.
- **b)** By a shift to the left in the AD curve.
- **c)** By a movement up on the AD curve.
- **d)** By a movement down on the AD curve.

30. How is the result of an increase in the money supply illustrated graphically?
- **a)** A shift to the right in the AD curve.
- **b)** A shift to the left in the AD curve.
- **c)** A movement up on the AD curve.
- **d)** A movement down on the AD curve.

31. Why is the equation MV = PQ an identity and not just an equation?
- **a)** Because M × V equals real GDP and P × Q equals nominal GDP.
- **b)** Because M × V equals nominal GDP and P × Q equals real GDP.
- **c)** Because both M × V and P × Q equal real GDP.
- **d)** Because both M × V and P × Q equal nominal GDP.
- **e)** Because the monetarists assume it to be so.

32. How does the interest rate effect help explain why the aggregate demand curve is downward-sloping?
- **a)** Because it suggests that a lower price level causes a higher interest rate and therefore a lower level of aggregate expenditures.
- **b)** Because it suggests that a lower interest rate causes a higher price level and therefore a lower level of aggregate expenditures.
- **c)** Because it suggests that a lower price level causes a lower interest rate and therefore a higher level of aggregate expenditures.
- **d)** Because it suggests that a lower interest rate causes a lower price level and therefore a higher level of aggregate expenditures.

Refer to **Figure 8.9** to answer questions 33, 34, and 35.

FIGURE 8.9

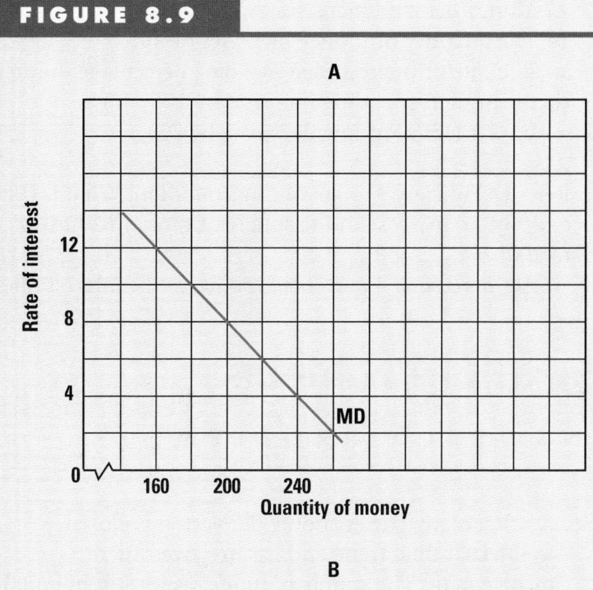

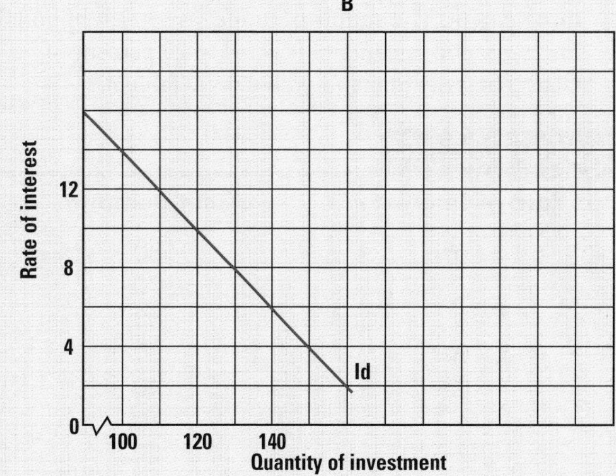

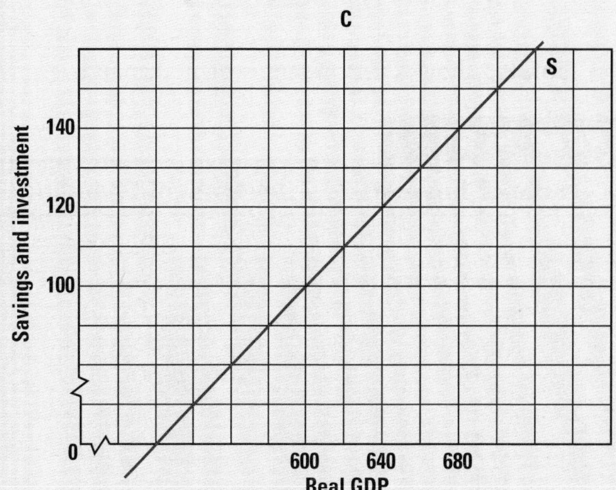

33. Refer to **Figure 8.9** to answer this question. What is the effect of an increase in the money supply of 20?
a) Money demand increases by 20.
b) The quantity of money increases by 40.
c) The rate of interest increases by 2 percentage points.
d) Investment spending increases by 10.
e) Investment spending decreases by 20.

34. Refer to **Figure 8.9** to answer this question. What is the effect of an increase in the supply of money from 160 to 200?
a) An increase of 4 percentage points in the interest rate.
b) A decrease in the transactions demand for money.
c) A decrease of 40 in investment spending.
d) A decrease in aggregate expenditures.
e) An increase of 40 in real GDP.

35. Refer to **Figure 8.9** to answer this question. What is the value of the multiplier?
a) 1.
b) 2.
c) 20.
d) 40.
e) Cannot be determined from this information.

Parallel Problems

ANSWERED PROBLEMS

36. Key Problem The economy of Everton is closed to international trade and has no government involvement. The supply of money is $90 (in billions), the transactions demand is equal to 20 percent of GDP. The asset demand is shown in **Table 8.2**.

TABLE 8.2

Rate of Interest	Asset Demand
6%	$80
7	70
8	60
9	50
10	40
11	30
12	20
13	10

Table 8.3 shows Everton's investment demand.

TABLE 8.3

Rate of Interest	Investment Spending
6%	$80
7	75
8	70
9	65
10	60
11	55
12	50
13	45

Finally, **Table 8.4** shows the savings function for Everton.

TABLE 8.4

GDP	Savings
$100	$45
150	50
200	55
250	60
300	65
350	70
400	75
450	80

a) If Everton's GDP is $350 and its interest rate is 11 percent, will there be a surplus or shortage of money? Will there be a surplus or shortage of goods and services?
Surplus/shortage: ________ of $________ of money.
Surplus/shortage: ________ of $________ of goods and services.
b) What must be the values of GDP and interest rate in Everton if both its product and money markets are in equilibrium?
GDP: $________ and interest rate: ________ %.
c) What is the total demand for money at equilibrium?
Total demand for money: $________ .
d) What will happen to the equilibrium values of GDP and interest rate if the money supply is increased to $110?
GDP: $________ and interest rate: ________ %.

e) In summary, what effects does an increase in the money supply have on the following variables? (Indicate with ↑ for increase and ↓ for decrease.)
Interest rate: ________ ; investment ________ ;
GDP: ________ .

Basic (Problems 37–42)

37. In the country of Sparta, the money supply equals 11 million drams, real GDP is 70 million drams, the price level is 1.1, and the velocity of money is 7.

a) What is the value of its nominal GDP? ________ .

b) If, in the next year, V remains constant and real GDP increases to 77 million drams, what must happen to the money supply in order to keep prices stable? ________ .

38. Suppose that the money supply in Hertha is 36 billion gelts, its real GDP is 420 billion gelts, and the price level is 1.2.

a) What is the value of the nominal GDP? ________ .

b) What is the value of the velocity of money?

________ .

c) If in the next year, the velocity of money stays the same and the money supply increases to 40 billion gelts, what will be the value of its nominal GDP?

________ .

39. In a recent year, Canada's money supply averaged $88.4 billion, real GDP was $873 billion, and the GDP deflator was 108.7. What was the value of the velocity of money? (Hint: you may need to rearrange the equation of exchange and divide by 100.) ________ .

40. In the country of Juventus, the money supply is equal to 40 (billion), the velocity of circulation is 5, and real GDP is 100 (billion).

a) What is the price level in Juventus, and what is the value of its nominal GDP?
Price level: ________ ; nominal GDP: ________ .

b) If the money supply increases by 20 percent, what will be the new values of the price level and nominal GDP, assuming that V and real GDP remain constant?
Price level: ________ ; nominal GDP: ________ .

c) What does this suggest about the connection between the money supply and the price level?

________ .

41. Justin's grandfather left him a $10 000 bond with exactly one year left until redemption. It pays a nominal interest rate of 8 percent. The current rate of interest on similar bonds is 5 percent. Unfortunately Justin has to sell this bond to raise money for tuition next semester. Ignoring brokerage fees and other transaction costs, approximately how much will Justin get for his bond?

________ .

42. Suppose that the economy of Celtic, depicted in **Table 8.5**, is a closed, private (no government) economy. Assume that the money supply is $100.

TABLE 8.5

Rate of Interest	Money Demand	Rate of Interest	Investment	GDP	Savings
12%	$60	12%	$60	$300	$60
11	70	11	65	350	70
10	80	10	70	400	80
9	90	9	75	450	90
8	100	8	80	500	100
7	110	7	85	550	110
6	120	6	90	600	120
5	130	5	95	650	130
4	140	4	100	700	140

a) If the interest rate is 10 percent, is there a surplus or shortage of money? Of how much? ________ .

b) If the interest rate is 10 percent, and GDP is $500, is there a surplus or shortage of goods and services?

____
Of how much? ________ .

c) What are the equilibrium values of GDP and the interest rate? ________ .

d) If the money supply is reduced to $80, what will be the new equilibrium values of GDP and interest rate? ________ .

e) If the full-employment level of GDP is $500, what must be the level of the money supply to produce this level of GDP? ____________________.

Intermediate (Problems 43–47)

43. Below, in Figure 8.10, is information on the economy of Tabriz, whose money market is in equilibrium.

FIGURE 8.10

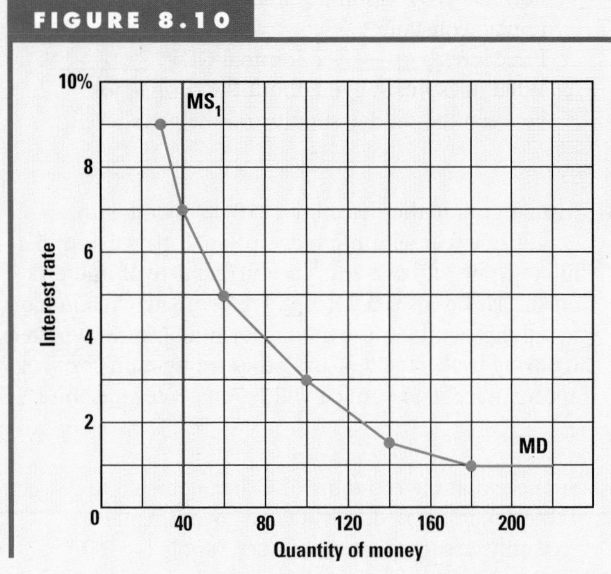

Rate of Interest	Investment Spending
8	$500
7	600
6	700
5	800
4	900
3	1000
2	1100
1	1200

a) What change in interest rates is required to obtain a $300 increase in investment spending? __________.

b) What change in the money supply is necessary to obtain this change in the interest rate? __________.

c) Given the results from a) and b), what increase in the money supply is required to increase investment spending by another $300? __________.

d) Is it possible to push interest rates below 1 percent? ____________________.

44. Figure 8.11 shows the situation in the economy of Hasik, where the money market is currently in equilibrium.

FIGURE 8.11

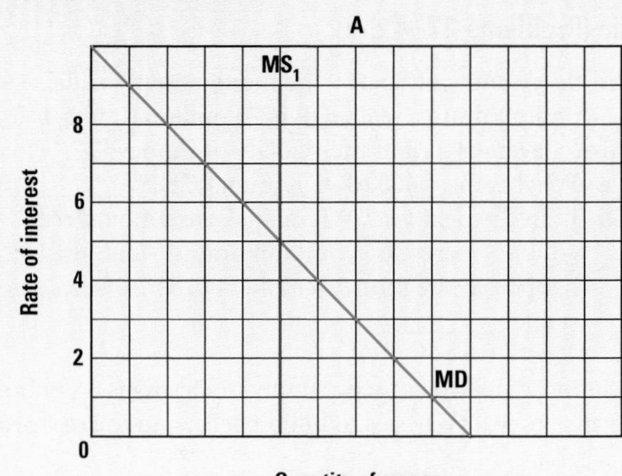

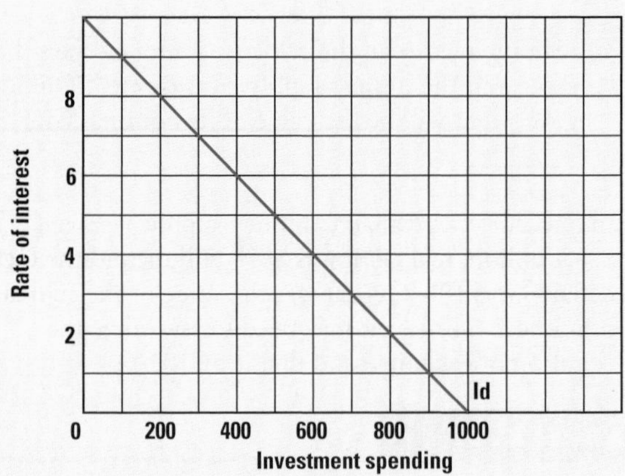

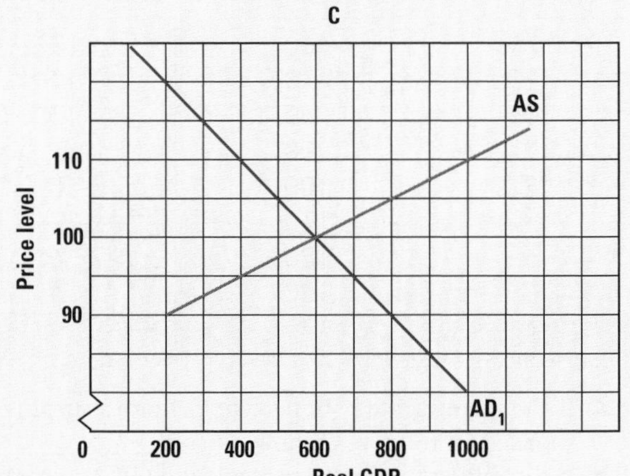

a) In Figures A and B, show the effect of a significant drop in prices, which results in an increase in the level of investment spending of $100.
b) What is the new equilibrium interest rate? ______.
c) Assuming that Hasik's multiplier is 2 and that the price decrease mentioned above was caused by an increase in aggregate supply, draw in the new AS_2 curve in Figure C, which results in equilibrium in the product market.
d) What was the percentage decrease in the price level? ______.

45. Below in **Figure 8.12** is information on the economy of Heart, which is a closed economy with no government.
a) In Figure A, illustrate the effect of an increase in the money supply which reduces the interest rate to 4 percent, and in B, the effect of the lower interest rate on the level of investment spending.
b) What is the new level of investment spending? ______.
c) Assuming that the multiplier in Heart is 2, show the effect of this change in investment spending in Figure C.
d) What is the new level of real GDP? ______.

FIGURE 8.12

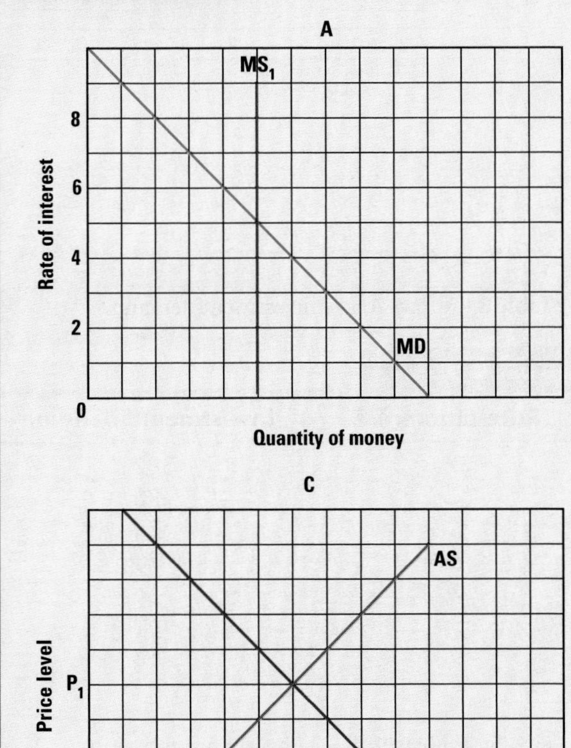

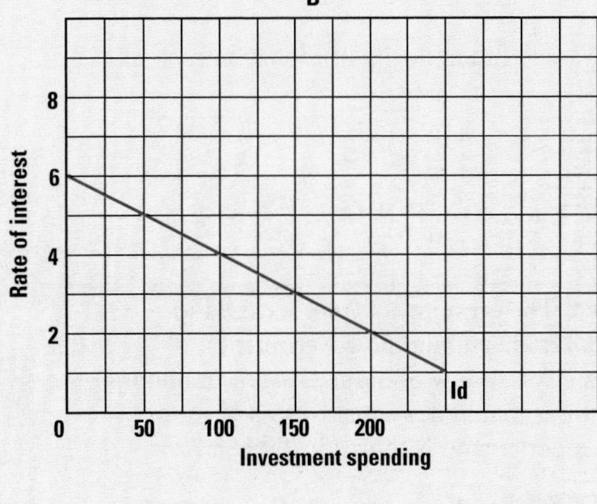

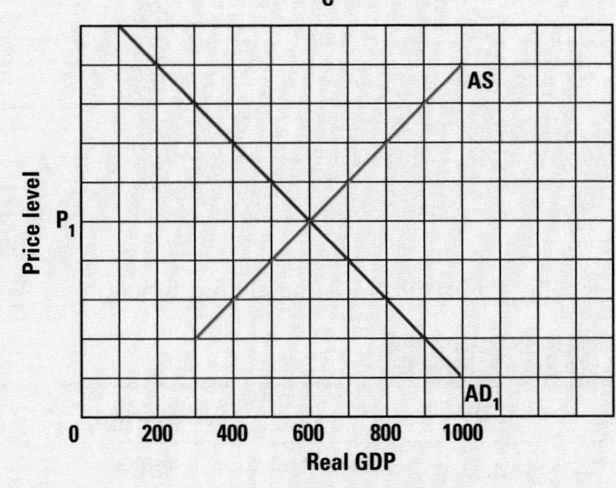

46. Explain why (or why not) each of the following will cause an increase in the transactions demand for money:
a) An increase in the price level: ______.
b) An increase in real income: ______.
c) An increase in nominal income: ______.
d) An increase in both the price level and nominal income by the same percentage: ______.

47. **Table 8.6** shows actual data for the Canadian economy for the period 1993–1997 (all money figures in $ billion). For each year, calculate the velocity of money. (Hint: You may need to rearrange the equation of exchange and divide by 100.)

TABLE 8.6

Year	M1	Price Level (1992 =100)	Real GDP (GDP at 1992 price level)
1993	48.3	101.2	716
1994	54.2	102.4	744
1995	57.1	105.1	760
1996	63.1	106.6	770
1997	73.5	107.1	798

What is the value of the velocity of money in each of the five years?
1993___; 1994 ___; 1995 ___; 1996 ___; 1997 ___.

Advanced (Problems 48–49)

48. In 2001, Canadian interest rates dropped to levels not seen for decades. What would Keynesians expect the asset demand for money to be at this point? What would monetarists expect?

____
____
____.

49. The story about the Malawian student earlier in the chapter made it clear that if the money supply is increased too quickly, severe inflation can result. So why increase it at all?

____
____
____.

UNANSWERED PROBLEMS

50. **Key Problem** The economy of Ajax is closed to international trade and has no government involvement. The supply of money is $50 (in billions), the transactions demand is equal to 10 percent of GDP. The asset demand is shown in **Table 8.7**.

TABLE 8.7

Rate of Interest	Asset Demand
3%	$28
4	26
5	24
6	22
7	20
8	18
9	16

Table 8.8 shows Ajax's investment demand.

TABLE 8.8

Rate of Interest	Investment Spending
3%	$82
4	78
5	74
6	70
7	66
8	62
9	58

Finally, **Table 8. 9** shows the savings function for Ajax.

TABLE 8.9

GDP	Savings
$220	$58
240	62
260	66
280	70
300	74
320	78
340	82
360	86
380	90

a) If Ajax's GDP is $300 and its interest rate is 9 percent, will there be a surplus or shortage of money? Will there be a surplus or shortage of goods and services?
b) What must be the values of GDP and the interest rate in Ajax if both its product and money markets are in equilibrium?
c) What is the total demand for money at equilibrium?
d) What will happen to the equilibrium values of the interest rate and GDP if the money supply is decreased to $42?
e) What is the effect of a decrease in the money supply on the interest rate, investment, and GDP?

Basic (Problems 51–56)

51. In the country of Taskent, the money supply equals 10.5 million dollars, real GDP is 70 million dollars, the price level is 1.2, and the velocity of money is 8.
a) What is the value of nominal GDP?
b) If in the next year V remains constant and real GDP increases to 84 million dollars, what must have happened to the money supply to keep prices constant?

52. Suppose that the money supply in Akkerman is 40 billion urts, its real GDP is is 600 billion urts, and the price level is 1.4.
a) What is the value of nominal GDP?
b) What is the value of the velocity of money?
c) If in the next year the velocity of money stays the same and the money supply increases to 42 billion urts, what is the value of nominal GDP?

53. In a recent year, Canada's money supply averaged $91.6 billion, real GDP was $892 billion, and the GDP deflator was 110.1. What was the velocity of money?

54. In the country of Srinagar, the money supply is equal to 60 billion, the velocity of circulation is 6, and real GDP is 240 billion.
a) What is the price level in Srinagar, and what is the value of its nominal GDP?
b) If the money supply were to increase by 10 percent, what would be the new values of the price level and nominal GDP, assuming that V and real GDP remained constant?
c) What does this suggest about the connection between the money supply and the price level?

55. Steffany's aunt left her with a $15 000 bond which pays $1050 a year. The bond has two years left until redemption. Steffany is going to cash in the bond to help put a down payment on a house. The current interest rate on similar bonds is 10 percent. Ignoring brokerage fees and other transaction costs, approximately how much will Steffany get for her bond?

56. The economy of Tayma, illustrated in **Table 8.10**, is a closed, private (no government) economy. Assume that the money supply is $120.

TABLE 8.10

Rate of Interest	Money Demand	Rate of Interest	Investment	GDP	Savings
10%	$90	10%	$90	$450	$65
9	100	9	95	500	80
8	110	8	100	550	95
7	120	7	105	600	105
6	130	6	120	650	120
5	140	5	135	700	135
4	150	4	150	750	150
3	160	3	165	800	165
2	170	2	180	850	180

a) If the interest rate is 5 percent, is there a surplus or a shortage of money? Of how much?
b) If the interest rate is 5 percent and GDP is $600, is there a shortage or surplus of goods and services? Of how much?
c) What are the equilibrium values of GDP and the interest rate?
d) If the full-employment level of GDP is $700, what must be the level of the money supply to produce this level of GDP?

Intermediate (Problems 57–61)

57. In **Figure 8.13**, is information on the economy of Basra, where the money market is in equilibrium.

FIGURE 8.13

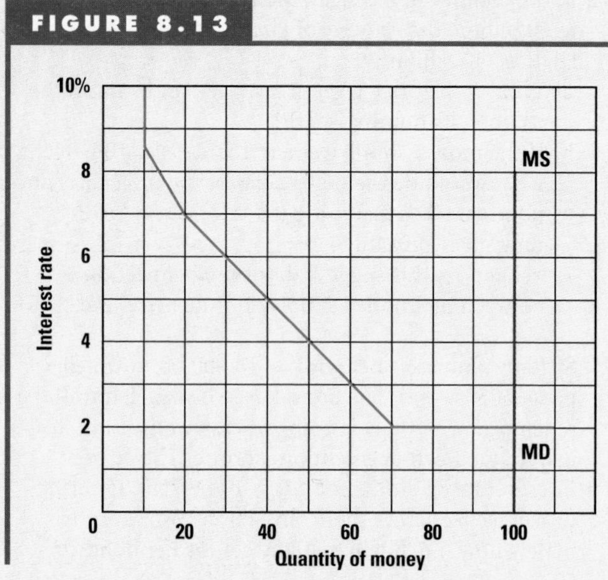

Rate of Interest	Investment Spending
8	200
7	400
6	600
5	800
4	1000
3	1200
2	1400
1	1600

a) What change in interest rates is necessary to obtain a $400 decrease in investment?
b) What decrease in the money supply is necessary to obtain this change in the interest rate?
c) Given the results from a) and b), what decrease in the money supply is necessary to decrease investment spending by another $400?
d) Is a zero interest rate possible?

58. **Figure 8.14** shows the situation in the economy of Suakin, where the money market is currently in equilibrium.
a) In Figures A and B, show the effect of an increase in prices which results in a decrease in the level of investment spending of $100.
b) What is the new equilibrium interest rate?
c) Assuming that Suakin's multiplier is 1.5 and that the price increase mentioned above was caused by a decrease in aggregate supply, draw in the new AS_2 curve in Figure C which results in equilibrium in the product market.
d) What is the percentage increase in the price level?

FIGURE 8.14

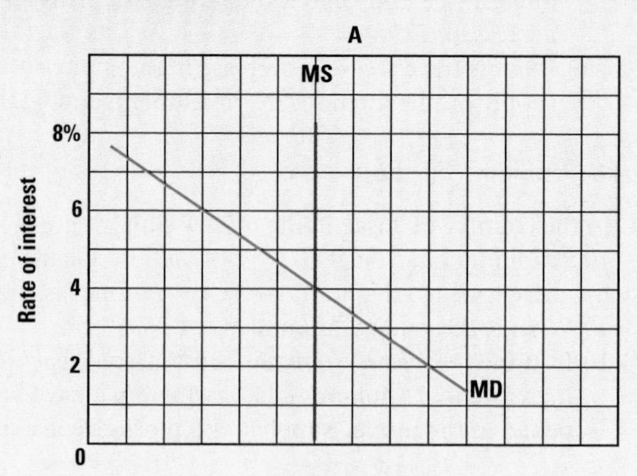

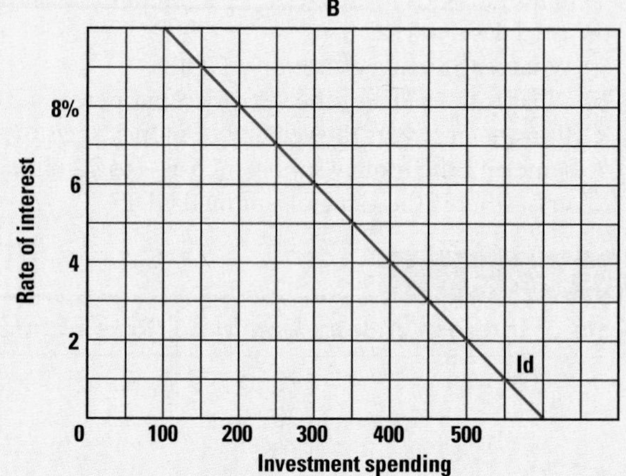

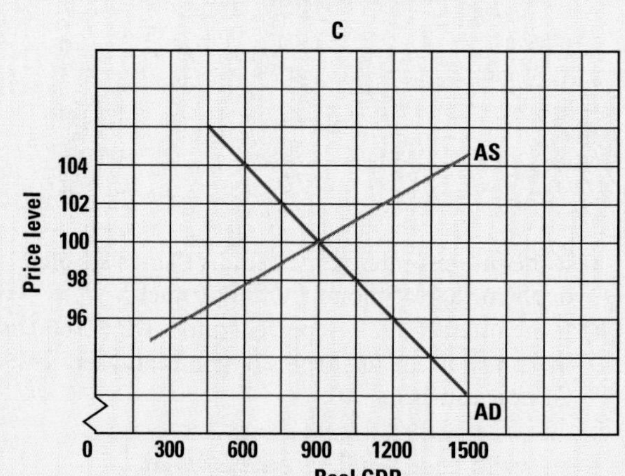

59. Below in **Figure 8.15** is information on the economy of Fustat, which is a closed economy with no government.

FIGURE 8.15

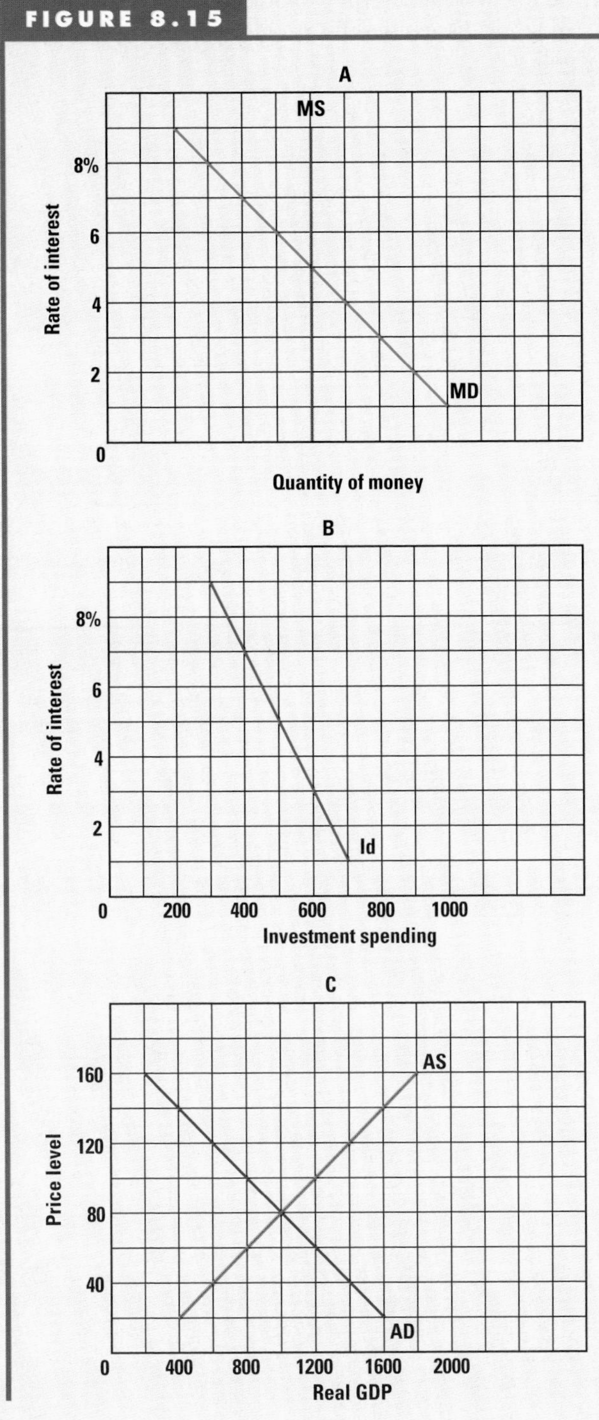

a) In Figure A, illustrate a decrease in the money supply which will increase the interest rate to 7 percent, and in B, the effect of the higher interest rate on the level of investment spending.

b) What is the new level of investment spending?

c) Assuming that the multiplier in Fustat is 2, show the effect on real GDP in Figure C.

d) What is the new level of real GDP?

60. Explain why (or why not) each of the following will cause a decrease in the transactions demand for money: a) a decrease in the price level; b) a decrease in real income; c) a decrease in nominal income; d) a decrease in both the price level and nominal income by the same percentage.

61. **Table 8.11** shows approximate data for the Canadian economy for the period 1997–2001 in billions of dollars.

TABLE 8.11

Year	M1	Price Level (1992 = 100)	Real GDP
1997	73.5	107.1	798
1998	77.9	108.0	821
1999	86.5	110.3	839
2000	93.8	112.6	856
2001	99.2	113.9	872

What is the value of the velocity of money in each of the five years?

Advanced (Problems 62–63)

62. In the early 1980s, interest rates in Canada rose to levels not seen in the twentieth century. What would Keynesians expect the asset demand for money to be at this point? What would monetarists expect?

63. What would be the effect of deflation of 4 or 5 percent on the money market?

Web-Based Activities

1. Go to **www.bank-banque-canada.ca/english/monetary/index.htm** and explain how monetary policy affects spending, production, and employment in the economy.

2. Go to **www.cato.org/pubs/books/money/money16.htm** and then discuss the effects of e-money on monetary policy.

CHAPTER NINE

International Trade

LEARNING OBJECTIVES

This chapter will enable you to:

LO1 **Explain why nations trade with each other.**

LO2 **Explain why nations import certain goods *even* though they can be made cheaper at home.**

LO3 **Explain how the gains from trade are divided between trading partners.**

LO4 **Describe why some groups win and others lose as a result of freer trade.**

LO5 **Identify some arguments for and against free trade.**

What's ahead...

We start by looking at the reasons why individuals and countries trade with each other, and discover that the reason in both cases is differences in endowment: each is endowed with resources not available to others but lacks things possessed by others. These differences lead to the cost advantages over others that some producers enjoy and is at the heart of Ricardo's theory of comparative advantage, which we investigate in the first part of the chapter. We then look at the concept of the terms of trade and show how this determines who gets what share of the increased production that results from trade. The chapter then looks at some of the arguments against free trade and ends with an investigation of how and why trade has often been restricted and impeded.

A QUESTION OF RELEVANCE...

Have you looked at the little tag on your jeans lately? Were they made in Canada? What about your camera? Your fishing rod? Your tennis racket? Your CD player? Does it concern you that they all might well have been made abroad? It probably won't come as a surprise to you that Canada imports approximately a quarter of all its products. Is this good for the country? Surely it would be in Canada's interest to produce its own goods. Or would it? This chapter looks at the question of whether Canada is better or worse off as a result of international trade.

People have traded in one form or another since the dawn of time, and most of the great powers in history have also been famous traders: the Phoenicians and the Greeks; medieval Venice and Elizabethan England; the early American colonies and modern Japan. It seems obvious that great benefits are obtained from trading, but there has always been the underlying suspicion that someone also loses as a result. For many, a great trading nation is one that consistently, and through shrewd practice, always manages to come out on top during trade negotiations. This "beggar thy neighbour" attitude was the cause of no great concern for writers immediately preceding Adam Smith, who thought it was part of the natural state of affairs that there are always winners and losers in trade. It was the job of policy-makers, they felt, to ensure that their own country was always on the winning side.

It took the mind of Adam Smith, however, to see that whenever two people enter into a voluntary agreement to trade, both parties must gain as a result. If you trade a textbook in exchange for your friend's new Guns 'n' Butter CD, you obviously want that CD more than the textbook, and your friend must want the textbook more than the CD. Trade is to the advantage of both of you, otherwise it would not take place. When we look at international trade between nations, all we are doing is simply looking at this single transaction multiplied a billionfold. It is not really nations that trade, but individual people and firms who buy from other foreign individuals and firms. In many ways the reason you trade with a friend is the same reason you buy products from a Toronto brewery, Winnipeg car dealer, or Tokyo fishing rod manufacturer: you hope to gain something as a result, and what you give up in return (usually money) is of less value to you than the thing you obtain in return.

All of which raises the question of why you personally (or a whole nation for that matter) would want to buy something rather than make it at home. In other words, why are people not self-sufficient? Why do they not produce everything that they personally consume? Well, Adam Smith had an answer for this (as for many things):

> It is the maxim of every prudent master of a family, never to make at home what it will cost him more to make than to buy.[1]

There, in essence, is the main argument for trade: why make something yourself if you can buy it cheaper elsewhere? If it takes Akio three hours to make a certain product, but he can buy it elsewhere from the income he gets from one hour's work in his regular job, then why would he bother? It would pay him to do his own job for three hours; he could afford to buy three units of the product. An additional consideration is the fact that there are many things that Akio is incapable of making (actually, most things), or that he could make only after extensive training and with the help of very expensive equipment.

9.1 Specialization and Trade

LO1
Explain why nations trade with each other.

Specialization is the cornerstone of trade. As we have seen in earlier chapters, big advantages can be gained from specialization. From an individual's point of view, each of us is better suited to one thing than to another. Rather than trying to grow all our own food, make our own clothes, brew our own beer, and so on, it makes more sense to specialize in our chosen occupation and, with the proceeds, obtain things that other people can make better and cheaper. Similarly, firms will be far more productive if they specialize in the production process, that is, make use of the division of labour. As we shall see in this chapter, there are also great benefits to be enjoyed by countries that specialize rather than trying to be self-sufficient.

[1] Adam Smith, *Wealth of Nations* (Edwin Cannan edition, 1877), pp. 354.

It follows that the result of more specialization is more trading. Specialization and trade go hand in hand. Modern nations, firms, and individuals have become increasingly specialized, and with this has come a huge increase in the volume of trade, domestically and internationally. But is there a limit to specialization? From a technical point of view, Smith thought not; but he did believe that specialization would be limited by the size of the market. The smaller the market, the less output and therefore the less opportunity or need for extensive specialization. The bigger the size of the market, the more specialization that can take place and the lower the cost of producing goods. The prime driving force behind the expansion of markets is that it enables firms to produce in higher volumes and at a lower cost. All things being equal (including demand), it is the cost of production and therefore the price of the product that induces trade. If you can produce a product cheaper than I can, then it will make no sense for me to try to produce it myself. And why are you able to produce certain products cheaper than I can? The answer presumably is that you possess certain advantages over me. Let us look at these advantages.

ADDED DIMENSION

Canada, the Great Trader

Canada is certainly one of the world's great trading nations, at least in relative terms. In 2001, for example, Canada exported $468 billion worth of goods and services and imported $412 billion from abroad. These figures represent about 40 percent of Canada's GDP. Only a few developed countries, such as Austria and the Netherlands, trade a larger fraction. The United States and Japan, in comparison, trade only about 12 percent of their GDPs (though, of course, in actual dollars this represents a lot more). In terms of Canada's trading partners, the United States is far more dominant than all other countries combined (buying approximately 80 percent of our exports). In fact, Canada sells three times as much to the United States as it does to all other countries combined, and buys approximately 76 percent of all its merchandise from our neighbour to the south.

Factor Endowment

One person has an advantage in production over others if he or she is endowed with certain natural or acquired skills, or has more or better equipment or other resources. Just as there are many explanations why some people are better gardeners or truck drivers or hockey players than others, so it is with countries, too. A country will have a great advantage in producing and trading pineapples, for instance, if it possesses the right type of soil and climate. But the same country may well be at a disadvantage in growing coniferous trees. Another country has an advantage in producing electronic equipment if it has the right capital, the technical expertise, and a well-educated labour force. It may not, however, be able to compete with other countries in raising sheep. All people are different. Although some are graced with certain advantages over others, they are often handicapped in other areas. So it is with countries; they are well endowed in certain areas, they are impoverished in others. Japan has a well-educated and motivated work force, possesses great technical expertise, and is highly capitalized, yet it is very poorly provided with arable land and possesses very few mineral resources.

It is often suggested that the prime reason a country trades is in order to buy resources that it does not naturally possess. Although there is some truth in this, it often obscures the main motivation. Canada, for instance, is not endowed with a warm and sunny climate throughout the year and is unable to produce bananas commercially. However, through the use of geodesic domes with artificial light and heating, it could grow its own bananas, though the cost would be enormous. The reason it does not grow bananas is not because it cannot, but because it is cheaper to buy them from countries that possess the necessary resources at lower cost. Most countries, then, can often overcome a resource deficiency by using different methods or other resources, but it does not make sense if this production method results in more expensive products than those obtainable from abroad.

Theory of Absolute Advantage

A country will gravitate to producing in those areas where, because of its own factor endowments, it possesses a cost advantage over other producing countries: Canada produces wheat, lumber, and minerals; Colombia produces coffee; Malaysia produces rubber; Japan produces electronic equipment; and so on. This is no more or less than what Adam Smith proposed when he put forward his *theory of absolute advantage*. Nations, like firms and individuals, should specialize in producing goods and services for which they have an advantage, and they should trade with other countries for goods and services in which they do not enjoy an advantage. Let us work through a simple example of this theory. We will concentrate on just two countries and suppose that they produce just two products. We will assume that the average cost of producing each product remains constant. In addition, to begin with, we will further assume that each country is self-sufficient and that no trade is taking place. **Table 9.1** shows the productivity per worker (average product) of producing wheat and beans in Canada and Mexico.

TABLE 9.1 **Output per Worker by Country and Industry**

	NUMBER OF BUSHELS PER DAY		
	Wheat		**Beans**
Canada	3	or	2
Mexico	1	or	4

We can see at a glance in **Table 9.1** that Canada is more productive than Mexico at producing wheat, whereas Mexico is more productive than Canada at producing beans. Let us examine the possibility of gains if both countries were to specialize—Canada in wheat and Mexico in beans.

Let's suppose that initially the two countries are self-sufficient and the working population in each country is 16 million, divided equally between the two industries. **Table 9.2** shows what the two countries are producing:

TABLE 9.2 **Total Outputs Before Trade**

	TOTAL NUMBER OF BUSHELS PER DAY (in millions)	
	Wheat	**Beans**
Canada	24	16
Mexico	8	32
Totals	32	48

For instance, there is half the working population of Canada—8 million workers—producing wheat. Since each person is capable of producing 3 wheat, the total production of wheat is 8 million times 3 or 24 million bushels. The other figures are similarly derived.

Now suppose that the two countries decide to enter into a free trade agreement, with each country totally specializing in what it does best: Canada producing wheat and Mexico producing beans. With the whole of the working population of 16 million in Canada producing wheat and all 16 million people producing beans in Mexico, the totals can be seen in **Table 9.3**.

TABLE 9.3 **Total Outputs After Trade**

	TOTAL NUMBER OF BUSHELS PER DAY (in millions)	
	Wheat	**Beans**
Canada	48	0
Mexico	0	64
Totals	48	64

As a result, the two countries combined could produce an additional 16 million wheat (48 minus the previous 32) *and* an additional 16 million beans (64 minus the previous 48). These are referred to as the *gains from trade*. Strictly speaking, the increased total production is really the result of increased specialization. But, of course, if a country is going to specialize, it will need to trade in order to obtain those products that it is not producing. Specialization, then, implies trade, and it would be impossible to have one without the other.

SELF-TEST

1. Suppose that the productivity per worker in the beer and wine industries of Freedonia and Libraland are as follows:

	Output in Hundreds of Litres		
	Beer		**Wine**
Freedonia	4	or	1
Libraland	3	or	4

a) Which country should specialize in which product?

b) Suppose that initially the working population of each country is 20 million, with 10 million working in each industry. What is the total output of the two countries?

c) Now suppose that each country decides to specialize in the product in which it has an advantage. What will be the total output of each product and what are the gains from trade?

9.2 Theory of Comparative Advantage

LO2
Explain why nations import certain goods even though they can be made cheaper at home.

The eminent economist David Ricardo, following in the footsteps of Adam Smith, agreed in principle with his mentor and added a subtle but important refinement to Smith's theory of trade. To see the effect of his modification, let's change our example to that of theoretical trade between the United States and the Philippines, but keep the same two products, wheat and beans. The output per worker in each country is shown in **Table 9.4**.

TABLE 9.4 **Output per Worker by Country and Industry**

	NUMBER OF BUSHELS PER DAY	
	Wheat	**Beans**
United States	6	4
Philippines	1	2

If we compare the United States' productivity in wheat, you can see from the table that it is six times as great as that of the Philippines; similarly, the United States is twice as productive as the Philippines in producing beans. If we were to follow Smith's dictum, then presumably the United States should produce both products itself. After all, how can it possibly be of any advantage to that country to trade with the Philippines, since it could produce both products cheaper? The heart of Ricardo's idea is that it is not *absolute* but **comparative advantage** that provides the mutual gains from trade. Let us see exactly what this means, through an example.

comparative advantage: the advantage that comes from producing something at a lower opportunity cost than others are able to do.

Suppose you happened to be the absolutely best lawyer in town. Not only that, but you are also its greatest secretary. Given this, why would you bother to hire a secretary to do your clerical work, since you are faster and, by all measurement, more efficient than anyone you could possibly hire? The answer is that you would still hire a secretary because you couldn't afford not to. The reason for this is that you are so productive. Your high productivity is both a blessing and a curse. It is a blessing because you earn a great deal as a lawyer; it is a curse because you sacrifice a great deal in not being a secretary. In other words, your opportunity cost of being a lawyer is the lost salary of not being a secretary. Your opportunity cost of being a secretary is your lost earnings as a lawyer. But because you can earn *comparatively* more as a lawyer than as a secretary, you would be advised to concentrate on that career and hire someone (admittedly less productive than yourself) to act as your secretary.

What Ricardo did with his idea of comparative advantage was, in a sense, to direct attention away from making comparisons between countries and instead focus attention on the comparison between products. In **Table 9.4**, for instance, what is the cost for the United States of producing wheat? One way to answer this would be to express it in dollars and cents. Knowing that the value of money varies over time and that it is often misleading to translate one currency into another, Ricardo was at pains to express costs in more fundamental terms. One way of doing this would be to express costs in terms of the number of hours it takes to produce something. For instance, if in our example the average worker in the United States can produce 4 bushels of beans in an average 8-hour day, then the cost of 1 bushel of beans would be 8/4, or 2 hours. In contrast, the cost of one bushel of beans in the Philippines would be 8/2, or 4 hours. So, it is twice as expensive in the Philippines. However, a better and more illuminating way of measuring costs is in terms of *opportunity costs*. This is the method Ricardo chose.

You will remember that the opportunity cost of producing one thing can be measured in terms of another thing that has to be sacrificed in order to get it. As far as the United States and the Philippines are concerned, the cost of producing more wheat is the sacrifice of beans, and the cost of increased bean production is the loss of wheat. Let us work out these costs for each country. The cost of employing a worker in the wheat industry is what that worker could have produced in the bean industry, assuming that the country is fully employed. In other words, for every 6 bushels of wheat that an American worker produces, the country sacrifices 4 bushels of beans. In per unit terms in the U.S.:

since 6 bushels of wheat costs 4 bushels of beans,

then, 1 bushel of wheat costs $4/6 = 0.67$ bushels of beans,

and since 4 bushels of beans costs 6 bushels of wheat,

then, 1 bushel of beans costs $6/4 = 1.5$ bushels of wheat.

Similarly, in the Philippines: the cost of 1 wheat is 2 beans and the cost of 1 bean equals 1/2 wheat. Let us summarize these figures in **Table 9.5**.

TABLE 9.5 **Opportunity Costs of Production**

	COST OF PRODUCING ONE UNIT	
	Wheat	**Beans**
United States	0.67 beans	1.5 wheat
Philippines	2 beans	0.5 wheat

Now you can understand the significance of comparative costs. If you measure the costs in absolute terms, using hours or dollars, beans are cheap to produce in the United States. But in comparative terms, they are very *expensive*. Why is that? Because to produce beans, the United States has to make a big sacrifice in the product in which it is even more productive: wheat. Similarly, although beans in absolute terms are very expensive in the Philippines, in comparative terms they are cheap, since to produce them the Philippines does not have to make much sacrifice in wheat production because productivity in the wheat industry is so low.

In this example then, as **Table 9.5** suggests, the United States should specialize in producing the product in which it has the comparative advantage—wheat—and the Philippines should specialize in beans, where it has the comparative advantage.

Let us extract some further insights by showing the production possibilities of the two countries on the assumption that the size of the labour force in the United States is 100 million, that of the Philippines is 80 million, and that unit costs are constant. Their respective production possibilities are shown in **Table 9.6**. The 600 wheat, under option A in the U.S., is the maximum output of wheat if all of the 100 (million) workers were producing 6 wheat each. Similarly, if the 100 million U.S. workers produced only beans, and no wheat, then they would produce 400 beans (100 million times 4 beans each) as seen under option E. The figures for B, C, and D are derived by calculating the output if 75, 50, and 25 million workers are employed in wheat production while 25, 50, and 75 million workers are, correspondingly, employed in bean production. The figures for the Philippines are similarly obtained, this time changing the number of workers by 20 million for each new option.

TABLE 9.6 **Production Possibilities**

	UNITED STATES: OUTPUT (millions of bushels per day)				
	A	**B**	**C**	**D**	**E**
Wheat	600	450	300	150	0
Beans	0	100	200	300	400
	PHILIPPINES: OUTPUT (millions of bushels per day)				
	A	**B**	**C**	**D**	**E**
Wheat	80	60	40	20	0
Beans	0	40	80	120	160

Suppose that initially the countries are self-sufficient and that both are producing combinations B. (There is nothing particularly significant about B; we just need a starting point.) Before specialization and trade, therefore, their joint totals are as shown in **Table 9.7**.

TABLE 9.7 Output of Both Countries Before Specialization and Trade

	TOTAL OUTPUT (millions of bushels per day)	
	Wheat	**Beans**
United States	450	100
Philippines	60	40
Total	510	140

If the two countries now specialize, the U.S. producing wheat and the Philippines producing beans, their output levels would be as shown in **Table 9.8**.

TABLE 9.8 Output of Both Countries After Specialization and Trade

	TOTAL OUTPUT (millions of bushels per day)	
	Wheat	**Beans**
United States	600	0
Philippines	0	160
Total	600	160

You can see by comparing the before and after specialization positions of the two countries that production of both products is now higher. **Table 9.9** outlines the gains from trade.

TABLE 9.9 Gains From Specialization and Trade

TOTAL OUTPUT (millions of bushels per day)	
Wheat	**Beans**
+90	+20

SELF-TEST

2. Suppose that the labour force in Freedonia is 10 million, of whom 6 million are producing apples, one of the two crops it produces; the other is pears. In contrast, Libraland's labour force is 16 million, half of whom are producing apples, and the rest pears. The labour productivity in the two countries is as follows:

Output per Worker (bushels per day)

	Apples		Pears
Freedonia	5	or	2
Libraland	1	or	3

Do a production possibilities table to Fredonia (from A to F) and for Libraland (A to E).

a) Which is Fredonia's present combination (A – F)?

b) Which is Libraland's present combination (A – E)?

Thus, we can conclude that:

As long as there are differences in comparative costs between countries, regardless of the differences in absolute costs, there is a basis for mutually beneficial trade.

What these examples show is that it is possible for both countries to gain from trade, but the remaining questions are: will they? How will the increased production be shared? Will it be shared equally, or will one country receive more than the other? Discussion of the terms of trade will help answer these questions.

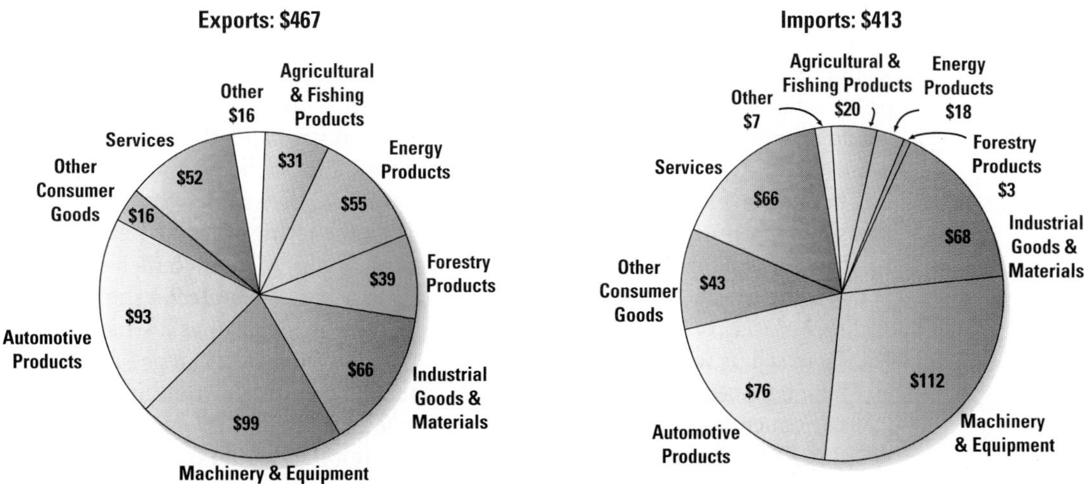

Source: CANSIM II, tables 228-0001-0003 and 376-0001-002.

REVIEW

1. How are trade and specialization related?
2. What is meant by the term *factor endowment*?
3. What is the theory of absolute advantage? Who introduced it?
4. What is the theory of comparative advantage? Who introduced it?

ADDED DIMENSION

The World after September 11, 2001

In the aftermath of the Second World War, the free nations of the world negotiated a series of trade agreements that reduced tariffs and other trade restrictions and increased the amount of trade between nations. This was done under the auspices of GATT (General Agreement on Trade and Tariffs), which has since been replaced by the WTO (World Trade Organization). As a result of this increased trade, nations have become more interdependent and the flow of people, as well as of goods, between countries has greatly increased. For Canada, the culmination of this trend was the NAFTA agreement with the U.S. and Mexico, which has dramatically increased Canadian exports and created hundreds of thousands of jobs within our borders. In the aftermath of the tragic events of 9-11-01, we may wonder whether this trend will reverse itself as borders become more difficult for goods and people to penetrate because of increased security concerns. If this does occur, then the events of that infamous day will reach far into the future and affect the entire world community.

9.3 Terms of Trade

LO3
Explain how the gains from trade are divided between trading partners.

terms of trade: the average price of a country's exports compared with the price of its imports.

The **terms of trade** refers to the price at which a country sells its exports compared with the price at which it buys its imports. StatsCan regularly measures Canada's terms of trade using the following formula:

$$\text{terms of trade} = \frac{\text{Average price of exports}}{\text{Average price of imports}} \times 100 \qquad [9.1]$$

If the worldwide demand for Canadian softwood lumber were to increase, for example, it would increase the average price of Canadian exports, with the result that the terms of trade would be said to have moved in Canada's favour. The result would be the same if Canadian prices remain the same but the price of imports drops. In either case, the sale of our exports would enable us to purchase more imports. On the other hand, the terms of trade would shift against Canada if Canadian export prices dropped and/or the price of imported goods rose.

In our previous United States–Philippines example, the simple answer as to which country gains most from trade is that it all depends upon the terms of trade. But let us look at what would be acceptable prices from the two countries' point of view. Remember that the United States is the wheat producer and exporter. A glance back at **Table 9.4** shows that: *in the U.S. 1 bushel of wheat costs 0.67 bushels of beans.* Given this we can ask: what price would it be willing to sell its wheat for? Presumably for as high a price as it can get, but certainly not for less than 0.67 beans. What about the Philippines? How much would it be willing to pay for wheat? Remember, **Table 9.5** tells us that: *in the Philippines 1 bushel of wheat costs 2 bushels of beans.* Therefore, we can conclude that the Philippines would certainly not pay any higher than this price and would be happy to buy it for less. You can see that as long as the price is above the U.S. minimum and below the Philippines' maximum, both countries would be willing to trade. In other words, trade is possible if the price of one unit of wheat is anywhere between 0.67 and 2 units of beans. We could have just as easily expressed things in terms of beans, and a glance back at **Table 9.5** shows that feasible terms of trade would be anywhere between 0.5 wheat to 1.5 wheat for 1 bushel of beans. Where the actual terms of trade end up will depend on the strength of demand in the two countries for these products.

Let us choose one particular rate among the many possible terms of trade and work out the consequences. Suppose, for instance, that the terms end up at: *1 bushel of wheat = 1 bushel of beans.* Let us now assume, since we need some point to start from, that the Philippines is quite happy consuming the 40 million bushels of beans that it was producing before it decided to specialize, as shown in **Table 9.6**. However, because of specialization it is now producing only beans and will therefore have 160 – 40 = 120 million bushels of beans available for export, which it sells to the United States at a rate of 1 bean for 1 wheat. It will receive back 120 million bushels of wheat and will finish up with 40 million bushels of beans and 120 million bushels of wheat. Because of trade, it will have gained an additional 60 million bushels of wheat, compared with its self-sufficient totals shown in combination B of **Table 9.6**. The United States will also gain. It was the sole producer of wheat, and of the total of 600 million bushels produced, it has sold 120 million bushels to the Philippines in exchange for 120 million bushels of beans. It will end up with 480 million bushels of wheat and 120 million bushels of beans, which is 30 million bushels of wheat and 20 million bushels of beans more than when it was producing both products as shown in combination B. All the numbers above can be a bit overwhelming, so let's summarize what we have just done in the **Table 9.10**. Recall that we are assuming that the Philippines consumes the same 40 million bushels of beans before and after trade.

Terms of Trade

5 Coho salmon @ $20 each

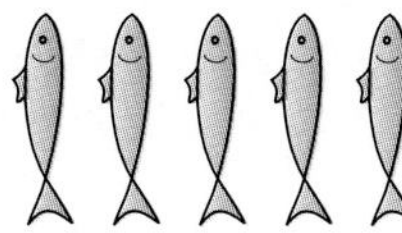

=

1 Daiwa fishing rod @ $100

If the price of Coho salmon increases to $40 each

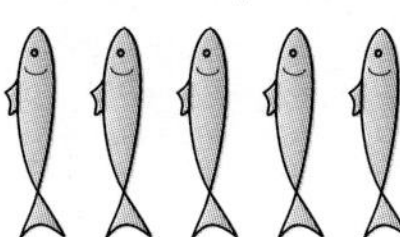

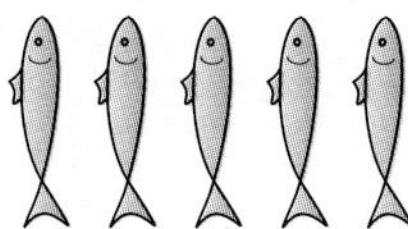

=

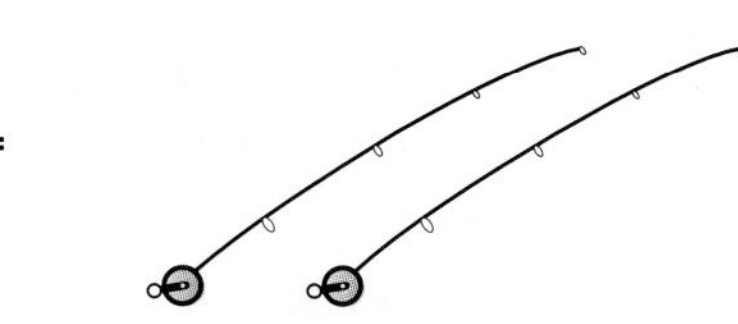

Or, if the price of Daiwa rods decreases to $50

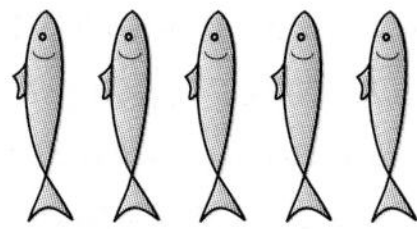

=

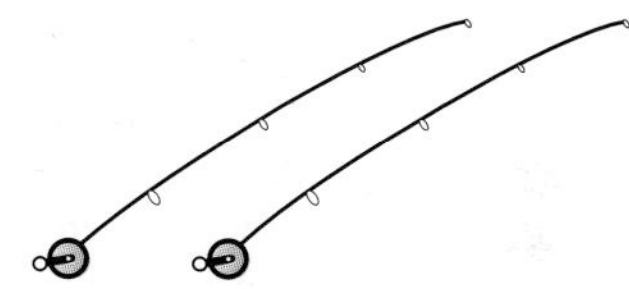

In either case, the terms of trade have moved in Canada's favour; that is, Canada now gets more imports for the same amount of exports.

TABLE 9.10

		PHILIPPINES	
		Before Trade	**After Trade**
	Beans produced	40	160
	Beans exported	0	−120
Beans consumed		**40**	**40**
	Wheat produced	60	0
	Wheat imported	0	+120
Wheat consumed		**60**	**120**
		Gain = 60 Wheat	
		UNITED STATES	
		Before Trade	**After Trade**
	Beans produced	100	0
	Beans imported	0	+120
Beans consumed		**100**	**120**
	Wheat produced	450	600
	Wheat exported	0	−120
Wheat consumed		**450**	**480**
		Gain = 20 Beans and 30 Wheat	

SELF-TEST

3. Suppose that the average productivity in Freedonia and Libraland is as follows:

Output per Worker (bushels per day)

	Apples		Pears
Freedonia	6	or	3
Libraland	3	or	2

a) Assuming the two countries wish to trade, would terms of trade of 1 pear = 2.5 apples be feasible? What about 1 pear = 1 apple? 1 pear = 1.75 apples?

Terms of Trade and Gains from Trade, Graphically

Let us now look at each country's trading picture separately. **Figure 9.1** shows the production possibilities curve for the United States. Before it decided to trade, this was also its consumption possibilities curve, since it could obviously not consume more than it produced. The slope of the curve is 1.5, which is the cost of 1 bean (that is, it equals 1.5 wheat). The curve to the right is its trading possibilities curve, which shows how much the United States could obtain through a combination of specializing its production and trading. Note that the slope of the trading possibilities curve is equal to 1. This is the terms of trade of 1 wheat for 1 bean established between the two countries. You can see from this graph that the United States, at one extreme, could produce the same maximum quantity of 600 million bushels of wheat as before and keep all of it. However, before trade, the maximum amount of beans available was 400. Now, if it wished, the United States could produce 600 million bushels of wheat and trade *all* of it, and receive in exchange 600 million bushels of beans. More likely, of course, it will opt to have a combination of both products, such as 480 million bushels of wheat and 120 million bushels of beans, as in our numerical example above.

FIGURE 9.1 **U.S. Production and Trading Possibilities Curves**

The slope of the production possibilities curve shows the cost of producing beans in the United States is equal to 1.5 wheat per bean. The slope of the trading possibilities curve shows the cost of buying beans internationally; that is, it is the terms of trade and equals 1 wheat per bean. The previous maximum obtainable quantity of beans was 400 million bushels, when the United States was self-sufficient. Its new maximum, as a result of trading, is now 600 million bushels, because it could produce, if it wished, a maximum amount of 600 million bushels of wheat and trade this output for 600 million bushels of beans.

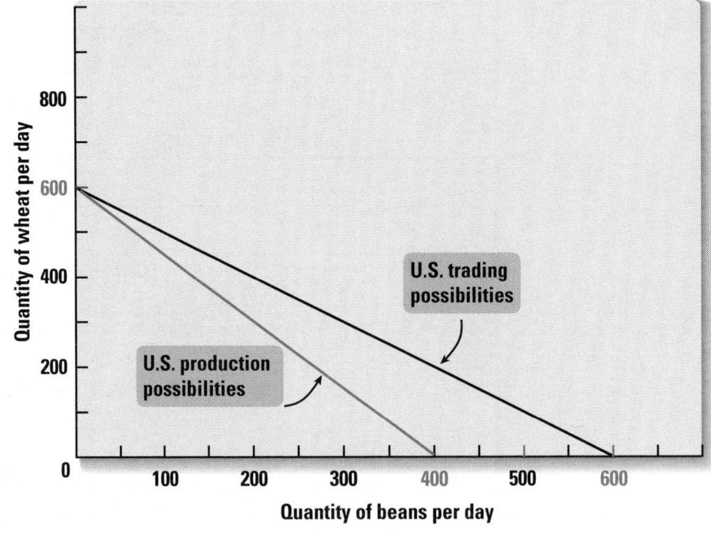

Figure 9.2 shows the situation from the point of view of the Philippines. The inside curve is its production (and therefore its consumption) possibilities curve, representing the maximum of both products that can be produced when the country is self-sufficient. The slope of the curve represents the cost of 1 bushel of beans and is equal to 0.5 bushels of wheat. The outer curve is the trading possibilities curve based on the terms of trade: 1 bean = 1 wheat. You can see that trading allows the Philippines as well to enjoy increased consumption. After specialization, the maximum amount of beans remains unchanged at 160 million bushels. However, the maximum amount of wheat has increased from 80 (if produced in the Philippines) to 160 (by trading away all its 160 million bushels of beans for this quantity of wheat).

FIGURE 9.2 **Philippines' Production and Trading Possibilities Curves**

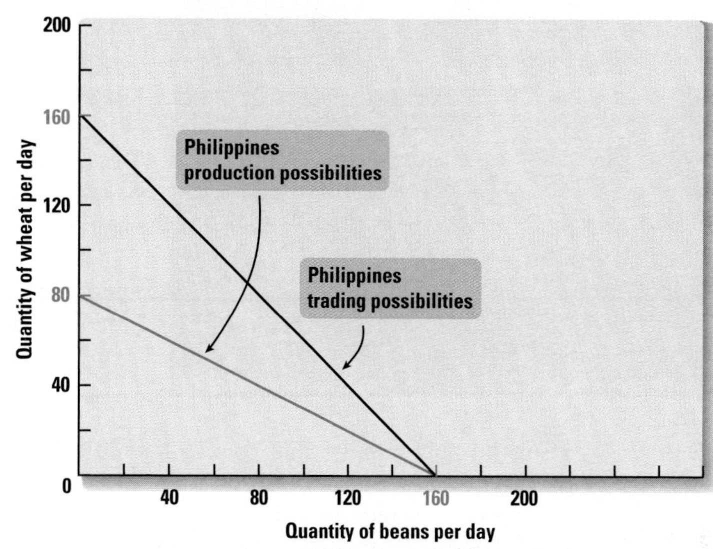

The Philippines specializes in the production of beans, and its trading possibilities curve lies to the right of the production possibilities curve. In other words, irrespective of whether it trades or not, the cost of beans remains the same; the cost of wheat, however, is now lower as a result of trade, since it can now obtain wheat at a cost of 1 bean per 1 wheat, whereas producing its own wheat costs 2 beans per 1 wheat.

SELF-TEST

4. From the data contained in Figure 9.1 or Table 9.6, how many beans can the United States obtain if it is self-sufficient and producing 450 million bushels of wheat? If, instead, it specializes in wheat production and can trade at terms of 1 wheat = 1 bean, how many beans could it have to accompany its 450 million bushels of wheat? What if the terms were 1 wheat = 2 beans?

Some Important Qualifications

Ricardo's theory of comparative advantage, which we have been looking at, is very important because it clearly highlights the major benefits of trade. Free and unrestricted trade allows nations and individuals the opportunity to sell in world markets, and this will, as a result, enable them to specialize in the products in which they enjoy a cost advantage over others. The result will be that products will be produced and sold at a *lower price* and in higher volumes, which translates into *higher incomes* and standards of living for all. In addition, the *variety of products* available when the world becomes one big market would presumably increase.

A final benefit of free trade is the fact that it is more difficult to be a world monopolist than it is to be a monopolist in the home market. In other words, it is often suggested that free trade *increases competition*. In summary, free trade has the following advantages:

- lower prices
- higher incomes
- a greater variety of products
- increased competition

CP/Moe Doiron

The then-minister for international trade, Art Eggleton (right), shakes hands with Israel's minister of industry and trade, Natan Sharansky, after the signing of the Canada–Israel Free Trade Agreement in 1996.

These are indeed powerful arguments in favour of free trade, but before we leave the topic, let us look at some of the qualifications that must be introduced. First, free trade is never free, because there will always be transport, insurance, and other freight charges, which must be added to the cost of production and which will usually reduce the trading advantage of foreign sellers. (However, in a country as large as Canada, it is often cheaper to transport products to American states bordering the country than it is to transport them from one end of the country to the other.) In addition, selling in a foreign country is always going to be more difficult (and usually, therefore, more expensive) than selling in the domestic market, because of the differences in language, culture, taxation, regulations, and so on. Besides cost differences, the analysis we have presented so far has assumed constant costs. This leads to the result in our examples that countries should specialize in, perhaps, a single product and produce that product to a maximum. However, as we learned in Chapter 1, if any country tries to concentrate on a single product, its production is subject to the law of increasing costs. This means that one country only enjoys a cost advantage over others *up to a point*. As it tries to push production levels higher, its cost will start to increase, so that it no longer enjoys a competitive advantage. This is the reason why few countries specialize entirely and why many countries both produce *and* import the same product. The presence of increasing costs will also lessen the advantages that one country enjoys over another in trade.

Even allowing for these cautions, it is still true that there are a number of benefits to be obtained from trade. This leads us to ask: why then does free trade tend to be the exception rather than the rule throughout history? Why does the question of free trade still divide countries and lead to such acrimonious debate? To understand part of the reason, let us look at the consequences of trying to restrict trade.

ADDED DIMENSION

Trade Organizations and Treaties of the World

Several international organizations exist today. The more important ones include the following.

WTO

The World Trade Organization (WTO) was established on January 1, 1995, and consists of more than 100 nations. It was formerly known as GATT (General Agreement on Tariffs and Trade) and is devoted to liberalizing world trade by reducing tariffs and quotas between nations. WTO regularly issues publications that document every aspect of its activities. Its secretariat is in Geneva.

OECD

The Organization for Economic and Cooperative Development (OECD) grew out of the Marshall Plan, which was designed to aid war-ravaged Europe at the end of the Second World War. This Paris-based inter-governmental organization's main purpose is to provide its 29 members with a forum in which governments can compare their experiences, discuss the problems they share, and seek solutions that can then be applied in their own national contexts. Each member is committed to the principles of the market economy and pluralistic democracy.

NAFTA

The North American Free Trade Agreement (NAFTA) is an agreement between Canada, the United States, and Mexico, implemented in 1994, whereby barriers to trade between the countries would be phased out over a 10-year period. In addition, it promotes fair competition and increased investment and provides protection of intellectual property rights. An important aspect of the treaty is a final and binding dispute-resolution mechanism that can be triggered by any one of the parties.

EU

The European Union (EU) currently has 15 member countries and grew out of the former European Economic Community, which was established in 1957. By 1993 it had evolved into a true common market, within which there is free movement of goods and services, capital, and labour. It is moving toward greater monetary union with the establishment of the euro currency in 1999 and, some believe, eventual political union. The inclusion of up to 13 additional member countries in eastern and southern Europe is under consideration.

G8

This group of eight nations consists of Canada, the United States, Japan, the United Kingdom, France, Germany, Italy, and, recently, Russia. It represents (along with China and Spain) the ten largest economies in the world. The heads of state of these eight countries hold summits in which the world's pressing economic, political, and social issues are discussed. Often a summit meeting is followed by the release of a position paper on policy objectives that all have agreed to pursue.

APEC

The Asia-Pacific Economic Cooperation (APEC) was formed in 1989 and includes Canada among its 18 members. Its goal is to advance Asia-Pacific economic dynamism and sense of community by encouraging the region's economic growth and development; encouraging the flow of goods and services, capital, and technology; and encouraging the reduction of barriers to trade in goods and services in a manner consistent with WTO principles.

9.4 The Effect of Free Trade

LO4
Describe why some groups win and others lose as a result of freer trade.

Let us set up a scenario in which, initially, we have two self-sufficient countries, France and Germany, each producing wine. The demand and supply conditions in the two countries are different, of course, with both the demand and supply being greater in France than in Germany, as is shown in **Table 9.11**.

TABLE 9.11 The Market for Wine in France and Germany (millions of litres per month)

FRANCE			GERMANY		
Price ($ per litre)	Demand	Supply	Price ($ per litre)	Demand	Supply
3	24	13	3	12	2
4	19	14	4	11	3
5	**15**	**15**	5	10	4
6	12	16	6	9	5
7	10	17	7	8	6
8	9	18	**8**	**7**	**7**

The equilibrium price in France is $5 per litre and the equilibrium quantity is 15. In Germany, the equilibrium price and quantity are $8 and 7 respectively. These are shown graphically in Figure 9.3.

FIGURE 9.3 Demand and Supply of Wine in France and Germany

In France, the demand and supply of wine are both higher than in Germany. The consequence is a greater quantity of wine traded in France: 15 million litres, compared with 7 million in Germany. The price of wine, however, is lower in France than in Germany.

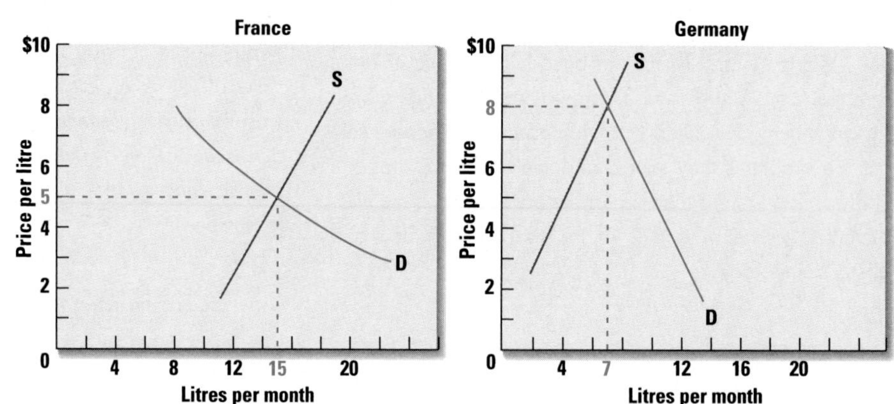

Now suppose that the two countries decide to engage in free trade. To keep things simple, let's assume there are no transport costs. If free trade is now introduced, what will be the price of wine in the two countries? Well, we know that at $5 per litre, the French winemakers were making a profit, so they should have no difficulty in competing with the German producers and presumably could easily undercut the German price of $8. Since we've assumed there are no transport costs, the price in the two countries should be the same. To find this price, all we need to do is look at the combined market of France and Germany. In other words, we need simply to add the demands and supplies of the two countries, as shown in Table 9.12.

TABLE 9.12 Deriving the Total Market Demand and Supply of Wine for France and Germany (in millions of litres per month)

	FRANCE		GERMANY		TOTAL MARKET	
Price ($ per litre)	**Demand**	**Supply**	**Demand**	**Supply**	**Demand**	**Supply**
3	24	13	12	2	36	15
4	19	14	11	3	30	17
5	15	15	10	4	25	19
6	12	16	9	5	**21**	**21**
7	10	17	8	6	18	23
8	9	18	7	7	16	25

Corel

Bottled wine ageing in storage.

The total market demand is obtained by adding together the French demand and the German demand at each price. For instance, at $3 per litre, the quantity demanded in France is 24 and in Germany it is 12, giving a total for the two countries of 36. Similarly, the quantity supplied at $3 is 13 in France and 2 in Germany, giving a total market supply of 15. This is done for all prices. The new market price (let's call it the world price) then, will be $6 per litre, and at that price a total of 21 million litres will be produced and sold.

Now let us look at the effect in each market. French winemakers are delighted at the situation because the world price for wine is higher and their volume of business is higher. French winemakers are now producing 16 million litres, up from the 15 million litres produced before trade and the price they receive is $6, up from $5. Note also that in France the quantity produced (16) exceeds the demand from French consumers (12). What happens to the surplus of 4 million litres? The answer is that it is being exported to Germany. And what is the situation in that country? Well certainly, German consumers are delighted, because the new world price of $6 is lower than the previous domestic price of $8. But we can imagine that the German winemakers are far from happy. The new lower world price has caused a number of producers to cut back production, and presumably some producers are forced out of business. At the world price of $6, German producers are only producing 5 million litres, below the German demand of 9 million litres. How is this shortage going to be made up? Answer: from the import of French wine. This simply means that the French export of 4 million litres equals the German import of 4 million litres. These points are illustrated graphically in Figure 9.4.

FIGURE 9.4 **Demand and Supply of Wine in France and Germany with Free Trade**

The new world price of wine is above the previous French price but below the previous German price. The result is a surplus of wine in France of 4 million litres but a shortage in Germany of 4 million litres.

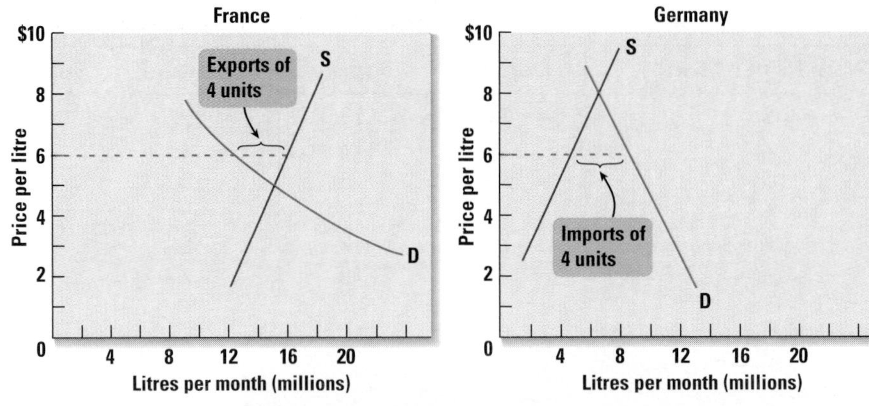

SELF-TEST

5. In Table 9.12, if the demand for wine in Germany increased by 5 (million litres) at every price, how much wine would now be produced in Germany, and how much would be imported from France?

So who are the losers and who are the gainers as a result of markets being opened up? The answer in our example is that both German wine consumers and French wine producers gain and French wine consumers and German wine producers lose. Free trade has cost French consumers $1 a litre, and it has cost German winemakers $2 per litre. Previously German winemakers were selling 7 million litres at $8 per litre, for a total revenue of $56 million. Now, they are selling only 5 million litres for $6 per litre, for a total revenue of $30 million. In total, then, these producers, of whom there may be fewer than 100, have collectively lost $26 million in revenue. It is easy to see why these producers may not be in favour of free trade! In fact, it would pay them to lobby their own parliament and to launch publicity campaigns in an attempt to keep out "cheap" French wines. If they are successful and efforts do not cost more than $26 million, they will be ahead of the game.

It is easy to see why powerful lobby and special interest groups have been very vocal throughout history in trying to persuade parliament and the public that it is in the country's interest to ban or curtail foreign imports. This is an activity that economists call *rent seeking*. Such **protectionism** can take many forms, which we need to look at.

protectionism: the economic policy of protecting domestic producers by restricting the importation of foreign products.

quota: a limit imposed on the production or sale of a product.

Imposition of Quotas

The most obvious restriction of imports is to ban them either entirely or partially, and this is exactly what is meant by a **quota**. A quota can take a variety of forms, ranging from a total restriction to a maximum limit being placed on each individual foreign exporter, or perhaps the requirement that each foreign exporter reduce its exports by a percentage of the previous year's sales. The essence of a quota is to reduce or restrict the importation of certain products. And what will be the effect of such restriction? Suppose in our wine example that German winemakers were successful in their efforts to keep out French wines, and the German government imposed a total ban on French wines. At the current price of $6 per litre, there will be an immediate shortage in Germany. The result of the shortage is to push up the price of wine. It will continue to rise, encouraging increased German production until the price returns to the pre–free-trade price of $8. In France, the immediate effect of the German quota will be to cause a surplus of French wine, which will depress the price of French wine until it too is back at the pre-trade price of $5 per litre.

Let's move on from our France/Germany example and look at trade from the Canadian perspective. The price of wine and of most products traded internationally is determined by the world's demand and supply. That is to say, for any one small country, such as Canada, the world price is a given; the country's action will have little impact on the world price. This situation is illustrated in Figure 9.5.

FIGURE 9.5 **The Effects of a Quota**

Initially the Canadian demand and supply is D_d and S_d and the world price is P_w. The quantity demanded in Canada at the world price P_w equals *c*, of which Canadian producers would produce *a* and foreign producers would export *ac* to Canada. A quota of *ab* would raise the price to P_q. As a result, domestic production will increase, and imports would drop to the amount of the quota.

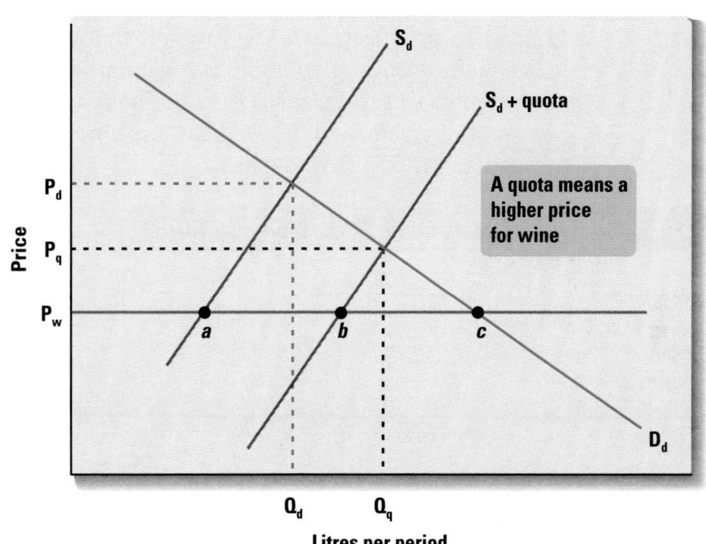

Figure 9.5 shows the domestic demand (D_d)and supply (S_d) of wine in Canada. P_d is the domestic price and Q_d is domestic production. Suppose that the world price is P_w and that Canada now freely allows imports into the country. This means that if the world price of P_w prevails within Canada, the amount produced by domestic Canadian producers is *a*, and the amount demanded is *c*. Since Canadian consumers want to purchase more than Canadian producers are willing to produce, the difference of *ac* represents the amount of imports. Now suppose that the Canadian government yields to pressure from Canadian wine producers and imposes a quota of *ab* on imported wine. In effect, the total supply is equal to the domestic supply plus the amount of the quota. This is represented by the new supply curve, S_d *plus quota*. Since the total available has now been reduced, the price will increase to P_q and the quantity will fall to Q_q.

From this, it can be seen that the losers will be Canadian consumers (who are paying a higher price and are having less quantity and variety of wines) and foreign winemakers whose exports are being restricted. The winners will be Canadian winemakers, who are producing more wine and receiving a higher price.

The Imposition of a Tariff

tariff: a tax (or duty) levied on imports.

A second way of restricting imports is by the use of a **tariff**, which is a tax on imports. It is a more frequently chosen method than quotas, because governments can derive considerable revenue from tariffs. The effects of a tariff are much the same as those of a quota because, in both cases, the price of the product will increase. With a quota, however, the domestic producers get the whole benefit of the higher price, whereas with a tariff, the benefit is shared between the domestic producers and the government. An additional benefit of a tariff over a quota is that a quota tends to treat foreign producers indiscriminately because each and every producer is treated in the same way, whereas with a tariff only the more efficient producers will continue to export, since only they will be able to continue to make a profit. A tariff discriminates against the less efficient producers, and therefore, from an efficiency point of view, it is superior to a quota. These points are illustrated in **Figure 9.6**.

In **Figure 9.6**, suppose again that we are describing the Canadian wine market. At the world price of P_w, Canadian producers are supplying *a* and Canadian consumers are buying *b*. The difference *ab* is the amount of imported wine. Suppose that the Canadian government imposes a tariff of *t* per unit. The price in Canada will rise to P_t. Note that at the higher price, Canadian producers, who will receive the whole price P_t, will increase production to Q_f. Canadian consumers will reduce consumption to Q_g. In addition, imports will fall to a level represented by the distance $Q_f - Q_g$. The result is very similar to what we saw in the analysis of quotas. Again, it is Canadian consumers and foreign producers who lose out, and Canadian producers who gain.

FIGURE 9.6 **The Effects of the Imposition of a Tariff**

The imposition of a tariff, *t*, will increase the price of wine in Canada to P_t from P_w. As a result, Canadian production will increase from Q_e to Q_f and imports will drop to $Q_g - Q_f$. The tax revenue to the government is equal to *t* times the quantity of imports, $Q_g - Q_f$, the shaded area.

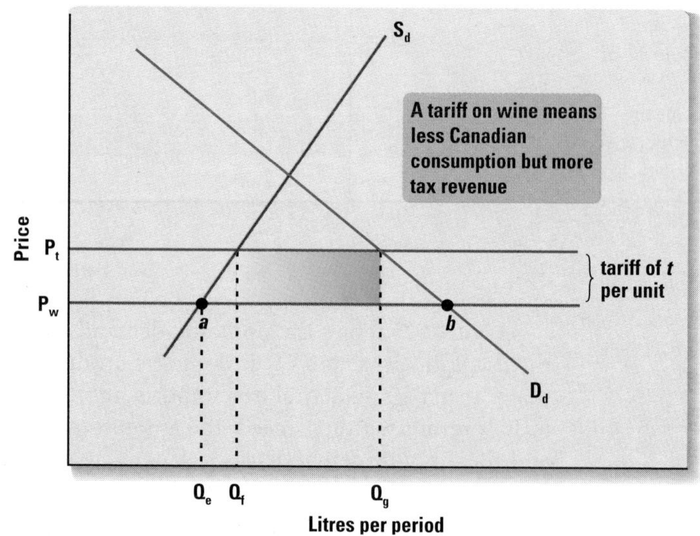

The other gainer in this scenario will be the Canadian government, which will receive tax revenue equal to the shaded rectangle in **Figure 9.6**.

Other Trade Restrictions

exchange controls: restrictions imposed by a government limiting the amount of foreign currencies that can be obtained.

Besides the two popular protectionist measures of tariffs and quotas, a number of other available methods deserve mention. **Exchange controls** are similar to quotas, but instead of a restriction being placed on the importation of a good, the restriction is placed on the availability of foreign currencies (that is, foreign exchange). The effect is the same because, since foreigners wish to be paid in their own currencies, if an importer is unable to get his hands on the appropriate currency, he will not be able to buy the foreign goods. The controls might be across-the-board restrictions or restrictions on particular currencies or on particular products or industries. The effect in all cases will be to increase the domestic price of the products affected, which will be to the benefit of the domestic producer at the expense of the domestic consumer. Another more subtle but often equally effective way of cutting imports is by way of *restrictions and regulations*. A government might make trade so difficult or time-consuming for the importer that the amount of trade is significantly reduced. For instance, the customs department of a particular country might tie the importer up with red tape by requiring that all imports must be accompanied by 10 different forms (all in triplicate) obtainable from 10 different government departments. Or perhaps the product must comply to certain very unrealistic standards of safety, or packaging, or hygiene standards that are not required for domestically produced items.

voluntary export restriction (VER): an agreement by an exporting country to restrict the amount of its exports to another country.

A more recent type of trade restriction is known as **voluntary export restrictions (VERs)**. Rather than imposing, say, tariffs and quotas, the importing country requests that the exporting country itself voluntarily restrict the amount being exported. In this way, the exporting country is given the power to administer the quotas, which will also prevent the importing country from receiving tariff revenue on the imports. Since the restrictions are voluntary, the exporting country does not have to comply. However, since the importing country has other weapons at its disposal, then...

9.5 Protectionism

LO5
Identify some arguments for and against free trade.

In this chapter we have tried to avoid making an outright declaration in favour of free trade, though the flavour of the chapter would suggest that there are many benefits to be derived from trade, and probably the majority of economists feel that the freer the trade, the better. But even a notable free-trader like the astute Adam Smith recognized that there *may* be occasions when a degree of protectionism in the way of tariffs and quotas might be called for. He suggested, for instance, that a country's strategic industries should be offered protection so that, for instance, the country does not become dependent on foreign manufacturers for the production of military hardware and the related technology. The problem with this *strategic industry argument*, however, is that most industries would claim that they are of "strategic importance" to a nation and therefore deserve similar protection from foreign competition. Also, the idea of hindering the production of military goods has appeal to many.

In addition, Smith suggests that in order for there to be a level playing field for both domestic and foreign producers, if the produce of domestic industry is being taxed, then foreign imports should be taxed by a similar amount. He also felt that if a foreign country is placing tariffs and quotas on your country's exports, then you should do likewise to its exports, but not, it should be noted, just for retaliation, but to help the foreign country to recognize the folly of its actions and to persuade it to restore free trade. Finally, Smith was prescient enough to realize that if a country has had a long history of protectionism, then the sudden arrival of free trade is likely to cause dramatic shifts of labour and capital away from industries that can no longer compete to those industries that find themselves growing. This dislocation may cause a great deal of suffering in the short term, so Smith felt that a wise government would introduce free trade gradually and would try to mitigate the suffering. This caveat is of particular importance in terms of the North American Free Trade Agreement discussions. Although many felt that there would be great long-term benefits for all the participating countries, it is equally certain that in the short term a great deal of suffering would be experienced by those industries, firms, and individuals who, through no fault of their own, found themselves unable to compete. This is why tariffs were reduced in stages over a ten year period.

In addition, it ought to be mentioned that some economists feel that certain "infant" industries should be given a helping hand by the government until they are sufficiently mature to compete with foreign competition. This *infant industry argument* is strongest when the government feels that undue reliance on the exportation of a few staple products would leave the country in a vulnerable position if a future change in demand or technology were to occur. In order to diversify the economy and develop other industries, many feel that these "infants" should be sheltered from competition. However, the trouble is, these infant industries often never grow up! In addition, even if there are persuasive arguments in favour of protecting or assisting certain industries, it may be better for the government to give this aid in the form of direct subsidies rather than by interfering with normal trading patterns through the imposition of tariffs and quotas.

A final argument against free trade is the *cultural identity argument*. This one is difficult to dismiss solely on economic grounds. Many commentators feel that free trade brings with it mass production and standardization, which may harm the importing country's sense of individuality and cultural identity. As a result, some are totally against free trade while others feel that it should not extend into areas like communications, health, and education. They firmly believe that a country's radio and television stations, its newspapers and magazines, its educational institutions and hospitals, should not be foreign-owned or -controlled. In summary, three arguments against free trade are:

- the strategic industry argument
- the infant industry argument
- the cultural identity argument

REVIEW

1. What is meant by the *terms of trade*?
2. In general, what could cause the terms of trade to move in Canada's favour?
3. What does the slope of the production possibilities curve indicate? What does the slope of the trading possibilities curve indicate?
4. List four major advantages of free trade.
5. What does *protectionism* mean?
6. List four ways to restrict imports.
7. List three arguments against free trade.

STUDY GUIDE

Review

CHAPTER SUMMARY

In this chapter you learned that the benefits of free trade are rooted in specialization and that a nation's comparative advantage determines what products it should export. The way that the gains from trade are divided between trading partners is determined by the terms of trade between them. You also learned that when a nation embraces free trade there are both winners, usually consumers, and losers, usually inefficient producers of certain products.

1. If trade is voluntary, then *both parties* to the trade must *benefit*.

2. Differences in factor endowments between nations and the *theory of absolute advantage* explain why, for example, Canada exports lumber and imports bananas.

3. The *theory of comparative advantage* explains why one nation is willing to trade with another nation even though it may be more efficient in producing both (all) the products involved.

4. The trade in any two products between any two nations will result in there being gains from trade unless the *opportunity costs* of production happen to be exactly the same in each country.

5. The way in which the gains from trade are divided between the trading partners is determined by the *terms of trade*, calculated as the average price of exports divided by the average price of imports times 100.

6. The major *benefits of free trade* are:
   - lower prices;
   - higher incomes;
   - a greater variety of products;
   - increased competition.

7. The two most common forms of *trade restrictions* are tariffs and quotas, both of which:
   - increase the domestic price of a product that is imported;
   - reduce the quantities traded of that product.

   While the other two types of restrictions are:
   - exchange controls;
   - voluntary exports restrictions.

8. Three arguments *against free trade* are the:
   - strategic industry argument;
   - infant industry argument;
   - cultural identity argument.

NEW GLOSSARY TERMS AND KEY EQUATION

comparative advantage 304
exchange controls 318
protectionism 316
quota 316
tariff 317
terms of trade 308
voluntary export restriction (VER) 319

Equation:

[9.1] $$\text{terms of trade} = \frac{\text{average price of exports}}{\text{average price of imports}} \times 100$$ page 308

STUDY TIPS

1. The argument for free trade is based on Ricardo's theory of comparative advantage. It is important that you fully understand the basic idea of opportunity costs that lies behind this theory. A good way to test yourself is to make up your own figures for a two-country, two-product world, draw the corresponding production possibilities curves, and work out which country has an advantage in which product and why.

2. Some students have difficulty understanding that if we are dealing with only two products and if a country has a comparative advantage at producing one product it must, by definition, have a comparative *disadvantage* in the other product.

3. To get an understanding of the terms of trade, again try to make up some numbers for yourself and plot them on a production possibilities diagram. For instance, start off with a country that could produce 30 units of wool or 20 computers and has an advantage in wool production. If it could trade at 1 wool = 1/2 computer, what combinations could it have? Try 1 wool = 1 computer, 1 wool = 2, 3, 5 computers and so on. Draw each resulting trading possibilities curve. Note that both the trading and production possibilities curves reflect opportunity costs. The former case shows what must be given up in trading; the latter case shows what must be given up in production.

4. To understand the idea behind world markets, note, as in **Figure 9.4**, that what one country is exporting, another country must be importing. This means that if one country produces a trade surplus, then the other country must be experiencing a trade deficit. In the exporting country, the world price must be higher than the domestic price. In the importing country, the world price must be lower than the domestic price.

5. You will get a good grip on the effects of tariffs and quotas by drawing a simple demand and supply curve and noting, first, the effect of a price set above market equilibrium (which is what a tariff produces) and second, a quantity below market equilibrium (which is what a quota produces). This approach suggests that the effect of both tariffs and quotas is to produce higher prices and lower quantities.

Answered Questions

Indicate whether the following statements are true or false.

1. **T or F** A country has a comparative advantage over another only if it is able to produce all products more cheaply.

2. **T or F** David Ricardo first introduced the theory of comparative advantage.

3. **T or F** If a country wishes to specialize its production, it will also want to engage in trade.

4. **T or F** If a country is able to produce all products more cheaply than any other country can, then there is no advantage in trade.

5. **T or F** The terms of trade relate to the laws and conditions that govern trade.

6. **T or F** If the prices of a country's exports decrease and the prices of imports increase, then the terms of trade will move in its favour.

7. **T or F** If a country's trading possibilities curve lies to the right of its production possibilities curve, there are no gains from trade.

8. **T or F** Protectionism is the economic policy of protecting domestic producers by putting restrictions on exports.

9. **T or F** A tariff is a tax on exports; a quota is a tax on imports.

10. **T or F** Domestic producers gain and domestic consumers lose as a result of the imposition of tariffs or quotas.

Basic (Questions 11–26)

11. What is the meaning of the term "gains from trade"?
   a) The surplus of exports over imports.
   b) The increase in output resulting from international trade.
   c) The fact that everyone gains from international trade.
   d) The increase in revenue that the government receives from tariffs.

12. What is a tariff?
a) It is a tax imposed on an import.
b) It is a tax imposed on an export.
c) It is a tax imposed on production.
d) It is a tax imposed on consumption.

13. What are the two largest categories of goods that Canada exports?
a) Energy and forestry products.
b) Agricultural and forestry products.
c) Forestry products and industrial materials.
d) Automotive products and machinery/equipment products.

14. What is the definition of "the terms of trade"?
a) It is the average price of a country's imports divided by the average price of its exports.
b) It is the average price of a country's exports divided by the average price of its imports.
c) They are the rules and regulations governing international trade.
d) The value of a country's currency compared to that of its biggest trading partner.

15. What does it mean if the opportunity costs differ between two countries?
a) Then comparative costs must be the same.
b) There can be no gains from trade.
c) It is possible for both countries to gain from specialization and trade.
d) Then absolute costs must be the same.

16. On what basis are the gains from trade divided between countries?
a) According to the terms of trade.
b) According to international trade agreements.
c) According to the quantity of resources possessed by each.
d) According to each country's comparative advantage.

17. Under what circumstances will there be no opportunity for mutually advantageous trade between two countries?
a) When the terms of trade are the same.
b) When comparative costs are the same.
c) When comparative costs are different.
d) When tariffs exist.

18. Suppose that originally the average price of Happy Island's exports was 180, and the average price of its imports was 120. Now, the price of its exports drops to 160, and the price of its imports drops to 100. What effect will this have on Happy Island's terms of trade?
a) There will be no change in the terms of trade.
b) The terms of trade have moved in Happy Island's favour.
c) The terms of trade have moved against Happy Island.
d) The terms of trade have both increased and decreased.

19. All the following, except one, are forms of protectionism. Which is the exception?
a) Import subsidies.
b) Tariffs.
c) Exchange controls.
d) Quotas.

20. Suppose that the cost of producing 1 unit of wine in Happy Island is 2 units of rice; in Joy Island, 1 wine costs 4 rice. What does this mean for the two countries?
a) Happy Island should specialize in and export rice to Joy Island.
b) Happy Island should specialize in and export wine to Joy Island.
c) Happy Island should specialize in rice but export wine to Joy Island.
d) Happy Island should specialize in wine but export rice to Joy Island.

21. Suppose that the cost of producing 1 unit of wine in Happy Island is 2 units of rice; in Joy Island 1 wine costs 4 rice. What might be possible terms of trade between the two countries?
a) 1 rice = 3/8 wine.
b) 1 rice = 3 wine.
c) 1 rice = 6 wine.
d) 1 wine = 1 rice.

22. What is the difference between a tariff and a quota?
a) A tariff causes an increase in the price, whereas a quota does not affect the price.
b) Both a tariff and a quota will affect the price, but a tariff has no effect on the quantity, whereas a quota will lead to a reduction.
c) Both a tariff and a quota will affect the price, but a tariff has no effect on the quantity, whereas a quota will lead to an increase.
d) A quota affects all foreign producers equally, whereas a tariff does not.
e) A tariff affects all foreign producers equally, whereas a quota does not.

Refer to **Figure 9.7** to answer questions 23–26.

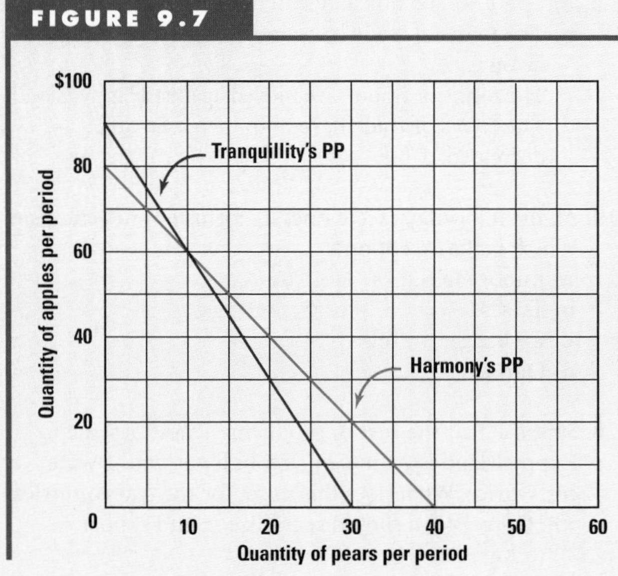

23. Refer to **Figure 9.7** to answer this question. What is the opportunity cost of producing 1 apple in Harmony and in Tranquillity?
a) 2 pears in Harmony and 3 pears in Tranquillity.
b) 1/2 pear in Harmony and 1/3 pear in Tranquillity.
c) 2 pears in Harmony and 1/3 pear in Tranquillity.
d) 1/2 pear in Harmony and 3 pears in Tranquillity.
e) 3 pears in Harmony and 2 pears in Tranquillity.

24. Refer to **Figure 9.7** to answer this question. What do the comparative opportunity costs in the two countries suggest?
a) That there are no advantages to be gained from trade.
b) That Harmony should specialize in apples but export pears.
c) That Tranquillity should specialize in apples but export pears.
d) That Harmony should specialize in pears but export apples.
e) That Harmony should specialize in pears and Tranquillity should specialize in apples.

25. Refer to **Figure 9.7** to answer this question. Suppose that both Harmony and Tranquillity are producing 20 pears; what will be the total gains from trade for the two countries?
a) 20 apples and 0 pears.
b) 30 apples and 10 pears.
c) 20 apples and 10 pears.
d) 20 apples and 30 pears.
e) 0 apples and 20 pears.

26. Refer to **Figure 9.7** to answer this question. What could be possible terms of trade between the two countries?
a) 1 apple = 0.25 pears.
b) 1 apple = 2.5 pears.
c) 1 apple = 3 pears.
d) 1 pear = 0.5 apples.
e) 1 pear = 2.5 apples.

Intermediate (Questions 27–31)

Refer to **Table 9.13** to answer problems 27–31.

TABLE 9.13

	AVERAGE PRODUCT PER WORKER		
Country	**Broomsticks**		**Swords**
Rings	1	or	4
Potter	6	or	3

27. Refer to **Table 9.13** to answer this question. What is the cost of producing one sword in Rings?
a) 4 broomsticks.
b) 0.25 broomsticks.
c) 0.67 broomsticks.
d) 1.5 broomsticks.

28. Refer to **Table 9.13** to answer this question. What is the cost of producing one broomstick in Potter?
a) 2 swords.
b) 0.5 swords.
c) 0.33 swords.
d) 3 swords.

29. Refer to **Table 9.13** to answer this question. Supposing that there are 200 workers in Rings, how many broomsticks could be produced if 200 swords were produced?
a) 40 broomsticks.
b) 50 broomsticks.
c) 150 broomsticks.
d) 160 broomsticks.

30. Refer to **Table 9.13** to answer this question. Supposing that there are 200 workers in Potter, how many swords could be produced if 540 broomsticks were produced?
a) 0 swords.
b) 110 swords.
c) 120 swords.
d) 330 swords.

31. Refer to **Table 9.13** to answer this question. Supposing that there are 200 workers each in Rings and Potter. If, originally, half the workers were employed in each industry, what would be the gains from trade if the countries completely specialized in the products in which they have a comparative advantage?
 a) +200 broomstics; – 100 swords.
 b) +200 broomstics; + 100 swords.
 c) +500 broomstics; + 100 swords.
 d) +700 broomstics; + 700 swords.

Advanced (Questions 32–35)

Refer to **Figure 9.8**, which shows the market for cloth in Smith Island, to answer questions 32, 33, and 34.

FIGURE 9.8

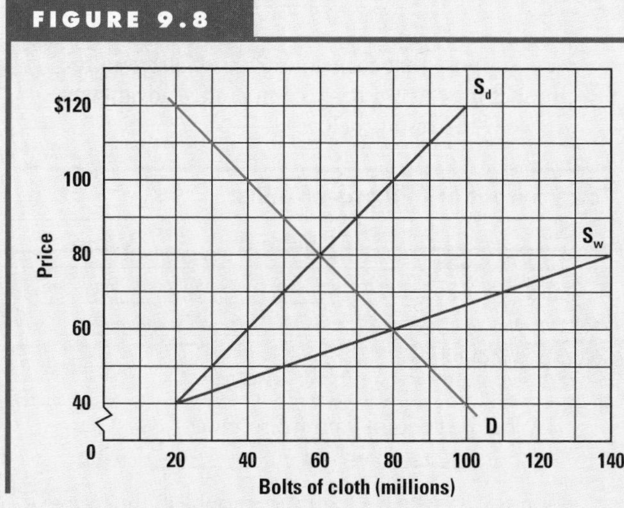

32. Refer to **Figure 9.8** to answer this question. At the world price, how much is Smith Island trading?
 a) It is importing 30 units.
 b) It is importing 40 units.
 c) It is exporting 30 units.
 d) It is exporting 40 units.

33. Refer to **Figure 9.8** to answer this question. If Smith Island introduced an import quota of 20, what would be the new price of cloth in Smith Island?
 a) $55.
 b) $60.
 c) $70.
 d) $90.

34. Refer to **Figure 9.8** to answer this question. If Smith Island introduced a tariff of $10 on cloth, how much would be imported?
 a) 0 units.
 b) 10 units.
 c) 20 units.
 d) 40 units.

Table 9.14 shows the output of kumquats per month. Refer to this table to answer question 35.

TABLE 9.14

		SMITHLAND	
Price ($ per kilo)	**Demand**	**Domestic Supply**	**Imports**
3	100	40	30
4	90	50	40
5	80	60	50
6	70	70	60

35. Refer to **Table 9.14** to answer this question. What is the world (free trade) price of kumquats, and what quantity of this product is being consumed domestically?
 a) $4 and 50 kilos consumed.
 b) $4 and 90 kilos consumed.
 c) $5 and 80 kilos consumed.
 d) $6 and 70 kilos consumed.
 e) $6 and 130 kilos consumed.

Parallel Problems

ANSWERED PROBLEMS

36. **Key Problem** Suppose that Richland and Prosperity have the output figures shown in **Table 9.15**.

TABLE 9.15

	AVERAGE PRODUCT PER WORKER		
Country	**Wheat**		**Wine**
Richland	4 bushels	or	2 barrels
Prosperity	2 bushels	or	6 barrels

Assuming that cost and productivity remain constant:

a) What is the opportunity cost of producing 1 bushel of wheat in Richland? ______________.

b) What is the opportunity cost of producing 1 barrel of wine in Richland? ______________.

c) What is the opportunity cost of producing 1 bushel of wheat in Prosperity? ______________.

d) What is the opportunity cost of producing 1 barrel of wine in Prosperity? ______________.

e) In what product does Richland have a comparative advantage? ______________.

f) In what product does Prosperity have a comparative advantage? ______________.

Suppose that the labour force in each country is 10 million.

g) Fill in the missing production possibilities data for both countries in **Table 9.16**.

TABLE 9.16

	RICHLAND'S PRODUCTION POSSIBILITIES (millions of units)				
	A	**B**	**C**	**D**	**E**
Wheat	40	30	20	10	0
Wine	____	____	____	____	____
	PROSPERITY'S PRODUCTION POSSIBILITIES (millions of units)				
	A	**B**	**C**	**D**	**E**
Wheat	____	____	____	____	____
Wine	0	15	30	45	60

Suppose that both countries are presently producing combination C.

h) Fill in the blanks below:

Total output in millions of units:		
	Wheat	**Wine**
Richland	________	________
Prosperity	________	________
Total: both countries	________	________

Now suppose that each country specialized in the product in which it has a comparative advantage.

i) Show the results below.

Total output in millions of units:		
	Wheat	**Wine**
Richland	________	________
Prosperity	________	________
Total: both countries	________	________

j) What is the joint gain from trade?
__________ wheat __________wine.

Suppose that the two countries establish the terms of trade at 1 wine = 1.5 wheat, and Prosperity decides to export 12 wine to Richland.

k) As a result, the two countries will share the gains from trade as follows:

Gains for each country in millions of units:		
	Wheat	**Wine**
Richland	________	________
Prosperity	________	________
Total: both countries	________	________

Basic (Problems 37–41)

37. If the terms of trade for the country of Onara equals 0.9 and the average price of its imports is 1.4, what is the average price of its exports? ______________.

38. In Onara, the average worker can produce either 5 bags of pummies or 3 kilos of clings, whereas in Traf the average worker can produce either 4 bags of pummies or 6 kilos of clings. Which country can produce pummies cheaper and which can produce clings cheaper? Show the cost in each country.

Pummies: ____________ ; cost: ______________ .
Clings: ____________ ; cost: ______________ .

39. The following shows the maximum output levels for Here and There:

	Cloth		Computers
Here	100	or	50
There	60	or	120

a) What is the cost of a unit of cloth and a computer in Here?
1 unit of cloth: ______________________ ;
1 computer: ______________________ .

b) What is the cost of a unit of cloth and a computer in There?
1 unit of cloth: ______________________ ;
1 computer: ______________________ .

c) In what product does each country have a comparative advantage?
Here: ______________________ ;
There: ______________________ .

d) What is the range of feasible terms of trade between the two countries?
1 unit of cloth: ______________________ ;
1 computer: ______________________ .

40. The following table shows the productivity for the countries of Yin and Yang:

	Machines		Bread
Yin	2	or	10
Yang	3	or	2

a) If the working populations of Yin and Yang are both 40 million, divided equally between the two industries in each country, how many machines and bread are currently being produced in Yin and Yang?

	Machines	Bread
Yin	______	______
Yang	______	______
Totals	______	______

b) If the two countries decide to specialize, in which product does each country have a comparative advantage?
Yin: ______________ ; Yang: ______________ .

c) If the two countries were to totally specialize, what would be the resulting totals?

	Machines	Bread
Yin	______	______
Yang	______	______
Totals	______	______

d) What are the gains from trade?

Machines	Bread
______	______

41. Table 9.17 shows the production possibilities curves for Concordia and Harmonia.

TABLE 9.17

CONCORDIA'S PRODUCTION POSSIBILITIES					
Product	**A**	**B**	**C**	**D**	**E**
Pork	4	3	2	1	0
Beans	0	5	10	15	20

HARMONIA'S PRODUCTION POSSIBILITIES					
Product	**A**	**B**	**C**	**D**	**E**
Pork	8	6	4	2	0
Beans	0	6	12	18	24

a) What are the costs of the two products in each country?
Concordia: 1 unit of pork costs ______________ .
1 unit of beans costs ______________ .
Harmonia: 1 unit of pork costs ______________ .
1 unit of beans costs ______________ .

b) What products should each country specialize in and export?
Concordia: ______________________.
Harmonia: ______________________.

c) If, prior to specialization and trade, Concordia produced combination C and Harmonia produced combination B, what would be the total gains from trade?
Pork: ______________.
Beans: ______________.

d) What would be the range of feasible terms of trade between the two countries?
______________________.

Intermediate (Problems 42–46)

42. The graph in Figure 9.9 shows the domestic supply of and demand for mangos in India.

FIGURE 9.9

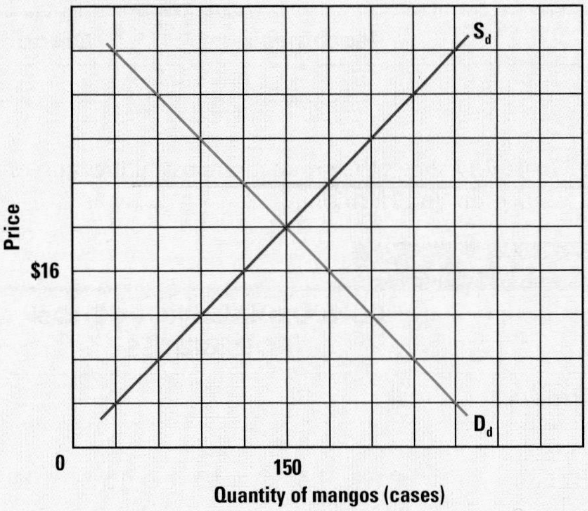

S_d
D_d
Price
$16
0
150
Quantity of mangos (cases)

The world price is $16 a case and India has free trade.

a) Will India export or import mangos? __________.

b) What quantity will domestic producers supply?
______________________.

c) What quantity will India export or import?
______________________.

d) What will be the price in India? ______________.

43. Table 9.18 shows the market for wool in Australia, which is closed to trade.

TABLE 9.18

Price per Tonne ($)	Quantity Demanded Domestically	Quantity Supplied Domestically
1700	145	45
1800	140	60
1900	135	75
2000	130	90
2100	125	105
2200	120	120
2300	115	135
2400	110	150

a) What is the present equilibrium price and domestic production?
Price: ______________________;
domestic production: ______________.

b) Suppose that Australia now opens to free trade and the world price of wool is $2000 per tonne. How much wool will Australia produce domestically, and how much will it import?
Domestic production: ______________;
imports: ______________________.

c) Assume that the Australian government, under pressure from the Australian wool industry, decides to impose an import quota of 20 tonnes. What will be the new price, and how much will the Australian industry produce?
Price: ______________________;
domestic production: ______________.

d) Now suppose that the Australian government, wishing to benefit from the trade restriction, decides to replace the import quota with a tariff. If it wishes to maintain domestic production at the same level as with a quota, what should be the amount of the tariff, and how much revenue will the government receive?
Tariff: $ ______________________;
tariff revenue: $ ______________.

44. **Table 9.19** shows the production possibilities for Canada and Japan. Prior to specialization and trade, Canada is producing combination D, and Japan is producing combination B.

TABLE 9.19

CANADA'S PRODUCTION POSSIBILITIES						
Product	**A**	**B**	**C**	**D**	**E**	**F**
Compact disc players	10	8	6	4	2	0
Wheat	0	4	8	12	16	20

JAPAN'S PRODUCTION POSSIBILITIES						
Product	**A**	**B**	**C**	**D**	**E**	**F**
Compact disc players	30	24	18	12	6	0
Wheat	0	6	12	18	24	30

a) On the graph (**Figure 9.10**, below), draw the production possibilities curve for each country, and indicate their present output positions.

b) Suppose that the two countries specialize and trade on the basis of 1 CD player = 1.5 wheat. Draw the corresponding trading possibilities curves.

FIGURE 9.10

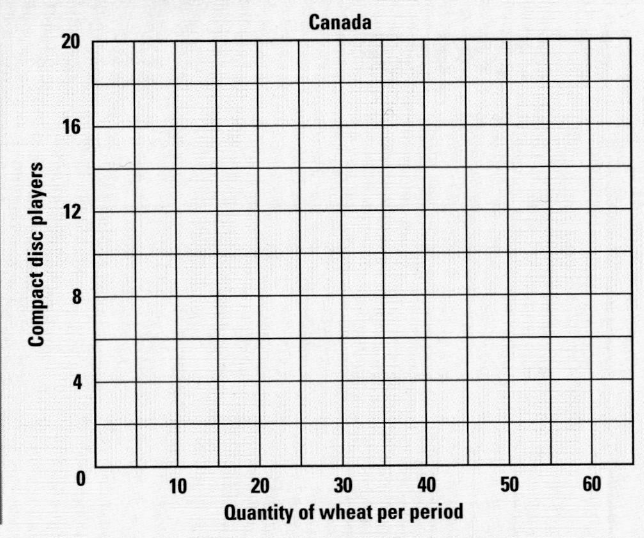

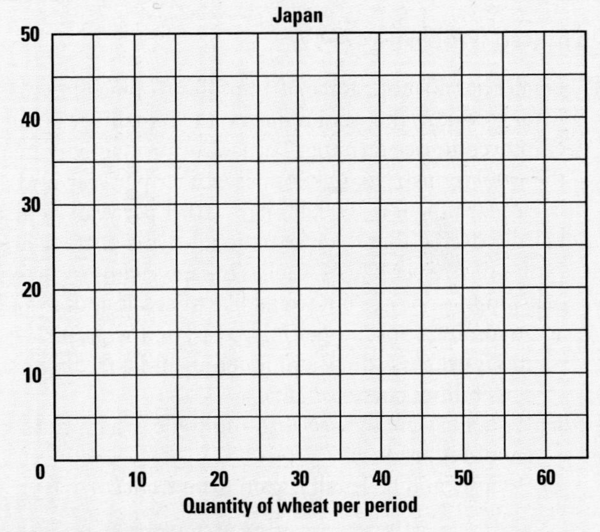

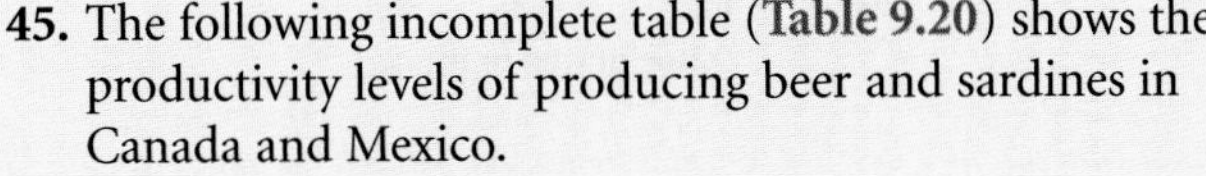

45. The following incomplete table (**Table 9.20**) shows the productivity levels of producing beer and sardines in Canada and Mexico.

TABLE 9.20

	PRODUCTION PER WORKER (average product)	
	Beer	**Sardines**
Canada	6	4
Mexico	3	______

In order for there to be no advantage to be gained from trade, what does the Mexican productivity per worker in the sardine industry need to be?

46. Suppose the Canadian demand for and the Japanese supply of cars to Canada is shown in **Table 9.21** (quantities in thousands).

a) The present equilibrium price is $ ______________ and quantity is ______________ (thousand).

b) Suppose that the Canadian government imposes a $2000 per car tariff on imported Japanese cars. Show the new supply in the last column above. The new equilibrium price is $ ______________ and quantity is ______________ (thousand).

c) The total revenue received by the government will be $ ______________ .

d) Assume, instead, that the government imposes an import quota of 100 000 cars. The new equilibrium price is $ ______________ and quantity is ______________ (thousand).

e) Does the government now receive any revenue? ______________ .

TABLE 9.21

Price($)	Quantity Demanded	Quantity Supplied (before tariff)	Quantity Supplied (after tariff)
$12 000	180	60	______
13 000	160	80	______
14 000	140	100	______
15 000	120	120	______
16 000	100	140	______
17 000	80	160	______
18 000	60	180	______
19 000	40	200	______

Advanced (Problems 47–49)

47. Latalia has a labour force of 12 million, one half of whom work in the wool industry, the remainder being employed in rice farming. The labour productivity in the wool industry is 40 kilos per worker per year, and in rice farming it is 100 kilos per worker per year. Latalia has discovered that the international terms of trade are 2 kilos of rice per kilo of wool. It is happy with its current consumption of rice but would like to obtain more wool.

a) Assuming constant per unit costs, on the graph in **Figure 9.11**, draw a production and a trading possibilities curve for Latalia.

b) If Latalia were to specialize and trade, what product should it produce? ______________ .

c) What would be Latalia's gain from trade? ______________ .

d) On the graph, indicate the consumption levels before and after trade.

FIGURE 9.11

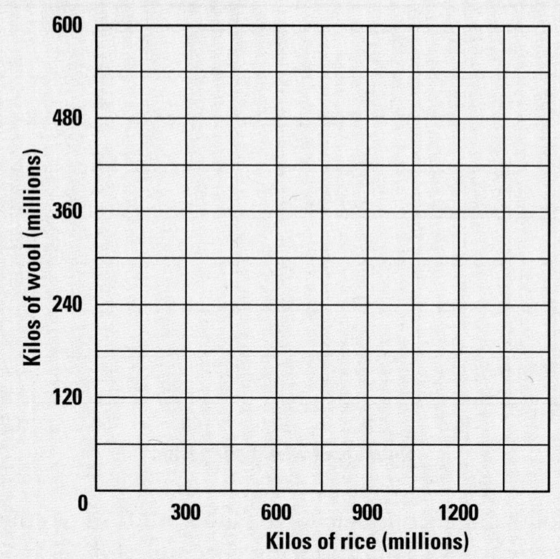

48. Suppose three countries have the productivity data shown in **Table 9.22**.

TABLE 9.22

	PRODUCTIVITY PER WORKER	
	Wheat	**Beans**
Alpha	1	2
Beta	4	2
Gamma	2	2

a) What is the cost of wheat in each country?
In Alpha, 1 unit of wheat costs ______________ .
In Beta, 1 unit of wheat costs ______________ .
In Gamma, 1 unit of wheat costs ______________ .

b) Which country can produce wheat comparatively the cheapest?

c) Which country can produce beans comparatively the cheapest? ______________ .

d) Suppose that the international terms of trade were 1 wheat = $\frac{3}{4}$ beans. Which countries would export wheat? ______________ .
Which countries would import wheat? ______________ .

e) Suppose instead that the international terms of trade were 1 wheat = $1\frac{1}{2}$ beans. Which countries would export wheat? ______________ .
Which countries would import wheat? ______________ .

49. If comparative cost is the basis for trade, why are Third World countries, which have very low wage rates, not the world's greatest trading nations? ______________ .

UNANSWERED PROBLEMS

50. Key Problem Suppose that Hopeland and Faithland have the output figures contained in **Table 9.23**, shown in terms of productivity per worker.

TABLE 9.23

	AVERAGE PRODUCT PER WORKER		
Country	**Wheat**		**Wine**
Hopeland	3 bushels	or	1 barrel
Faithland	1 bushel	or	2 barrels

Assuming that the costs and productivity remain constant:

a) What is the opportunity cost of producing wheat and wine in Hopeland and Faithland?

b) In which product does each country have a comparative advantage?
Suppose that the labour force in Hopeland is 20 million, and it is 10 million in Faithland.

c) Show, in a table with 5 columns, the production possibilities of each country.
Assume that each country is now producing 5 million barrels of wine.

d) What are their present joint output totals?
Now suppose that each country specializes in the product in which it has a comparative advantage.

e) What will be the new output totals, and what will be the gains from trade?

Suppose that the two countries establish the terms of trade at 1 wine = 2 wheat, and Hopeland decides to trade 15 wheat to Faithland.

f) What will be the consumption totals for the two countries?

Basic (Problems 51–55)

51. If the terms of trade for the country of Ono equals 1.1 and the average price of its exports is 13.2, what is the average price of its imports?

52. In Ono the average worker can produce either 10 bags of rice or 5 kilos of asparagus, whereas in Trafalgar the average worker can produce either 6 bags of rice or 4 kilos of asparagus. What is the cost of each product in each country?

53. The following, **Table 9.24**, shows the maximum output levels for Click and Klack.

TABLE 9.24

	Guns		**Butter**
Click	160	or	120
Klack	80	or	200

a) What is the cost of one gun and one unit of butter in Click?

b) What is the cost of one gun and one unit of butter in Klack?

c) In which product does each country have a comparative advantage?
d) What is the range of feasible terms of trade between the two countries?

54. The following table shows the productivity for the countries of Pin and Pang.

	Machines		Bread
Pin	4	or	3
Pang	3	or	8

a) If the working populations of Pin and Pang are both 6 million, divided equally between the two industries in each country, how many machines and bread are currently being produced in Pin and Pang?
b) If the two countries decide to specialize, in which product does each country have a comparative advantage?
c) If the two countries were to totally specialize, what would be the resulting combined totals?
d) What are the gains from trade?

55. Table 9.25 shows the production possibilities for Concordia and Harmonia.

TABLE 9.25

CONCORDIA'S PRODUCTION POSSIBILITIES

Product	A	B	C	D	E
Pork	4	3	2	1	0
Beans	0	5	10	15	20

HARMONIA'S PRODUCTION POSSIBILITIES

Product	A	B	C	D	E
Pork	8	6	4	2	0
Beans	0	6	12	18	24

Suppose that, before trading, Concordia experienced a doubling of productivity in the pork industry.
a) What are the costs of the two products in each country?
b) Which product should each country specialize in and export?
c) If, prior to specialization and trade, Concordia produced (the new) combination D and Harmonia produced combination B, what would be the total gains from trade for the two countries?
d) What is the range of feasible terms of trade between the two countries?

Intermediate (Problems 56–60)

56. The graph in Figure 9.12 shows the domestic demand and supply of apples in Canada.

FIGURE 9.12

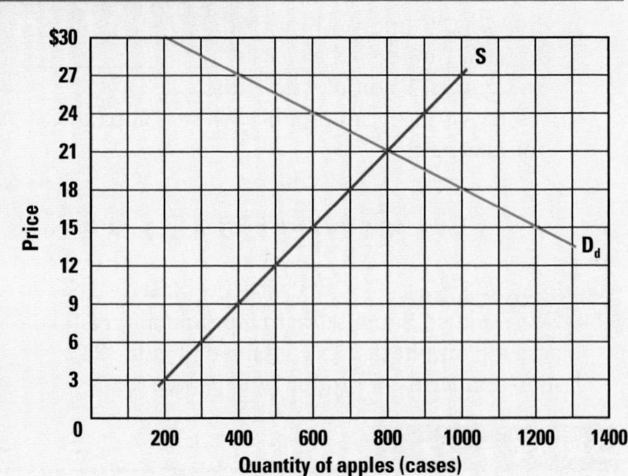

The world price is $15 per case and Canada is open to free trade.
a) How many cases will Canada import from abroad?

Suppose the government wishes to reduce imports by 300 cases per period.
b) What import quota should it impose, and what will be the effect on the price?
c) Alternatively, what tariff should the government impose, and what will be the total revenue from the tariff?

57. Table 9.26 shows the (hypothetical) annual demand and supply of cellular phones in Canada (in tens of thousands annually), where D is the quantity demanded by Canadian consumers, S_C is the quantity supplied by Canadian manufacturers, and S_J is the quantity supplied to the Canadian market by Japanese manufacturers.

TABLE 9.26

Price	D	S_C	S_J
$40	28	4	0
80	26	6	2
120	24	8	4
160	22	10	6
200	20	12	8
240	18	14	10
280	16	16	12
320	14	18	14

a) Add a final column showing the total quantity supplied in the Canadian market, labelled S_T.

b) If Japanese imports were totally banned, what would be the price and quantity of cellular phones in Canada?

c) If Canada was open to Japanese imports, what would be the price and quantity of cellular phones in Canada as a result?

d) Suppose that the Canadian government were to impose a quota on Japanese imports limiting them to 4 (tens of thousands) per year. What would be the price and quantity of cellular phones in Canada then?

e) To produce the same result as in d), alternatively, what amount of tariff would the Canadian government have to impose on Japanese imports?

58. Table 9.27 shows the production possibilities for Atlas and Globe. Prior to specialization and trade, Atlas is producing combination C, and Globe is producing combination B.

TABLE 9.27

ATLAS'S PRODUCTION POSSIBILITIES

Product	A	B	C	D	E	F
Cameras	25	20	15	10	5	0
Soybeans	0	4	8	12	16	20

GLOBE'S PRODUCTION POSSIBILITIES

Product	A	B	C	D	E	F
Cameras	20	16	12	8	4	0
Soybeans	0	5	10	15	20	25

a) On the graph (Figure 9.13), draw the production possibilities curve for each country and indicate the present output position of each.

b) Suppose that the two countries specialize in trade on the basis of 1 camera = 2 unit of beans. Draw the corresponding trading possibilities curves.

FIGURE 9.13

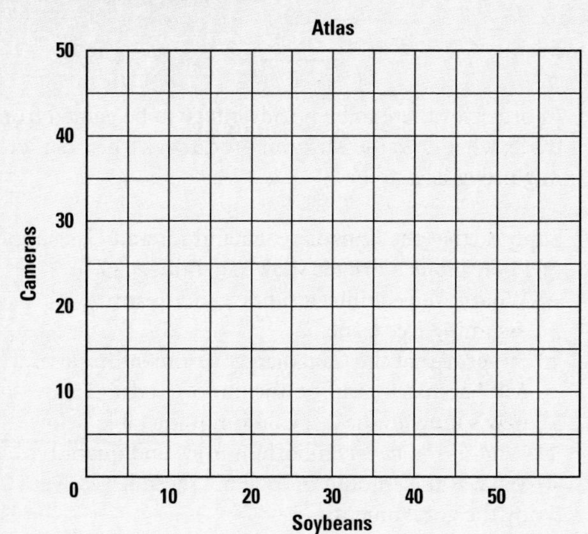

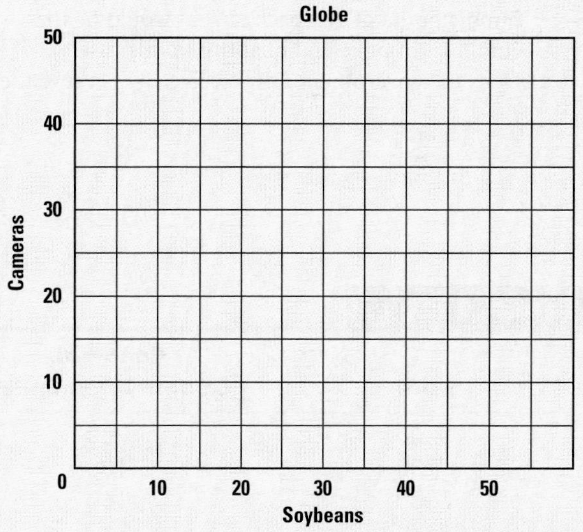

59. The following incomplete table (**Table 9.28**) shows the productivity levels of producing ginseng and corn in Canada and Mexico.

TABLE 9.28

	PRODUCTION PER WORKER	
	Ginseng	**Corn**
Canada	20	6
Mexico	_______	1.5

In order for there to be no advantage to be gained from trade, what does the Mexican productivity per worker in ginseng have to be?

60. Suppose that the Canadian demand for and U.S. supply of a new biotech drug is shown in **Table 9.29**.

a) What is the equilibrium price and quantity, assuming free trade?

b) Suppose that the Canadian government imposes a $300 per pack tariff on the imported drug. Show the new supply in the last column in the table below.

c) What is the new equilibrium price and quantity?

d) What is the amount of total tax revenue received by the government?

e) Assume, instead, that the government imposes an import quota of 100 packs. What would be the equilibrium price and quantity in this case?

f) Does the government now receive any tax revenue?

Advanced (Problems 61–64)

61. Germania has a labour force of 20 thousand, one quarter of whom work in the milk industry, while the remainder are employed in the production of widgets. Labour productivity in the milk industry is 100 litres per worker per year and in the widget industry it is 20 widgets per worker per year. Germania has discovered that the international terms of trade are 1 litre of milk for 0.8 widgets. It is happy with its current consumption of milk, but would like to obtain more widgets.

a) In what product should Germania specialize?

b) What would be Germania's gains from trade?

c) Draw Germania's production and trading possibilities curve and indicate its consumption levels before and after trade.

62. Suppose three countries have the productivity data shown in **Table 9.30**.

TABLE 9.30

	PRODUCTIVITY PER WORKER	
	Grain	**Beans**
Bravo	2	3
Charlie	3	3
Delta	2	1

a) Which country can produce grain the cheapest?

b) Suppose that the international terms of trade were 1 grain to 0.75 beans. Which countries would export grain? Which country would import grain?

c) Suppose, instead, that the international terms of trade were 1 grain to 1.75 beans. Which countries would export grain? Which country would import grain?

TABLE 9.29

Price	Canadian Quantity Demanded	U.S. Quantity Supplied (before tariff)	Quantity Supplied (after tariff)
$800	200	80	_______
900	180	90	_______
1000	160	100	_______
1100	140	110	_______
1200	120	120	_______
1300	100	130	_______
1400	80	140	_______

63. If Third World countries are unable to compete in world markets, why are so many North American corporations locating plants in these countries?

64. To what extent are the conclusions of the theory of comparative advantage affected if unit costs increase, rather than remaining constant, as output increases?

Web-Based Activities

1. Is free trade a good idea? Here are two views to help you answer this question: go to **www.cato.org** and then type "free trade" into the search box and open "Peace on Earth, Free Trade for Men." Next, go to **www.stopftaa.org** for quite a different view.

2. Go to **www.tradecompass.com** and enter "softwood lumber" into the search box. Then read the latest articles on the possible renewal (or not) of the softwood lumber agreement between Canada and the United States. Do you think that this issue is an example of the broad consumer gain versus small special interest loss that was discussed in this chapter?

CHAPTER TEN

Exchange Rates and the Balance of Payments

LEARNING OBJECTIVES

This chapter will enable you to:

LO1 **Calculate the value of the Canadian dollar in terms of other currencies.**

LO2 **Identify who wants to buy and sell Canadian dollars and why.**

LO3 **Explain why the value of the Canadian dollar fluctuates.**

LO4 **Compare flexible and fixed exchange rate systems.**

LO5 **Construct a balance sheet of international payments.**

LO6 **Understand what a balance of payments surplus and deficit means.**

What's ahead...

This chapter begins by giving a definition of the exchange rate and explains the meaning of an appreciation or depreciation in exchange rates. We then examine the causes of such changes and look at the different effects under a flexible exchange-rate system and under a fixed exchange-rate system. We see how each system interacts differently with the domestic economy. Finally, we explain exactly how international transactions are recorded in a country's balance of payments.

A QUESTION OF RELEVANCE...

Have you ever travelled abroad? If so, wasn't part of the excitement of a new country finding and purchasing goods and services that were really "cheap" by Canadian standards? Did you try to spend Canadian dollars? Did you have difficulty in calculating the exchange rate? Did this exchange rate change while you were in the foreign country? What caused it to change? On the other hand, didn't you find some things that were really "out of line" in terms of the prices that you are used to? So why are there such differences in prices around the world? This chapter will help clear up questions like these.

Suppose that a resident of Alberta buys a product that was made in Quebec. This involves an economic exchange that we all understand. The product is moved west and the money payment flows east, and that is that. But now suppose that the same Alberta resident buys a product that was made in Japan. How is this exchange any different? In one sense there is no difference, in that the product goes one way and the payment the other. But in another sense it is different—here, two currencies are involved. The Alberta resident will want to pay in Canadian dollars, and the Japanese seller will want to be paid in yen. This means that an exchange between the two currencies will have to occur as the one currency will be exchanged for the other. This exchange will involve at least one bank. As well, import and export regulations and procedures are also involved. Thus, international trade is more complicated than domestic trade, and the most obvious complication is the exchange rate itself. Let's now go to a discussion of exchange rates.

10.1 Exchange Rates

LO1
Calculate the value of the Canadian dollar in terms of other currencies.

For most people, an exchange rate is an enigma, yet it is nothing more than the comparative value of one currency in terms of another. It is, if you like, the relative price of a currency. Until comparatively recently, it was possible to state the value of a currency in terms of an international medium of exchange: gold. When countries were on the gold standard, each currency could be valued in terms of a comparative amount of gold. Today, however, if you want to know how much a Canadian dollar is worth, the answer can be expressed only in terms of how many American dollars, British pounds, Swiss francs, or some other currency it can buy.

Before we look at the determinants of exchange rates, let's make sure that you are able to easily convert one currency into another. For instance, if the Canadian dollar is worth, let's say, 0.70 American dollars, then how much is an American dollar worth in Canada? The answer is $1.43 (not $1.30). If you're not sure why, then ask yourself, what is the value of an American dollar if a Canadian dollar is worth $0.50 American—$1.50? $2? The answer is $2 Canadian. Both the $0.50 and $2 are **exchange rates**: Canadian for American, and American for Canadian. In general, to convert one currency into another we simply take the reciprocal:

exchange rate: the rate at which one currency is exchanged for another.

$$1 \text{ Canadian dollar} = \frac{1}{1 \text{ unit of foreign currency}} \qquad [10.1]$$

or

$$1 \text{ unit of foreign currency} = \frac{1}{1 \text{ Canadian dollar}} \qquad [10.2]$$

If a Canadian dollar is worth 5 Mexican pesos, then 1 Mexican peso is worth 1/5, or $0.20 Canadian. If a Canadian dollar is worth 0.50 British pounds, then a British pound would be worth 1/0.50, or $2 Canadian. And if the Canadian dollar is worth 0.70 American dollars, then an American dollar is worth 1/0.70, or 1.43 Canadian dollars.

CP/Jeff McIntosh

Most banks and exchange bureaus post the exchange rates on display boards so that they are readily accessible to travellers.

SELF-TEST

1. **a)** Assume that a French franc is worth 0.20 Canadian dollars. How much is a Canadian dollar worth in francs?

   b) Assume one Canadian dollar equals 70 Japanese yen. How much is a yen worth in Canadian dollars?

currency appreciation: the rise in the exchange rate of one currency for another.

currency depreciation: the fall in the exchange rate of one currency for another.

Exchange rates fluctuate, sometimes rising and sometimes falling. Such an increase or decrease is always in terms of another currency. For example, assume that instead of 1 British pound equalling $2 Canadian, it now equals $4 Canadian. How much is the Canadian dollar worth now? The answer is 0.25 pounds. In other words, when one currency **appreciates** in terms of another, the other currency automatically **depreciates** in value. This is not a case of cause and effect; it's simply true by definition.

Another point that's worth making is the fact that just because the Canadian dollar might be depreciating against the American dollar doesn't mean that it is also depreciating against other currencies. In fact, it may well be *appreciating* against the Japanese yen or against the euro.

ADDED DIMENSION

Strong Currencies

The international value of a currency is, unfortunately, regarded by some people (even, at times, by some economists) as an indicator of a country's economic strength and prestige on the international stage. Thus, when the Canadian dollar appreciates in value, it is sometimes described as a "stronger" dollar. Exchange rates are nothing more than the price (in terms of some other currency) of a currency, and how can one possibly talk of strong or weak prices? If this made any sense, we could certainly say that the price of beer is getting much stronger in Canada. Exchange rates appreciate and depreciate. They do not get stronger or weaker.

flexible exchange rate: a currency exchange rate determined by the market forces of supply and demand and not interfered with by government action.

fixed exchange rate: a currency exchange rate pegged by government and therefore prevented from rising or falling.

purchasing power parity theory: a theory suggesting that exchange rates will change so as to equate the purchasing power of each currency.

Two of the questions we need to answer in this chapter are: what determines the value of any given currency, and what are the causes of changes in this value? The exchange rate is simply the relative price of a currency, and that price may be determined by either the interaction of demand and supply in the marketplace, or it may be determined by government decree. In the first case, we are looking at **flexible** (or floating) **exchange rates**; in the second, at **fixed** (or pegged) **exchange rates**. We will look at each in turn.

Before we get into a detailed analysis of currency value determination, we should mention an old economic theory known as the **purchasing power parity theory** of exchange rates. This theory suggests that in the long run, exchange rates will adjust so as to equate the purchasing power of each country's currency. This means, for instance, that a pint of beer should have the same price in every country. (You will have to use a different currency in each, of course.) It also means that a thousand Canadian dollars should have the same spending power in Canada as the equivalent number of French francs in France, or Japanese yen in Japan.

On the surface, this seems difficult to accept. Most international jetsetters (and anybody who shops south of the border) realize that commodities in some countries are relatively cheap for Canadians and one can have a reasonably good time for very little (in parts of Africa and Asia, and in most Latin American countries, for example), whereas commodities in other countries are prohibitively expensive for the average Canadian (such as Japan, the Scandinavian countries, and Switzerland). So why on earth would anyone suggest that, over time, the cost of living in various countries should become comparable?

In answering this question, we'll work through a model in which we assume that transport costs are negligible and that each country produces products that are identical to those from other countries. For instance, suppose that France produces and sells coal at 1000 French francs a tonne; Canada also produces and sells coal for $200 a tonne. Further, suppose that the exchange rate is $1 Canadian = 5 French francs. The price of coal, therefore, is the same in both countries. Now, what would happen if the price of coal in Canada were to rise to $250 a tonne? If the exchange rate remained the same, everybody would buy their coal in France. But of course, the exchange rate would not remain the same. People would be demanding French francs in order to buy French coal. The French franc would appreciate (as would, in all likelihood, the price of French coal). But how much would it appreciate? Well, as long as there was a difference in prices, it would pay some enterprising company to buy coal in France, where it is cheap, and sell it in Canada, where it is expensive.

Assuming that the price of coal in France remains at 1000 francs a tonne, then the French franc will appreciate until the prices in Canada and France are the same; that is, until $250 is equal to 1000 francs. In other words, the French franc will appreciate until 1 Canadian dollar is worth only 4 francs instead of 5 francs.

Once again, the purchasing power parity theory says that if the same product is sold at different prices in different countries, it would be worthwhile buying it where it is cheap and selling it where it is expensive. But this action, by itself, will cause the exchange rates to adjust until there is no longer any difference in the relative prices.

Yet, prices are not the same worldwide—why? First, if the price of a haircut in Edmonton is only half the price of a haircut in New Orleans, we would not really expect a mass exodus of Edmontonians heading down to Louisiana to get their locks shorn. In other words, certain goods and services are not transportable, and therefore differences in the prices of these things may well persist over time between countries. Second, if transport and other shipping costs are taken into account, price differences might continue. Third, tariffs and quotas limit the quantity and increase the costs of trade and lead to price differences between countries. Fourth, products are not identical. Some people do prefer, say, Japanese cars over North American cars. Fifth, and finally, exchange rates don't equate the purchasing power among countries because they are also greatly affected by the international sale and purchase of financial assets. Sometimes there is a strong demand by foreigners for Canadian stocks and bonds. At other times, Canadians may have a strong demand for foreign stocks and bonds. The five factors that explain differences in purchasing power between countries are:

- the fact that many services, such as haircuts, are not traded internationally
- the existence of transportation and insurance costs
- the existence of tariffs and other trade restrictions
- the expression of particular preferences by consumers
- the effect on the value of currencies of trade in financial assets

Despite all these reservations, many economists still hold, however, that in the long run there is a tendency for exchange rates to move toward equalizing the purchasing power of currencies. Whether or not this is true, we still need to explain day-to-day and year-to-year fluctuations in exchange rates.

10.2 Flexible Exchange Rates and the Demand for the Canadian Dollar

LO2
Identify who wants to buy and sell Canadian dollars and why.

In the absence of government involvement, exchange rates are determined by the interplay of demand and supply in a free market. However, even when governments don't actually peg exchange rates, they still often feel it necessary to intervene in international exchange markets so as to influence the value of currencies. They become, therefore, active players in the game of buying and selling currencies. For the time being, however, we will ignore such involvement and concentrate on the determination of exchange rates entirely by market forces.

Apart from Canadians, who else wants to obtain Canadian dollars? The first and most obvious group are foreigners who want to obtain Canadian goods and services. The demand for Canadian exports, such as forest products and automobiles, therefore creates a demand for the Canadian dollar. Note, however, that some services can only be enjoyed in Canada. We are thinking here of restaurant, hotel, and other tourist services required by foreigners travelling in Canada. Tourism in Canada, therefore, represents a (significant) Canadian export. Conversely, spending by Canadians on imported goods or by travel abroad represents a Canadian import.

direct investment: the purchase of real assets.

portfolio investment: the purchase of shares or bonds representing less than 50 percent ownership.

A second demand for the Canadian dollar involves foreigners who want to purchase Canadian investments. These investments might include the purchase of Canadian real estate or real assets, which we call **direct investment**, or it might include the purchase by foreigners of Canadian shares or bonds, which we call **portfolio investment**. In either case, a demand for the Canadian dollar with which to purchase these investments is created. The level of portfolio investment in Canada by foreigners is partly driven by the interest rate paid on savings in Canada relative to that paid elsewhere. If Canadian bonds are paying an average of 6 percent while similar bonds in the U.S. are paying only 4.5 percent, then portfolio investment into Canada, and the demand for Canadian dollars, will be strong.

This brings us to the third group of people who demand Canadian dollars: Canadians who receive income, gifts, or transfers from abroad. This includes, for instance, people who have previously bought foreign investments. These people will be earning returns on these investments, which will be paid to them in foreign currencies. As Canadians, of course, they do not have much use for foreign currencies, and they will want to convert these currencies into Canadian dollars.

CP/Chuck Stoody

Railway trains carrying grain for export are constantly on the move at the United Grain Growers elevator in Vancouver.

A fourth group who want to buy Canadian dollars are speculators. Speculators who deal in foreign exchange are no different from other types of speculators. They hope to buy when the price is low and sell later when the price is high. Speculators buying Canadian dollars are therefore hoping for an appreciation of the Canadian dollar relative to foreign currencies some time in the future, when they will then sell. The level of currency speculation depends a great deal on the expectations that people hold towards the currency. If people expect the Canadian exchange rate to fall, then speculators will "sell the Canadian dollar short." This action will have the effect of pushing the actual value of the dollar down and thus fulfilling people's expectations.

There is another group of currency dealers who also buy and sell Canadian dollars, but for a different reason. They buy Canadian dollars (or any other currency) whenever they see a difference in quoted exchange rates on different international exchanges. For instance, let's say that the Canadian dollar is quoted at $0.715 U.S. on the Zurich exchange, but is being quoted at $0.718 on the Tokyo exchange. Then it would pay someone to buy Canadian dollars in Switzerland (where they are cheap) and sell them in Japan (where they are relatively more expensive). This is known as **arbitrage**. Notice that, unlike speculators, those engaged in arbitrage are not concerned with the future value of the Canadian dollar and are not holding them to sell at some later date; they are selling immediately.

arbitrage: the process of buying a commodity in one market, where the price is low, and immediately selling it in a second market where the price is higher.

To sum up, those who have a demand for the Canadian dollar are:

- foreigners who want to buy Canadian exports or who travel in Canada
- foreigners who want to purchase Canadian investments
- Canadians who receive income or gifts or transfers from abroad
- currency speculators

Finally, as noted above, governments also sometimes buy and sell currencies, but more on this later.

Now, remember what we mean by the demand for a currency. It's no different from the demand for any other product or service; that is, it is defined as the quantities that people are willing and able to buy at various prices in the foreign exchange market. As you would expect, the demand curve for the Canadian dollar is downward-sloping, as shown in **Figure 10.1**.

FIGURE 10.1 **The Demand for the Canadian Dollar**

The demand curve for the Canadian dollar is downward-sloping, reflecting the inverse relationship between the price of the currency and the quantity demanded. At P_1 the quantity demanded is Q_1.

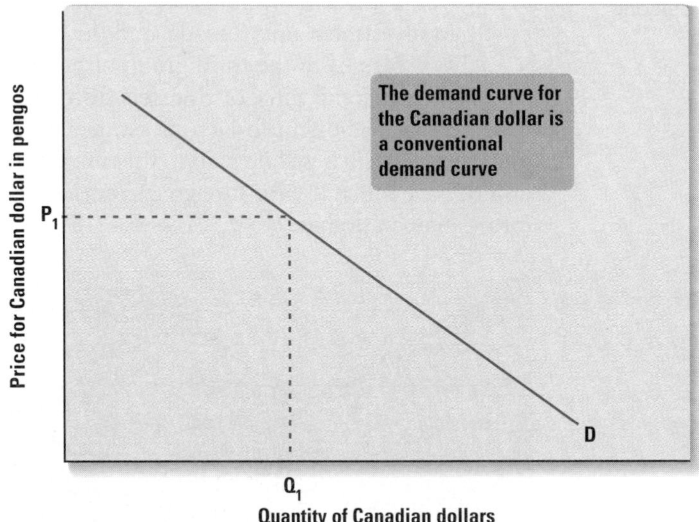

Note that on the vertical axis we need to express the price of the Canadian dollar in terms of another currency since, if you think about it, it would be a bit silly to express the price of the Canadian dollar in Canadian dollars, because then it would always equal one.

A Canadian dollar is always worth one dollar in Canada. It always was and always will be.

Whatever currency you choose to express it in, other than the Canadian dollar, is of no importance. On our graph, we have used the pengo, the currency of the mythical and fascinating country of Pengoland. The demand curve is of course downward-sloping, which implies that at a higher exchange rate the quantity of Canadian dollars demanded will be low; at a low exchange rate, the quantity demanded will be high. Now let's figure out why that should be so. Remember that the demand for the Canadian dollar comes, by and large, from foreigners buying our goods, services, and investments, that is, from Canadian exports in the broad sense.

Let's start off by assuming that the Canadian dollar is worth 1 pengo and that one of our major exports to Pengoland is smoked salmon, which is priced at $100 a box in Canada and therefore sells for 100 pengos in Pengoland. Now, what would happen if the value of the Canadian dollar were to appreciate so that $1 Canadian is now equal to 2 pengos? (Note that as the Canadian dollar appreciates, the pengo depreciates; it is now worth only 50 cents). The effect of such an appreciation is summarized in **Table 10.1**.

TABLE 10.1

Price of One Canadian Dollar	Price in Canada of a Box of Salmon	Price in Pengoland of a Box of Salmon
1 pengo	$100	100 pengos
2 pengos	$100	200 pengos

ADDED DIMENSION

The Effective Exchange Rate

There is no single commodity whose value remains constant and against which all currencies can be measured. This means the Canadian dollar might well be *depreciating* against one currency, such as the U.S. dollar, but at the same time *appreciating* against all other currencies. It is possible, however, to work out an average of what is happening to the Canadian dollar. This is what is referred to as the effective exchange rate. The effective exchange rate compares the value of the Canadian dollar in terms of the average value of the currencies of all the countries with which Canada trades. It is a weighted average, which means that the value of the U.S. dollar, for instance, would carry more weight than, say, the Swiss franc in calculating its value, since Canada does much more trade with the United States than it does with Switzerland. The effective exchange rate is also based on an index value of 100, assigned in the base year. Following are figures for the effective Canadian exchange rate for the last several years.

1992	100
1995	86.82
1996	88.21
1997	88.07
1998	82.70
1999	84.14
2000	82.85
2001	80.23

Source: Bank of Canada, *Quarterly Review*, Spring 2002.

Despite the fact that the price of smoked salmon in Canada remains unchanged, its effective price has increased as far as the Pengolians are concerned. Whereas before they paid 100 pengos, now they will have to pay 200 pengos for the same box. One would expect therefore that they would buy less smoked salmon. In other words, when the Canadian dollar appreciates, the effective price of Canadian exports increases, and total exports are likely to decline.

You can see why, therefore, a high Canadian dollar is likely to be unpopular among Canadian exporters and in the high-export provinces of Canada. For example, even a small increase in the Canadian dollar can have big implications in terms of sales, profits, and employment in the B.C. lumber industry, and is looked on with alarm. Not only that, but a higher Canadian dollar means that the effective price of Canadian financial investments will also be higher for foreigners, so that foreign investment is likely to decrease.

The depreciation of the Canadian dollar, on the other hand, has the opposite effect. Assume, for instance that, starting from $1 Canadian = 1 pengo, the Canadian dollar were to fall to $1 Canadian = 0.5 pengo. (The pengo now equals $2 Canadian; that is, it has appreciated). The same box of Canadian smoked salmon that used to cost the Pengolians 100 pengos can now be obtained for a mere 50 pengos. This will then cause exports of smoked salmon to increase. In general, therefore, when the Canadian dollar depreciates, the effective price of Canadian exports decreases, and total exports are likely to increase. Exporters will prefer a low Canadian dollar to a high Canadian dollar, since this makes Canadian products more competitive abroad.

We can summarize these results as follows:

When the Canadian dollar depreciates, the effective price of Canadian exports decreases and total exports are likely to rise.

and

When the Canadian dollar appreciates, the effective price of Canadian exports increases and total exports are likely to fall.

SELF-TEST

2. Given the events described below, indicate whether the demand for the Canadian dollar would appreciate, depreciate, or not change:

a) Canadian exports rise.

b) Toronto hosts the World Expo 2004.

c) IBM, ITT, and the provincial government announce the construction of a $2 billion data processing and informational transfer complex in Halifax.

d) Migration from the Maritime provinces to Ontario increases appreciably.

10.3 The Supply of Canadian Dollars

LO3
Explain why the value of the Canadian dollar fluctuates.

Let's now take a look at the other side of the coin, the supply of Canadian dollars on the foreign exchange market, and examine who exactly provides this supply. Most people would probably answer: the government or the Bank of Canada. Well, under certain circumstances that may be true, as we shall see later. However, in a free market system it's not really necessary for these institutions to supply Canadian dollars to foreigners, since through trade, dollars will be made available automatically on the world's money market. How does this come about? It is from the simple fact that if we Canadians wish to purchase foreign currencies, then we will use Canadian dollars to make these purchases. Thus, in obtaining foreign currencies, we must automatically supply Canadian dollars. In general, therefore, the supply of Canadian dollars comes from our demand for foreign currencies. This relationship between the supply of and demand for currencies is important enough to emphasize:

Quantity demanded of foreign currencies = Quantity supplied of Canadian dollars
Quantity demanded of Canadian dollars = Quantity supplied of foreign currencies

The supply of Canadian dollars is graphed in **Figure 10.2**.

FIGURE 10.2 **The Supply of the Canadian Dollar**

The supply of the Canadian dollar is upward-sloping, reflecting the direct relationship between the price of the currency and the quantity supplied. At price P_1 the quantity supplied is Q_1.

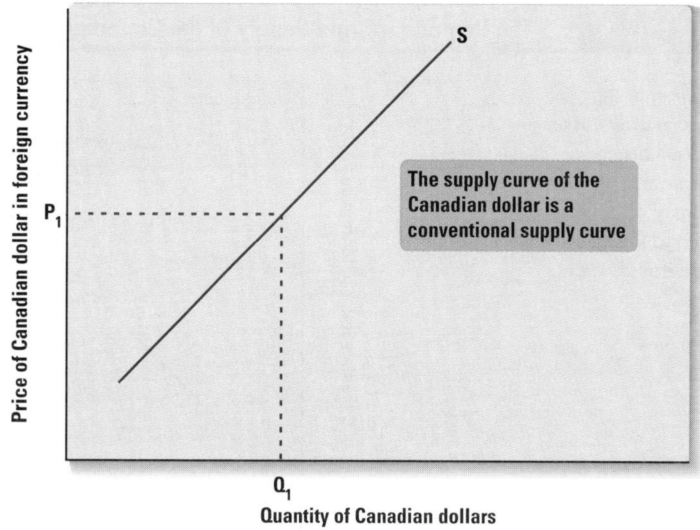

Why is the supply curve upward-sloping? It is for the usual reason, that an increase in the price (of a currency) will lead to an increase in the quantity supplied. Or, put another way, an appreciation of the Canadian dollar will lead to an increase in imports. Let's make sure that we understand this. Suppose that a Japanese car carries a price tag of 1 400 000 yen and that the exchange rate between the yen and the Canadian dollar is 80 yen for one Canadian dollar. A Canadian auto dealer would then sell this auto for $18 000 (1 400 000/80). (For simplicity, we are ignoring the dealer's mark-up, tariffs, transport costs, insurance, and so on.) Now, assume that the Canadian dollar appreciates so that one Canadian dollar buys 100 yen. Then, the auto dealer would likely set the price at $14 400 since he would sell more units of this auto at $14 400 rather than at $18 000. This increase in imports will increase the quantity of Canadian dollars supplied on the world market. We can summarize these results, as follows:

When the Canadian dollar appreciates, the effective price of Canadian imports decreases and total imports are likely to rise.

Conversely,

When the Canadian dollar depreciates, the effective price of Canadian imports increases and total imports are likely to fall.

From a Canadian importer's point of view, a high Canadian dollar is much preferred. This is also true from the average consumer's point of view: a high Canadian dollar makes foreign products much cheaper, and as a result one would expect more cross-border shopping by Canadians.

10.4 Equilibrium in Foreign-Exchange Markets

We now need to put together the supply and demand curves to obtain an equilibrium exchange rate, as is done in Figure 10.3.

FIGURE 10.3 The Demand for and Supply of the Canadian Dollar

The intersection of the demand and supply curves yields the equilibrium exchange rate: ER_1. At ER_1 the quantity of dollars demanded and the quantity supplied are equal.

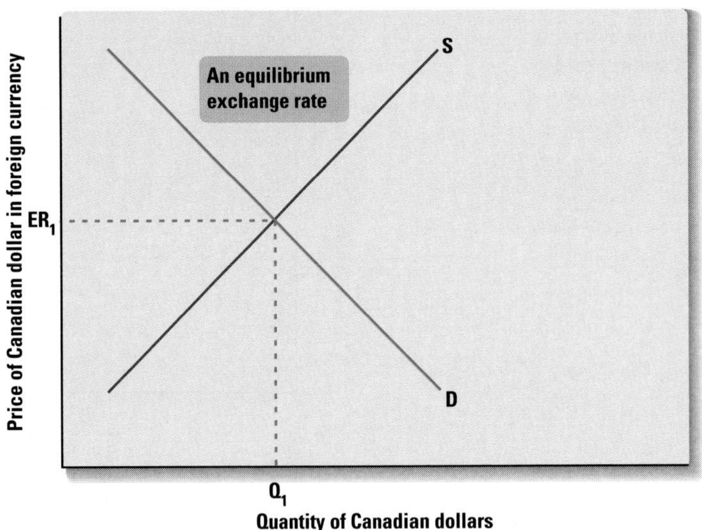

Note that at the equilibrium exchange rate, ER_1, the quantity demanded for the Canadian dollar is equal to the quantity supplied. The demand comes from foreigners (Canadian exports) and the supply comes from Canadians (Canadian imports). Can foreigners always get their hands on sufficient Canadian dollars to purchase Canadian goods? Certainly. It does not require any assistance from the Canadian government or from the Bank of Canada. With truly flexible exchange rates, sufficient Canadian dollars are made available by Canadians themselves, who automatically supply dollars when purchasing foreign currencies. Note also that at equilibrium, not only is the quantity supplied and the quantity demanded of Canadian dollars equal, but the quantities demanded and supplied of foreign currencies in Canada will also be equal. Remember that foreign currencies are made available to Canadians whenever a foreigner purchases Canadian products or investments, and at equilibrium such foreign currencies will just be sufficient to satisfy the demand by Canadians for these currencies.

ADDED DIMENSION

Real Exchange Rates

How would you feel about emigrating to the fictitious country of Albioni, where the average monthly salary is 20 000 albions? Before you could decide, you would probably want to know, among many other things, what 20 000 albions are worth. Suppose that you learned that 1 Albion equalled 1 Canadian dollar, would that help you decide? If you still cannot make up your mind, perhaps some more data would be helpful. An average meal in Albioni will cost you 200 albions per person, a pair of socks cost 20 albions, and a new car will cost you 200 000 albions. Now, a rational decision is easier to make. In other words, in order to compare the values of currencies we need to know not only the exchange rate but *also* the average price level in each country. This is what the real exchange rate measures. In terms of a formula, it is:

$$\text{real exchange rate} = \frac{\text{price level in Canada}}{\text{price level in other country}} \times \text{nominal exchange rate}$$

The nominal exchange rate is simply the value of the Canadian dollar, in the sense that we have been talking about throughout this chapter. As an example, suppose that a brand-new Toyota costs 1 400 000 yen in Japan and that an equivalent Ford car in Canada costs $20 000. If the exchange rate was equal to 70 yen per Canadian dollar, then you can see that the two cars have equivalent value, for example:

$$\text{real exchange rate} = \frac{20\ 000}{1\ 400\ 000} \times 70 = 1$$

The real exchange rate, therefore, measures the comparative purchasing power of a currency. The formula tells you, for instance, that the value of Canada's real exchange rate will increase if either the nominal exchange rate or the Canadian price level increases or if the Japanese price level falls. Now suppose that the price of a new Ford dropped to $15 000. The value of the real exchange rate would change to:

$$\text{real exchange rate} = \frac{15\ 000}{1\ 400\ 000} \times 70 = 0.75$$

In other words, a Canadian Ford owner is now poorer than a Japanese Toyota owner, since, if he sold his car and converted it into yen (obtaining 15 000 × 70 or 1 050 000 yen), he could only afford to buy 3/4 of a Toyota. The Toyota owner, on the other hand, could now buy 4/3 Fords. Given this, you can imagine that Japanese buyers will be flocking to buy Canadian Fords, which have become a real bargain. The result of this increased demand (for both Fords and for the Canadian dollar) is that both of them will increase. Can you figure out how far they will increase? The answer is, when the real exchange rate is again equal to 1. This is the reason why economists suggest that there is a long-run tendency for the purchasing power of all currencies to move toward par.

SELF-TEST

3. Imagine a flexible exchange rate that was temporarily above the equilibrium rate.

a) Would there be a surplus or a shortage of this currency?

b) As market forces push the exchange rate toward equilibrium, would the quantity demanded for the currency rise or fall? What about the quantity supplied?

REVIEW

1. Define *exchange rate.*
2. Contrast a *flexible exchange rate* with a *fixed exchange rate.*
3. What is the *purchasing power parity theory*?
4. Define *direct investment.* How does it differ from *portfolio investment*?
5. What is *arbitrage*?
6. Who supplies Canadian dollars on foreign exchange markets?
7. What happens to the effective price of Canadian products as the Canadian dollar appreciates? What happens to the volume of Canadian exports?
8. What happens to the effective price of Canadian imports as the Canadian dollar depreciates? What happens to the volume of Canadian imports?

10.5 Changes in Demand and Supply

Since the value of a currency is determined by the interplay of supply and demand, it follows that any change in supply or demand will change its value. We now focus on what could cause a change in demand or supply and how such a change will affect a currency's value. Let's start on the demand side. What could cause people to demand more Canadian dollars, even though there has been no change in the currency's value? Well, the first and most straightforward reason would be a rise in incomes in the countries that buy Canadian goods. It seems reasonable to suggest that if *foreign incomes* increase, then the demand for all available products, including Canadian ones, will increase. Let's trace through the effects on **Figure 10.4**.

The initial demand curve is D_1. The increase in foreign income and the resulting increase in the demand for Canadian exports will increase the demand for Canadian dollars. This is illustrated by the shift in the demand curve to D_2. The increase in demand creates a shortage of Canadian dollars, which results in the exchange rate rising from ER_1 to ER_2. At this higher exchange rate, we obtain a new equilibrium. This higher exchange rate means that the attractiveness of Canadian exports is reduced because they are effectively more expensive. However, the volume of trade has still increased, *despite* the higher Canadian dollar. Note that imports and exports have increased. Why have imports increased? Remember that the higher exchange rate, ER_2, makes imports cheaper and therefore more are bought. In other words, an increase in the demand for Canadian goods and services will increase Canadian exports, even though it has caused the Canadian dollar to appreciate. The amount of Canadian imports has also increased, but this is because of the appreciation.

FIGURE 10.4 **An Increase in the Demand for a Currency**

A rightward shift in the demand for the Canadian dollar will cause the equilibrium exchange rate to rise from ER_1 to ER_2 and the equilibrium quantity to increase from Q_1 to Q_2.

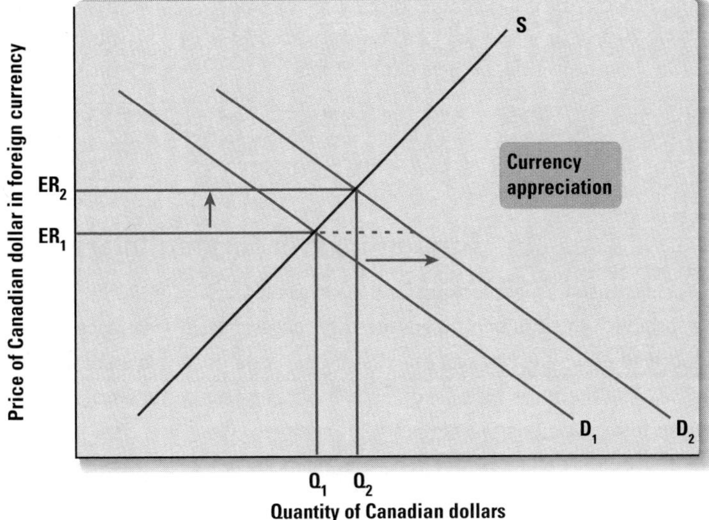

Perhaps a small reminder is in order: the level of Canadian exports is independent of Canadian income; it is determined by the level of foreign income. On the other hand, the level of Canadian imports definitely does depend on the level of our income: the greater our income, the more we import.

Other things besides an increase in foreign income will cause a change in the demand for Canadian dollars. For example, the *price of Canadian products that are traded abroad* will also have an impact on demand. A decrease in the price of these goods will cause the worldwide demand for such products to increase. It must be added, however, that it's not the absolute level of prices of traded goods that is important, but rather the relative level, compared with that of other countries. An increase in the prices of foreign goods that compete with Canadian exports will have the same effect on the demand for Canadian exports as would the decrease in Canadian prices.

A third factor affecting the demand for a currency is the view foreigners hold toward Canadian goods—in short, *foreigners' tastes*. For example, if tastes shifted away from wood-frame houses towards metal-frame houses, this could well decrease Canada's lumber exports.

A final factor affecting the demand for Canadian dollars is *interest rates*. When foreigners are deciding whether or not to put money into Canada, they will look at a number of factors, but the rate of interest that they can obtain is certainly one of the most important. Traditionally, rates of interest in Canada have been kept above those in the United States for the express reason of encouraging the inflow of American money and to discourage the outflow of Canadian dollars to the United States. Obviously, the higher the rate of interest, the higher the level of foreign currency flow into Canada. This will mean a higher demand for Canadian dollars. As with prices, it's not the absolute level of interest rates that is important, but the difference between Canadian rates and those in other countries. The demand for the Canadian dollar would therefore increase with a drop in interest rates abroad. In summary, the demand for the Canadian dollar is determined by:

- the level of foreign incomes
- the price of Canadian products relative to the price of foreign products
- foreigners' tastes
- comparative interest rates

SELF-TEST

4. Assuming flexible exchange rates, draw a graph that illustrates a decrease in the demand for the Canadian dollar. On the graph, identify the effect of the decreased demand on the exchange rate and the quantity of dollars bought and sold. Next, list four reasons why such a decrease might occur.

ADDED DIMENSION

Foreign Investment and Interest-Rate Parity

The amount of international funds looking for a good (profitable) home is enormous. International investors are constantly seeking opportunities where they can earn the highest returns on their funds. Hundreds of billions of dollars are traded every day in foreign-exchange markets. (In contrast, the demand for Canadian dollars to buy Canadian products is less than $1 billion per day.)

An investor buying foreign financial assets can earn a return from both the interest and from an appreciation in the value of the currency in which it is denominated. For instance, suppose I buy a French bond that has a value of 5000 francs and pays annual interest of 8 percent per annum. If the exchange rate is 5 French francs to the dollar, it will cost me $1000. At the end of the year, I receive 5400 francs. Now suppose that during the year the franc has appreciated to 4.5 francs to the dollar. Converting my francs back into dollars gives me $1200. I have therefore earned $200, or 20 percent on my original $1000. I earned 8 percent in interest and 12 percent from the appreciation of the franc.

This also means that if the currency I hold drops in value, the interest earned is wiped out by the loss on the exchange rate. Foreign investors therefore are concerned not only with interest to be earned but also with what might happen to the value of the foreign currency. This is the reason why there are often big differences in interest rates around the world.

Ask yourself this: if Canadians can earn only 5 percent interest in Canada but can earn 20 percent in Mexico, why wouldn't all the funds flow out of Canada and into Mexico? The answer is that in order to earn that 20 percent per year, you have to convert your dollars into pesos and leave it in pesos for a whole year. But many are fearful that during the year the value of the peso might fall against the dollar. How much does the average investor think it will fall? Presumably by 15 percent. Why this amount? Because they will earn a certain 20 percent on their funds but expect to lose 15 percent on the depreciation of the peso, netting them 5 percent—the same amount they can earn in Canada. In other words, if you take into consideration both the interest earned and the gain or loss on the foreign currency, the rate of return you can earn is more or less equal around the world. This is often referred to as *interest-rate parity*, though perhaps it would be better to refer to it as rate of return parity.

We now need to recognize that any change in the demand for the Canadian dollar will have effects on the domestic economy. If the demand for the Canadian dollar has increased because Canadian exports have increased, aggregate demand will also have increased. Whether this increase in exports is because of higher foreign incomes, lower Canadian prices, or a change in tastes in favour of Canadian goods doesn't matter. The higher exports mean greater aggregate demand. This is illustrated in **Figure 10.5**.

FIGURE 10.5 **The Effect of an Increase of Exports on Aggregate Demand**

An increase in Canadian exports increases aggregate demand, as illustrated by the shift from AD_1 to AD_2. This results in a rise in both the price level and in GDP.

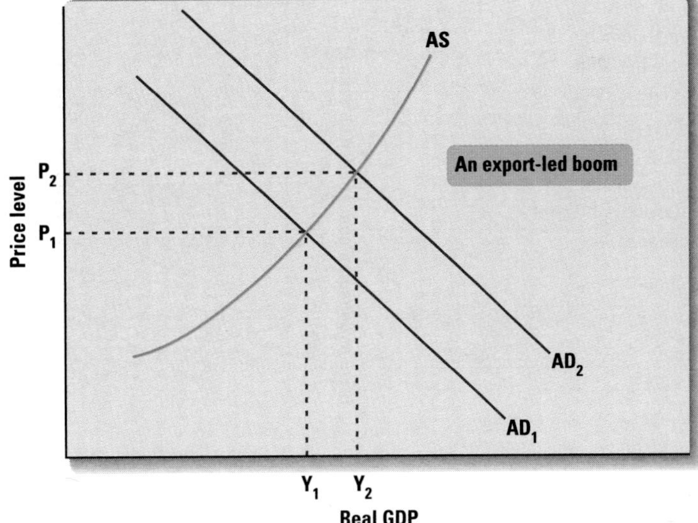

An increase in Canadian exports does indeed raise the value of the dollar (and also imports), but it also raises Canadian GDP (assuming that the increase in exports is greater than the increase in imports, which is almost always the case). This process is often given the name of an export-led boom. Foreigners buy more Canadian goods and this raises aggregate demand within Canada, creating new jobs, raising GDP and, finally, raising the price level.

You should also note that we can see here that this export-led boom may have the effect of reducing the size of the Canadian multiplier. This is because the boom will, as we just mentioned, likely increase the prices of Canadian products and, further, will raise the value of the Canadian exchange rate. Both of these effects will tend to dampen the effect of the initial rise in exports.

A very important point in all this discussion is that the exchange rate does not move in isolation from the domestic economy. What happens on the international market very much affects what happens internally. This fact has always been true, but it is becoming increasingly pertinent as the world's economies become more integrated. We will return to this theme in Chapter 13.

SELF-TEST

5. Assume that the demand for Canadian exports decreases. What would be the effect on:

a) The value of the Canadian dollar?

b) The level of aggregate demand?

c) The level of GDP?

d) The price level?

Let us now work through a situation that affects Canadians' demand for imported goods. Assume that Canada were to remove the tariffs on British products coming into Canada. To the Canadian consumer, this lowers the price of British products; and we would expect the quantity demanded of such goods by Canadians to increase. This means that the Canadian demand for the British pound increases, and this, in turn, implies that Canadians will be supplying more Canadian dollars on the world market. This last point is illustrated in **Figure 10.6**.

FIGURE 10.6 **An Increase in the Supply of Canadian Dollars**

An increase in the supply of Canadian dollars is represented by the shift from S_1 to S_2. As a result of this increase, the value of the Canadian dollar decreases and the quantity of Canadian dollars bought and sold increases.

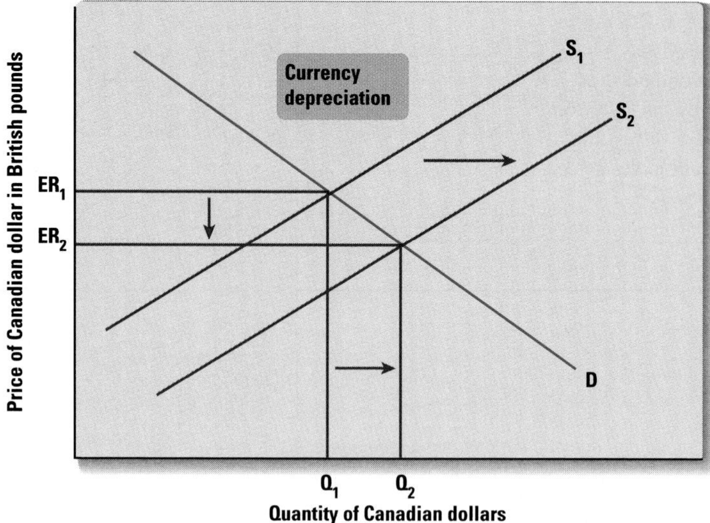

As Canadians demand more imports from the U.K. and thus more pounds, the supply curve of Canadian dollars shifts outward from S_1 to S_2. This will cause the exchange rate to drop to a lower level at ER_2. The removal of tariffs on British imports therefore will tend to lead to a depreciation of the Canadian dollar and, on the other side of the coin, an appreciation of the pound.

In other words, British exports to Canada will increase *despite* the higher pound. In addition, British imports of Canadian products will increase *because* of the higher pound. The total value of trade will therefore increase.

The intellectual appeal of market-determined flexible exchange rates is strong among most economists today. If the supply of, or the demand for, a currency changes for any one of a variety of reasons, the exchange rate itself changes and the economy adjusts automatically without any need for government policy and with a minimum of disruption to the domestic economy. Perhaps the best way to really understand all this is to now move to a discussion of fixed exchange rates and then to compare the two systems.

@-CONOMICS

The Changing Nature of Currency Markets

Between the middle of 1998 and 1999, the Canadian dollar fell from a little over 70 cents U.S. to record lows in the 63 to 66 cent range. The reasons for this were mainly global. First, demand for the U.S. dollar was very strong and this drove up its value while decreasing the value of the loonie. Second, the general price trend for natural resources continued to be down, and Canada is a major resource exporter. Third, Canadian interest rates were, at that time, lower than those in the United States, reflecting the Bank of Canada's attempt to stimulate economic growth and job creation.

What would have been the effect of higher interest rates? For as long as anyone can remember, high interest rates resulted in a country's currency appreciating. For example, in the first half of the 1980s, record-high interest rates in the U.S. attracted billions in foreign currencies and the U.S. dollar soared. While it is true that a country's economic health eventually asserts its influence on a currency, it was believed that in the short term it was interest rates that mattered most.

However, in an article in the February 21, 2000 issue of *BusinessWeek*, it is argued that in the recently termed new economy, equity flows—foreign stock purchases and cross-border merger deals—are becoming increasingly important and this is resulting in a major transformation of foreign-exchange markets. As an example, for over a year the Bank of Japan kept Japan's interest rate near zero to try to revitalize its economy, yet the yen rose in value against the U.S. dollar. Why? During the same period of time, Renault bought 35 percent of Nissan, GE Capital bought heavily into Japanese financial assets, a British company bought a large Japanese telecom company, and portfolio investors from the U.S. and Europe snapped up Japanese shares. The resulting inflow of dollars, pounds, and euros drove up the price of the yen despite Japan's very low interest rate.

10.6 Fixed Exchange Rates

LO4
Compare flexible and fixed exchange rate systems.

Fixed exchange rates have been the rule rather than the exception over the centuries. Up to the early 1970s, most governments throughout the world were persuaded that they needed to exercise control over the value of their own currency and not leave it open to the vagaries of international dealing. At that time, the Canadian dollar was fixed at $U.S. 0.925. Let's look at some of the reasons for this belief.

It is suggested that, by its very nature, international trading is fraught with problems and uncertainties. If, as a Canadian company, you want to trade with a firm in Japan, Germany or any other country, you need to understand the different commercial laws and government regulations, the language and culture, the customs and history, and a host of other factors. What you do not need is the addition of another problem: fluctuating exchange rates. After all, if you have spent a good deal of time and money negotiating a contract with some foreign firm, you do not want to run the risk of seeing all your profit wiped out by an unforeseen shift in exchange rates.

Fixed exchange rates do add a degree of certainty to international trade. Without this security, many feel that the volume of international trade would be considerably less. Remember that, if flexible exchange rates change, both exports and imports are immediately affected. This means that employment and profits in the firms within these sectors can take rather abrupt swings up or down. An appreciation of the exchange rate, for instance, will lead to a decline in exports and an expansion of imports. This will be good news for those firms that do the importing, but it will involve layoffs, the cancellation of contracts, and the postponement of investment plans for export industries. The import industries, on the other hand, will be gearing up for the higher volumes by hiring additional staff, buying new equipment, and expanding capacity. What happens if the exchange rate now starts to depreciate? Everything will be thrown into reverse, with the export industries now booming, but the import industries suffering. Thus, it is argued, flexible exchange rates can lead to a great deal of domestic disruption and make long-term planning very difficult. A corollary of this is the fact that flexible exchange rates can be affected by the actions of a small group of speculators. Why, it is asked, should the fortunes of many firms and the livelihoods of many people be in the hands of a few speculators who are out for private gain and cannot be held accountable for their actions?

Finally, it should be mentioned that in people's minds there is a great deal of national prestige tied up in exchange rates. They are often fixed at rates that do not reflect economic reality. Many people want to feel that their nation has a "strong" currency, despite the fact that, as we have mentioned, appreciating and depreciating currencies are neither good nor bad. Yet, many people in Canada feel that since we have only a "63 cent" dollar, the Canadian dollar is weaker than the American dollar. They do not seem to realize that we are dealing with two different countries and two separate currencies, and there is no reason why, except through coincidence, they should be at par. Hardly anyone would suggest that the Canadian dollar should be at par with the pound sterling or the German mark or the Japanese yen, yet the comparison of the Canadian dollar with the American dollar still persists. In summary, the arguments in favour of fixed exchange rates are that:

- they add a degree of certainty to international trade
- they prevent instability in the export and import industries
- they discourage currency speculation
- they appeal to people who tend to equate the exchange rate with national prestige

These are the arguments for a fixed exchange rate. Let us now delve deeper into how such a system would function. Assume that initially the government of Canada fixed the exchange rate. This means that anyone buying or selling Canadian dollars could only do so at the official rate decreed by the government. Let's begin with the rate fixed at the equilibrium market rate. Suppose that later, however, an increase in the demand for Canadian exports and thus the Canadian dollar occurs. The situation is illustrated in **Figure 10.7**.

FIGURE 10.7 **An Increase in Currency Demand under Fixed Exchange Rates**

An increase in the demand for the Canadian dollar does not lead to an appreciation of the Canadian dollar under a fixed-exchange-rate system. The result, therefore, is a shortage of Canadian dollars on the world market and an undervalued dollar.

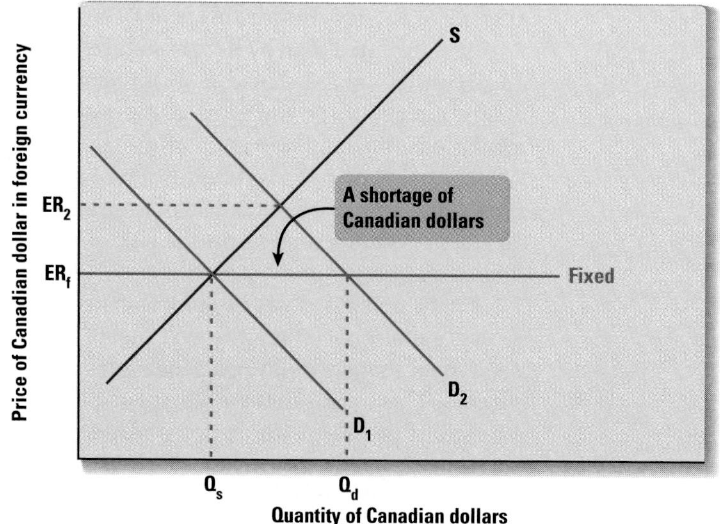

Given a fixed exchange rate, an increase in the demand for the Canadian dollar results in the dollar being undervalued, compared with what a free-market value would be (the market rate ER_2 is above the fixed rate, ER_f, in this case). Foreigners see Canadian goods as very attractive buys. At the fixed rate of ER_f, the quantity demanded (Q_d) of Canadian dollars exceeds the quantity supplied (Q_s). Since the government has fixed the exchange rate, it must ensure, for normal trading to continue, that enough Canadian dollars are made available. In other words, the Bank of Canada will have to supply this shortage by expanding the money supply. This strong demand for Canadian exports and the continual increase in money supply by the Bank of Canada will eventually be inflationary. Once this inflation occurs for a long enough time, the price of Canadian goods will rise, causing the export of these goods to fall. Eventually, this will reduce the demand for Canadian dollars back to equilibrium on curve D_1. However, during this period of adjustment, the economy will experience inflation.

Let's look now at the second scenario, which is in many people's view more serious for an economy and, for that reason, requires us to go into greater detail. Again, suppose that the Canadian government fixes the value of the Canadian dollar at ER_f. This time, however, the demand for the dollar drops, as shown in **Figure 10.8**.

The exchange rate is now above what would be the free-market equilibrium rate (the market rate ER_2 is below the fixed rate, ER_f), and thus there is a surplus of Canadian dollars on the world market. Let's examine what is happening. Before the change in demand, the quantity of dollars foreigners wanted to buy was equal to the quantity supplied of dollars on the foreign exchange market. Then the demand for the dollar dropped. Since foreigners are now buying fewer Canadian goods and services and therefore buying fewer Canadian dollars, the amount of foreign currencies available for Canadians to buy is reduced. Thus, this situation can be seen as either one of a surplus of Canadian dollars on the foreign exchange market or as a shortage of foreign currencies in Canada. Whichever way you look at it, the fixed exchange rate ER_f is overvalued. So, what happens next?

FIGURE 10.8 **A Decrease in Currency Demand under Fixed Exchange Rates**

A decrease in the demand for the Canadian dollar does not lead to a lower Canadian dollar under a fixed-exchange-rate system. The result is a surplus of Canadian dollars on the foreign exchange market and an overvalued dollar.

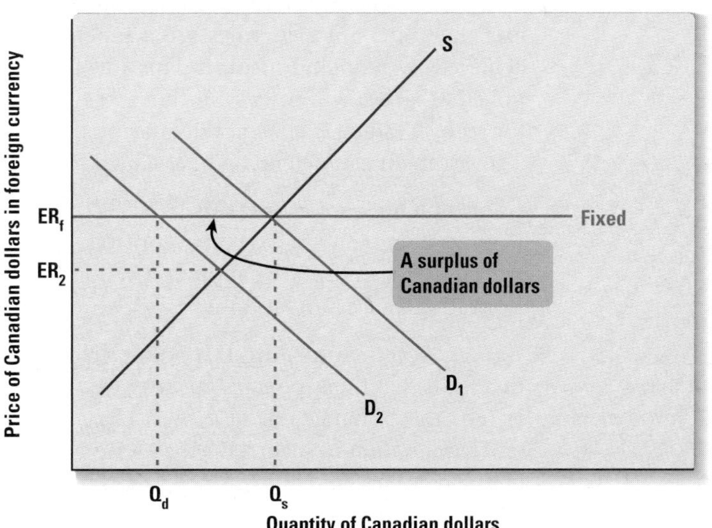

In instituting fixed exchange rates, the government must take responsibility for any surplus or shortage of currencies. Faced with an insufficient supply of foreign currencies from normal trading, the government, through the Bank of Canada, has got to make good the deficiency. One of the major assets of the Bank of Canada, apart from government bonds, is reserves of gold and foreign currencies. (At the end of December, 2001, for instance, these stood at approximately $396 million U.S., of which $392 million was in U.S. dollars.) These official international reserves, or at least as much as necessary, have to be made available to Canadians. So, along with an overvalued fixed exchange rate, as in **Figure 10.8**, comes the depletion of the central bank's foreign reserves. Canada, like all other countries, possesses only a limited amount of gold and foreign currencies. Because of this, the draining of foreign-currency reserves cannot continue indefinitely, and the government will, as a result, be forced to take some kind of action. There are few options open, and none of them are attractive.

subsidy: a payment by government for the purpose of increasing some particular activity or increasing the output of a particular good.

One possible tactic to stem the demand for foreign currencies would be to introduce quotas or tariffs. However, introducing such trade policies to try to reduce the amount of imports would violate international trade agreements and probably result in retaliation against Canadian exports. Direct **subsidies** to increase Canadian exports could, again, be in violation of trade agreements and would be expensive for the government.

A policy of introducing foreign-exchange controls has been used by some governments in the past. Here, instead of directly restricting imports, the government restricts the amount of foreign currencies available to Canadians. In other words, it rations the relatively scarce foreign currencies by saying: this is the amount of currency being made available by foreigners buying our goods and services, and this amount only can be obtained by Canadians. What this does, in effect, is restrict the amount of imports. These foreign-exchange controls can take many forms, including quotas on foreign currencies available for foreign travel, placing currency quotas on importing companies or industries, or giving preference to certain imports over others. The problem with foreign-exchange controls is that they distort trade and production, favour some importers over others, and restrict consumer choice.

Another alternative would be for the Canadian government to convince countries that are big exporters to Canada to agree to voluntary export restrictions. This would restrict imports to Canada. This is not often an easy option to exercise but has been achieved by a few countries recently.

There is only one other policy option for a government facing an overvalued fixed exchange rate. Since imports are a function of income, a reduction in imports could be achieved by reducing income. This involves reducing aggregate demand through specific policies that we will discuss in the next two chapters. In short, the adjustment mechanism for an overvalued exchange rate may be the deliberate creation of a recession. In summary, a government can defend an overvalued exchange rate in four ways:

- introducing quotas or tariffs
- introducing foreign-exchange controls
- negotiating voluntary export restrictions
- creating a recession at home

devaluation: the re-fixing by government of an exchange rate at a lower level.

A government that finds it politically impossible to impose any of the above policies, or that finds that those policies fail after being tried, will be forced to **devalue** its currency, that is, refix the exchange rate at a lower level.

Devaluation of a currency has serious political ramifications. It is often interpeted as a failure of a government to control its own destiny and, from that point of view, may lead to a loss of confidence generally in a government's economic policies. Furthermore, once even the possibility of a devaluation is recognized by the market, international currency dealers will ask only "when" and not "if." This lack of confidence by itself may make devaluation an inevitability, because dealers will not want to hold the currency when there is the possibility that it may be devalued. Their actions, in selling off the currency that is under siege, then become a self-fulfilling prophecy.

dirty float: an exchange rate that is not officially fixed by government but is managed by the central bank's ongoing intervention in the market.

In sum, the adjustment mechanism for an under- or overvalued fixed exchange rate is very painful and throws the economy into either an inflationary situation or into recession. For this reason, most economists favour the flexible exchange-rate system. In fact, fixed exchange rates have been rare in the past 30 years. However, truly flexible rates are almost as rare. Instead, most countries operate a system of managed exchange rates, or a **dirty float.** This means that the degree to which a currency is allowed to float (or fluctuate) is managed by the central bank in order to stabilize the exchange rate. In Canada's case, then, the Bank of Canada buys and sells foreign currencies to keep the value of the dollar within what it perceives to be permissible limits. In order to prevent too rapid a depreciation of the dollar, the government sells foreign reserves and buys dollars so as to hold up the demand for the dollar. Similarly, to keep the dollar from appreciating too quickly, the government will do the opposite and sell dollars in exchange for foreign currency. This hybrid of the fixed and flexible exchange-rate systems will probably continue to be the choice of governments for the foreseeable future.

SELF-TEST

6. Assume that the demand for the Canadian dollar increases. Describe the adjustment mechanism to this change, given: a) flexible exchange rates; and b) fixed exchange rates.

10.7 The Balance of Payments

LO5
Construct a balance sheet of international payments.

balance of payments: an accounting of a country's international transactions that involves the payment and receipt of foreign currencies.

current account: a subcategory of the balance of payments that shows the income or expenditure related to exports and imports.

capital account: a subcategory of the balance of payments that reflects changes in ownership of assets associated with foreign investment.

official settlements account: a subcategory of the balance of payments that shows the change in a country's official foreign exchange reserves.

Just like any other balance sheet, the **balance of payments** (or, more correctly, the international balance of payments) should always balance. But it is important to know where the dollars went and how they were spent. The balance sheet is divided up into three main sections: the **current account**, the **capital account**, and the **official settlements account**. In a sense, the balance of payments is a misnomer, since it is more like an income statement than a balance sheet. What it shows are the various categories of international buying and selling that involve the Canadian dollar during a year. **Table 10.2** is a simplified balance of payments for Canada for 2001.

PhotoDisc

Gold has been a means of international payment for centries

TABLE 10.2 **Canada's Balance of Payments 2001 ($ billions)**

Current Account		
Export of goods and services	+468	
Import of goods and services	−413	
= Balance of trade		+55
Investment income from abroad	+37	
Investment income paid abroad	−65	
Net investment income		−28
Transfers (net)		+2
= Current Account balance		+29
Capital Account		
Foreign investment in Canada	+81	
less Canadian investment abroad	−107	
= Capital Account balance		−26
Balance of Current Account and Capital Account		+3
Official Settlements Account		
Change in Canadian dollars (change in foreign reserves)		−3
Total Balance		
(Current Account + Capital Account + Official Settlements Account)		0

Source: Adapted from Statistics Canada, CANSIM Database, Table 376-0001 and 376-0002.

balance of trade: the value of a country's exports of goods and services less the value of its imports.

In a sense, the current account shows income and expenditures from international trading. The first two lines, exports and imports of goods and services, are self-explanatory. The difference between the two represents the **balance of trade** (what we called "net exports" in earlier chapters). Recall that imports create a supply of Canadian dollars; exports create a demand. However, when looking at the balance of payments, it is often more illuminating to look at the corresponding flows of foreign currencies. In other words, imports create a demand by Canadians for foreign currencies and exports produce a supply of foreign currencies. Traditionally, Canada has had a *positive* balance of trade. This means that trade in goods and services usually produces a net inflow of foreign currencies to Canada. In 2001, this inflow amounts to $55 billion.

The next line, investment income from abroad, includes the total amount of interest and dividends that Canadians received in this particular year from their previous foreign investments. This income produces an inflow of foreign currency into Canada. Investment income paid abroad represents an outflow of foreign currencies. Since, in the past, foreigners have invested more in Canada than Canadians have invested abroad, the income going abroad far exceeds the income flowing into Canada.

The last line in the current account, transfers, includes gifts and other remittances (pensions, for example) as well as foreign aid. In our example, more transfers came into Canada than went abroad.

The balance on the current account equals +29, which means that $29 billion more in foreign reserves came into Canada than left Canada. In recent years, the current account has had a positive balance.

The capital account shows the changes in international investment holdings during the year. Canadians purchased $26 billion more in the way of stocks, bonds (portfolio investment), and purchases of companies abroad (direct investment) than foreigners purchased in Canada during the year. The total of the current and capital accounts gives us a balance of payments surplus of $3 billion. This means that overall, foreigners were buying more

Canadian currencies than Canadians were buying foreign currencies. The resulting shortage of Canadian dollars from trading was made available by the Bank of Canada. This shows up in the final section of the balance of payments statement: the Official Settlements Account. This section shows the involvement of the Bank of Canada in international transactions. In 2001, there was an outflow (a negative balance) of $3 billion. However, this is an outflow of Canadian dollars, which means that the Bank of Canada received the equivalent of $3 billion Canadian in return in international reserves. A balance of payments surplus, then, means that foreign reserves are coming into the country. (A balance of payments deficit, on the contrary, means an outflow of foreign reserves leaving the country.)

The total balance of current, capital, and official settlements accounts sums to zero. This will always be the case, since it includes both private and government (Bank of Canada) currency dealings. If there is a deficit, the government will make up the shortage of foreign currencies; if there is a surplus, the government will make up the shortage of Canadian dollars. Only with complete, instantaneous flexible exchange rates will there be no government intervention and never a balance of payments deficit or surplus.

SELF-TEST

7. Fill in the blanks in the following hypothetical balance of payments statement:

Canada's Balance of Payments for 2004		
Current Account		
Export of goods and services	+164	
Import of goods and services	____	
= Balance of trade		+2
Investment income from abroad	+8	
Investment income paid abroad	____	
Net investment income		−15
Transfers (net)	____	
= Current Account balance		−17
Capital Account		
Foreign investment in Canada less Canadian investment abroad	+18	
= Capital Account balance		+18
Balance of Current Account and Capital Account		____
Official Settlements Account		
Change in Canadian dollars		____
Total Balance (Current Account + Capital Account + Official Settlements Account)		____

Let us now raise a new question. Since, with flexible exchange rates, the balance of payments automatically balances, can balance of payments problems ever arise? The answer is yes, because it really does make a difference what a country is importing and what it is exporting. Canada can earn foreign currencies by exporting goods or services, or by selling assets. Exporting goods and services does not lead to any future obligations on the part of anyone in Canada. However, selling off Canadian assets obligates some Canadians to pay out future income to foreigners and, in a sense, represents a drain on our foreign reserves in the future.

It is important that we clear up one particular myth relating to these flows. It is often suggested that Canada needs to encourage the inflow of foreign investment because we need this inflow to pay off the deficit that Canada invariably has on its current account. Perhaps you've figured out why this is a myth. The reason why Canada generally has a deficit on the current account is because of the amount of investment income that has to be paid abroad.

And the reason this is so high is the big amount of foreign investment in the past. If we express this in terms of the individual, it might make more sense. Picture a student who defends her excessive borrowing every year by pointing out that she needs to borrow because her expenditures always seem to exceed her income, so she is left with no choice. But the reason why her expenses are so high is because she's having to pay such huge interest payments on her previous loans. In a similar fashion, many people suggest that if Canada were to cut down its dependence on foreign investment, it would not have current account problems in the future.

REVIEW

1. If foreign incomes rise, what is likely to happen to the demand for Canadian exports?
2. If the price of Canadian goods rises, what is likely to happen to the demand for Canadian exports?
3. If Canadian interest rates rise, what is likely to happen to the demand for the Canadian dollar?
4. Define *tariff.*
5. What does it mean to devalue a currency?
6. What is a *subsidy?*
7. Define a *dirty float.*
8. Distinguish between the *balance of payments* and the *balance of trade.*
9. Distinguish between the *current account* and the *capital account.*

STUDY GUIDE

Review

CHAPTER SUMMARY

This chapter began with a discussion of the exchange rate and explained what is meant by the appreciation or depreciation of a currency. The main focus of the chapter was an examination of how exchange rates are determined under a flexible exchange rate system and how this contrasts with a fixed exchange rate system. The chapter concluded with a discussion of the balance of payments.

1. Purchasing power parity is the theory that the purchasing powers of different currencies will, over time, tend to become equal.

2. The factors that prevent this from happening are:
   - many services are not traded internationally;
   - the existence of transportation and insurance costs;
   - the existence of tariffs and other trade restrictions;
   - consumers often show a preference for the products of one particular country over another;
   - the value of currencies is affected by trade in financial assets.

3. The demand for the Canadian dollar on the international market comes from:
   - foreigners who want to buy Canadian exports or who travel in Canada;
   - foreigners who want to buy Canadian assets;
   - Canadians who received investment income from abroad;
   - currency speculators.

4. Changes in the demand for the Canadian dollar come from:
   - changes in the level of foreign incomes;
   - changes in the price of Canadian goods;
   - changes in foreigners' preferences;
   - changes in comparative interest rates.

5. The supply of Canadian dollars on the international market comes from Canadians' demand for foreign currencies and will increase if:
   - Canadians want more foreign goods;
   - Canadians buy more foreign assets;
   - foreigners receive more Canadian income.

6. The arguments for a fixed exchange rate are:
   - it adds a degree of certainty to international trade;
   - it prevents instability in the export and import industries;
   - it discourages currency speculation;
   - it appeals to people who tend to equate the value of the exchange rate with national prestige.

7. Many economists favour a flexible exchange rate system because:
   - it avoids the necessary adjustment of inflation which results when a fixed exchange rate is undervalued;
   - it avoids the necessary adjustment of recession which results when a fixed exchange rate is overvalued.

8. The balance of payments is an accounting of a country's international transactions and is made up of the:
   - Current account, which adds the balance of trade (export of goods and services minus imports), net investment income and transfers;
   - Capital account (the net flow of all changes in the ownership of international assets);
   - Official settlements account, which shows the movement of foreign reserves in and out of the Bank of Canada.

NEW GLOSSARY TERMS AND KEY EQUATIONS

arbitrage 342
balance of payments 357
balance of trade 358
capital account 357
currency appreciation 339
currency depreciation 339
current account 357
devaluation 356
direct investment 341
dirty float 357
exchange rate 338
fixed exchange rate 339
flexible exchange rate 339
official settlements account 357
portfolio investment 341
purchasing power parity theory 339
subsidy 356

Equations:

[10.1] $1 \text{ Canadian dollar} = \dfrac{1}{1 \text{ unit of foreign currency}}$ page 338

[10.2] $1 \text{ unit of foreign currency} = \dfrac{1}{1 \text{ Canadian dollar}}$ page 338

STUDY TIPS

1. A lot of this chapter is about the idea of price being determined by supply and demand, something that students have little difficulty in accepting. The price we are focusing on is that of currencies, and (given a flexible exchange rate system) a currency's price (exchange rate) is determined by the supply and demand for that currency. Just keep thinking of currencies as commodities, and don't get hung up on the fact that they are also moneys. You will find there is nothing unduly mysterious or difficult about the topic.

2. The value of any currency always has to be expressed in terms of another currency. The question, "What is the price of the Canadian dollar?" makes no sense. "What is the price of the Canadian dollar in yen?" is a sensible question.

3. It is quite important for you to keep in mind that (flexible exchange) rates are determined by the supply and demand for a currency, and *not* the other way around. Thus any question that starts with "if the exchange rate changes" has to be handled carefully, because one needs to know what caused the exchange rate to change in the first place.

Answered Questions

Indicate whether the following statements are true or false.

1. **T or F** If a Panamanian balboa is worth 0.20 Canadian dollars, then a Canadian dollar is worth 4 balboas.

2. **T or F** The purchasing power parity theory suggests that exchange rates adjust so as to equate the purchasing power of each currency.

3. **T or F** A major source of demand for the Canadian dollar in the international money markets is the desire by foreigners to buy Canadian exports.

4. **T or F** A resident in Canada receiving a British pension will have a demand for the British pound.

5. **T or F** An increase in Canadian interest rates will lead to an appreciation of the Canadian dollar.

6. **T or F** When the Canadian dollar depreciates, the effective price of Canadian exports increases and, as a result, total exports are likely to fall.

7. **T or F** If the Canadian dollar appreciates, cross-border shopping by Canadians will increase.

8. **T or F** If Canada were on a fixed exchange-rate system, an increase in the demand for the Canadian dollar would result in the dollar being undervalued.

9. **T or F** A fixed exchange rate above the market value will lead to an outflow of foreign currencies.

10. **T or F** An increase in imports will have a negative effect on the current account balance.

Basic (Questions 11–24)

11. What is the value of the euro in terms of dollars if a French importer can buy 8 dollars for 10 euros?
 a) $1.25.
 b) $0.8.
 c) $80.
 d) $2.

12. If the Canadian dollar appreciates in value against the Mexican peso, what happens to the value of the Mexican peso against the dollar?
 a) It appreciates.
 b) It depreciates.
 c) It might appreciate or depreciate.
 d) It remains unchanged.

13. An American resident who receives interest on the Canadian savings bond she holds will be be demanding what currency?
 a) Canadian dollars.
 b) U.S. dollars.
 c) Euros.
 d) British pounds.

14. What does arbitrage mean?
 a) The cost of shipping and insuring exported goods.
 b) The buying of a currency at one price and its immediate sale at another price.
 c) The cost of holding goods whose price is expected to increase in the future.
 d) Speculation on the future price of a currency.

15. If Canada and the United Kingdom are both on flexible exchange-rate systems, what would happen if the United Kingdom experiences rapid inflation, while prices remain steady in Canada?
 a) The Canadian dollar will depreciate.
 b) The British pound will depreciate.
 c) The British pound will appreciate.
 d) The exchange rate will not change.

16. Which of the following would result from an increase in Canada's GDP?
 a) Canadian exports would rise.
 b) Both Canadian exports and imports would rise.
 c) Canadian exports would rise, but imports would decrease.
 d) Canadian imports would rise.

Table 10.3 contains hypothetical data for Canada's balance of payments accounts for a particular year. (Figures are in $ billions.)

TABLE 10.3

Exports of goods and services	$150
Imports of goods and services	145
Investment income received from abroad	10
Investment income paid abroad	30
Net transfers	–5
Foreign investment in Canada	200
Canadian investment abroad	190

17. Refer to **Table 10.3** to answer this question. What is Canada's balance of trade?
 a) A surplus of $150 billion.
 b) A surplus of $5 billion.
 c) A deficit of $15 billion.
 d) A deficit of $10 billion.

18. Refer to **Table 10.3** to answer this question. What is Canada's current account balance?
 a) A surplus of $10 billion.
 b) A surplus of $15 billion.
 c) A deficit of $10 billion.
 d) A deficit of $20 billion.

19. Refer to **Table 10.3** to answer this question. What is Canada's capital account balance?
 a) A deficit of $10 billion.
 b) A surplus of $10 billion.
 c) A surplus of $5 billion.
 d) A surplus of $30 billion.

20. All of the following groups, except one, demand Canadian dollars. Which is the exception?
 a) An American tourist visiting Canada.
 b) Canadians who received dividends from American corporations.
 c) Texans who purchase Alberta beef.
 d) Americans who receive interest on their holdings of Canadian savings bonds.
 e) International speculators who think that the Canadian dollar will soon appreciate.

21. Which of the following would increase the supply of Canadian dollars on the international money market?
 a) Canadians travelling abroad.
 b) An American corporation investing in Canada.

c) A Canadian resident receiving interest payments on a foreign bond.
d) A Canadian exporter selling products abroad.
e) A retired American, living on Vancouver Island, receiving a pension cheque from U.S. Social Security.

22. If a country is suffering perennial balance of payments deficits, all except one of the following will help solve the problem. Which is the exception?
a) The introduction of quotas on imported goods.
b) An increase in interest rates.
c) The introduction of exchange controls.
d) The reduction in tariffs on imported goods.
e) An increase in subsidies to exporting industries.

23. What does a managed (or dirty) float mean?
a) That a country's currency is fixed to the price of gold.
b) That a country's currency is fixed to the value of the U.S. dollar.
c) That a country's balance of payments is persistently in deficit.
d) That the country's central bank fixes the value of its currency.
e) That a country's central bank buys and sells currencies in order to smooth out short-run fluctuations in its own currency.

24. What is purchasing power parity theory?
a) A theory suggesting that exchange rates will change so as to equate the purchasing power of each currency.
b) A theory suggesting that exchange rates tend to diverge over time.
c) A theory suggesting that all currencies will be, in time, at par.
d) A formula used to calculate the exchange rate of one currency for another.

Intermediate (Questions 25–31)

25. What will be the result of a change in exchange rates if fewer Mexican pesos are needed to buy a Canadian dollar?
a) Canadians will buy more Mexican goods and services.
b) Mexicans will buy fewer Canadian goods and services.
c) Canadians will buy fewer Mexican goods and services.
d) Mexicans will buy more Mexican goods.

26. Assuming a flexible exchange-rate system, what would happen to the value of the Canadian dollar and the Mexican peso if Canadian interest rates increase while Mexican rates remain the same?
a) The price of dollars in terms of the peso would increase.
b) The price of pesos in terms of dollars would increase.
c) The peso in terms of dollars would appreciate.
d) The Canadian dollar in terms of the peso would depreciate.

27. Which of the following statements is true about the supply curve for the Canadian dollar?
a) It is downward-sloping because a lower price for the dollar means Canadian goods are cheaper to foreigners.
b) It is downward-sloping because a higher price for the dollar means Canadian goods are cheaper to foreigners.
c) It is upward-sloping because a lower price for the dollar means foreign goods are cheaper to Canadians.
d) It is upward-sloping because a higher price for the dollar means foreign goods are cheaper to Canadians.

28. Assuming a fixed exchange-rate system, which of the following would contribute to a Canadian balance of payments deficit?
a) Bryan Adams and Anne Murray team up for a giant outdoor concert in Shanghai.
b) The number of Indian tourists visiting Canada increases significantly.
c) The United States increases its tariff on Canadian softwood lumber.
d) A wealthy Taiwanese family builds a mansion in Calgary.
e) Honda builds a new assembly plant outside Montreal.

29. All of the following, except one, would help to explain differences in purchasing power between countries. Which is the exception?
a) Many services are not traded internationally.
b) Financial assets are seldom traded internationally.
c) The existence of transportation and insurance costs.
d) The expression of particular preferences by consumers.
e) The existence of tariffs and other trade restrictions.

30. Refer to **Table 10.4** to answer this question. What is the price of one Canadian dollar in Year 2?
   a) 72 yen.
   b) 80 yen.
   c) 88 yen.
   d) Cannot be determined.

TABLE 10.4

	Price of one Canadian Dollar	Price in Canada of a Gallon of Maple Syrup	Price in Japan of a Gallon of Maple Syrup
Year 1	80 yen	$20	1600 yen
Year 2	______	$20	1760 yen

31. Refer to **Table 10.5** to answer this question. Which of the following statements is correct?
   a) The Canadian dollar has appreciated and the Japanese yen has depreciated.
   b) The Canadian dollar has depreciated and the Japanese yen has appreciated.
   c) The Japanese yen is now worth less in terms of the Canadian dollar.
   d) The Canadian dollar is now worth more in terms of the Japanese yen.

TABLE 10.5

	Price of one Canadian Dollar	Price in Canada of a Gallon of Maple Syrup	Price in Japan of a Gallon of Maple Syrup
Year 1	80 yen	$20	1600 yen
Year 2	72 yen	$20	1440 yen

Advanced (Questions 32–35)

32. What does it mean for a country that is on a fixed exchange-rate system to have a balance of payments surplus?
   a) The quantity supplied of its currency on the international money market will exceed the quantity demanded.
   b) The exchange rate is overvalued.
   c) There is an inflow of foreign currencies into the country.
   d) The balance of payments surplus is matched by a balance of trade deficit.
   e) There is an outflow of foreign currencies from the country.

Figure 10.9 shows the market for the U.S. dollar.

FIGURE 10.9

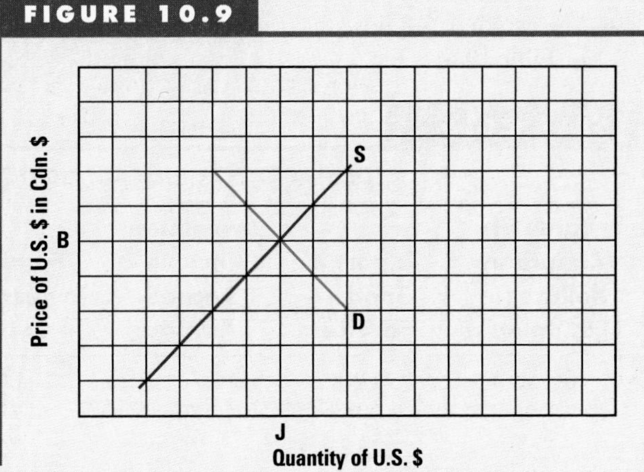

33. Refer to the graph in **Figure 10.9** to answer this question. What is the value of the U.S. dollar if a flexible exchange-rate system is in effect?
   a) 0J Canadian dollars for one U.S. dollar.
   b) 0B Canadian dollars for one U.S. dollar.
   c) 1/0B dollars for one Canadian dollar.
   d) 0J U.S. dollars for one Canadian dollar.
   e) 0B U.S. dollars for one Canadian dollar.

34. Assuming flexible exchange rates, which of the following would result in an increase in a country's exchange rate?
   a) The purchase by the central bank of its own currency.
   b) The purchase by the central bank of foreign currencies.
   c) The sale by the central bank of its own currencies.
   d) The central bank decreasing the country's interest rates.
   e) The government imposing an export tax.

35. The country of Lancore, which was on a fixed exchange-rate system and had an undervalued currency, has just adopted a flexible exchange-rate system. Which of the following statements is correct?
   a) Lancores's currency will depreciate and its exports will increase as a result.
   b) Lancores's currency will appreciate and its exports will increase as a result.
   c) Lancores's currency will depreciate and its exports will decrease as a result.
   d) Lancores's currency will appreciate and its exports will decrease as a result.

Parallel Problems

ANSWERED PROBLEMS

36. Key Problem Suppose that the international demand and supply of (in billions of) Canadian dollars is as shown in **Table 10.6.**

TABLE 10.6

	DEMAND FOR CANADIAN DOLLARS				SUPPLY OF CANADIAN DOLLARS			
Value of Canadian dollars (in U.S. dollars)	Export of Goods & Services	Investment Income Earned Abroad	Foreign Investment in Canada	Total	Import of Goods & Services	Investment Income Paid Abroad	Canadian Investment Abroad	Total
$0.56	120	70	180	____	80	67	146	____
0.58	119	70	175	____	83	67	148	____
0.60	118	70	170	____	86	67	150	____
0.62	117	70	165	____	89	67	152	____
0.64	116	70	160	____	92	67	154	____
0.66	115	70	155	____	95	67	156	____
0.68	114	70	150	____	98	67	158	____
0.70	113	70	145	____	101	67	160	____
0.72	112	70	140	____	104	67	162	____
0.74	111	70	135	____	107	67	164	____
0.76	110	70	130	____	110	67	166	____

This represents the total market for Canadian dollars (i.e., there are no transfers, speculation, or arbitrage).

a) Calculate and fill in the total demand and total supply columns.

Suppose that Canada is operating with a flexible exchange rate system.

b) What will be the equilibrium value of the Canadian dollar? __________.

c) What is the value of its balance of trade?

__________________________.

d) What is the value of its current account balance?

__________________________.

e) What is the value of its capital account balance?

__________________________.

f) What is the value of its total balance of payments (current and capital accounts)?

__________________________.

Now suppose that Canada fixes its exchange rate against the U.S. dollar at a value of 1 Canadian dollar equals 0.68 U.S. dollars.

g) What is the value of its balance of trade?

__________________________.

h) What is the value of its current account balance?

__________________________.

i) What is the value of its capital account balance?

__________________________.

j) What is the value of its total balance of payments (current and capital accounts)?

__________________________.

k) What is the balance on its official settlements account? ________________.

Basic (Problems 37–42)

37. If a Canadian hockey stick has a price of $42, how much does it cost in:

a) Europe, assuming an exchange rate of 1 euro = $1.40 Cdn.? ________________________.

b) the U.K., assuming an exchange rate of 1 pound = $2.10 Cdn.? ______________________.

38. Fill in the blanks below:

a) If one Canadian dollar equals 0.75 U.S. dollars, then one U.S. dollar equals ______ Canadian dollars.

b) If one Canadian dollar equals 80 yen, then one yen equals ______ Canadian dollars.
c) If one euro equals 1.6 Canadian dollars, then one Canadian dollar equals ______ euros.

39. Refer to the following list and explain who will be buying Canadian dollars and who will be selling.
a) A Canadian businesswoman visiting Japan. ______ .
b) A Russian tourist visiting Cape Breton. ______ .
c) An American corporation building a new plant in Saskatoon. ______ .
d) A Canadian bank expanding its operations in the United States ______ .

40. Refer to the following list and identify who would be hurt and who would benefit from an appreciation of the Canadian dollar.
a) An Italian father spending the summer with his daughter in Calgary. ______ .
b) A Canadian research scientist living in Washington, D.C., who is paid a monthly salary in Canadian dollars by his Ottawa employer. ______ .
c) A retired couple living in Ontario whose major source of income is from a U.K. pension. ______ .
d) A nurse living in Windsor who works at a hospital in Detroit. ______ .

41. What effect will the following events have on the value of the Canadian dollar versus that of the Mexican peso?
a) Canadian interest rates rise significantly above Mexican rates. ______ .
b) An especially bad winter causes tens of thousands of Canadians to escape to the Mexican Riviera for vacations. ______ .
c) A Canadian telecommunications firm sells equipment to the Mexican government.
______ .
d) The winter vegetable crop in Mexico is destroyed by unusually cold temperatures. ______ .

42. Arrange the following data into the form of a balance of payments for Etruria (all figures are in $ billions)

TABLE 10.7

Foreign investment in Etruria	90
Transfers (net)	+4
Investment income from abroad	11
Imports of goods and services	153
Exports of goods and services	157
Etruria investment abroad	68
Investment income paid abroad	29

a) What is the value of the balance of trade?
______ .
b) What is the value of the balance on the current account?
______ .
c) What is the value of the balance on the capital account?
______ .
d) Is there a balance of payments surplus or deficit? How much?
______ .

Intermediate (Problems 43–46)

43. Karen operates a small foreign-currency exchange business. She begins each day with three boxes of cash. Each box contains 10 000 units of Canadian currency and 10 000 units of another currency. **Table 10.8** shows Karen's holdings of each currency at the end of a day's business.

TABLE 10.8

Box 1	euros	8 000	and	$12 800 Cdn.
Box 2	Japanese yen	7 000	and	10 050 Cdn.
Box 3	U.S. dollars	6 400	and	15 000 Cdn.

What is the value of the Canadian dollar in terms of the three currencies?
Dollar in terms of the euro: ______ .
Dollar in terms of the yen: ______ .
Dollar in terms of the U.S. dollar: ______ .

44. A country that experiences a capital account surplus for many years will, eventually, experience many years of current account deficits. Explain.
______
______
______
______ .

45. Assume that the demand for the Canadian dollar increases because of a rising GDP level in the United States. What will happen to the value of the Canadian exchange rate, Canada's GDP, and the unemployment rate in Canada?
Exchange rate: ______ .
GDP: ______ .
Unemployment rate: ______ .

46. The graph in **Figure 10.10** illustrates hypothetical supply and demand curves for the Canadian dollar. Use the graph to answer the questions below.

a) What is the quantity of dollars exchanged, given D_1 and S_1? ______.

b) What is this quantity worth in U.S. dollars? ______.

c) If you increase the demand for the dollar by 20 (draw in D_2), what would be the dollar volume of exchange if the exchange rate is fixed? ______.

d) What is the quantity of Canadian dollars exchanged if the exchange rate is flexible? ______.

e) What is this quantity worth in U.S. dollars? ______.

FIGURE 10.10

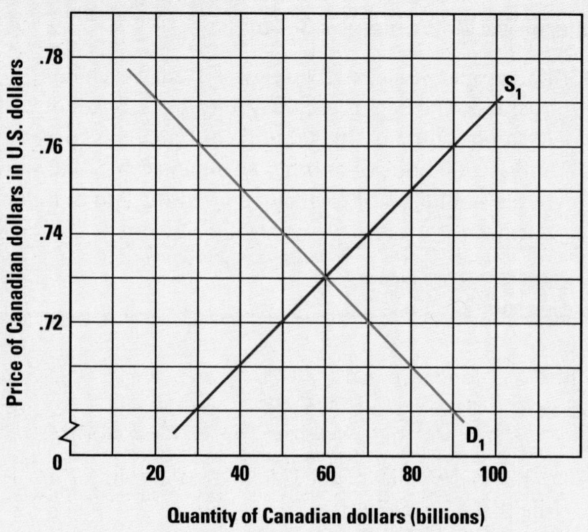

Advanced (Problems 47–49)

47. An increase in the demand for Canadian products will cause the Canadian dollar to appreciate. Yet an appreciation of the dollar causes the demand for Canadian products to fall. How can you reconcile these two statements? ______.

48. Explain why a country with a fixed exchange rate loses control over its money supply as an effective policy tool. ______.

49. Suppose that a certain type of SUV costs $32 000 in Canada, whereas it sells for 18 000 pounds in the U.K. Suppose that the nominal exchange rate is: one Canadian dollar is equal to 0.45 U.K. pounds.

a) What is the value of the real exchange rate? ______.

b) In which country is the SUV cheaper? ______.

UNANSWERED PROBLEMS

50. **Key Problem** Suppose that the international demand and supply of (in billions of) Canadian dollars is as shown in Table 10.9.

TABLE 10.9

Value of Canadian dollars (in U.S. dollars)	DEMAND FOR CANADIAN DOLLARS: Export of Goods & Services	Investment Income Earned Abroad	Foreign Investment in Canada	Total	SUPPLY OF CANADIAN DOLLARS: Import of Goods & Services	Investment Income Paid Abroad	Canadian Investment Abroad	Total
$0.60	90	30	150	____	56	40	97	____
0.62	89	30	145	____	59	40	99	____
0.64	88	30	140	____	62	40	101	____
0.66	87	30	135	____	65	40	103	____
0.68	86	30	130	____	68	40	105	____
0.70	85	30	125	____	71	40	107	____
0.72	84	30	120	____	74	40	109	____
0.74	83	30	115	____	77	40	111	____
0.76	82	30	110	____	80	40	113	____
0.78	81	30	105	____	83	40	115	____
0.80	80	30	100	____	86	40	117	____

This represents the total market for Canadian dollars (i.e., there are no transfers, speculation, or arbitrage).

a) Calculate and fill in the total demand and total supply columns.

Suppose that Canada is operating with a flexible exchange-rate system.

b) What will be the equilibrium value of the Canadian dollar?

c) What is the value of its balance of trade?

d) What is the value of its current account balance?

e) What is the value of its capital account balance?

f) What is the value of its total balance of payments (current and capital accounts)?

Now suppose that Canada fixes its exchange rate against the U.S. dollar at a value of one Canadian dollar equals 0.68 U.S. dollars.

g) What is the value of its balance of trade?

h) What is the value of its total balance of payments (current and capital accounts)?

i) What is the balance on its official settlements account?

Basic (Problems 51–56)

51. If a Japanese tennis racquet has a price of 3500 yen, how much does it cost in

a) Canada, assuming an exchange rate of $1 Cdn. = 70 yen?

b) the U.S., assuming an exchange rate of $1 U.S. = 100 yen?

52. Fill in the blanks below:

a) If one U.S. dollar equals 1.6 Canadian dollars, then one Canadian dollar equals ________ U.S. dollars.

b) If one Japanese yen equals 0.005 Canadian dollar, then one Canadian dollar equals ________ Japanese yen.

c) If one Canadian dollar equals 0 .75 euros, then one euro equals ________ Canadian dollars.

53. Refer to the following list and explain who will be buying Canadian dollars and who will be selling.

a) A Canadian student living in Rome who receives a Canadian scholarship.

b) A Honda dealer in Hamilton.

c) A German currency speculator who feels that the euro will depreciate against the Canadian dollar.

d) A resident of Hong Kong who is about to emigrate to Canada.

54. Refer to the following list and identify who would be hurt and who would benefit from a depreciation of the Canadian dollar.

a) A Quebec manufacturer of light rapid transit systems sold around the world.

b) A Nova Scotia couple who are thinking of buying a winter home in Florida.

c) An Ontario firm that imports items for sale in Canada.
d) A resident of Spain who travels to Canada frequently.

55. What effect will the following events have on the value of the Canadian dollar versus that of the Mexican peso?
a) Canadian firms increase their investment in Mexico.
b) The Mexican government greatly reduces the tariff on imports of softwood lumber from Canada.
c) The Mexican economy experiences big growth in its national income.
d) Pemex, the Mexican oil giant, makes a huge investment in Canadian Arctic oil exploration.

56. Given the following hypothetical data for the Canadian economy in **Table 10.10**:

TABLE 10.10

Exports of goods and services	$180
Foreign investment in Canada	45
Investment income from abroad	18
Imports of goods and services	173
Investment income paid abroad	36
Net transfers	+10
Canadian investment abroad	40

Calculate:
a) balance of trade;
b) current account balance;
c) capital account balance;
d) Is there a Balance of Payments surplus or deficit? How much?

Intermediate (Problems 57–60)

57. Kyle operates a small foreign-currency exchange business. He begins each day with three boxes of cash. Each box contains 5000 units of Canadian currency and 5000 units of one other currency. **Table 10.11** show's Kyle's holdings of each currency at the end of a day's business.

TABLE 10.11

Box 1	N.Z. dollars	3750	and	$5750 Cdn.
Box 2	U.K. pounds	14 000	and	1200 Cdn.
Box 3	Italian lira	2 525 000	and	2200 Cdn.

What is the value of the Canadian dollar in terms of each of the three currencies?

58. Canadians are now investing in foreign countries much more than ever before. This is good news for Canada's balance of payments in the future. Explain.

59. Assume that the U.S. experiences a big decrease in its GDP. What would you predict will happen to Canada's GDP, the value of the Canadian exchange rate, and the unemployment rate in Canada?

60. The graph in **Figure 10.11** illustrates hypothetical supply and demand curves for the Canadian dollar. Use the graph to answer the questions below.

FIGURE 10.11

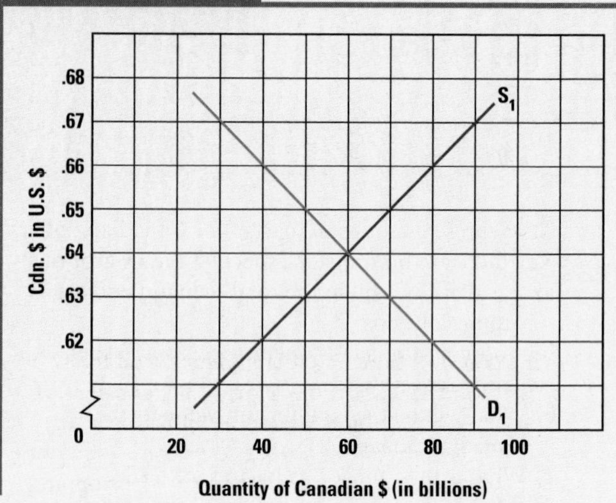

a) What is the quantity of dollars exchanged given D_1 and S_1?
b) What is this quantity worth in U.S. dollars?
c) If the demand for the Canadian dollar decreases by 20, what would be the dollar volume of exchange if the exchange rate is fixed?
d) What is the quantity of Canadian dollars exchanged if the exchange rate is flexible?
e) What is this quantity worth in U.S. dollars?

Advanced (Problems 61–64)

61. If the value of the Canadian dollar depreciates, it means that the demand for Canadian goods must have fallen. Yet a lower value of the Canadian dollar causes foreigners to buy more Canadian goods. Reconcile these two statements.

62. Explain how a fixed exchange-rate system may lead to painful adjustments in the domestic economy if there is an increase in the demand for its currency.

63. Suppose that a certain type of DVD player costs $300 in Canada, whereas it sells for 20 000 yen in Japan. Suppose that the nominal exchange rate is $1 Canadian is equal to 80 yen.

a) What is the value of the real exchange rate?

b) In which country is the DVD player cheaper?

64. Following are some hypothetical data concerning exchange rates and the price of a Big Mac in the summer of 2003. The Asian currencies are expressed in **Table 10.12** in Canadian dollars.

TABLE 10.12

Location	Big Mac Price	Exchange Rate
Montreal	2.80 Canadian dollars	/
Tokyo	280 yen	$1 = 90 yen
Singapore	3.00 Singapore dollars	$1 = 1.12 Sgp.
Hong Kong	10.20 Hong Kong dollars	$1 = 5.25 H.K.

The theory of purchasing power parity would predict that long-term exchange rates would change so that a Big Mac would cost the same in all countries.

a) Calculate exactly what the value of the Canadian dollar would be in terms of each of the other currencies in order for the price of a Big Mac to be the same in each of the three Asian countries as it is in Montreal.

b) Given your calculations in a) above, would you say that the three Asian exchange rates were undervalued or overvalued in terms of the PPP theory?

c) Given your answer in b) above, would you expect Asian exports to Canada would continue to grow or begin to decrease?

Web-Based Activities

1. What to do about the Canadian dollar? Read the two articles found at **www.cdhowe.org/pdf/buckaug.pdf and www.cdhowe.org/pdf/kbkool-2.pdf**. What was the cause of this depreciation? What could have been done to reverse the trend in the exchange rate? Is propping up the value of the dollar good for the economy? Why or why not?

2. Go to **www.x-rates.com** and look up the current value of the Canadian dollar in terms of five other currencies. Is your calculation higher or lower than it was one year ago?

CHAPTER ELEVEN

Fiscal Policy

LEARNING OBJECTIVES

This chapter will enable you to:

LO1 **See why the federal government's revenue depends on the rate of taxation, the size of the GDP, and its own spending.**

LO2 **Explain the pros and cons of a budget policy aimed at achieving full-employment equilibrium.**

LO3 **Explain the pros and cons of a budget policy aimed at achieving a balanced budget in each fiscal year.**

LO4 **Explain the pros and cons of a budget policy aimed at achieving both full employment and a balanced budget over the life of the business cycle.**

LO5 **Discuss the cause, size, and problems of the national debt.**

What's ahead...

This chapter focuses on fiscal policy, which is one of the more important economic policies used by the government. We begin by defining several important terms, including net tax revenue, budget deficits, surpluses, and the national debt, and then go on to explore what can cause each of these to change. We then proceed to examine two distinct approaches to the use of fiscal policy: counter-cyclical fiscal policy and balanced-budget fiscal policy. We explain the assumptions that lie behind each approach and explore criticisms of each. Then, a compromise between these approaches, the cyclically balanced-budget fiscal policy, is explained and briefly explored. The chapter ends with a discussion of national debt.

A QUESTION OF RELEVANCE...

Do you remember what you were doing the evening that the last federal budget was unveiled in Parliament? Probably not. Furthermore, you quite likely think that "it has nothing to do with me." Yet, the truth is that the government's annual budget affects you more than almost any other regularly scheduled event in your life, other than personal events such as birthdays and anniversaries. It determines the taxes you pay, the chances of your getting a job next summer, the likelihood of getting a student loan, and even the size of your classes next year. This chapter will help you learn more about the budget.

It is a truism that governments have to spend, and, therefore, they have to tax. So, what should the government's attitude toward its own spending and taxation be? How small or large should this spending and taxation be? Should the two be equal? Does the condition of the economy have anything to do with the answers to these questions? For example, when the economy is in the middle of a recession with high unemployment, what should the attitude of government be? Should the government decrease its own spending, increase it, or change nothing? Alternatively, should we expect it to cut taxes, to increase taxes, or to change nothing? These are the types of questions we will be looking at in this chapter. But first we need to define some terms.

11.1 Fiscal Policy and the Budget

LO1
See why the federal government's revenue depends on the rate of taxation, the size of the GDP, and its own spending.

fiscal policy: the government's approach toward its own spending and taxation.

Fiscal policy refers to the government's approach toward its own spending and taxation. When the minister of finance brings down the budget in Parliament each spring, this reveals the government's fiscal policy for the coming year. The annual budget contains estimates of the government's revenues and expenditures. Budget day is headline news, and TV screens across the country are filled with political comments about how good or bad the new budget is.

Table 11.1 shows the federal government's budget plan for the fiscal year beginning April 1, 2001. All figures are in billions of dollars.

TABLE 11.1 Federal Government's Budget Plan for Fiscal Year Beginning April 2001

REVENUES	
Personal income taxes	$84.3
E.I. premiums	17.8
Corporate income taxes	23.6
GST and excise taxes	37.2
Non-tax revenues	8.4
Total Revenues	171.3
OUTLAYS	
Transfers to persons	39.3
Spending grants to other levels of government	27.1
Public debt charges	40.7
Direct program spending	64.1
Total Outlays	171.3
Projected Budget Plan Surplus/Deficit	0

Source: Data derived by authors from information found in Department of Finance; Budget Plan, 2001.

Revenues are the government's total receipts which were projected to be $171.3 billion in the fiscal year 2001–2002, which began on April 1. This figure represents approximately 15.8 percent of Canada's projected GDP. These revenues do not include the CPP payments that are made by Canadians, since this program is administrated independently of the budget. By far the largest source of revenue is the *personal income tax* which is estimated to be $84.3 billion, while E.I. premiums, also paid by individual income earners, are $17.8 billion.

CP/Tom Hanson

Prime Minister Jean Chretien and Finance Minister John Manley acknowledge a standing ovation from the Liberal Caucus for the federal budget.

Corporate income taxes are taxes on profits paid by companies and totalled $23.6 billion. *GST and excise taxes* include the federal sales tax on consumption as well as excise taxes on gasoline, alcohol, and cigarettes plus tariff revenues on certain imports. *Non-tax revenues*, at $8.4 billion, include income from government crown corporations and other government investments, plus Bank of Canada earnings.

Total outlays were projected to be $171.3 billion. Transfers to persons are projected to be $39.3 billion and include payments towards Old Age Security, Guaranteed Annual Income Supplements, Spouse's Allowances, and the E.I. program. Once again, CPP payments are not included here. *Spending grants to other levels of government*, at $27.1 billion, are earmarked for spending on postsecondary education, health, and social assistance, as well as equalization payments, which are aimed at seven provinces (all but Ontario, Alberta, and B.C.). Aid to developing nations and dues to international organizations such as the U.N. are also included in this category. *Public debt charges*, at $40.7 billion, is the interest that is paid on the government's national debt and is also treated as a form of transfer payment in national income accounting. The last item, *direct program spending* of $64.1 billion, is part of the total spending on goods and services (G) that we first identified in the circular flow treatment in Chapter 3 and includes everything from computers for government offices to the civil servants working in those offices. The *projected plan* for this year is for the budget to be balanced with total government revenues projected to be equal to total outlays.

net tax revenue: total tax revenue received by government less transfer payments.

We now need to define **net tax revenue**, which is:

$$\text{NTR} = \text{tax revenue} - \text{transfer payments} \quad [11.1]$$

The government's budget balance is defined as the difference between net tax revenues and government spending; that is,

$$\text{budget balance} = \text{NTR} - \text{G} \quad [11.2]$$

budget surplus: net tax revenue in excess of government spending on goods and services.

budget deficit: government spending on goods and services in excess of net tax revenues.

national debt: the sum of the federal government's budget deficits less its surpluses.

A positive balance means a **budget surplus**, since net tax revenue would be greater than spending on goods and services. Conversely, a negative balance means a **budget deficit**, since net tax revenues would be lower than government spending. It is important to note that government tax revenues, spending, and the deficit (or surplus) are all flows, because they occur over a period of time. If we were to add up all the deficit flows over the years and then subtract the sum of all the surpluses over the same time period, we would get the **national debt**. The national debt, or, as it is sometimes called, the public debt, is a stock concept because it is a total outstanding at any particular point in time and is the summation of the flows of all deficits and surpluses. We will return to this topic at the end of the chapter.

Let's take a brief historical look at the government's budget balance by going to **Table 11.2**.

TABLE 11.2 Budget Surpluses/Deficits and the National Debt (current $ billion)

Year	Budget Surplus	Budget Deficit	National Debt
1940		0.1	5.1
1960		0.6	16.8
1969	0.1		34.8
1973		1.9	29.7
1983		23.9	138.6
1993		41.0	466.2
1994		42.0	508.2
1995		37.5	545.7
1996		28.6	574.3
1997		8.9	583.2
1998	3.5		579.7
1999	2.9		576.8
2000	12.3		564.5
2001	17.1		547.4

Source: Adapted from Department of Finance, Budget 2001 Budget Plan.

Deficits were a permanent feature in the 70s and 80s, and rose to over $40 billion per year in the early 90s. This led to increasing pressure on the government to change policy and balance the budget. The size of the deficit started to fall in 1995 and turned into a surplus in 1998. What was behind this rather dramatic turnaround? The answer is twofold. First, the government cut transfer payments to the provinces, which squeezed the delivery of health care and higher education services across the country, with the result that waiting lists for surgery grew and hospitals closed beds, while college and university classes grew in size and professors salaries were frozen. Second, despite the cut in government spending, the rate of economic growth, fuelled by increased exports to the U.S., accelerated and raised government revenues since more people were working and paying income tax, and total spending was up, which meant more GST revenue.

By the turn of the millenium, the government was feeling a new kind of pressure: debate over what to do with the projected budget surplus of approximately $50 billion over the coming five years. Some voices called for a dramatic increase in health and education spending, citing what they saw as a threat to the viability of Canada's health care system and a deterioration in the quality of higher education in the country. Others wanted the surpluses to go to a reduction in the national debt, which they felt was simply too large. A third group called for reductions in taxes, expressing concern over the growing gap in after-tax income between Canadians and Americans and evidence of a growing "brain-drain" to the United States. Perhaps not surprisingly, the then-minister of finance, Paul Martin, brought down budgets that did a little of all three.

Changes in the Economy and Government Revenues

It is important to emphasize the fact that changes in the economy can have an impact on government revenues. A prime example of this occurred between the budget years of 1996 and 1997. In those two years, the size of the budget deficit dropped from $28.6 billion to $8.9 billion. As we mentioned, while transfer payments did decrease a little, the decrease in the deficit was primarily because continued economic growth in the economy raised government revenues. In general, net tax revenues are directly related to the level of GDP. In addition, you may recall that we treat government spending on goods and services as autonomous of the level of real GDP. We put revenue and spending together in **Figure 11.1**.

FIGURE 11.1 **Government Deficits and Surpluses**

At real GDP level Y_2, government spending and net tax revenues are equal and, therefore, there is a balanced budget, as illustrated by point *c* in Figure 11.1A. In 11.1B, a balanced budget is also indicated by point *c*, which is where the budget line, BL, crosses the zero axis. At real GDP level Y_3, net tax revenues exceed government spending and, therefore, there is a budget surplus, indicated by *de* in either graph. Conversely, at real GDP level Y_1, there is a budget deficit of *ab*.

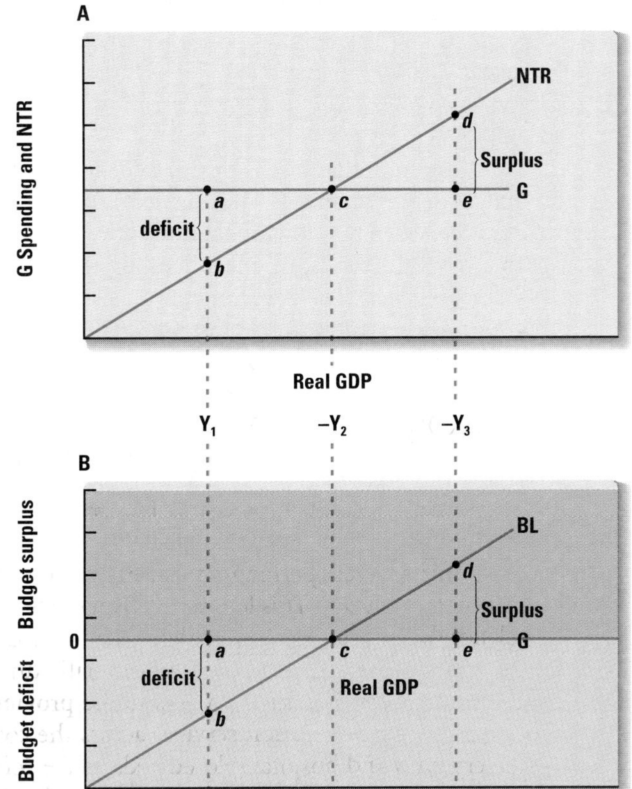

Since the government's tax revenue is greater and transfer payments are lower at higher levels of real GDP, net tax revenue (NTR) rises as the level of real GDP rises. We will assume that when GDP is zero, tax revenues and transfers are also zero, so that the NTR line begins at the origin and rises as GDP rises, as illustrated in **Figure 11.1A**. The horizontal line G reflects the autonomous nature of government spending on goods and services. At a GDP level of Y_1, NTR is less than the level of government spending and there would be a budget deficit equal to *ab*. At a GDP level of Y_3, NTR exceeds G and there would be a budget surplus equal to *de*. When GDP is at a level indicated by Y_2, there would be neither a budget surplus or deficit, as illustrated by point *c*. The effect of different levels of GDP on the budget is shown explicitly in **Figure 11.1B**, with the budget line, BL, showing the same deficit, *ab*, at GDP level Y_1 and the same surplus, *cd*, at GDP level Y_3. Point *c* on either figure is the situation of a **balanced budget**.

balanced budget: the equality of net tax revenues and government spending on goods and services.

Continuing with **Figure 11.1**, note that there are two things besides the level of GDP that will affect the government's budget and therefore the position of the budget line: a change in either the amounts of government spending or net tax revenues. An increase in government spending, for instance, will increase the amount of the budget deficit (or reduce the surplus) at every level of GDP and result in the budget line shifting down. An increase in tax rates (and thus the level of net tax revenues), on the other hand, will imply a reduced deficit (or increased surplus) at every level of GDP. This would be illustrated by an upward shift in the budget line and a change in the slope if NTR $= f(\text{GDP})$. The essential point is that:

The state of the government's budget depends on the level of GDP in the economy as well as on tax rates and its own spending.

SELF-TEST

1. Assume that current net tax revenues are $200 billion, government spending on goods and services is $180 billion, and the national debt at the beginning of the period was half the size of current net tax revenues. What is the size of the national debt at the end of the period?

A question that often springs to people's minds at this point is: how is the government's budget deficit financed? There is no mystery to the answer: it is financed by borrowing. For example, when an individual buys a government bond (such as a Canada Savings Bond or a Treasury Bill) she is, in effect, lending the government some of her savings so that it can finance a deficit. The government can also borrow from the Bank of Canada. In this case, the government would issue bonds and sell them to the Bank of Canada, which would increase the amount that the government had on deposit with it. The government would then write cheques that would clear through the banking system and ultimately get debited against that same account with the Bank of Canada. The effect of this is pretty well the same as the government printing money to pay its bills: it leads to an increase in the money supply. This method of borrowing, known as **monetizing the debt**, is not used to a great extent in Canada today but has been frequently used by desperate governments in the past to finance wars or to otherwise help a country survive extreme economic conditions.

monetizing the debt: the action by government of borrowing from its central bank to finance increased spending.

We now want to address one of the more important questions posed at the beginning of this chapter. What, if anything, should the government do when the economy faces unemployment, or for that matter inflation? There are two distinct schools of thought on this issue. On the one hand we have economists and policy makers, interventionists, who believe that the government needs to deliberately intervene in the economy and overspend, or underspend, from time to time in order to help the economy achieve the goals of full employment and stable prices. On the other hand there are those, the non-interventionists, who believe that these goals can be achieved only if there is no government intervention. Let's now look at each of these schools of thought in some detail.

11.2 Counter-Cyclical Fiscal Policy

LO2
Explain the pros and cons of a budget policy aimed at achieving full-employment equilibrium.

counter-cyclical fiscal policy: deliberate adjustments in the level of government spending and taxation in order to close recessionary or inflationary gaps.

The interventionists start with the premise that the modern market economy is unstable and thus prone to periods of unacceptably high levels of unemployment or inflation. Thus they advocate the use of **counter-cyclical fiscal policy**, a policy used by governments in many countries around the world since the Second World War. The main purpose of counter-cyclical fiscal policy is to close recessionary and inflationary gaps; that is, figuratively speaking, to lean against the prevailing winds. If, for example, aggregate demand is weak and a recessionary gap exists, expansionary policy should be used to deliberately stimulate demand with higher government spending or lower taxes (or both). On the other hand, if aggregate demand is so strong that an inflationary gap exists, then contractionary policy should be used to dampen down demand through cuts in government spending or increases in taxes. The recessionary gap situation is illustrated in **Figure 11.2**.

FIGURE 11.2 **Counter-Cyclical Fiscal Policy with a Recessionary Gap**

A recessionary gap exists if the current level of GDP is below the full-employment level as illustrated by $Y_{FE} - Y_1$. Counter-cyclical fiscal policy is aimed at increasing the level of aggregate demand by either increasing government spending or decreasing taxes. It shifts up the aggregate demand curve from AD_1 to AD_2 and closes the recessionary gap.

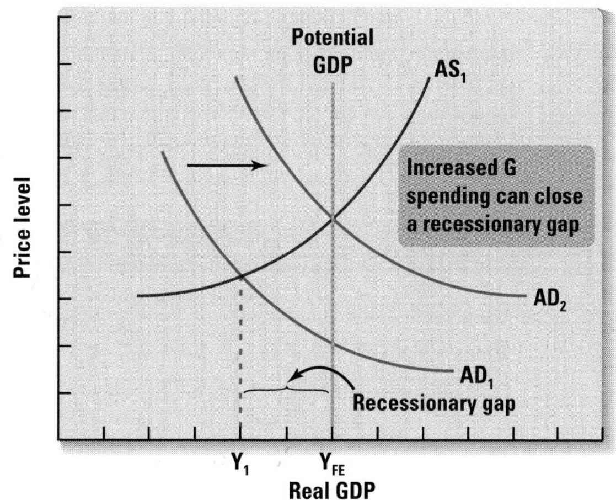

Given the current aggregate supply curve, AS_1, and the aggregate demand curve AD_1, equilibrium GDP is Y_1. Since this level of GDP is below potential GDP of Y_{FE}, we have a recessionary gap of $Y_{FE} - Y_1$. Counter-cyclical fiscal policy would call for either increased government spending or decreased taxes. This would increase aggregate demand, as indicated by the shift from AD_1 to AD_2. If such a policy was crafted well, aggregate demand would increase just enough to eliminate the recessionary gap by moving the economy to Y_{FE}.

Next, let's assume the economy is experiencing an inflationary gap. Here the appropriate counter-cyclical fiscal policy would be to decrease government spending or increase taxes in order to reduce the level of aggregate demand. This is illustrated in **Figure 11.3**.

FIGURE 11.3 **Counter-Cyclical Fiscal Policy with an Inflationary Gap**

If the economy is experiencing an inflationary gap such as $Y_1 - Y_{FE}$, then the appropriate counter-cyclical fiscal policy aimed at closing the gap is to lower the level of aggregate demand by either reducing government spending or increasing taxes. This is illustrated by a downward shift in the aggregate demand from AD_1 to AD_2.

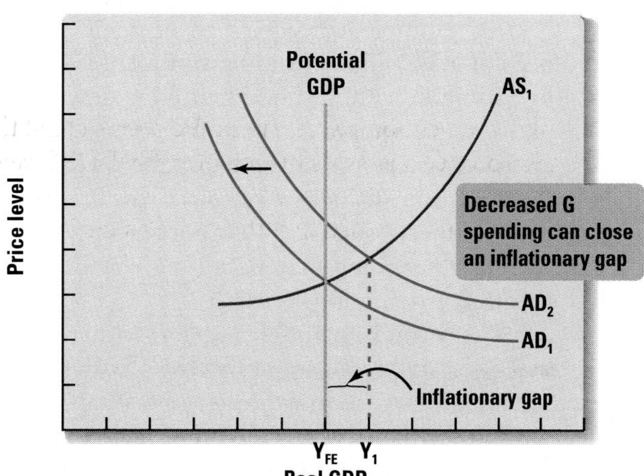

An inflationary gap is present because the equilibrium level of GDP, Y_1, is above the full-employment level, Y_{FE}. Closing the gap requires a lower level of aggregate demand, as illustrated by the shift from AD_1 to AD_2. This could be accomplished by the government reducing its spending or increasing taxes.

In summary, counter-cyclical fiscal policy means that:

- When aggregate demand is low and the economy is experiencing a recessionary gap, governments should spend and tax in a way that *increases* aggregate demand.
- When aggregate demand is high and an inflationary gap is present, governments should spend and tax in a way that *reduces* the level of aggregate demand.

In this way, government policy would be helping to stabilize the economy and take some of the sting out of the fluctuations in the business cycle.

SELF-TEST

2. In the following cases, indicate the direction toward which the aggregate demand curve will shift (right or left).

a) Taxes increase.

b) Government spending on goods and services decreases.

c) Counter-cyclical fiscal policy is used to close a recessionary gap.

d) Counter-cyclical fiscal policy is used to close an inflationary gap.

Criticisms of Counter-Cyclical Fiscal Policy

Counter-cyclical fiscal policy has come under a good deal of criticism in recent years. We will look at three potential problems associated with the use of counter-cyclical fiscal policy.

The first involves the fact that interventionists see the essence of counter-cyclical fiscal policy as that of fine-tuning the economy. This is done by adjusting government spending or taxation by just the right amounts to achieve a level of aggregate demand sufficient to bring about full-employment GDP. Critics, however, argue that, in practice, the use of counter-cyclical fiscal policy is like fine-tuning with a sledgehammer. Even if just the right amount of adjustment can be determined, counter-cyclical fiscal policy takes time to implement and is slow to take effect. This means that the economy may suffer from an overdose of spending when the policy does take full effect.

For example, consider a government that has just determined that the economy is in need of a $4 billion spending stimulant. This government cannot simply increase spending by $4 billion without first identifying how it is going to spend the money and then getting parliamentary approval for its fiscal plans. The next problem is that a number of procedures are necessary before the actual spending can begin, the most significant of which is putting out contracts for bids by various firms in the private sector. All of this takes time, and since major projects, such as a new port facility, may last a number of years, the full effect of the increased spending may be a long way down the road; by which time the need for such spending may no longer exist.

The second potential problem with counter-cyclical fiscal policy is that many believe that it is, quite simply, ineffective. Critics argue that the effect of increased government spending to try to close a recessionary gap may prove to be much less potent than expected, for two distinct reasons. The first is that any increase in government spending that is not financed through taxation may be inflationary. Suppose, for instance, that the government uses counter-cyclical fiscal policy to get an economy out of a recession. The result will be an increase in aggregate demand, as shown in **Figure 11.4**.

FIGURE 11.4 **The Effect of Counter-Cyclical Fiscal Policy on the Price Level**

If the economy is experiencing a recessionary gap, counter-cyclical fiscal policy will increase the level of aggregate demand. This is illustrated by the shift from AD_1 to AD_2. The recessionary gap closes as real GDP increases from Y_1 to Y_{FE}. However, the price level will also increase from P1 to P2.

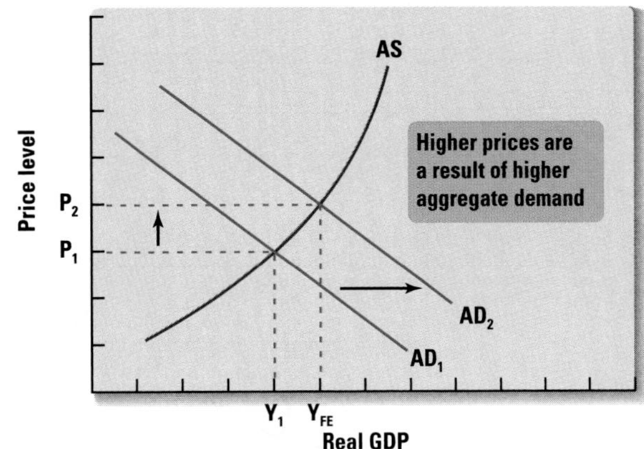

An increase in government spending (or a reduction in taxes) would shift the aggregate demand curve to the right, from AD_1 to AD_2. Clearly, the level of GDP increases from Y_1 to Y_{FE}. Unfortunately, the price level also rises, in this case from P_1 to P_2. Counter-cyclical fiscal policy therefore is inflationary, and the rate of inflation depends on how close the economy is to full employment. As you may recall from Chapter 6, as we approach the full-employment level of GDP, the rise in prices accelerates. This inflation will hurt consumers and investors and make Canadian goods and services less attractive to foreigners. This loss of international competitiveness has serious consequences for an economy like Canada's, which relies so heavily on exports.

crowding-out effect: the idea that government borrowing to finance a deficit crowds out private investment because it causes interest rates to rise.

The second reason why counter-cyclical fiscal policy may be ineffective is because of what is termed the **crowding-out effect**. As we just saw, counter-cyclical fiscal policy used to close a recessionary gap will increase the level of GDP. But as the level of GDP rises, so too will the money demand, as we learned in Chapter 8. Assuming no increase in the money supply, this increase in the demand for money will tend to push up interest rates, and this increase in interest rates will tend to reduce the level of, or crowd out, private investment spending. This is illustrated in **Figure 11.5**.

FIGURE 11.5 **The Effect of Counter-Cyclical Fiscal Policy on Money Demand**

Expansionary fiscal policy implies an increase in aggregate demand, shown as a shift from AD_1 to AD_2. If the price level remains constant at P_1, GDP would increase from Y_1 to Y_{FE}. However, the price level increases to P_2, and as a result the money demand and interest rates both increase as shown in Figure 11.5B. The higher interest rate reduces the level of investment spending, as seen in Figure 11.5C. The lower investment spending in turn reduces the aggregate quantity demanded (a movement along AD_2) in Figure 11.5A and thereby reduces real GDP to Y_3.

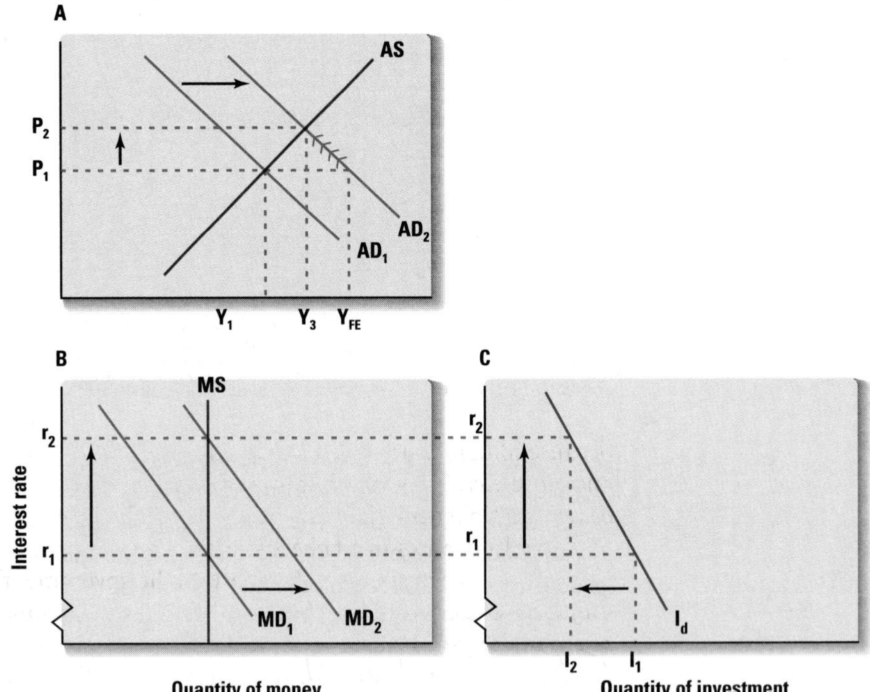

In **Figure 11.5A** we see that counter-cyclical fiscal policy results in the aggregate demand curve shifting from AD_1 to AD_2. If we could ignore the effect on the money market, then real GDP would increase from Y_1 to Y_{FE}. However, the consequent increase in the price level will increase the transactions demand for money, and therefore the money demand curve will shift out from MD_1 to MD_2, as seen in **Figure 11.5B**. This, in turn, increases the interest rate from r_1 to r_2. This higher interest rate reduces investment spending, as illustrated in **Figure 11.5C**, where investment falls from I_1 to I_2. This then reduces the aggregate quantity demanded (a movement up AD_2) as seen in **Figure 11.5A**. In summary, the increase in government spending pushes up aggregate demand and real GDP, but the subsequent decrease in investment spending causes the aggregate quantity to fall back a little.

We have just seen that counter-cyclical fiscal policy might push up interest rates and weaken the effect of fiscal policy through the crowding-out of private investment spending. There is another possible effect of higher interest rates that we need to consider. In an open economy with flexible exchange rates, like Canada's, the higher interest rates will pull money into the country as foreign money-fund managers buy Canadian dollars in order to make deposits in Canadian financial institutions. The effect of this inflow of foreign currencies is to increase the demand for the Canadian dollar and as a result cause the Canadian dollar to appreciate. As we know from Chapter 10, the higher exchange rate will reduce the level of Canadian exports (just as higher Canadian prices did) and increase Canadian imports.

The net effect of all this is that counter-cyclical fiscal policy may crowd out net exports. Thus we have two possible aspects to this crowding-out effect—on investment spending and on net exports—both of which combine to weaken the effectiveness of fiscal policy.

In summary, the effectiveness of counter-cyclical fiscal policy to close a recessionary gap may be reduced because:

- it increases the price level and decreases exports
- it increases interest rates, which crowds out investment spending, and it increases the exchange rate, which crowds out net exports.

As you can see, the use of fiscal policy has a number of possible undesirable side-effects, which leaves it open to criticism.

SELF-TEST

3. What effect will counter-cyclical fiscal policy aimed at closing an inflationary gap have on interest rates, the exchange rate, net exports, and prices?

There is another way to look at the possible ineffectiveness of counter-cyclical fiscal policy. You will recall that an increase in government spending will increase the level of national income by an amount determined by the multiplier. However, we have just seen that some of this increase in government spending is offset by a decrease in consumption spending because of higher prices, a decrease in investment spending because of higher interest rates, and a decrease in exports because of a higher exchange rate. The result of this is that the size of the multiplier is reduced.

The third, and some believe the most serious problem with counter-cyclical fiscal policy, is that it completely ignores the effect on the government's budget. Over the last half century Canada's counter-cyclical fiscal policy has been aimed mainly at attempting to close recessionary gaps. Such policy involves either higher levels of government spending or lower levels of taxation. Either of these will have a deficit-inducing effect on the current budget. The result will be an increase in the size of an already-existing budget deficit or a decrease in the size of an already-existing budget surplus. This is best illustrated with **Figure 11.6**.

FIGURE 11.6 **Effect of Counter-Cyclical Fiscal Policy on Budget Deficits**

Suppose the economy is originally at GDP level Y_1 with a budget deficit of *ab*. Counter-cyclical fiscal policy aimed at increasing aggregate demand from AD_1 to AD_2 will also shift the budget line down from BL_1 to BL_2. The result is a larger budget deficit, *cd*, at the new equilibrium income of Y_{FE}.

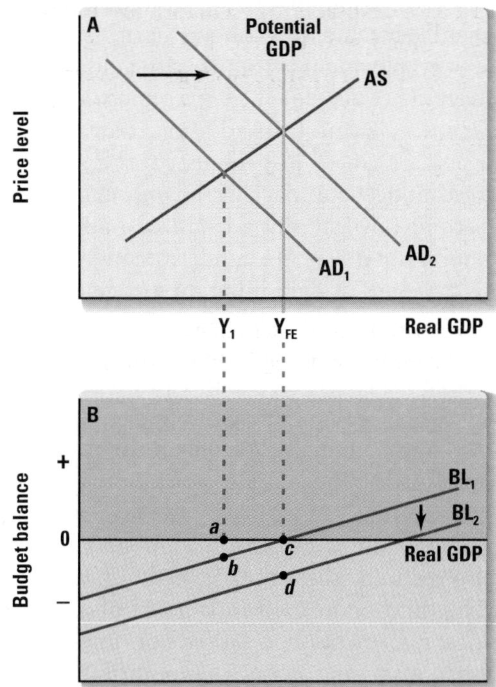

Suppose that the current level of GDP in **Figure 11.6A** is Y_1. This means that the economy is experiencing a recessionary gap equal to the distance between full-employment level of GDP, Y_{FE}, and the current level Y_1. We can also see, in **Figure 11.6B**, that at GDP level Y_1 the government has a budget deficit of *ab*. The recessionary gap can be closed by the use of counter-cyclical fiscal policy. This would imply an increase in government spending or a decrease in taxation. The effect, graphically, would be to shift aggregate demand from AD_1 to AD_2. However, the greater government spending or lower taxation would also increase the size of the government's budget deficit. This is illustrated in the downward shift in the budget line from BL_1 to BL_2. The overall result is the economy moving to full-employment equilibrium at Y_{FE}, but this would result in an even larger deficit of *cd*.

If the deficit-inducing effects occur often and are allowed to accumulate over a period of time, the size of the government's national debt will grow substantially. Increased deficits mean increased borrowing and this then requires that the government spend a larger percentage of its total spending on servicing its debt, leaving only a smaller percentage for conventional spending on things like health care and post-secondary education.

In summary, the three criticisms of counter-cyclical fiscal policy are that it:

- is subject to serious time lags
- is ineffective because it may be inflationary, crowds out private spending, and thus reduces the size of the multiplier
- can cause serious budget deficits

11.3 Balanced-Budget Fiscal Policy

LO3
Explain the pros and cons of a budget policy aimed at achieving a balanced budget in each fiscal year.

balanced-budget fiscal policy: the belief that a government's budget should be balanced in each budget period.

Some politicians and political commentators, and even a few economists, alarmed at the effect of counter-cyclical fiscal policy on the size of budget deficits, argue that the government should balance its spending and tax revenues in *each budget period*. This is known as a **balanced-budget fiscal policy**. Advocates of a balanced-budget fiscal policy use three observations to support their position. First, they contend that counter-cyclical fiscal policy is just as likely to do the economy harm as it is to help it. For example, they would argue that while unemployment insurance expenditures might help an immediate problem, they will adversely affect people's incentives and warp their sense of responsibility, which, in the long run, is quite harmful. In addition, they consider the three criticisms of counter-cyclical fiscal policy that we just discussed as a serious indictment of that approach and see the balanced-budget approach as the only alternative.

automatic stabilizers: provisions of tax laws and government spending programs that automatically take spending out of the economy when it is booming and put spending in when it is slowing down.

Second, advocates of a balanced-budget fiscal policy approach believe that because of **automatic stabilizers**, the modern economy has enough built-in safeguards to ensure that it avoids extremes of high inflation or unemployment. Automatic stabilizers are government programs that ensure that spending remains relatively stable even in times of rapid economic change. For instance, as we have seen, when an economy enters a recession, because of the progressive nature of taxes, disposable incomes don't fall by as much as GDP. In addition, the amount paid out in unemployment benefits and welfare assistance increases, and this buoys up disposable income and therefore consumption spending.

Automatic stabilizers also come into force when the economy is booming and in danger of "over-heating." In this case, the higher levels of GDP generate proportionately higher taxes, and, at the same time, the amounts paid out for unemployment benefits and welfare are also reduced. These both have the effect of dampening-down expenditures.

The third point used in support of a balanced-budget fiscal policy is by far the most significant. As mentioned earlier, non-interventionists believe that if either a recessionary or an inflationary gap exists (temporarily), then the economy is capable of returning to full-employment equilibrium by itself through a self-adjustment process, unaided by interventionist polices of any kind. We have touched on this self-adjustment process in Chapter 5, and we will examine it in depth in Chapter 13. For now we need only point out that if the self-adjustment process is effective, as the non-interventionists believe, then fiscal policy should be as neutral in its effects on the economy as is possible. The non-interventionists see such neutrality achieved through the use of a balanced-budget fiscal policy.

In summary, the arguments in support of a balanced-budget fiscal policy are that:

- the non-interventionist approach emphasizes incentives
- the economy has effective automatic stabilizers
- the economy is capable of returning to full-employment equilibrium through a self-adjustment process

Criticisms of Balanced-Budget Fiscal Policy

We now need to examine the economic effects of a government actually following a balanced-budget fiscal policy. In doing so we will find that the effects are significant but they are not at all neutral.

Suppose in **Figure 11.7A** that the economy is at income level Y_1. Since income is below potential GDP, the economy finds itself in a recession. As is often the case in a recession, because of falling tax revenues, the government is suffering a budget deficit, as shown by the distance *ab* in **Figure 11.7B**. If the government is intent on balancing the budget irrespective of the condition of the economy, then it will have no choice but to either reduce government spending and/or increase taxation. The result, graphically, will be an upward shift in the budget line from BL_1 to BL_2 in **Figure 11.7B**, so that at income level Y_1, the budget is, in fact, balanced. However, the effect of cutting government spending or increasing taxes will have an impact not only on the government budget but also on the economy. The result will be a reduction in aggregate demand. This is shown graphically in **Figure 11.7A** as a leftward shift in the aggregate demand curve from AD_1 to AD_2.

FIGURE 11.7 **Reduced Government Spending and the Deficit**

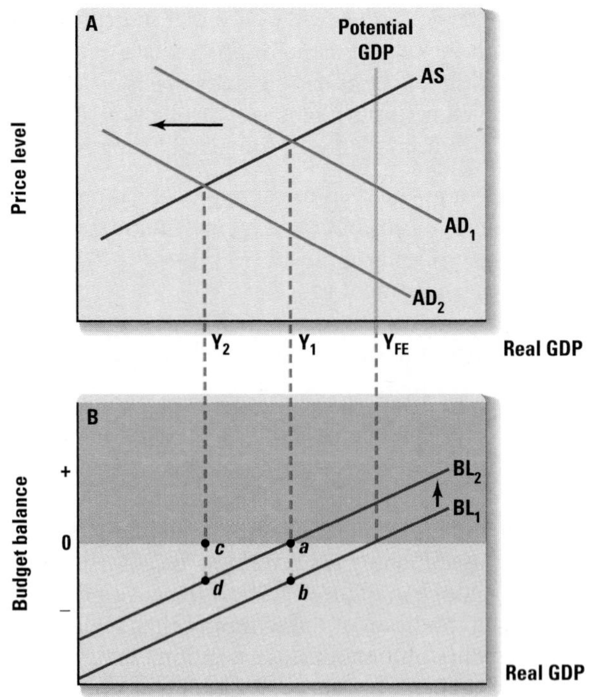

An attempt to eliminate the budget deficit that exists at Y_1 would call for a reduction in government spending or an increase in taxes. Thus, the budget line shifts up from BL_1 to BL_2, and the budget deficit appears to be eliminated (point *a*). However, this action reduces aggregate demand from AD_1 to AD_2, which causes the level of equilibrium GDP to decrease to Y_2 and at this lower level of GDP, there is still a budget deficit of *cd*.

The drop in aggregate demand will cause GDP to drop by a multiple of the decrease in aggregate expenditures. At the lower equilibrium level of Y_2, NTR will be smaller, with the result that the budget deficit (*cd*) will persist (although it is now smaller than it was at *ab*).

What we have just seen is that if the economy is experiencing a recessionary gap and a budget deficit, then the pursuit of a balanced-budget fiscal policy will be **pro-cyclical**. To understand this, note that a recession implies that there is unemployment in the economy. If the government takes action to try to eliminate the budget deficit, rather than the unemployment, then the level of unemployment will rise, since the level of GDP falls. In short, the business cycle has created a given level of unemployment and the government's fiscal policy, which was aimed at reducing the deficit, resulted in even *higher* unemployment.

pro-cyclical: action by the government that tends to push the economy in the same direction it is leaning in.

Would a balanced-budget fiscal policy result in the same pro-cyclical tendencies if the economy was experiencing an inflationary gap? The answer to this depends on the state of the budget associated with the gap. Recall that an inflationary gap is a result of high aggregate demand, which generates a level of income that is temporarily higher than the full-employment level of GDP.

Let's assume that this high GDP level generates sufficient tax revenue for the government to be running a budget surplus. Strict adherence to a balanced-budget fiscal policy would then necessitate that either taxes be lowered or spending increased to eliminate the budget surplus. Such fiscal policy action would *raise* aggregate demand and, thus, the level of GDP. This would increase the size of the inflationary gap, and we again see the pro-cyclical nature of a balanced-budget fiscal policy in this situation.

Let's review what we have here. A balanced-budget fiscal policy will likely be pro-cyclical in circumstances in which the economy is experiencing a recessionary gap, since the low levels of income will generate low levels of tax revenue, which create budget deficits. Similarly, such a policy will be pro-cyclical when the economy is experiencing an inflationary gap if the inflationary gap comes with a budget surplus.

The Arithmetic of a Balanced Budget

Let's now examine another aspect of the pro-cyclical nature of the balanced-budget philosophy in more detail. We will again assume that the budget is balanced and that the economy is at full-employment equilibrium. Next, assume that a new government, which promised lower government spending, is elected. This new government is intent on carrying out its promise of cuts in spending. However, in consideration of the already balanced budget and given the fact that the economy is at full employment, they also announce that taxes will be reduced by a similar amount. Since government spending and taxes are to be cut by the same amount, won't both the government's budget balance and the level of GDP be unaffected? That is to say, isn't it true that what the government takes out of the economy in the form of reduced spending is exactly offset by what it puts back into the economy in the form of reduced taxes? It comes as a surprise to most people that the answer to this question is no.

Suppose that the economy is at a full-employment equilibrium of \$1000, government spending is \$200, and taxes, which for simplicity we assume are entirely autonomous, are also \$200. Furthermore, suppose that the value of the multiplier is equal to 2 and that the portion of additional income that consumers spend (the MPC_D) is 0.8. As we know, a reduction in government spending will definitely reduce aggregate demand and, therefore, the level of GDP. Suppose government spending is cut by \$40. With a multiplier of 2, this will reduce GDP by \$80. Next, we know that the corresponding cut in taxes will increase aggregate demand and the level of the GDP. But how much will GDP increase? Will it increase by the same \$80?

Well, a cut in taxes of \$40 will immediately raise disposable income by the same \$40. Does this mean that consumers will spend all of this additional disposable income? The answer is no, since, with an MPC_D of 0.80, we know that the increase in spending will only be $0.8 \times \$40$, or \$32 (the other \$8 will be saved). This additional \$32 in spending, not the whole \$40 cut in taxes, is the amount that gets multiplied. Schematically, therefore:

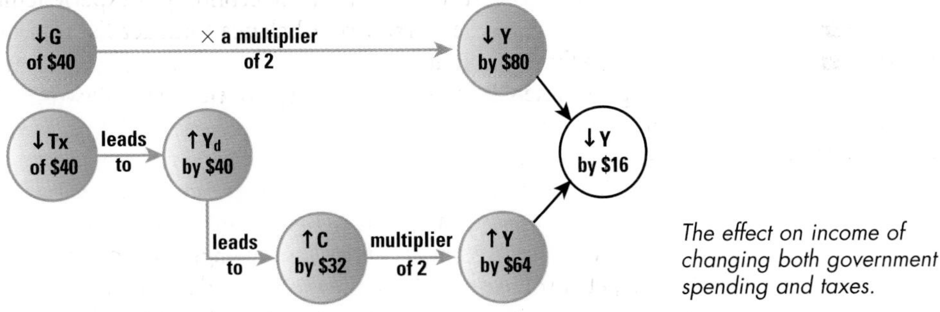

The effect on income of changing both government spending and taxes.

The cut in government spending reduces the level of GDP by \$80, whereas the cut in taxes increases it by only \$64. The net result is a drop in GDP of \$16. In short:

A policy of decreasing both government spending and taxes by the same amount results in a lower real GDP and higher unemployment.

We end this discussion of the two contrasting approaches to fiscal policy by noting that the essence of a counter-cyclical fiscal policy, which is aimed at the level of GDP and unemployment, is to use fiscal policy to address recessionary and inflationary gaps that might exist in the *economy*. In simple terms, it attempts to balance the economy, not the government's budget. By contrast, the essence of the balanced-budget fiscal policy, which is aimed at the government's budget, is to use fiscal policy to balance that *budget*, not the economy.

SELF-TEST

4. Assume that the economy is in a recession and that the government is experiencing a budget deficit. If fiscal policy is used to try to eliminate the deficit, what will happen to:

a) unemployment?

b) GDP?

c) NTR?

d) the deficit?

Next, assume the same conditions, but this time fiscal policy is used to try to reduce unemployment. How will your four answers above change?

5. Given the following data, and assuming all taxes are autonomous, calculate equilibrium income.

$C = 20 + 0.75Y_D$

$X_N = 60 - 0.25Y$

$I = 50$

$G = 80$

$T_0 = 80$

Next, assume that the government increases both its spending and autonomous taxes by 20. Calculate the new equilibrium income. Is this action by government neutral, or does it have some impact on income?

It is now clear that the issues regarding the use of fiscal policy to address recessionary gaps, inflationary gaps, and the question of the budget deficit are more complex than one would first imagine. It is true that some people object to counter-cyclical fiscal policy because such an approach ignores the issue of budget deficits and the associated level of the national debt. On the other hand, the balanced-budget fiscal policy has the potential problem of exacerbating the economy's situation because of its pro-cyclical tendencies. Is there another approach that could be used? In fact, the answer is yes. We now turn to a discussion of it.

11.4 Cyclically Balanced-Budget Fiscal Policy

LO4
Explain the pros and cons of a budget policy aimed at achieving both full employment and a balanced budget over the life of the business cycle.

Without overstating the obvious, one could ask, as far as budgets are concerned, what is so sacred about a year? Why not balance the budget each week, or each month, or, for that matter, each day? Well, a week or a month simply wouldn't be practical, because the government's flow of income and expenditures is not regular, so some weeks or months would have high deficits, while others would have high surpluses. Given this, and given the fact that a government's budget also depends on the level of GDP in the economy, some economists suggest that governments should instead try to balance the budget, not on an annual basis but *over the life of the business cycle.* A typical business cycle can last for several years so that the use of fiscal policy to smooth out the business cycle would be viewed from a longer perspective than just each budget period. In these circumstances, deficits might be big in some years, as the government uses its fiscal policy to close a recessionary gap. On the other hand, when fiscal policy is used to close an inflationary gap the result should be budget surpluses. This longer-view approach would continue to use counter-cyclical fiscal policy to lean against the prevailing winds, while addressing the concerns of many people about budget deficits and the size of the national debt.

In a sense, this policy is a compromise of the two approaches discussed above and is known as a **cyclically balanced-budget fiscal policy**. The exact definition of this term is the use of counter-cyclical fiscal policy with the aim of balancing the budget over the life of the business cycle. Such a policy would require governments to spend more (or tax less) at some times, but also to spend less (or tax more) at other times.

cyclically balanced-budget fiscal policy: the use of counter-cyclical fiscal policy to balance the budget over the life of the business cycle.

Although it sounds like a sound idea, there are two potential problems with this cyclically balanced-budget fiscal policy. The first is that there is no guarantee that the size and length of the recessionary gap, when the government is running a budget deficit, will be exactly offset by the size and length of the inflationary gap, when the government is running a budget surplus. As a result, the end of the business cycle may still show a net budget deficit. The second is a political problem: most governments find it easier to increase spending in bad times than to decrease it in good times. In short, pursuing a cyclically balanced-budget fiscal policy would take a remarkable amount of discipline on the part of the government. In addition, most business cycles are longer than the term of office of any particular government. This invites the existing government to leave the problem of balancing the budget to the succeeding government.

REVIEW

1. Define *fiscal policy.*
2. Explain the difference between a *budget deficit* and the *national debt.*
3. What is the primary goal of counter-cyclical fiscal policy? What are three criticisms of it?
4. What is the primary goal of a balanced-budget fiscal policy? What are three criticisms of it?
5. What is meant by a *cyclically balanced-budget fiscal policy*?

11.5 Fiscal Policy and the National Debt

LO5
Discuss the cause, size, and problems of the national debt.

The size of the national debt is a topic that has received a great deal of attention lately. The use of counter-cyclical fiscal policy usually leads to growth in the debt, and, thus, its use has created a lot of debate. Let's examine all this more closely by asking: just what's so bad about budget deficits and therefore a growing national debt?

First, let us establish to whom this debt is owed. Any Canadian individual, corporation, or bank who buys a Canada Savings Bond, a treasury bill, or other type of government bond is lending money to the government. The payment of interest and the redemption of the bond is the responsibility of the government. In this sense, it can be regarded as a debt that we Canadians owe to ourselves. However, one of the major problems with the debt is that the "we" and the "ourselves" in the last sentence do not refer to the same groups of people. We, the taxpayers, are responsible for paying off the interest and principal to ourselves, the bondholders. But while all bondholders are taxpayers, not all taxpayers are bondholders. And therein lies one of the problems: as the size of the debt increases, and with it the interest payments, increasing amounts must be raised in taxes, which will then get transferred to bondholders. Since it is normally the comparatively wealthy who hold the majority of bonds, while taxes are paid by rich and poor alike, the payment of interest on the national debt could represent a major *redistribution of income.*

CP/Jeff McIntosh

This national debt "clock" was on public display across the country in the mid- and late 1990s.

For another angle on this redistributional aspect, let's assume the debt is entirely internal and that in response to public pressure it was decided to repay all of the debt of approximately $547 billion (as of 2001). How could this be done? The most straightforward answer is for the government to raise $547 billion additional dollars through increased taxes, of which all Canadians would pay some small part. What then would Ottawa do with this incredible rush of additional revenue? Turn around and send it back to those Canadians who hold Canada Savings Bonds and those institutions holding the other bonds. The net effect: all Canadians pay $547 billion in additional taxes, and some Canadians receive $547 billion in bond repayments. Why bother, many might argue? Why not leave it where it was in the first place?

Twenty years ago, the above discussion might have ended at this point. Alas, the world is no longer so simple. In 2001, 21 percent of the national debt was held by foreigners. *External debt* is not just what we owe to ourselves, since a portion of the interest payments now require a transfer of Canadian real output to the outside world. The reason for this is easy to comprehend. Interest payments to a foreigner lead to an outflow of foreign currency, and the only way to earn that currency is to first sell real goods or services abroad. The amount of the national debt held by foreigners grew from less than $1 billion in 1975 to approximately $93 billion in 2001. While it is true that the Canadian economy benefited from this inflow at the time that it occurred, the needed outflow to pay interest on it must now be a consideration in the debate as to the seriousness of the debt.

Let's now turn to an examination of some statistics. Public discussion of the national debt often runs to hyperbole, and we hear mention of a "staggering" debt of "enormous" proportions as a result of "crippling" deficits. Dollar amounts in billions are certainly enormous from an individual's perspective, but one seldom hears the size of Canada's GDP described as staggering. We need therefore to put things in perspective. Just how big is our national debt? It might help if we look at it over a period of time. **Table 11.3** shows some figures for selected years.

TABLE 11.3 **Net Federal Debt (nominal $ billion)**

1926	1940	1946	1967	1991	2001
2.4	3.3	13.4	15.6	386.3	547.4

Source: Adapted from Statistics Canada, CANSIM database, Table 385-0010.

It certainly seems a "staggering" increase. But since the population of Canada has increased appreciably during this century, it might be better to show the figures in terms of *per capita* debt, as in **Table 11.4**.

TABLE 11.4 **Per Capita Net Federal Debt (nominal dollars in billions)**

1926	1940	1946	1967	1991	2001
263	287	1090	780	14 180	17 658

Source: Adapted from Statistics Canada, CANSIM database, Table 385-0010.

It still looks like a fairly staggering increase. But we need to make one further adjustment to allow for the effects of inflation over the years. So let's show the total debt, but this time in constant 1997 dollars, as in **Table 11.5.**

TABLE 11.5 **Net Federal Debt ($1997, billions)**

1926	1940	1946	1967	1991	2001
23.9	38.0	130.0	78.9	424.2	516.9

Source: Adapted from Statistics Canada, CANSIM database, Table 385-0010.

Finally, let's combine both factors in **Table 11.6** to give us figures in terms of constant dollars per capita.

TABLE 11.6 **Per Capita Net Federal Debt (in $1997)**

1926	1940	1946	1967	1991	2001
2474	3356	10 562	3945	15 714	16 674

Source: Adapted from Statistics Canada, CANSIM database, Table 385-0010.

This puts things in perspective. In real terms, the per capita debt increased 35 per cent in the fourteen years leading up to the Second World War; it more than tripled during the war, declined to less than half by 1967, but has more than quadrupled in the last 34 years.

These figures show clearly that one of the major causes of the growth of Canada's debt was the financing of the Second World War. During a major war, few nations are able to finance their military expenditures through taxation alone. They are often left with little choice but to borrow, and the majority of this borrowing is from the nation's own citizens. Most would feel this is a legitimate reason to increase the debt and might also agree that there are other legitimate reasons for the increased debt—for example, deficit financing to prevent or escape from a recession, or the financing of necessary infrastructure such as bridges and airports. The third explanation for the increased Canadian debt, especially since the early 1970s, has been the increase in the size of income-support programs. Here, controversy about whether this is a good reason for the debt to increase heats up; some have suggested that these programs are too generous in comparison with those of some other countries.

Finally, it should be noted that the very high interest rates between the mid-1970s and the 1990s have compounded the size of the debt. (As we saw, some economists suggest that the reason interest rates were so high in the first place was because of borrowing by governments, that is, the crowding-out effect. Complicated world, isn't it?) Leaving the statistics behind, let's examine some of the problems associated with the debt.

Well, we've already mentioned three of them. First, we have seen how borrowing by the government may well crowd out private investment and leave the economy with a smaller capital stock in the future. However, some would point out that this is a cost only if one assumes that private capital investment (say, another shopping mall) is superior to public capital investment (a hospital). It obviously depends on what investment is crowded out.

The second potential problem (as we just saw) involves the size of the foreign portion of the debt. Private financial agencies give ratings for government bonds sold around the world, as an aid to their clients for investing. The lower the rating given a particular government's bonds, the higher the interest payments that must be paid. In early 1995, there was a *perception* that Canada's national debt was too large. The result was a lower bond rating, and the outflow of interest payments on the foreign-held debt increased.

Third, we noted that payment of interest on the debt represents a big redistribution of income.

As a fourth point, the big interest payments also mean, from the government's point of view, that each year it has to earmark several tens of billions of dollars to be paid in interest before it can even start to consider other spending claims. This obviously curtails its ability to satisfy other demands in the economy. (The annual total interest payments in the 1990s were approximately $40 billion, which is higher than the annual deficits during the period.) This is a conundrum: if the government didn't have to pay these interest charges, then it could balance the budget. But because it didn't balance the budget in the past, it has to pay these interest charges.

A final criticism comes from the fact that a federal government has almost unlimited power to spend. Theoretically (and legally) there is no upper limit to how big a deficit can be. That doesn't mean that big deficits are not harmful to an economy; it simply means that a national government has supreme power to tax, to borrow, and to print money. This means that without checks on its spending, a government can become greedy and wasteful in its fiscal affairs. And for this we would all suffer.

In summary, the problems with high deficits and debt are:

- the potential crowding out of private investment spending and net exports
- the interest payments that must be paid on the foreign-held debt
- the income redistribution effects of large interest payments
- the reduced ability of government to meet the needs of its citizens
- the possible increased greed and wastefulness of government

Let's now take a brief look at what are sometimes seen as problems of the debt but really aren't.

One of these bogus arguments seeks to draw an analogy between a household or a business and the operations of the federal government. It suggests that, just like an individual or a business, if revenue falls short of expenses for a long enough period of time, then bankruptcy will follow. This just isn't a legitimate concern when applied to a federal government, which has unlimited powers of taxation and borrowing, and direct control over the nation's supply of money. Therefore, a federal government cannot go broke as a result of *internal* borrowing. The government of Germany went broke following the First World War, but this was a result of external debt imposed on it by the victors in war. A particular city might go broke in the sense of defaulting on interest payments on the bonds it sold to borrow money, if urban decay and high taxes drive many higher-income taxpayers and businesses out of the city. The same might be said, although this would be stretching it, of a particular province or state, but not about a country as large, and as desirable to live in, as Canada.

Another argument suggests that a big national debt means that we are encumbering future generations, who will eventually have to pay it. It is true that our children and grandchildren will inherit a larger debt and the interest charges associated with it. However, it is also true that future generations will inherit the Canadian-held portion of the assets (bonds) represented by that debt. That is, if our descendants have to pay extra taxes to service a larger debt, they also, as a generation, will get those same taxes back as the interest payments are made to whoever holds those bonds.

While it is true that the federal government is in debt to the tune of hundreds of billions of dollars, it is also true that the government owns assets—airports, military hardware, land, buildings, and so on—that also total a great deal. Is the debt too large relative to the assets owned? A similar question is: what is the size of the public debt relative to Canada's GDP? We do have figures on this. Canada's debt–to–GDP ratio was highest at the end of the Second World War, then steadily fell to approximately 25 percent in the 1960s, and has since risen to approximately 50 percent in 2001.

A Wrap-up and a Plea for Common Sense

A national debt that is internally held, is in the 40–50 percent range of GDP, and whose interest payments are in the 10–15 percent range of the government's annual budget, is nothing to worry about. It is unfortunate that, until recently, Canada's national debt had grown to be over 60 percent of GDP, with interest payments now over 25 percent of the budget. In addition, a large portion of the debt was held by foreigners. It would, however, be a mistake to overreact and impose rigid rules or laws on government policy in an attempt to bring the debt under control. Doing so would only rob the federal government of its counter-cyclical fiscal policy options. Instead it is important for government and the public to understand that curing any economic problem will often come at the expense of causing other problems. Deficits can be reduced but perhaps only at the cost of jobs and real economic growth. Decisions on issues like these are fundamental and should be made carefully.

SELF-TEST

6. Under what circumstances is it inappropriate for the government to run a budget deficit?

REVIEW

1. Explain how the *crowding-out effect* might affect private investment spending.

2. Explain how the *crowding-out effect* might affect exports.

3. Explain how paying off the national debt would redistribute income.

4. To whom does the federal government owe most of its debt?

5. Why is it practically impossible for a country like Canada to go bankrupt?

STUDY GUIDE

Review

CHAPTER SUMMARY

The focus of this chapter was on three distinct budget polices. The first is counter-cyclical policy aimed at closing any GDP gaps that may exist in the economy. The second is an annually-balanced budget policy aimed at balancing the budget each budget period. The third is called a cyclically-balanced budget policy and calls for the budget to be balanced over the life of the business cycle.

1. The state of the government's *budget* depends on:
   - its net tax revenues which, in turn, depend on both the rate of taxation and the size of the GDP;
   - its own spending.
2. *Counter-cyclical fiscal policy*:
   - increases the level of government spending or decreases the level of taxation when a recessionary gap exists;
   - decreases the level of government spending or increases the level of taxation when an inflationary gap exists.
3. There are three potential *problems* with counter-cyclical fiscal policy:
   - there are serious time lags involved in closing a GDP gap;
   - it may be inflationary and may crowd out both private investment spending and exports;
   - it can cause serious budget deficits.
4. *Balanced-budget fiscal policy* balances the government's revenues and overall spending each budget year and:
   - stresses the role of individual incentives and responsibility;
   - highlights the effect of automatic stabilizers;
   - argues that the economy is capable of achieving full-employment equilibrium through a self-adjustment process.
5. The *problem* with a balanced-budget policy is that it is usually pro-cyclical and therefore can make an existing economic problem, such as unemployment, more serious.
6. A cyclically-balanced budget policy attempts to meld the above two policies into one where the budget is balanced but only over the life of the business cycle and not in every budget year.
7. The size of the *national debt* should be viewed in terms of:
   - per capita debt in constant dollars;
   - a percentage of real GDP;
8. The potential *problems* with the national debt are:
   - the crowding out of private investment spending and net exports;
   - the interest payments that must be paid out on its foreign-held portion;
   - the income distribution effects of large interest payments;
   - the reduced ability of the government to meet the needs of its citizens;
   - the possible increased greed and wastefulness of government.

NEW GLOSSARY TERMS AND KEY EQUATIONS

automatic stabilizers 384
balanced budget 377
balanced-budget fiscal policy 384
budget deficit 375
budget surplus 375
counter-cyclical fiscal policy 378
crowding-out effect 381
cyclically balanced-budget fiscal policy 388
fiscal policy 374
monetizing the debt 378
national debt 375
net tax revenue 375
pro-cyclical 386

Equations:

[11.1] NTR = tax revenue – transfer payments page 375

[11.2] budget balance = NTR – G page 375

STUDY TIPS

1. Students sometimes have difficulty understanding the concept behind the word "pro-cyclical." It simply means a tendency to push things further in the direction that they are already moving. Try this: assume that, early in the morning, it has been determined that there are 100 new forest fires in a particular area as a result of a thunderstorm the previous evening. If the rest of the day turns out to be sunny and very hot with some wind, the weather will certainly add to the size of the fires; that is, it will be pro-cyclical. On the other hand, if the day turns out to be cool, with some rain and no wind, then the weather will be counter-cyclical.
2. You should realize that all governments have some kind of fiscal policy. Just what kind of policy a government has depends on its attitude toward spending, taxation, and budgets. No governments would ever set out to deliberately make an economy already in a recession even worse with a pro-cyclical policy that pushed down GDP and raised unemployment even more. However, if a government decided to balance its budget regardless of cost, pursuing a policy of reducing government spending (or increasing taxation) when the economy is in recession, then it would have the effect of doing just that.
3. It is probably useful to state outright that the cause-and-effect relationship between a change in taxes and GDP operates both ways. A change in the level of taxation will certainly have an impact on GDP. But it is also true that if GDP changes, then the tax revenue received by the government will change. To keep these effects clear, you need to focus on which is the cause and which is the effect. However, it's no different from saying that a change in income will affect consumption but also that a change in consumption will affect income. The distinction between induced and autonomous consumption and taxes is important here.

Answered Questions

Indicate whether the following statements are true or false.

1. **T or F** The national debt is the sum of the federal government's past budget deficits less its surpluses.
2. **T or F** Monetizing the debt is the action by the government of borrowing from the central bank to finance spending.
3. **T or F** If aggregate demand increases as a result of counter-cyclical fiscal policy, prices will rise and GDP will fall.
4. **T or F** Counter-cyclical fiscal policy aimed at closing an inflationary gap is illustrated graphically by the aggregate demand curve shifting to the left.
5. **T or F** Both net tax revenues and government spending on goods and services are a function of GDP.
6. **T or F** A decrease in government spending on goods and services will shift the budget line up.
7. **T or F** A decrease in autonomous taxes would pivot the NTR line up.
8. **T or F** Counter-cyclical fiscal policy is aimed at balancing the budget, whereas a balanced-budget fiscal policy is aimed at balancing the economy.
9. **T or F** If government spending on goods and services is increased by exactly the same amount that taxes are increased, the level of GDP will not change.
10. **T or F** In trying to cure a recession, counter-cyclical fiscal policy may crowd out both private investment and export spending.

Basic (Questions 11–24)

11. What is fiscal policy?
- **a)** It is the government's policy on spending.
- **b)** It is the government's policy on taxation.
- **c)** It is the government's policy on both spending and taxation.
- **d)** It is the central bank's policy on interest rates.

12. Which of the following will close an inflationary gap?
- **a)** An increase in government spending.
- **b)** A decrease in government spending.
- **c)** A decrease in taxes.
- **d)** An increase in exports.

13. The largest portion of the national debt is owed to what group?
- **a)** The Canadian public, that is, individuals, businesses, and banks in Canada.
- **b)** Foreign individuals, banks, and businesses.
- **c)** The Bank of Canada.
- **d)** The Government of Canada.

14. What is net tax revenue?
- **a)** It is the total of all taxes collected by the government.
- **b)** It is the total of all taxes collected by government less spending by government on goods and services.
- **c)** It is the total of all taxes collected by government plus transfer payments.
- **d)** It is the total of all taxes collected by government less transfer payments.

15. When does a government budget surplus exist?
- **a)** When government spending of all types exceeds net tax revenue.
- **b)** When net tax revenue is less than government spending of all types.
- **c)** When government spending on goods and services exceeds net tax revenue.
- **d)** When net tax revenue exceeds government spending on goods and services.

16. What is true about the national debt since the 1960s?
- **a)** It has grown both absolutely and as a percentage of GDP.
- **b)** It has grown absolutely but has declined as a percentage of GDP.
- **c)** It has grown absolutely but remained constant as a percentage of GDP.
- **d)** It has declined absolutely, but increased as a percentage of GDP.

17. What is the effect of a counter-cyclical fiscal policy?
- **a)** It intensifies changes in GDP caused by the business cycle.
- **b)** It dampens changes in GDP caused by the business cycle.
- **c)** It has no effect on changes in GDP caused by the business cycle.
- **d)** It allows the government to balance its budget.

18. What would cause the aggregate demand curve to shift to the right?
- **a)** An increase in taxes.
- **b)** A decrease in government spending on goods and services.
- **c)** An increase in net tax revenues.
- **d)** Counter-cyclical fiscal policy used to eliminate a recessionary gap.

19. What can cause an upward (left) shift in the budget line?
- **a)** An increase in GDP.
- **b)** An increase in taxes.
- **c)** An increase in government spending.
- **d)** A decrease in taxes.

20. Which of the following statements about counter-cyclical fiscal policy is correct?
- **a)** It is appropriate in situations of a recessionary gap but not when an inflationary gap exists.
- **b)** It is appropriate in situations of an inflationary gap but not when a recessionary gap exists.
- **c)** It involves only higher government spending.
- **d)** It involves only higher taxes.
- **e)** It is the use of spending or taxation policies by the government to push the economy in a direction opposite to the way it was moving.

21. What is the crowding-out effect?
- **a)** The idea that government borrowing to finance a deficit crowds out private investment because it causes interest rates to fall.
- **b)** The idea that government borrowing to finance a deficit crowds out private investment because it causes interest rates to rise.
- **c)** The idea that fiscal policy crowds out economic growth.
- **d)** The idea that balanced budgets crowd out economic growth.

22. What are automatic stabilizers?
- **a)** Imports and exports that automatically change with the state of the economy so as to stabilize the economy.

b) Investment spending which automatically changes with the state of the economy so as to stabilize the economy.
c) Tax provisions and government spending programmes that automatically put spending into the economy in a recessionary period and take it out in a boom period.
d) Consumption spending which automatically changes with the state of the economy so as to stabilize the economy.

23. What is a cyclically balanced-budget fiscal policy?
a) A policy of balancing the budget each fiscal year.
b) A policy of using the budget to balance the economy each fiscal year.
c) A policy of balancing the budget over the life of the business cycle.
d) A policy of using the budget to balance the economy over the life of the business cycle.

Refer to **Figure 11.8** to answer questions 24, 25, and 26.

FIGURE 11.8

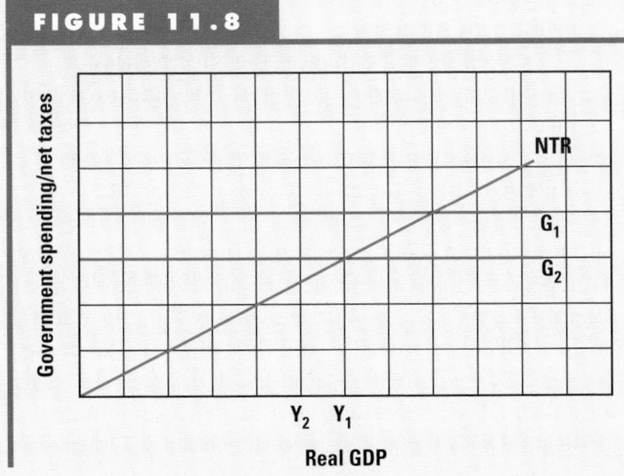

24. Refer to **Figure 11.8** to answer this question. Which of the following statements is verified by the graph?
a) A budget surplus exists if government spending is G_1 and real GDP is Y_1.
b) A budget deficit exists if government spending is G_1 and real GDP is Y_1.
c) If government spending was reduced from G_1 to G_2, the budget surplus at Y_2 would decrease.
d) NTR is a function of the level of government spending.

Intermediate (Problems 25–32)

25. Refer to **Figure 11.8** to answer this question. What is most likely to happen if the level of GDP is Y_1 and the government reduces its spending from G_1 to G_2 in an attempt to balance its budget?
a) The budget would be balanced at the new GDP level Y_2.
b) GDP would remain at Y_1, but the budget would be in deficit.
c) GDP would be Y_2, and the budget would be in deficit.
d) GDP would be Y_2, and the budget would be in surplus.

26. Refer to **Figure 11.8** to answer this question. If government spending is G_1 and GDP is Y_1, why won't a reduction in government spending by the size of the budget deficit eliminate the deficit?
a) Because GDP and NTR will decrease as a result of the decrease in government spending.
b) Because government spending is a function of income.
c) Because GDP will rise as a result of the decrease in government spending.
d) Because NTR will rise as a result of the decrease in government spending.

27. Which of the following statements concerning a budget deficit is true?
a) It is smaller if the economy is in the midst of a severe recession.
b) It is smaller if the economy is experiencing strong aggregate demand.
c) It reduces the size of the national debt.
d) It can be measured in terms of the amount of unemployment that it causes.

28. Which of the following is true if the government attempts to balance its budget when the economy is in a recession and the government is running a budget deficit?
a) Inflation would result.
b) The unemployment rate would decrease.
c) Government spending would have to increase.
d) GDP would increase.
e) The action would be pro-cyclical.

29. What is the effect of counter-cyclical fiscal policy on the price level?
a) It will increase in the case of a recessionary gap.
b) It will increase in the case of a inflationary gap.
c) It will decrease in the case of a recessionary gap.
d) It will have no effect in the case of a recessionary gap.
e) It will have no effect in the case of an inflationary gap.

30. An increase in government spending can result in crowding-out. Which of the following is a correct statement of the process?
   a) It leads to a decrease in savings, which leads to a decrease in investment spending.
   b) It leads to an increase in the money supply, which pushes interest rates up and causes a decrease in investment spending.
   c) It causes bond prices to increase, which pushes interest rates up and leads to a decrease in investment spending.
   d) It increases GDP and the demand for money, which causes interest rates to increase and investment spending to decrease.
   e) It leads to an increase in GDP and in savings, which increases investment spending.

31. All of the following, except one, are arguments *against* the use of counter-cyclical fiscal policy to close a recessionary gap. Which is the exception?
   a) Counter-cyclical fiscal policy can be inflationary.
   b) Counter-cyclical fiscal policy is subject to serious time lags.
   c) Counter-cyclical fiscal policy can increase interest rates and crowd out private investment spending.
   d) Counter-cyclical fiscal policy can reduce budget deficits, but this would also lower the exchange rate.

32. What is the result of using balanced-budget fiscal policy when both a recessionary gap and a budget deficit exist?
   a) The recessionary gap would be reduced and the budget deficit would fall.
   b) The recessionary gap would increase and the budget deficit would fall.
   c) The recessionary gap would be reduced and the budget deficit would rise.
   d) The recessionary gap would increase and the budget deficit would rise.

Advanced (Problems 33–35)

33. Suppose that counter-cyclical fiscal policy pushed up interest rates and the economy had a flexible exchange rate. Which of the following would be true?
   a) The exchange rate would fall, and exports would rise.
   b) The exchange rate would fall, and exports would fall.
   c) The exchange rate would rise, and exports would rise.
   d) The exchange rate would rise, and exports would fall.

34. If counter-cyclical fiscal policy causes crowding-out, which of the following statements is correct ?
   a) The crowding-out increases the effectiveness of fiscal policy by pushing up interest rates and reducing investment spending.
   b) The crowding-out reduces the effectiveness of fiscal policy by pushing up interest rates and reducing investment spending.
   c) The crowding-out reduces the effectiveness of fiscal policy by lowering interest rates and reducing investment spending.
   d) The crowding-out enhances the effectiveness of fiscal policy by lowering interest rates and increasing investment spending.
   e) The crowding-out reduces money demand and thereby reduces the effectiveness of fiscal policy.

35. Suppose that an economy is simultaneously experiencing a budget deficit and an inflationary gap. If the government attempts to balance the budget, what will be the effect?
   a) Real GDP will increase, and the deficit will increase.
   b) Real GDP will increase, and the deficit will decrease.
   c) Real GDP will decrease, and the deficit will increase.
   d) Real GDP will decrease, and the deficit will decrease.

Parallel Problems

ANSWERED PROBLEMS

36. **Key Problem** Figure 11.9 shows the aggregate demand/supply and the government budget line for the economy of Mahdi. The economy is presently at equilibrium. For every $1 change in government spending, aggregate demand changes by $3.

FIGURE 11.9

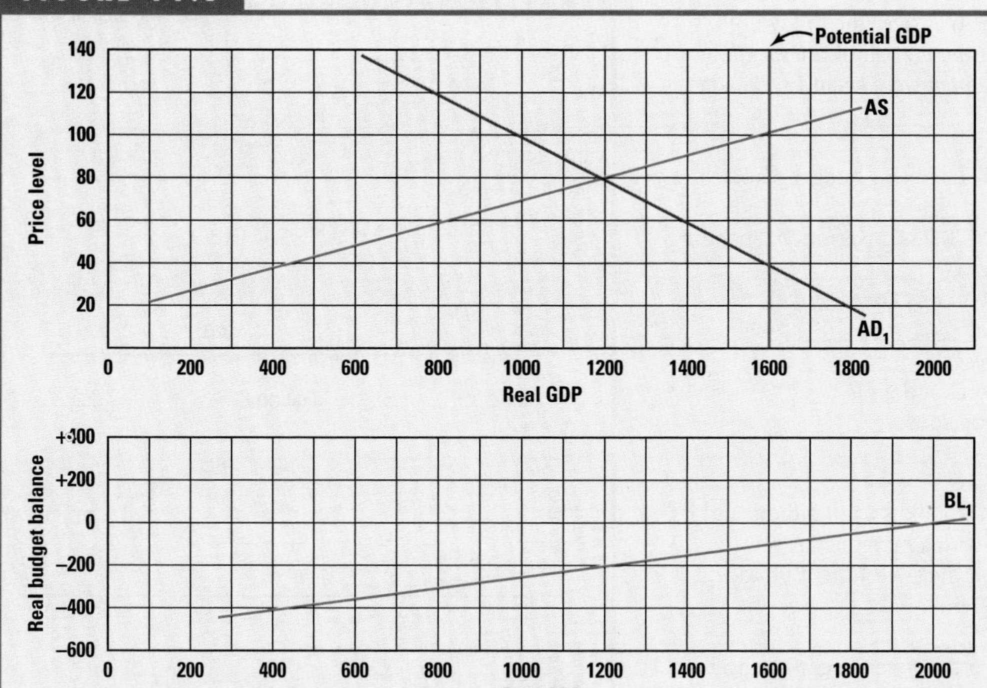

a) What is the present level of GDP and the price level in Mahdi?
GDP: ________________ ;
price level: ________________ .

b) Is there a recessionary or an inflationary gap? How much?
Gap: ________________ ;
amount: ________________ .

c) Does the government have a budget deficit or a surplus? How much?
Deficit or surplus: __________ ;
amount: ________________ .

d) By how much must aggregate demand increase or decrease in order to move the economy to full employment equilibrium? Draw in the new AD curve labelled AD_1.
Increase or decrease: ________ ;
amount: ________________ .

e) What change in government spending is necessary in order to move the economy to full-employment equilibrium?
Increase or decrease: ________ ;
amount: ________________ .

f) If the government makes the change in e), draw in the new budget line, labelled BL_2. What effect will this have on the level of GDP and the price level?
New GDP: ________________ ;
new price level: ________________ .

g) What will be the new value of the government's budget at this new GDP?
Deficit or surplus: ____________ ;
amount: ________________ .

Returning to the original equilibrium, suppose that the government is committed to a balanced budget.

h) What change in government spending is necessary in order to balance the budget at the present income level? Draw in the new budget line labelled BL_3.
Increase or decrease: ____________ ;
amount: ________________ .

i) What effect will the change in h) have on aggregate demand? Draw in the new curve labelled AD_3.
Increase or decrease: ____________ ;
amount: ________________ .

j) As a result of this change in aggregate demand, what will happen to the value of GDP and the price level?
New GDP: ________________ ;
new price level: ________________ .

k) What will be the new value of the government's budget at this new GDP?
Deficit or surplus: ____________ ;
amount: ________________ .

Basic (Problems 37–41)

Use **Table 11.1** in the chapter to answer the following questions. For simplicity, assume that all of the *spending grants to other levels of government* were spent in Canada on goods and services.

37. a) What are projected NTRs in this budget plan? __________ .

b) What is the value of NTR less government spending on goods and services (G)? ____________ .

What percentage of total revenue is:

c) personal income taxes? ________________ .

d) corporate income taxes? ______________ .

What percentage of total outlays is

e) transfer payments to persons? __________ .

f) public debt charges? __________________ .

38. Government spending in Robok is $140 billion, and its only tax is an income tax with a marginal tax rate of 0.35.

a) What is the balance on the government's budget at a GDP level of $360 billion?
Answer: ______________ .

b) What is the balance on the government's budget at a GDP level of $500 billion?
Answer: ______________ .

c) At what level of GDP will the economy of Robok have a balanced budget?
Answer: ______________ .

39. Figure 11.10 shows the economy of Tagara. Its aggregate demand is currently AD_1 and the budget line is BL_1.

FIGURE 11.10

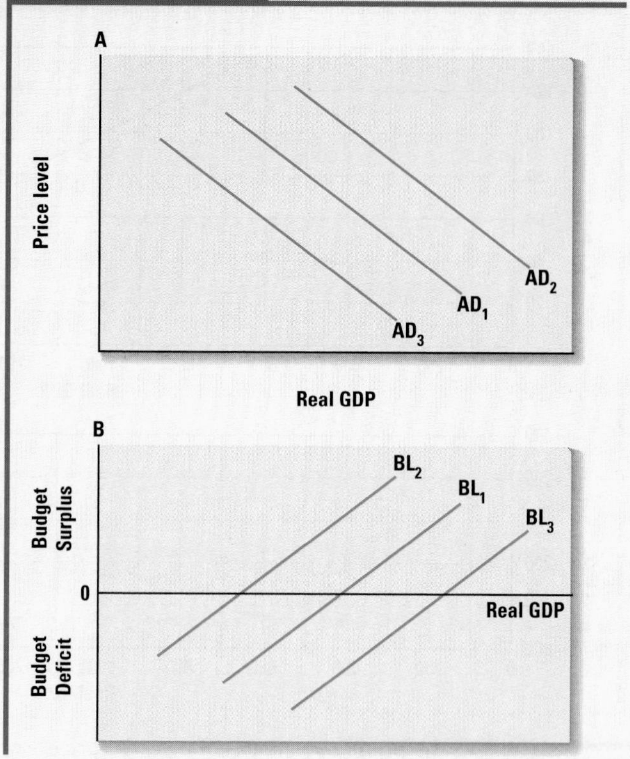

a) What effect would an increase in government spending have on each of the graphs:
Graph A: the aggregate demand curve would shift from ______ to ______ ;
Graph B: the budget line would shift from ______ to ______ .

b) What effect would an increase in taxes have on each of the graphs:
Graph A: the aggregate demand curve would shift from ______ to ______ ;
Graph B: the budget line would shift from ______ to ______ .

40. Suppose that a federal election is called at a time when the economy is experiencing a recessionary gap and there is a budget deficit. The leader of Party A promises, if elected, to immediately balance the budget by slashing government spending. The leader of Party B promises, if elected, to stimulate the economy with a tax decrease. What would be the effect of each party's proposed policy on each of the following:

a) The level of GDP. ________________________ .

b) The level of NTR. ________________________ .

c) The level of unemployment. ________________ .

d) The budget deficit. ______________________ .

e) The price level. ________________________ .

41. The economy of Morin is shown in **Figure 11.11**.

FIGURE 11.11

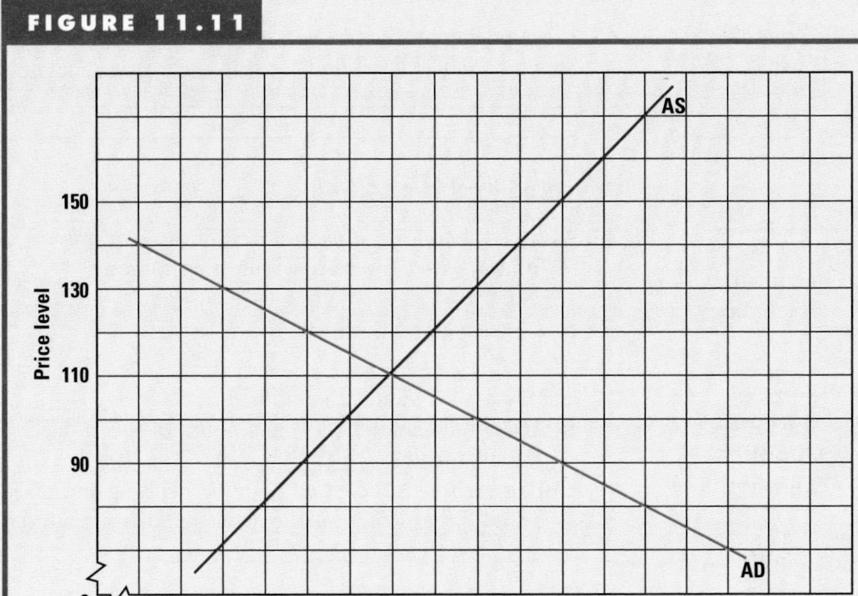

a) If potential GDP is $530, and the economy is presently in equilibrium, is there an inflationary or a recessionary gap? ______________ .
How much of a gap? ______________ .

b) By how much must aggregate demand increase in order to close this gap? ______________ .

c) If every $1 change in government spending leads to a $4 change in aggregate demand, what is the amount that government spending must increase?

d) Suppose that initially the government has a balanced budget. If the government increases its spending as in c) and tax revenues are 0.25 of real GDP, what will be the government's real budget surplus/deficit at the new full-employment equilibrium?
______________ of ______________ .

Intermediate (Problems 42–45)

42. Answer the questions below for the economy of Motak, using the graph in **Figure 11.12**.

FIGURE 11.12

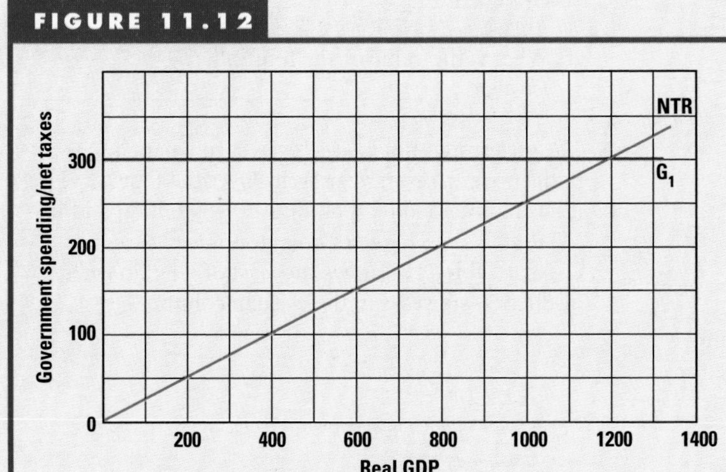

a) If GDP is $800 and government spending is G_1, what is the size of Motak's budget deficit?
Answer: ______________________.

b) If government spending is decreased by the size of the deficit in a), and the multiplier is 2, what is the new level of equilibrium GDP?
Answer: ______________________.

c) What is the size of Motak's deficit at this new level of equilibrium GDP?
Answer: ______________________.

43. The aggregate demand and supply for Cancum are shown in **Table 11.7**. Potential GDP is $1500 billion.

TABLE 11.7

Price	Aggregate Quantity Demanded	Aggregate Quantity Supplied
105	1600	400
110	1500	800
115	1400	1100
120	1300	1300
125	1200	1400
130	1100	1500
135	1000	1600
140	900	1650

a) If the economy is in equilibrium, is the economy experiencing an inflationary or recessionary gap? ______________ How much? ______________.

b) Suppose the government uses counter-cyclical fiscal policy to close the gap. By how much and in what direction would AD have to change in order to achieve full employment? ______________.

c) As a result of this change, what would be the inflation rate? ______________.

44. Given the following data for the economy of Moksha:

$C = 25 + 0.6Y$ $\quad G = 160$

$I = 60$ $\quad X_N = 55 - 0.1Y$

a) Calculate equilibrium GDP.

b) Calculate the multiplier.

c) If the tax function is : $T = 20 + 0.2Y$, calculate the size of the budget deficit or surplus.

d) Now change government spending by the amount of the surplus or deficit in an attempt to balance the budget. What will be the new equilibrium income?

______________________.

e) What is the budget surplus or deficit at the new equilibrium? ______________________.

45. Explain some of the problems associated with a counter-cyclical fiscal policy. ______________________

____

______________________.

Advanced (Problems 46–48)

46. Assume the following parameters for the economy of Tandor, where taxes are wholly autonomous:

$C = 40 + 0.8Y_D$ $\quad X_N = 107 - 0.1Y$

$G = T_O = 340$

$I = 100$

a) What is the value of equilibrium income? ________.

b) At equilibrium, what is the amount of the budget? Deficit/surplus ____________ of $ ____________.

c) If government increased both its spending and taxes by $60, what would be the new equilibrium income?

______________________.

47. Assume that the parameters for the economy of Tindor are:

$C = 60 + 0.8Y_D$ $\quad X_N = 700 - 0.2Y$

$T = 200 + 0.25Y$

$I = 600$

Further, assume that the government is constrained by law to maintain a balanced budget, that is, $G = T$ (where $T = 200 + 0.25Y$).

a) What is the value of equilibrium income?
Answer: ______________________.

b) What are the values of G and T at equilibrium income?
Answer: ______________________.

c) What is the value of X_N at expenditures equilibrium?
Answer: ______________________.

d) What is the value of the multiplier?
Answer: ______________________.

48. The government of Osiris believes in balancing its budget over a seven-year cycle. Over the first six years it has maintained its spending at $150 billion and its MTR at 0.25. (There are no autonomous taxes in Osiris.) **Table 11.8** shows the level of GDP in each of the first six years in the cycle in column 2.

TABLE 11.8

(1) Year	(2) GDP ($ billion)	(3) Deficit/Surplus
1	600	______
2	580	______
3	560	______
4	612	______
5	620	______
6	608	______

a) Fill in column (3), showing the actual amounts of the budget deficit or surplus for each year.

Suppose that the estimated level of GDP in year 7 is projected at $600.

b) What level of government spending (assuming no change in the tax rate) is necessary for the government of Osiris to end the seven-year cycle with its budgetary goal on target? Answer: __________ .

c) Alternately, what change in the tax rate (assuming no change in government spending) is necessary for the government of Osiris to end the seven-year cycle with its budgetary goal on target? Answer: ______________________________ .

UNANSWERED PROBLEMS

49. **Key Problem** Figure 11.13 shows the aggregate demand/supply and the government budget line for the economy of Kalam. The economy is presently at equilibrium and for every $1 change in government spending, aggregate demand changes by $3.

FIGURE 11.13

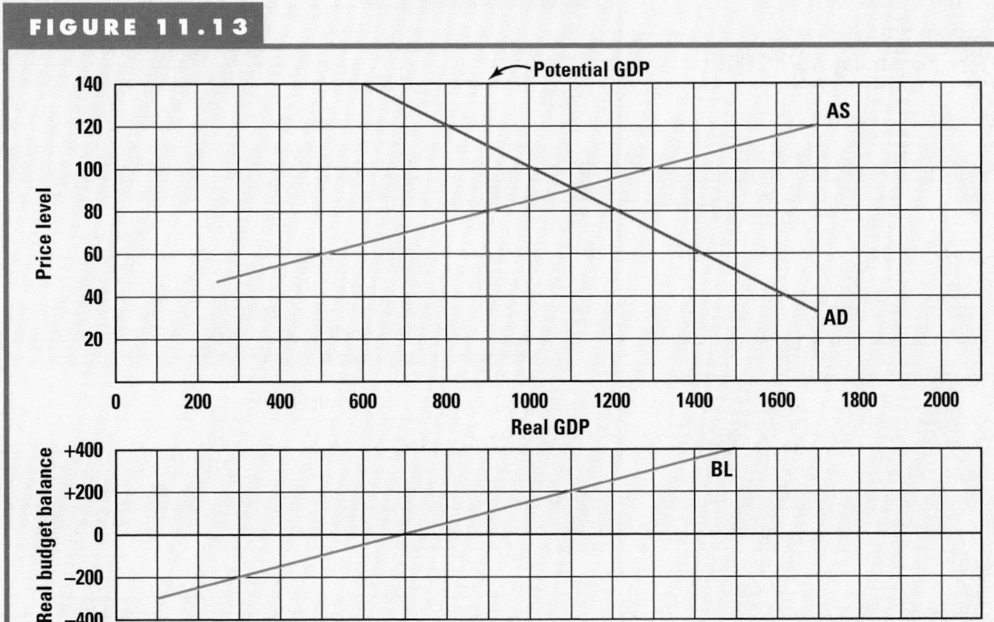

a) What is the present level of GDP and the price level in Kalam?

b) Is there a recessionary or an inflationary gap? How much?

c) Does the government have a budget deficit or a surplus? How much?

d) By how much must aggregate demand increase or decrease in order to move the economy to full employment equilibrium?

e) What change in government spending is necessary in order to move the economy to full-employment equilibrium?

f) If the government makes the change in e), what effect will this have on the level of GDP and the price level?

g) What will be the new value of the government's budget at this new GDP?

Returning to the original equilibrium, suppose that the government is committed to a balanced budget.

h) What change in government spending is necessary in order to balance the budget at the present income level?

i) What effect will the change in h) have on aggregate demand?

j) As a result of this change in aggregate demand, what will happen to the value of GDP and the price level?

k) What will be the new value of the government's budget at this new GDP?

Basic (Problems 50–54)

50. **Table 11.9** below shows the Revenue and Spending of the Canadian federal government in 2000–2001. For simplicity, assume that all of the *spending grants to other levels of government* were spent in Canada on goods and services.

TABLE 11.9 Federal Government's Budget Plan for Fiscal Year Beginning April 2000

REVENUES	
Personal income taxes	$79.2
E.I. premiums	18.2
Corporate income taxes	23.9
GST and excise taxes	33.5
Non-tax revenues	7.2
Total Revenues	**162**
OUTLAYS	
Transfers to persons	36.0
Spending grants to other levels	22.6
of government	42.0
Public debt charges	57.4
Direct program spending	
Total Outlays	**158**
Projected Budget Plan Surplus	**4**

Source: Data derived by authors from information found in Department of Finance; Budget Plan, 2000.

a) What are projected NTRs in this budget plan?

b) What is the value of NTR less government spending on goods and services (G)?

What percentage of total revenue is:

c) personal income taxes?

d) corporate income taxes?

What percentage of total outlay is:

e) transfer payments to persons?

f) public debt charges?

51. Government spending in Palara is $270 billion and its only tax is an income tax with a marginal tax rate of 0.3.

a) What is the balance on the government's budget at a GDP level of $800 billion?

b) What is the balance on the government's budget at a GDP level of $960 billion?

c) At what level of GDP will the economy of Palara have a balanced budget?

52. Aggregate demand is currently AD_1 in **Figure 11.14** for the economy of Colchi, and the level of government spending is G_1.

FIGURE 11.14

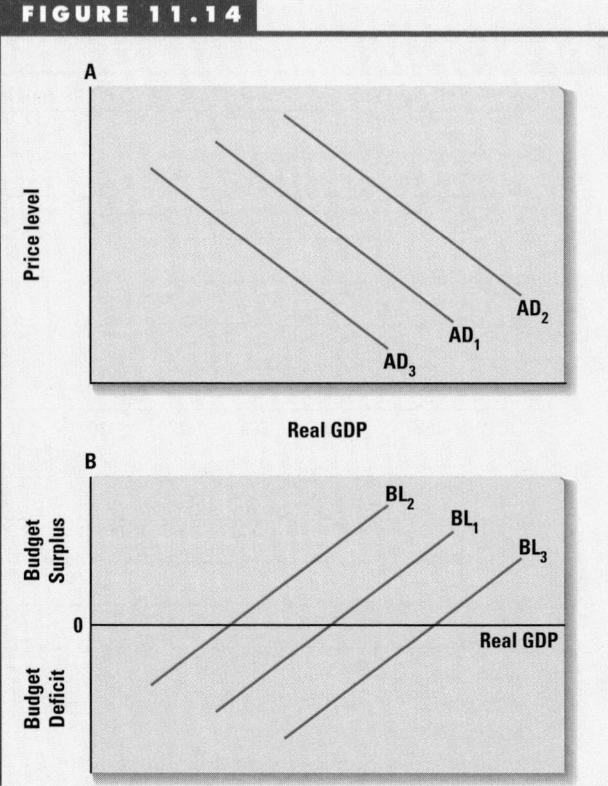

a) What effect would a decrease in government spending have on each of the graphs:
Graph A: the aggregate demand curve would shift from ______ to ______;

Graph B: the budget line would shift from _____ to _____.

b) What effect would a decrease in taxes have on each of the graphs:
Graph A: the aggregate demand curve would shift from _____ to _____;
Graph B: the budget line would shift from _____ to _____.

53. Suppose that a federal election is called at a time when the economy is experiencing an inflationary gap and there is a budget surplus. The leader of Party A promises, if elected, to immediately balance the budget by cutting taxes. The leader of Party B promises, if elected, to cut government spending to deflate the economy. What would be the effect of each party's proposed policy on each of the following:

a) The level of GDP.
b) The level of NTR.
c) The level of unemployment.
d) The budget surplus.
e) The price level.

54. The economy of Patna is shown in **Figure 11.15**.

FIGURE 11.15

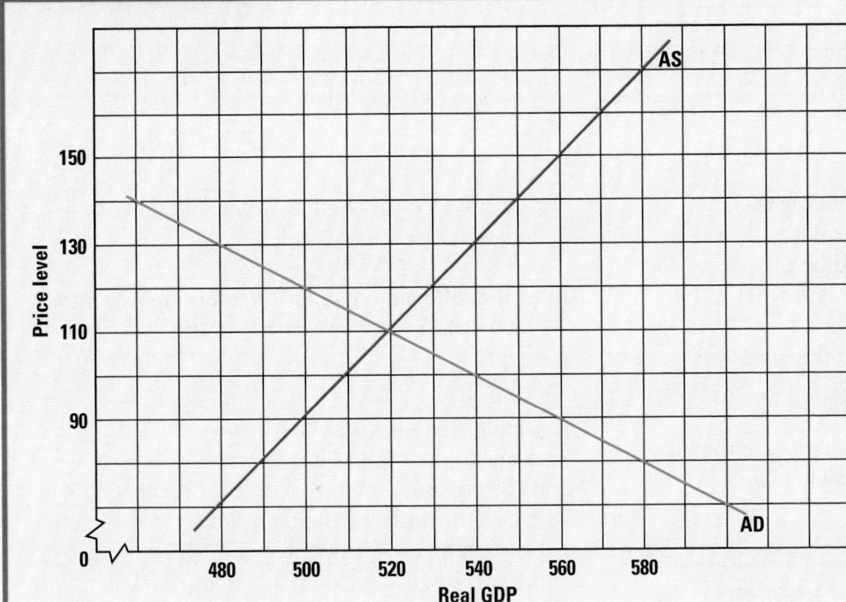

a) If potential GDP is $500, and the economy is presently in equilibrium, is there an inflationary or a recessionary gap and how large is this gap?
b) By how much must aggregate demand decrease in order to close this gap?
c) If every $1 change in government spending leads to a $2 change in aggregate demand, what is the amount that G must decrease?
d) Suppose that initially the government had a balanced budget. If government spending decreased as in c), and if tax revenues are 0.25 of real GDP, what will be the government's budget surplus/deficit at full-employment equilibrium?

Intermediate (Problems 55–58)

55. Answer the questions below for the economy of Qana using the graph in **Figure 11.16**.

FIGURE 11.16

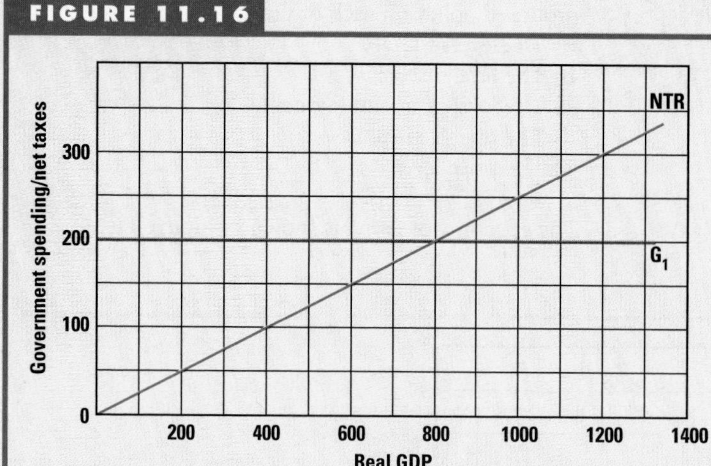

a) If GDP is 1000 and government spending is G_1, what is the size of Qana's budget surplus?
b) If government spending is decreased by the size of the surplus in a), and the multiplier is 2, what is the new level of equilibrium GDP?
c) What is the size of Qana's surplus at this new level of equilibrium GDP?

56. The aggregate demand and supply for Charax are shown below in **Table 11.10**. Potential GDP is $800 billion.

TABLE 11.10

Price	Aggregate Quantity Demanded	Aggregate Quantity Supplied
102	1000	800
104	950	850
106	900	900
108	850	950
110	800	1000
112	750	1050
114	700	1100

a) If the economy is in equilibrium, is it experiencing an inflationary or recessionary gap and what is the size of the gap?
b) Suppose the government uses counter-cyclical fiscal policy to close the gap. By how much, and in what direction, would AD have to change in order to achieve full employment?
c) As a result of this change, what would be the deflation rate?

57. Given the following data for the economy of Petra:
$C = 100 + 0.8Y$ $\quad X_N = 20 - 0.05Y$
$I = 200$
$G = 360$
a) calculate equilibrium GDP.
b) calculate the multiplier.
c) if the tax function is $T = 98 + 0.1Y$, calculate the size of the budget deficit/surplus.
d) Now change government spending, by the size of the surplus, or deficit, in an attempt to balance the budget and calculate the new equilibrium income.
e) Calculate the new budget deficit/surplus resulting from the new equilibrium income.

58. Explain some of the problems associated with a balanced-budget fiscal policy.

Advanced (Problems 59–62)

59. Assume the following parameters for the economy of Tandor, where taxes are wholly autonomous:
$C = 100 + 0.75Y_D$ $\quad G = T = 400$
$I = 200$ $\quad X_N = 300 - 0.15Y$
a) What is the value of equilibrium income?
b) At equilibrium, what is the amount of the budget deficit/surplus?
c) If government increased both its spending and taxes by $80, what would be the new equilibrium income?

60. Assume that the parameters for the economy of Tindor are:
$C = 80 + 0.75Y_D$ $X_N = 750 - 0.1Y$
$T = 200 + 0.2Y$
$I = 620$
Further, assume that the government is constrained by law to maintain a balanced budget, that is, $G = T$ (where $T = 200 + 0.2Y$).
a) What is the value of equilibrium income?
b) What are the values of G and T at equilibrium income?
c) What is the value of X_N at expenditures equilibrium?
d) What is the value of the multiplier?

61. The government of Ran believes in balancing its budget over a seven-year cycle. Over the first six years it has maintained its spending at $165 billion and its MTR at 0.2. (There are no autonomous taxes in Ran.) **Table 11.11** shows the level of GDP in each of the first six years in the cycle in column 2.

TABLE 11.11

(1) Year	(2) GDP ($ billion)	(3) Deficit/Surplus
1	800	______
2	820	______
3	850	______
4	835	______
5	825	______
6	860	______

a) Fill in column (3), showing the actual amounts of the budget deficit or surplus for each year.
Suppose that the estimated level of GDP in year 7 is projected at $900.
b) What level of government spending (assuming no change in the tax rate) is necessary for the government of Osiris to end the seven-year cycle with its budgetary goal on target?
c) Alternatively, what change in the tax rate (assuming no change in government spending) is necessary for the government of Osiris to end the seven-year cycle with its budgetary goal on target?

62. Assume that, in the economy of Ladush, the MPC is 0.75 and the multiplier is 4, and that both government spending and autonomous taxes are increased by 100. By how much, and in what direction, will equilibrium GDP change?

Web-Based Activities

1. Go to **www.fin.gc.ca/activity** and do a search for "Economy in Brief." How would you evaluate the performance of the Canadian economy based on the most recent statistics?

2. Go to **www.hoover.stanford.edu/presswebsite/flattax/chpts.html** and write a short essay on whether you think this type of tax reform would be fair.

3. A good source for details on the federal government's revenue and expenditures is: **www.statcan.ca/english/pgdb/state/govern.htm#rev**. Also take a look at the Department of Finance's web page at: **www.fin.gc.ca** and click on Budget info.

CHAPTER TWELVE

Monetary Policy

LEARNING OBJECTIVES

This chapter will enable you to:

LO1 **Describe the various functions of Canada's central bank—the Bank of Canada.**

LO2 **Understand the role of monetary policy and how the Bank of Canada influences interest rates.**

LO3 **Clearly understand why monetary policy is needed.**

LO4 **Describe the arguments for and against the activist approach to monetary policy.**

LO5 **Describe the arguments for and against the non-activist approach to monetary policy.**

LO6 **Realize why some argue that other direct controls are needed as alternatives to both fiscal and monetary policy.**

What's ahead...

We start this chapter by looking at the agency responsible for monetary policy, the Bank of Canada, and examine some of the tools it has available to effect changes in the nation's money supply. We then proceed to discuss what is appropriate monetary policy by exploring the activist approach to policy making. This approach has two versions—one uses monetary policy to attempt to achieve full-employment equilibrium in the economy, and the other uses it to achieve stability in the value of the currency. The other approach, that of the non-activist school, is then discussed. The chapter closes with a brief discussion of stagflation and the resulting need for policies beyond those of fiscal and monetary policy.

A QUESTION OF RELEVANCE...

Have you ever watched one of the many business or money shows on TV? Did you notice the emphasis that the analysts put on interest rates? "I expect the stock market to remain strong, as long as interest rates stay low," is a sentiment that was often expressed in the last few years on these shows. Low interest rates are certainly good for the stock market, but are they also good for the economy and for you and me? Generally the answer is yes. So, if low interest rates are so important, why aren't they always kept low? Is it because they have to be kept in line with those in the United States? Why is this? This chapter will help answer questions like these.

monetary policy: economic policy designed to change or influence the economy through changes in the money supply.

In Chapter 8 we saw that changes in the money supply can bring about real changes in the economy and move it toward full-employment equilibrium. The Bank of Canada is the main agent that effects such changes in the money supply, a process called **monetary policy**. And what is the appropriate goal of monetary policy—what should these changes be aimed at? Not many years ago the stated mandate of the Bank of Canada was "to assist the economy in achieving a full-employment, non-inflationary level of total output." Then a perceptible shift in this mandate began to emerge. Today, the Bank's stated goal is:

> **"To preserve the value of money... [since] stability in the value of money (a low rate of inflation) promotes economic prosperity by providing a framework in which households and businesses can make sound economic decisions."**

The Bank of Canada nowadays sees the role of monetary policy as a means of providing a healthy economic environment that will *assist* the economy in achieving the more specific goals of low inflation and low unemployment. We will be examining the role of monetary policy in greater detail later in this chapter, but first we look at the Bank of Canada's functions and the tools it uses to carry out monetary policy.

12.1 Functions of the Bank of Canada

LO1
Describe the various functions of Canada's central bank—the Bank of Canada.

In general, the Bank of Canada operates in a way similar to that of most other central banks throughout the world. Some central banks are state owned (for example, the Bank of Canada, the Bank of England); others are privately owned (such as the American central bank, known as the Federal Reserve Board). However, for all intents and purposes, ownership is unimportant. What is important are the things that central banks have in common. The following comments about the Bank of Canada apply equally, therefore, to most central banks.

As we noted in Chapter 7, one traditional function of the Bank of Canada is that it is the *sole issuer of currency*. In this regard, it tends to act as a reservoir, in that it will issue more currency to the banks when needed (just before Christmas, for instance) and at other times it will take back any surplus above the banks' and the public's requirements. You may recall that only the portion of the outstanding currency that is in the hands of the public is considered part of the money supply; the portion in bank vaults is excluded.

CP/Tom Hanson

A visitor to the currency museum in the Bank of Canada building in Ottawa looks at the half-burnt Canadian dollar. The display illustrates how old currency is disposed of.

A second traditional function is that the Bank of Canada acts as the *government's bank*. It is the institution that looks after the government's banking needs. More recently, however, individual government ministries have been given authority to deal with whichever commercial bank they choose, making this function of the Bank of Canada less important. However, the Bank of Canada also *manages reserves of foreign currencies* (and gold) on behalf of the government. This includes the buying and selling of Canadian dollars and other currencies, in consultation with the government and consistent with its policies.

Just as the Bank of Canada traditionally acted as the government's bank, so too did it act as the *bankers' bank*, in that each of the commercial banks has an account with the Bank of Canada to facilitate the borrowing and lending of funds between the two. The central bank stands prepared to make extraordinary loans to a commercial bank that is experiencing a liquidity problem to avert a loss of depositor confidence. In this respect, it is often known as the "lender of last resort."

The *Bank Act* also charges the Bank of Canada with the responsibility of acting as *auditor and inspector of the commercial banks*, and the latter are required to submit periodic reports to the Bank of Canada and to open their books and accounts for inspection and audit.

The final function of the Bank of Canada is the most important, and that is to *regulate the money supply*. It is interesting to note in this regard that although the federal government, through Parliament, has the power and the responsibility to effect fiscal policy, it does not itself directly control monetary policy: this is the prime function of the governor and the board of directors of the Bank of Canada. It is possible, therefore, at least in theory, for the government and the Bank of Canada to be in conflict regarding the direction in which they want to move the economy. In fact, there was such a conflict between the two in the late 1950s. Generally speaking, however, this does not happen often, not because the two always agree, but because a conflict in policies would be regarded as something of a political failure and thus something which the policy makers wish to avoid. In summary, the functions of a central bank, such as the Bank of Canada, are to act as:

- the issuer of currency
- the government's bank and manager of foreign currency reserves
- the bankers' bank and lender of last resort
- the auditor and inspector of commercial banks
- the regulator of the money supply

ADDED DIMENSION

The Bank of Canada and the Government

It is worth emphasizing that although the governor and directors of the Bank of Canada are appointed by the federal cabinet (through the governor general), their roles are meant to be non-political. Appointments are not politically motivated by patronage, but rather based on merit and expertise. In addition, their seven-year terms exceed the life of a government, and the governor's appointment can be terminated only by an act of Parliament. In these ways it is hoped that the bank will operate independently of government and pursue monetary policy without needing to consider short-term political considerations. The government could, through the minister of finance, attempt to formally dictate to the governor what policy it wished him (so far, all governors have been men, including the present governor, David Dodge) to follow. However, being forced to act openly in this manner signals a marked political failure for the government—which may well have negative economic repercussions—and is therefore rare.

Let's now look now at the way in which the Bank of Canada carries out monetary policy.

12.2 Tools of Monetary Policy

LO2
Understand the role of monetary policy and how the Bank of Canada influences interest rates.

expansionary monetary policy: a policy that aims to increase the amount of money in the economy and make credit cheaper and more easily available.

contractionary monetary policy: a policy in which the amount of money in the economy is decreased and credit becomes harder to obtain and more expensive.

open-market operations: the buying and selling of securities by the Bank of Canada in the open (to the public) market.

Let's assume that the Bank of Canada wishes to effect an **expansionary monetary policy** (also called an easy money policy). This involves increasing the money supply. How could this be done? Well, we know from Chapter 7 that if the Bank could increase the amount of cash reserves held by the commercial banks, then any reserves that banks consider in excess of their target reserves would be loaned out and, through the money multiplier process, would lead to an increase in demand deposits (the main portion of the money supply). **Contractionary monetary policy** (or a tight money policy) would imply the opposite.

One simple way for the Bank of Canada to increase the commercial banks' cash reserves would be simply to give them additional amounts of reserves. However, some of us might complain about a free gift of cash to the banks! The Bank of Canada therefore has to use a more subtle and businesslike process known as **open-market operations**, so called because it involves the Bank of Canada (or at least its agent) buying or selling bonds in a market that is open to anyone. In other words, the Bank of Canada buys and sells government bonds in the same way that any individual or corporation might do.

To better understand just how this market works, we need to understand the role of treasury bills. These are a type of short-term bond, or fixed-term debt, issued by the Bank of Canada, acting as the government's agent. Fortunately, from time to time, corporations, commercial banks, life insurance and pension fund companies, and other organizations find themselves with excess cash. Usually, this cash will be needed by these organizations in the near future, so the question of what to do with, say, $2 million for 60 days can arise. One of the most popular revenue-earning assets are treasury bills, or T-bills, which can be bought for either a three- or six-month term. These bills can be bought and sold quickly and easily in various amounts. They differ from longer-term government and corporate bonds in that they are short-term and do not pay interest. Instead, the return is earned on them because they are purchased at a discount (at a price below the face value) but are then redeemed at the end of the fixed term at face value.

If it wished to increase the amount of cash reserves of the commercial banks, the Bank of Canada would buy T-bills. The sellers of the T-bills would receive a cheque from the Bank of Canada, which they would then deposit in their bank accounts. At the end of the day, these banks would look to the Bank of Canada for collection. This could be effected by the Bank of Canada transferring the required amount of reserves to the commercial bank in question. Rather than doing this, however, the Bank of Canada simply credits the account of the appropriate commercial bank at the Bank of Canada. It, in effect, tells the commercial bank that the amount of credit it has "on reserve" at the Bank of Canada has been increased. The commercial banks' reserves have therefore increased, and this recently acquired surplus will be loaned out, thus leading to a multiple expansion of money in the economy, as we discussed in Chapter 7.

To reduce the money supply, the Bank of Canada would of course do the opposite and would sell T-bills to whoever wished to purchase them. These people would have to make payment to the Bank of Canada, and their bank account balances would be thus reduced, and so would the reserves of the commercial banks. As a result of this, banks would be forced to call in loans, and this would reduce the amount of money in the economy.

The sequence of events when the central bank uses open-market operations to expand the money supply.

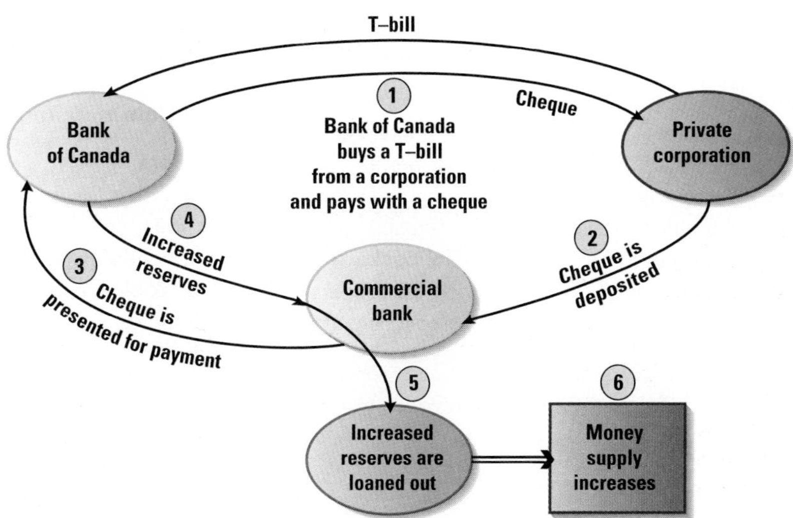

Open-market operations are not the only tool of monetary policy, but they are a frequently used and important method. This is because they can be initiated on short notice, take effect quickly, and can be done in any amount.

SELF-TEST

1. In terms of the banking system's ability to create money, what difference, if any, does it make if the Bank of Canada buys bonds from a commercial bank, rather than buying them from a member of the public?

ADDED DIMENSION

The Bank of Canada's Balance Sheet

The operations of the Bank of Canada affect the economy, but they, of course, also affect the balance sheet of the bank itself. The following table shows the Bank of Canada's balance sheet in simplified form as of December 31, 2001. All figures are in billions.

The biggest asset of the bank is its holdings of government bonds and treasury bills, and it is the sale and purchase of these that we term open-market operations. Notice also that the advances (loans) to members of the Canadian Payments Association (abbreviated as "banks, etc."), are the short-term loans, mentioned in Chapter 7, that banks take from time to time. The major liability of the bank, as you can see, is the amount of notes in circulation. Although these notes are assets to members of the public that own them, they represent a liability to the issuing bank, the Bank of Canada. The other major liability is the reserves that the commercial banks lodge with the Bank of Canada. Such reserves are, of course, an asset to the commercial banks, but a liability to the Bank of Canada.

Assets		**Liabilities**	
Treasury bills of Canada	$12.6	Notes in circulation	$38.8
Other securities	26.2	Government of Canada deposits	1.0
Advances to banks, etc.	0.6	Deposits of banks	1.3
Foreign currencies	0.4	Other liabilities	0.7
Other assets	2.0	Total	41.8
Total	41.8		

Source: Adapted from the *Bank of Canada Review*, Spring 2000.

SELF-TEST

2. What follows are the simplified (and hypothetical) balance sheets for the commercial banking system and for the Bank of Canada (all figures are in billions):
   a) Show the effects on the balance sheets of both the Bank of Canada and the commercial banks as a result of the Bank of Canada buying $2 billion worth of securities directly from the commercial banks.

All Commercial Banks		Bank of Canada	
Assets		**Assets**	
Reserves:		Securities	
In vaults	$70		$80
On deposit with the Bank of Canada	10		
Securities	120		
Loans	600		
Totals	800		80
Liabilities		**Liabilities**	
Deposit	800	Notes in circulation	65
		Deposits of banks	10
		Other liabilities	5
Totals	800		80

bank rate: the rate of interest payable by the commercial banks on loans from the Bank of Canada.

The second tool of monetary policy is a change in the **bank rate**. The bank rate is the official interest rate of the Bank of Canada. It is an "announced" rate that stays in effect until it is changed by the Bank of Canada and influences all other interest rates in the economy so that it is closely watched and is often referred to as the "trend-setting" rate. The bank rate establishes the upper limit of a one-half point range for what is called the *overnight loans rate*. This is the rate at which major financial institutions borrow and lend one-day funds to each other. The upper limit of this range is the rate at which the Bank of Canada will loan one-day funds to financial institutions, and the lower limit is the rate it will pay on one-day funds deposited by those same institutions. These standing offers to loan or accept deposits ensure that the overnight loans rate stays within the central bank's desired range. This particular tool of monetary policy is being used more frequently by the Bank of Canada today.

Since commercial banks must pay the upper limit of the overnight loans rate to the Bank of Canada on any loans they take out to cover temporary shortages of reserves, they regard this rate as a penalty rate, and any increase in it would cause them to want to restrict the amount of any such loans. Therefore, Canadian commercial banks have historically tried to keep these loans to an absolute minimum. Because of this, changes in the bank rate are a clear signal of interest-rate trends.

To the average consumer who is considering the purchase of a new house or car, the interest rate is one of the most important of all economic statistics. It has the power to shape the future of most of us, whether we are interest earners or interest payers. To a firm thinking of new capital investment, a change in interest rates—compared to its expected rate of return—will often tip the decision of whether or not to go ahead. It is important to realize that the bank rate is just one of the many rates that make up the whole interest-rate structure. For example, the rate that commercial banks charge their best customers, the prime rate, is a little higher than the bank rate. Moving up the scale, the mortgage rate would be next and then, above that, the personal loan rate. All the various rates on savings would be below the bank rate, with the rate on large sums of money that are committed for a long time paying the highest savings rate and small sums for short periods the lowest. When we speak of a change in the interest rate, we are referring to the whole interest-rate structure.

A drop in the bank rate signals expansionary policy, which, we just saw, means that credit is more freely available and cheaper. Contractionary policy, which means less money in the economy, is reflected in a higher bank rate. What this means is that:

The supply of money and interest rates are inextricably linked, and it is impossible to change one without at the same time changing the other.

ADDED DIMENSION

Bond Prices and Interest Rates

To understand the connection between the price of bonds and interest rates, consider the issuance of a T-bill at the face value of $100 000 that will be redeemable in 91 days from issuance for the same amount. Since no one would pay $100 000 for a bill that will give them $100 000 later, these bills are sold at a discount.

A bill that is sold at a discounted price of $97 500 and is worth $100 000 in 91 days means that anyone purchasing this bill would earn a return of $2500 in just three months. As a percentage of the investment outlay, this represents ($2500/$97 500) × 100, or 2.56 percent. Annualized, this comes to 2.56 × 4, or an annual rate of 10.24 percent. Now, what would happen if the purchaser had received a bigger discount and only had to pay $96 000 for the bill? In this case, she would be earning a return of ($4000/$96 000) × 100 × 4, or 16.67 percent per annum. From this, it can be seen that the lower the price (the higher the discount), the greater will be the rate of return (in effect, the rate of interest) that can be earned.

Another feature of treasury bills is that they can be bought or sold, through a broker, at any time during their 91-day life. In fact, a particular bill may have gone through three, four, or more owners between its original purchase and the time of redemption. The closer the maturity date, the closer to the face value will be its selling price. Thus, institutions that have excess cash will be T-bill buyers, and 20, 40, or 60 days later—when they need the cash—they will be T-bill sellers.

A bond shares many of the characteristics of a treasury bill. A bond is another type of IOU issued by the government (and others). It differs from a T-bill in that it has a longer term and pays a fixed interest annually. A prospective buyer of a previously issued bond will take into account the interest receivable as well as the possible increase or decrease in the value of the bond. A purchaser willing to pay only $98 for an 8 percent, $100 bond redeemable in one year will, therefore, receive a $2 capital appreciation as well as $8 in interest. The return (the effective rate of interest), therefore, is $10, or 10 percent. If that same purchaser were forced to pay $103 for the bond, then the rate of return would only be approximately 5 percent (a capital loss of $3 plus interest of $8). Again, the actual rate of interest earned depends on the price of the bond. A higher bond price means a lower rate of interest.

Another way the Bank of Canada can affect the money supply is by *switching government deposits.* If the Bank of Canada wants to contract the money supply, for instance, then it can, with approval of the finance ministry, transfer some of the government's deposits from a commercial bank to the Bank of Canada. It does this by, in effect, writing a cheque on the government's account at the commercial bank made payable to the Bank of Canada. The effect of switching deposits is similar to open-market operations. In both cases, demand deposits and reserves are affected. Switching deposits has become an increasingly popular monetary tool for the Bank of Canada.

SELF-TEST

3. Suppose that the banking system's target reserve ratio is 10 percent and the Bank of Canada switches $100 million of government funds from the government's account with the Bank of Canada to an account at a commercial bank. Since neither the government's accounts with commercial banks nor the commercial banks' reserves are considered to be part of the money supply, how could such a switching of funds have any effect on the money supply?

A final tool of monetary policy is given the euphemistic title of *moral suasion*. This simply means that the Bank of Canada informs the financial community, by way of pronouncements, public or private discussions, and by other means, of the direction it would like to go. The heads of financial and government agencies constitute a relatively small and fairly exclusive group. Communication among them is ongoing and informal, so it is not difficult for the Bank of Canada to let members of this community know in what direction it would like them to proceed. Usually, the banks are happy to concur. Even if they are not happy, they still usually concur! In summary, the four tools of monetary policy are:

- open-market operations
- setting the bank rate
- switching government deposits
- moral suasion

By these various ways the Bank of Canada is able, directly and indirectly, to control the supply of money in the economy. Changes in the *supply* of money, as we saw in Chapter 8, will lead to important changes in the economy. We will now turn to an examination of the way these changes can affect various macroeconomic aggregates.

REVIEW

1. List the functions of the Bank of Canada.
2. What is the biggest asset of the Bank of Canada? What is its biggest liability?
3. What do we mean when we say a bond is sold at a "discount"?
4. What are the four tools of monetary policy?
5. Describe what is meant by the term *open-market operations*.
6. If the Bank of Canada switches government bank balances from itself to a commercial bank, does the money supply increase or decrease?

12.3 Is Monetary Policy Needed?

LO3
Clearly understand why monetary policy is needed.

In Chapter 7 we looked at some of the characteristics of money and noted that it should be reasonably scarce (stones or seashells would not be a good form of money) but not so scarce that people had to wait their turn to use it. What this means is not only that an economy can have too much money, but that it is also possible for it to have too little money. Let's look at this aspect in more depth by asking:

What would happen if the Bank of Canada increased the money supply too much?

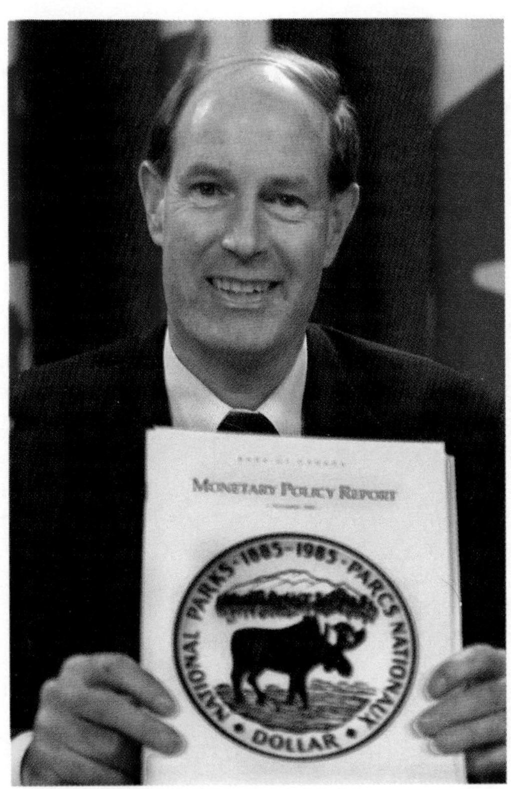

CP/Fred Chartrand

David Dodge, governor of the Bank of Canada, discusses the contents of the bank's monetary policy report.

You will recall from Chapter 8 that an increase in the money supply will reduce the interest rate, which will, in turn, raise the level of investment spending. The increase in investment spending will increase the level of aggregate demand. As aggregate demand increases sufficiently to push the economy to full employment and beyond, real GDP would be unable to rise any further and the full impact of the increase in the money supply would be on the price level. What this means is something most people are well aware of:

If the money supply is increased too much, the result will be inflation.

Remember that this is what we earlier characterized as too much money chasing too few goods—a description of demand-pull inflation. History is filled with examples of what happens when a nation's money supply is increased too fast, resulting in serious inflation. For example, in the seventeenth and eighteenth centuries, European countries tied their money supply to the amount of gold reserves held by governments. Thus, when shipload after shipload of Spanish gold bullion began arriving from the New World, inflation was triggered and continued for a long time. In the 1920s, because of the treaty that ended the Second World War, Germany's Weimar Republic felt it had little choice but to increase the money supply very rapidly in order to pay its bills. This triggered the hyper-inflation that we looked at in Chapter 4. A contemporary example is that of the Russian government, which began a rapid increase in its money supply in late 1998 after the collapse of its fixed exchange rate, which, predictably, led to inflation.

If such increases result in these types of problems, why increase the money supply at all? In other words, let's now turn to the other side of the question and ask:

What would be the effect of the Bank of Canada not increasing the money supply?

We know that increases in the level of real GDP increase the demand for money. In other words, normal economic growth results in increased demand for money. If, at the same time, the money supply does not increase but, instead, is held constant, the result will be a higher interest rate. This will reduce investment spending, and thus aggregate demand, which brings the economy's growth to a halt and, in extreme cases, could cause real GDP to fall. Something like this in fact happened in the early 1930s, when the American Federal Reserve Board *contracted* the money supply in the face of falling aggregate demand. This made the fall in GDP even worse. In addition, we would also expect the price level to fall. This is in fact what happened in both the United States and Canada in the early 1930s. In Canada's case, the decrease in prices between 1929 and 1933 was 23 percent. This leads us to the conclusion that:

If the money supply is not increased sufficiently, the result will be a recession and low economic growth.

These two examples bring out something very fundamental. The health of an economy depends on the money supply growing, but not too quickly or too slowly. Since it is the Bank of Canada that controls the growth of the money supply through its actions, it is clear that some kind of monetary policy is needed. This being the case, what kind of policy should this be?

In Chapter 11, when we asked what kind of fiscal policy should be used, we saw that there were two distinct schools of thought on the question. Exactly the same situation applies here to the question of what kind of monetary policy should be used. The first school of thought we will call the activist school, which is analogous to the interventionists of the previous chapter, and the second we will call the non-activist school, which is analogous to the non-interventionists.

The Bank of Canada's policies can influence the money supply, interest rates, and the exchange rate. The bank's goal is to create the right mix appropriate for the economy.

Money and Monetary Policy in Canada. Toronto: Canadian Council for Economic Education, 1994. Cartoon by Kelly Brine.

12.4 The Activist Approach to Monetary Policy

LO4
Describe the arguments for and against the activist approach to monetary policy.

There are two versions of activist monetary policy. The first is Keynesian monetary policy, which, until approximately 20 years ago, dominated most monetary policy making. The second version is anti-inflationary monetary policy, which surfaced in the late 1970s and early 1980s. We will look at each in turn.

Keynesian Monetary Policy

Keynesian monetary policy envisions an active process of setting goals and then adjusting policy to achieve those goals. As an example, the Bank of Canada used *Keynesian monetary policy* for some time after it was established in 1935. Its mandate then was:

> to regulate credit and currency in the best interest of the nation. . .and to mitigate by its influence fluctuations in the general level of production, trade, prices, and employment.

As you can see, implied here is the use of monetary policy to assist in achieving four separate goals:

- steady growth in real GDP
- an exchange rate that ensures a viable balance of trade
- stable prices
- full employment

However, economists know that no single policy tool can be expected to simultaneously achieve multiple goals. Thus, we can see that in this situation what was called "policy making" often involved deciding which goal, or goals, should be given priority. For three or four decades following the Second World War, most economists and policy makers took it for granted that monetary policy should be activist. Further, they felt that the two goals it should focus on were stable prices and full employment.

SELF-TEST

4. Which of the above goals are in conflict with each other, and which are compatible?

Achieving these twin goals seemed reasonable enough at the time, since unemployment and inflation were seen as opposite ends of the spectrum. That is to say, if aggregate demand was too low to achieve full employment, then there would be little or no inflationary pressure. Similarly, if aggregate demand was so high as to create inflation, then there would be little or no unemployment. In short, it was believed that an economy might suffer from an unemployment problem or from an inflation problem, but never from both problems at the same time. It followed then that monetary policy could be used to address the one problem that was present at that time, be it inflation or unemployment. This point is illustrated in the next two figures.

FIGURE 12.1 **The Effect of Contractionary Monetary Policy**

Given an aggregate demand of AD_1, there exists an inflationary gap equal to the distance $Y_E - Y_{FE}$. If contractionary monetary policy reduced aggregate demand to AD_2, then the inflationary gap would be closed.

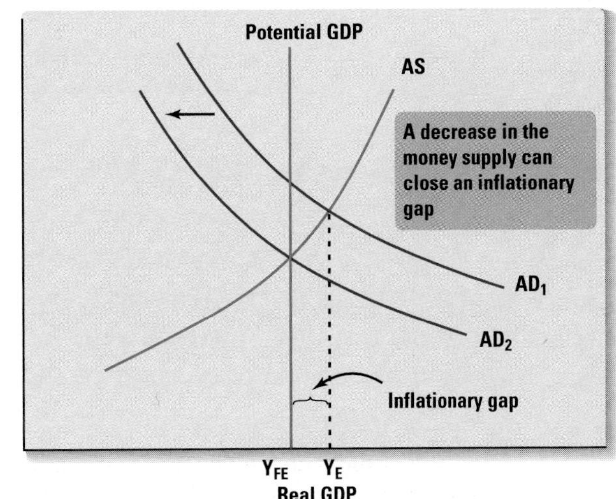

In **Figure 12.1**, if aggregate demand is AD_1 and full-employment national income is Y_{FE}, then there is an inflationary gap equal to $Y_E - Y_{FE}$. Keynesian monetary policy would call for contractionary monetary policy in this case. You will recall that this means reducing the money supply and making credit tighter, which increases the interest rate. The higher interest rate means a lower level of investment spending. Furthermore, the higher interest rate will encourage foreigners to send their savings to Canada, which increases the demand for the Canadian dollar on the international money markets and pushes the exchange rate up. This leads to a decrease in exports, which reinforces the decrease in investment spending. The combined effect of lower investment spending and lower exports reduces the level of aggregate demand to AD_2 and closes the inflationary gap.

SELF-TEST

5. If the Bank of Canada wanted to decrease the money supply, should it buy or sell government bonds?

Let's turn now to **Figure 12.2**. Once again, the level of aggregate demand is AD_1, and equilibrium national income is YE. However, in this situation there is a recessionary gap, since Y_E is less than Y_{FE}, the full-employment level of GDP. Here, Keynesian monetary policy would call for the use of expansionary monetary policy, which means increasing the money supply and making credit more readily available. This would lower the interest rate, which would increase the level of investment spending. In addition, a lower interest rate discourages foreigners from holding Canadian bonds and savings-account balances and encourages Canadians to send their savings abroad in search of higher interest rates. This pushes down the exchange rate, which increases exports. The combination of higher investment spending and higher exports would increase aggregate demand, from AD_1 to AD_2, and this would close the recessionary gap by increasing national income from Y_E to Y_{FE}.

FIGURE 12.2 **The Effect of Contractionary Monetary Policy**

Given AD_1, a recessionary gap equal to the distance $Y_{FE} - Y_E$ exists. Expansionary monetary policy that increases aggregate demand to AD_2 would close the recessionary gap.

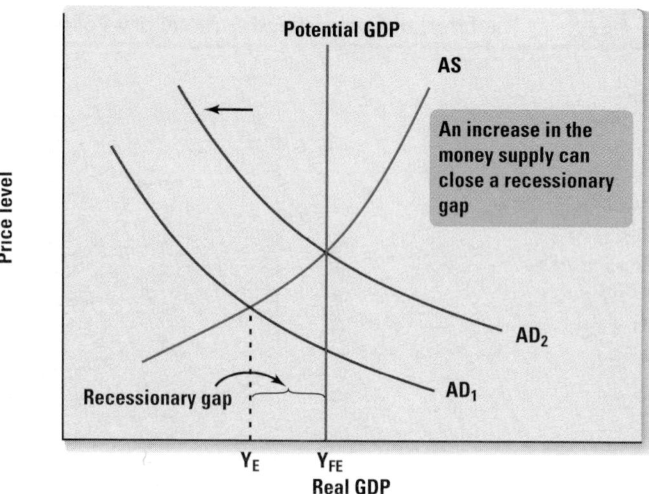

In summary, Keynesian monetary policy aims to keep the level of spending in the economy stable. If the economy is under-spending and a recessionary gap exists, then expansionary monetary policy would be used to raise spending. Similarly, if the economy was over-spending, then contractionary monetary policy would be used to reduce spending.

Criticisms of Keynesian Monetary Policy

The major problem with Keynesian monetary policy, as economists later came to realize, is that the twin goals of full employment and stable prices are sometimes incompatible and it may not be possible to achieve them together. This point was first explored in the early 1960s by A.W. Phillips, a British economist, who looked at the possibility of an economy achieving both goals simultaneously. He concluded that there was no evidence of this occurring in Britain in all of the previous century. In fact, it seemed to him that there was a "trade-off" between the two goals. This means that while it may be possible to achieve full employment, it would only be at the expense of higher rates of inflation. Similarly, stable prices could be achieved, but only at the cost of higher unemployment. Under these circumstances, the best that a central bank can do is achieve a delicate balance between the two without ever attaining either goal. For instance, it might be able to help the economy achieve a modest amount of inflation combined with a not-too-high level of cyclical unemployment. Any attempt to reduce inflation further would likely provoke unacceptably high rates of unemployment. Similarly, expansionary monetary policy designed to reduce unemployment would cause an acceleration in inflation rates. A central bank is caught therefore between "a rock and a hard place."

ADDED DIMENSION

The Phillips Curve

In 1958, British economist A.W. Phillips confirmed what many economists had long suspected, namely, that curing the twin evils of unemployment and inflation simultaneously may be not only difficult, but, in fact, impossible. Phillips did a time-series analysis of unemployment and inflation rates (actually, yearly changes in wage rates) for the British economy for the previous 100 years. He discovered that there were very few years of both low unemployment and low inflation rates. In fact, it seemed to be the case that when there was low unemployment, inflation was high; and vice versa—when inflation was low, unemployment was high. In other words, there appeared to be a "trade-off" between the two. A simple table of hypothetical data will illustrate the idea:

Unemployment Rate	Inflation Rate
4%	12%
6	8
8	5
10	3
12	2

Not only are low unemployment rates associated with high inflation rates and high unemployment with low inflation, but the cost of trying to fully achieve either of these goals becomes more and more expensive for society. In other words, to reduce unemployment by 2 percentage points when the economy is suffering 12 percent unemployment "costs" society a 1 percentage point increase in inflation, from 2 percent to 3 percent. But to reduce unemployment by a similar 2 percentage points when the economy is close to full employment, say from 6 percent to 4 percent, "costs" the country 4 percentage points in inflation.

While the idea seemed like a major breakthrough at the time, in hindsight, the Phillips curve does nothing more than confirm the shape of the aggregate supply curve: that it is upward-sloping and gets steeper as we approach the full-employment level of GDP. You can validate this in your own mind by picturing what would happen as aggregate demand increases. The answer is that it would result in both higher GDP (lower unemployment) and higher prices (inflation). Additionally, as you move closer to full-employment GDP, the increase in the price level is greater than the increase in GDP.

Over the last two decades, the Bank of Canada, along with a number of other central banks around the world, have concluded that the task of simultaneously curing both unemployment and inflation simply isn't possible. As a result, the bank has refocused its mandate toward the more attainable goal of maintaining the value of the Canadian dollar.

Anti-Inflationary Monetary Policy

In contrast to Keynesian monetary policy, the Bank of Canada now sees its role as preserving both the internal and external value of the currency. This means that the bank uses monetary policy to affect both inflation rates and the value of the Canadian dollar. Its recent target has been to keep inflation rates at between 1 and 3 percent per year. In this, it has been markedly successful. Recent inflation rates are in stark contrast to the experience of most of the 1970s and 1980s. Following the OPEC-imposed oil price increases of the early 1970s, inflation rates around the world, including Canada, were in the range of 8 to 12 percent per year. In addition to holding the rate of inflation down, the bank is also concerned with the external value of the currency (the exchange rate), with an eye to maintaining its stability.

Those who support this new role for monetary policy argue that the underlying purpose of preserving the internal and external value of a country's currency is to create the right atmosphere for investment. Price stability is the key condition for stimulating investment and thus in maintaining the highest possible levels of productivity, real incomes, employment, and global competitiveness. This is because, as we saw in Chapter 4, the worst enemy of new investment is uncertainty. High rates of inflation, or even unpredictable changes in the inflation rate, create an atmosphere of uncertainty. Foreign investors in particular need the assurance that both the external value (the exchange rate) and the internal value (the price level) of a currency will not be changing dramatically in the near future. Sudden, unpredictable changes in either are undesirable. In short, uncertainty and the lower levels of investment spending that go with it reduce the rate of economic growth and the prosperity of the nation.

Given this, the federal government and the Bank of Canada made a joint statement in December 1993 attempting to generate confidence in the economy. They announced their objective of keeping inflation within a target range of 1 to 3 percent for the period 1995 to 1998. Later, in February 1998, it was announced that this inflationary-control target was extended to the end of 2001. Furthermore, the government and the bank made it clear that more target-range announcements would be forthcoming in the future.

We have already seen that controlling inflation means preventing aggregate demand from becoming too strong, and this is done by keeping the pace of monetary expansion in line with economic growth and, occasionally, by using contractionary monetary policy.

Let's now turn to the other part of the Bank of Canada's new mandate—preserving the value of Canada's flexible exchange rate. Is this possible if the bank is focused primarily on an anti-inflationary monetary policy? In fact, not only is it possible, but these two goals are quite compatible. The most noticeable effect of a tight monetary policy is a higher interest rate. These same higher interest rates, which dampen spending and keep inflation low, also encourage foreigners to hold Canadian securities, which increases the demand for the Canadian dollar and strengthens its value on international money markets. We know that a higher Canadian dollar will decrease Canadian exports and cause an increase in imports. Net exports, then, will decrease. Because of flexible exchange rates, monetary policy becomes a far more effective anti-inflation tool. Schematically, this can be shown as follows:

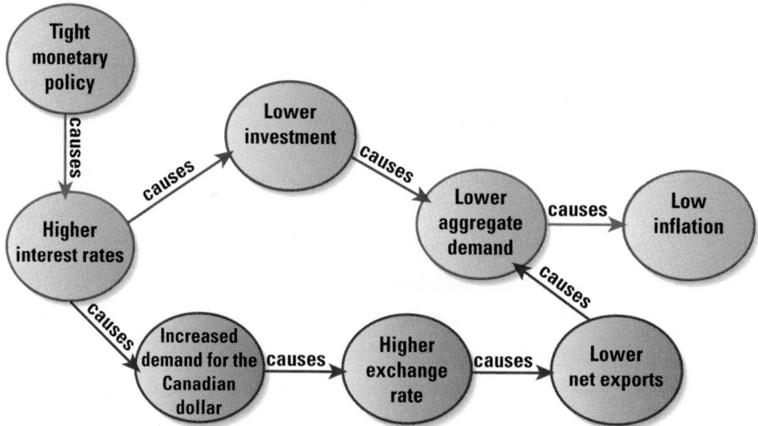

Contracting the money supply results in lower inflation.

We have just seen how pro-active monetary policy is quite effective under a flexible exchange-rate regime. But what happens if a country has a fixed exchange rate? Can it still use monetary policy to preserve the internal and external value of its currency? Well, the policy of a fixed exchange rate takes care of the latter task, since its value is being held constant by decree. But there is a price to pay for this. As we saw in Chapter 10, if an economy operates with a fixed exchange rate, then its central bank is obliged to maintain that value by buying and selling its own currency and its holdings of foreign currencies on the international money market. There is more to it than this, though. In order to maintain a fixed value of its currency, a central bank must also keep its interest rate at par with that of its trading partner(s). This is because, freed from any concern over fluctuations in the value of currencies, investors only need to look at which country is paying the highest interest rates. A difference of only 1/2 percent in interest rates might be enough to cause a huge amount of money to flood out of the country which has the lower interest rate. In essence, the country fixing the value of its currency to that of another must also fix its interest rates. This means that it relinquishes an independent monetary policy. If, for instance, the major partner increases its interest rates, it must do the same; if the other country lowers the interest rate, it must follow suit. If the economic conditions in the two countries are similar, this doesn't present a problem. However, if economic circumstances differ between the countries, a fixed exchange rate can have unfortunate repercussions. For instance, it could be that the major country, faced with an inflationary boom, decides to cut spending in the economy by increasing interest rates. The smaller country must do the same, despite the fact that its economy may be facing a recession and would like instead the stimulus of lower interest rates.

So, although fixed exchange rates do introduce certainty, that certainty comes with a cost.

ADDED DIMENSION

A Fixed Exchange Rate for Canada

In the fall of 1998, professors Tom Courchene of Queen's University and Richard Harris of Simon Fraser University proposed that a small country like Canada has a better alternative to flexible exchange rates, which is a fixed exchange-rate regime with its major trading partner. They recognized that fixing Canada's exchange rate to the U.S. dollar would essentially let U.S. monetary conditions set Canadian interest rates and would give Canada a long-term inflation rate equal to that in the United States. However, they argued that since the U.S. business cycle drives the Canadian business cycle anyway, monetary independence is overrated.

And what would be the advantage of such a policy? Stability and the encouragement of investment in plant and equipment and in human capital. Such investment is undermined by large swings in the Canadian–U.S. exchange rate. For example, following the 12–14 percent fall in the exchange rate in 1998, many, mostly young, highly skilled Canadians migrated to the United States, where wages, measured in U.S. dollars, were much higher. If these people do not return to Canada, this will prove to be a serious loss to Canada for the next 40 years.

Harris and Courchene pointed out that Austria and the Netherlands did with Germany exactly what they proposed that Canada should do with the United States. They noted that these two fixed exchange rates held, even under the most turbulent of conditions, including the global inflation crisis of the early 1980s.

SELF-TEST

6. Explain what will happen to the interest rate and to aggregate demand if the Bank of Canada increases the money supply and the country has a fixed exchange rate.

Criticisms of Anti-Inflationary Monetary Policy

The most serious criticism of anti-inflationary monetary policy is that, because the Bank of Canada is overly concerned about controlling inflation, it will lose sight of other equally valid goals such as economic growth and low unemployment.

An example of this concern can be found in a study done by professor Pierre Fortin of the University of Quebec. Fortin points out that between 1981 and 1989 real short-term interest rates were about 1 percent higher in Canada than in the United States, but between 1990 and 1996 the gap rose to 3.6 percent. He attributes these higher interest rates to the zeal with which the Bank of Canada pursued an anti-inflationary monetary policy. Further, Fortin and others argue that these high interest rates cost the Canadian economy dearly in the form of lost GDP and higher unemployment. Along the same lines, a recent U.S. study argues that a modest amount of inflation, say 2 percent to 3 percent, is a necessary lubricant for economic growth.

The second criticism of anti-inflationary policy is that, by using high interest rates to control inflation, the central bank has helped to increase the cost of servicing the national debt. Just a 1-percentage point difference in interest rates translates into a $5 billion difference in the annual interest payments that the government has to make. Many observers have suggested that, especially in the early 1990s, the Bank of Canada could have reduced interest rates significantly without triggering inflation. The benefit of doing so would not only have meant higher growth and employment as previously mentioned, but also lower budget deficits and debt.

Perhaps more seriously, other critics of activist monetary policy, especially critics of the Keynesian version, have argued that monetary changes have an uncontrollable impact on the economy. They therefore suggest that the money supply should not be left in the hands of central bank authorities, to be changed at their whim in an effort to fine-tune the economy. Instead, they feel that certain monetary rules should be followed. Let's explore this idea further.

12.5 The Non-Activist School

LO5
Describe the arguments for and against the non-activist approach to monetary policy.

A number of economists of the monetarist school that we looked at in Chapter 8 view the use of activist monetary policy with alarm. They believe that, because changes in the money supply can have such a powerful effect on the economy and are subject to significant lags, it is better if the central bank's role is restricted to that of following certain established rules. The focus of this group, the non-activist school, is on ensuring that the quantity of money supplied is kept equal to the quantity of money demanded. This would imply a constant interest rate. This is illustrated in **Figure 12.3**.

FIGURE 12.3 **Monetary Policy Aimed at Achieving a Constant Interest Rate**

Money demand will increase over time as a result of economic growth, as seen by the shifts from MD_1 to MD_2 to MD_3. If monetary policy accommodates each of these increases in demand with equal increases in supply, as seen by the shifts from MS_1 to MS_2 to MS_3, then the interest rate will remain unchanged at r_1.

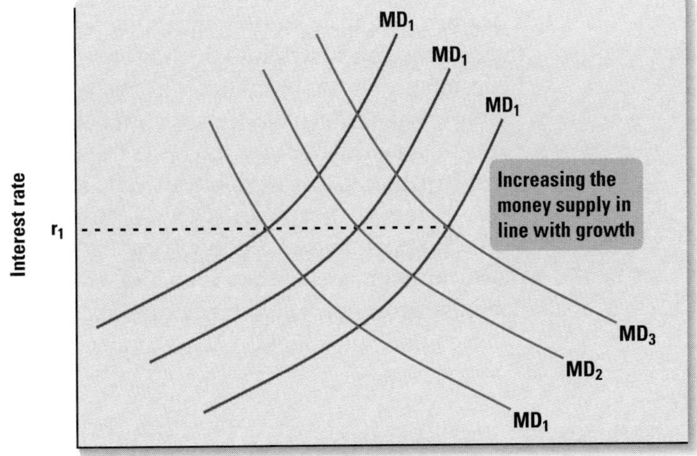

Figure 12.3 shows increases in the demand for money, as illustrated by the shifts from MD_1 to MD_2 to MD_3. These increases are an inevitable result of growth in real GDP, since higher levels of income imply a higher transaction demand for money. If the monetary policy of the central bank is to maintain a steady interest rate, then it would accommodate each of the increases in demand with equal increases in the supply of money, as seen by the shifts from MS_1 to MS_2 to MS_3.

Advocates of a fixed interest-rate policy think that not only should rates be held constant but that the target rate should be announced to the world. They believe that a stable interest rate will allow people and businesses to make rational decisions about savings, investment, and spending that will maximize the benefits to both individuals and to society. Thus, they believe that the appropriate monetary policy for the central bank to pursue is to continuously adjust the growth in the money supply in order to maintain a constant, pre-announced interest rate.

A variation on this same approach would be for the central bank to maintain a constant, pre-announced pace of monetary expansion and have the interest rate adjust to maintain the balance between the quantities of money supplied and money demanded. Advocates of this variation argue that this will result in maximum growth in the economy.

Irrespective of which of these two variations is used, the underlying philosophy of the non-activist school is that the central bank should take what amounts to a very passive role in making monetary policy by setting either an interest-rate target or a money-supply-growth target. Either of these variations, they feel, would enhance the performance of the economy by allowing it to adjust to these well known, long-term targets. In effect, non-activists believe that policy makers should be guided by rules rather than allowed to make decisions at their own discretion. This is analogous to the advocates of non-activist fiscal policy, who believe that the government should be constrained to obey the rule of a balanced budget rather than being allowed to run up budget deficits or surpluses at their own discretion.

Criticisms of the Non-Activist School

We have just seen that advocates of monetary rules suggest that this is the best way to achieve a degree of stability and predictability for the economy. Critics of setting fixed rules argue that, on the contrary, while the objective is stability in money markets, the result may well be instability in the economy. The reason for this is that fixing the growth in the money supply is not of much use if you cannot also control the demand for money. And a changing money demand will cause interest rates to change unpredictably. In short, a stable money supply might cause an unstable interest rate. Nor does it make much difference if the interest rate, rather than the money supply, is targeted for stability. A fixed interest rate of 6 percent, for instance, is neither a good nor a bad target in itself. If the economy is in a recession, 6 percent might well be too high a rate and help to prevent a recovery. But if, on the other hand, the economy is suffering from inflation, it might be that 6 percent is far too low a rate and is not doing enough to help dampen spending.

12.6 Beyond Fiscal and Monetary Policy

LO6
Realize why some argue that other direct controls are needed as alternatives to both fiscal and monetary policy.

stagflation: the simultaneous occurrence of high inflation and unemployment.

We need first to set the stage for this discussion. In 1973, OPEC (the Organization of Petroleum Exporting Countries), which controls a large portion of the world's oil exports, put quotas on the amount of crude oil being exported from the member countries. This reduction in supply led to a quadrupling of the price of crude oil on world markets. Since most of the major industrial nations were net importers of oil, this rise in price increased the cost of production of most goods and services. The effect of this was to usher in a period of **stagflation**—simultaneous stagnation (high unemployment) and inflation. Until 1973, governments generally had only to deal with one of the twin evils at a time. Now Canada, along with most other countries, found itself fighting an economic war on both the inflation and unemployment fronts.

In terms of our aggregate demand–supply model, there is only one explanation of what could cause stagflation: a decrease in the aggregate supply, as shown in **Figure 12.4**.

FIGURE 12.4 **The Cause of Stagflation**

A significant increase in the price of imported resources (such as oil in 1973) will decrease aggregate supply, causing it to shift left as seen by AS_1 to AS_2. The result will be a higher price level P_1 to P_2 and a lower level of real GDP, Y_1 to Y_2.

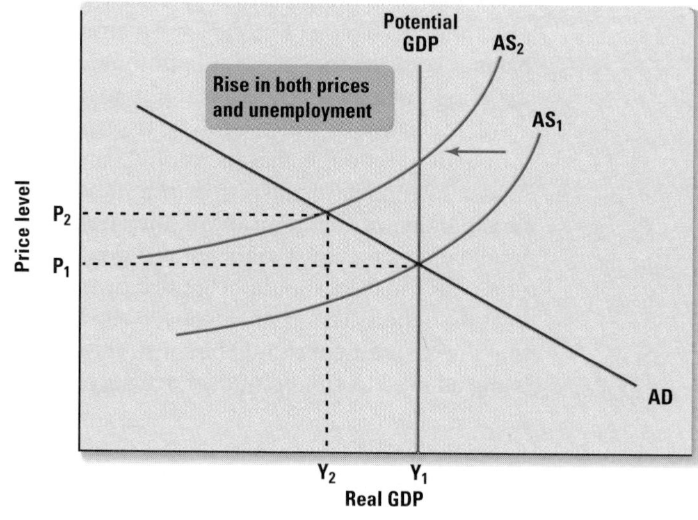

The 1973 increase in the price of imported oil caused a decrease in the short-run aggregate supply, as seen by the shift from AS_1 to AS_2, in **Figure 12.4**. The result of this was to increase the price level in Canada, from P_1 to P_2, and cause unemployment to rise, as is seen by the drop in real GDP from Y_1 to Y_2.

Inflation and unemployment rates remained high in Canada throughout the 1970s and early 1980s, peaking in 1982, when inflation hit 10.8 percent and unemployment was 11 percent. What was most alarming about stagflation when it first appeared was the fact that no one, including economists, was able to explain it, or offer remedies to cure it. The reason for this failure was the fact that the majority of economists were wedded to the idea that economic events could only be explained in terms of changes in *aggregate demand*. Although economists recognized the existence of aggregate supply, it was thought to be a very passive ingredient in the economy. After all, firms would never produce unless there was a demand for their products. If demand increased, firms would meet the increased demand by producing more; if demand decreased, firms would react by producing less. What more needs to be said about supply?

Unfortunately, this blind spot of most economists in the 1970s meant that they were unable to correctly diagnose the problem of stagflation and, worse, offered the wrong sort of remedies. This can be seen in **Figure 12.5**.

FIGURE 12.5 **Aggregate Demand and Stagflation**

The economy is in a stagflationary situation with a high price level, P_1 (inflation), and a low level of real GDP, Y_1 (high unemployment). Expansionary policy, either fiscal or monetary, will shift the aggregate demand curve from the present AD_1 to AD_2. The result will be a higher level of GDP, Y_2, but unfortunately this will cause even higher prices, P_2. Alternatively, the government could use contractionary policy to curb inflation. This will result in a leftward shift in aggregate demand from the current AD_1 to AD_3. This will cut prices to P_3 but with the unfortunate result of reducing real GDP to Y_3, thus causing even higher unemployment.

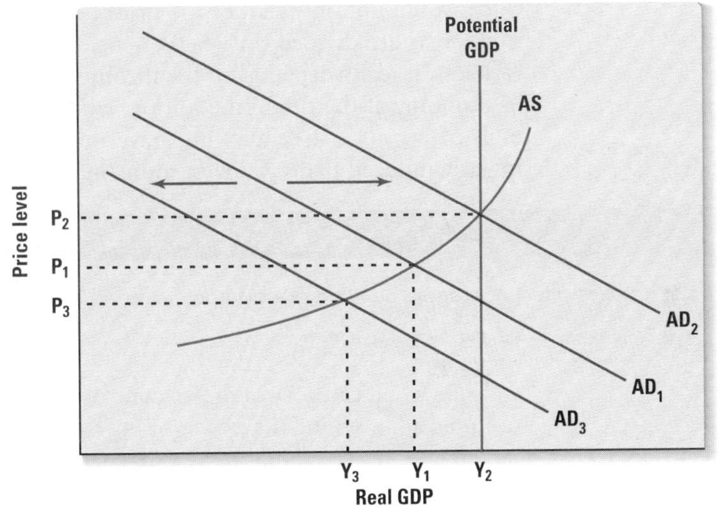

Neither expansionary fiscal nor monetary policies are able to cure the simultaneous problems of high unemployment and inflation. Such policies will increase aggregate demand, as shown by the rightward shift in the aggregate demand curve, from AD_1 to AD_2 in **Figure 12.5**. This will increase real GDP and therefore reduce unemployment. Unfortunately, it will also have the effect of pushing up prices, from P_1 to P_2. Contractionary fiscal or monetary policy is no better. It will cause a decrease in aggregate demand, from AD_1 to AD_3, which will reduce prices from P_1 to P_3. However, it will also cause an increase in unemployment, since GDP will fall.

In fact, the only way that production and employment can be boosted and prices reduced at the same time is through policies designed to increase aggregate supply. Faced with this apparent failure of traditional policies, governments were forced to propose alternative policies which all aim to increase aggregate supply. It is these we turn to now.

Direct Controls

Direct controls take the form of specific laws, rules, and regulations designed to modify the way people behave. Often these controls tend to have an impact on the supply side of the market, though in some cases they may also affect the demand side.

Direct-control policies can be grouped into three different categories, all of which are thought to help make the economy work more competitively and more productively. The first of these are called *tax incentive programs.* These include any tax changes that help stimulate people's incentives to work and save, and businesses to invest more. They include such things as reductions in personal and corporate income taxes, a decrease in capital gains tax, tax changes to allow bigger depreciation allowances (allowing firms to write off assets over a shorter period, thus stimulating investment), and bigger write-offs for spending on research.

The effect of a reduction in tax rates may well induce some people to work longer hours, take second jobs, postpone retirement, or remove themselves from the unemployment rolls. For others it could mean that they now need to work fewer hours than before to earn the same income. If successful, the policy would have the effect of increasing aggregate supply, which would not only reduce the price level, but would also boost GDP and employment. Economists are divided on whether such tax reductions cause people to work more or to work less; it really depends on the income level, the size of the tax cut, and the condition of the economy at the time. In addition, while people may have the desire to work more as a result of tax cuts, they may not have the opportunity unless an appropriate tax cut has similarly induced firms to invest more, increase output, and thus hire more people.

SELF-TEST

7. Will a cut in taxes affect aggregate demand or aggregate supply? Why?

The second category of direct-control policies are termed *pro-competition policies.* These are aimed at loosening the power of big corporations and trade unions in order to make the marketplace more competitive and enable it to more easily and rapidly adjust to the changing pattern of demand and technology. Particular policy proposals in this area include anti-monopoly or anti-combine legislation. A similar approach would be the increased deregulation of industry to make it easier for new firms to enter and compete; or the privatization of many government services so as to make them open to competition. Also, we need to mention the policy option that is becoming more significant as international trade continues to grow in both volume and in people's awareness. There is no question that freer trade results in greater competition within the economies involved. For example, both the Canadian and the Mexican economies are more competitive as a result of NAFTA.

The third category of direct-control policies available to governments are called *employment policies*. These include policies designed to increase the amount of employment and to reduce the natural rate of unemployment. Specific programs in this area include improved job retraining and allowances to help workers relocate, a better system of making unemployed people aware of job and career prospects through better information, and legislation to promote equality of job opportunities and the outlawing of any type of discrimination in the workplace. All of these, it is thought, will help to reduce the amount of time people spend looking for jobs.

In summary, the three categories of direct controls are:

- tax-incentive policies
- pro-competition policies
- employment policies

Finale

This chapter and Chapter 11 complete our look at the two significant policies available to governments: fiscal and monetary policies. The efficacy of these tools involves a degree of both economic and political faith. How well, if at all, we can expect these policy tools to work depends essentially on how we think the economy operates. Those who advocate interventionist fiscal policy and activist monetary policy believe that the economy is essentially unstable and needs the direction of policy to steer a course of successful, healthy economy. Other economists believe in the ability of the economy to automatically adjust to problems that arise and argue that the fiscal and monetary policy should be non-activist and neutral. In addition, they argue that unless changes are made to the basic structure of an economy, the effects of interventionist, activist policies will not be sustainable and may even be harmful. They would argue that increases in productivity as a result of the application of improved technology, better capital equipment, and a more adaptable and better-educated work force are likely to produce bigger dividends for the economy in the long run. The question of whether the economy is self-adjusting and the contrast in policy prescriptions between those who think it is and those who do not is the subject of the next chapter.

REVIEW

1. What is the effect of a too-rapid pace of monetary expansion?
2. Explain how expansionary monetary policy works to affect the economy.
3. Why does contractionary monetary policy imply a leftward shift in the aggregate demand curve?
4. Explain the two versions of activist monetary policy.
5. What are the two different targets of the non-activist school of monetary policy?
6. What does *stagflation* mean?
7. What are the three types of direct controls?

STUDY GUIDE

Review

CHAPTER SUMMARY

This chapter looked at the functions of the Bank of Canada and then defined monetary policy and examined two distinct approaches in its application.

1. The Bank of Canada *functions* as:
   - the issuer of currency;
   - the government's bank and manager of foreign currency reserves;
   - the bankers' bank and lender of last resort;
   - the auditor and inspector of commercial banks;
   - the regulator of the money supply.
2. The *tools* used by the Bank of Canada to affect monetary policy are:
   - open-market operations;
   - setting the bank rate;
   - switching government accounts;
   - moral suasion.
3. *Monetary policy* is needed simply because the money supply must grow as the level of GNP grows in order to maintain stability in the level of prices.
4. The Keynesian version of the *activist approach* to monetary policy is analogous to counter-cyclical fiscal policy and advocates see these two policies as a means of intervening in the economy to achieve:
   - full employment;
   - low inflation.
5. The major *criticism* of the Keynesian version of activist monetary policy is that the twin goals of full employment and low inflation are not compatible.
6. The *anti-inflationary version* of the activist approach to monetary policy has the goal of maintaining both the internal and the external value of the currency.
7. The major *criticism* of the anti-inflationary version of activist monetary policy is that when the Bank of Canada becomes overly concerned about the threat of inflation, both economic growth and the level of employment may suffer.
8. Advocates of the non-activist version of monetary policy:
   - view the activist approach with alarm because they believe that monetary changes are too powerful to be left in the hands of policy makers;
   - believe in a policy of changing the money supply in accordance with a pre-set rule and letting interest rates adjust accordingly or, alternatively, announcing a pre-set interest rate and adjusting the money supply to maintain this rate.
9. *Criticism* of the non-activist approach argues that such rule-making ignores cyclical swings in the rate of growth in GDP and employment and, therefore, could lead to economic instability.
10. Some economists, pointing to the failure of traditional policy (fiscal or monetary) to deal with stagflation, advocate the use of three alternative types of *direct controls*:
    - tax incentive programs;
    - pro-competition policies;
    - employment policies.

NEW GLOSSARY TERMS

bank rate 414
contractionary monetary policy 412
expansionary monetary policy 412
monetary policy 410
open-market operations 412
stagflation 426

STUDY TIPS

1. Though the idea of open-market operations at first seems unnecessarily subtle and complicated, it involves nothing more than the transfer of cash for bonds between the Bank of Canada and anyone who wants to buy or sell bonds. But since the central bank is doing the buying and selling, the effect is a little different from normal trading. For instance, if I buy a bond from you, I will have less money but you will have more. The net effect on the economy's money supply is zero. However, when money goes into the Bank of Canada, the nation's money supply is reduced, and when money comes out its money supply is increased.

2. Try not to confuse the primary sale of bonds (or any other security) and the secondary sale of bonds. When an institution (including the government) "floats" a new issue, that institution receives the proceeds of the sale. Any subsequent sale of the same bond is a private transfer and, apart from registering the name of the new owner, does not involve the issuing institution at all. The sale of government bonds by the Bank of Canada is a primary sale, and the proceeds go to the government. Open-market operations involve mostly the buying and selling of "pre-owned" bonds; that is, they are secondary sales.

3. Do not interpret the fact that there are two approaches (one with two versions) to monetary policy as evidence that economics is unnecessarily complicated or that economists never agree with each other. What you are seeing is a natural evolution in policy making as economic circumstances change over time.

Answered Questions

Indicate whether the following statements are true or false.

1. **T or F** The most important function of the Bank of Canada is to regulate the money supply.

2. **T or F** One way that the Bank of Canada can increase the money supply is to purchase bonds in the open market.

3. **T or F** The biggest asset on the balance sheet of the Bank of Canada is notes in circulation.

4. **T or F** A decrease in the bank rate is part of contractionary monetary policy.

5. **T or F** Activist monetary policy can take two forms.

6. **T or F** Contractionary monetary policy will result in a rightward shift in the AD curve.

7. **T or F** Expansionary monetary policy is more effective with a fixed rather than a flexible exchange rate.

8. **T or F** Policies aimed at influencing the level of aggregate demand include monetary but not fiscal policy.

9. **T or F** Stagflation means an increase in both inflation and unemployment levels.

10. **T or F** Direct controls usually affect aggregate supply.

Basic (Questions 11–24)

11. What is the effect of expansionary monetary policy?
   a) The money supply increases and interest rates rise.
   b) The money supply increases and interest rates fall.
   c) The money supply decreases and interest rates rise.
   d) The money supply decreases and interest rates fall.

12. Stagflation is the simultaneous occurrence of both:
   a) A recession and deflation.
   b) A recession and inflation.
   c) Inflation and rapid growth in GDP.
   d) Recession and rapid growth in GDP.

13. What is the name of the interest rate that the Bank of Canada charges to the commercial banks?
   a) The prime rate.
   b) The commercial rate.
   c) The bank rate.
   d) The loan rate.

14. In Canada, who controls the supply of money?
   a) The Department of Finance.
   b) The Bank of Canada.
   c) The market.
   d) The Canadian Mint.

15. All of the following, except one, are tools of monetary policy. Which is the exception?
   a) Switching government deposits between the Bank of Canada and the commercial banks.
   b) Changing the target reserve ratio of the commercial banks.
   c) Selling bonds in the open market.
   d) Changing the bank rate.

16. Which of the following is the most important function of the Bank of Canada?
   a) The collection and clearing of cheques among commercial banks.
   b) Regulating the supply of money.
   c) Holding the reserves of commercial banks.
   d) Issuing new currency.

17. Suppose that the Bank of Canada buys $5 million of government bonds from the commercial banks. What will happen to the reserves of the commercial banks as a result?
   a) They would decrease by $5 million.
   b) They would increase by $5 million.
   c) They would increase by $4.5 million.
   d) They would increase by $50 million.

18. What effect does expansionary monetary policy have on the aggregate demand curve?
   a) It causes it to shift right.
   b) It causes it to shift left.
   c) It causes a movement down the aggregate demand curve.
   d) It causes a movement up the aggregate demand curve.

19. All of the following, except one, are direct controls. Which is the exception?
   a) Interest-rate policies.
   b) Tax-incentive programs.
   c) Pro-competition policies.
   d) Employment policies.

20. All of the following, except one, are tools of monetary policy. Which is the exception?
   a) Switching government deposits between commercial banks and the Bank of Canada.
   b) Moral suasion.
   c) Changing the bank rate.
   d) Changing tax rates.
   e) Open-market operations.

21. What is the purpose of a tight money policy?
   a) To increase investment spending.
   b) To raise interest rates and restrict the availability of credit.
   c) To increase aggregate demand.
   d) To fight recessions.
   e) To lower the exchange rate.

22. Advocates of Keynesian monetary policy see all of the following, except one, as goals that monetary policy can help achieve. Which is the exception?
   a) Steady interest rates.
   b) Steady growth in real GDP.
   c) Stable prices.
   d) Full employment.

23. Which of the following would be appropriate if the economy was experiencing an inflationary gap?
   a) A tighter monetary policy that decreased the money supply.
   b) An easy monetary policy that increased the money supply.
   c) Lower interest rates.
   d) A lower exchange rate.

24. Which of the following would be appropriate if the economy was experiencing a recessionary gap?
   a) A tighter monetary policy that decreased the money supply.
   b) An easy monetary policy that increased the money supply.
   c) Higher interest rates.
   d) A higher exchange rate.

Intermediate (Questions 25–32)

25. Suppose that the government wishes to affect the level of aggregate demand in the economy. Which of the following are *not* consistent policy measures?
   a) A tax increase and an increase in the money supply.
   b) A tax reduction and an increase in the money supply.
   c) An increase in government spending and an increase in the money supply.
   d) A decrease in government spending and a decrease in the money supply.

26. If Canada wishes to maintain the value of the dollar relative to the American dollar, then what should it do?
   a) Keep the money supply constant.
   b) Continually adjust the money supply to keep interest rates in line with American rates.
   c) Increase the money supply whenever the American dollar starts to appreciate against the Canadian dollar.
   d) Purchase American dollars.

27. What happens when the Bank of Canada buys government bonds in the open market?
a) The demand deposits of the commercial banks remain the same, but their reserves increase.
b) The demand deposits and the reserves of the commercial banks both decrease.
c) The demand deposits of the commercial banks remain the same, but their reserves decrease.
d) The demand deposits and the reserves of the commercial banks both remain the same.
e) The demand deposits and the reserves of the commercial banks both increase.

28. Which of the following best describes the consequences of contractionary monetary policy?
a) An increase in the interest rate, an increase in investment spending, and an increase in nominal GDP.
b) An increase in the interest rate, an increase in investment spending, and a decrease in nominal GDP.
c) An increase in the interest rate, a decrease in investment spending, and a decrease in nominal GDP.
d) A decrease in the interest rate, an increase in investment spending, and an increase in nominal GDP.
e) A decrease in the interest rate, a decrease in investment spending, and a decrease in nominal GDP.

29. What is the most serious criticism of the anti-inflationary version of activist monetary policy?
a) Monetary policy is probably ineffective in fighting inflation.
b) Over-emphasis on controlling inflation comes at the expense of the equally valid goals of low unemployment and economic growth.
c) Maintaining internal price stability means losing control of the exchange rate.
d) The monetary rules implied by this version of monetary policy are too rigid.

30. What would be the effect if the Bank of Canada maintained the money supply at its current level and did not increase it at all in the future?
a) Prices would remain steady at their current level.
b) Interest rates would rise over time and economic growth rates would slow down.
c) Interest rates would fall over time and economic growth rates would increase.
d) The threat of inflation would increase.

Figure 12.6 refers to a closed, no-government economy (investment is the only injection, and savings is the only leakage).

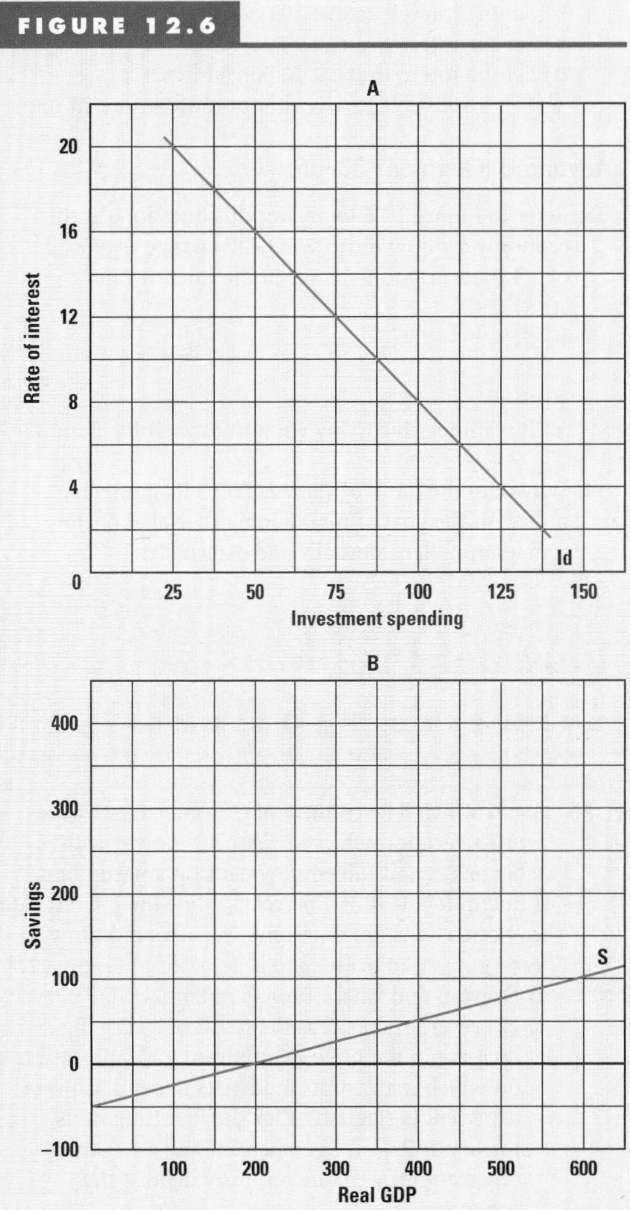

31. Refer to **Figure 12.6** to answer this question. If potential GDP in this economy is $400, what action should the central bank take?
a) Set the interest rate at 8 percent.
b) Set the interest rate at 10 percent.
c) Set the interest rate at 14 percent.
d) Set the interest rate at 16 percent.
e) It is impossible to say without more information.

32. Refer to **Figure 12.6** to answer this question. If potential GDP in this economy is $600, what action should the central bank take?
   a) Set the interest rate at 8 percent.
   b) Set the interest rate at 10 percent.
   c) Set the interest rate at 14 percent.
   d) Set the interest rate at 16 percent.
   e) It is impossible to say without more information.

Advanced (Questions 33–35)

33. Refer to **Figure 12.6** to answer this question. In this economy, by how much will GDP change as a result of a 4 percent point change in the interest rate?
   a) $12.50.
   b) $25.
   c) $50.
   d) $100.
   e) It is impossible to say without more information.

34. Why does the Bank of Canada focus its monetary policy on the goal of maintaining the value of the Canadian dollar internally and externally?
   a) Because it believes that a monetary rule approach to monetary policy is the best way to go.
   b) Because it believes that this approach will also achieve full employment.
   c) Because it believes that this approach will help achieve a balanced budget.
   d) Because it believes that interest rates must remain stable.
   e) Because it believes that the twins goals of stable prices and low unemployment are not compatible.

35. How does expansionary monetary policy affect exchange rates?
   a) It increases interest rates, which leads to an appreciation of the exchange rate.
   b) It decreases interest rates, which leads to an appreciation of the exchange rate.
   c) It increases interest rates, which leads to a depreciation of the exchange rate.
   d) It decreases interest rates, which leads to an depreciation of the exchange rate.
   e) It increases the price level, which leads to an appreciation of the exchange rate.

Parallel Problems

ANSWERED PROBLEMS

36. **Key Problem** The country of Corona has, over the last two decades, achieved vigorous growth with stable prices and full employment (at a natural rate of unemployment of 4 percent), while the interest rate has been a constant 5 percent. Corona's economy in year 1 is in equilibrium and is depicted in **Figure 12.7**.
   a) Draw in and label Corona's potential GDP curve. However, in year 2, as the result of a very big increase in the price of imported malt, a resource on which many of its industries depend, Corona experiences stagflation for the first time in its history. Inflation of 10 percent and a negative 5 percent growth rate seriously depress the economy.
   b) Shift the appropriate curves, labelled with 2, to denote Corona's year 2 economy. What are the new level of real GDP, the new price level, and the amount of the recessionary gap?
   New level of real GDP: $ ________________;
   new price level: ________________;
   recessionary gap: $ ________________.

FIGURE 12.7

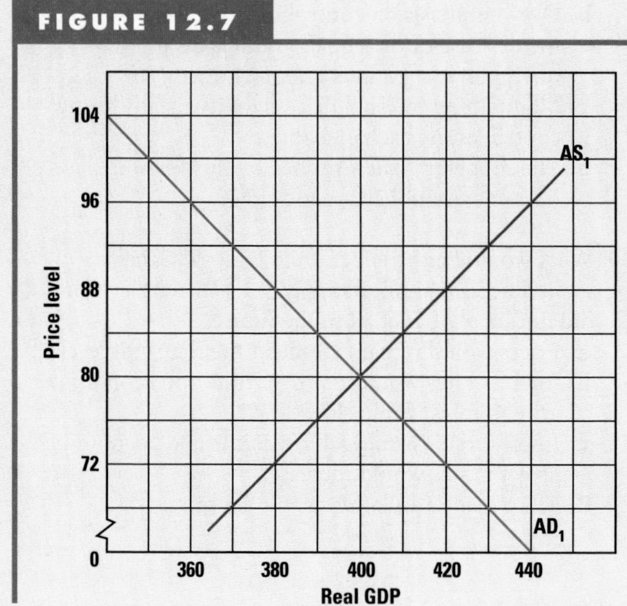

Alarmed at events in the republic, the president of Corona calls in the governor of the Bank of Corona and the secretary of the Corona Labour Congress to ask for their advice. The governor wants to focus on prices and suggests that the way to bring them down to the year 1 levels would be through the use of contractionary monetary policy. As a result of research done at the bank, he has concluded that for every 1-percentage-point change in interest rates, aggregate demand will change by $10 billion.

c) What new interest rate would bring price levels back to the year 1 level?
New interest rate: ____________________ %.
The secretary of the labour congress, while not disputing these figures, vehemently denounces the governor's plan. She argues that if successful, the contractionary monetary policy would undoubtedly cure inflation, but it would further increase the unemployment problem. The secretary points out that, according to Okun's Law, for every 2 1/2 percent that the actual GDP falls below potential GDP, unemployment rises by 1 percentage point.

d) If the secretary's fears are well-founded, what will be the rate of unemployment in Corona if the bank governor's plan is adopted?
Unemployment rate: ____________________ %.
Instead, the secretary implores the president to stimulate the economy so as to get the unemployment rate down. She recommends that the government of Corona immediately embark on an expansionary fiscal policy, which will have a multiplier effect on the economy. The aim, she suggests, is to boost aggregate demand by $40 billion. The governor of the Bank of Corona is outraged at the idea. To him, it means simply throwing taxpayers' money at the problem. While he agrees that an increase in aggregate demand of $40 billion will indeed produce full employment, he adds, pointedly, that it will also increase prices even more.

e) What will be the effect on the level of real GDP and the price level of increasing AD_1 by $40?
New level of real GDP: $ ____________________;
new price level: ____________________.
The president, angered by what he feels to be petty bickering and lack of consensus between the two (and also concerned that this Key Problem is getting far too long!), dismisses them both. Unacquainted with Okun and other esoteric economic laws, he feels that the solution to the problem of stagflation is simplicity itself. The Coronan people must take a pay cut. The effect of this would be to shift the aggregate supply curve.

f) What shift in the AS is necessary to return the economy to full employment, and what will be the resulting price level?
Shift in the AS curve: $____________________;
price level ____________________.

Basic (Problems 37–41)

37. The economy of Carlsberg is presently in equilibrium but is suffering a recession as depicted in **Figure 12.8.**

FIGURE 12.8

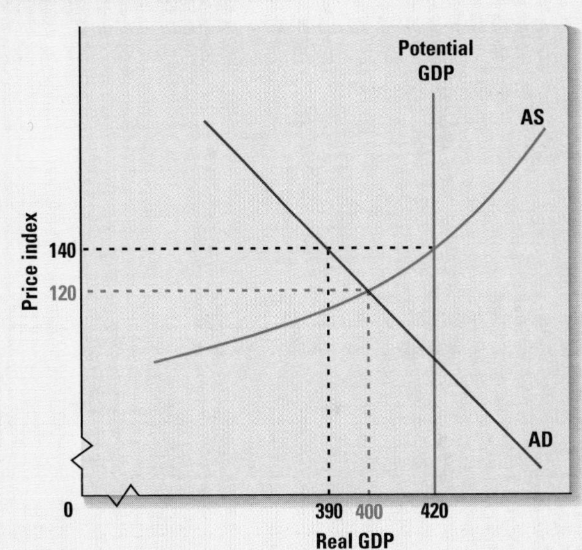

The Central bank of Carlsberg is introducing an expansionary monetary policy to get the economy back to the full-employment level of real GDP.

a) What increase in aggregate demand is necessary to achieve this?
Answer: ____________________.

b) If successful, what will be the growth rate?
Answer: ____________________.

c) If successful, what will be the inflation rate?
Answer: ____________________.

38. Suppose that the commercial banks' target reserve ratio is 10 percent and the Bank of Canada buys $100 million in bonds in the open market.

a) What immediate impact does this have on the money supply? _____________ .

b) What effect does it have on the money-creating potential of the banking system? _____________ .

39. **Table 12.1 A)** shows abbreviated balance sheets for the central bank in the country of Beckland. **Table 12.1 B)** shows tables for its whole commercial banking system. The target reserve ratio for the banks is 10 percent. (All figures are in $ billions.)

a) Suppose that the Bank of Beckland buys $1 billion of government securities (T-bills) from the commercial banks. Show the immediate effects of this transaction on the balance sheets in column (1) of **Table 12.1 A)** and **B)**.

b) What effect does this transaction have on the money supply of Beckland?
Change in the money supply: _______________.

c) What effect does the transaction have on the banking system's excess reserves?
____
_______________________________________ .

d) If the banks were to fully loan up, show the result in column (2) of the banking system's balance sheet.

e) By how much has the money supply now changed?
Change in the money supply: +/– _________ of $ _______ .

40. **Figure 12.9** illustrates the money demand and investment demand for the economies of Pabst and Kokanee.

a) If the money supply is increased by 10, what will be the new interest rate?
Pabst: __________ ; Kokanee: __________ .

b) What will be the increase in investment spending as a result of this new interest rate?
Pabst: __________ ; Kokanee: __________ .

c) If the multiplier is 2 in each economy, what will be the increase in GDP?
Pabst: __________ ; Kokanee: __________ .

d) In which economy would monetary policy be more effective in closing a recessionary gap?
______________________________ .

TABLE 12.1

A) Central Bank of Beckland

Assets		(1)	Liabilities		(1)
Treasury bills	190	_____	Notes in circulation	185	_____
Advances to banks	5	_____	Government deposits	6	_____
		_____	Deposits of banks	4	_____

B) Beckland's Banking System

Assets		(1)	(2)	Liabilities		(1)	(2)
Reserves: in vaults	8	_____	_____	Deposits	120	_____	_____
in Bank of Beckland	4	_____	_____				
Securities	30	_____	_____	Advances from Bank of Beckland	5	_____	_____
Loans to customers	90	_____	_____	Equity	7	_____	_____

FIGURE 12.9

Pabst

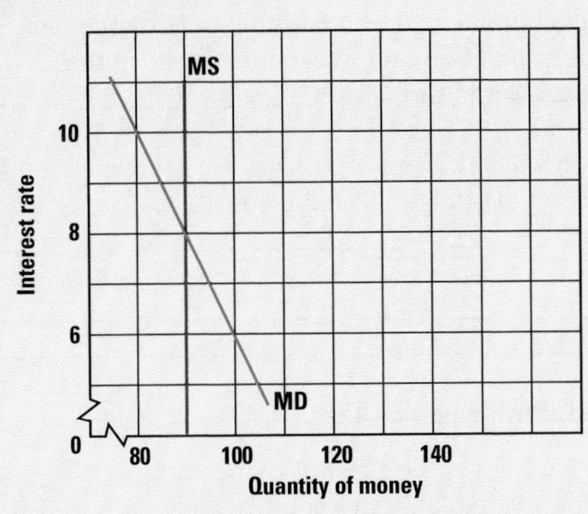

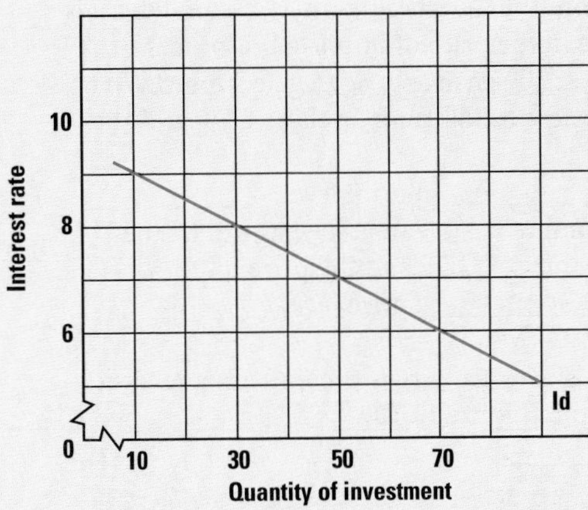

Kokanee

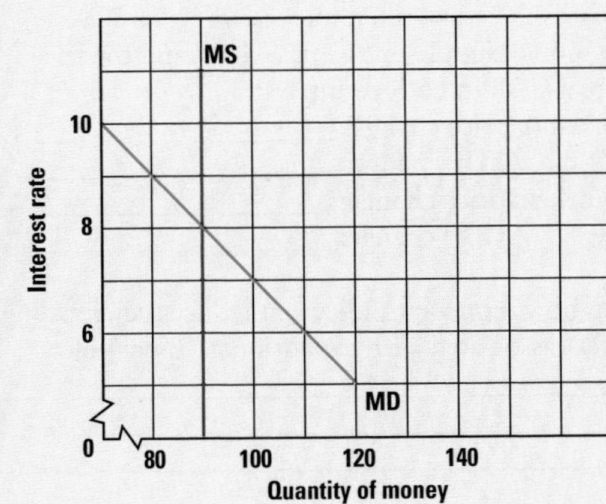

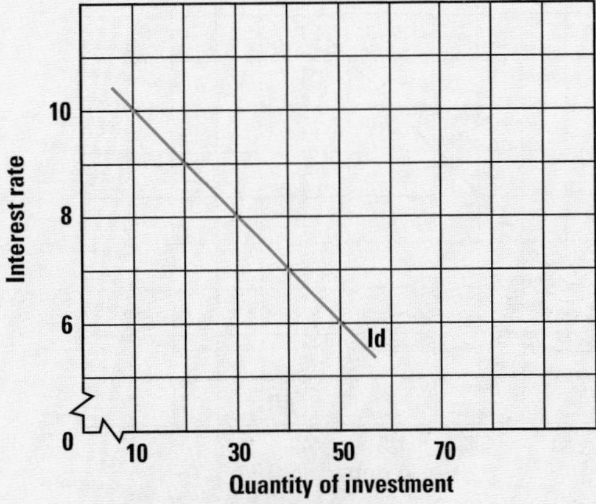

41. Explain how the use of monetary policy could close an inflationary gap.

____

______________________________.

Intermediate (Problems 42–45)

42. Assume that the original price of a three-month treasury bill with redeemable value of $100 was $96, and one month later it was sold for $96. What is the change in the rate of return on this bill?

____

______________________________.

43. Table 12.2 shows the aggregate demand and aggregate supply for the economy of Mackeson, which is in equilibrium at its potential level of GDP.

TABLE 12.2

Price	Aggregate Quantity Demanded	Aggregate Quantity Supplied
$90	1000	700
95	950	750
100	900	800
105	850	850
110	800	900
115	750	950

a) What are the values of equilibrium GDP and the price level?
GDP ____________; price level ____________.

b) Assume that the money supply expands, causing an increase in aggregate demand of $100 at every price level. What will be the new equilibrium levels of GDP and the price level?
GDP ____________; price level ____________.

c) Assuming flexible wages, what will be the long-run values of GDP and the price level?
GDP ____________ ; price level ____________ .

d) Starting from the initial values in a), assume there is an increase in the price of imported resources leading to a $100 change in aggregate supply. What will be the new equilibrium levels of GDP and the price level?
GDP ____________ ; price level ____________ .

e) Again, assuming flexible wages, what will be the long-run values of GDP and the price level?
GDP ____________ ; price level ____________ .

44. The economy of Kronenburg is presently in a recession and is depicted in **Figure 12.10**.

FIGURE 12.10

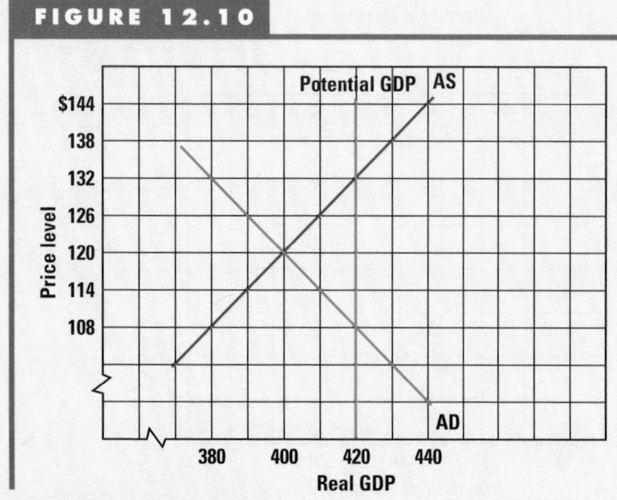

The governor of the Bank of Kronenburg favours a recovery program by increasing the money supply. However, he insists that it is in the long-run interest of the economy to keep inflation low. His target is a 5 percent inflation rate. What growth rate in the economy would this permit? ________________ .

45. Explain why the effect of expansionary monetary policy on net exports might be ambiguous.

____

____

____

____ .

Advanced (Problems 46–47)

46. **Table 12.3** shows the effect of changes in various economic variables in two countries, Beckland and Heineken.

a) What is the effect of an increase of $10 million in the money supply on the price level and the level of real GDP in both countries?
Beckland: price change: ________________ ;
GDP change: ________________ .
Heineken: price change: ________________ ;
GDP change: ________________ .

47. Explain how monetary policy can reduce the crowding-out effect associated with expansionary fiscal policy.

____

____

____

____ .

TABLE 12.3

	Beckland	**Heineken**
For every $10 million change in money supply:	Interest rates change by 1% point.	Interest rates change by 2% point.
For every 1% point change in interest tates:	Investment spending *and* net exports change by a total of 20 million.	Investment spending *and* net exports change by a total of $10 million.
For every $10 million change in expenditures:	Aggregate demand changes by $20 million.	Aggregate demand changes by $30 million.
For every $10 million change in aggregate demand:	The price index changes by 1 point; *and* real GDP changes by $5 million.	The price index changes by 2 points; *and* real GDP changes by $3 million.

UNANSWERED PROBLEMS

48. **Key Problem** The country of Anoroc has, over the last two decades, achieved vigorous growth as well as price stability. It is in equilibrium and at potential GDP (at a natural rate of unemployment of 7 percent), and its interest rate is 10 percent. Its president decides that her country's future success lies in increasing the level of productivity. Furthermore, she is convinced that success requires hard work. She therefore issues a presidential decree that forthwith the workers of Anoroc will work a six-day week (they now work a four-day week).

a) Assuming that this change causes an increase in aggregate supply of 300, draw the new curve (AS_2) and the new potential GDP curve on **Figure 12.11.**

b) What will be the new equilibrium level of GDP and the price level as a result of this shift?

Three months later, the president of Anoroc is visited by the angry governor of the Bank of Anoroc and by the secretary of its labour congress. They point out to the president (politely, of course) that her actions, far from leading the country to prosperity, have instead led it into a recession.

c) Are they right? Is there a recession in Anoroc? How much of a recession?

The secretary of the labour congress points out that although most people are working harder than ever, there are now more people unemployed than before. Assuming that, in Anoroc, for every 2 percent that actual GDP falls below potential GDP, unemployment is 1 percentage point above its natural rate.

d) What is the present unemployment rate in Anoroc?

Furthermore, the governor of the bank points out, prices have taken a tumble. For once, the governor and the secretary are in agreement. They both insist that demand must increase in order to boost prices and to encourage firms to hire more workers. Monetary policy must be changed immediately, they insist. Interest rates need to fall. In Anoroc, the governor informs them, a 1-percentage-point change in interest rates changes aggregate demand by $100 billion.

e) What interest rate is necessary to bring the country back to full employment?

FIGURE 12.11

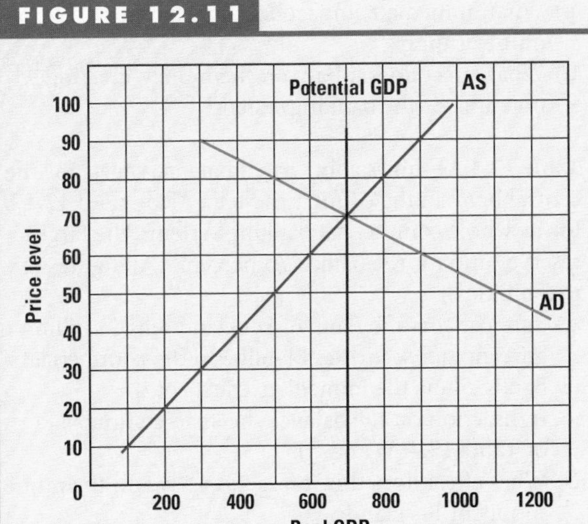

Basic (Problems 49–53)

49. **Figure 12.12** depicts the present situation in the economy of Red Eye.

FIGURE 12.12

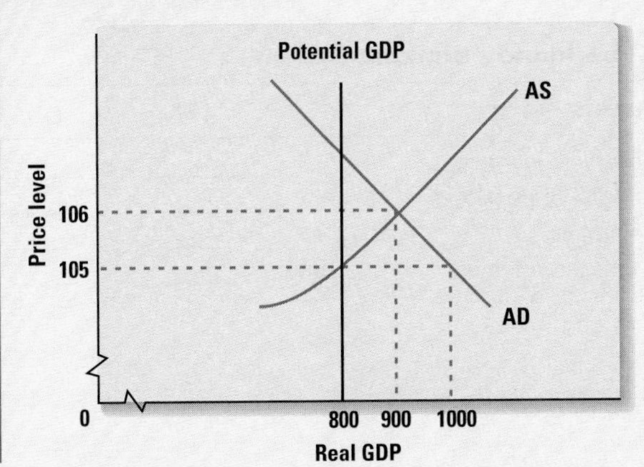

The central bank of Red Eye is introducing contractionary monetary policy to move the economy to the potential level of real GDP.

a) What change in aggregate demand is necessary to achieve this?

b) If successful, what will happen to the level of real GDP?

c) If successful, what will happen to the price level?

50. Suppose that the commercial banks' target reserve ratio is 10 percent and the Bank of Canada sells $200 million in bonds directly to the commercial banks.
  a) What immediate impact does this have on the money supply?
  b) What effect does it have on the money-creating potential of the banking system?

51. **Table 12.4 A)** shows abbreviated balance sheets for the central bank in the country of Stella Artois, and **12.4 B)** for its whole commercial banking system. The target reserve ratio for the banks is 5 percent. (All figures are in $ billions.)
  a) Suppose that the Bank of Beckland sells $1 billion of government securities (T-bills) to the commercial banks. Show the immediate effects of this transaction on the balance sheets in columns (1) of **Table 12.4 A)** and **B)**.
  b) What effect does this transaction have on the money supply of Beckland?
  c) What effect does the transaction have on the banking system's reserves?
  d) If the banks were to fully loan up, show the result in column (2) of the banking system's balance sheet.
  e) By how much has the money supply now changed?

52. **Figure 12.13** illustrates the money demand and investment demand for the economies of Miller and Budwieser.
  a) If the money supply is decreased by 10, what will be the new interest rate in the two countries?
  b) What will be the decrease in investment spending as a result of this new interest rate in the two countries?
  c) If the multiplier is 3 in each economy what will be the decrease in GDP in the two countries?
  d) In which economy would monetary policy be more effective in closing an inflationary gap?

53. Why might monetary policy be ineffective in combating stagflation?

TABLE 12.4

A) Central Bank of Beckland

Assets		(1)	Liabilities		(1)
Treasury bills	95	____	Notes in circulation	90	____
Advances to banks	1	____	Government deposits	4	____
		____	Deposits of banks	2	____

B) Beckland's Banking System

Assets		(1)	(2)	Liabilities		(1)	(2)
Reserves: in vaults	3	____	____	Deposits	100	____	____
in Bank of Beckland	2	____	____				
Securities	14	____	____	Advances from Bank of Beckland	1	____	____
Loans to customers	86	____	____	Equity	4	____	____

FIGURE 12.13

Miller

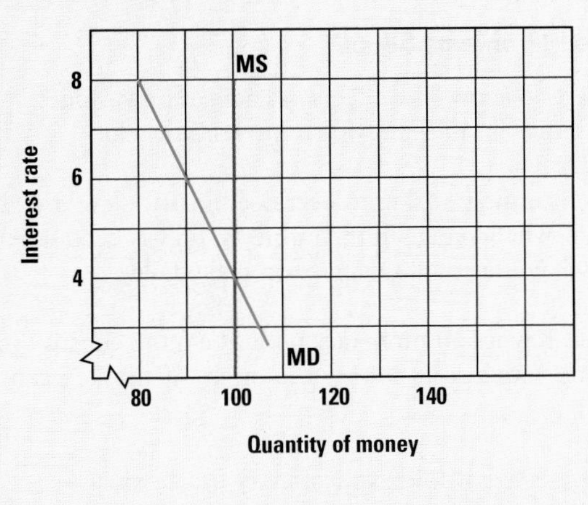

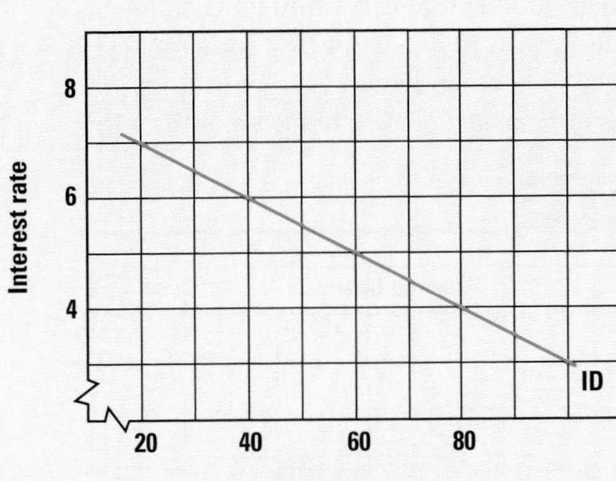

Budweiser

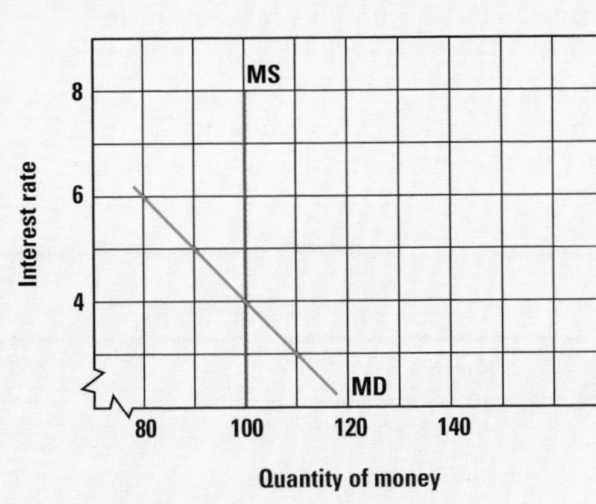

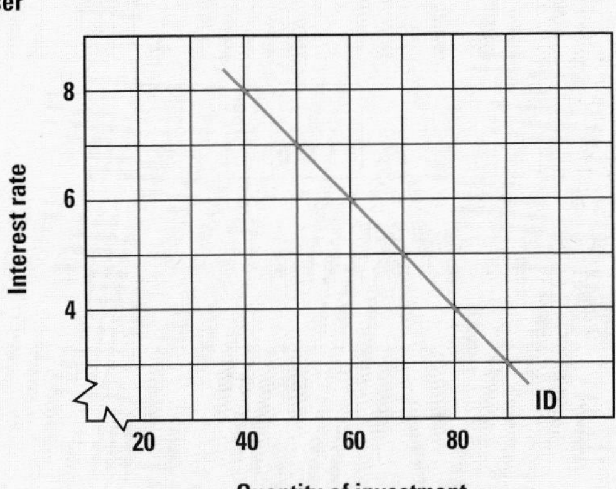

Intermediate (Problems 54–57)

54. Assume that the original price of a three-month treasury bill with a redeemable value of $1000 was $970, and two months later it was sold for $980. What is the change in the rate of return on this bill?

55. **Table 12.5** shows the aggregate demand and aggregate supply for the economy of Mackeson, which is in equilibrium at its potential level of GDP.

a) What are the values of equilibrium GDP and the price level?

b) Assume that the money supply contracts, causing a decrease in aggregate demand of $600. What will be the new equilibrium levels of GDP and the price level?

c) Assuming flexible wages, what will be the long-run values of GDP and the price level?

d) Starting the original values in a), assume that there was an decrease in the price of imported resources leading to a $300 change in aggregate supply. What will be the new equilibrium levels of GDP and the price level?

e) Again, assuming flexible wages, what will be the long-run values of GDP and the price level?

TABLE 12.5

Price	Aggregate Quantity Demanded	Aggregate Quantity Supplied
$99	8000	7100
100	7800	7200
101	7600	7300
102	7400	7400
103	7200	7500
104	7000	7600

56. Use **Figure 12.14** to answer this question. The economy of Kronemburg is presently in a recession. The government wishes to achieve full employment and yet keep inflation down to 5 percent by a judicious mixture of aggregate demand and aggregate supply policies. What shift in each curve does it recommend?

FIGURE 12.14

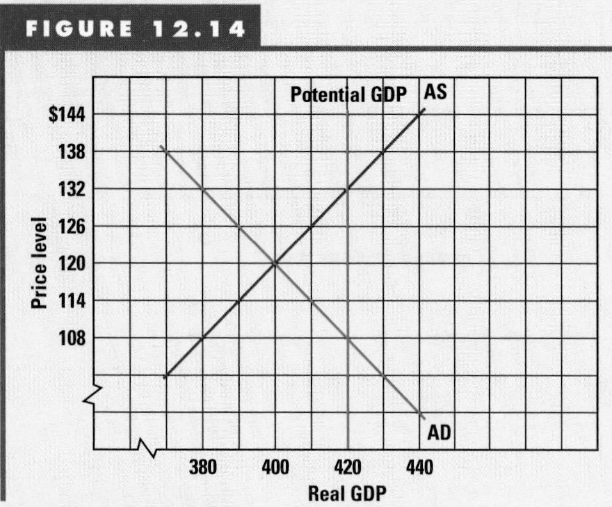

57. A country with fixed exchange rates cannot have a monetary policy. Explain.

Advanced (Problems 58–60)

58. **Table 12.6** shows the effects of changes on various economic variables in two countries: Michelob and Kirin.
If each country wishes to decrease the price level by 12 points, what change in the money supply is necessary, and what effect will this have on real GDP?

59. Would Keynesian monetary policy be more effective in dealing with a recessionary gap or an inflationary gap? Why?

60. How effective would expansionary fiscal policy be, and what would happen to the interest rate if:
   a) the Bank of Canada holds the supply of money constant.
   b) the Bank of Canada "accommodates" the fiscal policy by also increasing the supply of money.

TABLE 12.6

	Michelob	Kirin
For every $10 million change in money supply:	Interest rates change by 1% point.	Interest rates change by 2% point.
For every 1% point change in interest rates	Investment spending *and* net exports change by a total of $20 million.	Investment spending *and* net exports change by a total of $10 million.
For every $10 million change in expenditures:	Aggregate demand changes by $20 million.	Aggregate demand changes by $30 million.
For every $10 million change in aggregate demand:	The price index changes by 1 point; *and* real GDP changes by $5 million.	The price index changes by 2 points; *and* real GDP changes by $3 million.

Web-Based Activities

1. Read the article found at **www.bmo.com/economic/special/bocwatch.htm.** Briefly explain what factors the Bank of Canada monitors to help it determine monetary policy.

2. Should price stability be the only goal of the central bank? Read **www.worldbank.org/fandd/english/1296/articles/0101296.htm**, and write a short essay on the pros and cons of making price stability the primary goal of the central bank.

CHAPTER THIRTEEN

A Walk Through the Twentieth Century and Beyond

LEARNING OBJECTIVES

This chapter will enable you to:

LO1 Understand how economic ideas affect, and are affected by, world events.

LO2 Understand why neoclassicists believe the economy will automatically achieve full-employment equilibrium.

LO3 Understand why Keynesian economics challenged accepted beliefs on curing economic depression and maintaining prosperity.

LO4 Understand how the stagflation of the 1970s gave rise to supply-side economics.

LO5 Appreciate the significance of the new economy.

What's ahead...

This chapter examines the evolution of economic theory by looking at specific periods of the twentieth century. We begin by looking at the classical world of Say's Law in the context of the first years of the 1900s. We then move to the First World War and its aftermath, which saw the evolution of neoclassical thought and the belief that economies are capable of self-correction. Keynesian economics emerged with the Great Depression and prevailed until the 1970s. Then we look at the stagflation of the 1970s and the rise of supply-side economics. We then look at Canada at the turn of the new millennium and, finally, take a brief look at the future.

A QUESTION OF RELEVANCE...

Imagine that you are looking for an entry-level job as a graphic artist. Given your training and background, you decide to ask for $15 per hour. After three months of job searching, you have gotten nowhere: not a single interview, let alone a job offer. What went wrong? Do you think that the cause of your problem is personal, because you don't have the right qualifications or perhaps are asking for too high a wage? Or is it the fault of businesses for their unwillingness to create enough jobs? Or is it, instead, a problem to be laid at the doorstep of the government for not pursuing policies that would ensure that the economy created enough jobs?

We want to do two main things in this chapter. First, using the Canadian experience, we want to examine the ways in which contemporary events and economic theory are interrelated. We will look at six significant periods in the twentieth century, each of which had a profound influence on economic thinking and on the evolution of economic theory. At the same time, we will look at how these same economic theories, and the policies they generated, later helped shape some of the major events of this century. In addition, we will take a brief look at the future.

The second thing we want to do is to refocus on a question that we have touched on throughout this text and that has claimed the attention of political commentators, economists, and many others for over two centuries:

What is the appropriate role of government in ensuring a successful economy?

In answering this question, we will discover that there are two schools of thought, with different views on the question. Let's now turn to the first of our six time periods.

13.1 Canada at the Start of the Twentieth Century and the Aftermath of the First World War

LO1
Understand how economic ideas affect, and are affected by, world events.

At the beginning of the twentieth century, Canada stood at the threshold of a new era, one filled with the promise of growth and prosperity. A major source of that confidence was the Canadian Pacific Railway, which had linked the East and the West. More especially, the railway had opened up the vast prairie lands of the West, and new immigrants were pouring in. All this led Prime Minister Wilfrid Laurier to declare: "A new star has risen upon the horizon. And it is to that star that every immigrant...now turns his gaze." The "Canadian miracle," as it was called, led to the construction of more railways in the West (the Canadian Northern, the Grand Trunk, and the National Continental), to a huge increase in wheat production and wheat exports, and to the birth of two new provinces, Alberta and Saskatchewan, in 1905. Fuelled by British and American investment, the economy of this "new star" boomed. Rapid growth in the demand for Canadian products combined with low transportation costs—especially declining ocean-freight rates—caused many things to increase: production, incomes, jobs, and immigration. Perhaps the most significant statistic was that in the first 20 years of the century, Canada's population grew from just over 5 million to almost 9 million.

Classical Economics and Say's Law

As Canada was prospering, so too was the rest of the world. The new century was alive with promise, and this was echoed in the ideas of economists. Despite some earlier gloomy predictions, capitalism was alive, well, and flourishing. Although there was a certain amount of government intervention, this was a period in which the laissez-faire approach was dominant. Economists, policy makers, and indeed most of the public, believed that the government that governed least governed best. Furthermore, the prevailing belief was that those who earned above-average incomes deserved them because they must somehow be better than other people; otherwise they would not have earned those high incomes. Similarly, the majority believed that the poor suffered from some failing of character or were unwilling to work hard enough to avoid poverty. In short, people probably took on responsibility for many things for which they were not responsible.

However, a laissez-faire economy also meant an unplanned economy, and this was a source of disquiet for some. They wondered if it wasn't possible for such lack of planning to result in an economy producing more than people would be willing and able to consume. They asked: isn't capitalism likely to experience periodic bouts of overproduction? And wouldn't such overproduction, and the resulting increase in inventories, lead to firms reducing output and laying off workers? In short, isn't capitalism prone to recessions?

These questions were not new; almost a century before, the loud and clear voice of David Ricardo, one of the giants of the classical school, had answered "no" to them. Ricardo's answers relied on what is known as **Say's Law**, which states, "Supply creates its own demand." What this means is that:

Say's Law: the proposition that "supply creates its own demand"; that is, production (supply) creates sufficient income and thus spending (demand) to purchase the production. (Attributed to French economist Jean-Baptiste Say.)

- **The act of production (supply) requires the use of factors of production, which must be paid.**
- **Such payments are incomes to those who supply the factors, and these incomes are subsequently spent.**
- **This spending automatically creates enough demand to buy the supply.**

This is actually a restatement of the simple circular flow of income that we looked at in Chapter 3. Supply creates income, and this income creates enough demand to purchase the supply. If supply increases, then, income and, it was assumed, demand increase by an equal amount. Furthermore, if supply decreased, incomes and demand would also fall. That is, *supply is active*, and demand is the passive result.

With Ricardo's endorsement of Say's Law, the prevailing view of the classical economists was that it ensured that all that was produced would be bought. In short, equilibrium (the equality of supply and demand) in the economy was both automatic and normal.

This last statement does need some qualification. It was conceded that if demand patterns changed, then temporary surpluses and shortages of specific goods were possible. For example, if demand changed so that a shortage of beaver hats and a surplus of cloth hats occurred, then there would be unemployment among those who made cloth hats and an increase in the demand for labour to make beaver hats. This would lead to wage rates and prices in the cloth industry quickly falling while those in the beaver-hat industry rose. That is, a surplus in one industry will create a shortage in another industry, but there is a normal adjustment between the two. Thus, we can again state the conclusion of the majority of classical economists of the nineteenth century:

Equilibrium occurs automatically and is the normal state of affairs in a market economy.

This optimistic view was shared by most economists in the first decade of the twentieth century. This sense of confidence was, however, shaken by "the war to end all wars": the "Great War."

The First World War and After

In 1914, Canada entered the First World War as one of the Dominions of the United Kingdom. As a result of the enormous contribution Canada made to the Allied war effort, the country ended the war four years later a far more confident nation with a more independent frame of mind. Furthermore, relatively cheap credit, combined with a pent-up demand for consumer goods that had been in limited supply, fuelled an immediate postwar boom during which prices rose.

Despite the boom, the transition to a peacetime economy proved difficult, and when the bubble burst it led to a rapid contraction of the economy and a drop in prices. Returning

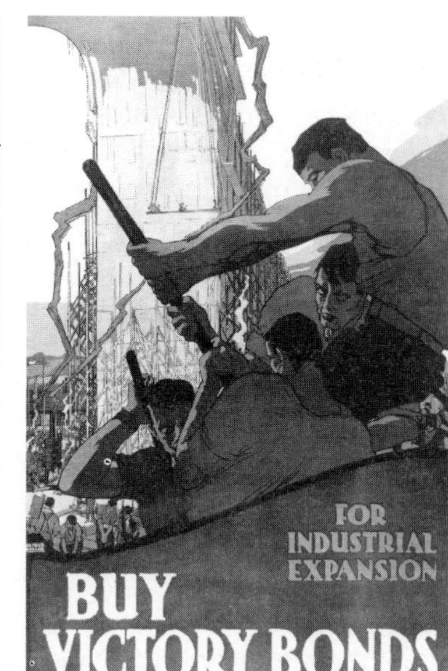

This First World War poster encouraged Canadian citizens to invest in the struggling economy.

soldiers, and workers who had been forced to make big sacrifices for the war effort, found that the promised rewards of victory were scant and a long time coming. A widespread and bitter strike broke out in Winnipeg, followed later by strikes in Halifax and Vancouver. Particularly hard hit were the Prairies and the Maritimes, as the price of wheat, for example, fell by 60 percent. By December 1923, unemployment reached 17 percent and many workers were forced to roam the country in search of work—a taste of what was to come less than a decade later.

Then, slowly, the Canadian economy improved, in tandem with a worldwide economic recovery. Fuelled by American investment (which surpassed that of Britain by 1921), Ontario in particular experienced a boom in industrial investment. Quebec saw a dramatic increase in the development of hydroelectric power, while the West enjoyed a recovery in world prices of grains and other resources. By the mid-1920s, the production of newsprint became the second-largest industry, next to agriculture, in Canada. It seemed like the long-awaited time of plenty had arrived, and Canadians were determined to make the most of it.

Neoclassical Economists and Aggregate Demand and Supply

Neoclassical economists of the time could rejoice in the recovery taking place and remained as confident as Ricardo that market economies could recover quickly from dislocations, even those caused by world wars. In short, they believed that market economies were self-adjusting. In fact, they went even further, and with the addition of three specific propositions they built an argument that concluded that prolonged recessions were an impossibility in a market economy.

The first of these propositions we already examined in Chapter 5. In terms of aggregate supply and demand analysis, neoclassical economists believed that any temporary overproduction (surpluses) or underproduction (shortages) would disappear through price changes. That is, flexible prices would ensure that the quantities demanded and supplied in the product market would be equal. Surpluses cause prices to drop; shortages cause prices to increase. This flexibility means that any change in aggregate demand will translate into a change in the price level but not a change in real GDP. This is illustrated in **Figure 13.1**.

FIGURE 13.1 A Change in Demand in the Neoclassical Model

An increase in aggregate demand will cause a rightward shift in the aggregate demand curve from AD_1 to AD_2. The effect will be an increase in the price level from P_1 to P_2, but the level of real GDP will remain unchanged at Y_{FE}.

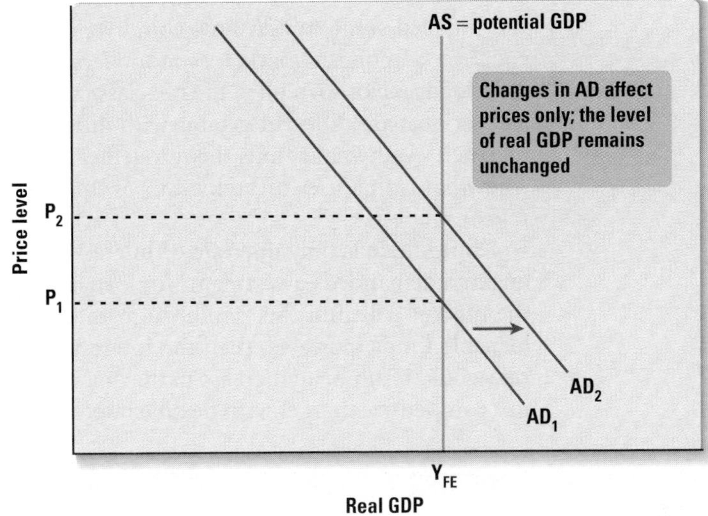

If prices are truly flexible, then aggregate supply would be determined by resource availability, productivity, and the current state of technology. This is to say, the current price level for goods and services, or any change in that price level, would have no effect on aggregate supply. Thus, an increase in demand, from AD_1 to AD_2 in **Figure 13.1**, would increase the price level and consequently wage levels, but it would not change aggregate supply. Similarly, a decrease in aggregate demand would decrease the price level and the wage level, but would not change aggregate supply. In short, since prices and wages adjust rapidly, neoclassicists make no distinction between the long and the short run. In terms of our Chapter 5 model, such an increase in aggregate demand would immediately cause a decrease in aggregate supply as the wage rate rises to adjust to the higher prices. The net result of this immediate adjustment of wages to prices is that there is only one supply curve, which is synonymous with potential GDP. Of course, any change in resources, productivity, or technology would change aggregate supply, and this would shift the AS curve to the left, or to the right. However, it would always be vertical. In short,

In the neoclassical model, the level of real GDP is unaffected by changes in aggregate demand.

SELF-TEST

1. Why did the neoclassical economists feel that the aggregate supply curve is vertical at the full-employment level of GDP?

Theory of Loanable Funds

To understand the neoclassicists' second proposition, we need to return to Ricardo's support of Say's Law. His argument also contained the proposition that any funds that were saved would automatically be invested, that is, spent in a different form. Recall that Ricardo wrote in context of the early nineteenth century, where most savers were profit-earning business owners who were quite willing to turn their savings into investment with an eye toward even greater profits in the future. However, by the early twentieth century, the incomes of a large percentage of working people had risen sufficiently so that savers (householders) and investors (businesses) had become different groups with different motivations.

This led some to ask: how could we be certain that savings and investment would be equal in a modern market economy? Surely their equality could come about only by coincidence? Not so, replied the neoclassical economists. After all, buyers and sellers of goods and services are different groups with different motivations, yet they are still able to "come together." And what brings them together? A commonly agreed upon price of the product. And what is the price of savings, or as they called them, loanable funds? The answer is the rate of interest.

Since there is only one rate of interest at which the quantity supplied (savings) and the quantity demanded (investment) for loanable funds is equal, if interest rates are truly flexible, the market will find this equilibrium rate automatically. For example, if the demand for loanable funds increases, then the interest rate would rise, and this increase in the interest rate would result in an increase in the quantity of savings to satisfy the higher demand. Thus, in a competitive market with flexible interest rates, what is saved must equal what is invested.

SELF-TEST

2. According to neoclassical economists, what two things could cause a decrease in interest rates?

The Supply of Labour and the Demand for Labour

The third and final proposition of neoclassical theory in support of the idea that an economy is capable of self-adjusting was the claim that any unemployment that might exist is temporary. This conclusion was arrived at by applying supply-and-demand analysis to the labour market. It was reasoned that there is only one equilibrium wage level at which the quantity supplied and the quantity demanded for labour are equal. Once this rate is achieved, there would be no surplus or shortage of labour, that is, no unemployment. Then how can the fact that unemployment exists be explained? As **Figure 13.2** illustrates, unemployment can occur only if the prevailing wage rate is above the equilibrium wage rate.

FIGURE 13.2 **A Surplus of Labour**

If the wage level is above equilibrium, there will be a surplus of labour. At wage level W_2, the number of workers demanded by firms, quantity *a*, would be less than at equilibrium. On the other hand, the number of workers seeking jobs would be higher, quantity *b*. The distance *ab*, therefore, represents the surplus of labour, that is, unemployed labour.

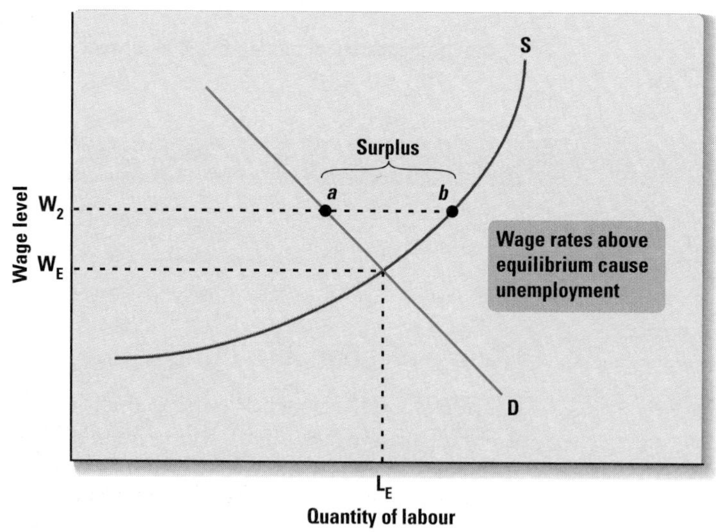

At wage rate W_2, the number of workers demanded and therefore employed is quantity *a*. The number of workers who would like a job at this rate, however, is quantity *b*. The distance *ab* then represents the quantity of unemployed labour, those people who would like jobs but are unable to obtain them. We can see that unemployment is a result of the prevailing wage rate being above equilibrium. However, such unemployment cannot continue indefinitely. Competition for jobs among the employed and the unemployed will force wage rates down and in doing so will induce firms to hire more workers. Flexible wage rates therefore ensure full employment. This means that if there are unemployed workers, then they must be voluntarily unemployed, because if they were willing to offer their services at a lower wage, they would be able to obtain a job. If, instead, they are holding out for a better wage, they must be doing so voluntarily.

In summary, neoclassicists built their view of how the macroeconomy works on four pillars:

- the validity of Say's Law
- the flexibility of prices
- the flexibility of interest rates
- the flexibility of wages

Given these four factors, neoclassical economists were convinced that serious or long-lasting recessions were an impossibility. Flexible prices, flexible wages, and flexible interest rates would all ensure that the macro market would quickly return to its normal equilibrium, and, further, this equilibrium was at full employment, or what we could also call potential GDP. This view remained the prevailing view of most economists until the Great Depression of the 1930s.

SELF-TEST

3. The following table shows the labour demand and supply in a hypothetical economy:

a) What is the equilibrium wage rate, and how many workers would be employed?

b) Suppose that the wage rate increases to $8.50. How many workers are employed? How many are unemployed?

c) How many of the unemployed are workers who have lost their jobs? Why is this figure less than the total number of unemployed?

Labour Demand (in millions)	Wage Rate ($)	Labour Supply (in millions)
12.8	6.00	11.0
12.4	6.50	11.5
12.0	7.00	12.0
11.6	7.50	12.5
11.2	8.00	13.0
10.8	8.50	13.5
10.4	9.00	14.0
10.0	9.50	14.5

13.2 The Great Depression and the Aftermath of the Second World War

LO2
Understand why neoclassicists believe the economy will automatically achieve full-employment equilibrium.

The Depression

In the fall of 1929, Wall Street's stock market crashed and, during the next three years, the American economy experienced such a severe depression that many observers at the time felt that it signalled the death throes of capitalism itself. Production in the United States dropped by 42 percent between 1929 and 1933, 85 000 businesses failed, 5000 banks closed their doors,

CP/Toronto Star

Thousands of unemployed men from British Columbia, Alberta, and Saskatchewan climbed aboard freight trains in an on-to-Ottawa protest against conditions in depression-era job camps in 1935.

and unemployment increased from 3 to 25 percent. The American experience spread quickly to Canada and was soon repeated in economies around the world. Clearly something had gone wrong with the market economies.

What had caused such a calamity? It is easy to point the finger at the Wall Street crash, but the North American economies were in trouble before the crash. In Canada, the main reason for this was the fact that a significant expansion in world production capacity in several of Canada's key industries in the last half of the 1920s had depressed commodity prices. The first reaction of neoclassical economists to the sudden downturn was that, whatever had caused this drastic turn of events, the prognosis was clear and obvious: the economy should be left alone to cure itself. They felt that prices would soon drop, which would encourage people to buy more, and this would stimulate production; that interest rates would soon fall, thus stimulating investment; and that wage rates would soon drop, encouraging firms to increase hiring. The Canadian experience in these early years of the Great Depression can be used to show how right and how wrong the neoclassicists were. Between 1929 and 1933, prices in Canada did drop by 23 percent. But production continued to fall. Wage rates also dropped by approximately 20 percent, but unemployment continued to hover around the 20 percent mark. Interest rates dropped to 2 percent, but gross investment remained low, and in 1933 net investment actually became negative.

It would be difficult to overstate the fear and pain experienced by Canadians during these dark years. The beginnings of a social security net was in place, but this was hardly enough to cushion the fall into unemployment and poverty—no unemployment insurance, a very limited pension plan, very limited and localized welfare payments (with the exception of a national war-widows benefits plan), no baby bonus cheques, no subsidized medical plan, and no subsidized housing. The freight trains that pulled into any one of many Canadian cities carried dozens of men riding the empty boxcars in search of a new place that might have some work. The problem was that the trains leaving that same city heading in the other direction had just as many unemployed souls hoping that the next stop might offer something better. And it wasn't just the unemployed who were suffering. Those still working often faced the prospect of pay cuts, which they were in no position to argue about because they might be laid off next. And those in business faced falling sales and meagre profits.

ADDED DIMENSION

Too Much or Too Little?

This extract from *Canada's Illustrated Heritage Series* neatly sums up the times: "The strange and terrifying thing about the depression was that there was too much of almost everything. Too much food. In Prince Edward Island, potatoes were left rotting in the ground, and on the prairies wheat was burned because it was not worth shipping. Too many houses. There were vacant houses on every street and you could rent a good-sized one for $10 a month. Too many automobiles. Factories could turn out 400 000 a year but only 40 000 were bought in 1932. Too many men for the jobs that needed doing. There was too much of everything, in fact, except jobs and money."

Through all this there was a nagging question that continued to go unanswered: why wasn't the economy adjusting in the way the neoclassicists thought it would? It took Keynes and his *General Theory* to finally provide some answers.

The Keynesian Response to the Neoclassicists

We have already studied the ideas of Keynes on how the macroeconomy works, but let's do a quick summary. Keynes disagreed with the neoclassical economists as to how the economy adjusts if production exceeds spending and a recessionary gap threatens. Where the neoclassicists saw prices falling, Keynes saw prices that were "sticky" and would fall only slowly, if at all. The reason why the neoclassicists and Keynes saw the question of the flexibility of prices so differently is because each built their models on different assumptions. The neoclassicists assumed perfect competition in both the product and the labour markets. Keynes, on the other hand, argued that the product market was dominated by large oligopoly firms with the power to set their own prices. A more practical explanation of why prices are inflexible downward lies in the fact that for a firm to change prices is both time-consuming and expensive, since existing labels, catalogues, advertisements, inventory valuations, and billing codes all have to be changed in order to institute a price change.

Given this, what was the economy's response to a decrease in demand? The answer was that firms would cut back on production and lay people off. This increases the level of unemployment but does not lead to much downward pressure on wages because, like prices, they too are "sticky downwards." The reason for sticky wages, Keynes argued, was the existence of trade unions, which had the power to resist wage cuts once labour contracts had been signed. But, besides that, even non-union workers would resist the idea of wages that fluctuate along with the employer's fortunes, since in the modern world most wages are fixed in the short run and are reviewed only periodically, say once a year. In short:

Keynes saw the adjustment process in terms of a fall in production and employment rather than a fall in prices and wages.

To emphasize the contrast between the neoclassical and Keynesian viewpoints, we can use a metaphor. Suppose there are two firms, Classical Cookies and Keynesian Kandies, both of whom face a downturn in business. The manager of Classical Cookies calls a meeting of her staff and informs them that she has some good news and some bad news: "Despite the 20 percent reduction in orders this month, you'll be pleased to learn that we are proposing no layoffs. You will all keep your jobs. Unfortunately, we have no choice in the circumstances but to reduce your pay by 20 percent. We will, however, maintain production levels, but it does mean—please note, sales department—that in order to do so, we will be cutting prices by 20 percent starting tomorrow."

Meanwhile, over at Keynesian Kandies, another meeting is taking place between its manager and staff and, similarly, there is both good and bad news: "Despite the 20 percent reduction in orders this month, you'll be pleased to learn that we are not proposing any pay cuts for our staff. Unfortunately, we have no choice in the circumstances but to lay off 20 percent of you, starting tomorrow. We will, however, maintain present prices, but it does mean—please note, production department—that production levels will be cut by 20 percent."

Another point that Keynes disagreed with the neoclassicists over was the way in which the equality of savings and investment in the economy is brought about. To Keynes, this occurs as a result of a painful adjustment of production and income and not by changes in the interest rate, as suggested by the neoclassicists. If savings are greater than investment, the value of total production must be greater than aggregate expenditures. This will lead to a cut in production, income, *and* savings until once more savings and investment are equal. This is a reflection of Keynes's belief that changes in the interest rate have very little effect on the level of total savings, which are, instead, determined by the level of income. Finally, Keynes believed, as we saw in Chapter 8, that interest rates are determined by the demand and supply of money, and not by the interaction of total savings and investment demand in the economy.

SELF-TEST

4. Explain why Keynes felt that the level of savings is not affected greatly by changes in interest rates.

In summary, if, as Keynes believed, prices and wages do not adjust quickly, if at all, to a decrease in aggregate demand, then an economy can fall into a recession and remain there indefinitely. In these situations, only active government intervention will get the economy on the road to recovery. This point is illustrated in **Figure 13.3**.

FIGURE 13.3 **A Recessionary Gap with Sticky Wages and Prices**

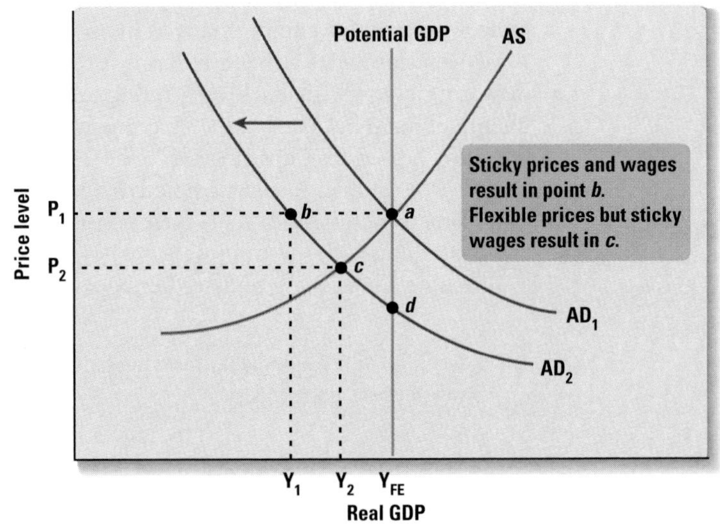

Originally, the economy is at full-employment equilibrium, as illustrated by point *a*. If aggregate demand decreases, then we have a shift from AD_1 to AD_2. If prices remain at (or near) P_1 and wages don't fall much either, then the economy could get stuck at point *b* and income level Y_1. If prices fall to P_2 but wages remain sticky downwards, then equilibrium at point *c* and GDP level Y_2 could become a permanent state of affairs. Point *d* occurs only if wages are completely flexible, which would shift the AS curve to the right.

Let's begin with the economy at full-employment-equilibrium income, Y_{FE}, with a price level of P_1. As the recession worsens, aggregate demand decreases from AD_1 to AD_2. If the price level is sticky downwards and remains at P_1—and if wages exhibit the same resistance to falling—then the economy could get stuck at *b* with a GDP level of Y_1. But we know that prices and wages in the Great Depression did fall some. However, if wages don't fall enough, then the intersection of AS and AD_2 at point *c* is an equilibrium that could persist indefinitely. What we have just described is, of course, the recessionary-gap situation that we looked at in Chapters 11 and 12.

Since Keynes reasoned that sticky wages prevent aggregate supply from shifting to the right and achieving full-employment GDP at point *d*, then the only way out of such a recessionary trap was for aggregate demand to increase, enabling the economy to return to *a*. If the circumstances of fear, uncertainty, high unemployment, and excess plant capacity result in neither households nor businesses being likely to increase their spending—and if exports don't go up—then the only way to increase aggregate demand is through increased government intervention and spending.

SELF-TEST

5. According to Keynesian theory, will an increase in aggregate demand cause an increase in real GDP, nominal GDP, or both?

In a sense, Keynes put Say's Law on its head by proposing that demand creates its own supply. The engine of change for Keynes was aggregate demand. If people are willing to spend, firms will be happy to produce. Therefore, anything that cuts spending will simply worsen a recession. In other words, instead of cutting back during a recession, people should spend more. Yet, this seemed to go against common sense. It would mean, for instance, that firms working well below capacity and in danger of being forced out of business should start to spend more on investment. Or, alternatively, it implied that governments should cut tax rates or increase their own level of spending at a time when they were already facing big budget deficits as a result of falling tax revenues. You can see why Keynes was regarded as a heretic. He was suggesting that when times are bad, people should spend more; and when they are good, they should spend less. Of course, as we have seen in earlier chapters, there is a lot more to the basic expenditure theory than this, but:

Spending and *aggregate demand* lie at the heart of Keynesian analysis.

So, how did governments initially react to these ideas of Keynes? In most cases the reaction was negative. It is true that the Canadian government did spend more to provide some limited relief for many of its impoverished citizens. For example, in 1932, the government established work camps run by military officers and under the control of the Department of National Defence. However, this was as much to stem the possibility of violent protest as to aid the unemployed. Wearing army fatigues, those in the work camps, mostly young men, worked on roads, bridges, historic sites, and so on. They received food, clothing, lodging, and 20 cents a day. Needless to say, the camps were not too popular. There was also some direct relief in the form of money or vouchers, but the amounts were small. In rural Quebec, for instance, a family of five received a food allowance of $3.25 per week. Despite the small amounts, the government was often criticized for its generosity. In a 1934 article, for instance, *Maclean's* magazine complained that total spending of all governments—municipal, provincial, and federal—had reached the incredible figure of $1 billion! Despite all this, the Canadian government did not spend a fraction of what would have been needed to pull the economy out of the depression. Furthermore, most governments of the time regarded Keynes as a radical who had dangerous ideas about the economy. Validation of his theory had to await the arrival of an event even more traumatic than the Great Depression: the Second World War.

The Aftermath of War

Canadians entered the Second World War in a far more sombre mood than they had entered the First World War. They had lived through a decade of despair, and the optimistic patriotism of the earlier age had given way to a grim realization that the task ahead, however necessary, might not yield a quick and easy victory.

War meant mobilization on all fronts. The Canadian government, in line with other governments around the world, suddenly opened the spout, and out flowed massive government spending on military goods, all in the name of the defence of democracy. Economies responded very quickly to this dramatic increase in aggregate demand. In

Canada, the war quickly converted a surplus of labour into a shortage. By 1941, the unemployment rate had fallen from the double-digit rates of the 1930s to 4.1 percent, and by 1944 it was down to 1.2 percent. Factories that had been standing idle for years were now humming, turning out Bren guns, military aircraft, tanks, and ships. The rate of growth of GDP hit double digits—14.1 percent in 1940 and a whopping 18.6 percent by 1942. In addition, as Keynesian theory would suggest, such increases were accompanied by inflation: from the deflation of 0.9 percent in 1939, prices rose by 4 percent in 1940 and 6.3 percent in 1941. This is illustrated in **Figure 13.4**.

FIGURE 13.4 **Return to Full Employment**

The increased government spending on the war effort greatly increased aggregate demand, as illustrated by the shift of the aggregate demand curve from AD_1 to AD_2. In addition, the price level increased from P_1 to P_2.

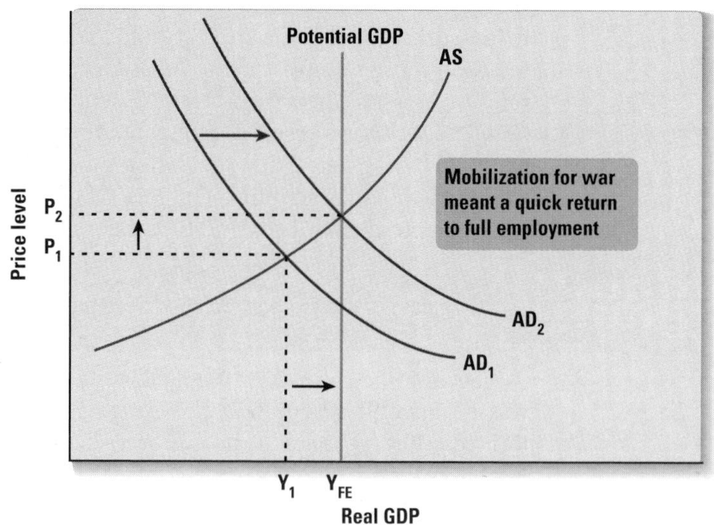

The depression was over, and it was massive increases in government spending that had ended it. This fact resulted in a growing recognition that Keynes was probably right about how the macroeconomy works.

Keynesian Economics in the Postwar Years

Following the end of the Second World War, there was a widespread sentiment among politicians, a growing number of economists, and a majority of the population that the experience of the Great Depression should never be allowed to happen again. Prime Minister Mackenzie King, who had led Canada in wartime, was re-elected in 1945 partly on the strength of his "New Social Order," which promised social and economic policies designed to prevent a recurrence of the economic woes of the 1930s. The cautious beginnings of Keynesian counter-cyclical policies, which had started in 1940 with the introduction of an unemployment scheme, were augmented by a system of family allowances that, combined with the Old Age Pension Plan, laid the foundation of the welfare state. In addition, measures were introduced to promote home building, to provide work for demobilized war veterans, and to increase aid to health care.

Such measures were not unique to Canada. In fact, governments around the world passed legislation that could be described as "full-employment acts." It was becoming accepted ideology that governments had a responsibility to use activist policies to ensure that the economic goal of full employment and stable prices was maintained. The doctrine of laissez-faire was replaced with the ideology of interventionism, dressed in the clothes of Keynesian economics.

For the 25 years following the Second World War, the ideas of Keynes reigned supreme in most countries in Europe and North America. Economies were now "managed" by governments using counter-cyclical fiscal and monetary policy to "fine-tune" them. During this time, the Canadian economy entered a period of remarkable stability. Between 1945 and 1970, apart from four years, the unemployment rate was never above 6 percent and inflation was consistently held below 5 percent. The trick, it seemed, was to steer the ship of state at a steady pace while not getting too close to the banks of inflation, or the reefs of unemployment. If the economy was a little sluggish and in danger of falling into a recession, then a dose of expansionary fiscal and/or monetary injection was called for. If, on the other hand, it looked like the economy was overheating and a period of inflation threatened, the solution was a measure of contractionary fiscal and/or monetary policy.

It became apparent that economic stabilization might be even more effective if the two policies were operating in tandem. After all, one of the drawbacks of using expansionary fiscal policy is the fact that it crowds out both private investment and net exports by pushing up interest rates. This makes fiscal policy less effective. But what if interest rates could be held down in the face of the increased demand for money? Then the crowding-out effect would be eliminated. And how could this be achieved? Simply by increasing the money supply. This combination of fiscal and monetary policy produced a very powerful mixture and was used often in Canada. Occasionally, however, a conflict of policies occurred, as in the late 1950s, when the government wanted to pursue expansionary fiscal policy while the Bank of Canada was intent on using contractionary monetary policy. Fortunately, such instances proved to be rare.

Nonetheless, as successful as Keynesian policy was in reducing both unemployment and inflation in postwar Canada, it became clear, as a result of the work of Phillips (which we looked at in Chapter 11), that achieving both goals *simultaneously* may not be possible. As **Figure 13.5** shows, there definitely seemed to be a trade-off between the two. For instance, the low unemployment rates in 1947 and 1948 were accompanied by high rates of inflation, and the low inflation rates of 1958 through 1961 were achieved at the cost of the highest unemployment rates since the Second World War. Apart from the single year of 1953, Canada had never seen inflation below 2 percent, and unemployment below 4 percent *at the same time.*

FIGURE 13.5 **Unemployment and Inflation in Canada, 1946–69**

Using actual data from the Canadian experience, it is clear that a trade-off existed between the level of inflation and that of unemployment in this period.

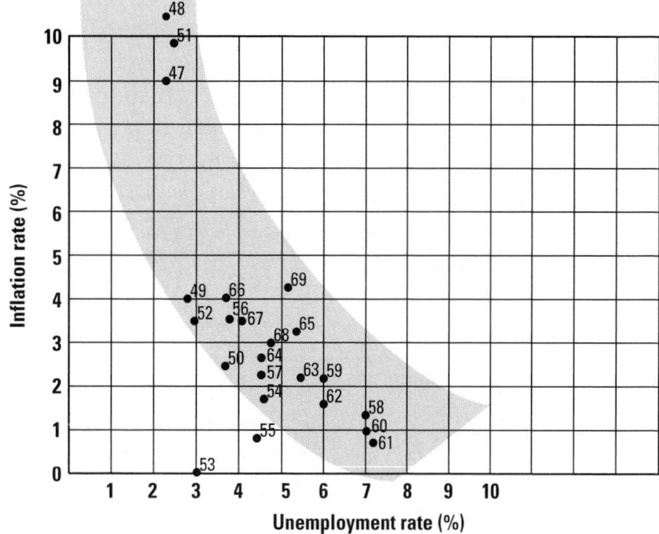

In summary, the quarter century following the end of the Second World War was a period of comparative prosperity for Canada, in which the size of the public sector grew significantly. However, the Phillips curve analysis meant that economists were beginning to realize that perhaps there were limits to what could be achieved with Keynesian policy. Its supremacy was to be seriously challenged by the events of the early 1970s.

REVIEW

1. What is Say's Law?
2. Describe economic conditions in Canada in the 1920s.
3. According to the neoclassicists, what is the shape of the AS curve?
4. Why is unemployment voluntary, according to neoclassical theory?
5. What four factors, according to neoclassical theory, ensure that a long-lasting recession is impossible?
6. When was the Great Depression?
7. Why are wages and prices sticky, according to Keynes?
8. How do Keynesians see the economy adjusting to a reduction in aggregate demand?
9. When was Canada's longest period of relative stability in the macroeconomy?

13.3 The Age of Anxiety: Canada in the 1970s and 1980s

LO3
Understand why Keynesian economics challenged accepted beliefs on curing economic depression and maintaining prosperity.

By the early 1970s, the certainties of the postwar era had started to fade. The United States devalued its currency by abandoning a fixed gold price at about the same time that its defeat in Vietnam seemed inevitable. The countries that would later be called the Asian Tigers were beginning to challenge established industries in both Canada and the United States. And in Canada, despite strong exports of prairie wheat to the U.S.S.R. as well as of British Columbia and Alberta coal to Japan, total exports began to falter. This was also the time when three million baby boomers began entering the labour market.

Then, in 1973, the Arab-state-dominated Organization of Petroleum Exporting Counties (OPEC), angered by the falling value of the dollars that its members received for their oil and by the West's support for Israel during the Yom Kippur War, decided to reduce its exports of oil. The result was a quadrupling of prices in less than 16 months. The shock was felt around the world. The Liberal government of Pierre Trudeau tried to insulate Canada from this shock by providing subsidies for eastern Canadian oil imports, financed by a special tax on western Canadian oil exports to the United States. This created intense antagonism in the West and seriously intensified regional tensions in Canada.

The main problem facing the Canadian government, as well as other governments around the world, was how to deal with the OPEC-induced stagflation. With the increase in both inflation rates and unemployment rates, Canadian policy makers faced a dilemma they had never experienced before. Unemployment rose from a low of 4.1 percent in 1967 to over 7 percent by the mid-1970s. Worse still, inflation reached double digits and stood at 12.6 percent in 1974. Feeling that the latter was the more serious of the two problems, the Trudeau government introduced wage and price controls in October 1975, whereby the newly created Anti-Inflation Board could roll back price and wage increases it felt were excessive. However, despite the best of intentions, this was a little like trying to control inflation by making it illegal! The problem with this approach, called incomes policies, is that, although it may curb inflationary expectations, it is really treating the symptoms rather than the disease itself.

In another attempt to protect Canadians from the ravages of inflation, the government tied the wages it paid, government pensions benefits, and welfare payments to a rising consumer price index. Furthermore, it also indexed tax exemptions to that same price index, which guaranteed that tax revenue would not rise as fast as government spending. These measures laid the groundwork for the huge budget deficits that followed in the late 1970s and 1980s.

We saw in Chapter 12 that trying to cure stagflation through traditional fiscal and monetary policy is impossible. As a result of this failure, many turned to a new school of thought that came to prominence at that time: supply-side economics.

The Rise of Supply-Siders

This new school of thought felt that the Keynesian approach put far too much emphasis on curing economic problems solely through manipulating aggregate demand, an approach that had come to be known as demand management. Supply-siders argued that the only cure offered by the interventionists was to throw more money at the problem, whatever the problem might be. While at times this might be an effective approach, especially in the short run, in many situations it simply created more problems by stifling investment and international competitiveness through burdening the country with large budget deficits. In the period following the OPEC-induced stagflation, these supply-side economists felt that attention must be focused on the underlying malaise crippling North America's economies: falling rates of productivity. Supply-siders argued that it is only through increased productivity that a country can lay the foundation for dealing with both inflation and unemployment.

Like the neoclassicists earlier in the century, supply-side economists believed that the aggregate supply was not simply a passive element that responded to changes in aggregate demand, but was itself a prime mover of economic activity. Their diagnosis of the stagflation of the 1970s was straightforward. It was caused by the high price of imported oil and further accentuated by declining productivity rates. Both of these factors caused a decrease in aggregate supply. Similarly, they felt that the cure was equally straightforward: an increase in aggregate supply. This is shown in **Figure 13.6**.

FIGURE 13.6 **Increasing Aggregate Supply to Fight Stagflation**

Assume that the economy is at a price level of P_1 and a GDP level of Y_1. An increase in aggregate supply will shift the aggregate supply curve from AS_1 to AS_2. The result will be a lower price level, P_2, as well as a higher level of GDP, Y_2, the latter implying a lower unemployment rate.

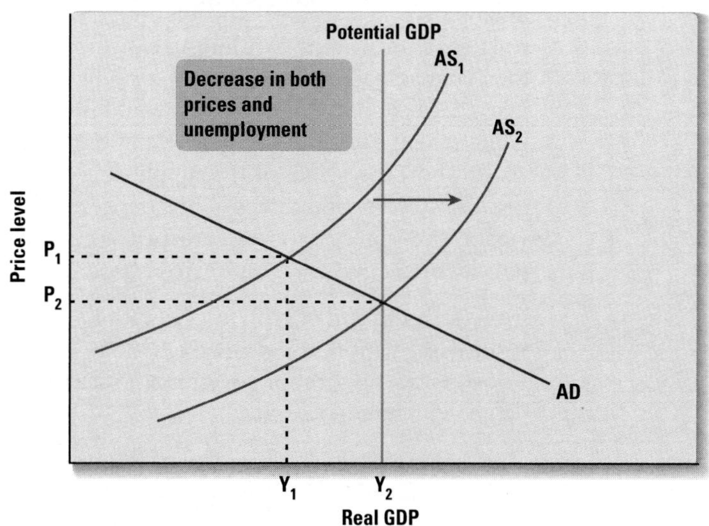

An increase in aggregate supply shifts the aggregate supply curve from AS_1 to AS_2. This results in a reduction in the price level from P_1 to P_2 *and* an increase in GDP from Y_1 to Y_2, which will result in reduced unemployment. Supply-siders believed that modern governments had stifled initiative and productivity through high levels of taxation and government bureaucracy. At different times in the 1980s, this argument caught the attention of a number of governments around the world, including the Brian Mulroney government in Canada, the Ronald Reagan government in the United States, and the Margaret Thatcher government in the United Kingdom.

What policies might be used to increase aggregate supply and stimulate the production of goods and services? The first was the *privatization* of many functions of government in the name of exposing these functions to the competition of the marketplace and thereby improving their efficiency. It was during this time, for example, that Air Canada and Canadian National [Railways] ceased to be crown corporations and were privatized. Second, a policy of *deregulation* was instituted, which aimed, again, at using the competitive marketplace to increase efficiency. The most dramatic example here is that of the deregulation of the airline industry in the United States, which resulted in some long-established airlines going broke and other new airlines entering the industry. Most would argue that this has proved successful because it has resulted in lower airfares and increased consumer choice on the most popular routes. (However, on other, less travelled routes, higher fares resulted.) Canada also deregulated both its airline and trucking industries, but not so completely.

A third policy aimed at increasing aggregate supply was the *contracting-out* of specific government services in the name of reducing the costs of these services and thus the costs of running the government. An example of this was the contracting-out by Canada Post of its retailing function to firms that put this service into local drugstores and convenience shops.

The fourth and most significant plank in the supply-siders' platform involved *cutting tax rates* on business profits and on individual incomes. The aim was to increase incentives for people to work more, save more, and invest more. The result, it was believed, would lead to an increase in aggregate supply. If income tax rates were cut, many workers would work longer hours, since high marginal tax rates tend to deter people from working overtime. Additionally, many unemployed workers would seek employment with more enthusiasm, while some homemakers and retired people would be tempted to return to the labour force. These results would be further enhanced if the social security net of welfare payments, unemployment coverage, and lifetime disability income were restructured to aid those in real need rather than providing an easy income for those who didn't deserve it. Furthermore, total savings would increase, since a cut in personal taxes would increase disposable income. Likewise, a cut in corporate taxes would provide increased profits for firms, who would then plough them back into the business in the form of new investment.

In short, advocates of the supply-side position saw the above policies as necessary steps to undo 40 years of interventionist polices that, they believed, had sapped the economy of its vigour and ability to grow, prosper, and adjust to change. In summary, the four major policies of supply-side proponents are:

- the privatization of crown corporations
- the deregulation of industry
- the contracting-out of government services
- the reduction of tax rates

The promised benefits of all of this are very attractive. Greater competition, more work effort, increased investment spending, and greater willingness to accept risk would result in higher economic growth—thus creating jobs, lowering unemployment, increasing output, and easing inflation.

There was a fly in the ointment, however. In advocating lower tax rates, supply-siders did leave themselves open to accusations that they too (like the Keynesians) were proposing big government deficits as a way of curing stagflation. It was at this point (the late 1970s) that a Californian economist named Arthur Laffer put forward the intriguing argument that a cut in tax rates in North America, far from decreasing the government's tax revenues, would in fact increase them.

Laffer curve: the graphical representation of the idea that, in terms of tax revenue, there is an optimal tax rate; above or below this rate, tax revenue would be less.

The Laffer Curve

The essentials of Laffer's argument are contained in **Figure 13.7**. The curve (henceforth known as the **Laffer curve**) shows the amount of tax revenue received by the government at various tax rates.

FIGURE 13.7 The Laffer Curve

If the economy is at point *a* on the Laffer curve, then a drop in tax rates will cause an *increase* in tax revenues, pushing the economy to position *b*.

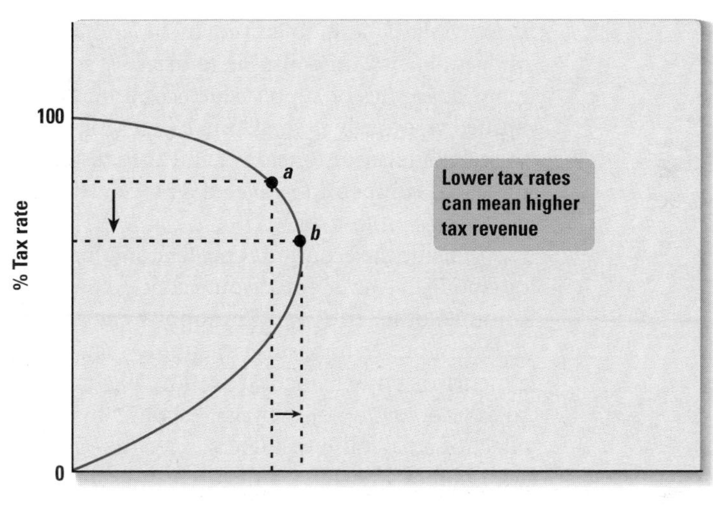

With a zero tax rate, tax revenue would of course be zero. At the other extreme, with a tax rate of 100 percent, presumably no one would work, and tax revenue would again be zero. In between these extremes, there is a particular relationship between the tax rate and tax revenue. Over the years of Keynesian-type interventionism, tax rates had been pushed higher and higher, so that many countries found themselves at a point represented by *a* in **Figure 13.7**. What was needed, argued Laffer, was a massive cut in tax rates, which would increase incentives so that production, and therefore income, would increase so much that tax revenues would actually go up to, say, a point represented by *b* on the Laffer curve. So, although tax rates are lower, tax revenues are higher.

SELF-TEST

6. Shown here are several different average tax rates (ATR) associated with various levels of GDP. Calculate the total tax revenue at each level of GDP and indicate the tax rate that would maximize the government's tax revenue.

ATR	GDP	Tax Revenue
0.30	$2000	______
0.35	1900	______
0.40	1700	______
0.45	1500	______
0.50	1300	______
0.55	1100	______

If Laffer's argument was correct, then a government could, figuratively speaking, have its cake and eat it too. Appropriate tax cuts could increase work, savings, and investment and thereby slash both unemployment and inflation. And on top of this, the government's budget deficit would also be reduced. It sounded very persuasive. The pity of it all was that many advocates of supply-side economics didn't stop there. Among other things, they also pushed vigorously in the United States for massive cuts to social programs (while leaving the military budget untouched), and for curtailing the power of trade unions (in the name of increased competition). Needless to say, this led to a backlash, both inside and outside the economics profession.

Outside the economics profession, this backlash took on a political character. Within the discipline, however, the dispute centred on the supposed stimulative effect of tax cuts. Many commentators criticized the supply-side argument on the grounds that a tax cut was likely to have a bigger impact on spending than on productivity. The average person in receipt of a higher disposable income is more likely to spend most of it, rather than work more hours so as to obtain an even bigger income. In economic terms, this means that the substitution effect of a pay raise will likely exceed the income effect of such an increase. Similarly, firms with higher after-tax profits are just as likely to pay higher dividends as they are to use the increased earnings to reinvest in their companies. In short, the criticism of many economists was not that tax cuts do not provide incentives to people, but that the effect on spending and aggregate demand will be far greater than the effect on the supply side. All this means that aggregate demand would rise more than aggregate supply, and not only would GDP increase but so too would inflation. Nonetheless, the supply-side position, with its overtones of laissez-faire, was given a boost by a relatively new idea in economics in the late 1970s: rational expectations.

SELF-TEST

7. Supply-side economists say that a cut in tax rates will lead to an increase in real GDP. Keynesians agree with this, but for different reasons. In what ways do they differ?

Rational Expectations

Many of the adherents to this theory were later labelled "new" classicists. Their main focus was a dissatisfaction with the prevailing view that people's future expectations are solely guided by past experience. As an example of this prevailing view, suppose that wage contracts were based solely on recent experience, and inflation rates had been running at 10 percent. Logic would dictate that unions would attempt to negotiate wage increases in excess of 10 percent. If these wage demands were successfully achieved, inflation would intensify and the chances of ever reducing people's inflationary expectations would seem remote. This led to many arguing that inflation might well have a self-generating aspect to it, and therefore could only be cured by a strong dose of unemployment. In other words, the only way of reducing inflation would be for the government to intervene with contractionary fiscal or monetary policy.

Adherents of the theory of rational expectations felt that such a conclusion is misguided and that the expectations of consumers, investors, and firms are formed not only by recent experience but also by their predictions of the likely response by the government and the central bank. In other words, they felt that rational individuals make use of all available information when making future plans. Thus, if the current rate of inflation is 10 percent, it does not mean that everybody expects it to remain at that level. People will take into consideration other indicators, such as unemployment levels, as well as their predictions of possible policy action to be taken by policy makers. This might well result in their lowering their expectations of future inflation rates. What all of this suggested was that inflation might be cured more quickly and less painfully than many economists believed. If this is so, then the economy could return to its "natural" state of full employment with stable prices, without the need for heavy-handed, recession-creating action by government.

13.4 Canada at the Start of the Twenty-first Century: A Time of Uncertainty

LO4
Understand how the stagflation of the 1970s gave rise to supply-side economics.

The decade of the 1990s may well go down in history as one of the most significant of the twentieth century. It began with the collapse of the Soviet Union and, with it, the birth of over a dozen new nations—a well-spring of hope and some anxious expectations. This was the time when China began seriously experimenting with the market system, and the world witnessed the enormous success of the Asian Tigers. All of this seemed to clearly say that the market system was likely to reign supreme forevermore.

For Canada, the decade began with a brief but sharp recession that affected Ontario and Quebec more than it did the West or the Maritimes. Once again, as with the much more serious recession of the early 1980s, some economists felt that this was a recession induced by the very tight monetary policy of the Bank of Canada, which seemed almost obsessed with holding inflation rates below 2 percent. For this reason, the then-governor of the Bank of Canada, John Crow, was not a popular man in the eyes of many Canadians. Thus, one of the first things that a new Liberal government did when it came to power in 1993 was to take advantage of the fact that Crow's first term as governor had just expired and replace him with Gordon Thiessen. Many thought this might signal a new direction for monetary policy. As events transpired, the change of governors didn't produce any change in policy. The Bank of Canada remained fixated on fighting inflation by keeping interest rates high.

On the fiscal side of policy, the big issue of the day was the federal government's budget deficits. The federal government had been running budget deficits for nearly 20 years straight, and these deficits were increasing year by year. The reasons for these huge deficits were at least threefold. First was the government's own attempt to shield Canadians from the effects of the inflationary 1970s. Second was unusually high interest rates in the early 1980s, which raised the interest payments on the public debt. Third was the simple fact that the size of government was much bigger than that of 20 years earlier. All this led to a growing chorus of political commentators, joined by some economists, who called for reduced deficits, or even balanced budgets, regardless of the costs of achieving this. Finance Minister Paul Martin responded by instituting massive cuts in federal government transfers to the provinces, in the form of cuts to health and education spending. By the fiscal year

1997–1998, the federal government's budget showed a modest surplus followed by larger surpluses in the ensuing years.

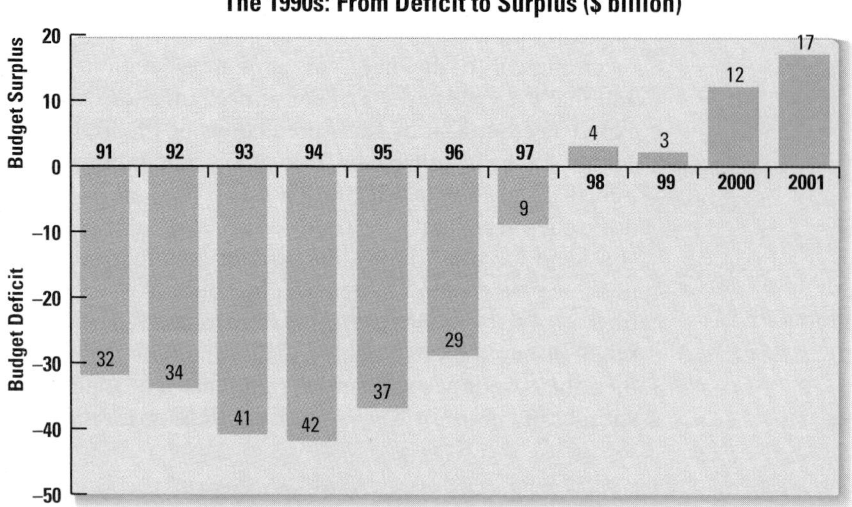

Despite the high level of exports, the Canadian dollar was on the decline for most of the decade and fell to historic lows in the early twenty-first century. A long-term downward trend in commodity prices and an economic crisis in Asia were certainly two reasons for this. Perhaps more significant was the fact that long-term foreign investment into Canada slowed considerably in the mid-to-late 1990s. The reasons for this include political uncertainty about Quebec, and a growing international perception that Canada had a restrictive business environment and high taxes. Finally, we should note that the U.S. dollar has risen against most other currencies of the world as well as against the Canadian dollar.

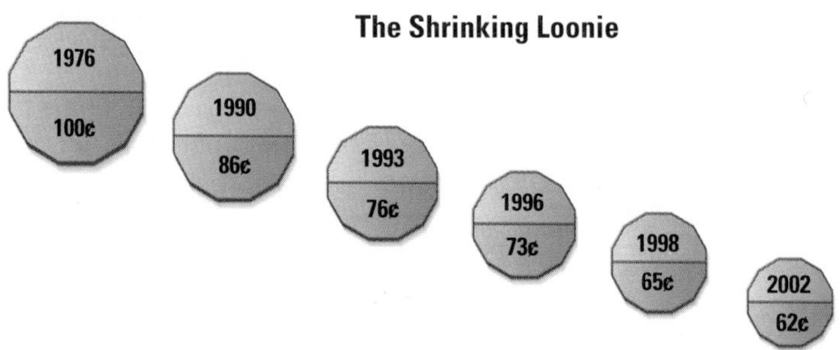

One thing that this brief overview of the twentieth century shows is that the economic goals that Canadians are concerned with are a reflection of the times they live in and are very much subject to change. At the beginning of the century, the problems of nation building and economic growth were at centre stage. By the 1920s, there was growing concern that the benefits of economic growth were not always shared equitably among people. The 1930s understandably put full employment at the top of everyone's list of economic goals. The postwar period saw the balancing of the twin goals of full employment and stable prices come into sharp focus. In the 1970s, Canadian concerns went in two very different directions. First there was increasing anxiety about stagflation, and second there was an increasing worry over resource depletion and environmental degradation. In the 1980s, bigger government deficits and debt became the major issue for many. This worry continued into the 1990s, then faded to be replaced by alarm over the depreciating Canadian dollar.

There is a clear message in all this: what is seen as the most important goal today is unlikely to remain as important tomorrow. Problems arise and then get dealt with, only to be replaced with some new problem that attracts people's concerns and attention. That is why the study of economic principles must remain broad and flexible. Too much focus on any one problem or any one issue is myopic, and could prove to be counter-productive, since a student's perspective for a lifetime is often formed in a few short years.

13.5 A Look at the Future

LO5
Appreciate the significance of the new economy.

symbolic knowledge: knowledge that encompasses data and information that is then systematically improved and refined into a form that has direct application to defining problems or creating solutions.

symbolic analyst: an individual who uses symbolic knowledge to identify problems, create solutions, and then present those solutions in a systematic form.

We are all aware that the Industrial Revolution, beginning in about 1750, swept around the world and resulted in almost everything changing—people's lifestyles, the means of producing wealth, transportation systems, forms of government, prevailing customs, values, and much more. This enormous transition took place over a period of approximately 150–200 years.

A growing number of people today are convinced that the rise of the information age signals a second revolution that will prove to be just as significant as the first and will usher in the "new economy." The difference this time, however, will be that we are probably looking at a transition period of only 50 years or so.

The Industrial Revolution took production out of the rural cottage and into the urban factory. Steam power, the electric motor, and other major innovations created the possibility for massive economies of scale in production, from which sprang the large corporation as the primary organizational form for the wealth-creation process. A vast array of durable goods then became affordable for ordinary consumers, and manufacturing became the driving force behind the powerful, rich economies of the world. What emerged was the "basic economy" that we are all familiar with.

To help us understand the nature of the new economy, we will make extensive use of two concepts. The first, used by Alvin Toffler in his book *Power Shift*, is called **symbolic knowledge**, and the other is what Robert Reich, in *The Work of Nations*, refers to as the **symbolic analyst**.

Symbolic knowledge is defined as facts and data that have been classified into meaningful categories and refined into a form that has direct application to defining problems or creating solutions. Much of today's symbolic knowledge comes in the form of symbols—either in mathematical form, or computer configurations, or in the form of new words and phrases that convey a unique combination of ideas. Reich's symbolic analysts are those individuals who, using symbolic knowledge, make a living identifying problems of method, efficiency, information gathering, or interpretation, then create solutions for those problems, and, finally, present those solutions in some systematic form. An example here is that of a young woman who has successfully combined the technique of designing questionnaires and the analytical ability to interpret answers with the intuition needed to draw conclusions, such that her market research for clients produces valuable information that was previously simply not available.

Symbolic knowledge is expanding at breakneck speed and is being shared and exchanged nearly as fast. The result is that the basic economy's bureaucratic managers are in fast retreat from a growing army of risk-taking, creative symbolic analysts who exhibit an entrepreneurial spirit in small companies that lie outside the world's multinational corporations.

National Archives of Canada

The basic economy.

The most significant aspect of the growing importance of both symbolic knowledge and the work of the symbolic analyst is the inability of anyone to control, restrict, or own knowledge, at least for very long. In the basic economy, capital was at the centre of production, and capital could be accumulated, controlled, and then transformed into the basis for monopoly control: one family, or even one individual, could control, say, a huge steel mill. In the new economy, symbolic knowledge is at the centre of the wealth-creation process, and it cannot be amassed and controlled in the same way as capital. No single firm, and certainly no individual, can control the vast array of new software programs that pour onto the market each year.

All of this has very interesting implications for where the centres of power in society lie. When the Industrial Revolution and the system of capitalism first started to sweep across Europe, we witnessed a struggle for power between the established landed gentry and the young, spirited, rising capitalists. As capitalism matured and production became organized around, and concentrated in, large corporations, we saw the struggle between capital and labour emerge. In the new economy, capital is waning in importance and, therefore, so too is the power of the large corporations as well as that of organized labour, whose members are centred within such corporations. Just who the protagonists will be in the future power struggles isn't clear, but the symbolic analyst will be on one side with, possibly, government regulators on the other.

The Changing Nature of Production

With the rise in importance of symbolic knowledge and the emergence of the new economy, it is clear that our conventional categories of the four factors of production—land, labour, capital, and enterprise—may soon become inadequate. Not only will knowledge have to be added to the list, but it is rapidly becoming the most important factor. Let's look at some specific examples of how symbolic knowledge is taking the place of other inputs.

The first example is the substitution of symbolic knowledge for financial capital. The widespread use of computers has allowed business to adopt just-in-time inventory control systems, with the result that the amount of materials that producers must carry in stock (or in storage) has been reduced to a minimum. As a result, tens of billions of dollars worth of inventory, once financed with borrowed money (the interest on which is added to the cost of production), is simply no longer needed.

Looking at symbolic knowledge as a substitute for real capital, the examples are almost endless. Robotics are reducing the capital–output ratio in thousands of different contexts. Fibre-optic cables are reducing the amount of needed capital per transatlantic phone call. Superconductivity and giant batteries are eliminating the need for extra power plants that handle peak-load demand. Fuel cell technology, to replace the internal combustion engine in automobiles as well as generate clean power, is only a few years away. More significant than any one example, however, is what Robert Thurow describes in *Head to Head* as the emerging reality of new *process technology* starting to replace *product technology*. In the basic economy, changing a product was expensive. It required large inputs of highly-paid machinists, tool-and-die makers, and lots of downtime with no production. Hence the reliance on the production of standardized products that were mass-produced in order to capture economies of scale. In the new economy, computer-driven manufacturing technology is producing customized products aimed at niche markets. As a result, we see the substitution of *high-value-added production* for *high-volume production*. What's more, these customized semi-personal products are not so expensive as to be beyond the budget of most consumers. To an increasing extent, customers are willing to pay a (not-so-high) premium for products that exactly meet their needs; and because such products cannot be easily duplicated by high-volume competitors, high-value output is where the firm's competitive advantage in the new economy lies. In short:

Just as the Industrial Revolution shifted production from small-scale handicraft production to standardized mass production, the new economy is reinventing the handicraft product in customized form.

In a sense, this shift from an emphasis on product technology to process technology is being forced on firms in the advanced economies. Product technology can be easily copied by firms in the newly industrial countries, such as South Korea, Taiwan, Hong Kong, and Singapore (the four Asian Tigers), where routine labour is cheap. To survive, the firms in the advanced economies of Europe, North America, and Japan must begin to do different things that cannot be easily copied. Below is a list of the industries that will likely be key to North America's changing economic role:

- microelectronics
- biotechnology
- the new-materials industries
- fuel cells
- telecommunications
- robotics
- computer software

These are all brain-power industries that will employ a large percentage of the symbolic analysts. Almost all the firms in these categories, and the jobs that go with them, could be located anywhere in the world. There is little natural advantage to any particular location. New economy jobs will go to those societies that organize themselves around the realities of the information age and are also able to offer the individuals involved the most desirable lifestyle opportunities.

As a point of contrast, you should realize that in the *basic* economy, a nation's comparative advantage lay in:

- abundant natural resources
- a high level of capital accumulation
- a disciplined labour force that was experienced in product production so that economies of scale could be captured

On the other hand, the *new* economy's comparative advantage is entirely human-made—with knowledge, human creativity, and flexibility being the key ingredients.

The Changing Nature of Work

Digital Vision/Getty Images

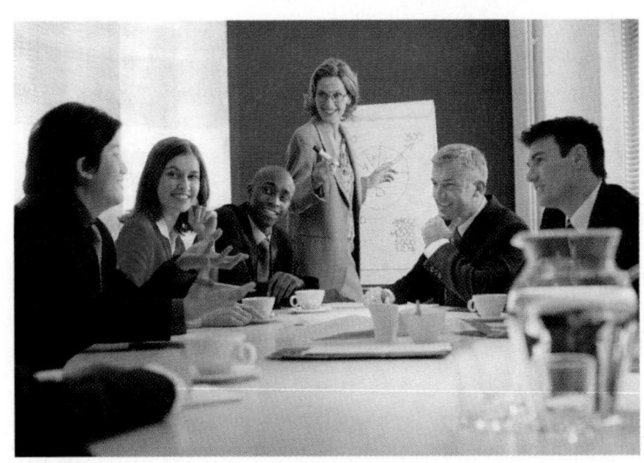

Problem solving exemplifies the new economy.

The French physiocrats of the eighteenth century were sure that wealth sprang from land. Marx, in the nineteenth century, was sure that it sprang from labour. Neoclassical economists, at the turn of the twentieth century, emphasized the role of capital formation in increasing an economy's production possibilities. As we look into the future, knowledge, information, and human creativity will play key roles in creating wealth and employment. For example, employment in the U.S. in small companies rose 34 percent in the years 1991–1995, while employment in Fortune 500 companies declined by 3.6 percent.

Let's emphasize this point by now looking at ways in which symbolic knowledge acts as a substitute for labour, and at the profound implications this has on the changing nature of work. Alvin Toffler reports that the Florida plant of a large electronics firm turns out customized radio pagers in production runs as small as one of a kind. Twenty-seven robots do the physical work. Of the 40 employees at the plant, only one actually touches the product. It is interesting to note that 24 highly specialized symbolic analysts worked (in teams, at very odd hours, and on weekends) for 18 months to design the product, engineer the plant and equipment, and plan the strategy for the marketing of the product. Their work done, this group was shuffled and reassigned to other similar projects.

There are hundreds of other similar examples, but the point is that the nature of work itself is changing. Here, we will rely on Reich for our framework once again. He sees three broad categories of work emerging in the new paradigm. The first is *routine production services*, which range from blue-collar assembly-line workers and supervisors who do repetitive checks on subordinates' work, to the makers of computer circuit-boards. This group makes up about 25 percent of today's work force, but this percentage is declining. The second category is *in-person services*, ranging from retail sales workers, bank tellers, and nursing aides, to real estate agents. This category makes up about 30 percent of the labour force and is growing. The third category is that of the *symbolic services*, which includes all problem-identifying, problem-solving, and strategic-brokering activities that involve the manipulation of data, words, and oral or visual representations. Like the products produced by the routine production workers—but unlike those of the in-person service worker—the output of the symbolic analyst can be traded worldwide. Examples of occupations in this category are design engineers, public relations consultants, film editors, energy consultants, systems analysts, and textbook authors and editors. They make up about 20 percent of today's work force. The remaining 25 percent of the work force is in agriculture and mining, and in government employment. To some extent, those within government could be sorted into the same three categories. In summary, Reich's three categories of work are:

- routine production services
- in-person services
- symbolic services

Focusing on these three categories of work, one can discern certain future trends in employment. Routine production workers may well have to accept lower real wages or see their jobs disappear. In-service production work may be either very routine and low paid ("MacJobs"), or specialized and fairly highly paid (realtors or nurses). Systems analysts will be specialized, highly skilled, and very well paid. Increasingly, workers will have only two things to sell: cheap routine labour or highly specialized skills. Often, those in the latter category will shun employment with large corporations and, instead, form small, highly specialized businesses of their own. Thus we find the number and variety of firms multiplying and forming clusters around a specific function or type of service.

Such clusters are held together by the free flow of information and data transfer and by the stimulus to creativity that personal interaction brings. Often, a major educational institution is at the core of such clusters. This last point emphasizes the fact that today's comparative advantage is human-made and not naturally endowed. This is a point we made earlier but needs emphasis:

Firms, industries, and economies with the best environment for symbolic analysts to work in will be the successful ones.

Physical products, whatever they may be, can be manufactured anywhere in the world, and here the cheapest labour will win out. But the process that identifies the unique needs of the customers and designs a specialized response to those needs will capture most of the value added in production.

To say it again: in the basic economy, capital is concentrated and owned by capitalists who hired interchangeable units of labour, and who in turn produced standardized goods. In the new economy, capital is less important and less concentrated because of its mobility and abundance and because of the decreasing importance of standardized production. The most powerful wealth-creating tools are the symbols, ideas, and imagination inside the heads of the symbolic analysts. These workers, therefore, own a critical, irreplaceable, share of the means of production.

The Rise of E-Commerce

The railway, invented in 1829, mastered distance. This explains why, more than any of the other inventions of the Industrial Revolution, the railway changed the economy and nature of the workforce. It also changed humanity's mindset, its horizon, and its "mental geography." Time may well prove that the most significant aspect of the new economy is the growing importance of e-commerce, which doesn't merely master distance, but eliminates it. For the first time in history, the Internet allows buyers and sellers to come together without regard to geography. Not only that, but most of tomorrow's markets will be like today's Wall Street market, where buyers and sellers have access to the same information and where prices fluctuate freely based on the forces of supply and demand.

The Internet is making it possible for companies to lower costs dramatically, take customer service to undreamed of levels, enter markets from which they were previously excluded, create new revenue streams and, ultimately, redefine the very nature of their business.

Consumer purchasing on the Internet is the most visible aspect of e-commerce—and not without reason: *business to customer* e-commerce went from $8 billion in 1999 to an estimated $108 billion in 2003, a 13-fold increase in just 4 years. In basic business structures, selling is still seen and organized as a servant to production. In the new economy, companies will sell what they can deliver quickly and efficiently; those that do this best will win the competitive race. Even more interestingly, the consumer purchase may, in itself, be electronic—a software program, trade on a stock market, music, or an article—and there will be no delivery problem since the "product" will simply be an entry in a computer's memory. The product will have a legal existence but no physical existence. As a result, it may prove difficult for governments to tax such purchases.

But far more significant is the *business to business* activity that is already well established. For example, it is reported that *85 percent* of U.S. businesses ordered products via the Internet in 1999. This amounted to $43 billion. Estimates for 2003 are for $1.3 trillion, an increase of over 30 times in, again, just 4 years.

And how far could all this go? Ford is giving serious consideration to outsourcing all its manufacturing, thus stripping the company down to the essentials of product development, brand management, and customer service, using the Internet as the conduit to its customers. If this were to happen, one could imagine that the thousands of unionized production jobs would not be part of the outsourcing. In fact, it is interesting to note that, in 1999, there were more individual stockholders in the U.S. than there were unionized workers. Others are pointing out the fact that the government's ability to tax is being squeezed from three directions: the rise of e-commerce and the resulting difficulty of governments to collect taxes on such activity; electoral resistance to increases in taxation; and the movement away from compulsory state-funded pension plans to privatized plans, as already seen in Singapore and Chile, and which is currently being seriously considered in Germany and the U.S. If all of this proves to be a valid trend, the year 2000 may well have marked the reversal of a long-established historical trend of higher taxes. Stretching things even further, some are predicting the evolution of an e-commerce currency that may bring to an end the role of central banks while others are even predicting the advent of on-line voting on most major policy issues of government, which may mark the beginning of the end of elected representatives of government.

Globalization and Beyond

French historian Fernand Braudel notes that, by the 1400s, the weekly market had become a powerful engine in certain parts of Europe's communities, linking the serfs of the small feudal estates with their (slowly growing) urban neighbours through "thousands of humble points of intersection." A small market of 100 people might generate trade among 6 or 7 times that many people. Yet, it wasn't the market itself that was new. Instead it was the fact that many pieces of a puzzle were beginning to take shape in simple forms—local markets, recognized coin and currency, stocks, double-entry bookkeeping, and banking, that subsequently matured into more sophisticated tools in the marketplace in a tightly defined geographical area and in a relatively brief period of a few hundred years. For the first time, economic life began to play a dominant role in everyday life, nudging out the religious focus that had so long prevailed. It was through this first "gateway" that capitalist society was born.

By the early twentieth century, the fundamental security of property, rule of law, democratic institutions, and stable central governments had pushed most of the European countries, North America—and later Japan—through the second gateway, and capitalism was well established.

By the end of the twentieth century, the third gateway had opened under the banner of globalization. The characteristics of this trend include relatively stable currencies, growing international trade, low rates of inflation, privatization, deregulation, and the lowering of the barriers to the movement of goods, capital, and people. Several countries are in the process of entering this stage; but there may well be many struggles, conflicts, acts of terrorism and much second guessing before the full effects of globalization are fully understood and accepted, if, indeed, they are.

Some commentators are now speaking of a fourth gateway, involving changes in government's approach to business, which they feel are needed to accommodate the fluid entrepreneurship and rapid capital development of the new scientific–technical revolution that is the essence of the new economy. The argument here is that government policy needs to recognize the inherent nature of venture capital markets, which are sometimes quite rewarding but also quite risky. A small, but typical, example of what is at issue here is the fact that, if the German law forbidding directors or officers of bankrupt companies from serving in such roles for 10 years prevailed in the U.S., then the Silicon Valley would not exist.

It is necessary to point out that there is no general agreement that globalization and all that might be entailed in this fourth gateway is for the good of all humankind. Some fear that this trend, as clear as it presently may be, is a road to the rule of large corporations rather than elected governments, and that while some will benefit greatly, far too many will be left completely out of the sharing of the increases in productivity and income. The first Industrial Revolution certainly had its victims—a fact that led to the rise of socialist/communist ideology. It is certainly possible that a similar reaction could occur again.

What is Canada's future in all this? Canada's options *could be* quite bright. The country is already strong in the things that are difficult to achieve, such as a stable, constitutionally-based government, good rates of entrepreneurial company formation, established capital markets that are open to venture capital financing, a well-educated population, and good science and technology educational institutions. In addition, this country's very diverse and multicultural population provides important links to many parts of the globe. On the other hand, there is the increasingly frequent claim by some that Canada's taxes are too high, that its economy is over-regulated, and that there is gross underfunding of higher education.

An interesting question is whether this fourth gateway will open wide within the context of the established international organizations of today—NAFTA, ASEAN, and the WTO—or not. At least some observers are answering "no" to this question. These organizations are attempting to achieve significant economic integration among nations with vastly different social, political, economic, and demographic profiles. Within the context of these organizations, agreements on the free movement of people, common commercial law, and science and technology cooperation will be hard to forge.

Let's return to the fifteenth-century French market and ask what questions the vendors of the day were asking themselves. Who has the right to set up a table and what position is optimal? Do customers have to line up, or can they wave their money and shout out a price? If you, the customer, band together with your neighbour to buy twice as many tomatoes, will you get a better price? Do merchants have to show all their tomatoes or can they impose an artificial scarcity? Will anyone pay more for Pierre's tomatoes than they will for Jean's because they trust Pierre more? Is anything fixed? Is anything free? In short, just *what are the rules* of this new marketplace? These are exactly the same questions that face us all as nations begin to pass through the third, and then the fourth, gateway. Interestingly, the circle seems to be closing.

Economic Goals Revisited

Just as the new economy is changing the very structure of the economy, so will it change what are perceived as the important economic goals. Let us give some tentative indications of how these are likely to change in the future.

As we have seen, the goal of full employment hinges on the very *definition* of employment and what is meant by "work." In the basic economy, full employment usually meant working away from home for a 40-hour week, Monday to Friday, for a single employer, at a fixed wage on a long-term basis. In the new economy, none of these parameters will remain fixed. More and more people will be working flexible hours at home on short-term contracts for a number of companies located around the world. This is not to suggest that all traditional forms of employment will disappear; there will still be a demand for routine production services, but even these types of jobs are bound to feel the effects of change. What all this means is that the level of employment achieved by the economy will very much depend on how we choose to redefine just what we mean by the term.

Turning now to the goal of economic growth, the conventional view of growth will likely evolve into something quite different. The shift from the high-volume production of standardized products to high-value customized products is well underway. This is a reflection of increased affluence and more discriminating taste being expressed on an individual level in the private markets. If this trend begins to express itself on a more collective level, we could see a growing concern about the composition of overall production. People could well begin to be more concerned about *how* growth meets their wants rather than just in growth itself. Product quality and uniqueness could be more important than just having more of the same. Improvements in more abstract goods, such as access to skiing and jogging trails or unique cultural and entertainment events, could become more important than another factory or more trees allocated for logging. In short:

We can see some definition of the right *kind* of growth beginning to take precedent over the size of the growth *rate*.

Tied up in all this will undoubtedly be a growing awareness of what we are doing to our environment. This issue is rising higher on most people's list of important goals.

Let's turn now to the future prospects of maintaining an equitable distribution of income. As we mentioned earlier, it may well be the case that some Canadians will do very well in the new economy, while others probably will not. This could easily translate into a widening income gap between those who reach the status of symbolic analyst and those who get mired in the status of routine-production-service worker, or low-skilled in-person service worker, or, even more seriously, those who become unemployable. Will government policies of income redistribution be able to counter any such tendency so that all Canadians can benefit from the success of some? To try to answer this question would propel us into a detailed discussion of perceived moral responsibility, political philosophy, and some sort of perceived sense of fairness as well as an analysis of new power structures. All of this is, indeed, a slippery slope. To put it bluntly, the question will become: does a successful software designer in Toronto, for example, have an obligation to subsidize an unemployed East Coast fisher? Suffice it to say that:

The issue of an equitable distribution of income and, in fact, the very definition of this term are likely to be at the centre of public consciousness and debate.

And what of the other three conventional economic goals—the control of inflation, maintaining a viable balance of payments, and the national debt?

It is more than likely that concern over these goals will start to fade, not so much because of changed perceptions, but simply because they become less pressing in comparison to the goals of employment, income distribution, and ensuring a liveable environment. Inflation has been tame for several years now and, in the absence of policy mistakes or war, we see this trend continuing. A truly flexible exchange rate could take the possibility of balance-of-payments problems off the table. A manageable national debt depends on the success of government policies in keeping increases in government spending rates below increased revenues. The accomplishment of this goal in Canada has recently been achieved, and we see no reason for it to slip away.

Finale

So what might be in your future?

The very optimistic scenario is one that sees inflation, the national debt, and balance-of-payment concerns fading into non-issues, while robust economic growth better allows us to redefine, and then deal with, the problems of unemployment, maintaining an equitable distribution of income, and creating a liveable environment.

To achieve this golden age will take imaginative government policies, a strong faith in human ingenuity, and a will to succeed that is free from rigid ideology. Above all, it will require all of us to take responsibility for our own actions as they affect both our fellow human beings and this small planet we call home.

We hope that you now have gained enough confidence in your study of economics to better accept such responsibility and to begin to appreciate this most challenging and fascinating discipline.

REVIEW

1. What is the Phillips curve?
2. What was the main cause of the inflation of the 1970s?
3. What did the supply-siders see as solutions for the economic problems of the 1970s and the 1980s?
4. What did Arthur Laffer think would be the effect of a reduction in tax rates?
5. Define the term *symbolic knowledge*.
6. Which economic goal is likely to be the most contentious in the future?

STUDY GUIDE

Review

CHAPTER SUMMARY

This chapter used six significant periods in twentieth-century Canada to illustrate the interaction between contemporary events and the development of macroeconomic theory. In the process, it discussed the role of government in a modern capitalist economy. The chapter ended with a brief look into the future.

1. At the turn of the last century, Say's Law and the philosophy of laissez-faire prevailed. In the years following the First World War, the *neoclassicists* were convinced that full-employment equilibrium was automatic because of:
   - the flexibility of prices;
   - the flexibility of interest rates;
   - the flexibility of wages.

2. The Great Depression led to the development of *Keynesian economics*, which argued that:
   - the economy could get trapped in a long-term depression;
   - the solution was an increase in aggregate demand.

3. Keynesian economic *policies prevailed* in the quarter century following the Second World War, which proved to be the longest period of relative stability in the macroeconomy of the century. Nonetheless, it was recognized that a trade-off existed between full employment and inflation, and that it may prove impossible to attain both goals simultaneously.

4. The oil price shocks of the 1970s lead to the development of *supply-side economics*, which sees the solution to the stagflation of this period as:
   - the privatization of crown corporations;
   - the deregulation of industry;
   - the contracting-out of government services;
   - the reduction of tax rates.

5. The 1990s proved to be prosperous despite a recession at the beginning of the decade. Concern over the low value of the Canadian dollar persisted, but large budget deficits came to an end.

6. Many observers are convinced that the world is in the middle of profound changes in the economy that will rival those of the Industrial Revolution, which ushered in the market system. Out of these changes will emerge a *new economy* that will show its effects in changes in every aspect of our lives.

NEW GLOSSARY TERMS

Laffer curve 459
Say's Law 445
symbolic analyst 463
symbolic knowledge 463

STUDY TIPS

1. It is important to realize that the different schools of thought examined in this chapter are products of their times: neoclassical theory is rooted in an era of buoyant growth and low unemployment; Keynesian theory was the product of the depression years, when unemployment was, by far, the most serious economic issue; and supply-side economics came into existence as a result of mainstream economics being unable to offer any clear solutions to the problem of stagflation.

2. It would be a mistake to leave this chapter with the idea that every economist, past or present, "belongs" exclusively to one or another of these schools of thought. The different schools are starkly delineated

here in order to clarify their contrasting viewpoints. In reality, few economists give their total allegiance to any one school.

3. In a similar vein, the different schools of economic thought are often characterized in political terms, with the Keynesians leaning left on the political spectrum and the other schools leaning to the right. But, as usual, all generalizations can be misleading (including this one). It is possible to be a Keynesian and also to be concerned about the size of the national debt, or to be a neoclassicist and still have compassion for the underprivileged and so on.

4. There is a great deal of pessimism about the future among young people today. This comes out in the form of questions such as, "will there be any jobs left when I am ready to enter the labour force full-time?" and "will I be able to earn enough income to live at least as well as most people today?" We think that this pessimistic outlook is misplaced. The world is entering a very exciting period in which opportunities for eager, creative, self-motivated young people will be greater than at any time in history. Finding those opportunities will not be easy, and those who try will inevitably make mistakes, but the rewards in terms of creative outlet, income, and a sense of accomplishment will be enormous. Oh, to be young again!

Answered Questions

Indicate whether the following statements are true or false.

1. T or F Say's Law suggests that supply creates its own demand.

2. T or F According to neoclassical theory, the aggregate supply curve is horizontal at the prevailing price level.

3. T or F According to neoclassical theory, an increase in the level of saving will cause the rate of interest to fall.

4. T or F According to Keynesian theory, a change in aggregate demand might have little or no effect on the price level.

5. T or F Neoclassical economists believe that market economies can achieve full employment through self-adjustment.

6. T or F Aggregate demand policies are effective in curing the problems of stagflation.

7. T or F The Phillips curve is based on the stable relationship between tax rates and the amount of tax revenue.

8. T or F One of the major criticisms of the supply-siders' emphasis on using tax cuts to stimulate the economy is that such cuts affect aggregate demand more than aggregate supply.

9. T or F Monopoly tendencies will intensify in the new economy with the maturing of the information age.

10. T or F The achievement of an equitable distribution of income will, in future, be the least contentious of Canada's economics goals.

Basic (Questions 11–24)

11. Which of the following is a statement of Say's Law?
a) Demand creates its own supply.
b) Supply creates its own demand.
c) The costs of production decrease as output increases.
d) The costs of production increase as output increases.

12. Which school of thought believed that long-run equilibrium occurs automatically and is the normal state of affairs in a market economy?
a) Keynesians.
b) Neoclassicists.
c) Supply-siders.
d) Symbolic analysts.

13. What do Keynesians believe?
a) Saving depends on the level of the interest rate.
b) Saving depends on the level of income.
c) Investment is stable.
d) Government policies should be neutral.

14. What ensures the equality of savings and investment, according to neoclassical theory?
a) Flexible prices.
b) Flexible interest rates.
c) Flexible wages.
d) Say's Law.

15. When did the Great Depression occur?
  a) At the beginning of the twentieth century.
  b) In the seven years following the First World War.
  c) During the decade of the 1930s.
  d) In the five years following the Second World War.

16. What characterized the decade of the 1970s in Canada?
  a) Prosperity and strong economic growth.
  b) Stagflation.
  c) Economic recovery from the 1960s depression.
  d) Low unemployment and high inflation.

Refer to **Figure 13.8** to answer question 17.

FIGURE 13.8

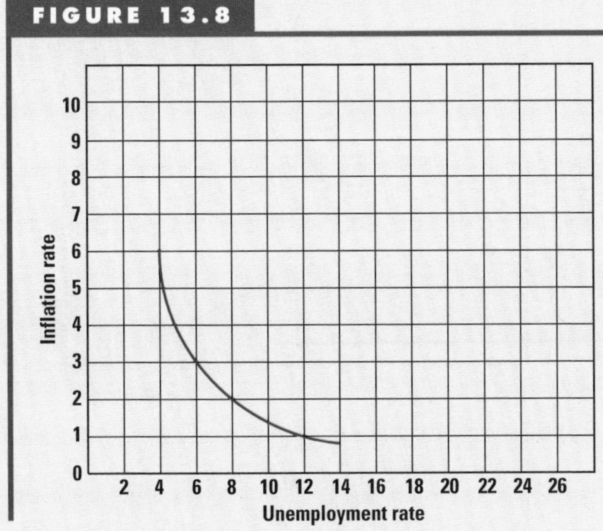

17. Refer to **Figure 13.8** to answer this question. What is the name of the curve shown here?
  a) Phillips curve.
  b) Aggregate supply curve.
  c) Laffer curve.
  d) Production possibilities curve.

18. Which of the following represents one of the basic problems portrayed by the Phillips curve?
  a) That the inflation rate tends to decrease as the economy moves closer to full employment.
  b) That the inflation rate tends to increase as the economy moves closer to full employment.
  c) That the unemployment rate tends to decrease as the economy moves toward price stability.
  d) That high levels of unemployment tend to accompany high rates of inflation.

19. According to Keynes, what determines interest rates?
  a) The level of saving.
  b) The level of investment.
  c) The velocity of money.
  d) Both saving and investment.
  e) The interaction of the demand and supply of money.

20. All of the following, except one, are pillars on which neoclassical theory is built. Which is the exception?
  a) The flexibility of production.
  b) The validity of Say's Law.
  c) The flexibility of prices.
  d) The flexibility of interest rates.
  e) The flexibility of wages.

21. According to supply-siders, what is one of the keys to curbing stagflation?
  a) Increasing the money supply and cutting government spending.
  b) Using income policies to increase productivity.
  c) Shifting the AD curve to the right.
  d) Convincing people to buy domestic rather than foreign-produced goods.
  e) Lowering taxes.

22. Which of the following statements is correct about symbolic knowledge?
  a) While it is powerful, it adds to the costs of production.
  b) It is bound to make mass markets even larger.
  c) It will shift the emphasis of production to product technology.
  d) It often proves to be a substitute for real capital.
  e) It has been most widely adopted and used in the newly industrial nations such as Asia's Four Tigers.

23. Which of the following statements about the source of wealth is correct?
  a) Marx said that it was land.
  b) The French physiocrats said it was capital.
  c) The neoclassicists said it was labour.
  d) Economists who embrace the new paradigm say it is knowledge, information, and human creativity.

24. What characterized the decades of the 1950s and 1960s?
  a) Low growth and high unemployment.
  b) Low unemployment and high inflation.
  c) Stagflation.
  d) Economic stability with reasonably low unemployment and inflation.

Intermediate (Questions 25–30)

25. Which of the following did neoclassical economists believe?
  a) That, in equilibrium, the leakage of savings from the circular flow would always be matched by an equal amount of investment.
  b) That if savings exceed investment, the interest rate will fall.
  c) That surplus output would lead to a fall in prices.
  d) All of the above.

26. How might monetary policy be used to overcome the crowding out effect?
  a) Contractionary monetary policy used together with expansionary fiscal policy.
  b) Contractionary monetary policy used together with contractionary fiscal policy.
  c) Expansionary monetary policy used together with contractionary fiscal policy.
  d) Expansionary monetary policy used together with expansionary fiscal policy.

Refer to Figure 13.9 to answer question 27.

FIGURE 13.9

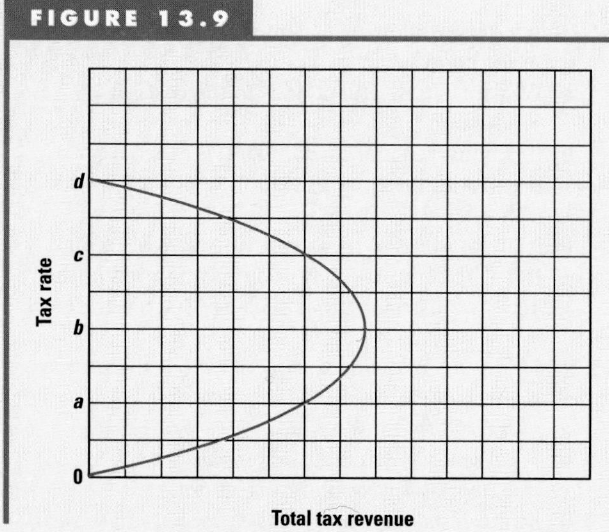

27. Refer to Figure 13.9 to answer this question. According to supply-side economists, at what level are present tax rates in Canada?
  a) At some level like 0*a*.
  b) At some level like 0*b*.
  c) At some level like 0*c*.
  d) At 0*d*.

28. According to neoclassical economists, what would happen if total spending was less than total output?
  a) Product prices would rise, but wage rates would fall.
  b) Product prices would fall, but wage rates would rise.
  c) Nominal GDP would rise, but real GDP would remain constant.
  d) Both product prices and wage rates would fall.
  e) Both product prices and wage rates would rise.

Refer to Figure 13.10 to answer questions 29 and 30.

FIGURE 13.10

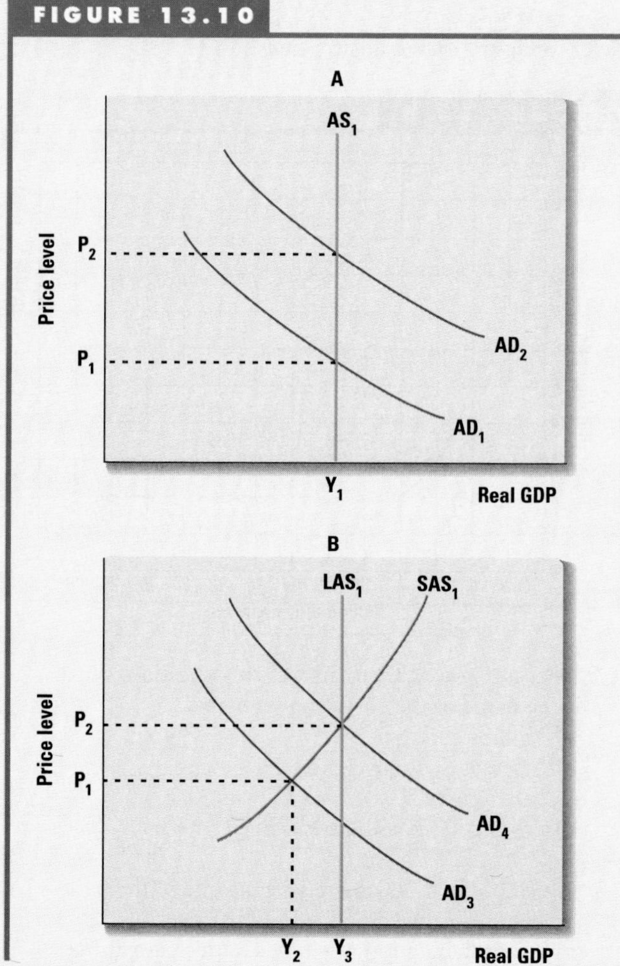

29. Refer to Figure 13.10 to answer this question. According to neoclassicists, which of the following is true?
  a) The horizontal axes of both graphs A and B show nominal GDP.
  b) It is not possible for an economy to be at Y_2 in graph B.
  c) The shift from AD_3 to AD_4 is caused by an increase in the price level.

d) Graph A illustrates that changes in aggregate demand have no effect on the price level.
e) Graph B illustrates a Laffer-curve-type trade-off.

30. Refer to **Figure 13.10** to answer this question. According to the Keynesians, which of the following is true?
a) The horizontal axes of both graphs A and B show nominal GDP.
b) The shift from AD_3 to AD_4 illustrates what should have happened in the 1930s but did not.
c) Graph B illustrates a Phillips-curve-type trade-off.
d) A shift from AD_1 to AD_2 is the result of contractionary fiscal and monetary policy.
e) The economy is always automatically at income level Y_1.

Advanced (Questions 31–35)

31. What is the essential difference between the Keynesian and the Neoclassical views about the macroeconomy?
a) The Keynesian view is that the economy is capable of automatically adjusting to economic changes because of the flexibility of wages, prices, and interest rates, while the Neoclassical view is that the economy could get stuck in a recessionary gap because of their inflexibility.
b) The Neoclassical view is that the economy is capable of automatically adjusting to economic changes because of the flexibility of wages, prices, and interest rates, while the Keynesian view is that the economy could get stuck in a recessionary gap because of their inflexibility.
c) While both views agree on the automatic adjustment ability of the economy, the Keynesian view sees wages as flexible but the Neoclassical view does not.
d) While both views agree on the automatic adjustment ability of the economy, the Neoclassical view sees wages as flexible but the Keynesians do not.

32. How might Neo-Keynesians explain the stagflation of the 1970s?
a) The Phillips curve shifted to the right.
b) The Laffer curve contracted.
c) Potential full-employment output expanded too quickly.
d) The oil-price shocks caused the AS curve to shift to the right.

33. Which of the following statements is likely to be true in the future?
a) Unemployment will continue to be a problem for some individuals despite an overall strong and growing economy.
b) Inflation is likely to remain low.
c) Income distribution patterns will show increased gaps between the rich and the poor, despite a strong and growing overall economy.
d) All of the above.

34. What would be the most reliable sign that the new economy is a phenomenon of real historical significance?
a) Rising real GDP.
b) Falling unemployment.
c) Low inflation.
d) Rising productivity over a sustained period of time.

35. How is a historical look at the macroeconomy of Canada beneficial?
a) It assures us that the real issues of the day do not change.
b) It enables us to realize that the views of economists about the issues of the day are very similar over time.
c) It helps us to identify the relationship between economic events and changes in macroeconomy theory.
d) It establishes the unchanging nature of macroeconomic theory.

Parallel Problems

ANSWERED PROBLEMS

36. Key Problem The economy of Copland is in equilibrium but is suffering from a recessionary gap of $10 billion. Its aggregate demand and supply curves are shown in **Figure 13.11**.

FIGURE 13.11

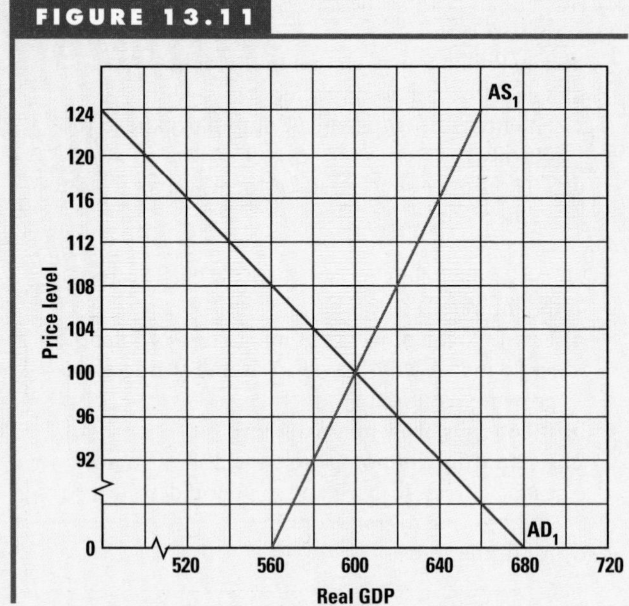

a) Draw in the potential GDP curve and label it I. Both demand-side and supply-side economists in Copland have been advising the government to reduce taxes in order to cure the recession. Independent economic research has determined that, for every 1 percent change in taxes, aggregate demand changes by $20 billion.

b) Assuming that the government decides to cut taxes by 6 percent, and that aggregate supply is unaffected, draw in and label the new curve AD_2 in **Figure 13.11**.

c) At the new equilibrium, by *how much* has real GDP and the price level changed?
Change in real GDP: (+/–) $ ______________ ;
change in price level: (+/–) ______________ .
Independent economic research has also determined that every 1 percent cut in tax rates in Copland, because it stimulates productivity, will increase aggregate supply by $5 billion.

d) For the same 6 percent cut in taxes, draw in and label the new aggregate supply curve, AS_2 and the new potential GDP curve II, in **Figure 13.11**.

e) Assuming that aggregate demand *did not* change, by how much would real GDP and the price level change?
Change in real GDP: (+/–) $ ______________ ;
change in price level: (+/–) ______________ .

f) Finally, assuming that the change in tax rates affect *both* aggregate demand and aggregate supply, add together the changes in b) and d):
Total change in real GDP: $ ______________ ;
total change in price level: (+/–) ______________ .

g) Is Copland's economy now at full employment? If there is a gap, what type is it, and how much?
Type of gap: ______________ of
$ ______________ .

Basic (Problems 37–40)

37. **Figure 13.12** shows the savings and investment of loanable funds for the very classical economy of Gluckland.

FIGURE 13.12

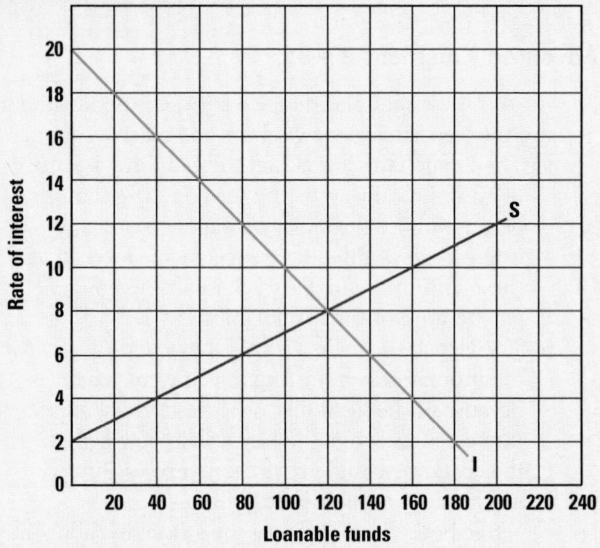

Rate of interest: 0, 2, 4, 6, 8, 10, 12, 14, 16, 18, 20
Loanable funds: 20, 40, 60, 80, 100, 120, 140, 160, 180, 200, 220, 240
S
I

a) What is the equilibrium rate of interest in Gluckland?
Rate of interest: ______________ %.

b) According to the graph, what rate of interest would induce the people of Gluckland to save $100 billion?
Rate of interest: ______________ %.

c) According to the graph, what rate of interest would induce the firms of Gluckland to invest $100 billion?
Rate of interest: ______________ %.

d) What change in savings would reduce the interest rate to 6 percent from its present equilibrium, and how much would savings and investment be as a result?
Change in savings: $ ______________ ;
new level of savings/investment $ ______________ .

e) Starting at the original equilibrium in **Figure 13.12**, what change in investment would reduce the interest rate to 6 percent, and how much would savings and investment be as a result?
Change in investment: $ ______________ ;
new level of savings/investment $ ______________ .

38. Match each item in the left-hand column with a related idea or event in the right-hand column by placing a letter in each blank.

A. laissez-faire	1. Keynesians	______
B. demand management	2. OPEC-induced oil price increases	______
C. tax cuts as a stimulus to aggregate supply	3. supply-siders	______
D. stagflation	4. neoclassicist	______

39. In the queendom of Frankland, GDP is currently $500 million. Production in Frankland is unaffected by changes in tax rates until the rate hits 35 percent. Thereafter, for each 5 percent increase in the tax rate, GDP drops by $40 million.

a) Complete Table 13.1 for the government of Frankland.

TABLE 13.1

% Tax Rate	GDP	Tax Revenue
0	$500	______
5	______	______
10	______	______
15	______	______
20	______	______
25	______	______
30	______	______
35	______	______
40	______	______
45	______	______
50	______	______
55	______	______
60	______	______
65	______	______
70	______	______

b) In Figure 13.13, graph Frankland's tax revenue curve.

FIGURE 13.13

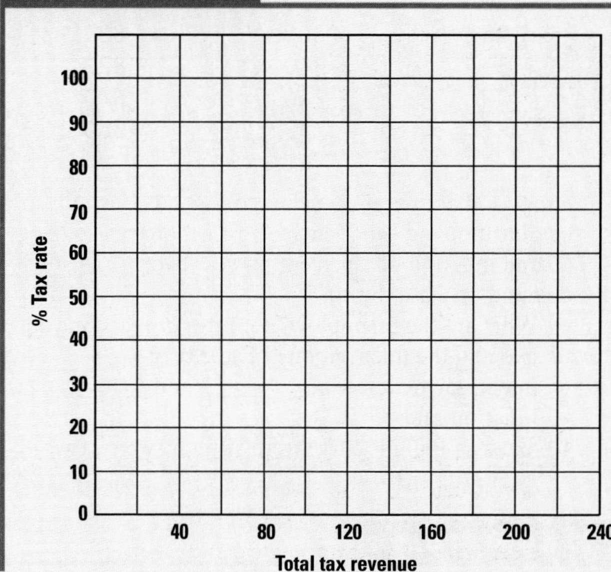

c) At what tax rate will the tax revenue be maximized? What will be the amount of tax revenue?

% tax rate: ________________;

tax revenue: $ ________________.

40. Decide which of the three categories of work (routine production services, in-person services, or symbolic services) each of the following occupations best fits into.

a) Coffee house waiter: ________________

b) Pulp mill worker: ________________

c) Cable TV installer: ________________

d) Computer systems consultant: ________________

e) Auto plant supervisor: ________________

f) Market research analyst: ________________

Intermediate (Problems 41–43)

41. The data in Table 13.2 shows Haydn's aggregate demand and aggregate supply. In this economy, the natural rate of unemployment is 6 percent, and for each $10 of recessionary gap, cyclical unemployment is 1 percent.

TABLE 13.2

Price Index	Aggregate Quantity Demanded	Aggregate Quantity Supplied
110	860	740
115	840	760
120	820	780
125	800	800
130	780	820
135	760	840
140	740	860

Suppose that in year one, the economy of Haydn is in equilibrium and experiencing a recessionary gap of 60 and inflation of 1 percent. In year two, aggregate demand increases by 40.

a) What are the unemployment rates in years one and two and the inflation rate in year two?
unemployment rates: _________ and _________;
inflation rate: _________ .

b) Sketch a Phillips curve from your answers in a), in **Figure 13.14**.

FIGURE 13.14

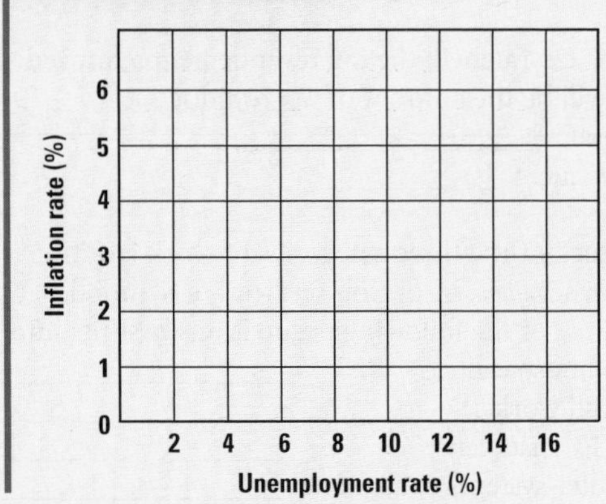

42. Assume that **Figure 13.15** is referring to the 1930s. Describe in words what actually occurred that enabled the economy to return to full-employment equilibrium.

FIGURE 13.15

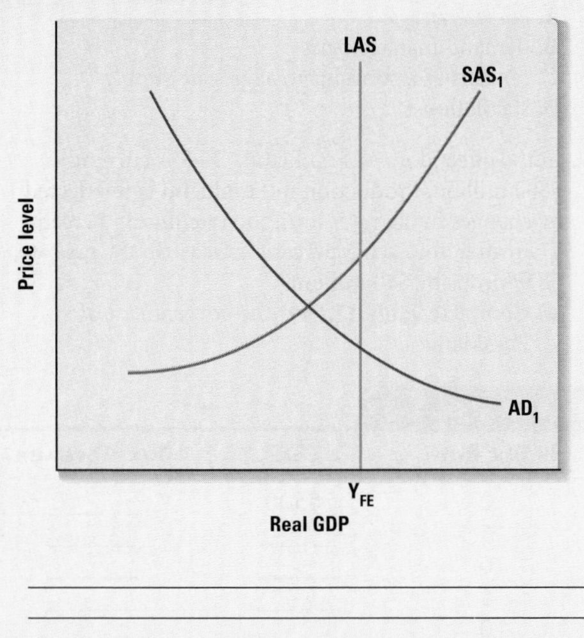

____
____
____.

43. Using AD/AS curves, on the graphs below, illustrate—in A) a small; in B) a larger; and in C) a very large—increase in the price level, resulting from expansionary fiscal (or monetary) policy.

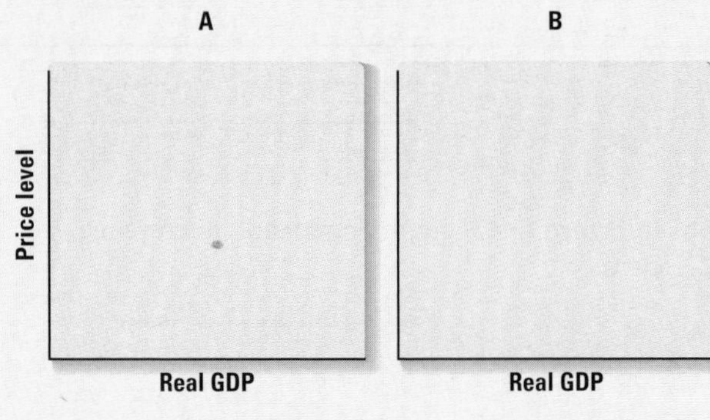

Advanced (Problems 44–47)

44. **Figure 13.16** shows the aggregate demand for the economy of Bachland. Its potential GDP is $350.

FIGURE 13.16

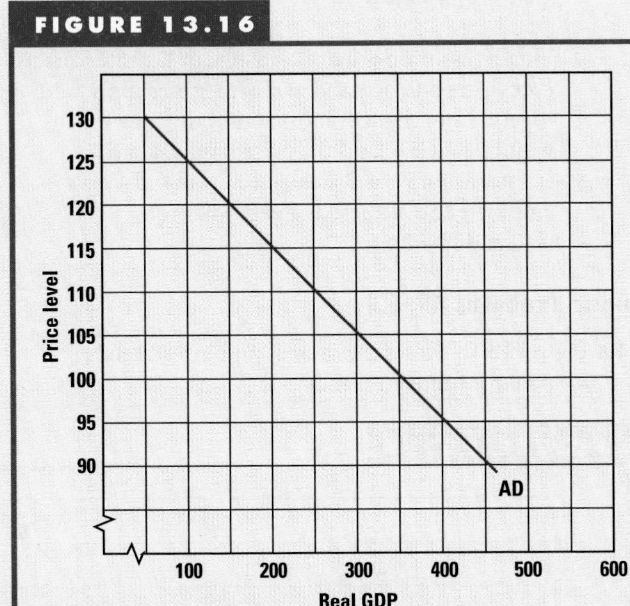

According to neoclassical theory:

a) If the price level is 110, is the economy of Bachland currently in equilibrium? If not, what might happen?

____

____.

b) If *instead* the economy of Bachland were in equilibrium, what would happen to GDP and the price level if aggregate demand were to increase by $50?

____.

According to Keynesian theory:

c) If the present price level is 110 and the economy of Bachland is in equilibrium, what is the level of real GDP?

______________.

d) If the economy of Bachland were in equilibrium at a price of 110 and a GDP of 250, what would happen to GDP and the price level if aggregate demand were to increase by $50?

____.

45. If you were a Keynesian, how would you explain the effect of an increase in savings on the economy? What if you were a neoclassicist?

____

____

____.

46. How might a Keynesian argue that fiscal policy could be made effective despite the existence of the crowding-out effect?

____

____

____.

47. Explain the circumstances in which economic policy might increase real GDP without affecting the price level.

____

____

____.

UNANSWERED PROBLEMS

48. **Key Problem** The economy of Bruchland is in equilibrium but is suffering from a recessionary gap of $10. Its aggregate demand and supply curves are shown in **Figure 13.17**.

FIGURE 13.17

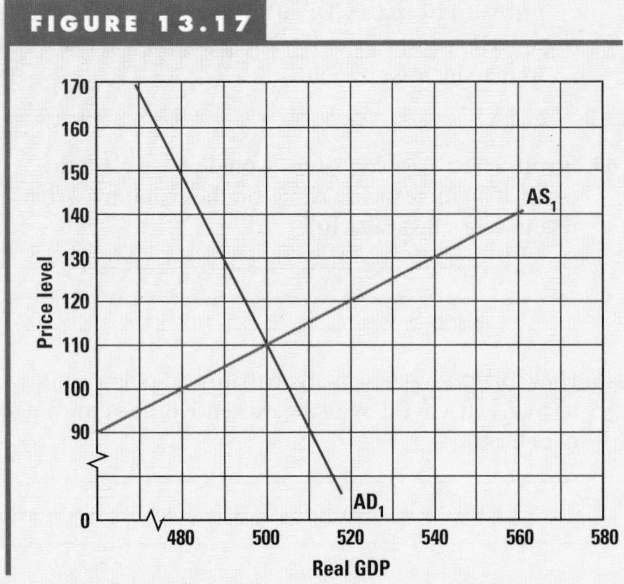

a) Draw in the potential GDP curve and label it I.

Both demand-side and supply-side economists in Bruchland have been advising the government to reduce taxes in order to cure the recession. Independent economic research has determined that for every 1 percent cut in taxes, aggregate demand increases by $5 billion.

b) Assuming that the government of Bruchland decides to cut taxes by 10 percent, and that aggregate supply is unaffected, draw in and label the new AD curve, AD_2, in **Figure 13.17**.

c) At the new equilibrium, by *how much* has real GDP and the price level changed?

Independent economic research has also determined that for every 1 percent change in tax rates, aggregate supply changes by $5 billion.

d) Assuming the same cut in taxes, draw in and label the new AS (AS_2) and the new potential GDP (II) curve in **Figure 13.17**.

e) Assuming that aggregate demand *did not* change, by how much would real GDP and the price level change?

f) Finally, assuming that the change in tax rates affects *both* aggregate demand and aggregate supply, add together the changes in b) and d). By how much would real GDP and the price level change?

g) Is the economy of Bruchland now at full employment? If there is a gap, what sort is it, and how much?

Basic (Problems 49–52)

49. **Figure 13.18** shows the savings and investment of loanable funds in Handel.

FIGURE 13.18

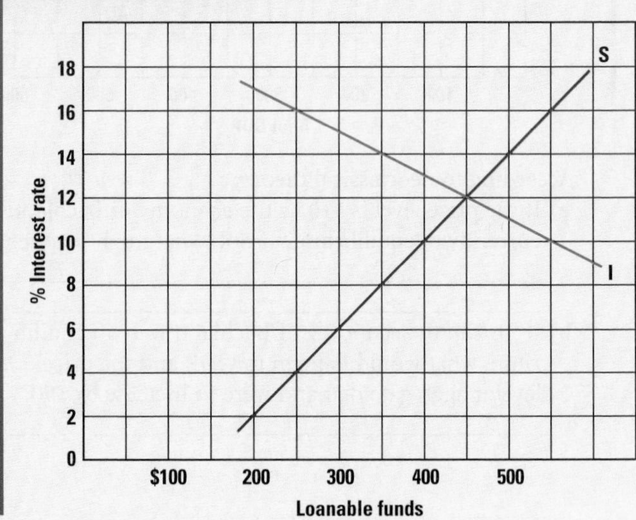

a) What is the equilibrium interest rate?

b) What rate of interest will induce savers to save $350 million?

c) What rate of interest will induce firms in Handel to borrow and invest $350 million?

d) What change in savings would reduce the interest rate to 10 percent from its present equilibrium?

e) What change in investment would reduce the interest rate to 10 percent?

50. Match each item in the left-hand column with a related idea or event in the right-hand column by placing a letter in each blank.

A. supply creates its own demand
B. recessions
C. rational expectations
D. the level of saving depends on interest rates

1. peoples' reactions to changes in policies ______.
2. Say's Law ______.
3. theory of loanable funds ______.
4. 1930s, early 1980s, and early 1990s ______.

51. In the kingdom of Rachmaninoff, GDP is currently $900 billion. Production in Rachmaninoff is unaffected by changes in tax rates until the rate hits 20 percent. Thereafter, for each 10 percent increase in the tax rate, GDP drops by $80 billion.

a) Complete **Table 13.3** for the government of Rachmaninoff.

TABLE 13.3

% Tax Rate	GDP	Tax Revenue
0	$900	______
10	______	______
20	______	______
30	______	______
40	______	______
50	______	______
60	______	______
70	______	______
80	______	______
90	______	______
100	______	______

b) In **Figure 13.19**, graph Rachmaninoff's tax revenue curve.

FIGURE 13.19

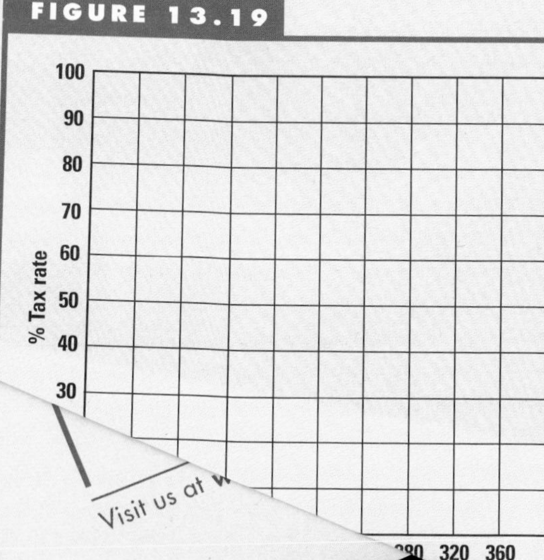

c) At what tax rate will the tax revenue be maximized? What will be the amount of tax revenue?
% tax rate: ________; tax revenue: $ ________.

52. Identify whether each of the following are associated with the basic economy (B) or the new economy (N):

a) a high level of capital accumulation;
b) human creativity;
c) a disciplined labour force;
d) knowledge;
e) abundant natural resources;
f) globalization.

Intermediate (Problems 53–55)

53. The data in **Table 13.4** below is for the economy of Bizet, where the natural rate of unemployment is 4 percent and, for each $10 of recessionary gap, cyclical unemployment is 1.5 percent. Potential GDP is $960.

TABLE 13.4

Price Index	Aggregate Quantity Demanded	Aggregate Quantity Supplied
111	950	860
114	940	880
117	930	900
120	920	920
123	910	940
126	900	960

Suppose that in Year one, the economy of Bizet is at equilibrium and has an inflation rate of 2 percent. In Year two, aggregate demand increases by 30.

a) What are the unemployment rates in Years one and two and the inflation rate in year two?
b) Sketch a Phillips curve using your answers from a).

54. Assume that **Figure 13.20** is referring to the early 1970s. Describe in words what actually occurred to cause stagflation.

FIGURE 13.20

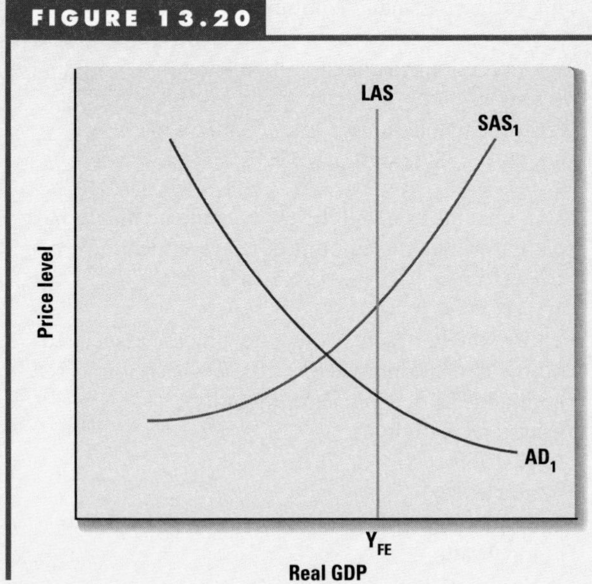

55. Using three separate AD/AS curve graphs, show how prices could rise, fall, or remain unchanged as a result of a tax cut that affects both the AD and the AS curves.

Advanced (Problems 56–59)

56. Figure 13.21 shows the aggregate demand for the economy of Vivaldi. Its potential GDP is $800.

FIGURE 13.21

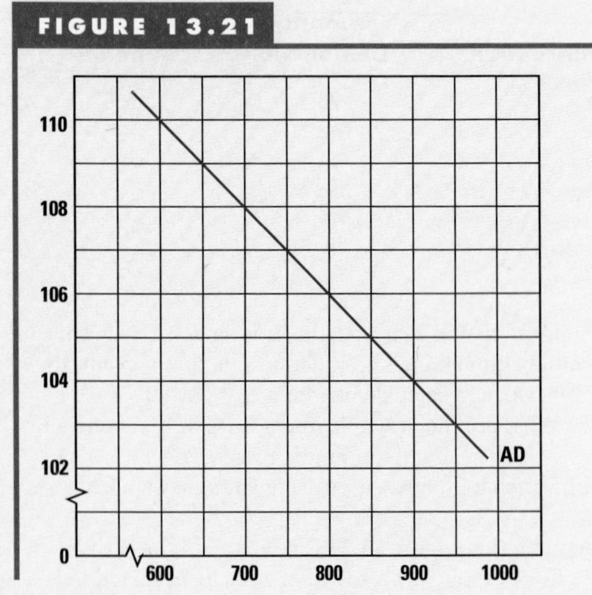

According to neoclassical theory:

a) If the price level is currently 108, is the economy of Vivaldi currently in equilibrium? If not, what might happen?
b) If *instead* the economy of Vivaldi were in equilibrium, what would happen to GDP and the price level if aggregate demand were to decrease by $100?

According to Keynesian theory:

c) If the price level is currently 108 and the economy in equilibrium, what is the level of GDP?
d) If the economy of Vivaldi were in equilibrium at a price of 108 and a GDP of $700, what would happen to GDP and the price level if aggregate demand were to increase by $100?

57. Explain the main differences between neoclassicists and supply-siders.

58. Both Keynesians and supply-siders agree that if taxes are cut, then GDP will rise. So what is the difference between the two concerning the effect of a decrease in taxes?

59. Location theorists in economics and geography argue that the location of (almost) every city in the world has a specific explanation involving either a national transportation factor (for example, two rivers merging) or the presence of a nearby natural resource such as a coal or iron ore deposit. What do you think might replace these factors as the main determinant of the fastest-growing population centres in the information age, and what areas in North America do you think will grow the quickest?

Web-Based Activities

1. Go to **http://www.fin.gc.ca/susdev/sds2001e.html #_Toc506359762** and scroll down to what are identified as four "Key Issues" concerning the future of Canada. How do these issues fit with the section in this chapter entitled "Economic Goals Revisited"?

2. Go to **http://www.cato.org/current/globalization/index.html** and read the brief description of the concept of "globalization" and then identify what this group feels is the big dividend of this trend.

Glossary

A

aggregate demand: the aggregate quantity of goods and services demanded by all buyers at various price levels.

aggregate expenditures: total spending in the economy, divided into the four components: C, I, G, and (X – IM).

aggregate supply: the aggregate quantity of goods and services produced by all sellers at various price levels.

arbitrage: the process of buying a commodity in one market, where the price is low, and immediately selling it in a second market where the price is higher.

asset demand for money: the desire by people to use money as a store of wealth, that is, to hold money as an asset.

assets: the part of a company's balance sheet that represents what it owns or what is owed to it.

automatic stabilizers: government policies and programs that automatically change with the state of the economy so as to stabilize the economy.

autonomous consumption: the portion of consumer spending that is independent of the level of income.

autonomous spending: the portion of total spending that is independent of the level of income.

B

balanced budget: the equality of net tax revenues and government spending on goods and services.

balanced-budget fiscal policy: the belief that a government's budget should be balanced each budget period.

balance of payments: an accounting of a country's international transactions that involves the payment and receipts of foreign currencies.

balance of trade: the value of a country's export of goods and services less the value of its imports.

bank rate: the rate of interest payable by the commercial banks on loans from the Bank of Canada.

bank rate: the rate of interest that the Bank of Canada charges a commercial bank for a loan.

budget deficit: government spending on goods and services in excess of net tax revenues.

budget surplus: net tax revenue in excess of government spending on goods and services.

business cycle: the expansionary and contractionary phases in the growth rate of real GDP.

C

capital: all human-made resources that can be used to produce goods and services.

capital account: a subcategory of the balance of payments that reflects changes in ownership of assets associated with foreign investment.

change in demand: a change in the quantities demanded at every price, caused by a change in the determinants of demand.

change in supply: a change in the quantities supplied at every price, caused by a change in the determinants of supply.

change in the quantity demanded: the change in the quantity that results from a price change. It results, graphically, in a movement along a demand curve.

change in the quantity supplied: the change in the amounts that will be produced as a result of a price change. This is shown as a movement along a supply curve.

commodity money: a type of money that can also function, and is useful, as a commodity.

comparative advantage: the advantage that comes from producing something at a lower opportunity cost than others are able to do.

complementary products: products that tend to be purchased jointly and whose demands, therefore, are directly related.

consumer goods and services: products used by consumers to satisfy their wants and needs.

consumer price index: a measurement of the average level of prices of the goods and services that a typical Canadian family consumes.

consumption: the expenditure by households on goods and services.

contractionary monetary policy: a policy in which the amount of money in the economy is decreased and credit becomes harder to obtain and more expensive.

cost–push inflation: inflation caused by an increase in the costs of production or in profit levels, with the effect being on the supply side.

counter-cyclical fiscal policy: deliberate adjustments in the level of government spending and taxation in order to close recessionary or inflationary gaps.

crowding-out effect: the idea that government borrowing to finance a deficit crowds out private investment because it causes interest rates to rise.

currency appreciation: a rise in the exchange rate of one currency for another.

currency depreciation: the fall in the exchange rate of one currency for another.

current account: a subcategory of the balance of payments that shows the income or expenditures related to exports and imports.

cyclical unemployment: unemployment that occurs as a result of the recessionary phase of the business cycle.

cyclically balanced-budget fiscal policy: the use of counter-cyclical fiscal policy to balance the budget over the life of the business cycle.

D

demand: the quantities that consumers are willing and able to buy per period of time at various prices.

demand–pull inflation: inflation that occurs when total demand for goods and services exceeds the economy's capacity to produce those goods.

demand schedule: a table showing the various quantities demanded per period of time at different prices.

devaluation: the re-fixing by government of an exchange rate at a lower level.

direct investment: the purchase of real assets.

dirty float: an exchange rate that is not officially fixed by government but is managed by the central bank's ongoing intervention in the market.

discouraged worker: an individual who wants work but is no longer actively seeking it because of the conviction that no opportunities exist.

disposable income: the personal after-tax income of people.

E

economic growth: an increase in an economy's real GDP per capita or an increase in the economy's capacity to produce.

employed: those who are in the labour force and hold paid employment.

enterprise: the human resource that innovates and takes risks.

equation of exchange: a formula that states that the quantity of money times the velocity of money is equal to nominal GDP (price times real GDP).

equilibrium: a state of balance of equal forces with no tendency to change.

equilibrium price: the price at which the quantity demanded equals the quantity supplied such that there is neither a surplus nor a shortage.

equilibrium quantity: the quantity that prevails at the equilibrium price.

excess reserves: reserves in excess of what the bank wants to hold as its target reserves.

exchange controls: government-imposed restrictions limiting the amount of foreign currencies that can be obtained.

exchange rate: the rate at which one currency converts into another.

expansionary monetary policy: a policy that aims to increase the amount of money in the economy and make credit cheaper and more easily available.

expenditure equilibrium: the income at which the value of production and aggregate expenditures are equal.

exports: goods and services produced in one country and sold to another country.

F

factor market: the market for the factors of production.

factors of production: the productive resources that are available to an economy, categorized as land, labour, capital, and enterprise.

financial security: any claim on assets that usually takes the form of a bond or certificate of deposit or similar financial instrument.

fiscal policy: the government's approach toward its own spending and taxation.

fixed exchange rate: a currency exchange rate pegged by government and therefore prevented from rising or falling.

flexible exchange rate: a currency exchange rate determined by the market forces of supply and demand and not interfered with by government action.

foreign-trade effect: the effect that a change in prices has upon exports and imports.

fractional reserve system: a banking system whereby banks keep only a small fraction of their total deposits on reserve in the form of cash.

frictional unemployment: that part of total unemployment caused by the fact that it takes time for people to find their first job or to move between jobs.

full employment: the situation in which there is only frictional and structural unemployment, that is, where cyclical unemployment is zero.

G

GDP deflator: a measure of the price level of goods included in the GDP, calculated by dividing the nominal GDP by the real GDP and multiplying by 100.

GDP gap: the difference between potential GDP and actual GDP.

gross domestic product (GDP): the value of all final goods and services produced in an economy in a certain period.

gross national product (GNP): the total market value of all final goods and services produced by the citizens of a country regardless of the location of production.

H

human capital: the accumulated skills and knowledge of human beings.

I

imports: goods and services that are bought from other countries and that reflect a leakage from the circular flow of income.

income: the earnings of factors of production expressed as an amount per period of time.

induced consumption: the portion of consumer spending that is dependent on the level of income.

induced spending: the portion of spending that depends on the level of income.

inferior products: products whose demands will decrease as a result of an increase in income and will increase as a result of a decrease in income.

inflation: a persistent rise in the general level of prices.

inflationary gap: the difference between actual real GDP and potential real GDP when the economy is temporarily producing an output above full employment.

injection: any spending flow that is not dependent on the current level of income.

interest: the payment made and the income received for the use of capital.

interest-rate effect: the effect that a change in prices, and therefore interest rates, has upon investment; for example, higher prices cause higher interest rates, which leads to lower investment.

investment: spending on capital goods.

investment demand: the relationship between investment spending and interest rates.

L

labour: human physical and mental effort that can be used to produce goods and services.

labour force: members of the labour-force population, whether employed or unemployed.

labour-force population: the total population in a country, excluding those under 15 years of age, inmates of institutions, those in the armed forces, and residents of Indian reserves or the territories.

labour productivity: a measure of the amount of output produced per unit of labour input (per unit of time).

Laffer curve: the graphical representation of the idea that in terms of tax revenue there is an optimal tax rate; above or below this rate, tax revenue would be less.

land: any natural resource that can be used to produce goods and services.

law of increasing costs: as an economy's production level of any particular item increases, its per unit cost of production rises.

leakage: income received within the circular flow that does not flow directly back.

liabilities: the part of a company's balance sheet that represents what it owes.

loanable funds: the portion of wealth that is available for loan through financial intermediaries.

long-run aggregate supply: the aggregate quantity of goods and services produced after all prices and wages have adjusted; that is, the full-employment level of real GDP.

M

M1: currency in circulation plus demand deposits.

M2: M1 plus all notice and personal term deposits.

M3: M2 plus non-personal term deposits known as certificates of deposit.

macroeconomic equilibrium: a situation in which the quantity of real GDP demanded equals the quantity of real GDP supplied.

macroeconomics: the study of how the major components of an economy interact; it includes the topics of unemployment, inflation, interest rate policy, and the spending and taxation policies of government.

marginal leakage rate: the ratio of change in leakages that results from a change in income.

marginal propensity to consume: the ratio of the change in consumption to the corresponding change in disposable income (MPCD) or national income (MPCN).

marginal propensity to expend: the ratio of the change in expenditures that results from a change in income.

marginal propensity to import: the ratio of the change in imports that results from a change in national income.

marginal propensity to save: the ratio of the change in savings to the corresponding change in disposable income (MPSD) or national income (MPSN).

marginal tax rate: the ratio of the change in taxation as a result of a change in income.

market demand: the total demand for a product by all of its consumers.

market supply: the total supply of a product offered by all producers.

medium of exchange: something that is accepted as payment for goods and services.

microeconomics: the study of the outcomes of decisions by people and firms through a focus on the supply and demand of goods, the costs of production, and market structures.

monetarism: an economic school of thought that believes that cyclical fluctuations of GDP and inflation are usually caused by changes in the money supply.

monetary policy: economic policy designed to change or influence the economy through changes in the money supply.

monetizing the debt: the action by government of borrowing from the central bank to finance increased spending.

money: anything that is widely accepted as a medium of exchange and therefore can be used to buy goods or to settle debts.

money multiplier: the increase in total deposits that would occur in the whole banking system as a result of a new deposit in a single bank.

multiplier: the effect on national income of a change in autonomous expenditures, such as I, G, or X.

N

national debt: the sum of the federal government's budget deficits less surpluses.

national income equilibrium: that level of income where total leakages from the circular flow equal total injections.

national income (Y): total earnings of all the factors of production in a certain period.

natural rate of unemployment: the unemployment rate at full employment.

near-banks: financial institutions, like credit unions or trust companies, which share many of the functions of commercial banks but are not defined as banks under the Bank Act (they are also known as non-bank financial intermediaries).

net domestic income: incomes earned in Canada (equals the sum of wages, profits, interest, farm, and self-employed income).

net exports: total exports minus total imports of goods and services which can be written as (X – IM) or as Xn.

net national product (NNP): gross national product less capital consumption (or depreciation).

net worth: the total assets less total liabilities of a company—also called equity.

nominal GDP: the value of GDP in terms of prices prevailing at the time of measurement.

nominal income: the present-dollar value of a person's income.

normal products: products whose demand will increase as a result of an increase in income and will decrease as a result of a decrease in income.

O

official settlements account: a subcategory of the balance of payments that shows the change in a country's official foreign exchange reserves.

Okun's law: the observation that for every 1 percent of cyclical unemployment an economy's GDP would be 2.5 percent below its potential.

open-market operations: the buying and selling of securities by the Bank of Canada in the open (to the public) market.

opportunity cost: the value of the next-best alternative that is given up as a result of making a particular choice.

P

participation rate: the percentage of those in the labour-force population who are actually in the labour force.

personal income: income paid to individuals before the deduction of personal income taxes.

pro-cyclical: action by the government that tends to push the economy in the same direction that it is leaning.

product market: the market for consumer goods and services.

production possibilities curve: a graphical representation of the various combinations of maximum output that can be produced.

profit: the income received from the activity of enterprise.

protectionism: the economic policy of protecting domestic producers by restricting the importation of foreign products.

portfolio investment: the purchase of shares or bonds representing less than 50 percent ownership.

purchasing power parity theory: a theory suggesting that exchange rates will change so as to equate the purchasing power of each currency.

Q

quota: a limit imposed on the production or sale of a product.

R

real-balances effect: the effect that a change in the value of real balances has on consumption spending (the value of real balances is affected by changing price levels).

real GDP: the value of GDP measured in terms of prices prevailing in a given base year.

real income: the purchasing power of income, that is, nominal income divided by the price level.

real interest rate: the rate of interest measured in constant dollars.

real wage: nominal wage divided by the price level; that is, the amount of goods and services that can be bought from a given nominal wage.

recessionary gap: the difference between actual real GDP and potential real GDP when the economy is producing below its potential.

rent: the payment made and the income received for the use of land.

S

savings: the portion of income that is not spent on consumption.

Say's Law: the proposition that "supply creates its own demand"; that is, production (supply) creates sufficient income and thus spending (demand) to purchase the production. (Attributed to French economist Jean-Baptiste Say.)

short-run aggregate supply: the quantity of goods and services produced at various price levels assuming that factor prices remain constant.

stagflation: the simultaneous occurrence of high inflation and unemployment.

store of wealth: the function of money that allows people to hold and accumulate wealth.

structural unemployment: the part of total unemployment that results from structural changes in an economy's industries.

subsidy: a payment by government for the purpose of increasing some particular activity or increasing the output of a particular good.

substitute products: any product whose demand varies directly with a change in the price of a similar product.

supply: the quantities that producers are willing and able to sell per period of time at different prices.

supply schedule: a table showing the various quantities supplied per period of time at different prices.

symbolic analyst: an individual who uses symbolic knowledge to identify problems, create solutions, and then broker those solutions in a systematic form.

symbolic knowledge: knowledge that encompasses data and information that is then systematically improved and refined into a form that has direct application to defining problems or creating solutions.

T

target reserve ratio: the portion of deposits that a bank wants to hold in cash.

tariff: a tax (or duty) levied on imports.

terms of trade: the average price of a country's exports compared with the price of its imports.

transactions demand for money: the desire of people to hold money as a medium of exchange, that is, to effect transactions.

transfer payments: one-way transactions in which payment is made, but no good or service flows back in return.

transmission process: the Keynesian view of how changes in money affect (transmit to) the real variables in the economy.

the spread: the difference between the rate of interest a bank charges borrowers and the rate it pays savers.

U

unemployed: those who are in the labour force and are actively seeking employment, but do not hold paid employment.

unemployment: the situation in which persons 15 years old and over are actively seeking work but do not have employment.

unemployment rate: the percentage of those in the labour force who do not hold paid employment.

unit of account: the function of money that allows us to determine easily the relative value of goods.

unplanned investment: the amount of unintended investment by firms in the form of a build-up or run-down of inventories.

V

value of production: the total receipts of all producers.

velocity of money (or circulation): the number of times that the average unit of currency is spent (or turns over) buying final goods or services.

voluntary export restrictions (V.E.R.s): an agreement by an exporting country to restrict the amount of its exports to another country.

W

wages: the payment made and the income received for the use of labour.

wealth: the sum of all valuable assets less liabilities.

wealth effect: the effect of a change in wealth on consumption spending (a direct relationship between the two).

Index

D

N

O

P